Joan Mitchell

~~Rules~~ 'for Joyce' & Feeling

To dare to love — action

Something anything — a flower — a piece of music — a picture.

(not of course who loves you or doesn't)

Example - Gisèle's love for her garden — The flowers themselves.

Of course to dare to love & feel it will necessarily make you know what death is all about — a loss.

a ... when Gisèle's flowers die.

(but she planted others for me until late Oct.)

Painting is made with feeling.

One has to have the guts to feel & love outside oneself.

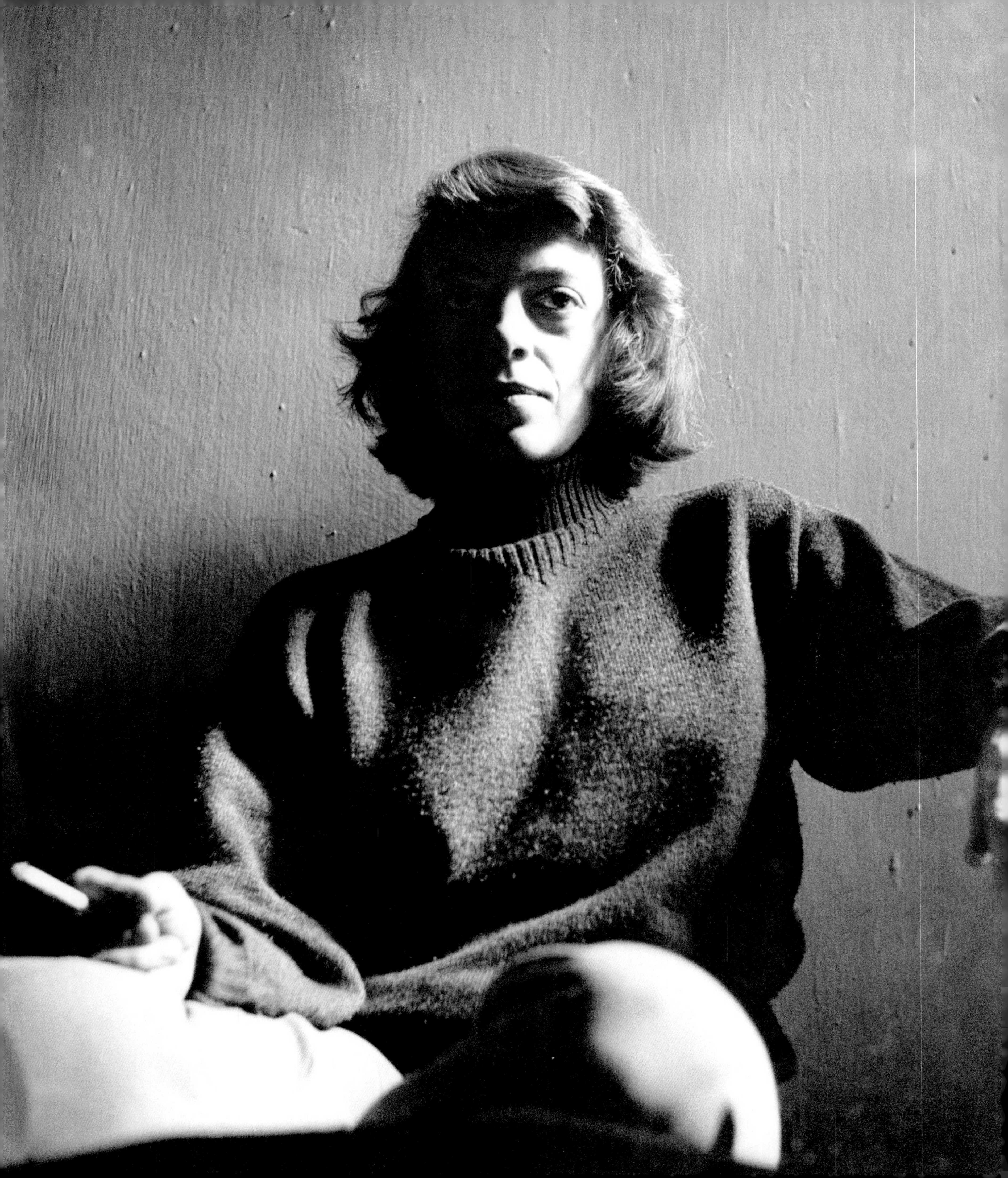

Joan Mitchell

Edited by Sarah Roberts and Katy Siegel

Published to accompany the exhibition co-organized by
The Baltimore Museum of Art and the San Francisco Museum of Modern Art

SAN FRANCISCO MUSEUM OF MODERN ART IN ASSOCIATION WITH YALE UNIVERSITY PRESS, NEW HAVEN AND LONDON

Contents

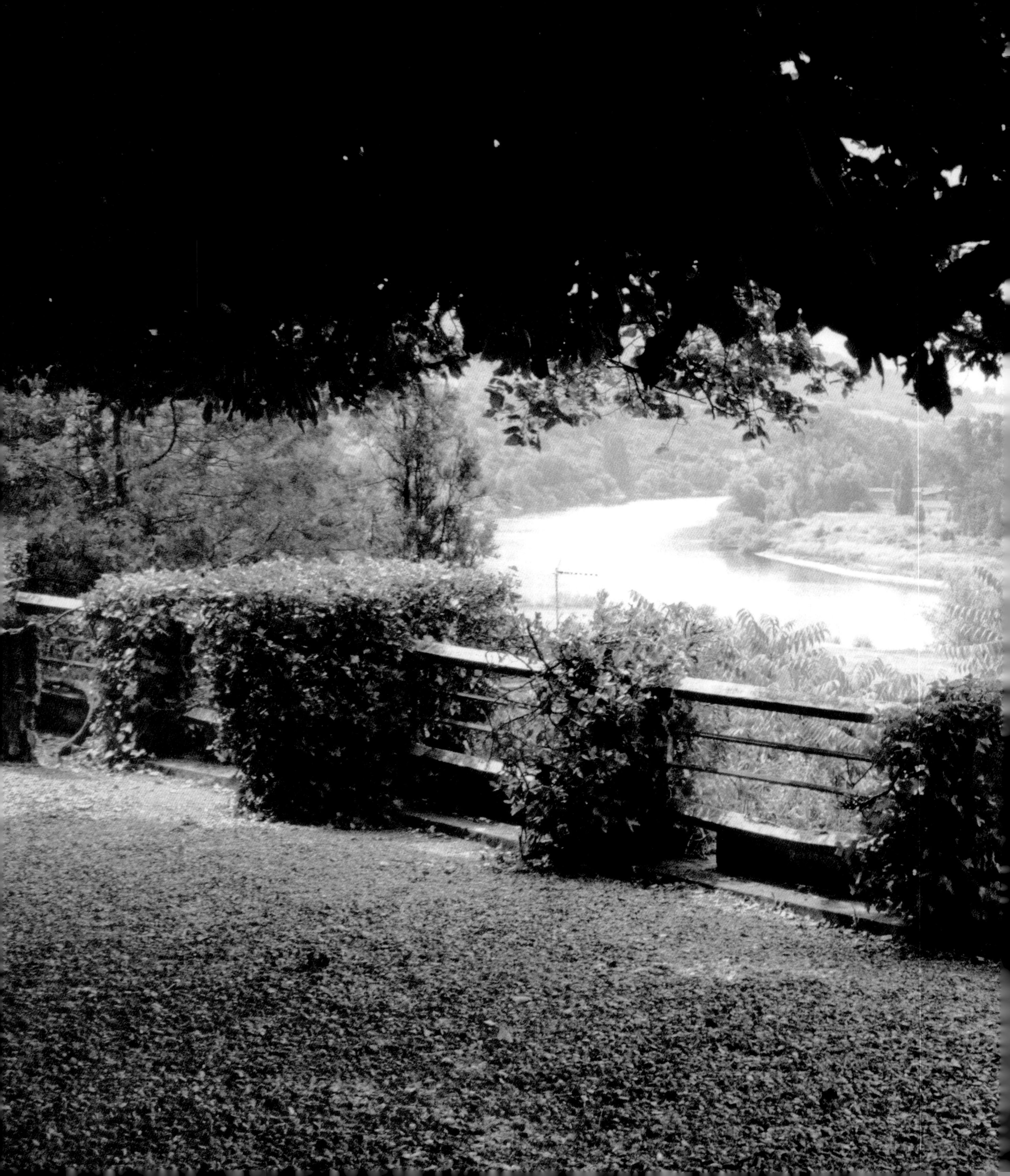

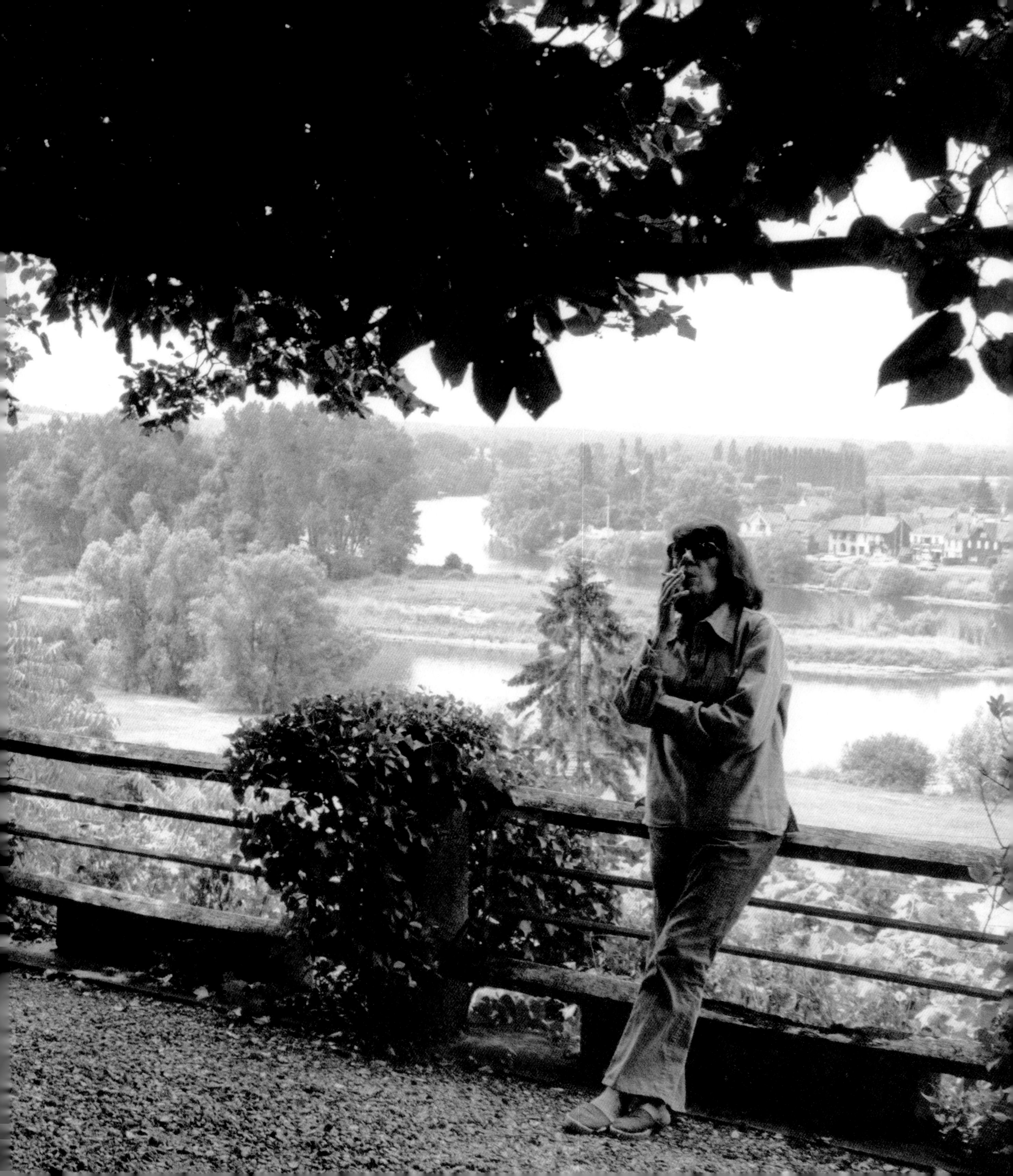

Foreword

Joan Mitchell has long been recognized as a formidable figure. A rare woman who managed to succeed in the male-dominated New York art circles of the 1950s, she later settled in France. There she continued for nearly four decades to produce a remarkable body of work that redefined abstraction with its unparalleled beauty, strength, and emotional intensity. Mitchell's independent sensibility makes her a riveting subject today. Yet during her own lifetime this great artist often found herself pushing against the constraints of her gender and social status, never receiving the recognition that came more easily to her male peers.

The Baltimore Museum of Art (BMA) and the San Francisco Museum of Modern Art (SFMOMA) are pleased to present this unprecedented reconsideration of Mitchell's art and its significance to postwar painting on both sides of the Atlantic. At the BMA, this exhibition was conceived as part of *2020 Vision,* an initiative encompassing exhibitions, acquisitions, and public programs that recognizes a range of extraordinarily talented female-identifying artists. Coinciding with the centennial of the passage of the Nineteenth Amendment, a landmark in the history of the struggle for women's rights in the United States, *2020 Vision* extends the museum's ongoing transformation, which seeks equity, diversity, and social justice in every facet of its existence, from exhibitions and programs to our board and staffing. At SFMOMA, *Joan Mitchell* is the latest in a run of significant presentations of the work of women artists, following Julie Mehretu's atrium commission HOWL, *eon* (I, II) and the monographic exhibitions *Vija Celmins: To Fix the Image in Memory* and *Suzanne Lacy: We Are Here*. This project also builds on an existing collection focus: SFMOMA's holdings include an exquisite early work on paper and five exceptional paintings, among them Mitchell's stunning multipanel work *Bracket* (1989, plate 119), which has been a keystone of the fourth-floor galleries devoted to The Doris and Donald Fisher Collection since 2016. That painting will now be part of this retrospective, the first special exhibition to be mounted in the Fisher Collection galleries since SFMOMA's post-expansion reopening.

At the heart of this undertaking are the research and scholarship of Katy Siegel, Senior Programming and Research Curator at the BMA and Eugene V. and Clare E. Thaw Endowed Chair in Modern American Art at Stony Brook University, New York; and Sarah Roberts, the Andrew W. Mellon Foundation Curator and Head of Painting and Sculpture at SFMOMA. We could not be prouder of their commitment and the remarkable exhibition and publication it has yielded. Over the years, incredibly varied understandings of Mitchell's work have developed in the U.S. and France. Grounded in more than two years of archival research and firsthand review of her paintings and drawings, *Joan Mitchell* not only considers these different perspectives on the artist but also reconciles them. The result is a more complete picture of Mitchell and the inner landscape that her extraordinary art explores. We salute Katy and Sarah, and thank them for their groundbreaking work.

An ambitious, yearslong project such as this would not have been possible without the support of a variety of institutions and individuals. Presenting support for the catalogue and the Baltimore and San Francisco presentations of the exhibition is provided by the Henry Luce Foundation. The research central to this project could not have been realized without the exceptional generosity of the Terra Foundation for American Art, which supported early curatorial travel and a critical convening of scholars in Paris, along with the exhibition's presentation in Paris. The Baltimore presentation is sponsored by Bank of America. Generous support is provided by The Alvin and Fanny B. Thalheimer Exhibition Endowment Fund and supported in part by an award from the National Endowment for the Arts. Additional support is provided by the Sigmund M. and Mary B. Hyman Fund for American Art, The Stoneridge Fund of Amy and Marc Meadows, and Komal Shah and Gaurav Garg. At SFMOMA, leadership support is provided by Helen and Charles Schwab. Major support is provided by Sanford Robinson. Generous support is provided by Richard and Mary Jo Kovacevich, the Bernard and Barbro Osher Exhibition Fund, and Komal Shah and Gaurav Garg. The Joan Mitchell Foundation generously supported both SFMOMA's production of the catalogue and exhibition research efforts at the BMA. Generous support for the publication was also provided by the Wyeth Foundation for American Art.

In an interview conducted by Yves Michaud in 1986, Mitchell observed: "Painting is a means of feeling 'living.' . . . Music takes time to listen to and ends, writing takes time and ends, movies end, ideas and even sculpture take time. Painting does not. It never ends, it is the only thing that is both continuous and still." This poetic statement hints at much of what is captivating about the experience of encountering Mitchell's work in person. But while the experience of great art can be transcendent, no exhibition is organized outside of its time. And as we navigate the unprecedented challenges posed by the COVID-19 pandemic, we are profoundly grateful to the lenders who have remained committed to making this project possible. We join the curators in heartily thanking all those named on pages 371–72, many of whom agreed to share their works with more than one venue as the exhibition traveled from Baltimore and San Francisco to Paris. At the Fondation Louis Vuitton, we thank Bernard Arnault, president; Jean-Paul Claverie, advisor to the president; Suzanne Pagé, artistic director; and Sophie Durrleman, executive director. We are also deeply grateful to the many BMA and SFMOMA staff members acknowledged on pages 373–74, whose indispensable efforts helped make this project a success, both at our own institutions and throughout the exhibition tour.

The Joan Mitchell Foundation, under the leadership of executive director Christa Blatchford, has been an outstanding partner throughout the development of this exhibition and publication, and its support and dedication have enriched this project immeasurably. Our greatest appreciation, however, is reserved for Joan Mitchell, whose indelible impact on postwar painting is only now, at last, coming into full view. The BMA and SFMOMA are proud to have been at the vanguard of bringing greater recognition to the achievements of this remarkable artist.

CHRISTOPHER BEDFORD
Dorothy Wagner Wallis Director
The Baltimore Museum of Art

NEAL BENEZRA
Helen and Charles Schwab Director
San Francisco Museum of Modern Art

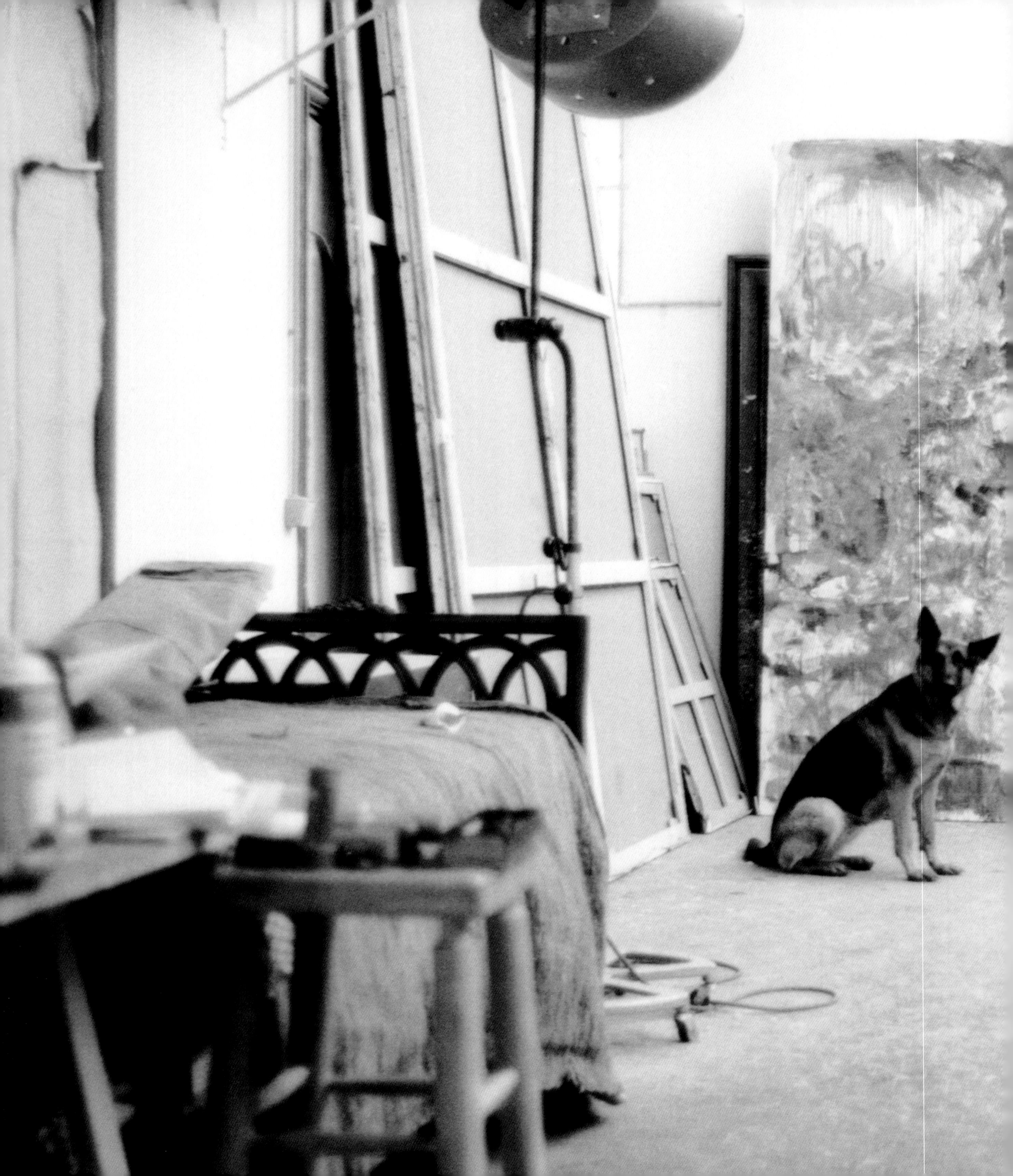

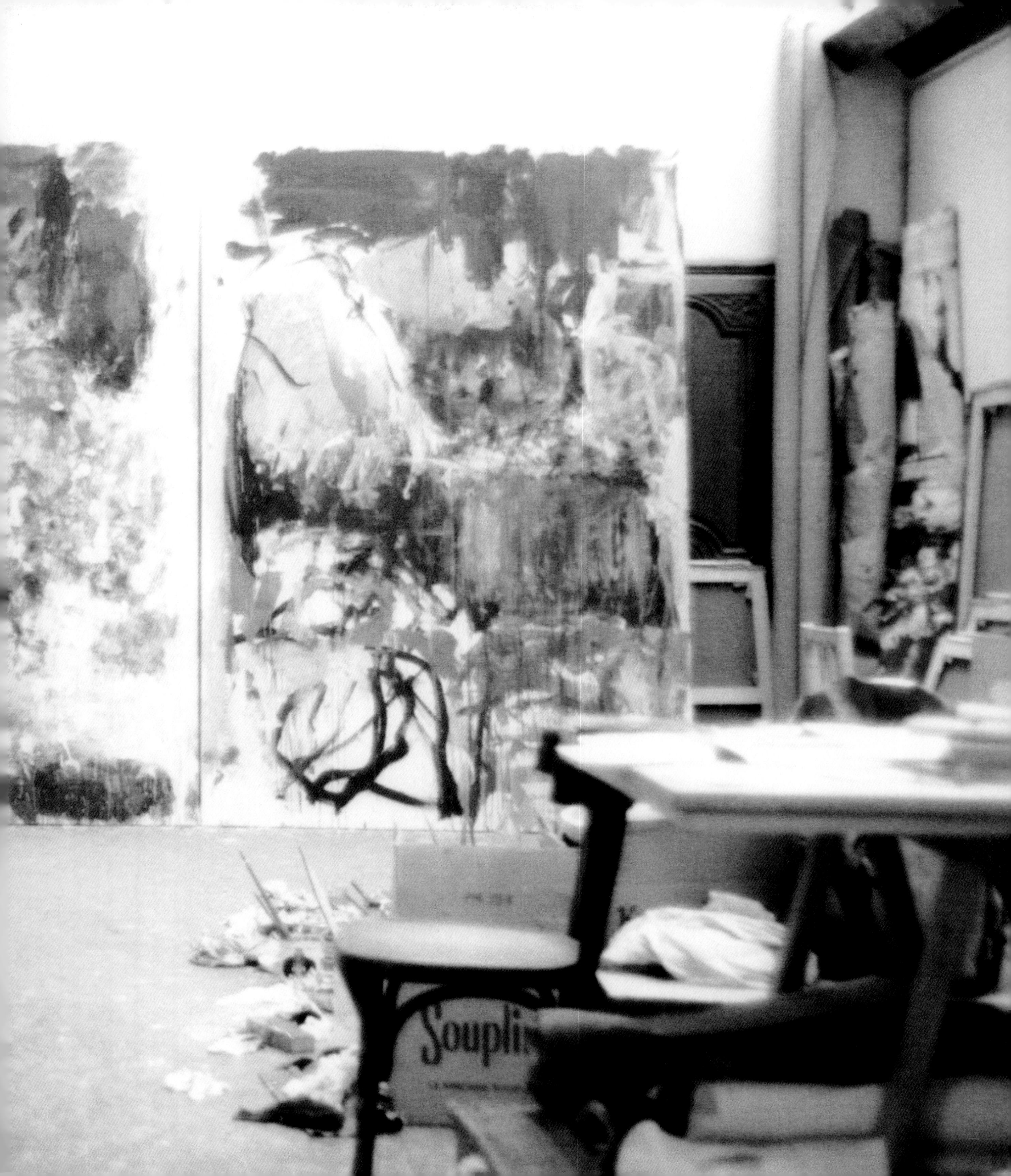

Beautiful Weed

Sarah Roberts and
Katy Siegel

History is full of women: overlooked women, difficult women, unloved women, forgotten women, unrealized women, overshadowed women.[1] With this book and the exhibition it accompanies we wanted to tell the story of a woman who, while perhaps all or many of these things, was foremost and without qualification a great artist. To see Joan Mitchell this way is to acknowledge not only the monumentality of what she accomplished but also the nature of her own desire. She never aspired to anything less than greatness—as it was understood and pursued in her historical moment (a time when such terms were rarely applied to women) and, ultimately, as she came to define it for herself.[2]

Joan Mitchell seeks to recognize what Mitchell achieved by bringing to her art the deep scholarly consideration it has always called for, the kind that has been largely reserved for a tiny number of white, male artists. Grounded in extensive archival research and an exhaustive firsthand review of Mitchell's work, this project centers on an attentiveness to her lifelong exploration of the material world as experienced from a specific view. The dance between object and subject, their meeting and parting, generated what Mitchell called "feeling." For her, a painting with feeling embodied largeness of purpose: to encounter the world with honest emotion and sensation. Mitchell recognized this impulse as the driver of a grand tradition that included Vincent van Gogh, Paul Cézanne, Claude Monet, Franz Kline, and Willem de Kooning; she both embraced that tradition and expanded its terms. Her work is difficult to categorize in that it disregarded contemporary critical pieties in favor of complexity and profundity; in throwing fresh light on Mitchell's art we also hope to offer new ways to think about postwar abstraction and its relation to representation, to nature, and to the self.

Mitchell's is not a progressive story but one of returns and stillnesses, moving in and out of sync with mainstream art history. Our primary goal is to understand her work in relation to the changing historical contexts spanned by her career, with attentiveness to the specificities of her cyclical approach to painting. More than two years of thought, research, and discussion with our exceptional research team led us to organize this book in ten chronological chapters that center on moments when Mitchell's concerns crystallize and emerge in closely related suites of canvases. Because so much of her life directly or indirectly shaped her art, we have interwoven elements of Mitchell's biography to a greater extent, perhaps, than is typical in many traditional art historical accounts, while mindful of concerns around biographical method and female artists. We wanted to deliver a more complex portrait of her as both an artist and a person—and of the imbrication of these roles—than that offered in the existing literature. Each chapter studies paintings that embody the highest achievement of a given suite but also shows Mitchell working her way into and out of ideas by picking up dropped threads, using drawing to experiment with process and representation, or emphatically disrupting an established vocabulary of marks and colors. Each chapter essay is complemented by a concise text illuminating particular works. In-depth essays by scholars Éric de Chassey, Jenni Quilter, and Richard Shiff present new historical models for understanding Mitchell's work in relationship to painting in Paris during the 1950s and 1960s; poetry; and nineteenth-century French Romanticism, respectively. And finally, texts by writer Paul Auster, composer Gisèle Barreau, poet and essayist Eileen Myles, artist Joyce Pensato, and painter David Reed in dialogue with conservator Jennifer Hickey offer artistic and literary responses to Mitchell's work.

We hoped that in treating Mitchell as the great painter she so clearly is, we would also discover something specific and possible—rather than solely limiting and exhausting—about being a woman artist. Mitchell and Simone de Beauvoir first wrestled with the question of how to live as a woman artist at almost the same moment.[3] The latter warned against narrow self-expression, rendered in descriptions of the confines of conventional female life. Mitchell's specter was not precisely the domestic but rather the triviality and stultification of the Social Register, the upper-class social circle to which her family belonged, which had constrained the writing and life of her mother, poet Marion Strobel. Politeness, sentiment, and pretension were all anathema to Mitchell, embodying the threat that she herself would fall prey to the minor mode if she did not rigorously avoid that life.

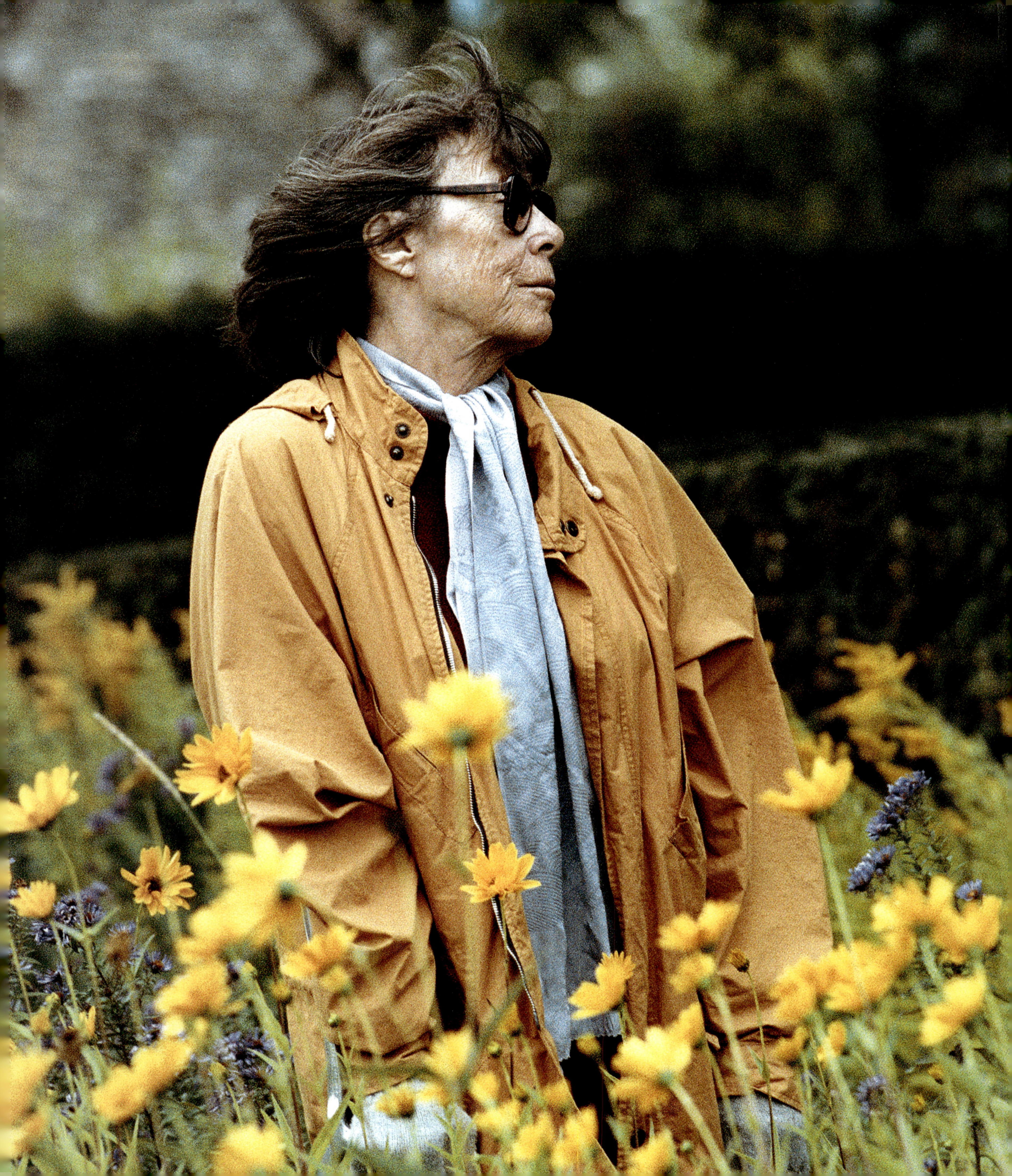

Most broadly, at the high point of postwar debates about the nature of the human, women artists were constrained by their less-than status. For Beauvoir, "As long as she still has to struggle to become a human being, she cannot become a creator."[4] If women's art lacked sweeping social relevance or "metaphysical resonances," it was because women themselves lacked the defining human quality: freedom. To be excluded from adventure and expansion was crippling:

> How could van Gogh have been born a woman? A woman would not have been sent on a mission to the Belgian coal mines in Borinage, she would not have felt the misery of the miners as her own crime, she would not have sought a redemption; she would therefore never have painted van Gogh's sunflowers. Not to mention that the mode of life of the painter—his solitude at Arles, his frequentation of cafés and brothels, all that nourished van Gogh's art in nourishing his sensitivity—would have been forbidden her.[5]

Mitchell painted sunflowers all her life; how did she manage?

Fortified by family money (no guarantee of artistic achievement) and an intense will to live and paint without constraint, Mitchell refused to accept that either cafés or solitude were forbidden to her. She traded in Smith College for the Cedar Tavern and the Café du Dôme, sought sex and passion, late nights and drinking—adventure. And she established absolute privacy in her studio on St. Mark's. Still, especially as a young woman, she spent a certain amount of energy bending herself toward and away from social expectations, accommodating and resisting. Even today, a conversation about Joan Mitchell almost always begins with stories of her behavior and misbehavior, some of it destructive and fueled by alcohol. In adulthood, Mitchell, like most women, struggled with conventional female roles—wife, mistress, hostess, homemaker, and (surrogate) mother—and with prescribed standards of beauty and femininity. Over time she cast off social conformity. She had survived, and even occasionally enjoyed the role-playing; midlife made room for intense friendships that supported new patterns for daily life, new heights of artistic ambition, and metaphysical resonance to burn.

At mid-century, Beauvoir believed that until she was recognized as human, woman could only be the other; Mitchell came to a version of this, concrete and vivid, seeing herself as a "mauvaise herbe"—a weed.[6] To her, dandelions were weeds, but so were daisies and even sunflowers—any plant, large or small, that was taken for granted or seen as unruly, out of place according to imposed classifications, or beautiful only when seen with the right eyes. She reenvisioned the negatives of the designation "weed" as positives. Mitchell often said that words failed her, leaving her to cursing and arch wordplay in her letters, to evasive actions in interviews, to the capacious ambiguities of poetry in her reading (and of poets in her friendships), and to music. Most profoundly, words failed to account for her: there was no name, no category in which she could recognize herself. As her lover Jean Paul Riopelle once teased, she was, impossibly, "un maître au feminin."[7] In the French, even the name for "feminine" here is masculine—there are no words.

Was there any drawback to being a male artist? In the 1950s and 1960s, Edrita Fried, Mitchell's Vienna-trained analyst, warned against the apparently male tendency toward narcissism, a narrowness masquerading as greatness that obscured the texture and value of real life.[8] In their work together, Fried reinforced Mitchell's drive to connect to the world, to love something "outside" herself, applauding her ability to alternately amplify and turn down the volume on her specific self. Eileen Myles argues that female reality compulsorily consumes and, therefore, is structured by but also *encompasses* male reality.[9] Might this condition open a multiplicity of perspectives not available to a man? Might a woman create works that comprehend both her own singular subjectivity and those of manifold imagined others, including those of another artist, a dog, a tree, a sunflower? Over the course of her lifetime, the scoring of traits as masculine or feminine seemed increasingly irrelevant to Mitchell. She settled into and fully inhabited a hardheadedness, angular athleticism, and single-minded dedication to painting that conflicted with traditional femininity, and she did not find any of this incommensurate with making frankly beautiful paintings or experiencing the full range of emotions, tenderness included.

The transnational nature of Mitchell's existence is yet another manifestation of her refusal to be categorized. New York and Paris have variously claimed her, fracturing her image in two: the 1950s painter vs. the 1980s painter, the belated daughter, respectively, of Abstract Expressionism or of Impressionism. In truth, she moved back and forth, on airplanes and in her mind, never losing touch with either place or moment. A wave of recent scholarly research on transatlantic cultural exchange has offered a cosmopolitan antidote to nationalism, valuing complexity over exceptionalism and the nuanced lives of individuals over the clumsy, violent projections of governments. Rather than *both,* the transatlantic condition can also mean *neither,* and suggest never feeling completely at home, as was certainly the experience of many postwar émigré and expatriate artists in New York, London, and Paris. Mitchell, who always had her blue suitcase packed, had a near-constant sense of being unsettled; like much of her generation, she felt compelled by what T. S. Eliot called the "poésie des départs."[10] And perhaps, for a woman, to be not at home had a special allure.

Mitchell's life story is compelling, both for its singular details—champion figure skater; owner of Monet's Vétheuil cottage; friend, lover, and valued interlocutor to renowned painters, writers, and composers—and because many of its pressures, including sexist gatekeepers, overbearing lovers, unwanted and absent pregnancies, and self-doubt are shared by other women. With this study we wanted to attend to how her personal experience mattered to the work, and to chart a life with art at its center—an existence that was neither desirable nor possible for all women, but was certainly the life that Mitchell pursued. The scale of her paintings, the views they imply, and the materials she used are all shaped by the places she lived and worked and the people she loved. Mitchell's greatness encompasses ambition, discipline, freedom, bodily experience, masterful technique, and heedless experiment, along with the smallest and largest natural phenomena, eternal life, and love.

1

Painter Sarah Roberts

The snow came down like stars tonight
Over the city silently.

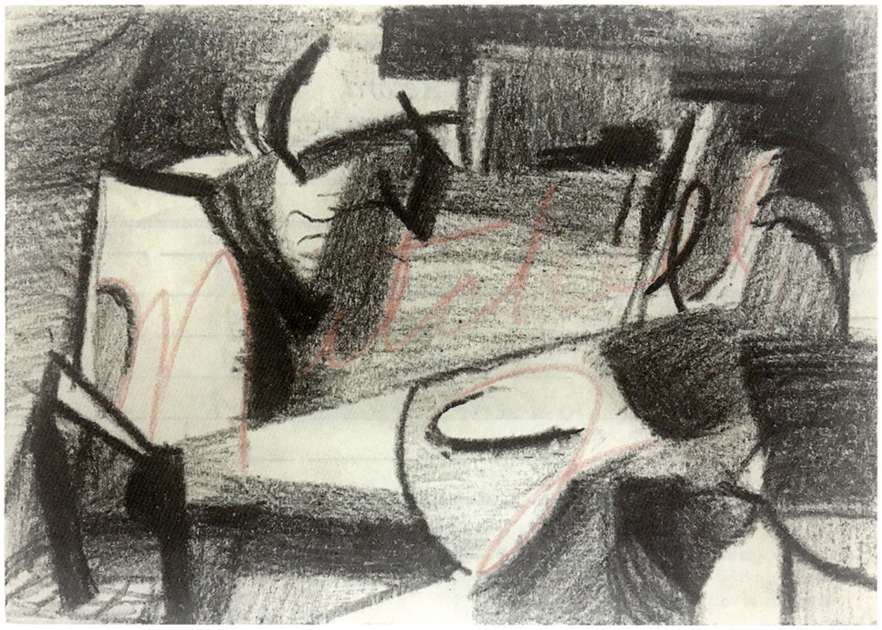

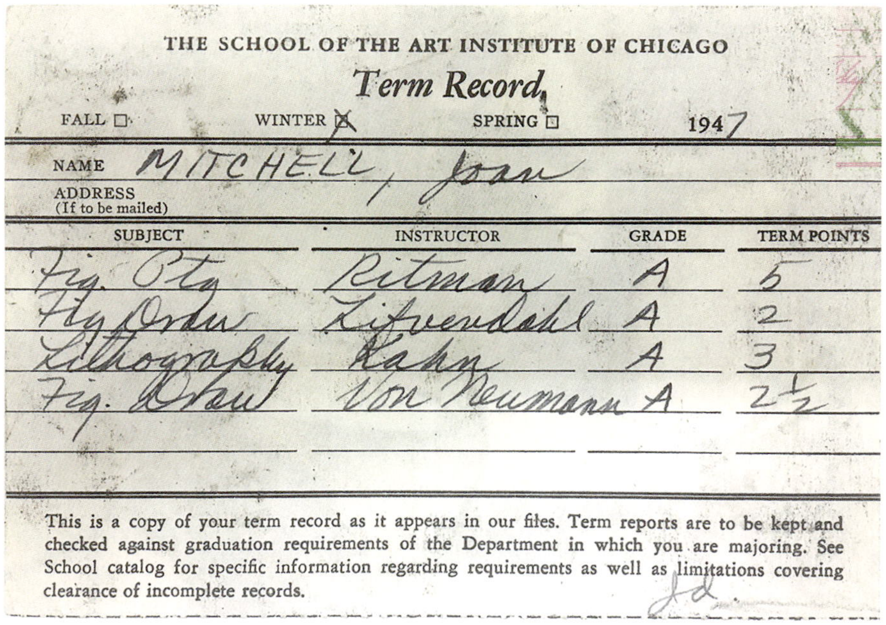

THE SCHOOL OF THE ART INSTITUTE OF CHICAGO

Term Record

FALL ☐ WINTER ☒ SPRING ☐ 1947

NAME MITCHELL, Joan

ADDRESS
(If to be mailed)

SUBJECT	INSTRUCTOR	GRADE	TERM POINTS
Fig. Ptg	Ritman	A	5
Fig Order	Lifvendahl	A	2
Lithography	Kahn	A	3
Fig. Draw	Von Neumann	A	2½

This is a copy of your term record as it appears in our files. Term reports are to be kept and checked against graduation requirements of the Department in which you are majoring. See School catalog for specific information regarding requirements as well as limitations covering clearance of incomplete records.

The air, like a great glittering tree,
Bloomed noiselessly with light. —GEORGE DILLON, "FALL OF STARS"

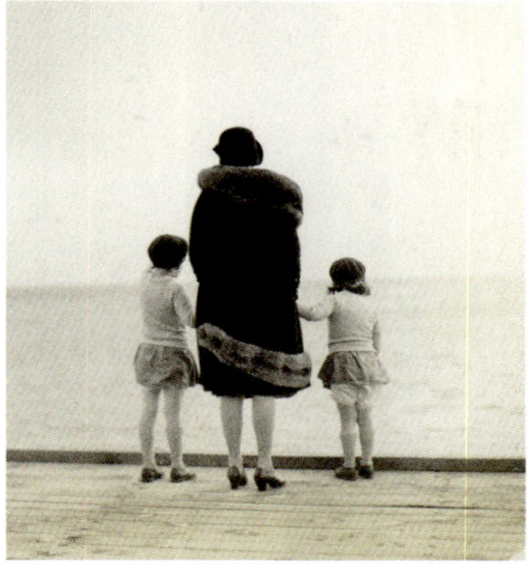

1.1

"We had wind coming down … unbroken wind. And the vast flatness. And the Lake."[1] Joan Mitchell was often mercurial in her statements about her work and life. Yet she consistently acknowledged Lake Michigan's centrality to the development of her sensibility as an artist and its role as a lifelong source for her art. "The very wild winters. I watched it all the time … at first from our early apartment where my big sister's room had the view of the Lake and I had the alley … and then, later on, when it was I who had the view."[2] The Lake. Its shifting colors, seasonal tempers, fluctuating surface, buffeting winds, and boundless expanse. A constant presence, yet endlessly mutable. And the view.

Hers was a remarkable childhood steeped in culture—reading and writing poetry, attending ballet and symphony performances, exploring the halls of the Field Museum of Natural History, and wandering through art galleries. Such pursuits were characteristic of her family's upper-class social circle, but her parents' drive to raise refined daughters and Mitchell's immersion in poetry and painting were distinctive. Her mother, Marion Strobel,[3] served as associate editor of *Poetry* magazine from 1920 to 1925; the journal's founder, Harriet Monroe, was known to young Joan and her sister, Sally, as "Aunt Harriet." The Mitchell sisters grew up in a thicket of books, with their mother reading to them frequently, poetry on every shelf, and authors including Thornton Wilder and T. S. Eliot regularly visiting the family at home. Books opened a vivid world apart from the rigid formality of her childhood, which was marked by strict schedules, dressing for dinner, and long days of silence due to her mother's partial deafness. After *Poetry* published ten-year-old Joan's poem "Autumn" in 1935, poet George Dillon sent her a note. Her reply related one of his poems to a performance by the Ballets Russes that she had recently seen and complimented his poem "Fall of Stars" for its lines "The air, like a great glittering tree, / Bloomed noiselessly with light."[4] Poems infused her daily life and became an enduring source of inspiration and, later, a stimulus to her own work.

Mitchell's early exposure to painting was no less extraordinary. Beginning with Saturday art classes at the Art Institute of Chicago in second grade, she benefited from a steady and sophisticated course of art instruction,

FRONTISPIECE
Joan Mitchell's School of the Art Institute of Chicago term record, winter 1947, with sketch on the verso. Joan Mitchell Foundation Archives, New York

FIG 1.1 Left to right: Sally Mitchell (later Perry), Marion Strobel, and Joan Mitchell looking at Lake Michigan, Chicago, ca. 1930. Courtesy Sally Perry both formal and informal. Weekend outings with her father, James Herbert Mitchell, regularly included painting watercolors together *en plein air* in parks or at the zoo, or excursions to the Art Institute to linger in the galleries. Although her family occasionally took in the more avant-garde exhibitions at the Katherine Kuh Gallery and Arts Club of Chicago on their weekend outings, they habitually returned to the venerable Art Institute. Her visits began as the last of six historic gifts from Chicago collectors arrived,[5] resulting in stunning holdings of French Impressionism and Post-Impressionism that quickly became synonymous with the museum and intimately tied to the cultural identity of Chicago itself. Asked near the end of her life how she learned about art, she replied, "I learned in Chicago, at the Art Institute. When I was young I had lessons in the basement under the halls of the museum. And in the galleries, Seurat, Cézanne, van Gogh, Lautrec, Monet... When I was a child, I thought all painting was French, because of these names."[6] She took in how each artist used color, light, and shadow to infuse landscapes, still lifes, and portraits with feeling. Possessed of an exceptional ability to absorb and retain sensory experiences—what she later referred to as her "valise" of memories—Mitchell could remember precise details of the Art Institute's collection for the rest of her life.[7] She later recalled that Vincent van Gogh was her "first passion";[8] her ardor grew from these regular visits and close looking at works like *The Poet's Garden* (1888), *The Bedroom,* and *Madame Roulin Rocking the Cradle (La berceuse)* (both 1889).[9]

When Mitchell was eleven years old, her father compelled her to choose between writing poetry and painting rather than risk mediocrity at both. "So I decided, painting."[10] Having declared herself and shown aptitude, she began studying art at an advanced level, enrolling in summer courses for adults and taking advantage of the flexible high school curriculum at the Francis Parker School to focus on art. There, her charismatic art instructor, Malcolm Hackett, took a lax approach to teaching, but encouraged experimentation and introduced students to Pablo Picasso, Georges Braque, Joan Miró, and German Expressionism.[11] Mitchell reflected, "I was crazy about Hackett. He wasn't much of a painter. But he was talking about Kokoschka in 1939."[12] Hackett impressed her with his declaration that "to become an artist you had to go through poverty and passion,"[13] and with his sharp disregard for the snug social conventions of the school's families. He instilled in Mitchell an awareness of and unease with the inherent tension between the comforts and privileges of her own upbringing and his Romantic model artist, who must find individual truth through poverty and travail. Mitchell's mother inherited money from her father, a successful engineer who notably built a number of bridges in the Midwest, while Mitchell's father had a lucrative practice as a dermatologist. Both valued and cultivated their family's position on the Social Register of Chicago, but Mitchell bridled at the expectation that she would keep to their path. She would later say of Hackett's influence, "Well, partly because of him but partly just because of the way I was, I turned my back against all the dancing school business."[14] The friction between her family background and expectations for what it meant to be an artist persisted, driving Mitchell's rebelliousness in young adulthood and lingering in her self-conception and descriptions of her life to its end.

Mitchell's parents pushed her and her sister to excel in multiple endeavors. She contended in (and frequently won) diving, swimming, tennis, and equestrian events before specializing in ice-skating. Her high school years were split between painting and successfully competing as a figure skater at the regional and national level.[15] Though she chafed at an early review that related her brushwork to the slicing movement of figure skating, later in life Mitchell acknowledged that the movement of one's body in any sport becomes part of one's physical coordination.[16] In addition to the athleticism of skating, the sport required of Mitchell an intense commitment of time, physical and mental focus, and perseverance, and fostered a particular kinetic and spatial awareness of her body in motion, all in the same period that she was learning to paint. The physicality of the sport shaped Mitchell's musculature and spatial sensibility; those elements—combined with her own innate, electric wiriness, visible in films of her throughout her life—surely affected the sweep of her arm and the specific nature of the energy she brought to bear on the surface of every canvas.

Around the time that she graduated from Francis Parker in spring 1942, Mitchell turned away from skating, both to escape her father's insufferable overinvestment in her athletic achievement and to focus on painting. Her father had been vocal since her birth about his disappointment that Mitchell had not been a boy, not an uncommon behavior among men of his generation and social class, but it impacted her sense of self, nonetheless. His driving her toward athletic prowess was colored by this sexism, leaving her with the unshakable sense that, as a woman, she would never measure up. Her choice of painting also collided with gender and class conventions. Though her parents had celebrated her precocity[17] and pushed her to specialize, a bohemian artist's life was not what Mitchell's mother had in mind for her well-bred daughter: "As I began to really commit myself to painting and to becoming an artist, mother became very worried and said, 'Oh Joanie, you're going off the deep end.' 'Joanie, you're so neurotic and high strung.'"[18]

FIG 1.2 **Joan Mitchell**
Untitled, ca. 1943. Watercolor, opaque watercolor, and graphite on paper, 14⅝ × 21⅞ in. (37.2 × 55.6 cm). Joan Mitchell Foundation Archives, New York

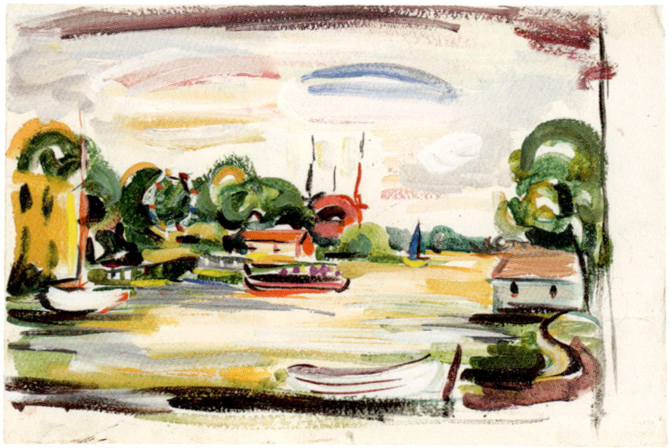

1.2

Her parents continued to control her path, insisting she attend Smith College over her first choice, Bennington College, which her father did not find academically rigorous enough.[19] Smith proved to be a culture shock—an odd atmosphere that, at that time, mixed high-society values with the omnipresence of the war and daily tragedy as classmates received news of casualties among friends and family. She loved her studies and made several lifelong friends, including Joanne Von Blon, but felt out of place and miserable in the larger college community. Although she took art classes at Smith, her 1943 and 1944 courses at Ox-Bow, the Art Institute's summer school of painting in Saugatuck, on the eastern shore of Lake Michigan, had far greater impact. "I couldn't wait to get up to paint.... It was heavenly, I mean, really, I never felt like that, before or since.... In the morning we painted the nude outside, which is a very strange experience, you know. Oh fantastic and the afternoon, landscape, whatever you wanted to do.... [I]t was just beautiful. It was romantic, it was everything."[20] Away from the stifling silence and formality of her parents' apartment and the social demands of Smith, Mitchell found a release in the natural beauty, freedoms, and friendships of Ox-Bow (see page 28, no. 3). Above all, the school gave Mitchell the opportunity to dedicate herself fully to painting for the first time.

Works from her time at Ox-Bow reveal Mitchell's emerging adventurous sense of color and an expressive approach to landscape; both are remarkably sophisticated for a teen artist. The distinctive red facade of the historic Saugatuck Dance Pavilion (now destroyed) appears in an untitled watercolor (fig. 1.2). Mitchell elongated its twin spires (rather squat in reality) with thin lines like exclamation points stretching into a sky stroked

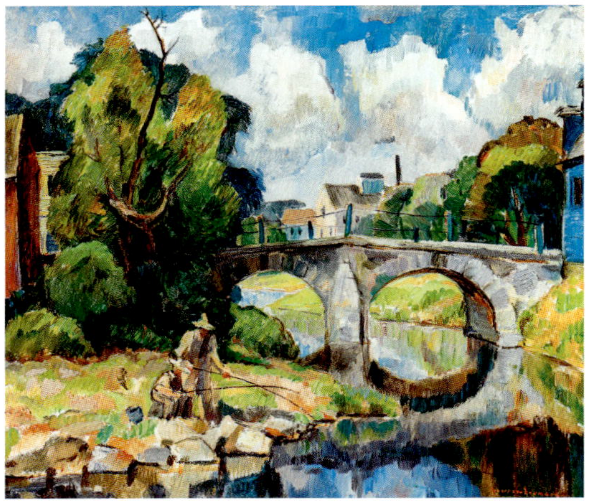

1.3

with blues, pinks, ochers, grays, and even a deep burgundy, bold uses of color and brush possibly informed by her hours spent looking at van Gogh, Pierre-Auguste Renoir, and Claude Monet. Near the center of the sheet, a risky combination of vivid violet and lemon-yellow staccato strokes represent figures in a boat. This cluster of contrasting color both animates and anchors the composition, a delicate balance of opposing purposes that Mitchell would perfect in later work.

The Ox-Bow experience convinced her that she was wasting her time at Smith, so she withdrew and enrolled in fall 1944 at the School of the Art Institute of Chicago (SAIC). Like every SAIC student, Mitchell began with foundation courses in composition, art history, and drawing and painting from the figure and plaster casts—the legacy of the school's long history as a classical Beaux-Arts academy. After the first year, she settled into a steady schedule dedicated to figure drawing and painting. Of the environment, she later stated, "The Art Institute was largely French and Art, with a Capital-A was French."[21] Her primary instructors, Louis Ritman (1889–1963) and Robert Von Neumann (1888–1976), both painted landscapes in styles rooted in nineteenth-century French art (fig. 1.3),[22] and many weekly lessons were taught in the galleries among the French paintings Mitchell already knew so well. Her surviving paintings from this period show a student hard at work learning to articulate the volumes of the human figure convincingly in space. But they also demonstrate her careful examination of historical precedents, thinking her way through them with her brush. Shades of other artists flickered in and out as she tried on and digested techniques and ways of seeing—a face rendered with the solidity and heavy round eyes of a Picasso; bare arms and legs delicately layered with color echoing Renoir; a still life placed in front of an open window pulsing with Henri Matisse's contrasting hues.

FIG 1.3 **Robert Von Neumann** *Menomonee Falls, Wisconsin,* ca. 1940. Oil on canvas, 24 × 28 in. (61 × 71.1 cm). Courtesy White Crow Fine Paintings, Milwaukee

Against this backdrop of historical French painting, Mitchell also keenly felt the impact of World War II, with high school friends going off to fight and the conflicting politics of her family, teachers, and classmates leading to heated conversations at school and at home. A stream-of-consciousness letter sent to her Smith friend Martha Bertolette early in her SAIC years lays bare the extent of Mitchell's struggle with the discordant priorities, politics, and philosophies of art churning around her:

> What are the Surrealists mirroring—that's important or constructive except to themselves—or the cold abstractionists—except to that sterile world of pure form.... Where is it all getting us until you look at a Renoir and then it seems to be everything, or you go to a concert and music becomes the reality—not the war—at times I see the old communist outlook—bring art to the people & other times I fear them ... they seem in their very positivism to leave no room for that reality which is music or just the sun coming through a window.[23]

Wrestling with abstraction, Renoir, and communism, she insists on making space for the "reality" of musical and visual pleasures. Such sensory realities and her memories of them are the foundation of what she later referred to as "feeling," which would become a central element of her approach to abstraction.

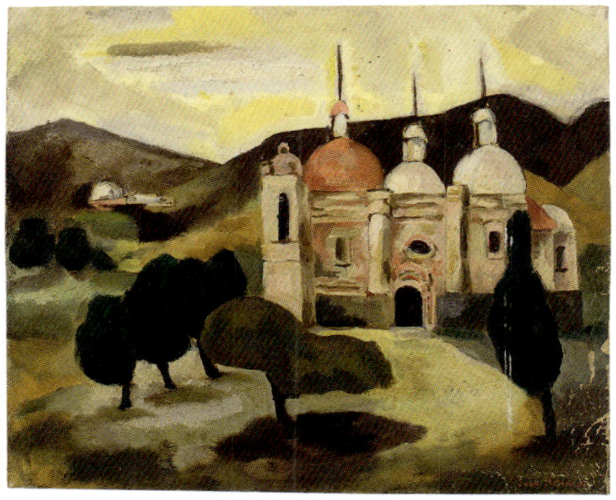

1.4

FIG 1.4 **Joan Mitchell**
Untitled, ca. 1945. Oil on canvas, 24 × 30⅛ in. (61 × 76.5 cm). Joan Mitchell Foundation, New York

Mitchell took two extended trips with her Ox-Bow friend Zuka Booyakovitsch (later Mitelberg, who painted under the name Zuka) to Guanajuato, Mexico, in the summers of 1945 and 1946, a choice that disconcerted her parents because they thought it unsafe. During the war, many of Mitchell's teachers at Ox-Bow and SAIC had spent time in Mexico, including Richard (Dick) Bowman, a young instructor she began dating shortly after his return from Mexico in 1944, who urged her to go. Between her Smith College experiences and spending time with Bowman, a Trotskyist, Mitchell developed an interest in and began attending meetings of communist student organizations, eventually becoming a "begrudging communist" herself.[24] However, her attention to politics did not run deep (and never would). Her fleeting involvement with communism was in keeping with the attraction the ideology held for many well-educated, left-leaning young people in the late 1930s and early 1940s.[25] Tellingly, and indicative of her family's station, she met leftist artists in Mexico not through political channels, but via a formal letter of introduction to Diego Rivera and José Clemente Orozco written by Daniel Catton Rich, the director of the Art Institute, at the request of her mother.[26]

Although Mitchell and Zuka did briefly meet Orozco and David Siqueiros, the real benefit of the trip was the chance to paint without interruption, away from the intervention of instructors. Zuka later noted, "Joan always worked. In Mexico, the minute there was light, we were painting."[27] They generally painted in their room to avoid the clamor of the street; Mitchell's Mexican scenes were painted from views out their windows or from memory. Two canvases depicting the distinctive Iglesia San Diego demonstrate the extent to which she began mixing observed landscapes with imagined ones. In the first untitled view (ca. 1946), the bell tower and tallest dome fill the upper-left quadrant, with the angled building facade across the street framing a narrow roadway between the structures. Mitchell elided and simplified details but remained relatively faithful to the actual cityscape. The second view depicts the urban church, with its identifiable triple domes, set in an enveloping green landscape that was entirely imagined (fig. 1.4). Mitchell eliminated all the surrounding buildings and selected a palette of

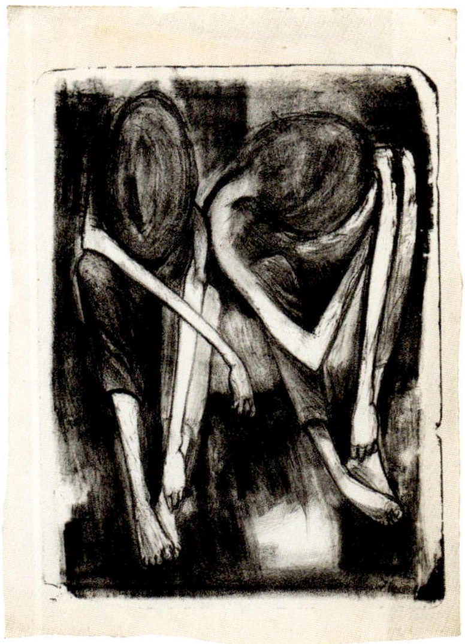

1.5

FIG 1.5 **Joan Mitchell**
Tired Children, ca. 1947. Lithograph, 27¾ × 20 in. (70.5 × 50.8 cm). Joan Mitchell Foundation Archives, New York

simmering ocher and rich umbers and greens, enlivened with touches of salmon. The effect is a serene pastoral scene that feels somber yet suggestive of heavy summer air—an early attempt to imbue a landscape with feeling rather than depict its reality.

On her return to Chicago in 1947, Mitchell won a printmaking prize for her lithograph *Tired Children* (fig. 1.5), which was based on a painting done in Mexico.[28] Free to paint figures of her own creation rather than models in classroom poses, she gravitated to animated and even dramatic postures like those of the curled waifs in *Tired Children*. An *Art News* reviewer described the prize-winning print as "in the Kollwitz tradition," a reference that likely pleased Mitchell. Käthe Kollwitz's death in 1945 was marked by articles in the art journals that Mitchell regularly read, as well as a February 1947 exhibition at the Renaissance Society in Chicago, which she likely saw.[29] Multiple references to Kollwitz pop up in Mitchell's 1947–48 letters to Barney Rosset, another former Francis Parker student whom she began dating in early 1946 and would later marry: "Right now I'd draw you a picture only I'm thinking it was mean of God not to let me draw like Kollwitz so I just won't draw at all."[30] Mitchell's interest ran parallel to broader public enthusiasm at the time for Kollwitz's work, which was seen as emblematic of individual suffering and endurance under political tyranny. Still, the emotional pull of Kollwitz's sensitive drawing clearly impacted and attracted Mitchell, perhaps because it departed so sharply from the staid realism that prevailed at SAIC.

Rosset had joined her briefly in Mexico in the summer of 1946, and their relationship accelerated back in Chicago as she completed her degree. Rosset moved to New York in January 1947, and after visiting him over her spring break, Mitchell poured a swirl of multisensory memories and physical longing into a letter: "It's all squashed together—the little boat—the tremendous curve of the bridge and you—semi yellow against the blue walls making eggs—naked and with big slippers—the night noises—the bus—the fog horns & train whistles, and always so damn warm against me in the little white room was Barney."[31] The language points to a full physical and psychological experience of the urban environment—visual, tactile, auditory, and vividly remembered. Determined to return to Rosset, Mitchell finished her classes in June 1947 and collected one of the school's coveted and highly competitive travel fellowships. While waiting for conditions to improve in postwar France, her ultimate fellowship destination, she moved to Brooklyn, eager to immerse herself in the New York landscape.

Mitchell certainly was aware of the art world in New York, and had been urged by her teachers to spend time there, but her initial contacts were tentative, the efforts of a student exploring a city rather than those of an artist seeking peers.[32] She visited the Fifty-Seventh Street galleries, later recalling exhibitions of works by Arshile Gorky at Julien Levy Gallery, Roberto Matta at Pierre Matisse Gallery, and Jackson Pollock at Art of This Century.[33] At her teacher Von Neumann's suggestion, she tested the waters at Hans Hofmann's studio but lasted just one or two classes, leaving intimidated and stupefied by his teaching methods. Instead, her education in New York came through extended time spent looking—looking at art, looking at the streets, looking at the rivers, skyscrapers, and bridges.

Life was centered in Mitchell and Rosset's intimate apartment, with the Brooklyn Bridge angling toward Manhattan just outside their window (see page 28, no. 4). The bridge dominated her view and, like Lake Michigan, became a full-time occupant of her imagination that seeped into her work even when she was not drawing or painting the bridge itself (as discussed by Karli Wurzelbacher on pages 26–27). Some two dozen photos that Rosset took of paintings made in that year show Mitchell working in a semiabstract style variably informed by Surrealism, Cubism, and Futurism, and tackling figures, still lifes, and landscapes studded with buildings and bridge forms.[34] Three years later, Rosset sketched ideas for a novel based on their time in Brooklyn: "Painting the bridge can be used as a symbol. She is trying to bridge the gap between wanting to be a painter and being a painter."[35]

Moving from wanting to being a painter meant spending time in Paris. Mitchell finally sailed in July 1948, following generations of U.S. artists who sought direct contact with the grand history of French painting as well as with its living masters—in this era, Matisse and Picasso. Reality did not meet her expectations. Six months into her Paris stay, she wrote her Smith College friend Von Blon:

> France has sort of disappointed me. I guess I was just a little romantic. I'm not even sure what I expected but I don't like it or the French much—yes beautiful & old but no guts—sort of sold out & living on a 1900 reputation & a frightening nationalism—(yes I suppose understandable in view of the Marshall plan). In Paris I live in the Latin quarter like I'm supposed to, Notre Dame out my window, rats in my corridor & cold water & a standup john on the stairs & a coal stove (looks like a Braque) . . . what can I say except that I prefer the East River & the Brooklyn Bridge.[36]

FIG 1.6 Joan Mitchell and Barney Rosset in Mitchell's studio and apartment at 73 rue Galande, Paris, 1948. Joan Mitchell Foundation Archives, New York. The stove is visible on the left.

In spite of her disappointment, she consoled herself with her view of Notre Dame (see page 29, no. 5) and by socializing with a small circle of fellow Americans, some of whom lived nearby, like Zuka, and others who just passed through, including Philip Guston. In the studio, she continued largely as she had in New York, painting steadily and showing her work to almost no one.

In December 1948, Mitchell wrote her mother that she had painted eighteen paintings, several of them focused on the Braque-like stove,[37] which also appears in photographs of her rue Galande studio (fig. 1.6). Although she claimed to have "avoided like the plague" any influence of Picasso,[38] like so many artists in the 1940s (Gorky, Pollock, Robert Motherwell, Lee Krasner), Mitchell clearly grappled with Picasso and elements of Cubism as she experimented with ways of thinking about space in a painting. In an untitled painting of her stove (1948, plate 4) and two related sketches (see plate 2), she employs differing means of opening up the forms of the stove and nearby coal bin, lantern, table, and chair, relaxing their volumes and planes and melding them with the space around them. Lines originating in concrete facts—the window frame or furniture parts—extend beyond their real bounds, lacing together the composition and

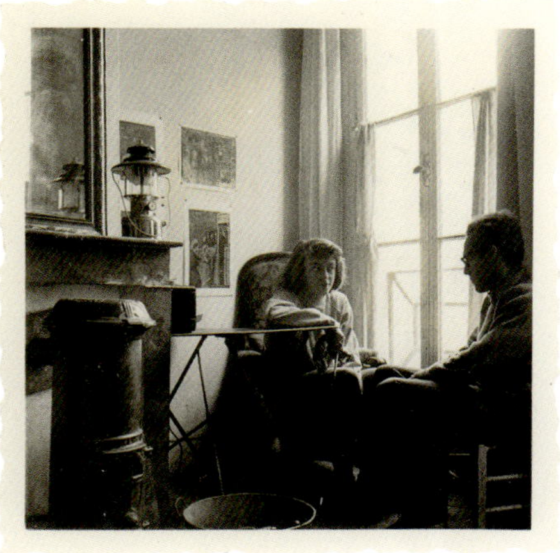

1.6

breaking down distinctions between foreground, middle ground, and background. She would later more freely acknowledge the connection to Cubism, describing her paintings from France as "moving Cubistically, whatever you would call it, into abstraction. Sort of cubed-up landscapes, things like that."[39]

Rosset visited Mitchell for a month in the summer of 1948 and then returned in November. After several weeks of travel around Europe, they escaped the harsh Paris cold, moving to the village of Le Lavandou on the Mediterranean for Mitchell's remaining nine months overseas. "The south—Arles looks just like van Gogh & Aix like Cézanne & this place like nobody—I'm on the sea—yellow mimosa blooming & fisherman & nets & colored boats—my house has 11 rooms & I eat lunch on the terrace in the sun & I paint all day & it's like no place—no country."[40] The colorful landscape she knew so well through paintings at the Art Institute now filled the view from her window. Yet Mitchell's paintings remained largely internally focused, as she intuitively pushed the formal dynamics already at play in her work, rather than moving in any new direction as a result of her surroundings. The only noticeable shift between her Paris and Le Lavandou works came in her palette, which turned toward a particular combination of purples, yellows, and blue-greens.[41] Rosset described the urgency with which Mitchell painted at Le Lavandou and her drive to contend with formal problems in this period:

> I was trying to force her to be more political, socialist realist. Then I began to understand that I didn't understand what she was doing. She was very powerful, believe me. And she couldn't stop herself. She could not stop.... I became aware of the importance of space in the paintings ... of the difference of trying to make the background come up to the foreground. Problems like that which became much more important to her than any message.[42]

As she had in Paris (and Brooklyn and Mexico before that), Mitchell painted what she saw out her window or remembered from her local explorations—the fishermen and their nets, games of boules, an unforgettable passing of cyclists in the Tour de France.[43] She abstracted from, but stayed close to, observed realities. She did not radically distort forms or figures, nor did she portray them from multiple vantage points. Instead, she stripped her figures and objects of specific features, pared them to physical and, increasingly, psychological essences, and sank them into webs of lines and planes, developing a complex spatial sensibility that would carry on and structure her work for the rest of her life. *The View from Window* (fig. 1.7), one of very few representations of a purely natural landscape from this period, shows the coast and surrounding hills of Le Lavandou as seen from their terrace (see page 29, no. 7), rendered as a complex spread of interlocking shapes in dusky teal, green, and umber. The town's two distinctive promontories jut left into a blue-green sea; the water is indicated with a sideways zigzag stroke, Mitchell's shorthand for movement and reflection that would later become a frequent motif. Though somewhat ungainly, the effort here seems less about formal decisions and more about capturing a specific sensory experience of a particular view, distance, moment, and cooling light—an endeavor that would soon define her approach to painting.

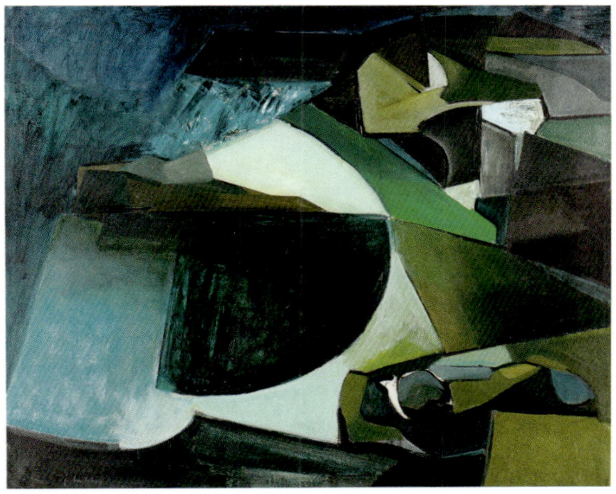

1.7

FIG 1.7 **Joan Mitchell**
The View from Window, 1949. Oil on canvas, 28½ × 36¼ in. (72.4 × 92.1 cm). Private collection

Mitchell would later describe 1948–49 as "a bad period" when she "painted terribly,"[44] perhaps reflecting the fact that the work from Brooklyn, Paris, and Le Lavandou circles the same set of problems without arriving at a fully satisfying solution. Newly married, Mitchell and Rosset left France for New York in September 1949, feeling she needed both a change of environment and more contact with like-minded artists in order to move forward. Initially, she continued to puzzle through the same, but increasingly conflicting, impulses—to work from observed reality, to develop a complex spatial composition, and to inject a painting with feeling. The gentle geometries of the Paris stove painting and undulating planes of *The View from Window* shattered into smaller mosaic-like shapes in paintings made shortly after her return, like *Figure and the City* (1949–50, plate 5). In the latter, an inward-looking female form is fully merged with her surroundings, her curved body and hanging head representing an expressive note more than a person. Soon, Mitchell would finally make the turn from abstracting reality to creating abstraction.

Sketchbook drawings, ca. 1948

Karli Wurzelbacher

Sketchbook drawings from this period are illustrated as plates 1–3.

FIG 1.8 **Joan Mitchell**
Sketchbook, ca. 1948. Pages 88 and 89 of 182. Graphite on machine-made wove paper, open: 10¼ x 15¾ in. (26 × 40 cm). Joan Mitchell Foundation Archives, New York

FIG 1.9 **Joan Mitchell**
Sketchbook, ca. 1948. Pages 84 and 85 of 182. Graphite on machine-made wove paper, open: 10¼ x 15¾ in. (26 × 40 cm). Joan Mitchell Foundation Archives, New York

Looking out the windows of her second-floor apartment and studio at 1 Fulton Street in Brooklyn, Mitchell could follow the sweep of the Brooklyn Bridge stretching over the East River to Manhattan (see page 28, no. 4). In a sketchbook that she began in 1947 or 1948, she used a graphite pencil to trace the bridge's "tremendous curve" in two dozen drawings that explore varying approaches to abstraction.[1] One example from the middle of the book shows the bridge through the frame of a window (fig. 1.8). A second transforms the iconic landmark into an airy network of verticals, arcs, webs, and shaded shapes (fig. 1.9). Mitchell had grown up in Chicago overlooking rooftops and a lake vista that expanded to the horizon, but it was in Brooklyn, with the lattice of the bridge filtering her impressions of the sky, that the artist first translated the view outside her window into abstract drawings and paintings.

Just steps from the river, the apartment allowed Mitchell and Barney Rosset, with whom she shared it for about a year, to enjoy watching the bridge and Manhattan's downtown skyline in changing light and weather. The area bustled with workers and traffic from nearby shipyards, warehouses, and factories, and the waterway teemed with boats. Mitchell dedicated her days to painting and sketching. In the evenings, the couple went for drives across the city's bridges; months later, in Paris, the artist would recall "the space & blueness & lights."[2] Like Mitchell, Rosset was enthralled with the Brooklyn Bridge, as both an architectural form and a symbol. He often photographed the structure and even tried his hand at painting it. The two also collaborated on an unrealized filmscript, drafts of which survive in Mitchell's sketchbooks. One scene directs the protagonist, an artist, to sink down at the water's edge "staring in wonder & relaxation at bridge forms abstract against sky."[3]

Mitchell's sketchbook drawing of the Brooklyn Bridge seen through a window speaks to her interest in working from the view immediately before her. With a few quick strokes, she situated herself within a spare, shallow interior anchored by the outline of a table. The planes of the tabletop and the window frame interlock and recede into a darkened landscape. Lines at the top of the paper suggest blinds. Mitchell has distilled the bridge into the upright rectangle of the westernmost tower, the shadowed underside of the arcing roadway, and the corresponding slope of the suspension cables. Rather than indicate skyscrapers or the river, she penciled in low-rise buildings. The juxtaposition of interior and exterior that Mitchell achieved in this composition of a table before a window is as true to her daily experience as it is an engagement with a classic art historical convention.

In the more abstract drawing, Mitchell's view dissolves into elemental shapes that tumble across the space of the page. Her shorthand for the bridge—an angle created by the intersection of a straight line and a curve—repeats throughout. Slender peaked forms evoke the bridge's Gothic arches and skyscrapers in profile, while the parallel marks at the bottom right may be patterned after wooden pilings. The high horizon and tessellated space of the drawing also distinguish Mitchell's canvases of the period (see plate 4). In paintings of the bridge, however, she filled every facet with color, differentiating flat areas of blue and green water from intense pink or yellow skies. The sketchbook drawings served as intermediaries between the artist's direct observation of the view and some of the earliest abstract paintings she created.

Mitchell used her early sketchbooks sporadically, over months or years, flipping to blank sheets at random. The volume in which bridge views predominate features other imagery executed in an array of styles: portraits and figure studies are interspersed with drawings of the human body dissected into shards and heavily cross-hatched; recognizable still lifes and city scenes follow compositions with no discernible subject. Mitchell also covered pages of the sketchbook in French vocabulary exercises and jotted addresses, including those for Stanley William Hayter's printmaking studio, Atelier 17, and galleries on Fifty-Seventh Street. In July 1948, she carried the multipurpose book with her to France, where she made studies related to paintings, including *Bicycle Race, Tour de France* (1949) and *Billiards* (1949). The heterogeneous, nonlinear nature of the sketchbook's contents attests to the young artist's rapid development and to her efforts to challenge herself through experimentation, as well as through exposure to new experiences and to the latest art.

Once in Paris, Mitchell looked in vain for landscapes as compelling and complex as her view of the Brooklyn Bridge from 1 Fulton Street. Writing to Rosset from her rue Galande studio, she bemoaned "this view I know by heart & have no desire to see anyway."[4] That summer and fall she returned to painting interiors and figures, and she drove more than four hundred miles (644 kilometers) south to Avignon, in part to draw its bridges. Missing the Brooklyn Bridge, she dreamed about it.[5] Her ca. 1948 sketchbook drawings show that her initial abstractions of her view in Brooklyn were based on a visible external referent, yet her longing for New York while in Paris may represent a turning point in her growing conception of abstraction as feeling, memory, and multisensory experience. Not until 1968, when Mitchell moved to Vétheuil, France, would she again enjoy a home and studio with a powerful and generative landscape view, one that would sustain her painting for decades.

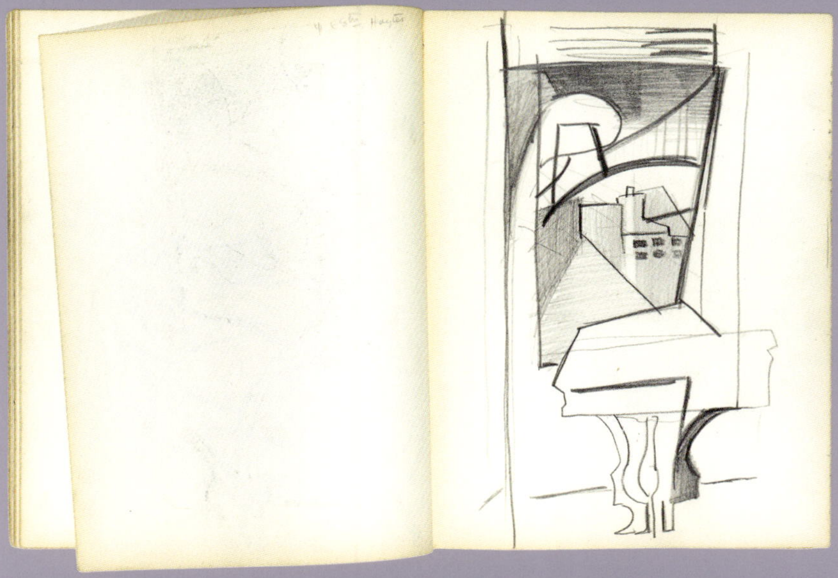

1.8

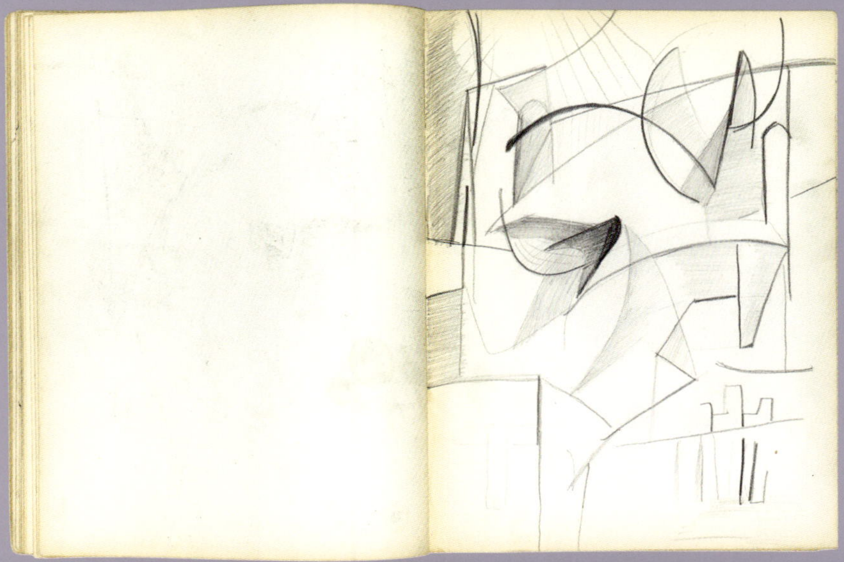

1.9

VIEWS 1925–49

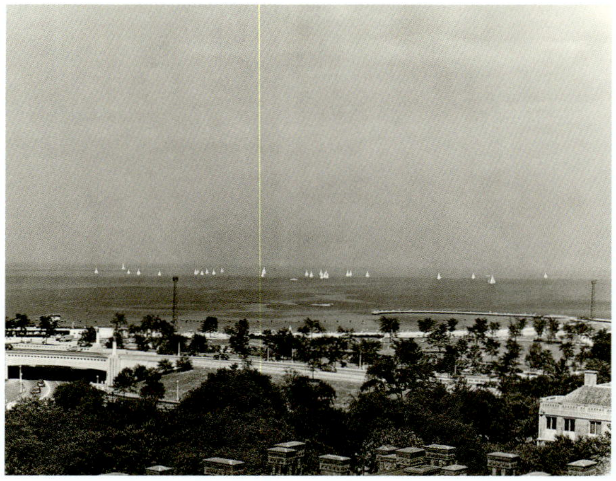

1

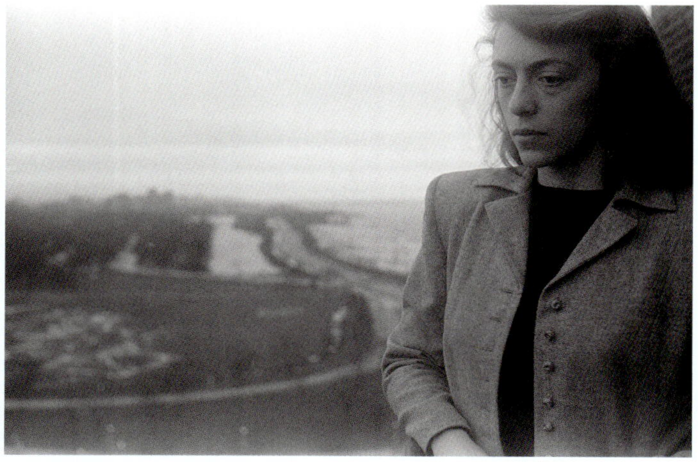

2

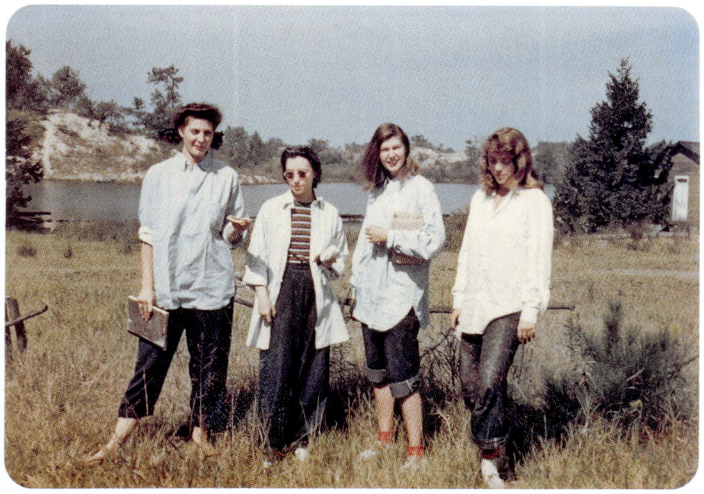

3

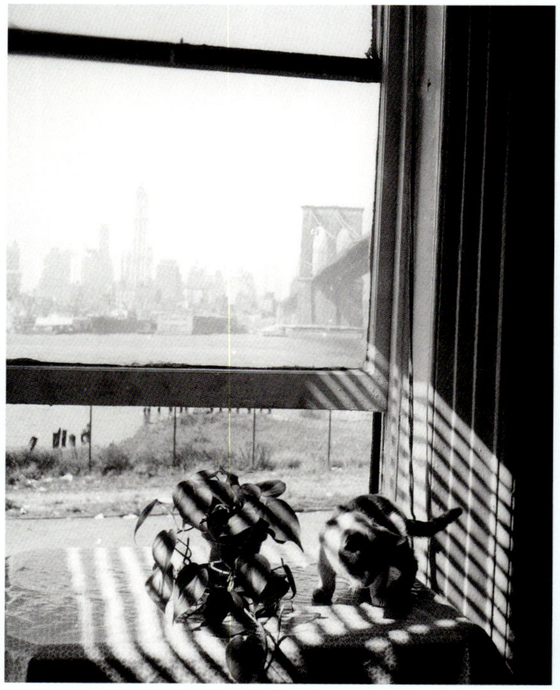

4

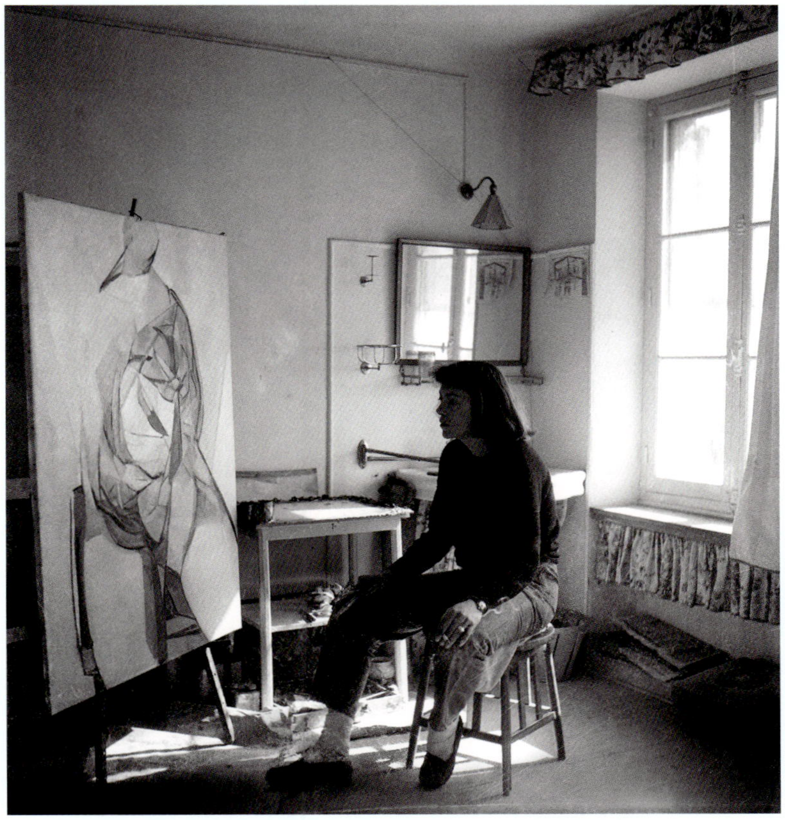

6

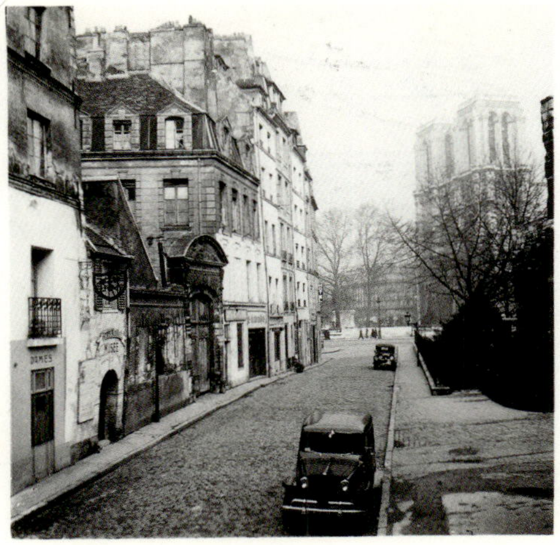

5

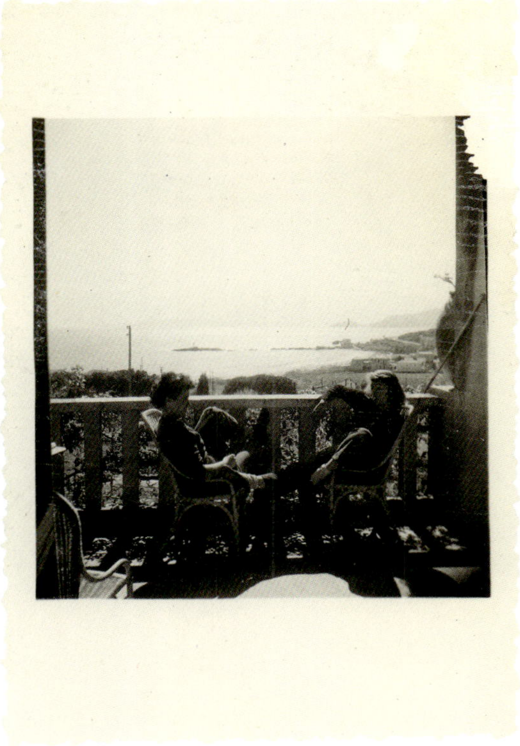

7

1 View of Lake Michigan from the Mitchell family's apartment at 1530 North State Parkway, Chicago, n.d. Courtesy Sally Perry

2 Joan Mitchell on the balcony of her childhood residence at 1530 North State Parkway, Chicago, ca. 1946. Joan Mitchell Foundation Archives, New York. Photograph by Barney Rosset

3 Zuka Booyakovitsch and Joan Mitchell (far right) with unidentified fellow students at Ox-Bow School of Art, Saugatuck, Michigan, ca. 1943. Courtesy Sally Perry

4 View of Brooklyn Bridge from Joan Mitchell and Barney Rosset's apartment at 1 Fulton Street, New York, ca. 1947. Joan Mitchell Foundation Archives, New York. Photograph by Barney Rosset

5 View of Notre Dame Cathedral from Joan Mitchell's studio and apartment at 73 rue Galande, Paris, 1948. Joan Mitchell Foundation Archives, New York. Photograph by Barney Rosset

6 Joan Mitchell at Villa Le Pin, 21 avenue Van Rysselberghe, Le Lavandou, France, ca. 1949. Joan Mitchell Foundation Archives, New York. Photograph by Barney Rosset

7 Joan Mitchell and an unidentified person overlooking Plage Crique Saint Clair in Le Lavandou, France, ca. 1949. Joan Mitchell Foundation Archives, New York

2
St. Mark's Katy Siegel

So speak to me of love
In words so tender
Let the rhapsody of life begin

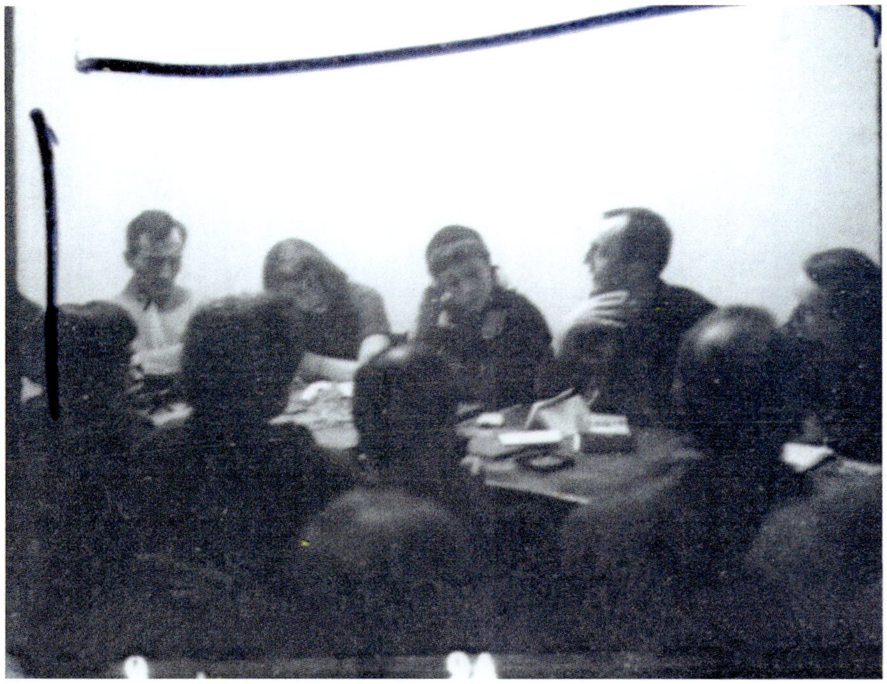

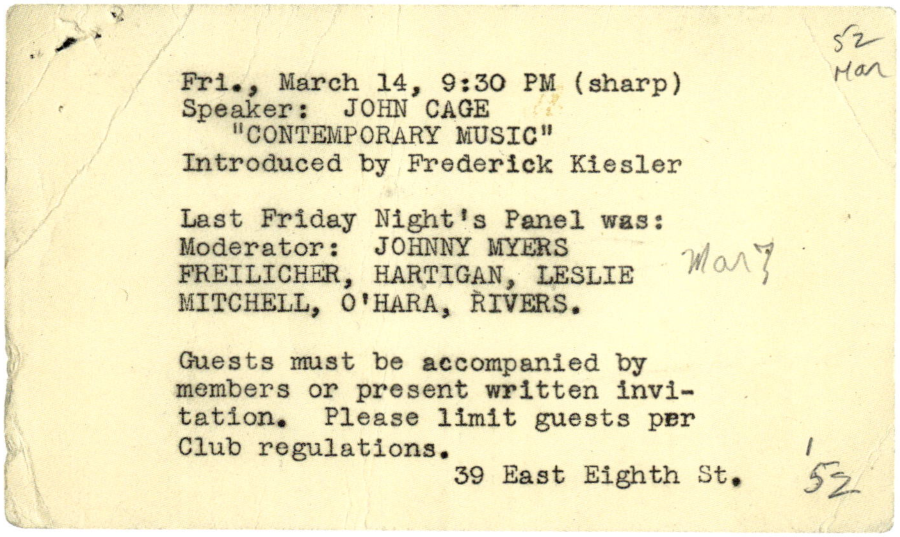

52 Mar

Fri., March 14, 9:30 PM (sharp)
Speaker: JOHN CAGE
"CONTEMPORARY MUSIC"
Introduced by Frederick Kiesler

Last Friday Night's Panel was:
Moderator: JOHNNY MYERS
FREILICHER, HARTIGAN, LESLIE
MITCHELL, O'HARA, RIVERS.

Mar 7

Guests must be accompanied by
members or present written invi-
tation. Please limit guests per
Club regulations.
39 East Eighth St.

I could give my heart in sweet surrender
It's the mood I'm in. —ABNER SILVER AND AL SHERMAN, "THE MOOD THAT I'M IN," PERFORMED BY BILLIE HOLIDAY

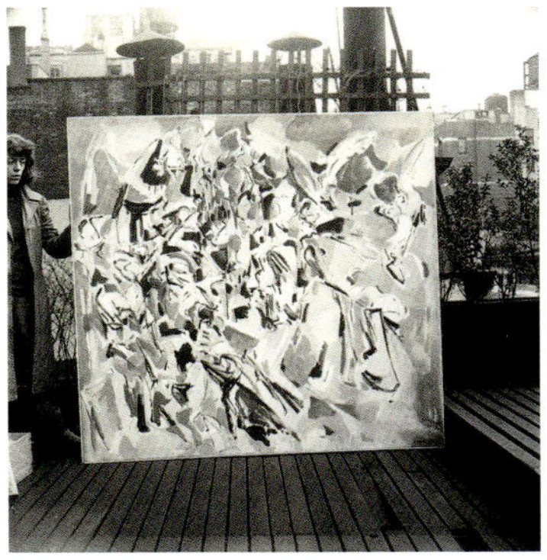

2.1

"I knew it was the last figure I would ever paint. I just knew. And it was."[1] *Figure and the City* (1949–50, plate 5) marked the end of Mitchell's first stay in France and her fresh start in New York; after that punctuation, "the paintings became the city."[2] In a photograph likely from the following year (fig. 2.1), Mitchell appears on a Greenwich Village rooftop with a ca. 1950 canvas that, although titled *Landscape* at one point, looks abstract. The "figure"—Mitchell herself—now stands outside the painting's world, not its occupant, but its viewing and making subject. Artist and painting alike are surrounded by yet another landscape: New York's strong, square profile, piles of tenements and lofts, bracketed by sky and water. The work she held on the rooftop would appear in 1951's Ninth Street Show, a landmark exhibition curated and organized by the senior figures among the artists who had so recently made New York a center for abstract painting. From 1950 to 1955, finding her place in this world would preoccupy Mitchell.

When Mitchell and Barney Rosset returned to New York, she immediately threw herself into every facet of modern art, from coursework in art history at Columbia University to the firsthand study of European modern painters in New York museums and galleries, with an emphasis on Piet Mondrian, Henri Matisse, and Wassily Kandinsky (as detailed by Tracey Bashkoff on pages 38–39). She also made a social life in established artists' gathering places like the Cedar Tavern and among artists and poets her own age. In this milieu, the most significant person for Mitchell was painter Michael Goldberg, with whom she began an intense romantic relationship almost as soon as she arrived in the city, before her 1952 divorce from Rosset. Goldberg—his hipster persona, his taste for jazz in downtown clubs, his swaggering artistic pronouncements, and the idea of him—would color her experience of New York and painting in these years.[3]

Central to Mitchell's self-education,[4] grounded in her years of looking at nineteenth-century painting at the Art Institute, was her exacting commitment to only the very best painting, which she immediately identified as being made by Willem de Kooning and Franz Kline, with Philip Guston close behind.[5] Unlike her first time in

FRONTISPIECE
Top: "Abstract Expressionism IV," panel discussion at The Club, New York, March 7, 1952. Left to right: Larry Rivers, Joan Mitchell, Elaine de Kooning, Frank O'Hara, and Grace Hartigan. Larry Rivers Papers, Fales Library and Special Collections, New York University. Bottom: Announcement for "Contemporary Music," lecture by John Cage at The Club, New York, March 14, 1952. Philip Pavia and Natalie Edgar Archive of Abstract Expressionist Art, Stuart A. Rose Manuscript, Archives, and Rare Book Library, Emory University, Atlanta

FIG 2.1 Joan Mitchell with *Untitled* (ca. 1950), ca. spring 1951. Joan Mitchell Foundation Archives, New York

New York, Mitchell did not hesitate to engage: she went to their studios and shows, and they came to hers (figs. 2.2 and 2.3);[6] she had dinner and drinks with them, in company and alone, talking painting materials and great art. Unlike many of their peers, the three older painters did not cast themselves as harbingers of the new, but as participants in a longer and larger history of art, and yet these artists eschewed the pretentiousness of artist-theorists like Robert Motherwell and Barnett Newman.[7] The first time Mitchell went to Kline's studio, in 1950, she and Goldberg simply walked in off the street; inside the old loft, she was "overwhelmed" by the unstretched paintings tacked to the brick walls, the drawings on pages from the telephone book scattered on the floor.[8] The directness, even "crudeness" of the imagery and feeling in Kline's painting, which Mitchell found beautiful, came to represent one side of what she sought in her own work: honesty and emotional power.[9] The counterpart was "accuracy," which she saw above all in the work of de Kooning, whose precision and skill with paint handling was an endless mystery and resource.[10] De Kooning himself paid homage to Arshile Gorky, and Mitchell (with Goldberg) visited the Whitney's early 1951 Gorky memorial exhibition on a weekly basis (see pages 50–51). For decades, Mitchell would use turpentine to achieve transparency, an effect that Gorky perfected.[11] She found his lushness and range of colors more sympathetic than New York painting's often rough surface and limited palette, largely dictated by the prohibitive cost of oil paint in tubes.[12]

These experiences all registered in Mitchell's first solo exhibition in New York, which opened in January 1952 at the New Gallery, operated by Eugene Thaw over the Oak Room of the Algonquin Hotel.[13] Thaw had extended the offer to show her work by September 1951, and she worked with the grand space in mind, creating an ambitious suite of "heroic-size" paintings with titles that recall Mexico, New York, France, and the Midwest, crowned by the enormous *Cross Section of a Bridge* (1951, plate 9).[14] The works deploy a focused formal vocabulary, with black-outlined colored shapes and thin, medium-value grays rubbed into the canvas that reflect Mitchell's admiration for de Kooning and Gorky.[15] The contrast in value is accentuated by the contrast between matte surface and shiny passages of commercial black enamel or glossy art paint, applied almost like a highlight.[16] Mitchell experimented to a lesser degree with composition; the exhibition's most radical was *Lyric* (ca. 1951, plate 8), broken open by a centrifugal swirl.[17]

The New Gallery exhibition was widely reviewed, and generally well. The most significant recognition was a call to appear at The Club, an invitation-only gathering in a loft on Eighth Street for discussion—and drinking and dancing—among artists and a few select poets, musicians, and critics. One of few female members, Mitchell became a regular, appearing on panels a half dozen times throughout the 1950s, and attending many Friday nights. On that first panel, in March 1952, she was alone among a "Tibor" stable of artists—Jane Freilicher, Grace Hartigan, Al Leslie, Larry Rivers—and their supporter Frank O'Hara; Tibor de Nagy Gallery director John Bernard "Johnny" Myers moderated (see page 30). Mitchell's exclusion from the gallery was a painful omission that she registered as primarily social; even though de Nagy showed several women, Mitchell felt that competition, rather than solidarity, between female artists was the standard.[18] Her work at the New Gallery also looked different from that of her peers, which appeared more spontaneous (Leslie), or somehow lighter (Rivers, Helen Frankenthaler). Noted poet and critic John Ashbery, taken to Mitchell's show by Freilicher, recalled "an energy that seemed to have other things in mind than the desire to please."[19] Private assessments of her

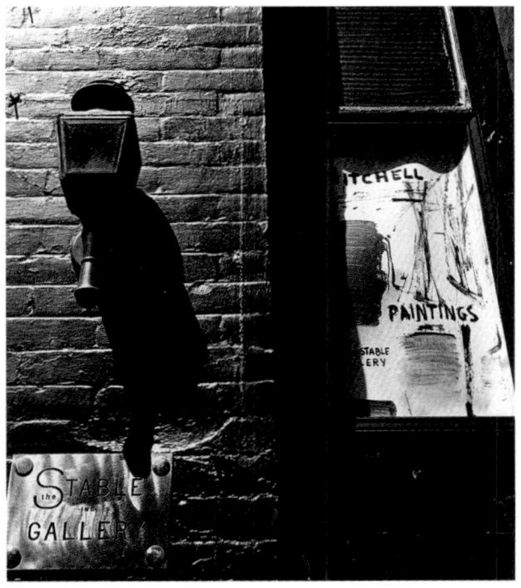

2.2

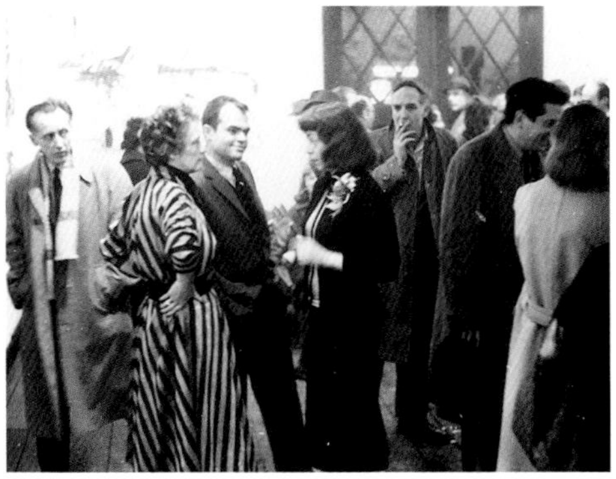

2.3

apparent strength could be caustic: to influential critic Clement Greenberg, the exhibition was "too perfect," and Hartigan sharply noted, "Joan Mitchell's show yesterday—a fantastic display of youthful talent and virtuosity, without the real thing."[20] Mitchell seemed to be aware of the sentiment: a few years later, she recounted, "I used to be called 'Tasty French.'"[21] The put-down could have alluded to her time in Paris; it certainly bought into Greenberg's well-known characterization of French painting as fussy, formulaic *cuisine*.[22]

Equal in importance to Mitchell's debut at The Club was finding a room of her own that spring: a studio at 60 St. Mark's Place, which she would keep through the early 1980s, and which lived on in her memory even after she lost the lease.[23] Whether set free within this private territory or stung by the accusations of perfection, Mitchell pushed herself to take risks in the second half of the year. In December 1952, she wrote her Smith College friend Joanne Von Blon to say, "Recently I've done some sort of decent pale paintings—different & more meaningful I think—(anyway to me)."[24] These works were exhibited in April 1953 at the Stable Gallery, an actual former stable where friends Elaine de Kooning and Janice Biala also showed. Mitchell's mother came for the opening, and praised the new paintings as "freer-er yet more controlled, more you," noting that many other viewers felt the same.[25] The works speak of Mitchell's energetic physicality: critics stressed the "cyclone," "whirl," and "whirlwind" nature of the compositions, accented by the active brushwork, as in *Untitled* (ca. 1953, plate 10).[26] Experimenting in paintings such as *Untitled* (1952–53, plate 11), Mitchell discovered soon-to-be signature marks: alongside the scribble used to indicate water and reflection, she framed the canvas with right-angled marks near its edges and short, emphatic horizontal strokes that often drip. She finished the painting with a declaration—a large green *X*, the second stroke challenging the energy of the first. Mitchell countered this apparent immediacy with the calculated use of white paint to restore a sense of openness, a practice that would become central to her work.

Where to go next was a constant question for Mitchell during the early 1950s, and she moved continually through painting's possibilities. In the summer of 1953, she went to Long Island, renting a cottage with painters

FIG 2.2 Exterior view of the Stable Gallery, New York, during the exhibition *Joan Mitchell,* 1953. Joan Mitchell Foundation Archives, New York

FIG 2.3 Opening of *Joan Mitchell Paintings* at the Stable Gallery, New York, 1957. The Miriam and Ira D. Wallach Division of Art, Prints, and Photographs, New York Public Library, The Walter Silver Collection, gift of George and Carole Silver, 2000. Mitchell and Eleanor Ward are in the foreground; Philip Guston is in the background. Mitchell's *The Bridge* (1956) hangs on the back wall.

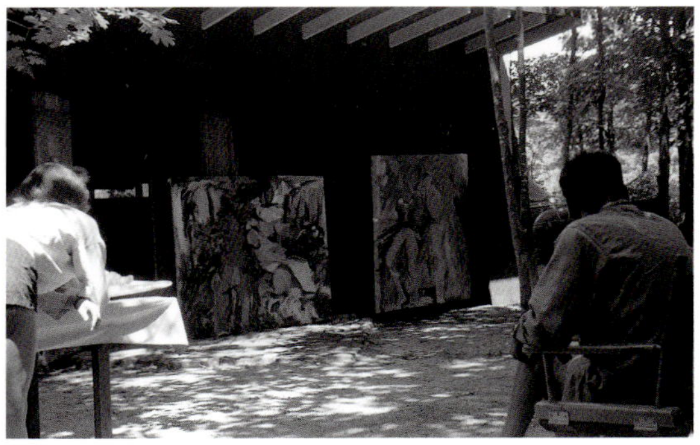

2.4

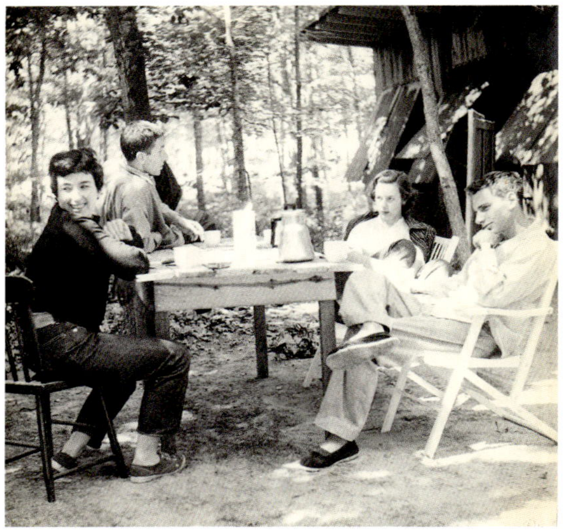

2.5

Miriam Schapiro and Paul Brach, with Goldberg very often in residence and Hartigan and other friends making short visits. They painted outdoors, under the eaves of the house (figs. 2.4 and 2.5). In *Rose Cottage* (1953, plate 12), Mitchell punctuated the canvas with blots of black paint made using a brush loaded with diluted pigment to press a mark on the surface, which she then either pulled into a vector or allowed to run down the canvas. As she continued to work through fall 1953 and winter 1954, whites, grays, and umbers supplanted the black, and the architectonic structure of the strokes gave way to a woven quality—short horizontals and verticals crossing again and again. From these hatched layers a central form almost, but not quite, coalesces, as in *Untitled* (1953–54, plate 13). If, in the New Gallery paintings, the artist's compositional strategy—the piecing together of space and plane—first becomes evident, in these heavily stroked and later crosshatched paintings of 1953–54, Mitchell's preoccupation with facture emerges. These works also respond to the Charles Egan Gallery's January–February 1953 exhibition of works by Guston (see page 50, no. 5), an artist with whom Mitchell had an admiring although ambivalent relationship.[27] While the two painters conjured similar atmospheres, both using relatively small, regular strokes to build structure, their differences are clear. Guston subtracted, scraping and repainting, while Mitchell added and even subtracted by adding, using white to return to the memory of the white ground and a previous stage of the work. Guston tended to paint in single, consuming sessions, while Mitchell's lifelong process was to move in and out of paintings, back and forth in space, and in and out of her own head.[28]

Guston's exhibition collided with a growing sense of a new direction for New York painting, which had been consumed with the self and, to a lesser degree, with art about art. It is not that gestural painters turned back to figuration as such, but that abstraction itself expanded, dropping the opposition to representation as a primary impulse. In his review of the Egan show, critic and artist Fairfield Porter describes a trajectory that would become a theme for artists and critics in the 1950s: "The color gets pinkish and translucent, like a bit of sky from a landscape by Sisley or Pissarro.... He seems to have gone behind Cézanne to Impressionism and to be developing what could be called an essential of this style."[29] Porter's friends (who were also Mitchell's) O'Hara, Elaine de Kooning, and Thomas B. Hess expressed similar ideas, arguing that New York artists were moving away from earlier purist positions around form to allow for content, both explicit and allusive.[30] Although Greenberg would focus on late Monet to establish a lineage for the flat, low-value contrast painting of Barnett Newman, Clyfford Still, and Mark Rothko, the other critics were writing before the Museum of Modern Art acquired *Nymphéas* (1914–26), driven not solely by reappraisals of Monet but also by exhibitions of Édouard Vuillard, Pierre Bonnard, Matisse, and Vincent van Gogh.[31] De Kooning and O'Hara insisted that what attracted contemporary artists to these earlier painters was not their supposed anticipation of abstraction but their capacity for *subject*—the emotional timbre of a Vuillard interior (echoed in the work of Porter, Freilicher, and Alex Katz) or the beauty of a van Gogh landscape.

For O'Hara, subject matter meant nature, broadly and deeply conceived: in the mid-twentieth century, the man-made and the natural worlds were no longer two separate categories.[32] This thinking applied to (or was adopted by) Mitchell, as in her insistence that "We don't have to go back because we never left. Man made a city; nature grows. I see it all as nature. I look at it all as what I see."[33] In her private letters too, "nature" was all the apparently mundane stuff of the world—a green tree, a red brick wall, daisies, a blue shirt, and orchids—a discovery of beauty in the quotidian shared with poets O'Hara, Barbara Guest, and James Schuyler (as detailed by Jenni Quilter and Erin Kimmel on pages 188–97 and 206–7).[34] Mitchell poked fun at grandiose statements about nature, but she never tired of the word "landscape," as both title and guiding principle.[35] Landscape was grounded in a "conservative" painting tradition, a favorite self-description for Mitchell and her work from 1957 on.[36] It presumes a viewing subject, an "I" that doesn't attempt to supplant nature (like Jackson Pollock) but observes and reciprocally finds itself within it.[37]

Mitchell's sensitivity to attempts to group or name extended above all to painting; she made fun of the voluble Brach for holding forth on art history, of Hartigan for her incessant cataloguing of painters.[38] This characteristic, while shared with others like Willem de Kooning, was distinguishing enough that art critic Irving Sandler would start his famous 1957 "Mitchell Paints a Picture" article with an excerpt from her statement to him on this topic, quoted here at greater length from Sandler's interview notes: "However I paint, I don't think is *the* way to paint. There is no one way to paint. There can't be. There is no single answer. And if people want to find it there is none."[39] One might say that for de Kooning, this distaste for prescriptive categories was motivated by a rejection of poisonous wartime ideology, and for a younger painter like Mitchell, by a *lack* of ideology, refusing the either/or oppositions of gesture and field, figuration and abstraction. The discomfort with labeling might be still stronger for a woman who was always doing things the "wrong" way; from her school days at Francis Parker to the end of her life, Mitchell felt herself on the edge of groups, the generally marginal status of women heightened by uneasiness with the mores of her upper-class background and her particular refusal to compromise.

FIG 2.4 Joan Mitchell and Paul Brach looking at Miriam Schapiro's paintings in Springs, New York, ca. 1953. Joan Mitchell Foundation Archives, New York. Photograph by Barney Rosset

FIG 2.5 Left to right: Miriam Schapiro, Michael Goldberg, Grace Hartigan, and Paul Brach at Rose Cottage, New York, 1953. Miriam Schapiro Papers, Special Collections and University Archives, Rutgers University Libraries, New Brunswick, New Jersey

By the summer of 1954, Mitchell was once more struggling to make new work; she was in "the duck shed" behind a house on Bossy Springs Road on Long Island, and complaining to Goldberg (who had remained in New York) that "my hand doesn't always feel and my eye sees just clichés."[40] She wanted the paintings for her early 1955 Stable Gallery exhibition to make a decisive statement, a wish for an individual identity made urgent by the increasingly crowded condition of New York painting. All of downtown seemed to have migrated to Long Island that summer, traveling from house to shack to studio, looking and talking. It was becoming clear to Mitchell that, for her, any such statement entailed embracing color, moving toward the nineteenth century, nature, and her early watercolors, and away from the emphasis of New York painting on force alone.[41]

As she wrote in July 1954, "Jean [Steubing, girlfriend of painter Milton Resnick] brought me flowers—blue & orange & deep red—like the Fauve book—if I could make a painting with color—& then it becomes a pressure & I want to deny it."[42] Two weeks later, she had begun, but still felt unsure under that collective eye: "I distrust my painting in color—I think it's because people said I ought to—& I distrust the others because I can't use color."[43] Related to this unsettled question of color was the relationship between intensity and control, with

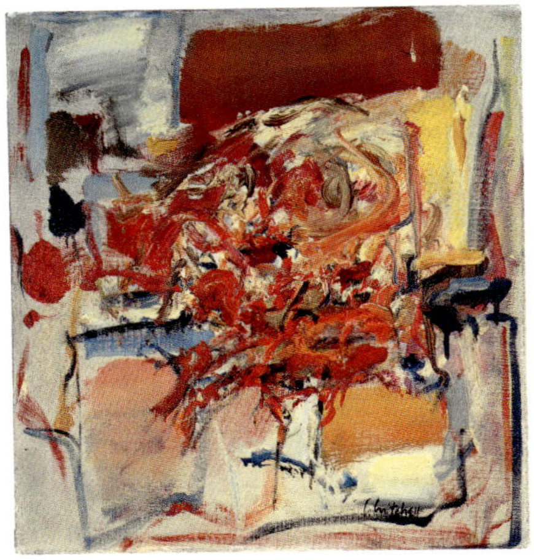

2.6

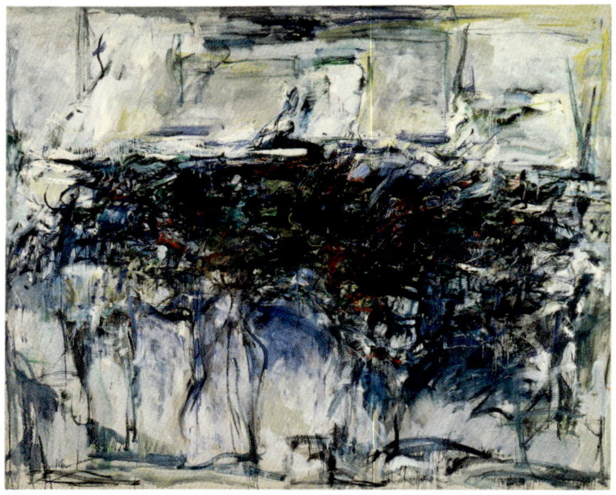

2.7

FIG 2.6 **Joan Mitchell**
Untitled, ca. 1955. Oil on canvas, 18⅛ × 17 in. (46 × 43 cm). Private collection

FIG 2.7 **Joan Mitchell**
The Lake, 1955. Oil on canvas, 80 × 100¼ in. (203.2 × 254.5 cm). Shizuoka Prefectural Museum of Art, Japan

van Gogh on one end representing passion, opposite Cézanne and Beethoven representing structure: "It's impossible to enclose things so completely—a monument—so very still like the damn blue horizon." In the end, Mitchell went for "excitement," deciding that she "better put in a red red line."[44] The line—fierce, disruptive—would complicate the beauty of the picture; such disruptions would become a constant motif through her very late paintings (as discussed by Richard Shiff on pages 282–91). These marks created an emotional friction analogous to what her psychoanalyst Edrita Fried saw as Mitchell's need for "discord" to feel alive.[45]

As she struggled with her work and emotions, Mitchell reported to Goldberg that Rosset's second wife, Loly, "brought me a yellow sunflower. We should grow them behind your place. It's like having the sun in here—an absolute head light. I like what van Gogh made of that starry night—to animate something—insanity & fanaticism."[46] A small, related work dated ca. 1955 (fig. 2.6), and recorded as having been in the collection of Rosset,[47] features a bristly texture, using small brushes to make curving lines and stippled surfaces, that would resurface in her 1969 paintings of sunflowers. The need to fully realize herself as a painter was resolved—or at least began to be resolved—in some fusion of feeling, color, nature, materiality, and faith that she associated with van Gogh and his sunflower. Emotions could be painful as well as thrilling. That August, amid conflict with Goldberg, Mitchell took an overdose of pills. She signed her suicide letter, "Te quiero—all colors," meaning the full spectrum of feelings, negative and positive, as well as of paint and nature.[48] Recounting the episode to former boyfriend Evans Herman just ten days later, she folded together van Gogh's strong color and his strong emotion.[49]

Mitchell consciously left behind the suicidal gesture but held on to the ideal of intensity in the works painted during the second half of 1954 and into 1955. In reviews of her solo show at the Stable Gallery in February 1955, critics celebrated the "full-blooded color" of these paintings, which included what was perhaps Mitchell's first exhibited "green" painting; the single work reproduced in a magazine review features flaming red,

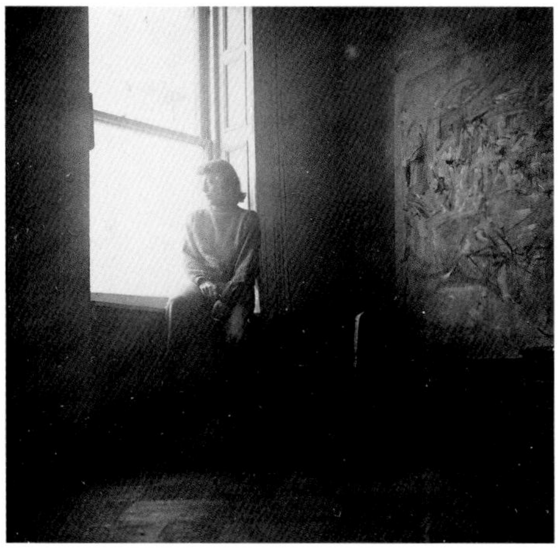

2.8

yellow, orange, and blue.[50] Missing from the reviews was the kind of sexist, coded language that dogged Frankenthaler and other women; Mitchell managed to foreground color and feeling without being typecast as feminine, quite an achievement in the intensely sexist 1950s.[51] And she managed to join structure with color and intensity in several major works. The tumultuous summer on Long Island, capped by a trip to Chicago, had jolted her memory: "I once loved looking across the lake—fuck the other side. I keep painting a blue stripe—no not like Al Leslie—its [*sic*] horizontal."[52] In the Stable Gallery solo show, as well as subsequent group exhibitions that year, paintings with this centering horizon/mass—three of which would be titled *City Landscape* (all 1955, including plate 14), and one *The Lake* (fig. 2.7)—received instant critical approval.[53] They had the light tops and bottom corners of earlier works, now clearly evoking the mutual reflection of sky and water, bracketing a monumental center of strokes that mass and tangle. In some, red or blue dominate, and in a few, the brilliant colors span an outrageous spectrum that embraces not only red, blue, and orange, but yellow, pink, and maroon, and hints of green.

These paintings are representational and also abstract. As landscapes, they sit at a distance from us—cities seen from afar—and they are also, of course, accumulations of paint, applied at no more than arm's length. More central than this dualism to Mitchell's thinking was the exchange between self and world: Chicago, seen across Lake Michigan; Manhattan, rising up behind the Brooklyn Bridge; the vast blue ocean stretching out from the beaches of Long Island; and perhaps the skyline across the East River, visible from a rooftop. All these views came with Mitchell to her St. Mark's studio (fig. 2.8), where the distance to the horizon was the twenty-three feet between the studio's far wall and her painting, hanging opposite.[54]

FIG 2.8 Joan Mitchell in her studio at 60 St. Mark's Place, New York, ca. 1954. The Miriam and Ira D. Wallach Division of Art, Prints, and Photographs, New York Public Library, The Walter Silver Collection, gift of George and Carole Silver, 2000

Untitled, ca. 1950

Tracey Bashkoff

Untitled (ca. 1950) is illustrated as plate 7.

FIG 2.9 **Wassily Kandinsky**
Painting with White Border, 1913. Oil on canvas, 55¼ × 78⅞ in. (140.3 × 200.3 cm). Solomon R. Guggenheim Museum, New York, Solomon R. Guggenheim Founding Collection, by gift

FIG 2.10 **Piet Mondrian**
Tableau No. 2/Composition No. VII, 1913. Oil on canvas, 41⅜ × 45 in. (105.1 × 114.3 cm). Solomon R. Guggenheim Museum, New York, Solomon R. Guggenheim Founding Collection

In interviews and letters from the 1950s and later, Mitchell raises her own pantheon of artists. In 1958, when Irving Sandler asked her if today's artist was "with or against the past," Mitchell cited a wide-ranging list of influences: Vincent van Gogh, Henri Matisse, Paul Cézanne, Pierre-Auguste Renoir, Édouard Manet, Francisco de Goya, Titian, Jean Baptiste Chardin, Chaim Soutine, and Wassily Kandinsky.[1] In some cases, Mitchell differentiates between interest and influence, and in others she specifies what she was drawn to—the scenery of Orozco or "Mondrian's trees, cathedrals and piers."[2] As if to equalize all influences and commit to none, she describes some of her fascinations as "a minor attachment," fleeting and open-ended: "Art keeps changing for me. One day I look at something I previously adored and it doesn't mean anything. I don't think much of Cézanne today and I used to like him. I may again."[3] Painted at the start of the decade, Mitchell's *Untitled* (plate 7) appears sensitive to the diversity of Modernism's roots, but the black and colored lines, patches, and choppy washes most markedly invoke the innovations of two pioneers of abstraction from her list in particular: Kandinsky and Piet Mondrian.

Before 1942, Mitchell encountered works by Kandinsky at the Art Institute of Chicago—fine examples from a 1931 gift from Arthur Jerome Eddy, one of the artist's earliest collectors in the United States. She could also have seen the fifty-three works in the *Wassily Kandinsky Memorial Exhibition* at the Chicago Arts Club in November 1945, organized by Hilla Rebay, director of the Museum of Non-Objective Painting in New York (the forerunner of the Solomon R. Guggenheim Museum).[4] Beginning in 1939, many of those same works and more would have been regularly on view in the galleries of the Museum of Non-Objective Painting, known for its fanatical dedication to the work of the master Modernist and his followers. Kandinsky also featured in special exhibitions in 1949 and 1952.[5]

Opportunities to see Mondrian's work in Chicago may have been limited during Mitchell's student years, though the Museum of Modern Art's (MoMA) 1945 memorial exhibition was widely covered in the art press.[6] In 1950–51, following her move to New York, Mitchell's interest in Mondrian heightened through the influence of others who admired the artist—primarily Willem de Kooning and Philip Guston. In a letter to Michael Goldberg, she recounted her first conversations with de Kooning: "We talked about Stuart Davis & Gorky & Mondrian & color and I missed you horribly."[7] Beginning in 1948, Mondrian's work was frequently on view in gallery exhibitions and museum collections throughout the city.[8] In addition to its permanent collection displays, MoMA presented paintings by Mondrian in 1951 and 1952 exhibitions.[9] Mitchell may have even had private access by special arrangement to the Guggenheim's Mondrian canvases.[10]

While both Kandinsky and Mondrian were adherents of theosophy, a quasi-religious and esoteric movement dating from the turn of the twentieth century, Mitchell, like many of her postwar peers, was likely less attracted to the spiritual aspects of their theories and practice than to the sense of the radical expressed through their words and paint.[11] Kandinsky's early expressionist landscapes, in which he creates a sense of place with a few quick, bright brushstrokes, may have been a source of inspiration for Mitchell.[12] *Untitled* (ca. 1950), however, is more visually aligned with Kandinsky's canvases from the 1910s, such as *Painting with White Border* (fig. 2.9), made as he was purging references to the external world from his works. Frequently on view at the Museum of

Non-Objective Painting, this imposing canvas records the artist's fondness for Moscow through abstracted remnants of favored Russian motifs, such as a troika (three-horse drawn sled) and a dragon. Kandinsky even replaces traditional perspective with a radical, allover composition that appears unmoored, or created from an unlikely aerial viewpoint.[13] At the same time, Mondrian was making groundbreaking canvases that pushed the planes of Analytic Cubism to the point of abstraction. His *Tableau No. 2/Composition No. VII* (fig. 2.10), also at the Museum of Non-Objective Painting, depicts a tree reduced to interlocking black lines and a palette of ocher and gray. While cubist works celebrate illusionistic volume with their simultaneous views of objects, Mondrian avoided it, painting lines that fade as they reach the edges of the canvas.

Mitchell around 1950, like Kandinsky and Mondrian in 1913, is emptying her canvases of representation but not of content. *Untitled* (ca. 1950) may be inspired by meaningful locations, yet it is freed from the task of realistically depicting the physical landscape. Her strokes of black, ocher, and bright primaries emerge from and merge with the roiling white ground. There is energy, movement, direction, and force without gravity. The composition is activated by what Kandinsky described in his own work as an "inner boiling" that emerged from the way "black smudges rotate within the white."[14] Mitchell's remarkable move away from student exercises and figurative experimentation is informed and inspired by those who came before her, but the bravura is all her own.

For Mitchell, grappling with the past did not mean residing there: "History is a continually changing thing. Different centuries find different artists of the past. Good art survives, but it goes up and down."[15] Art of the past becomes relevant through its use by later artists. Cézanne may have fallen out of favor for Mitchell in 1958 when she replied to Sandler's query, but he remained close, ready to be drawn on again, and newly relevant when drawn upon. Mitchell's days in museums may have informed her work, but she understood that the legacy of art history was not a simple one-way transmission of lessons, one generation to the next: "The past becomes more meaningful because of our tastes today."[16] Mitchell saw her work as of her time and part of a continuum that flowed both ways, a generative and generous way of looking at how artists communicate and live on.

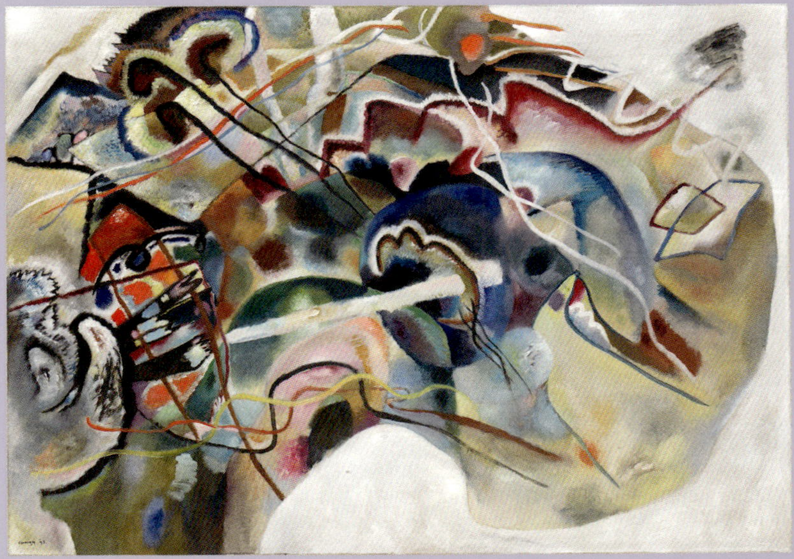

2.9

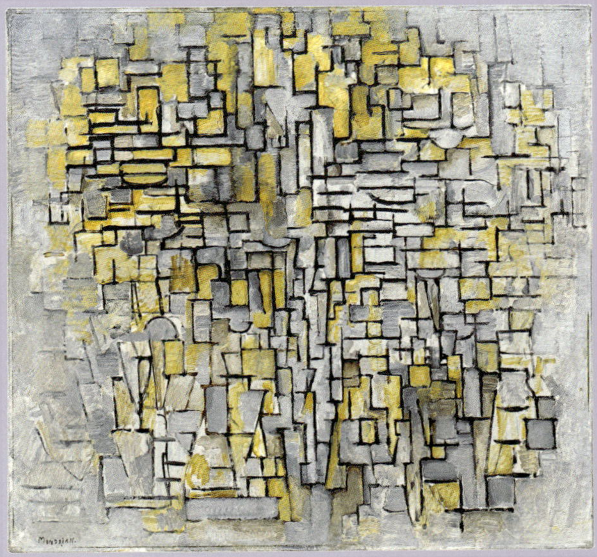

2.10

3
Par Avion Katy Siegel

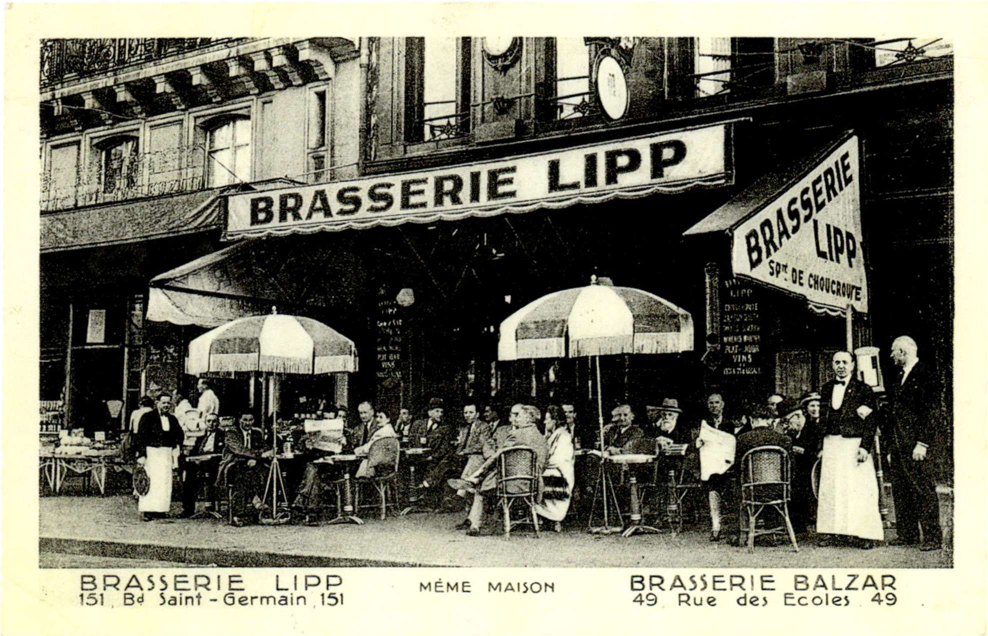

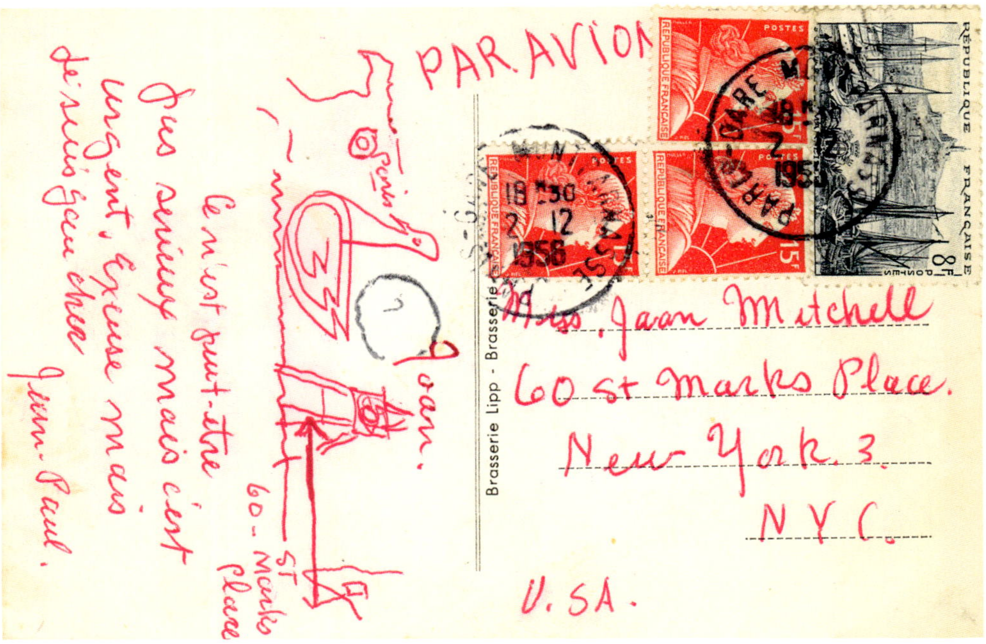

—RENÉ CHAR, "À ***," TRANSCRIBED BY FRANK O'HARA IN A LETTER TO JOAN MITCHELL

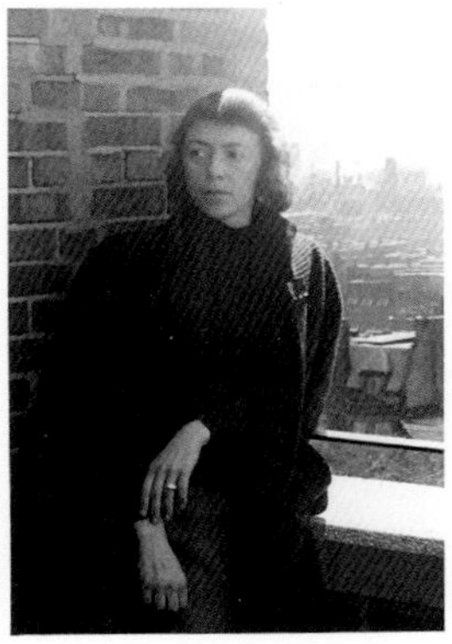

3.1

"I've moved—26 rue Jacob—Paris 6—very nice with large trees out the window—I've covered the wall with white paper—bought out that bastard Lefèbvre-Foinet and *la vie en rose* begins—and so I come all the way to Paris to tack some canvas on the wall & step back & swear."[1] In the years 1955–59, Mitchell would go back and forth between New York and Paris at least once a year. While she roughly divided the year into summer/fall in Paris, winter/spring in New York, she never established a fixed rhythm, and often shuttled between the two more frequently. Place and time and also feelings are tracked by a flutter of paper: amusing, affectionate postcards, tickets and telegrams, checks cashed at the Cedar Tavern or written to hold a studio, airmail in letters alternately arch and desperate.[2] The Paris/New York dialectic was punctuated by short trips elsewhere: to the outskirts of Paris to swim and drive with the Canadian painter Jean Paul Riopelle, her lover in France, with whom she also visited Canada; to Long Island in the summer; to Chicago to see her parents; to Santa Barbara to see her sister; to the Mediterranean coast to sail. As critic Dore Ashton (herself a Francophile and frequent traveler between New York and Paris) wrote in 1955, "Mitchell gives me the impression of a person in transit."[3]

That first departure, in May 1955, was personal and professional at a moment when the two seemed inseparable. Edrita Fried, Mitchell's therapist, counseled her to leave Michael Goldberg, her off-and-on lover of several years, with whom she remained intensely engaged throughout the 1950s and sporadically friendly across her life. The pleasure of her thriving career, meanwhile, was blunted by discomfort with an overripe art scene where individual struggle was giving way to the safety of signature style and commercial success. Mitchell clearly felt what one of her friends, influential *Art News* critic Thomas B. Hess, described as the wish to escape "inter-communication, social pressure, the 'crowded vision.'"[4] Paris promised respite: "I think it would be easier to live the life of a painter here—the continual working & not showing for years—it's accepted & has a dignity."[5] Still, Mitchell recognized that there was an art world in Paris, and immediately set about assessing both art and world. She was brutal in reviewing École de Paris painting but prided herself on speaking French

FRONTISPIECE
Postcard (recto and verso) showing the Brasserie Lipp, Paris, sent by Jean Paul Riopelle to Joan Mitchell, December 2, 1956. Joan Mitchell Foundation Archives, New York

FIG 3.1 Joan Mitchell, ca. 1955. Joan Mitchell Foundation Archives, New York and, unlike her first trip in 1948–49, breaking out of expatriate circles. Soon after arriving, Mitchell met American West Coast painter Sam Francis and his close friend Riopelle (fig. 3.2), both of whom had lived in Paris for a number of years; largely through them, she would enter a cosmopolitan Paris art world that included Marisol Escobar, Simon Hantaï, Shirley Jaffe, Judit Reigl, Kimber Smith, Zao Wou-Ki, Alberto Giacometti, and Samuel Beckett, as well as socially powerful French critics ("the gods") Michel Tapié and Georges Duthuit,[6] and dealers including Pierre Matisse, Jacques Dubourg, Jean Fournier, and Aimé Maeght (see pages 50–51).

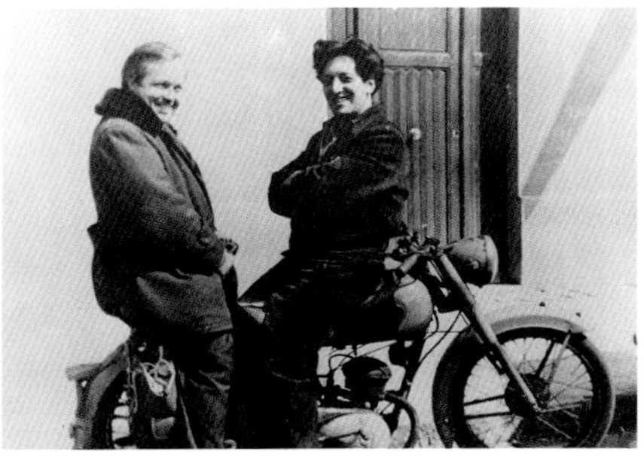

3.2

Mitchell ranged widely across Paris from May to November that first year, when she lived and worked in at least five successive apartment-studios in different neighborhoods, found through friends and word of mouth.[7] This peripatetic existence entailed a litany of issues, as detailed in a letter to Barney Rosset sprinkled with French:

> I've just spent an hour writing Fried—asking can I or should I stay & as I wrote I began to think it was stupid to stay. I've moved & I have this place for a month (*un vraie atelier*) and after I have another, gratuit, in Auteuil for October—& yet moving around—enormous, wet paintings is *emmerdant* & each place I have to get a *femme de ménage* to clean & I do put paint around. . . . I like the place I'm in now—far from St. Germain—I work & work—if I stayed I suppose I could get a show—one can make lots of money here eventually—but I would stay because of the man & he won't live in America & to get him to go there would take time & then it probably wouldn't work.[8]

FIG 3.2 Sam Francis and Jean Paul Riopelle in Paris, ca. 1953. Sam Francis Foundation

"The man" was Riopelle, with whom she had begun a volatile romance that would stabilize somewhat at the end of the 1950s and last another two decades. The other conditions inventoried here preclude definitive understanding of whether individual works were made in New York or Paris; Mitchell's unsettled state also meant that she made fewer paintings, and fewer that survived, in 1955. Even during subsequent more productive years she was rolling canvases—dry, wet, and blank—and planning to "float" them to New York, occasionally destroying them, or regretfully leaving the best ones behind because of the expense of shipping.[9] Exacerbating the puzzle, Mitchell showed actively in New York during the 1950s but would not have a solo exhibition in a Paris gallery until 1960.

Her relative anonymity in Paris gave her freedom, a pleasure tempered by the loss of a familiar artistic context in which to locate herself. Mitchell was also adapting to new materials, and she complained about the different paint colors in France—even the strangeness of their names—and particularly their lack of transparency (perhaps a result of the different dyes and mineral pigments used as coloring agents in Europe).[10] She worked primarily on small canvases in 1955, experimenting with isolated, emphatic marks in ultramarine blue with ocher, including paintings she called "Klines."[11] But over the course of her moves she managed to paint several large works as well, including "a large mess with a sky on top like my show," possibly the painting photographed by Francis in artist Kimber Smith's Batignolles studio, which Smith lent Mitchell in June–July (figs. 3.3 and 3.4).[12] The horizontal masses of the roughly contemporary city landscapes feather out from the center, the

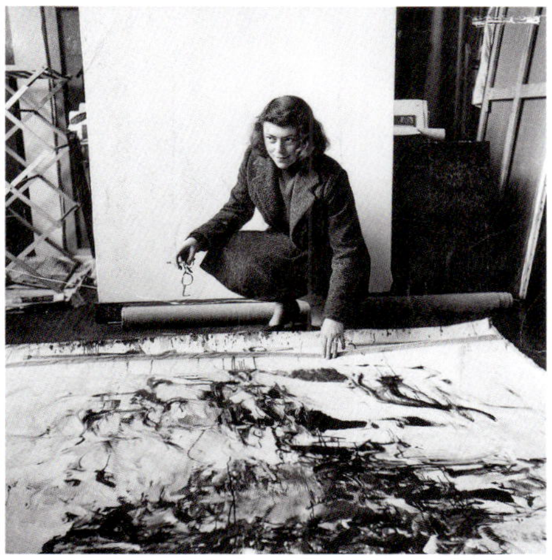

3.3

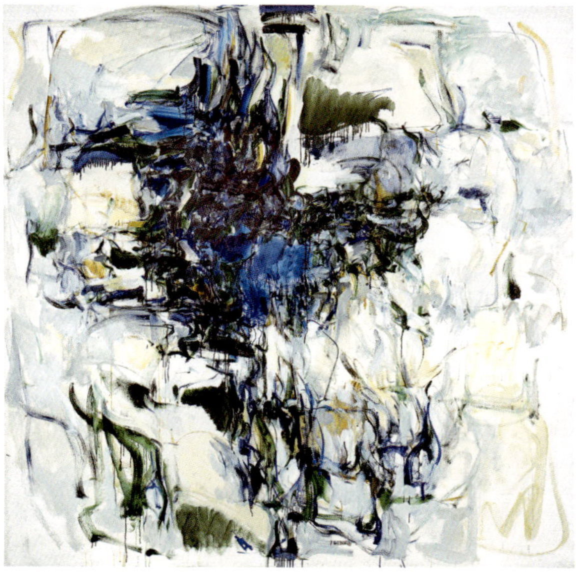

3.4

unfurling brushstrokes visibly seeking transparency. The effect is contrasted by a final, emphatic opaque white horizontal mark, apparently laid down with a palette knife—Riopelle's signature tool—an early appearance of a technique she would use frequently by the early 1960s.

Toward the end of her stay in 1955, Mitchell seemed to be laboring to make marks that added up to a composition. However unresolved, these works would feed the fully achieved paintings made in the months following her November return to New York, under the pressure and pleasure of a high-profile, blue-chip gallery appearance: "I hear I'm to be in a 3 man show at Sidney Janis—elegance & more elegance—& so need some pictures for such a fancy place."[13] Here, the transparency she had longed for in Paris returned full force, perhaps even increasing after her time with Francis, who also relied on turpentine, layering wet and dry—in the liquid washes of *East Ninth Street* (1956, plate 17), and still more diaphanous in *Hudson River Day Line* (1955, plate 15).[14] And yet, at almost the same moment, she painted *Monongahela* (1955, plate 16), which encompasses a vast range of hues and values, and a layered thickness. Using different means, all three paintings use paint's materiality to realize the feel of coursing water, making common cause of abstraction and representation. In the coming years, Mitchell would alternate between these various effects, and also work to incorporate varied textures, including thick and thin, in striking relation to each other in a single canvas.

When she returned to Paris in summer 1956, building on this success and a more settled studio arrangement, Mitchell found a confident new direction. Photographs from rue Daguerre for a *Life* magazine article on women artists show a room full of paintings, including a suite of new works.[15] Most have brightly colored strokes; in *Soldats de bois* (1956, plate 21), they are deployed in precise, accelerating gestures ("whiplash lines") that skate across expanses of white paint, punctuated by Prussian blue periods made with the push of a brush. Mitchell continued to open her paintings with delicate decisiveness, here retaining exposed ground rather than returning to white through overpainting, as she did in 1953–54. Riopelle would write to her that he saw

FIG 3.3 Joan Mitchell in Kimber Smith's studio, Paris, 1955. Sam Francis Papers, Getty Research Institute, Los Angeles

FIG 3.4 **Joan Mitchell** *Untitled,* 1955. Oil on canvas, 76 × 76 in. (193 × 193 cm). Private collection

Soldats de bois at Lefèbvre-Foinet (a firm that framed, stored, and shipped paintings in addition to making paint), applauding the work of a "maître au feminin." He was likely playing on the slippage between the idea of a female master and *maîtresse,* meaning "mistress."[16] The painting apparently appealed to French taste; according to Mitchell, *Soldats de bois* was met with approval when shown in a 1957 group exhibition, a step in the slow growth of her public presence in Paris: "I saw Tapié very briefly with Eleanor [Ward]. He said—'my reputation mounts secretly.'—& 'it's much better that way.'"[17]

That fall and winter of 1956, Mitchell turned back to landscape, manifested in the paintings' strong greens and also their titles: *October Island* and *Hemlock* (plate 24). While both first appeared in the May 1957 Stable Gallery exhibition, she likely made the former in Paris and the latter in New York, after traveling to rural Mont-Saint-Hilaire, Quebec, with Riopelle in the late autumn of 1956.[18] Mitchell titled the second painting *Hemlock* after the "dark and blue feeling" of the Wallace Stevens poem "Domination of Black."[19] The wooded setting of Mont-Saint-Hilaire, combined with the intensity of her time alone with Riopelle, clearly captured her imagination; she associated him with the color green, both "Ricard green" and "a J.-P. forest"—colors of their favorite drink and, more significantly, of the trees and his many paintings of them, including *Forest Blizzard* (1953), shown at Pierre Matisse Gallery in 1954 and seen by Mitchell at the Museum of Modern Art (MoMA) the following year (see page 51, no. 6).[20] Writing at Christmas, she remembers "The Tree" as a landmark in a shared romantic and erotic experience, and muses that "my paintings will perhaps really turn green."[21]

Riopelle's work fit the emerging French discourse around a "new nature," reconciling landscape traditions with postwar artistic currents to render what critic Michel Ragon called "paysagisme abstrait."[22] There were strong parallels in the United States, where the earlier thoughts about nature and painting of Fairfield Porter, Frank O'Hara, et al. continued to gain ground; like that of Riopelle, Mitchell's painting suited the critical conceit, and *Hemlock* was featured in the Whitney Museum of American Art's 1958 exhibition *Nature in Abstraction*. The exhibition catalogue was typical in moving quickly from contemporary painting to the return of late nineteenth-century facture and subjects; similarly, in Paris, critic Georges Limbour sought to redefine the École de Paris as a "new Impressionism."[23] Revivals of Impressionism had obvious appeal in these years, conveniently leaping backward over the awkward wartime associations of mid-century European art, and examples of Monet's *Nymphéas* paintings were installed at the Musée de l'Orangerie in 1953 and acquired by MoMA in 1955. The private interests of painters such as Francis and Riopelle, both of whom paid overt homage to *Nymphéas,* were solidified and made public in exhibitions like Lawrence Alloway's 1958 *Abstract Impressionism* in London, which prominently featured Mitchell's *Hudson River Day Line*.[24]

Riopelle and Francis exceeded these fashions. Georges Duthuit, a frequent writer for Galerie Maeght and one of Paris's most significant critical voices (as discussed by Éric de Chassey on pages 90–92), celebrated the "boundless vitality" of Riopelle's palette knife, rhapsodizing about the artist's presence, "like a trapper fresh from the Canadian solitudes."[25] Francis, too, had a signature sense of the environment—almost the inverse of Riopelle's thick materiality—that fluctuated between limpid surface and deep space (see page 51, no. 7). If Francis saw this space in painterly terms, observing, "I am surrounded in color-space=color," together with Duthuit and other critics he also cast it as aerial and even cosmic—like Riopelle's wilderness, an unbounded space.[26] Both the paintings and the talk surrounding them were unabashedly transcendent and almost comically gendered in their contrast with Mitchell's work and its criticism. Although ambitious, her version of landscape pointed to the everyday—flower, brick wall, city park—and although her view of the horizon was from on high, it was grounded in a specific vantage—a tenth-floor apartment in Chicago, a rooftop in New York's East Village, a room on rue Jacob. What Riopelle, Francis, and Mitchell *did* share was an intense relation to their surroundings, a way of being in the world.

The artists' physicality resonated with the current philosophical and phenomenological concerns of Jean-Paul Sartre, Simone de Beauvoir, and Maurice Merleau-Ponty.[27] Beyond the general vogue for existentialism in Paris and New York, their work specifically shaped the thinking of Duthuit, his protégé Pierre Schneider, art critic and philosopher Rachel Jacobs, Hess, and Harold Rosenberg, all of whom were actively writing on and socializing with artists in the 1950s and 1960s, and also traveling back and forth between Paris and New York.[28] If Sartre's emphasis on consciousness shaped the art criticism of the time (for instance, Rosenberg's formulation of action painting[29]), so, too, did the concept of embodied experience in Beauvoir and Merleau-Ponty. Both described a vision in which the operations and information of the senses were a single, unfragmented thing; as Merleau-Ponty put it, a "sensorium commune."[30] Mitchell's predilection for fusing sound, look, and feel ("It's all squashed together," as she wrote Rosset[31]) has led some writers to diagnose her with synesthesia, but the terms of contemporary phenomenology are a better match. Merleau-Ponty cast experience as concrete and detailed, based in the body's encounter with the rich texture of everyday life, a view sympathetic to Mitchell's green tree in New York, blue plush fabric in a Parisian bedroom, red tulip on Long Island—another kind of "accuracy" relative to the generalized transcendence of Francis and Riopelle. The philosopher's vision of the relationship between self and world, a mutual calling into existence that blurred the line between them, illuminates Mitchell's ability to empathize with and dissolve herself in a landscape, in painting, even in the yellow curtains of her childhood.[32] Merleau-Ponty believed that perception *was* expression, and this too resonates with Mitchell and her sophisticated play with conventional labels, confounding their interior/exterior thrust: "I want to express myself about my impressions."[33]

This "I" was suffused with, even constituted by, the past, constantly reactivated in the present.[34] The vivid availability of her memory going back to childhood sets Mitchell apart from artists like Pollock and Barnett Newman, for whom the past meant cave paintings and ancient symbols, and also from the general tendency to idealize immediacy of experience.[35] The presence of the past is evident in paintings that invoke specific locations and specific moments in Paris, in New York, and on Long Island: *August, rue Daguerre*; *Evenings on 73rd Street* (plate 26); and *George Went Swimming at Barnes Hole, but It Got Too Cold* (plate 25, hereafter *George*) (all 1957).[36] The first invokes a narrow, high-ceilinged Paris studio (borrowed from sculptor Day Schnabel) in a month of beautiful sunlight and empty streets; the second, nights spent in the lively company of younger writers and artists at her friend Hal Fondren's apartment. The third painting, of Mitchell's poodle, Georges du Soleil, was key to Mitchell's most extended account of what this remembering meant to her, in a series of interviews Irving Sandler conducted for an article in the famous *Art News* series "X Paints a Picture." The essays were all predicated on the centrality of process; for her feature, Mitchell began *Bridge* (1957), a large, single-panel painting, and then, frustrated with her progress, started *George*.[37] But the photographs (figs. 3.5 and 3.6) were likely staged (the artist always hated to be watched while she worked), and Mitchell's understanding of process is less about paint application and more about generating the will to paint.[38] In Sandler's interview notes for the essay, Mitchell unfolds her famous remark, "I carry my landscapes around with me," revealing the imbrication of outside world and artist.[39] She begins with an "image of love"[40]—the Brooklyn Bridge or her dog—used, like a record or a poem, to inspire feeling. That feeling must first be soaring, fierce emotion—a "state of joy" rather than "nostalgia" or "slop."[41] Feeling is also kinesthetic, the bridge generating "a spanning" sensation.[42] Finally, feeling becomes visual, and fully present: "You put color down and you look at it. This has to do with seeing.... Once I start painting I make a painting. Painting takes over at one point."[43]

Mitchell's visual memory encompassed past paintings. For example, she began the single-panel *Bridge* painting for the article shortly after completing a diptych on the same subject (1956, plate 18), one she had drawn and painted for at least a decade (as discussed by Marin Sarvé-Tarr on pages 48–49).[44] While she hated to copy herself ("Never feel you're making a picture of a painting"[45]), Mitchell remembered and learned from previous work. For example, if the diptych *The Bridge* occupies the linear end of a spectrum, and *Harbor December* (1956, plate 20) lies at the opposite, "painty" end, she aimed to land "midway" with her subsequent work.[46] Early photos of the rejected single-panel *Bridge* reveal long, dryish lines; in later stages, they are shored by shorter strokes loaded with paint in deeper, slightly darker, and more saturated colors. In *George,* these "painty" marks carry directional force and also become shapes, balancing positive and negative space, an intentional mark making to which she applied her term of praise, "accurate."[47]

This vocabulary would become still more assertive and sophisticated in *To the Harbormaster* (1957, plate 27), much like *Cross Section of a Bridge* (1951, plate 9) at the 1952 New Gallery solo show, sharing almost exactly the same dimensions. *To the Harbormaster* picks up the marine quality and range of blues in *George,* sky and water refracting, and also extending to the top and bottom of the canvas, with an expansiveness just shy of all over, structured by strong red strokes that feel more declarative than discordant. Her precision is unusual: individual bold, scaled-up marks are each carefully considered, broken by the butt end of a paintbrush, or by another stroke, to create a precise rhythm—no hunting for a picture, no rolling the dice. As Mitchell told her mother, Marion Strobel, her goal was to create paintings that were "strong and lyrical"; Strobel would have understood this in relation to the lyrical tradition in poetry (as detailed by Jenni Quilter on pages 188–97).[48] As a painter, Mitchell would also have been aware of the slightly negative and decorative connotation "lyrical" had in New York, which she deliberately offset by pairing it with "strong."[49] Over the decades, lyricism would become increasingly important to her as an inclination in painting, poetry, and music that was historically sweeping and also countered what she saw as the prevalent irony and conceptualism of contemporary art.

In works such as *Ladybug* and *Piano mécanique* (1957 and 1958, plates 28 and 29), Mitchell continued to develop the force and density of the marks found in *Harbormaster,* now using a broader color range.[50] In the final paintings of the 1950s, she would deploy these strokes in vertical heaps, playing on both the compositional resemblance to Monet's haystacks and the paintings' serial nature in their wry titles: *Cercando un Ago* (Looking for a Needle) or *Cherchez l'aiguille* (Look for the Needle).[51] Those 1958–60 paintings were made as

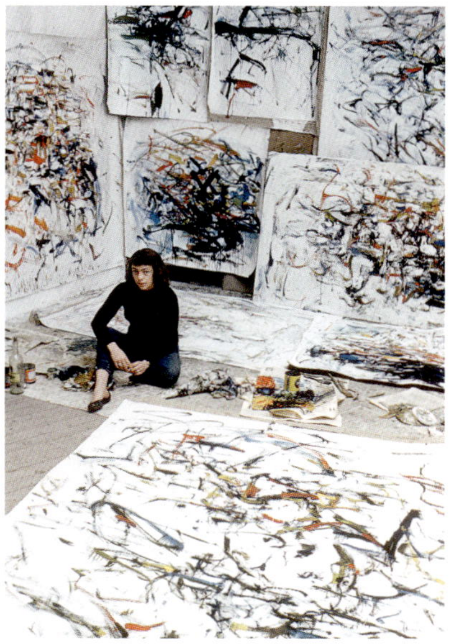

3.5

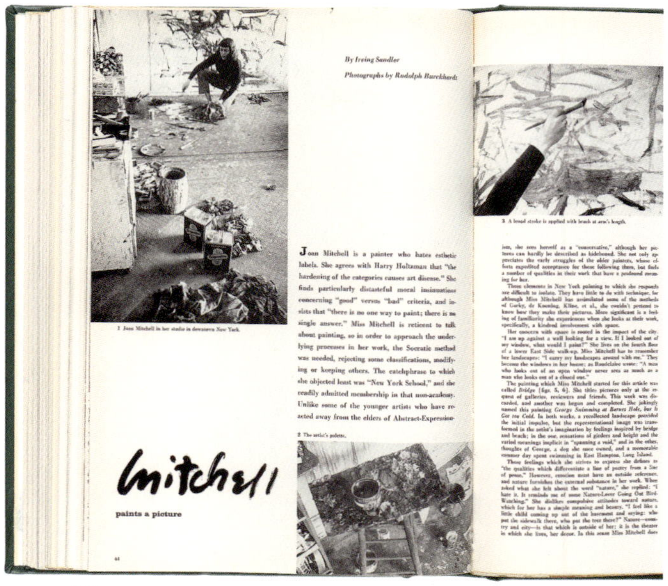

By Irving Sandler

Photographs by Rudolph Burckhardt

Mitchell paints a picture

Joan Mitchell is a painter who hates esthetic labels. She agrees with Harry Holtzman that "the hardening of the categories causes art disease." She finds particularly distasteful moral insinuations concerning "good" versus "bad" criteria, and insists that "there is no one way to paint; there is no single answer." Miss Mitchell is reticent to talk about painting, so in order to approach the underlying processes in her work, the Socratic method was needed, rejecting some classifications, modifying or keeping others. The catchphrase to which she objected least was "New York School," and she readily admitted membership in that non-academy. Unlike some of the younger artists who have reacted away from the elders of Abstract-Expression-

2 The artist's palette.

3.6

Mitchell's success in New York peaked, and as she gradually became a no-longer-"secret" presence in Europe. During these years, her paintings appeared in a string of high-profile international exhibitions, including the Osaka exhibition *International Art of a New Era: Informel and Gutai*; the 29th Venice Biennale; *Vitalità nell'Arte* at the Palazzo Grassi in Venice, traveling to the Kunsthalle in Recklinghausen, Germany, and the Stedelijk Museum in Amsterdam; the V Bienal do Museu de Arte Moderna, São Paulo; the Whitney Annual; a group show at the Galleria dell'Ariete in Milan; and *Documenta II* in Kassel.[52] Her work circulated among a network of American, French, German, Italian, Swiss, Japanese, and Dutch figures—primarily dealers, but increasingly critics and museum curators.[53] As France attempted to jettison outdated nationalism in favor of a cosmopolitan identity, Mitchell's work was included in the 1959 Biennale de Paris as that of a French artist.[54]

FIG 3.5 Joan Mitchell in her studio at 77 rue Daguerre, Paris, 1956

FIG 3.6 Joan Mitchell in her studio at 60 St. Mark's Place, New York, in Irving Sandler, "Mitchell Paints a Picture," *Art News* 56, no. 6 (October 1957): 44

The paradox of mobility paired with settling down characterized Mitchell's life at the end of the 1950s. As curators increasingly chose her paintings for international exhibitions, she selectively traveled to the openings, as well as to Greece, Turkey, and Corsica. She also settled decisively in Paris (although she would keep the lease on her St. Mark's studio for decades). Riopelle left his wife, and Mitchell secured an apartment for them on rue Frémicourt in 1959—finally, something she could consider all "mine"—which would remain her base in Paris until 1975.[55] O'Hara captured this duality with an appropriately aerial and bilingual image in his 1959 poem "Adieu to Norman, Bon Jour to Joan and Jean Paul," sent—again fittingly—in a letter from New York, addressed to Mitchell at her new home in Paris, commemorating visits both remembered and anticipated:

> yesterday I looked up the rue Frémicourt on a map
> and was happy to find it like a bird
> flying over Paris et ses environs.[56]

The Bridge, 1956

Marin Sarvé-Tarr

The Bridge is illustrated as plate 18.

FIG 3.7 Irving Sandler, "Is Today's Artist with or against the Past? Interviews with David Smith, Frederick Kiesler, Franz Kline, Joan Mitchell," *Art News* 57, no. 5 (September 1958): 41

In a September 1956 photograph (see fig. 3.5), Mitchell sits in her Paris studio at 77 rue Daguerre below the vertical panels of her first known diptych, *The Bridge*. Instead of the blooming masses of marks on surrounding unstretched canvases, the artist concentrated sparser clusters of streaking horizontal lines with dispersed diagonals to suggest a visual movement across the composition. Like Mitchell herself, who continually navigated between cities and continents, this work was painted in Paris but first exhibited in New York (see fig. 2.3) and encompasses a body of transatlantic travels and experiences.[1] Named for a subject that recurred in her painting until 1960 and made in a multipanel format that the artist returned to in the 1960s, *The Bridge* spans space and time in its theme and structure, capturing the importance of mobility and memory in Mitchell's abstraction.

Mitchell's work thrived on her transatlantic movement as she distilled flowing impressions of lived experiences into the fixed medium of paint. "Travelling around is a way of finding things which actually find me," she explained to critic Irving Sandler in 1957. "I paint what makes me want to get up in the morning."[2] Remembered views served as a point of departure that carried over in reaching brush marks and titles. That spring, she recalled from New York, "I went to Europe with that landscape feeling.... There were line drawings in the book [I was reading] of the Brooklyn Bridge.... I got homesick and nostalgic, and felt the image of the bridge come back and I painted [the] diptych. These images come and go."[3] Anchored in the artist's mobility, *The Bridge* stemmed from a corpus of embodied perceptions of foreign and familiar landscapes.

Grounded in an evolving amalgam of memories, the bridge motif emerged in the tension between a straddling horizontal armature and a pronounced vertical rise. *The Bridge* embodied for Mitchell a "feeling of space and freedom ... space—structure—color. [The] diptych will be used not only in terms of remembered images but remembered paintings."[4] She painted this diptych the same year that the Van Buren Street bascule bridge in Chicago designed by her grandfather was removed, the historic structure having remained in place during the construction of the new one. This striking fusion of past and present echoes the ways bridges could reference her native Chicago and her early New York apartment below the Brooklyn Bridge, or her first Paris studio on rue Galande, across the Pont au Double from Notre Dame Cathedral (see pages 28–29). As she described from Paris in 1948, "I walked the length of the Seine ... looking at the low squat bridges, looking vainly for something like the Brooklyn Bridge.... The closest thing to the Bridge is Notre Dame."[5] This slippage between bridges and cathedrals resurfaced in a 1958 interview that juxtaposed *The Bridge* with a tourist-like snapshot of a twelfth-century basilica in Burgundy, France (fig. 3.7). As Mitchell said, "I don't want to see a Romanesque cathedral every day.... It's there like Rikers. I can't close my eyes or limit my experiences."[6] This transatlantic description condenses forms and sensations from disparate monuments that each inflect the subject and matter of her paintings.

Mitchell's fluid fusion of the arcing extension of bridges and the sweeping reach of cathedrals forms the underlying structure of *The Bridge*. On a textured white ground touched with grays, the bold central forms framed by thin, sketchy blue, red, and black lines capture a vivid architectural monumentality in both the spanning sense of movement across the panels and the rising trajectory of ascending marks. The architectonic composition and strong flat lines build on an early touchstone motif that Mitchell recalled decades later as a "bridge picture."[7] Taken from views, paintings, or poems, bridges first appeared as straddling constructions across vast swatches of color in early figurative works or in the undulating scaffolding of abstract marks driving diagonally upward in *Cross Section of a Bridge* (1951, plate 9).[8] In *The Bridge,* nested lines of thickly layered marks in different colors trace over past brushstrokes, subtly inscribing the temporal process of making. On the left, broad streaks of white and sky blue mask thin black and olive lines, while the central beam on the right is built up of intricately woven touches of red, ocher, yellow, green, blue, and black made with brushes, fingers, paint tubes, and controlled drips.

Itself rooted in memory, *The Bridge* remained in Mitchell's mind when she flew back to New York and Chicago by December 1956. "I'm sitting in a DC6 missing you horribly," she wrote Jean Paul Riopelle. "Outside there are all those clouds you love so and maybe someday we'll be in a plane together. I started a large diptych before I left."[9] The rhythmic, mnemonic repetition of forms across the two panels of *The Bridge* reflects the artist's movement and anticipates her 1960s polyptychs like *Girolata Triptych* (1963, plate 39). These works transform the vertical format of each canvas into a horizontal sequence, creating a panoramic spatial and temporal succession. "Painting is a still thing," Mitchell explained in 1957. "It doesn't move in time like music or a novel, and the images of memory which are so important to me find their expression in my painting."[10] With its accumulated lines that disperse across the panels, this pivotal painting bridges her early and later work, fixing in paint a progression of transitory images that, like the artist herself, "come and go" across time, space, and place.

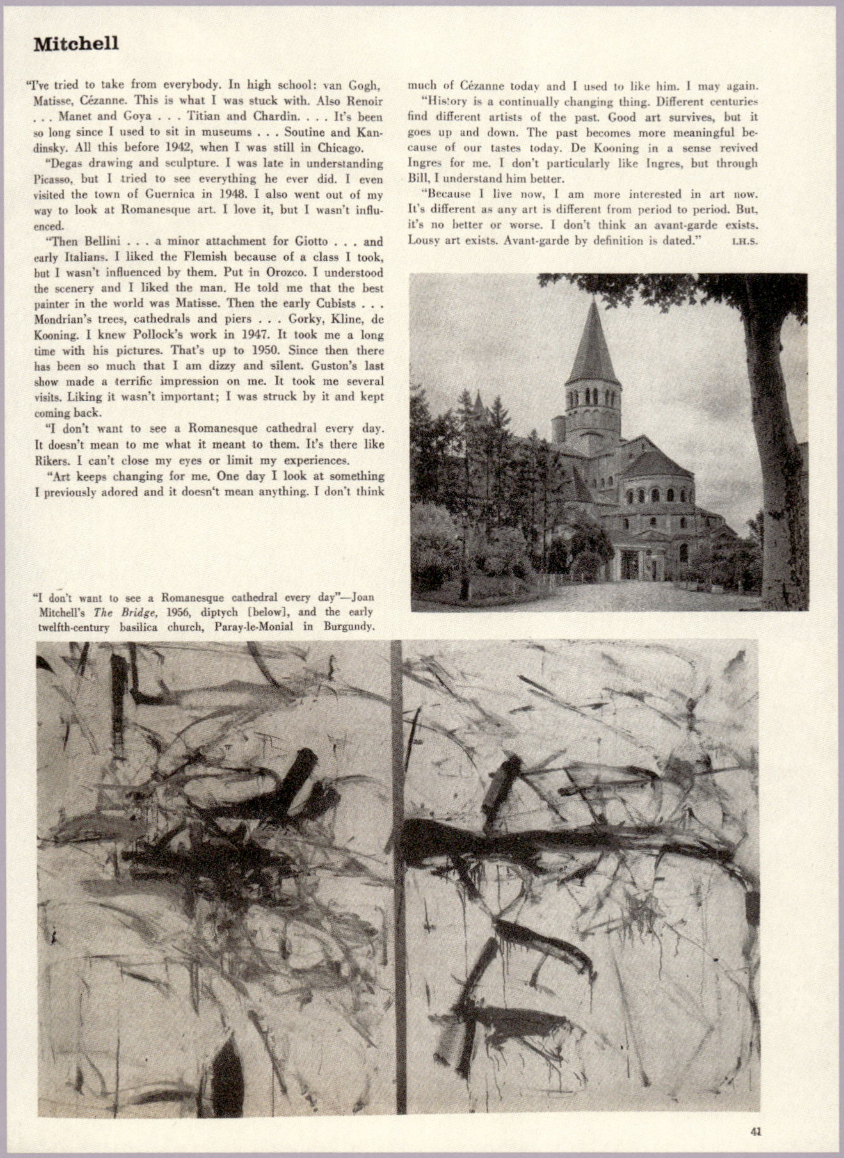

Mitchell

"I've tried to take from everybody. In high school: van Gogh, Matisse, Cézanne. This is what I was stuck with. Also Renoir . . . Manet and Goya . . . Titian and Chardin. . . . It's been so long since I used to sit in museums . . . Soutine and Kandinsky. All this before 1942, when I was still in Chicago.

"Degas drawing and sculpture. I was late in understanding Picasso, but I tried to see everything he ever did. I even visited the town of Guernica in 1948. I also went out of my way to look at Romanesque art. I love it, but I wasn't influenced.

"Then Bellini . . . a minor attachment for Giotto . . . and early Italians. I liked the Flemish because of a class I took, but I wasn't influenced by them. Put in Orozco. I understood the scenery and I liked the man. He told me that the best painter in the world was Matisse. Then the early Cubists . . . Mondrian's trees, cathedrals and piers . . . Gorky, Kline, de Kooning. I knew Pollock's work in 1947. It took me a long time with his pictures. That's up to 1950. Since then there has been so much that I am dizzy and silent. Guston's last show made a terrific impression on me. It took me several visits. Liking it wasn't important; I was struck by it and kept coming back.

"I don't want to see a Romanesque cathedral every day. It doesn't mean to me what it meant to them. It's there like Rikers. I can't close my eyes or limit my experiences.

"Art keeps changing for me. One day I look at something I previously adored and it doesn't mean anything. I don't think much of Cézanne today and I used to like him. I may again.

"History is a continually changing thing. Different centuries find different artists of the past. Good art survives, but it goes up and down. The past becomes more meaningful because of our tastes today. De Kooning in a sense revived Ingres for me. I don't particularly like Ingres, but through Bill, I understand him better.

"Because I live now, I am more interested in art now. It's different as any art is different from period to period. But, it's no better or worse. I don't think an avant-garde exists. Lousy art exists. Avant-garde by definition is dated." L.H.S.

"I don't want to see a Romanesque cathedral every day"—Joan Mitchell's *The Bridge,* 1956, diptych [below], and the early twelfth-century basilica church, Paray-le-Monial in Burgundy.

41

3.7

PAINTING 1950–58

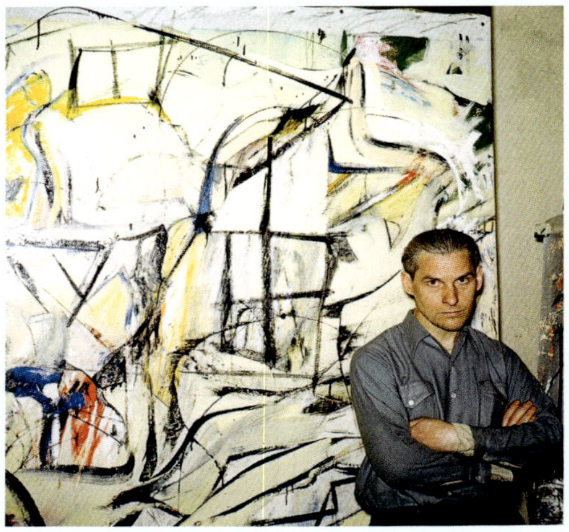

1

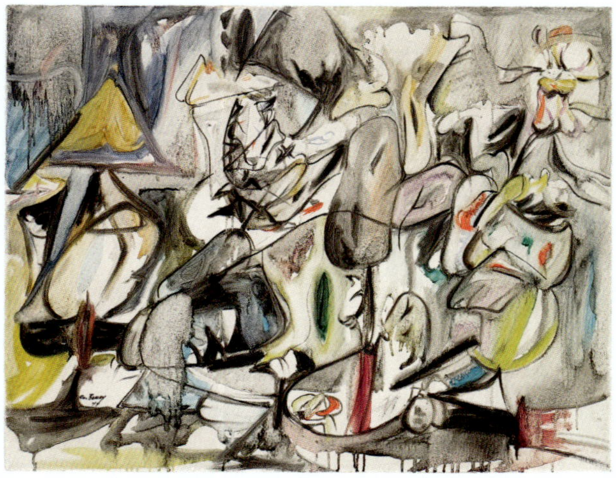

2

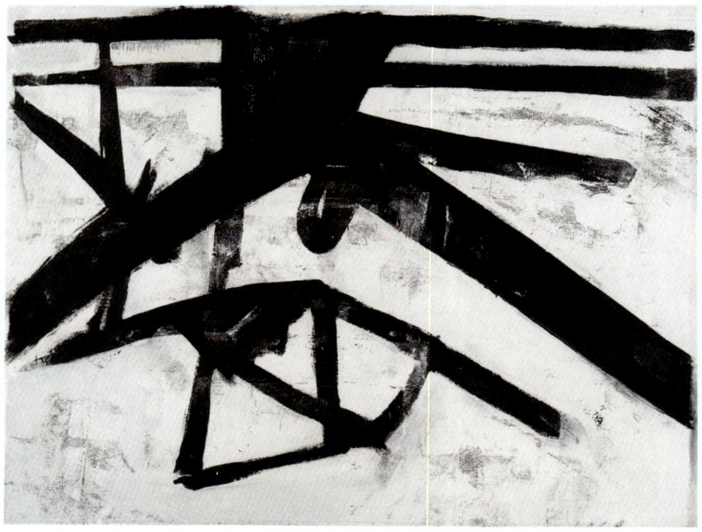

3

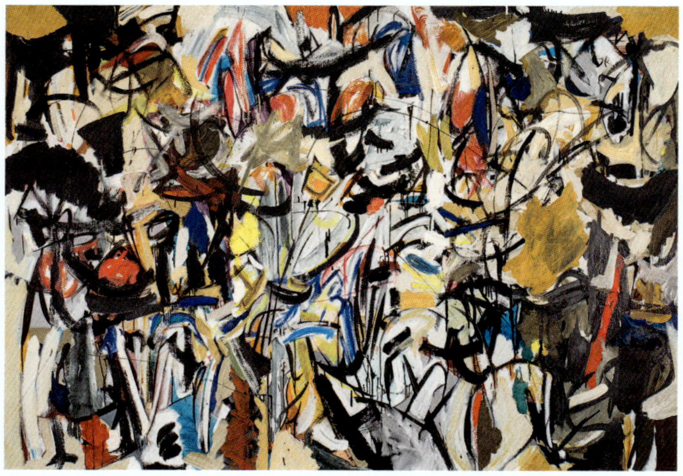

4

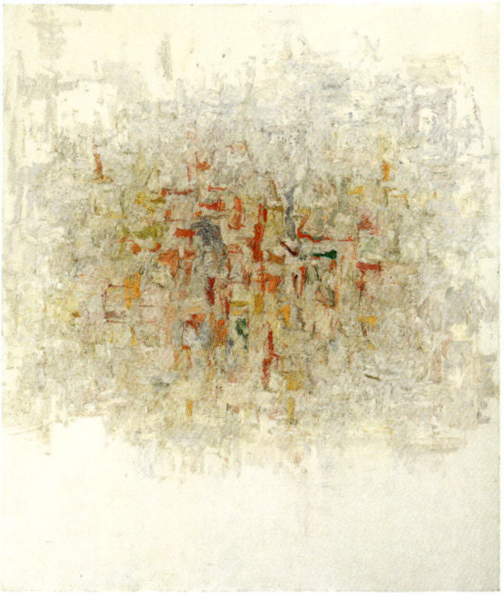

5

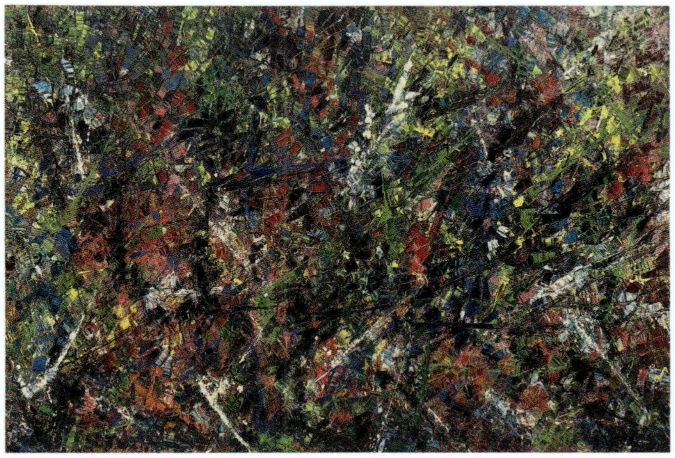

6

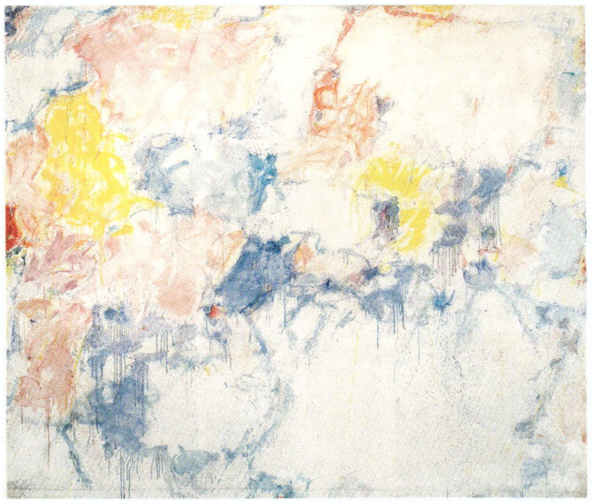

7

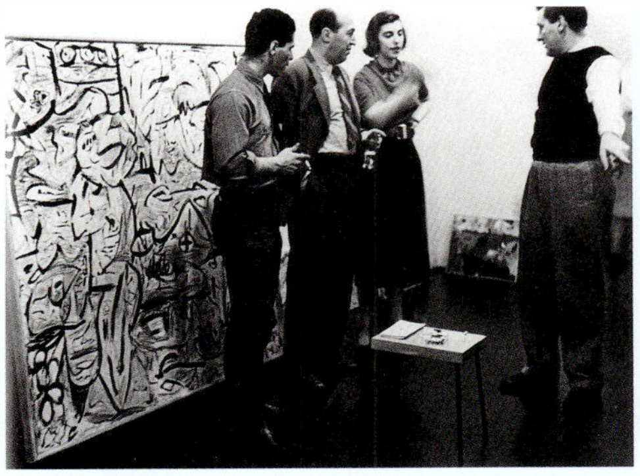

8

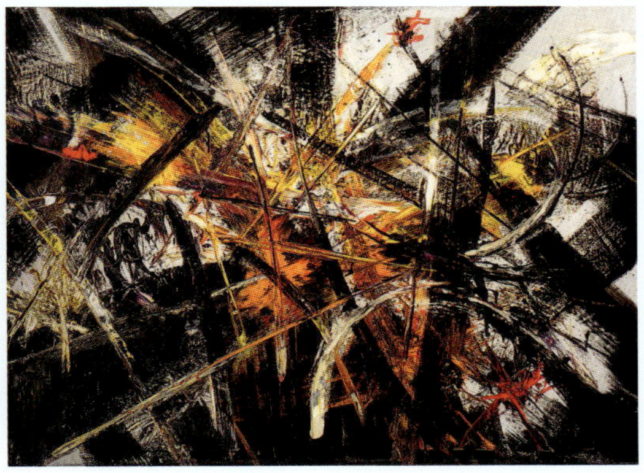

9

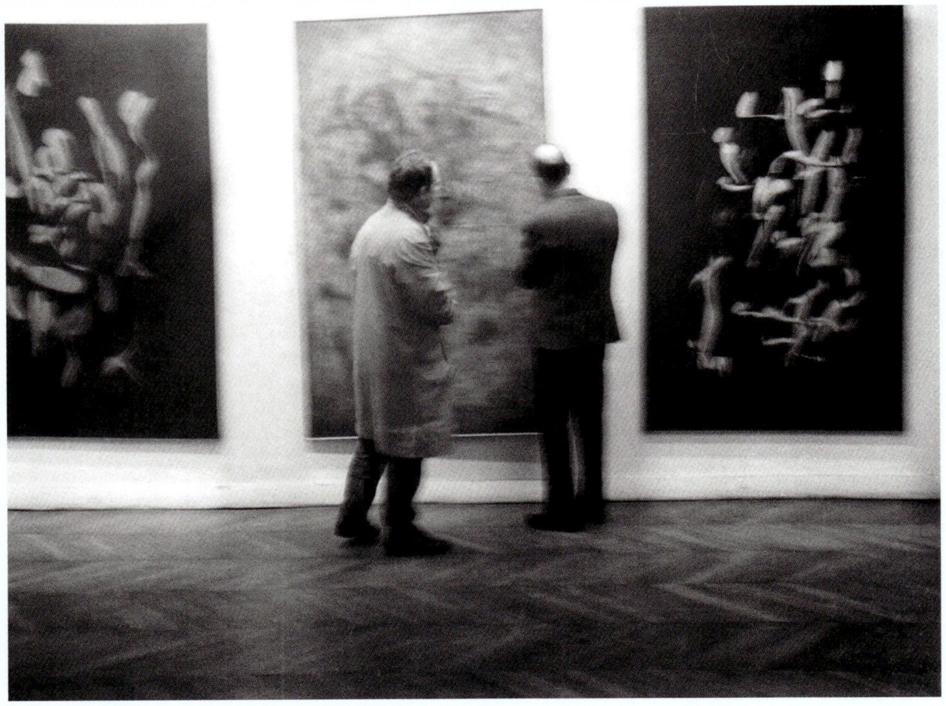

10

1 Willem de Kooning in his studio at 85 Fourth Avenue, New York, with an early version of *Excavation* (1950)

2 Arshile Gorky, *The Leaf of the Artichoke Is an Owl,* 1944. Oil on canvas, 28 × 35⅞ in. (71.1 × 91.2 cm). The Museum of Modern Art, New York, Sidney and Harriet Janis Collection Fund

3 Franz Kline, *High Street,* 1950. Oil on canvas, 58⅛ × 77½ in. (147.6 × 196.9 cm). Harvard Art Museums/Fogg Museum, gift of Lois Orswell

4 Michael Goldberg, *Untitled,* 1951. Oil on canvas, 51½ × 76 in. (130.8 × 193 cm). Courtesy Michael Rosenfeld Gallery LLC, New York

5 Philip Guston, *#5,* 1952. Oil on canvas, 46 × 41 in. (116.8 × 104.1 cm). The Metropolitan Museum of Art, New York, gift of Mrs. Lawrence Sophian, 1990

6 Jean Paul Riopelle, *Forest Blizzard,* 1953. Oil on board, 67⅛ × 100¼ in. (170.5 × 254.7 cm). The Museum of Modern Art, New York, gift of Mr. and Mrs. Ralph F. Colin

7 Sam Francis, *In Lovely Blueness No. 2,* 1955–56. Oil on linen, 122 × 144 in. (309.9 × 365.8 cm). Art Institute of Chicago, Mr. and Mrs. Frank G. Logan and Flora Mayer Witkowsky purchase prize funds; through prior gifts of Wallace L. DeWolf, Albert A. Munger, and the Charles H. and Mary F. S. Worcester Collection; gift of Lannan Foundation

8 Al Leslie, Clement Greenberg, Helen Frankenthaler, and John Bernard Myers installing *Helen Frankenthaler,* Tibor de Nagy Gallery, New York, 1951

9 Judit Reigl, *Outburst,* 1955. Oil on canvas, 39½ × 58 in. (101 × 147 cm). Courtesy Janos Gat Gallery, New York

10 Simon Hantaï and Jean Fournier at the Galerie Kléber, Paris, 1958. Galerie Jean Fournier, Paris

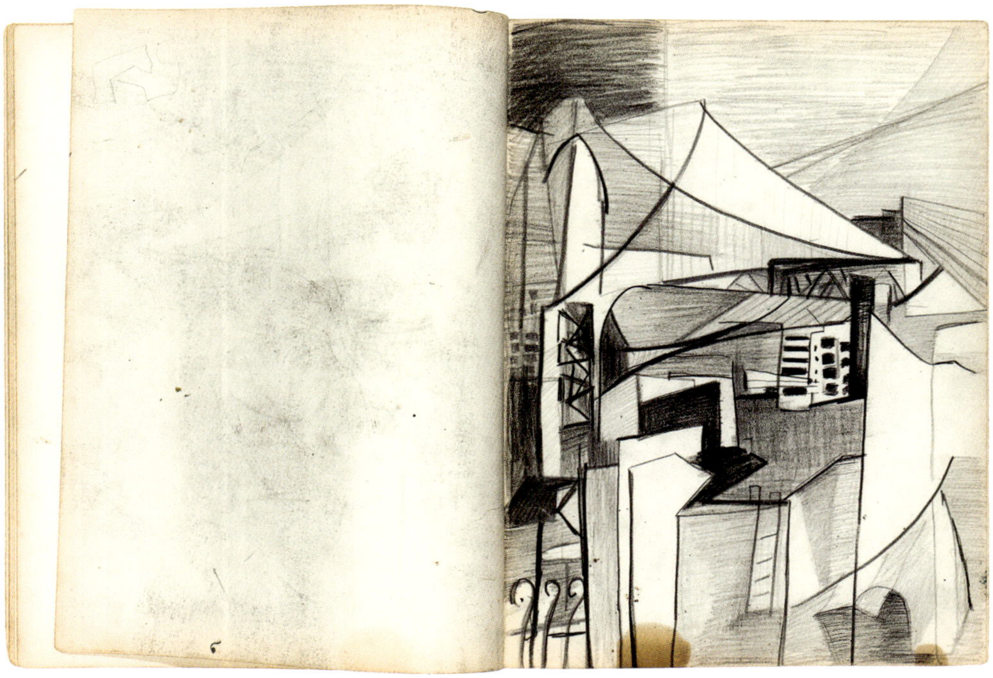

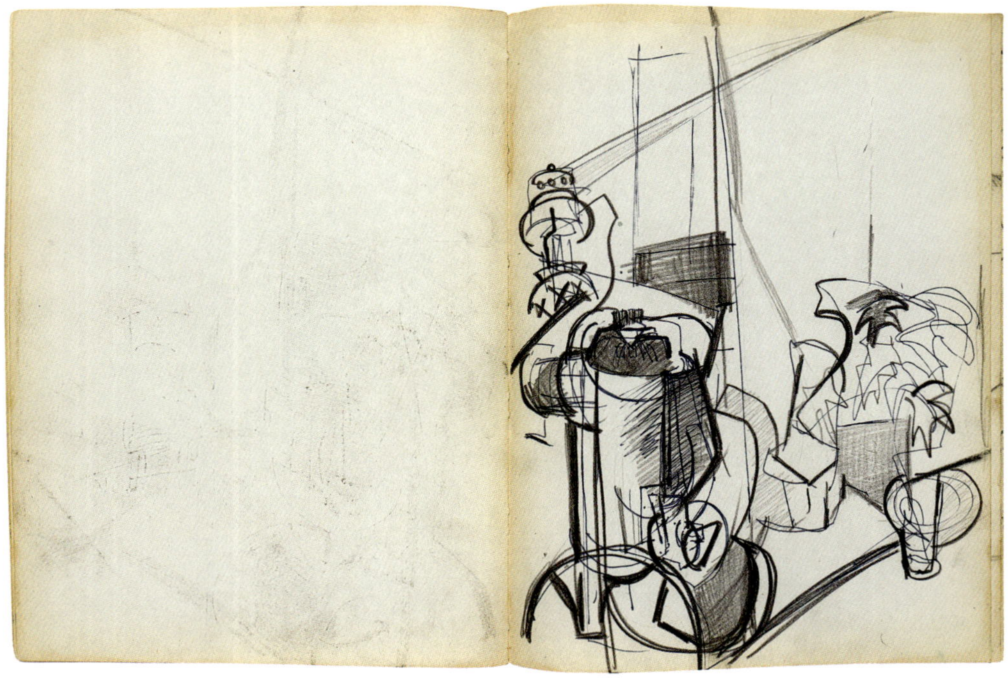

Sketchbook, ca. 1948. Pages 58 and 59 of 182. Graphite and wax crayon on paper, open: 10¼ × 15¾ in. (26 × 40 cm).
Joan Mitchell Foundation Archives, New York

Sketchbook, ca. 1948. Pages 52 and 53 of 142. Fabricated graphite pencil, pen, and ink on paper, open: 10³⁄₁₆ × 15⅝ in. (25.9 × 39.7 cm).
Joan Mitchell Foundation Archives, New York

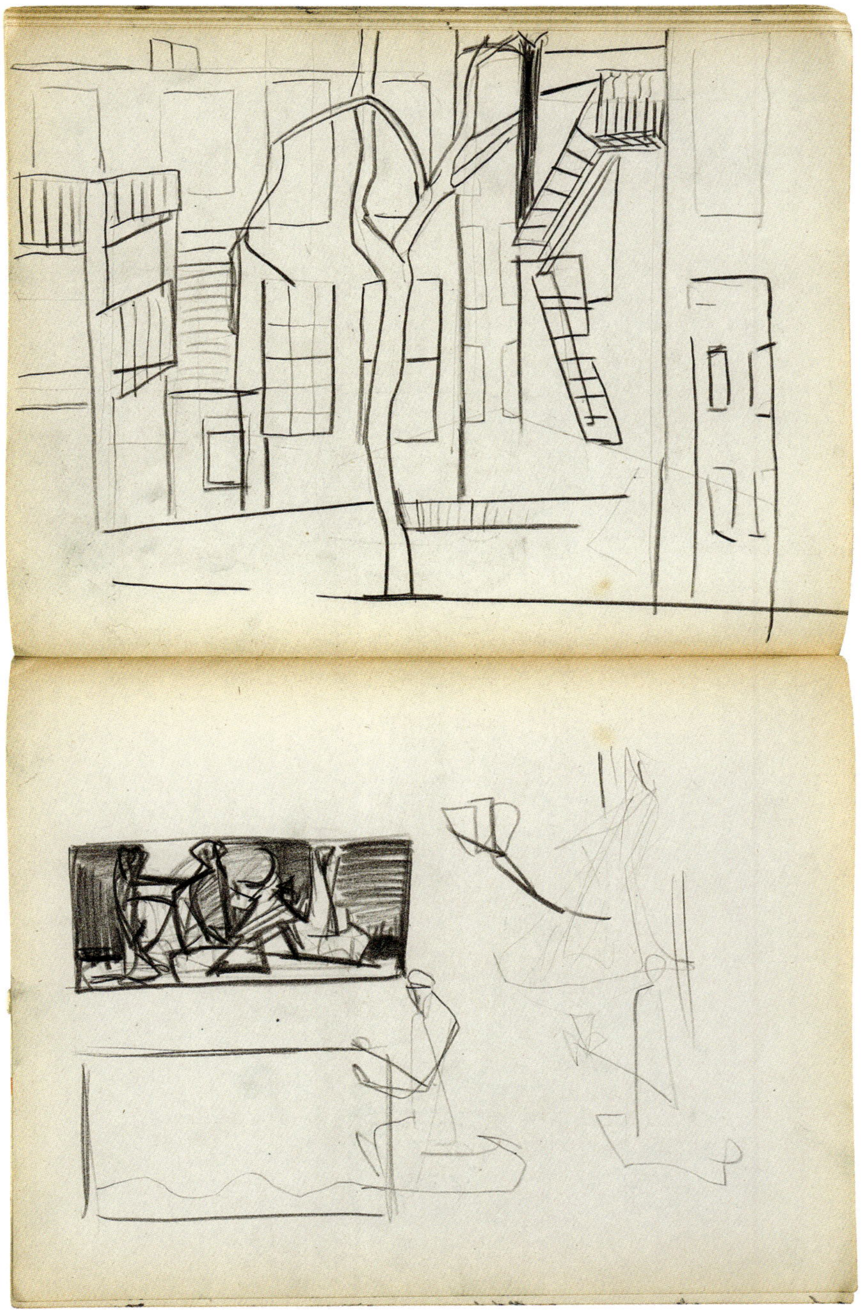

Sketchbook, ca. 1949. Pages 112 and 113 of 150. Wax crayon on paper, open: 10³⁄₁₆ × 15¾ in. (25.9 × 40 cm) (horizontal).
Joan Mitchell Foundation Archives, New York

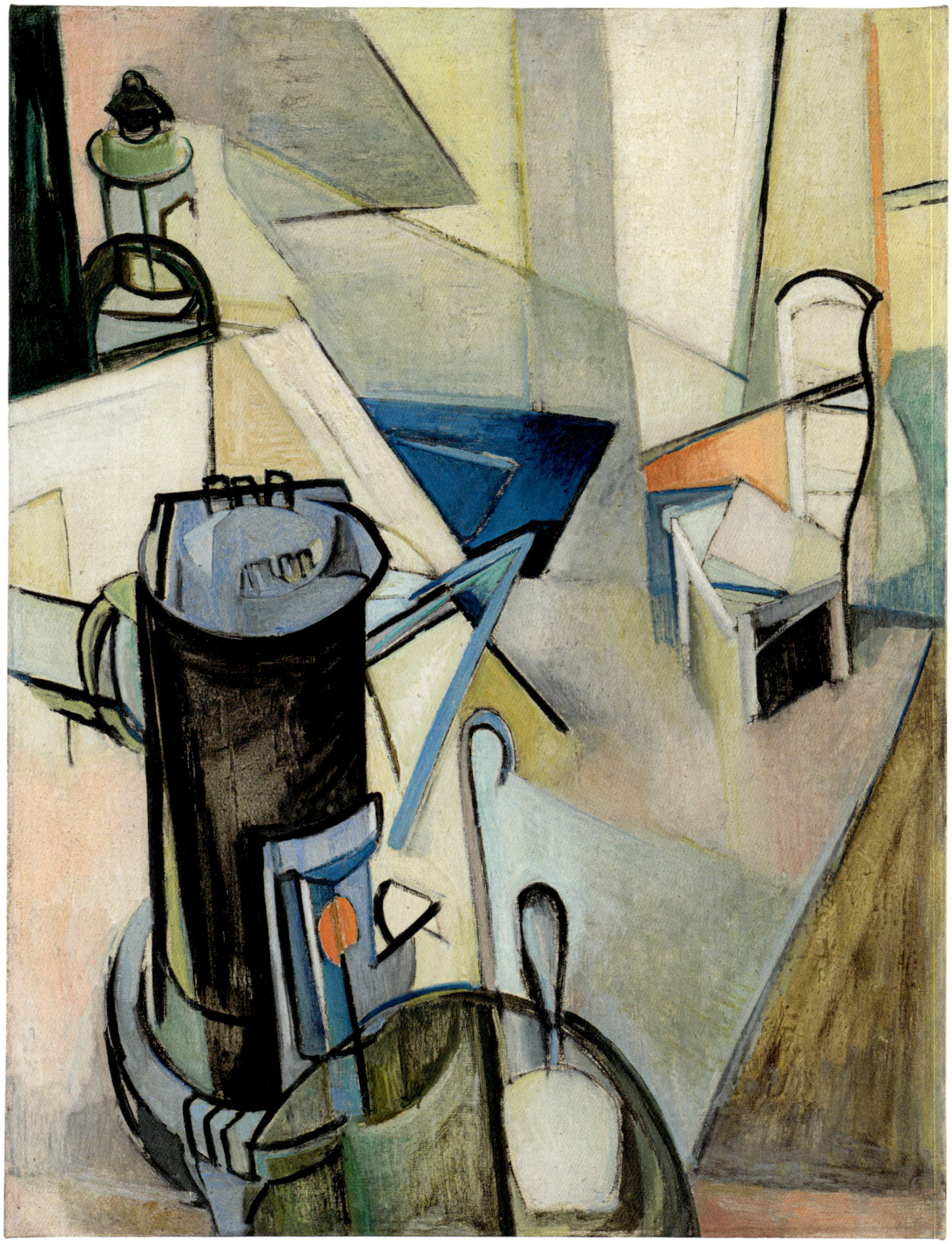

Untitled, 1948. Oil on canvas, 45¼ × 34¾ in. (114.9 × 88.3 cm). Joan Mitchell Foundation, New York

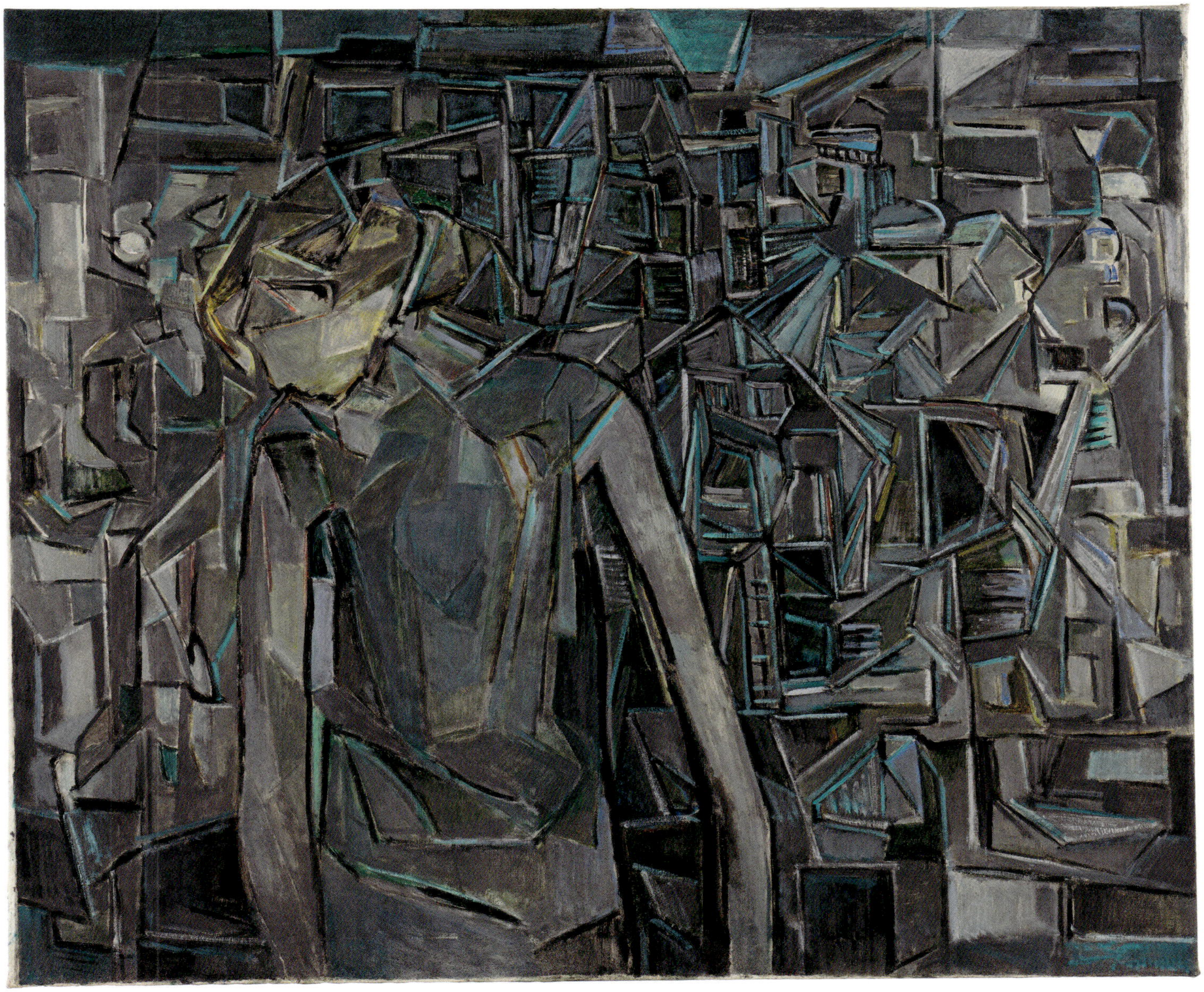

Figure and the City, 1949–50. Oil on canvas, 40¼ × 49 in. (102.2 × 124.5 cm). Joan Mitchell Foundation, New York

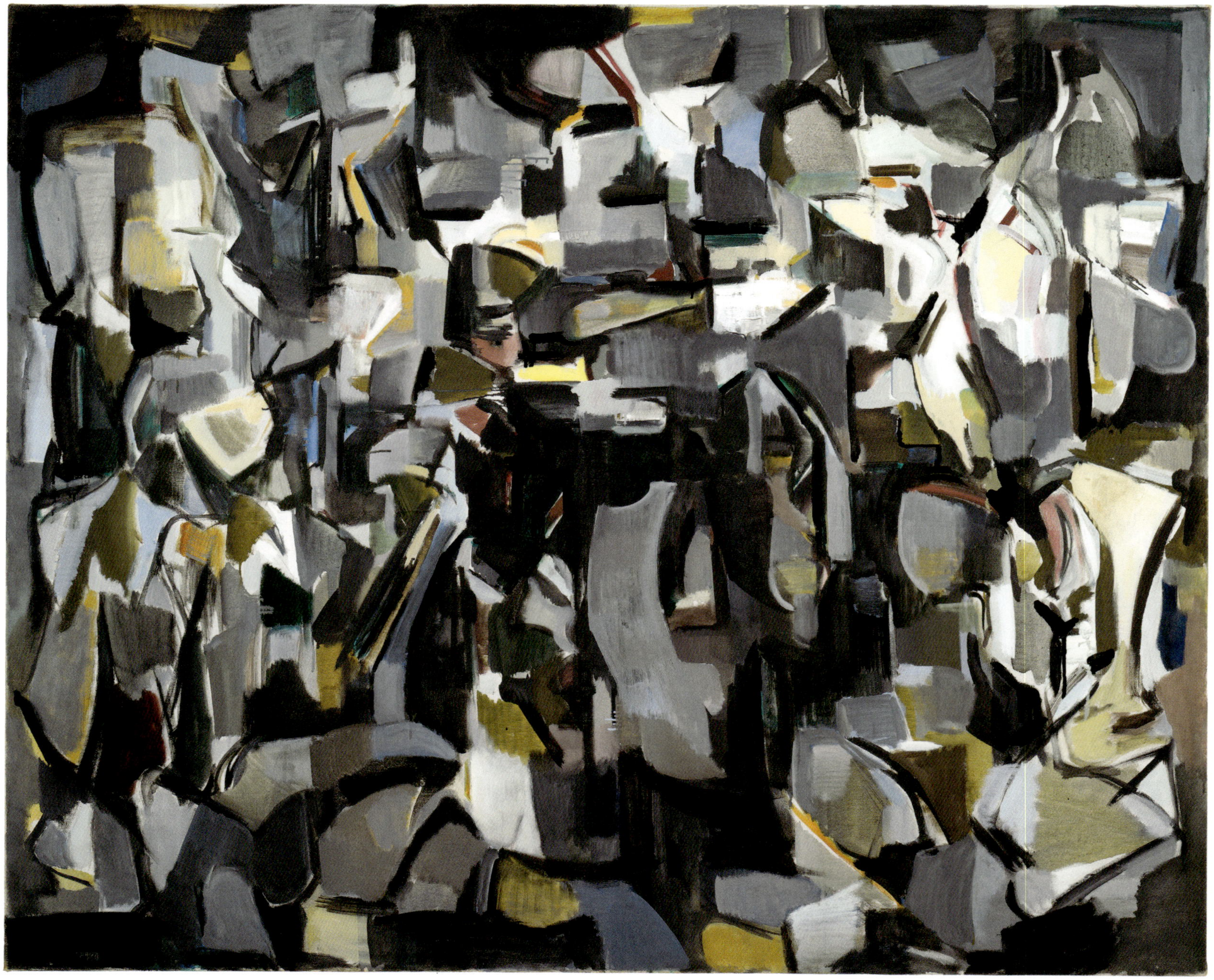

Untitled, ca. 1950. Oil on canvas, 51 × 63¾ in. (129.5 × 161.9 cm). Private collection

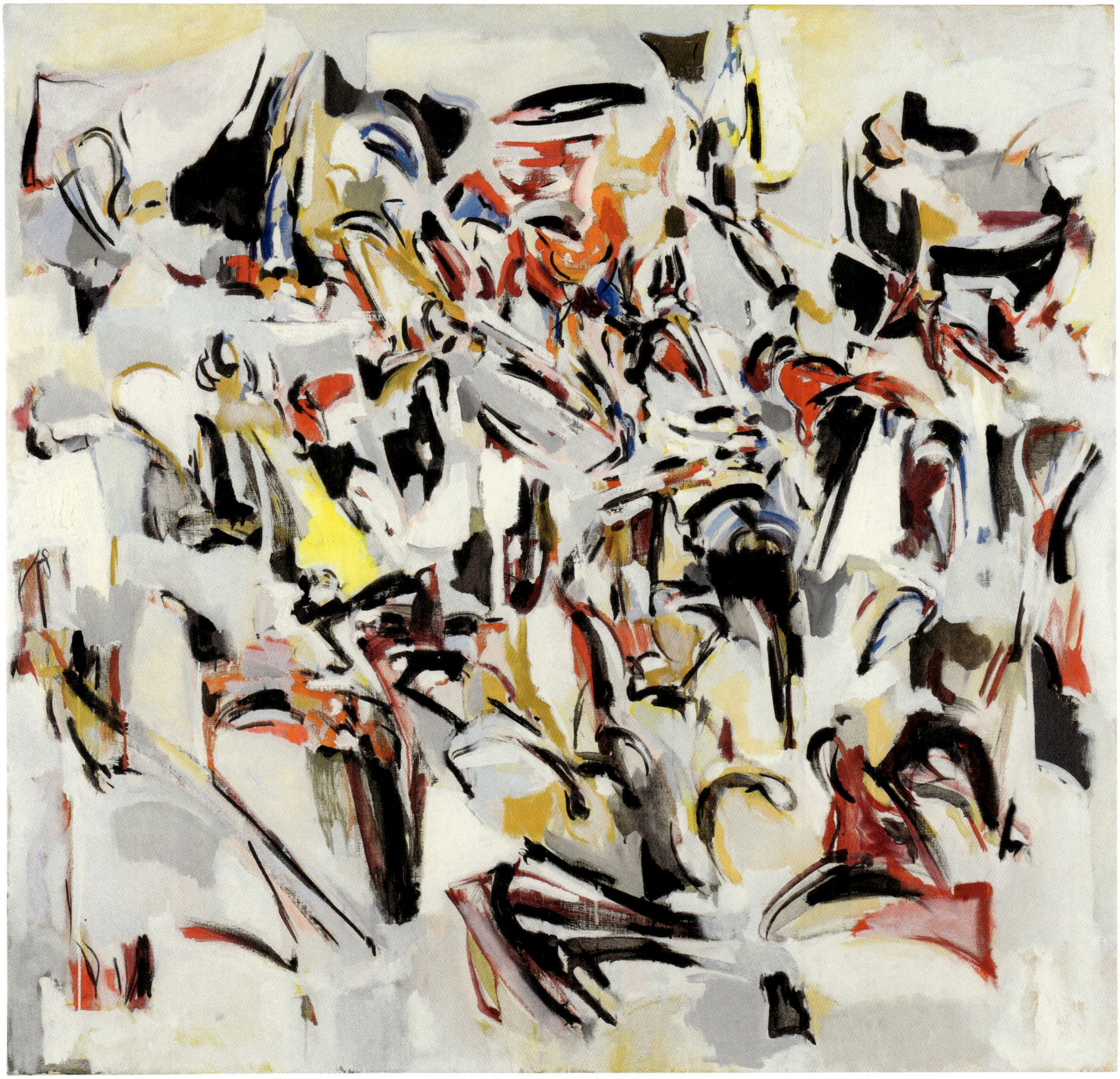

Untitled, ca. 1950. Oil on canvas, 52½ × 54⅝ in. (133.4 × 138.7 cm). Joan Mitchell Foundation, New York

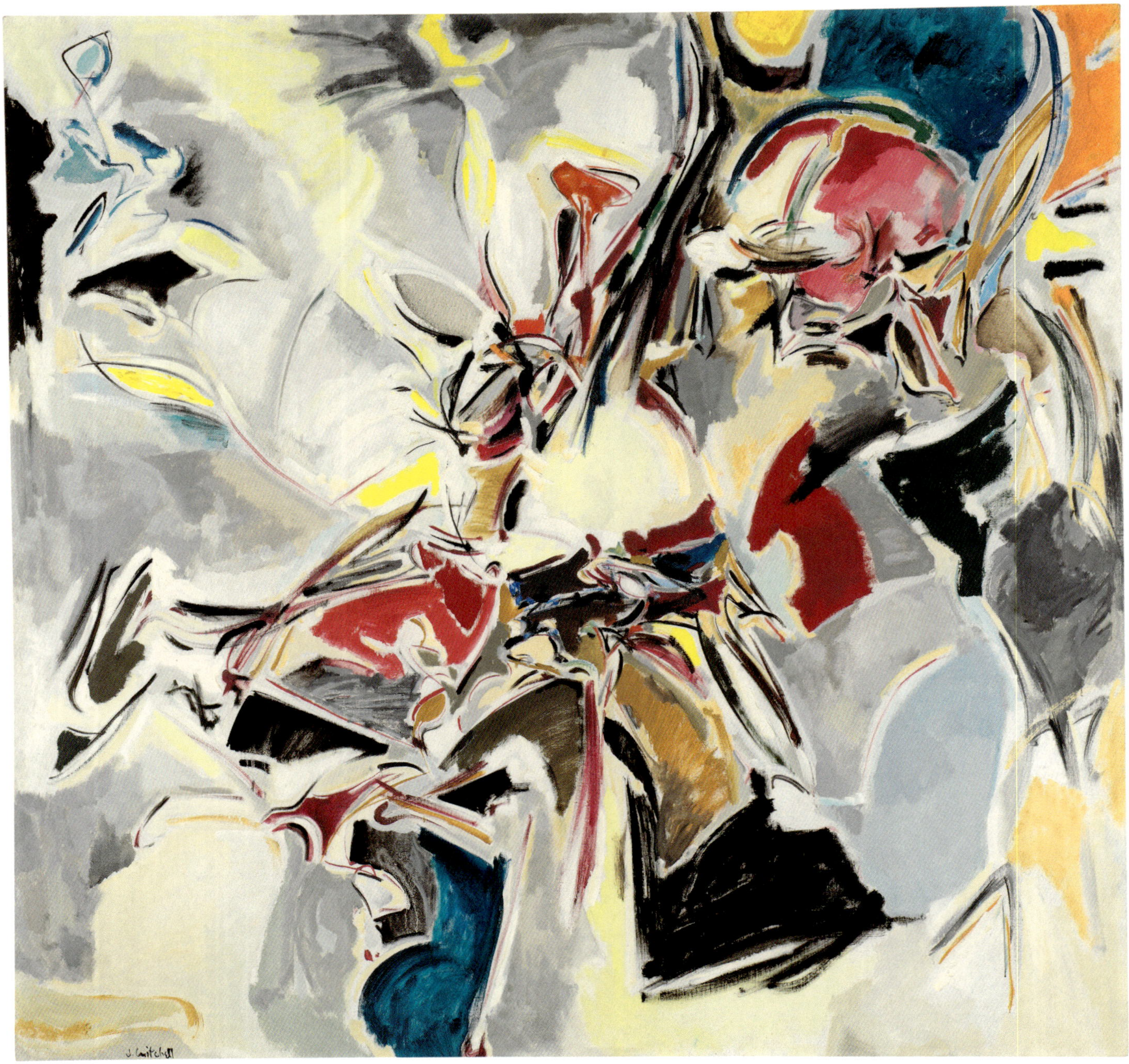

Lyric, ca. 1951. Oil on canvas, 68 × 72¾ in. (172.7 × 184.8 cm). Frances Lehman Loeb Art Center, Vassar College, Poughkeepsie, New York, gift of William Rubin

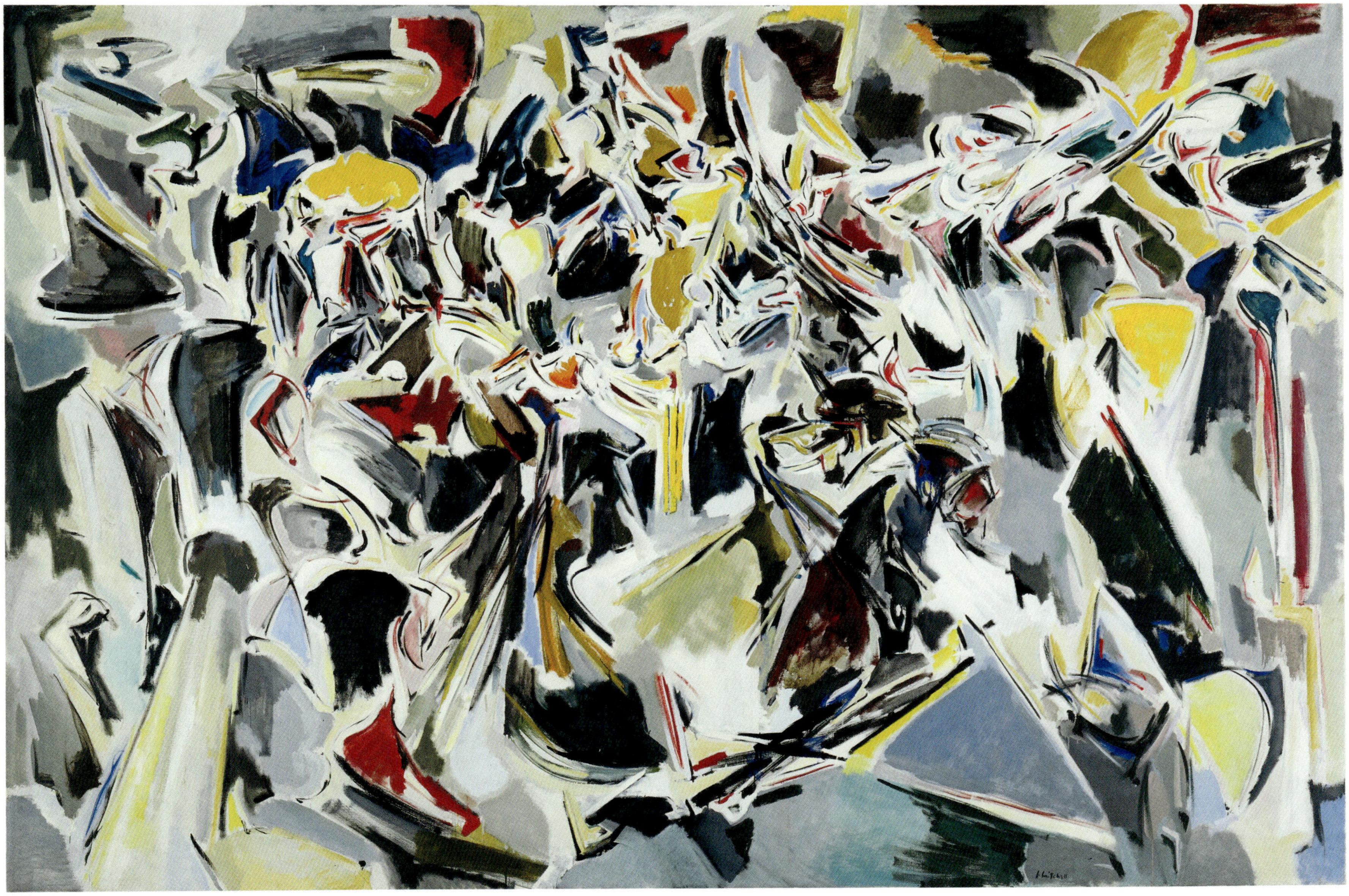

Cross Section of a Bridge, 1951. Oil on canvas, 79¾ × 119¾ in. (202.6 × 304.2 cm). Nakanoshima Museum of Art, Osaka, Japan

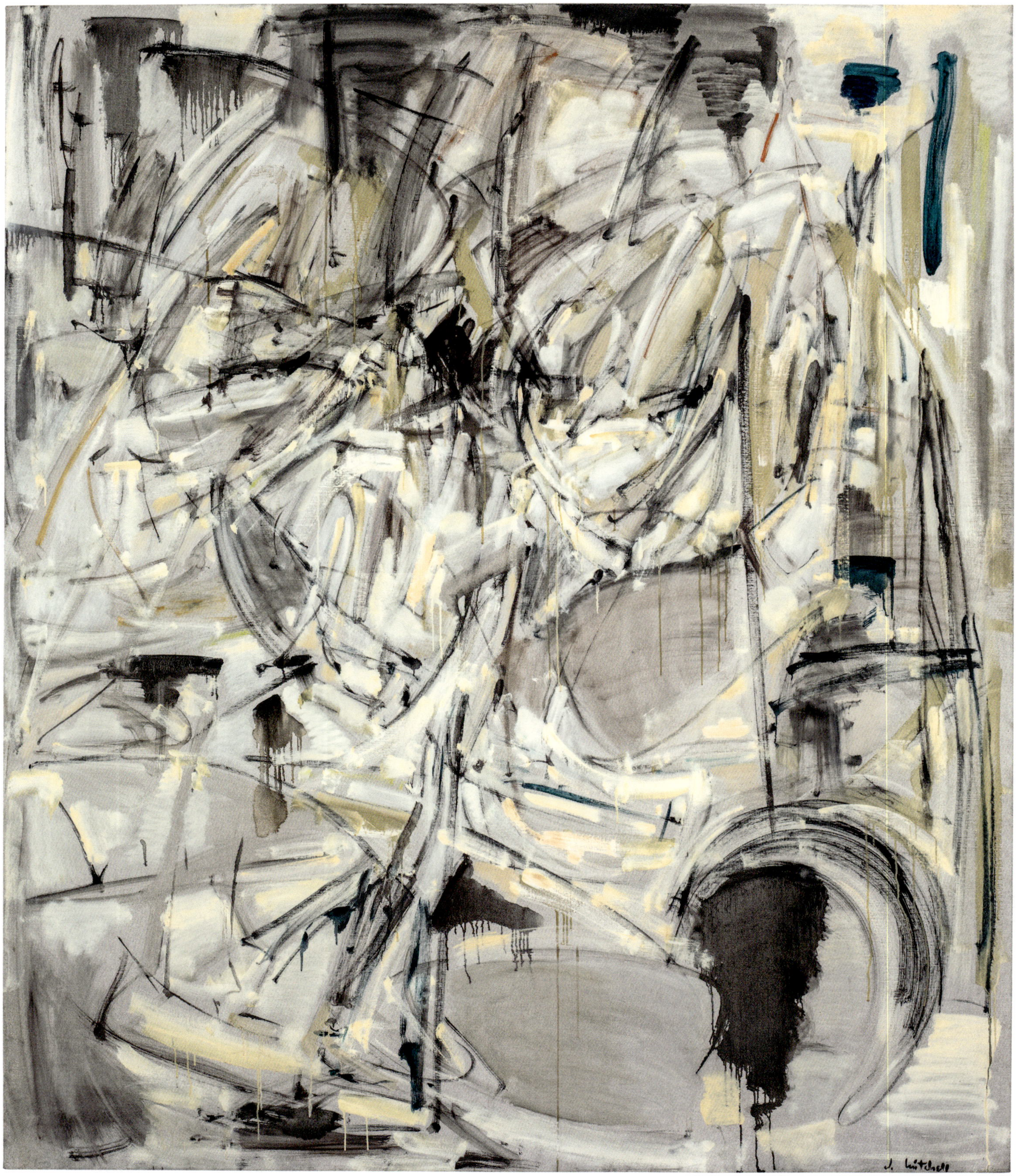

Untitled, ca. 1953. Oil on canvas, 80 × 70 in. (203.2 × 177.8 cm). Private collection

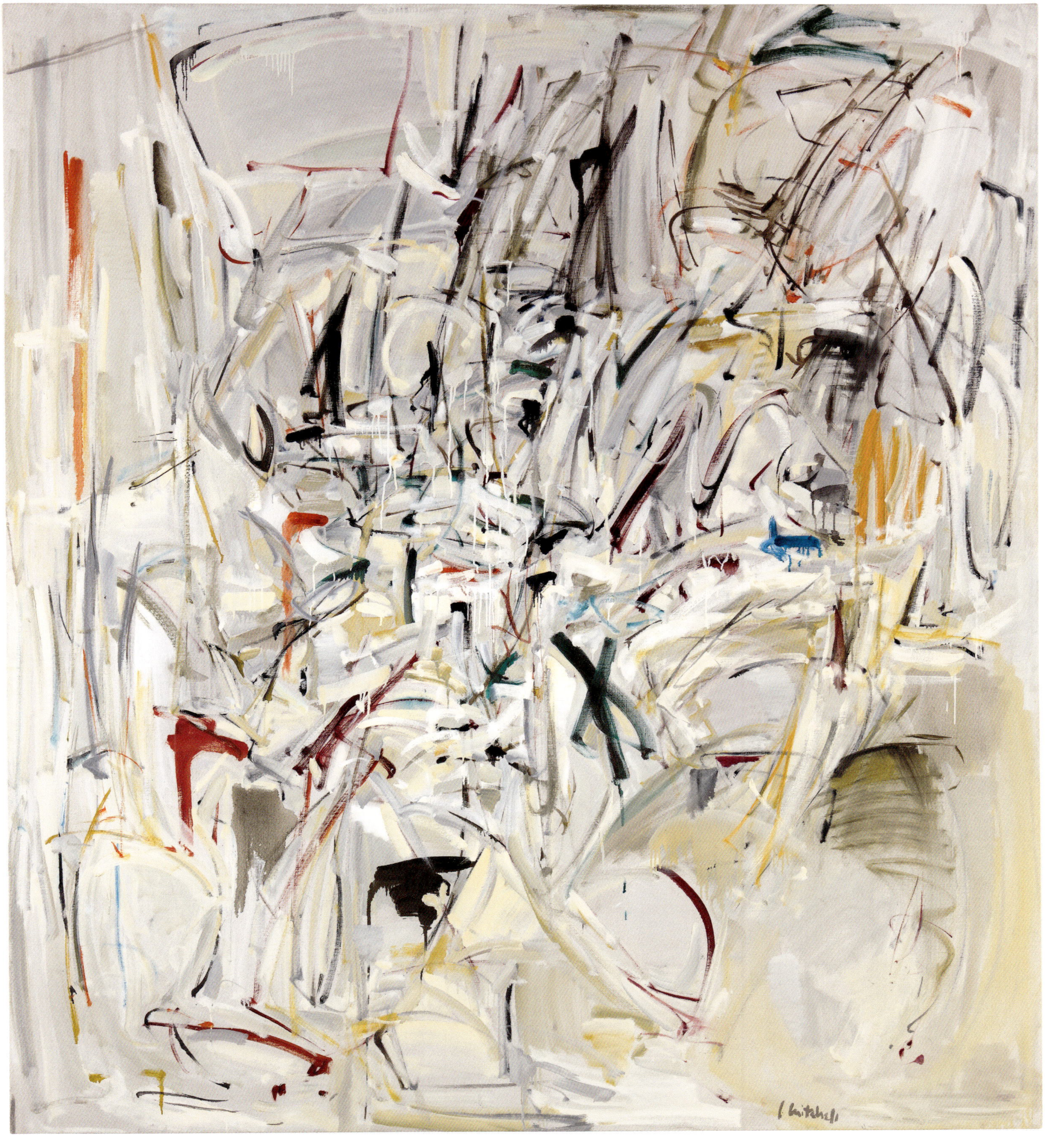

Untitled, 1952–53. Oil on canvas, 77½ × 71⅝ in. (196.9 × 181.9 cm). Promised gift to Crystal Bridges Museum of American Art, Bentonville, Arkansas

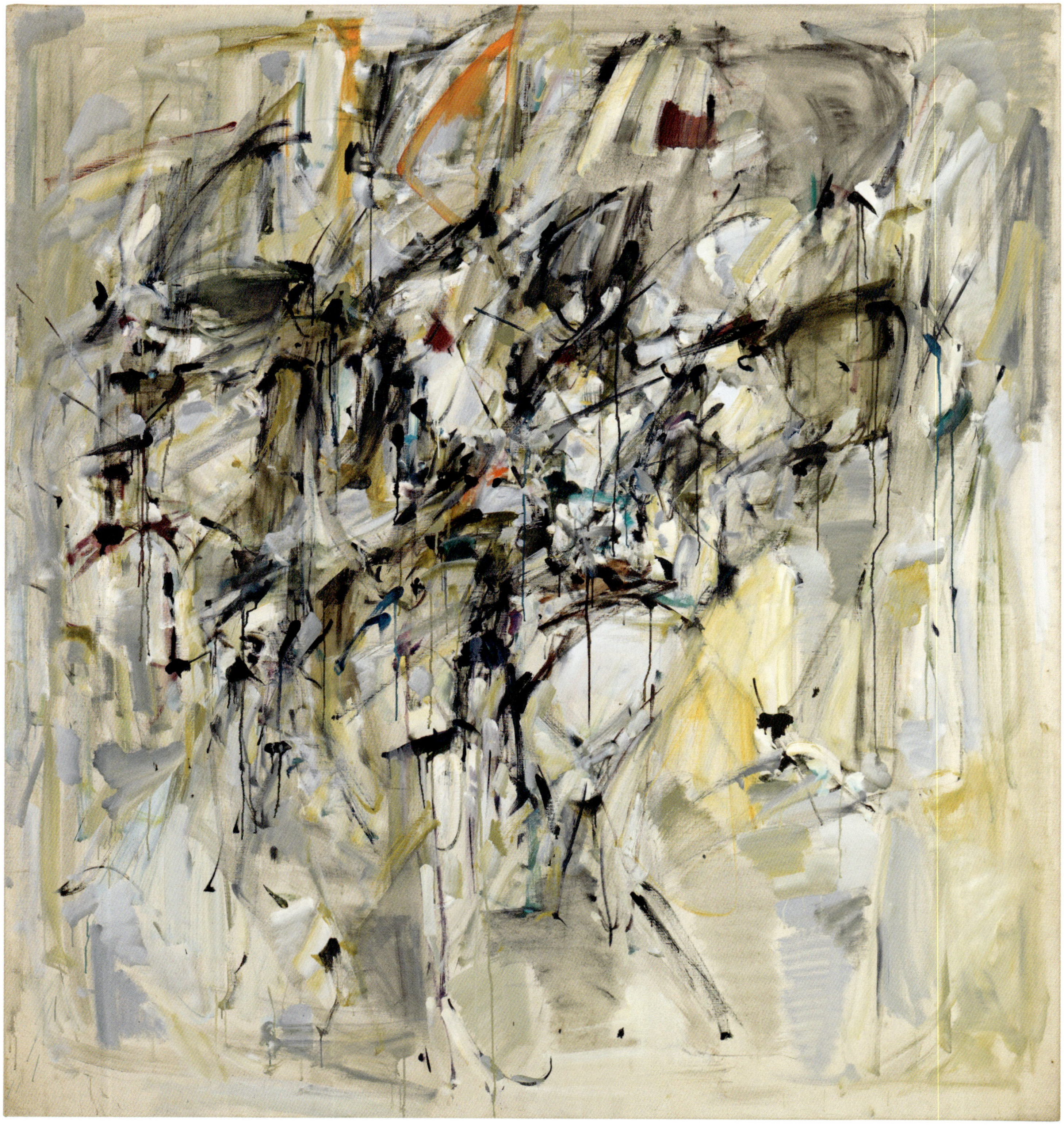

Rose Cottage, 1953. Oil on canvas, 71⅞ × 68½ in. (182.6 × 174 cm). Private collection

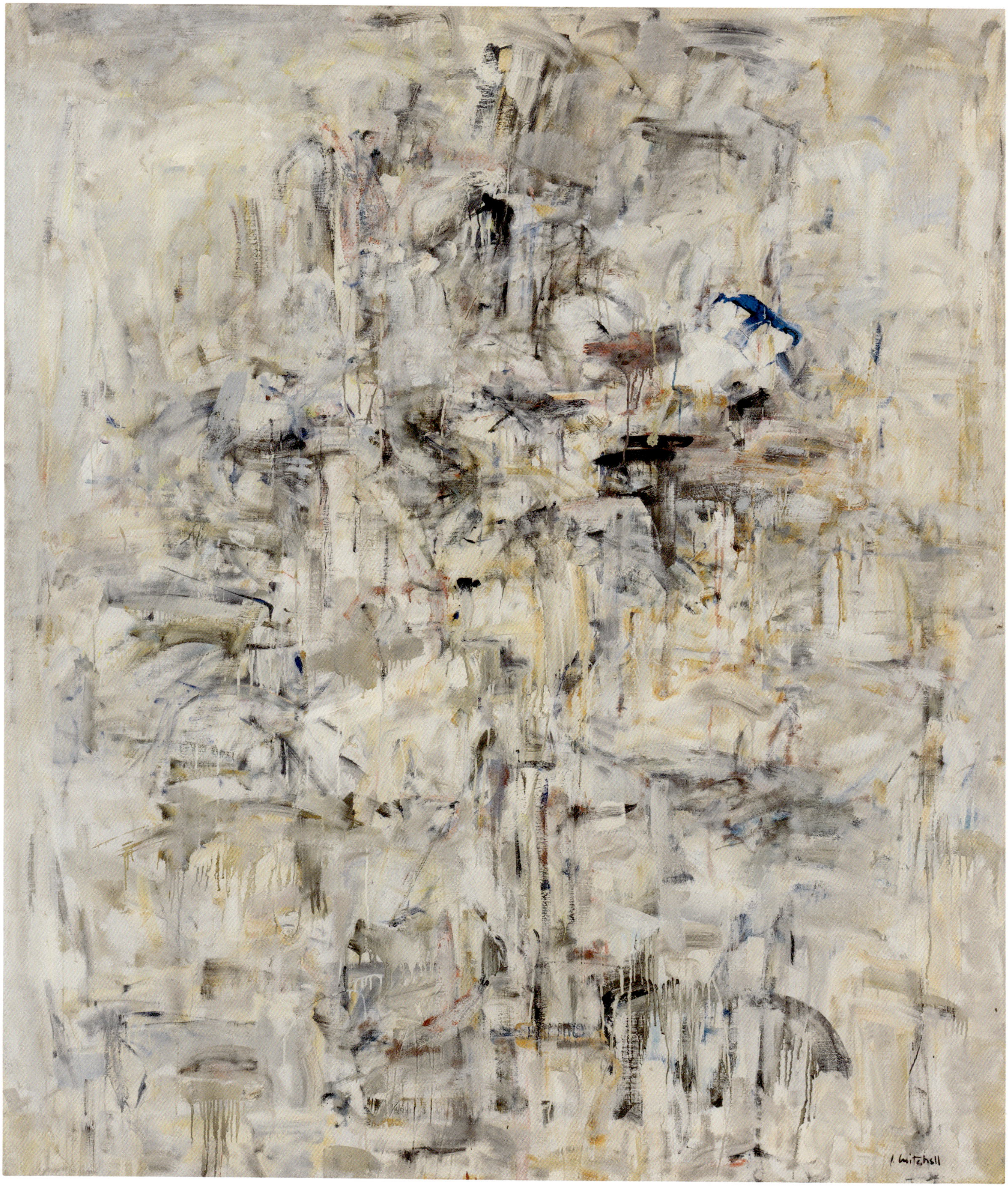

Untitled, 1953–54. Oil on canvas, 80⅝ × 69⅜ in. (204.8 × 176.2 cm). Private collection

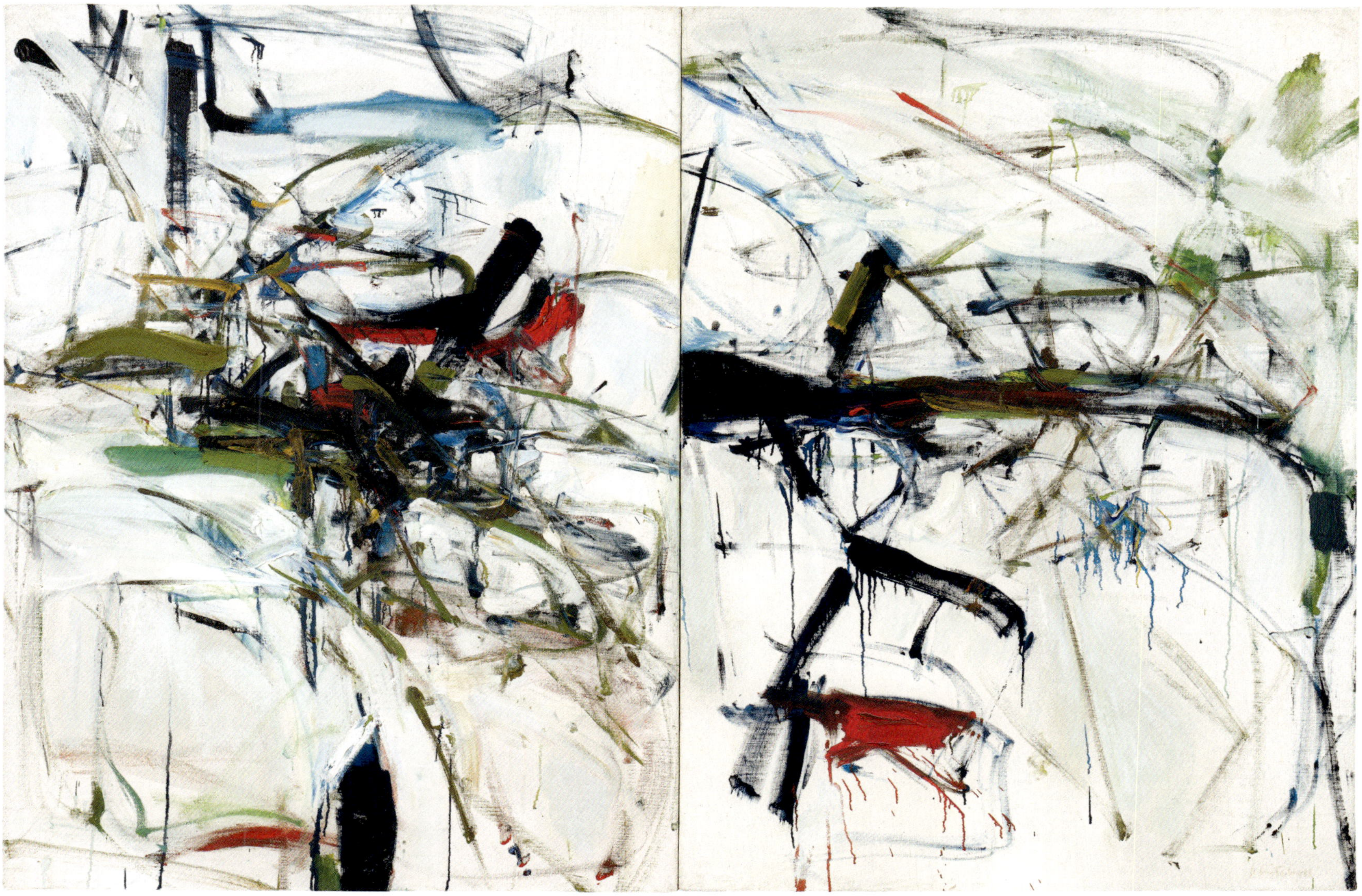

The Bridge, 1956. Oil on canvas, 45¾ × 70⅜ in. (116.2 × 178.8 cm). Private collection

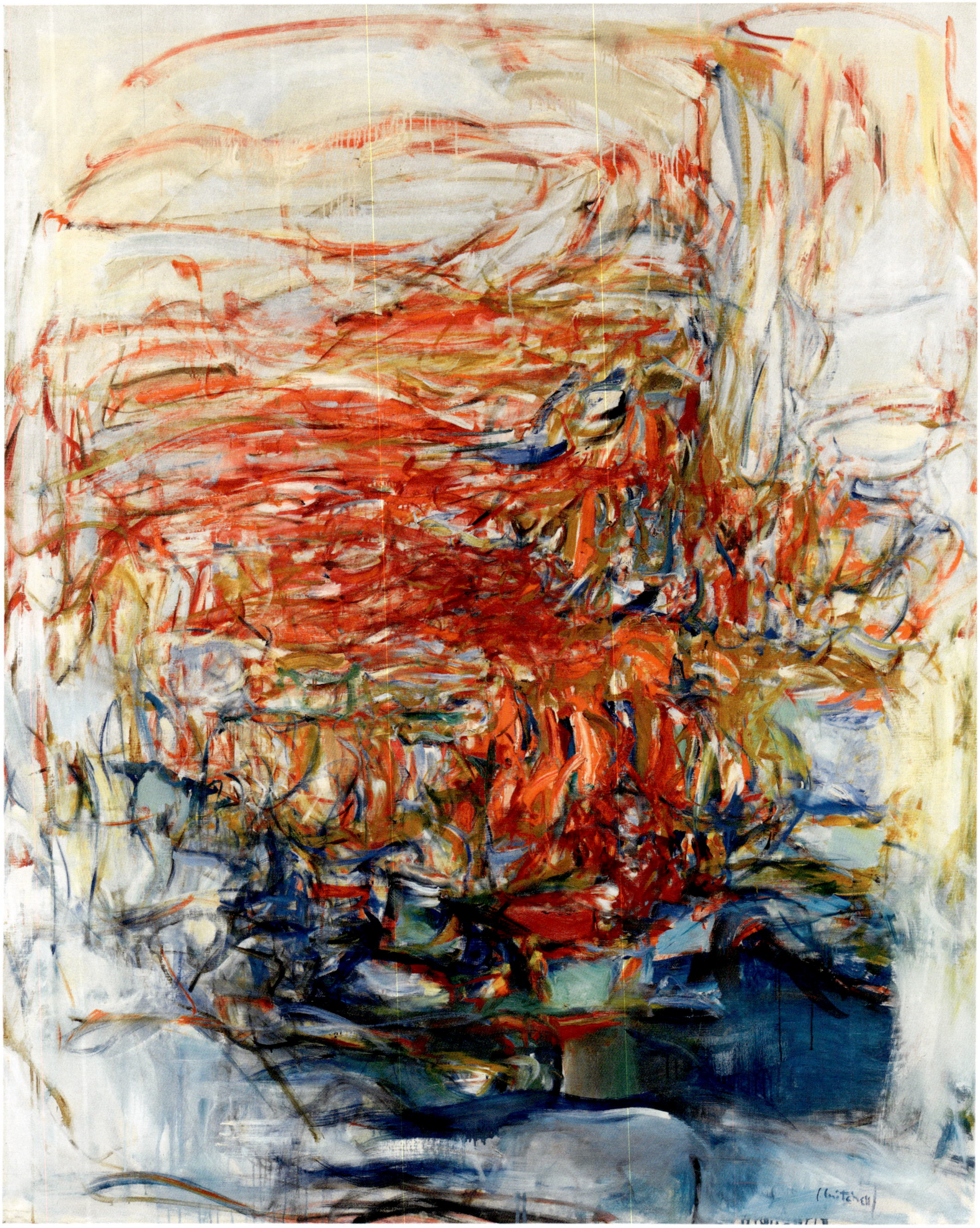

East Ninth Street, 1956. Oil on canvas, 80 × 64 in. (203.2 × 162.6 cm). Los Angeles County Museum of Art, gift of William Heller, Inc.

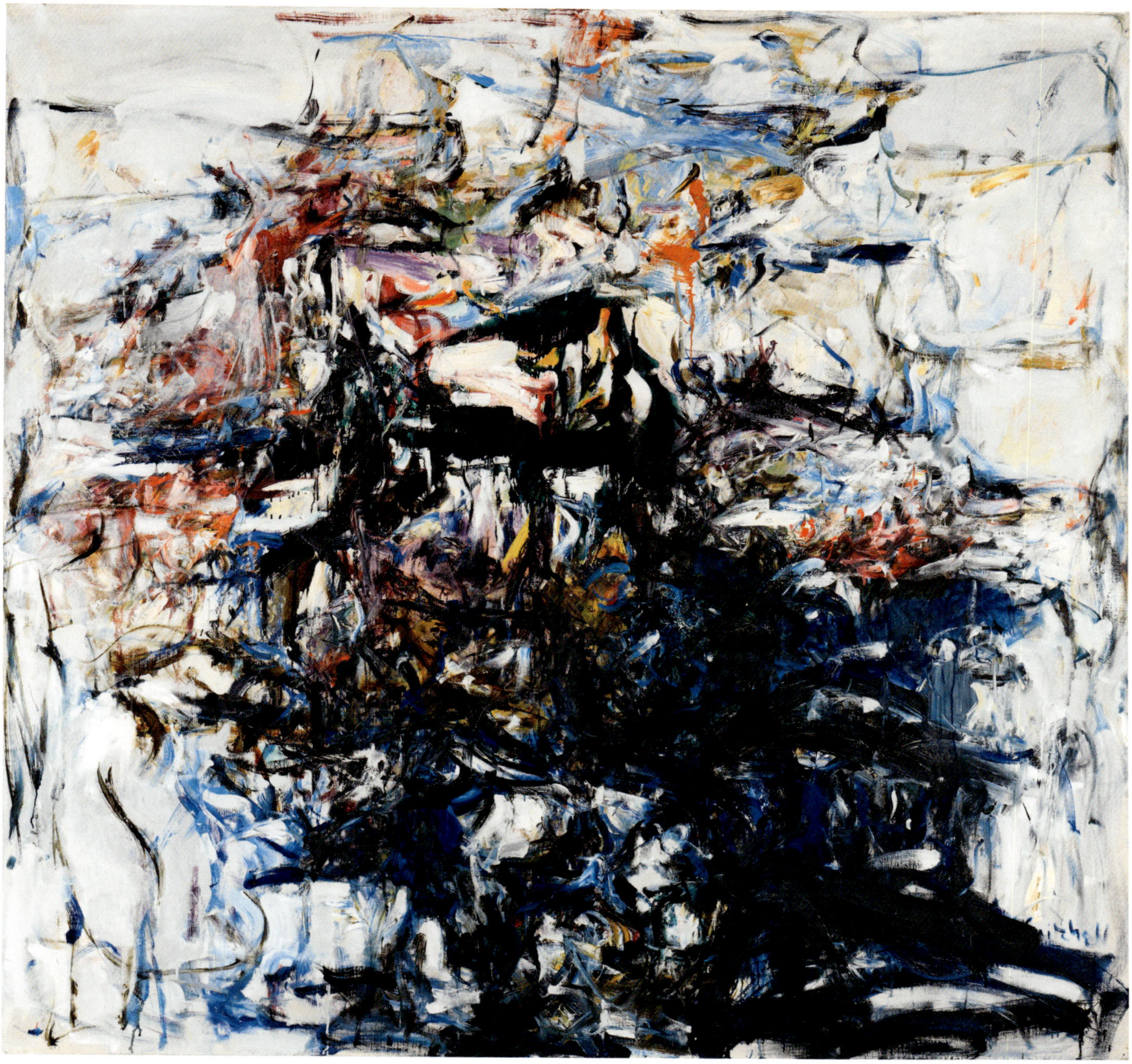

Monongahela, 1955. Oil on canvas, 71¾ × 78 in. (182.2 × 198.1 cm). Collection of Deborah DeCotis

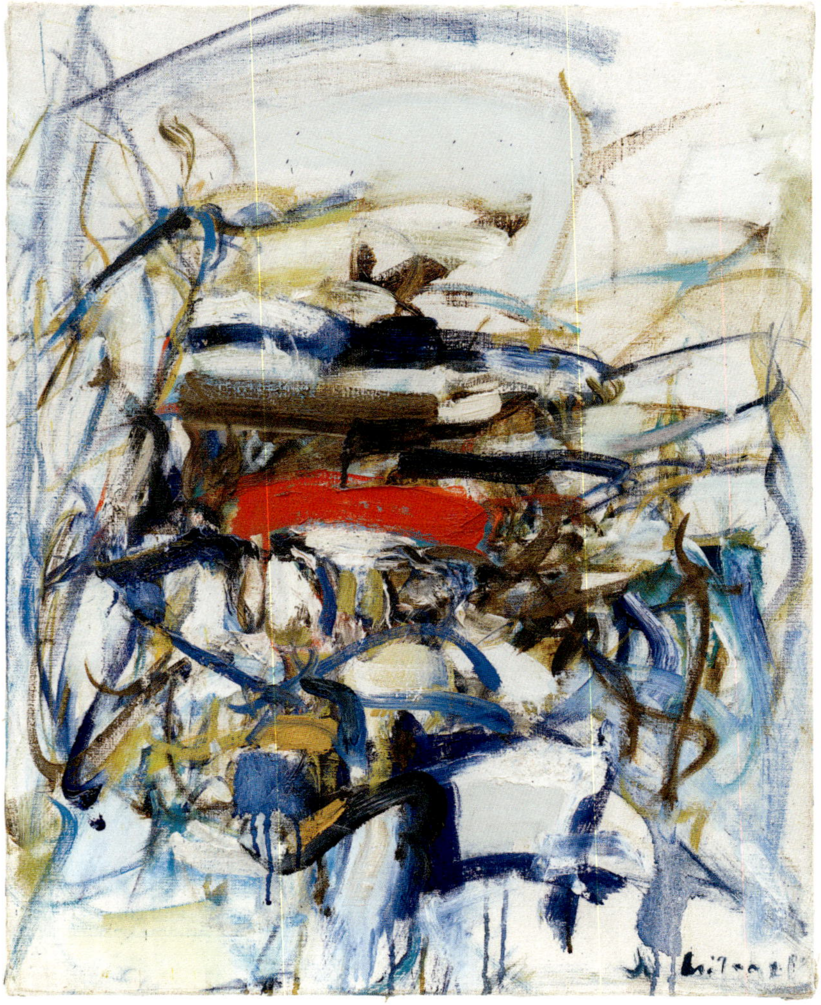

Untitled, 1956. Oil on canvas, 24 × 19¾ in. (61 × 50.2 cm). San Francisco Museum of Modern Art, gift of Sam Francis

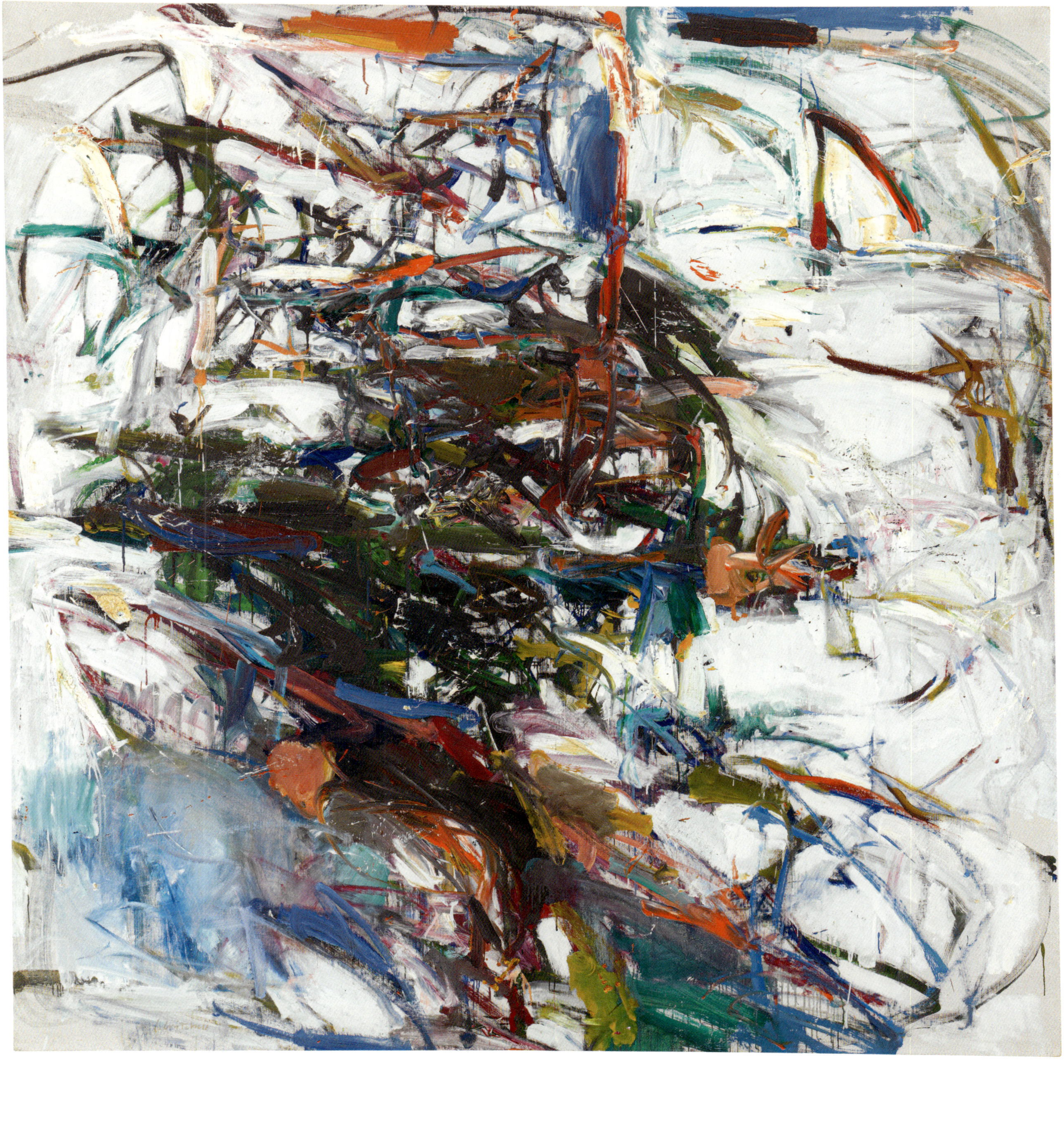

Harbor December, 1956. Oil on canvas, 80 × 80 in. (203.2 × 203.2 cm). Private collection, New York

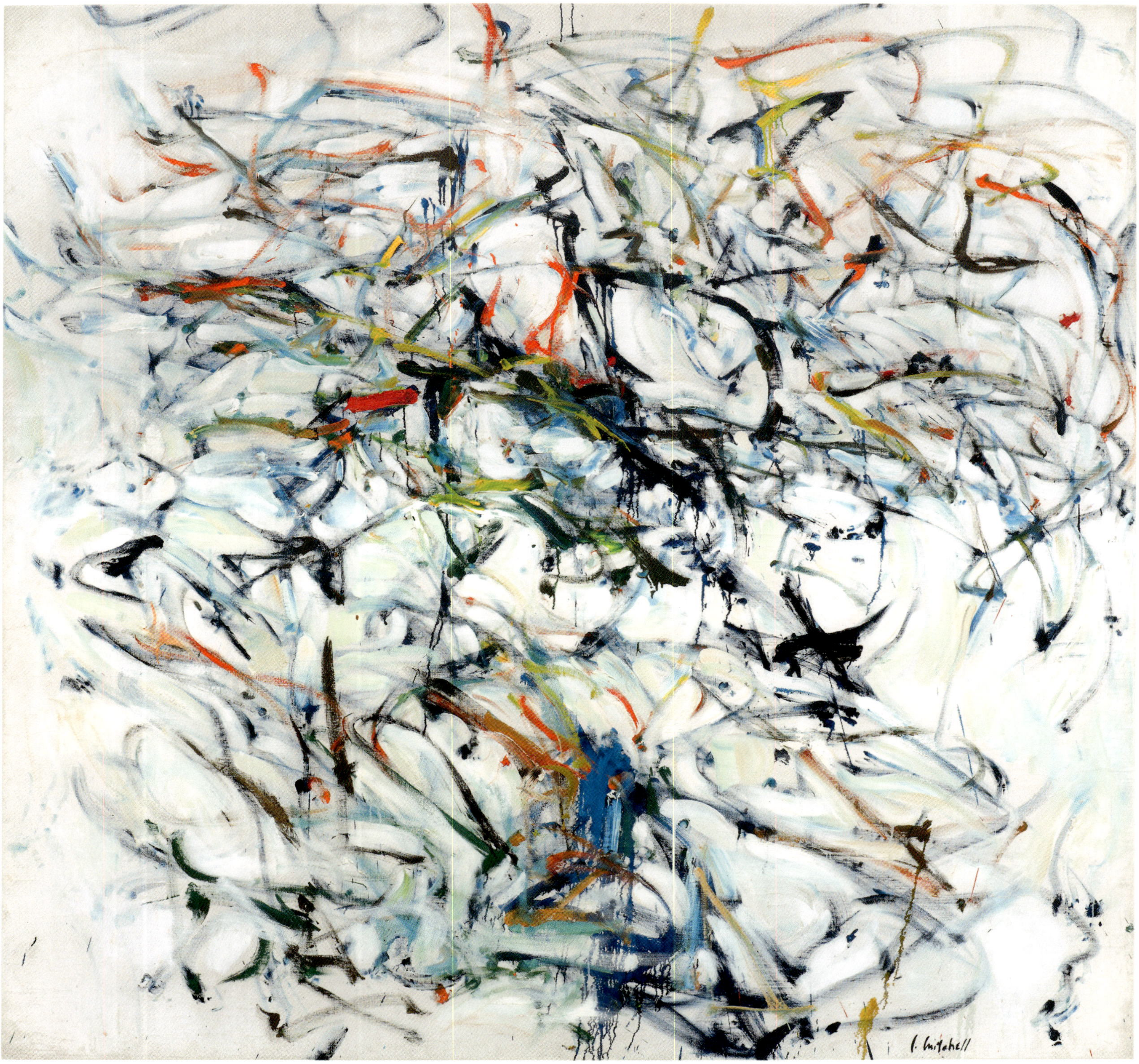

Soldats de bois, 1956. Oil on canvas, 71⅞ × 77⅝ in. (182.6 × 197.2 cm). Heithoff Family Collection

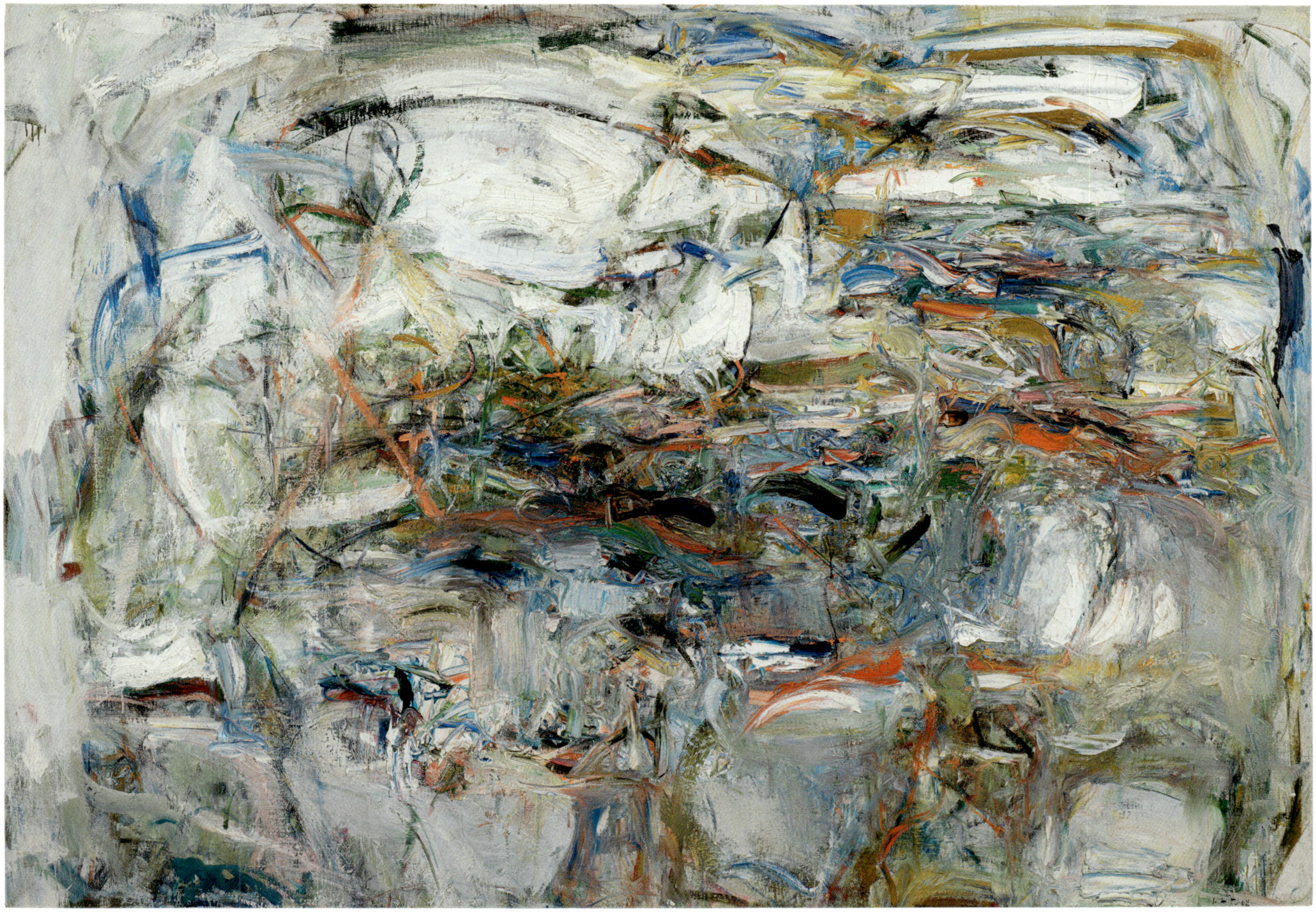

Swamp, 1956. Oil on canvas, 63 × 91½ in. (160 × 232.4 cm). Private collection

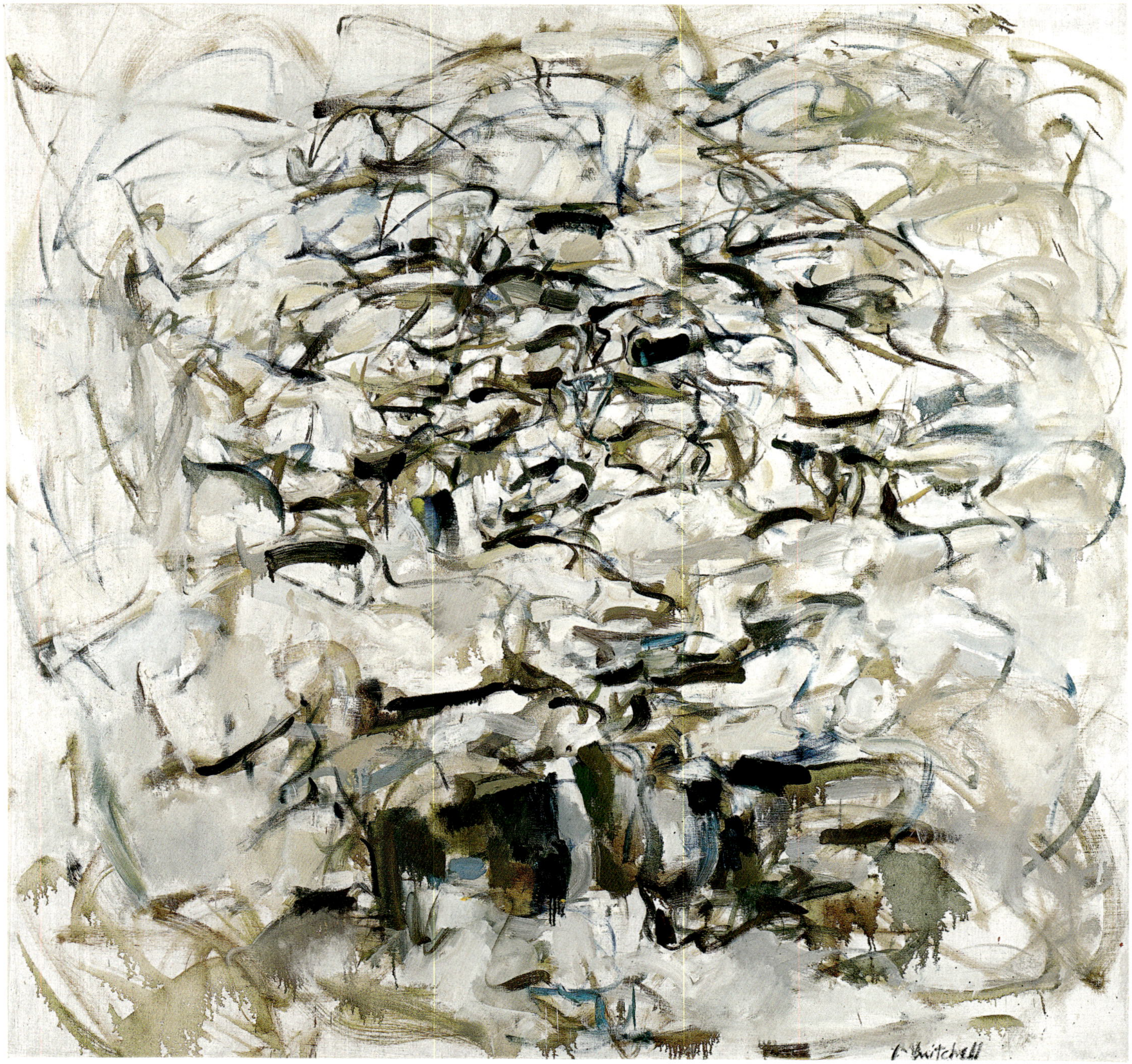

Marie Stadler Artichaud, ca. 1956. Oil on canvas, 67½ × 72 in. (171.5 × 182.9 cm). The Doris and Donald Fisher Collection at the San Francisco Museum of Modern Art

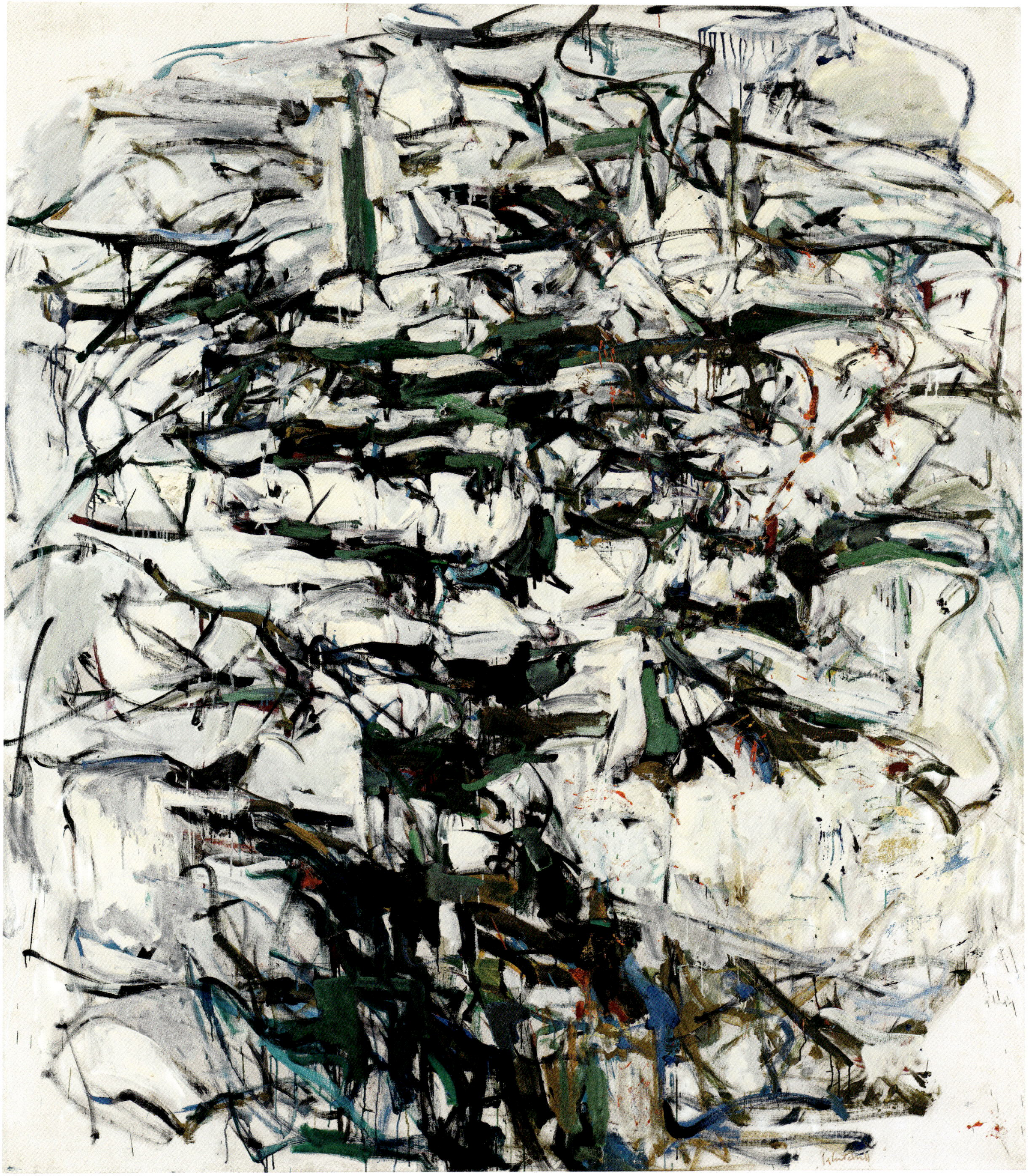

Hemlock, 1956. Oil on canvas, 91 × 80 in. (231.1 × 203.2 cm). Whitney Museum of American Art, New York, purchase, with funds from the Friends of the Whitney Museum of American Art

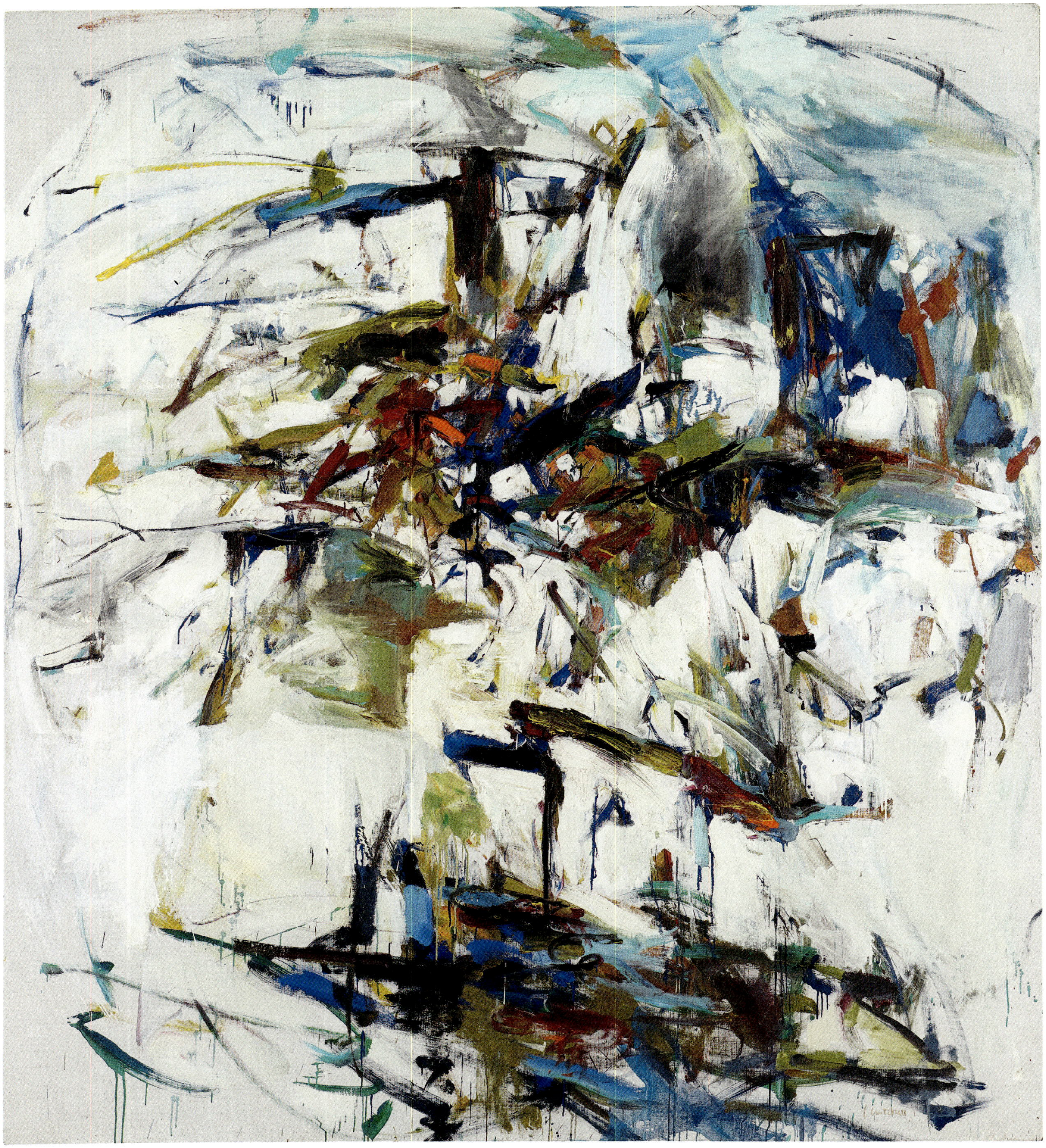

George Went Swimming at Barnes Hole, but It Got Too Cold, 1957. Oil on canvas, 87¾ × 78¼ in. (222.9 × 198.8 cm).
Albright-Knox Art Gallery, Buffalo, New York, gift of Seymour H. Knox, Jr.

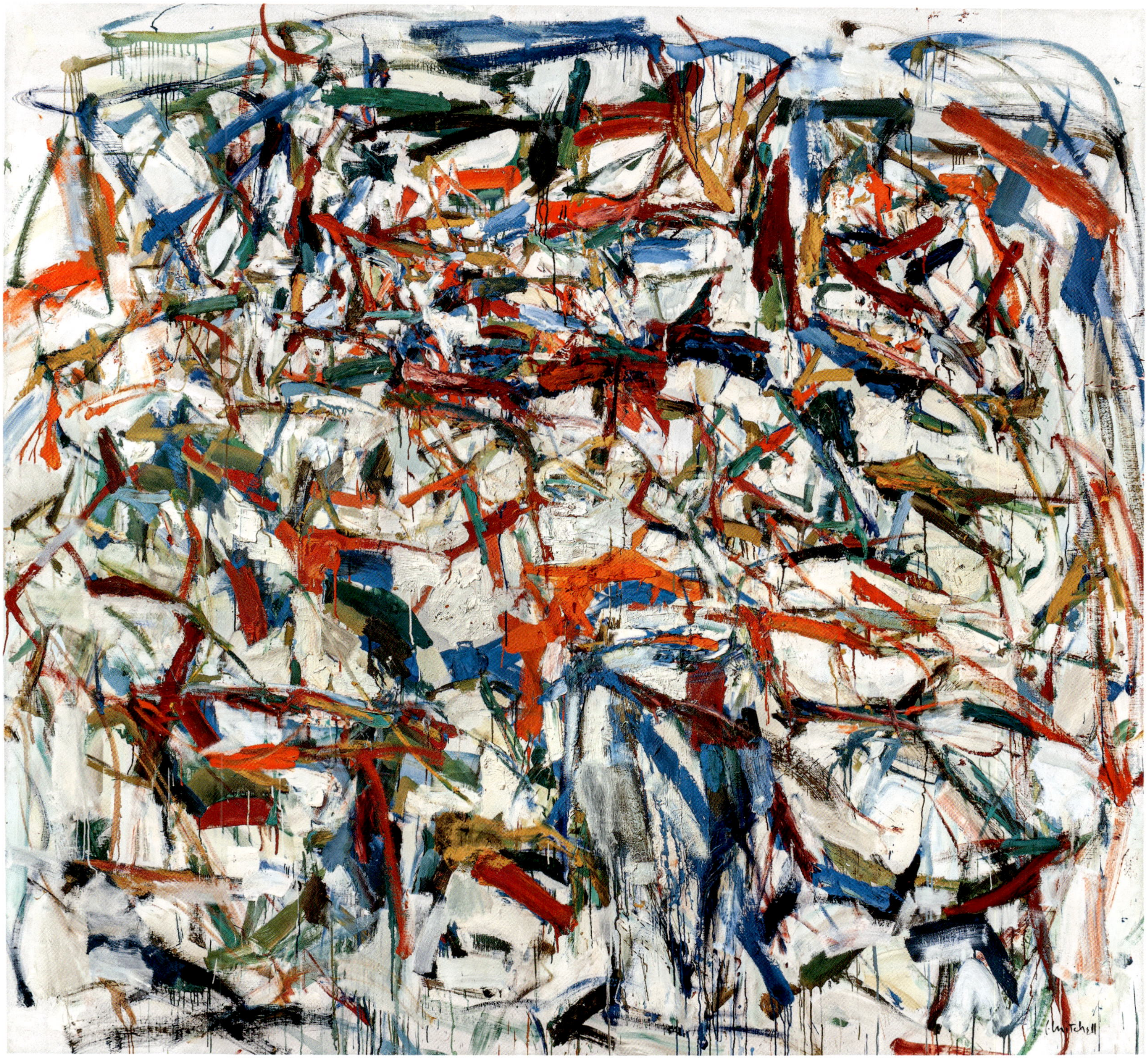

Evenings on 73rd Street, 1957. Oil on canvas, 75 × 85 in. (190.5 × 215.9 cm). Private collection, courtesy McClain Gallery, Houston

PLATE 27

To the Harbormaster, 1957. Oil on canvas, 76 × 118⅛ in. (193 × 300 cm). AKS Art

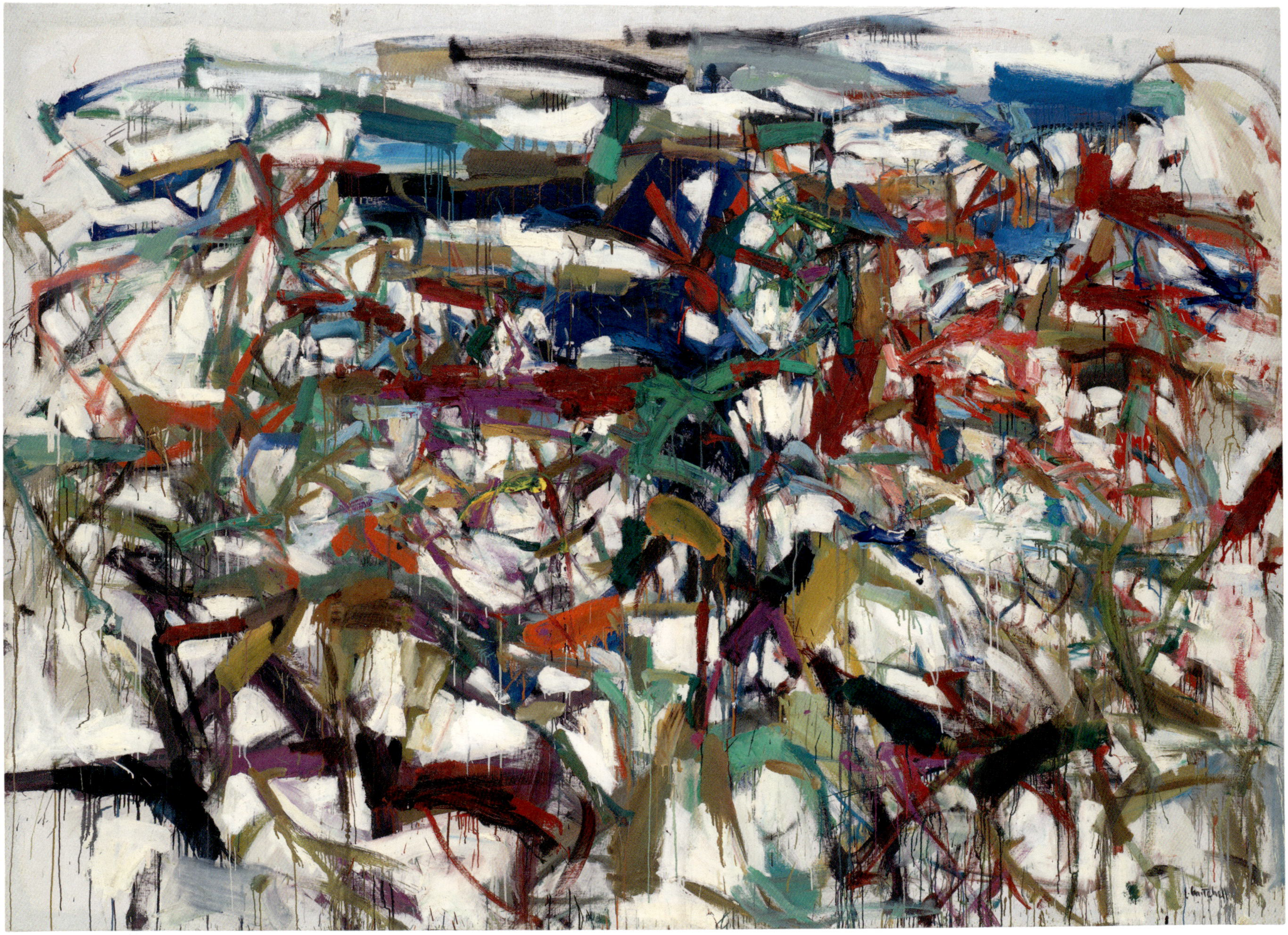

Ladybug, 1957. Oil on canvas, 77⅞ × 108 in. (197.8 × 274.3 cm). The Museum of Modern Art, New York, purchase

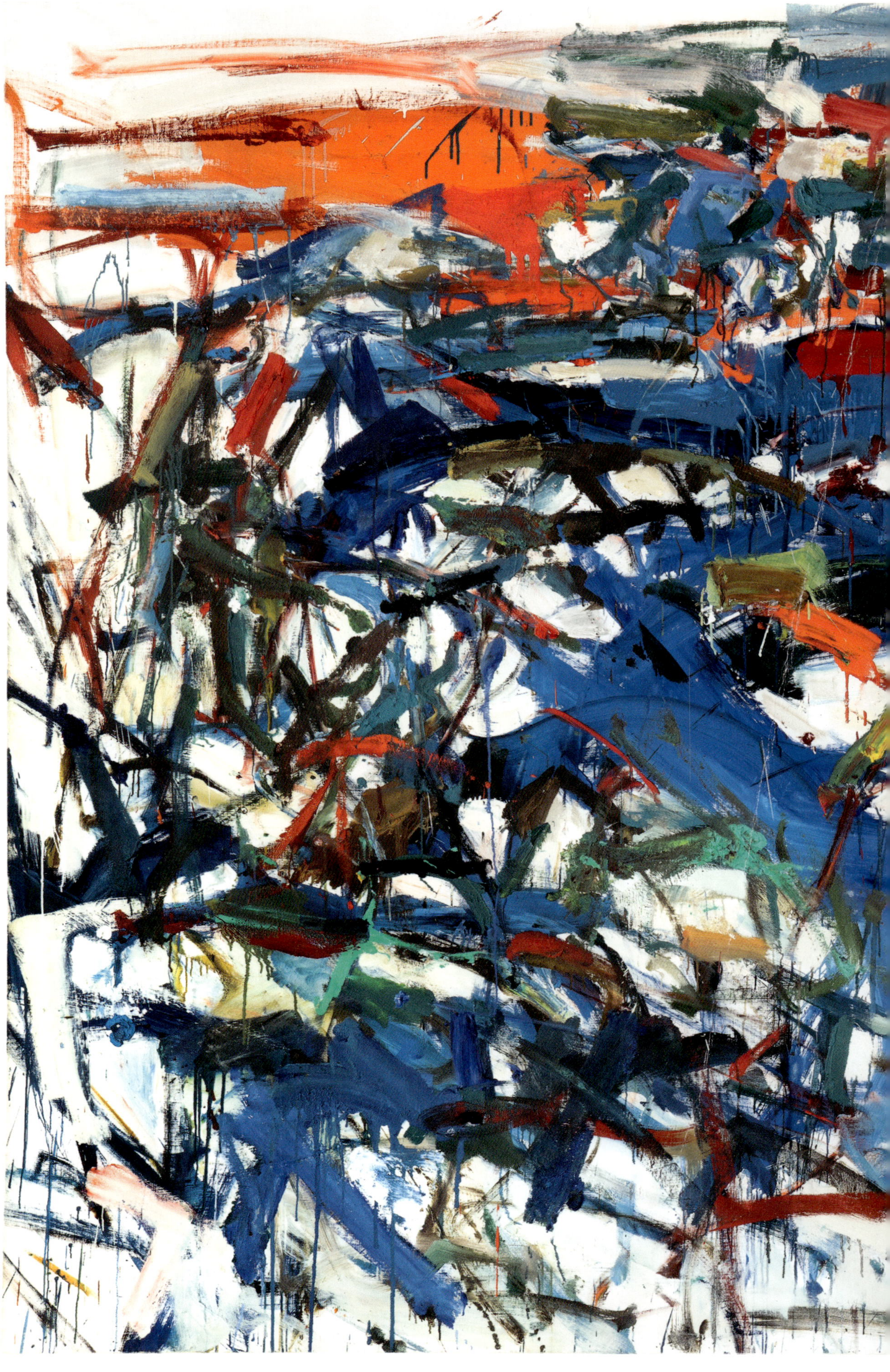

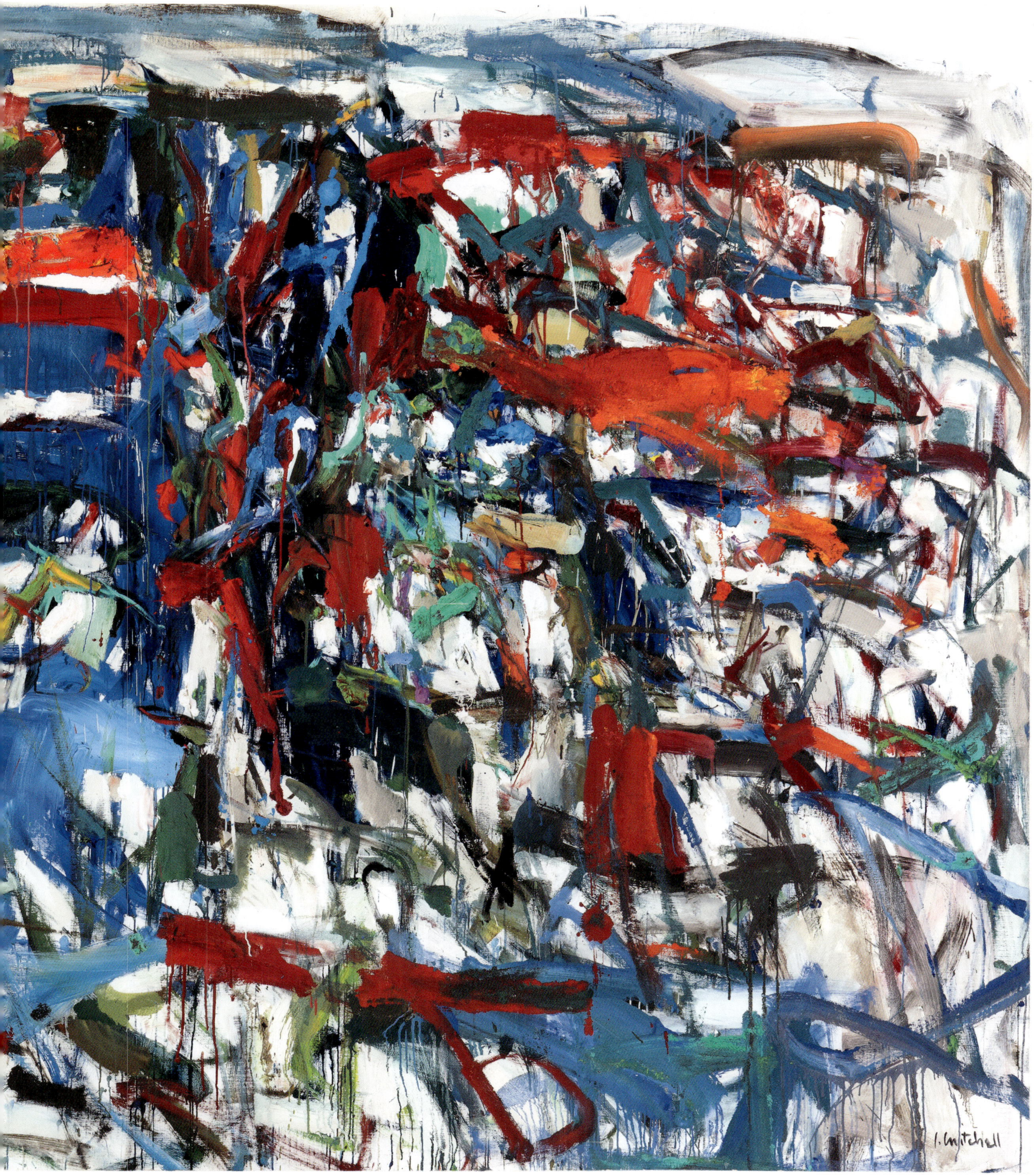
J. Mitchell

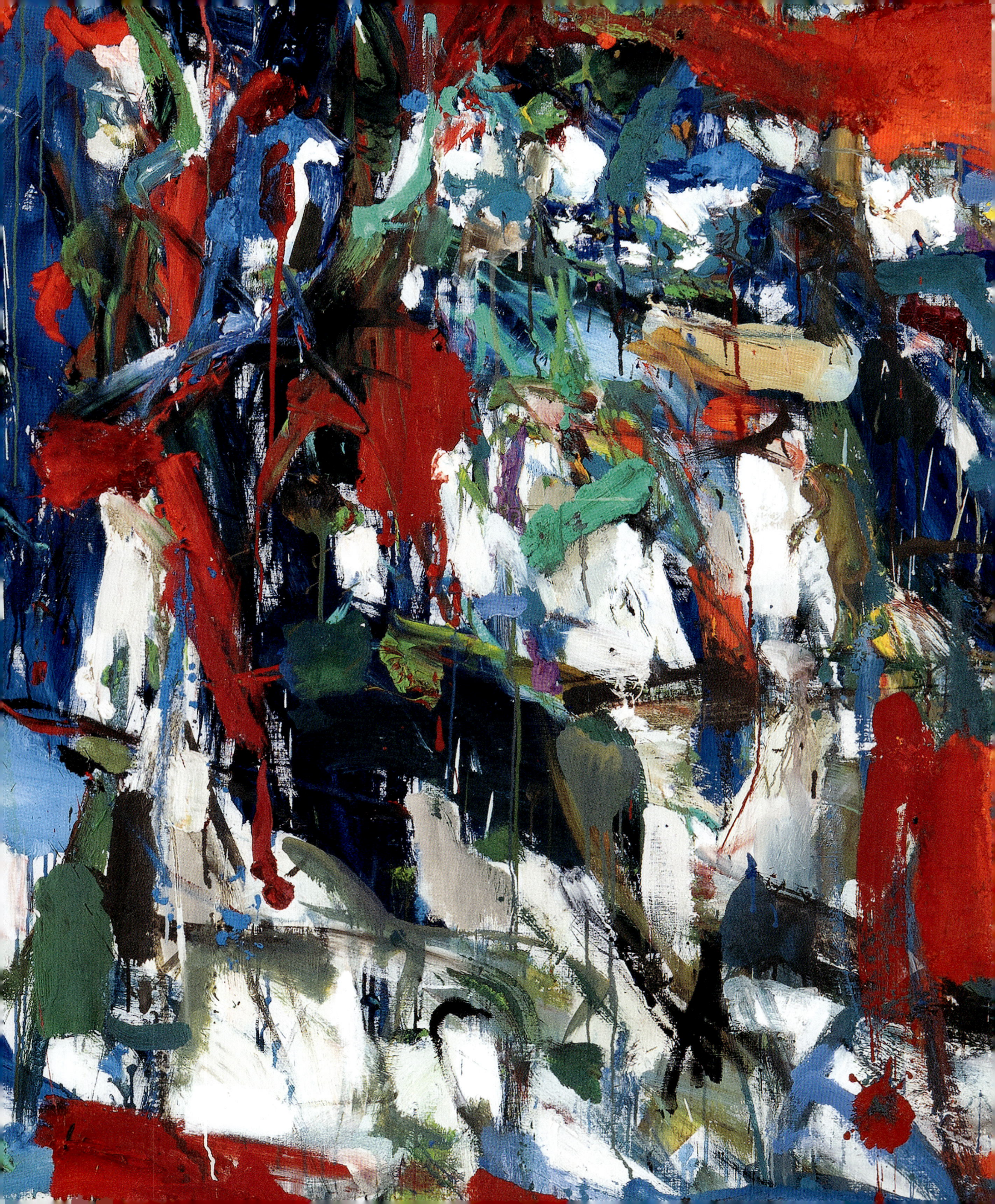

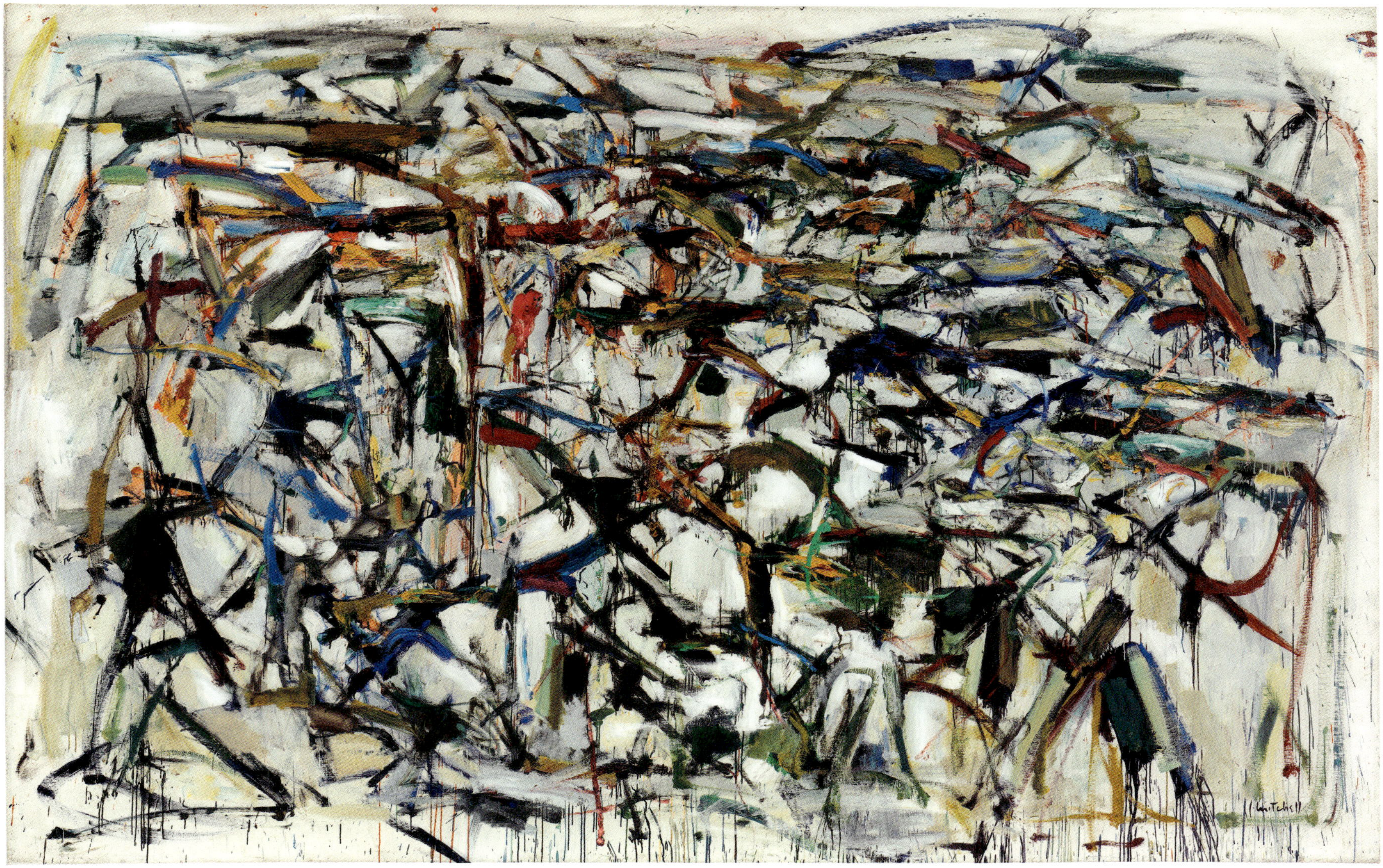

Piano mécanique, 1958. Oil on canvas, 78 × 124⅞ in. (198.1 × 317.2 cm). National Gallery of Art, Washington, D.C., gift of Addie and Sidney Yates

Untitled, ca. 1959. Oil on canvas, 70¾ × 63¼ in. (179.7 × 160.7 cm). Collection Jon Shirley

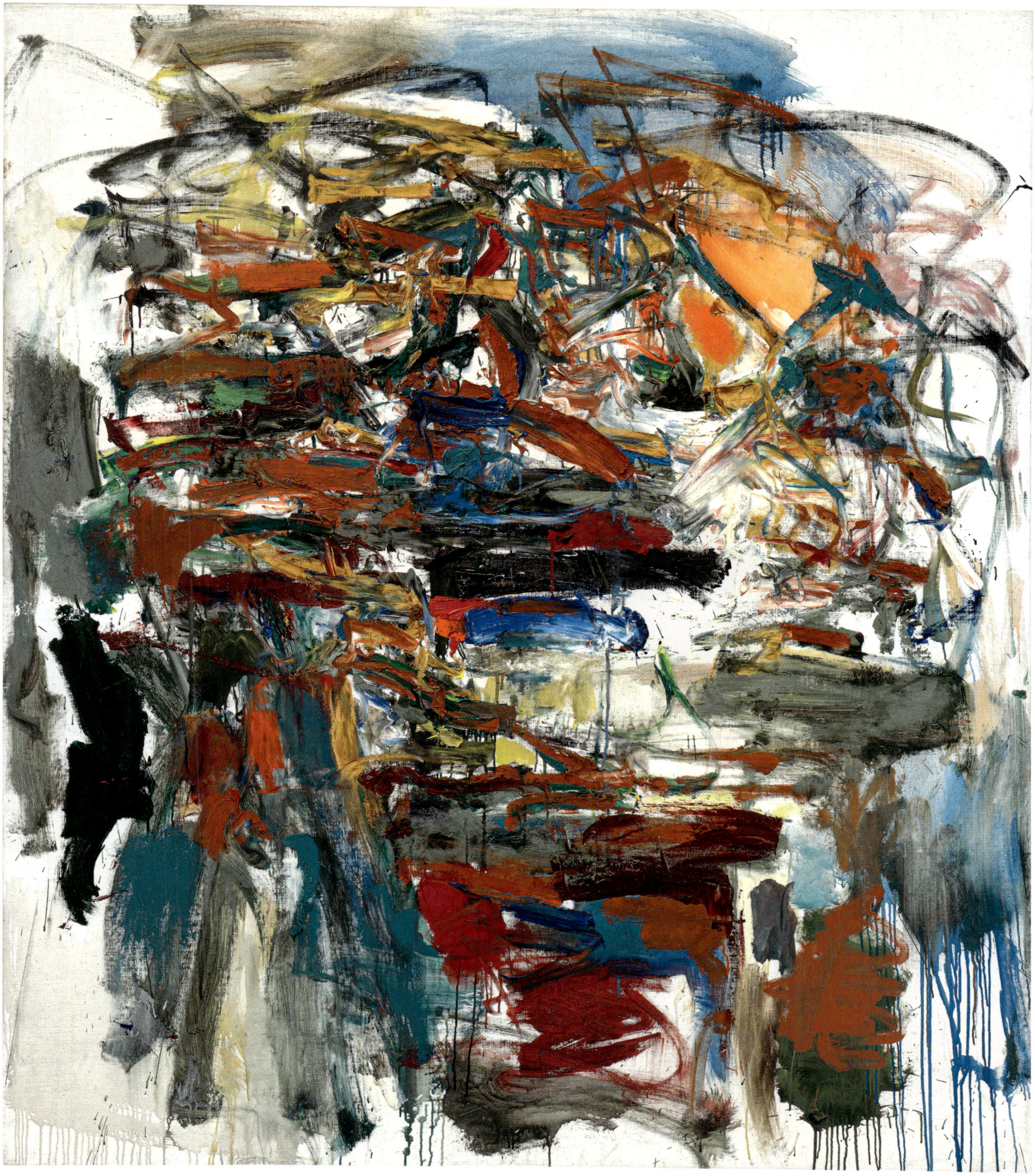

A Country of Her Own:

Joan Mitchell and France, 1948–1967

Éric de Chassey

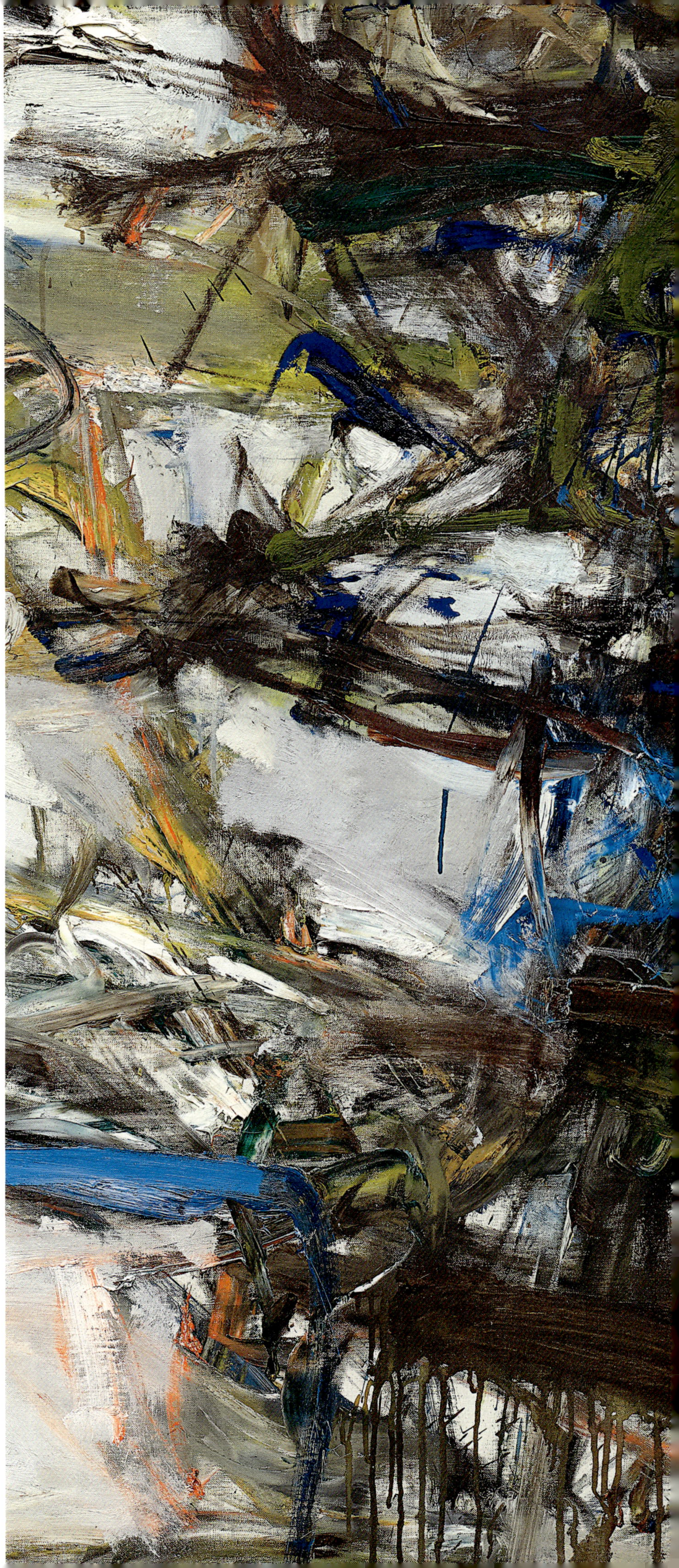

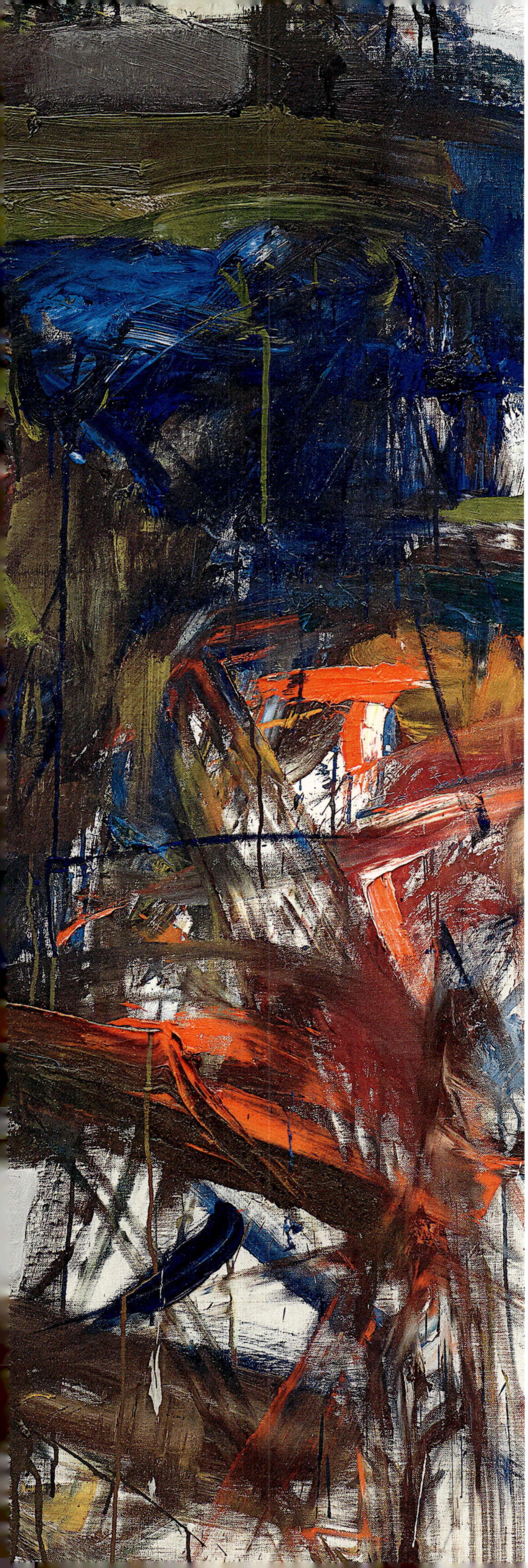

Born in the United States and first recognized as an important artist there, Joan Mitchell spent more than half her life in France. But it is difficult to find anything positive about this country in her statements, public or private. For anyone as attached to psychoanalysis as Mitchell—she even dedicated one of her paintings to her analyst, Edrita Fried—it would be hard not to suspect a case of Freudian denegation or denial. In a way, France epitomized everything Mitchell and the art world of which she was a part (albeit reluctantly) rejected, in New York but also, paradoxically, in Paris. Her first experience of this country, when she arrived in the harbor of Le Havre, in 1948, was clouded: she saw "sunk ships . . . war, war, war, war,"[1] and when she arrived in Paris, she felt that "it's so old and I see why Picasso had to destroy I think. It's hard to find the structure of things underneath the charm. It's hard to find things that mean something to me."[2] When she returned, in 1955, she felt, "Mmm, I don't like France,"[3] and when she wrote home that "it would be easier to live the life of a painter here," it was not for terribly positive reasons: "the continual working & not showing for years—it's accepted & has a dignity."[4] In what might have been her last interview, in 1992, after having settled in France for thirty-five years, she put the final nail in the coffin: "Why did I come? Certainly not because of the French people. . . . Of course, there are other advantages here: the landscapes, the *bistrots,* everything you call quality of life [*la qualité de la vie*]."[5]

For Mitchell, France seemed to have only been a repository of landscapes and objects of the past—"Lautrec people, Cézanne houses, Monet churches etc."[6] She constantly denied having any "particular affinity with [current] French painting,"[7] or any connection to the French art world that surrounded her: "I am not involved at all in the French scene. I am not

Joan Mitchell
Untitled (La Fontaine), 1957 (detail).
See fig. 3.

part of any group. My relationship with the art world is remote . . . I know New York much better than here [Paris]."[8] France was nevertheless a major part of the rich experience that fed into her paintings. I will not delve into the way she infused them with perceptions and feelings that she experienced there, but will rather try to see how her work from the 1950s and 1960s was conditioned, to a certain extent, by the French artistic context of its creation and reception—a context toward which she avowed indifference, but with which she did entertain a fruitful dialogue, sometimes consonant, sometimes dissonant.

Non-figuration

In 1948, Mitchell came to Paris as a budding Modernist, producing still lifes, landscapes, or figures in interiors, contrasting primary and secondary colors within a geometric structure. These works looked rather similar to some of those shown at Galerie Maeght in April 1947 under the title *Introduction à la peinture moderne américaine,* which gathered works by William Baziotes, Romare Bearden, Byron Browne, Adolph Gottlieb, Carl Holty, and Robert Motherwell, and which had been chastised by the French critics as merely accommodating and synthetizing various French influences.[9] Her *Untitled* (1948, plate 4) could indeed have been painted by a French artist of Mitchell's generation, emulating the works of Édouard Pignon and his fellow *Jeunes peintres de tradition française* (Young Painters in the French Tradition)—such as Jean Bazaine, who had held the forefront of attention (and official recognition) since they first exhibited under this moniker in 1941—blending a cubist structure with a fauvist palette.

As was common for a young foreign artist, she settled in a little apartment on the Left Bank, rue Galande. Her neighbors included U.S. artists like Robert Rosenwald and Herbert Katzman, who, soon after Mitchell's departure for New York, in late 1949, would be among the founders of Galerie Huit, a cooperative gallery located at 8 rue Saint-Julien-le-Pauvre, on the corner of rue Galande.[10] She befriended the Hungarian exile Simon Hantaï—with whom she would later entertain an interesting, if underrecognized, artistic dialogue—and his wife, Zsuzsa. Also typically, she made occasional trips to the "province" to see the masterworks of the past, especially Romanesque architecture. When she found Paris unbearable, Mitchell moved to the Côte d'Azur, choosing the picturesque harbor of Le Lavandou (in December 1949, Ellsworth Kelly would stay nearby, in Sanary-sur-Mer).

Mitchell's return to New York, in September 1949, is (and was) generally seen in terms of her prompt engagement with New York Abstract Expressionism and as a turning away from anything French, as she fashioned her own brand of gestural abstraction. She was soon classified as "one of the most vital of the younger New York artists around de Kooning."[11] Thus, when she started returning to Paris in 1955 before finally settling permanently there in 1959 (with many short trips back to the United States and Canada), she came as a fully fledged U.S. Abstract Expressionist. Indeed, almost all the critical texts written about her work in France or by French writers have since insisted on the fact that Mitchell was a U.S. painter, in the midst of a Paris/New York feud that only escalated from the mid-1950s to the 1960s.[12]

Despite that, the paintings Mitchell made in New York in the early 1950s were notably similar to the kind of non-figurative work produced in Paris at the same time, albeit without any actual influence, as the latter were mostly ignored in the United States. In fact, Mitchell's works were part of an international trend that should be considered a global Abstract Expressionism, with local inflections (if art historians ever get over the chauvinism and mutual ignorance to which they naturally stick). I take it as a happy coincidence that Mitchell made Le Lavandou her last residence in France during her first stay there, because it was also where Nicolas de Staël, certainly the most influential French painter of the turn of the 1940s–1950s, would, in 1952, create one of his first series of paintings—abstract landscapes, so to speak—that signaled his will to avoid being "too close or too far from subject,"[13] stirring heated debates. Moreover, Mitchell's paintings from the early 1950s are especially close in spirit and in form to the work of two female painters of foreign origins who were active in France and had clearly been influenced by de Staël: Maria Helena Vieira da Silva from Portugal[14] and Natalia Dumitresco from Romania, whose large-scale abstractions (fig. 1) use a "splintering of surface" (to quote Dumitresco[15]) to evoke feelings of urban landscapes, blended with memories of their native countries.

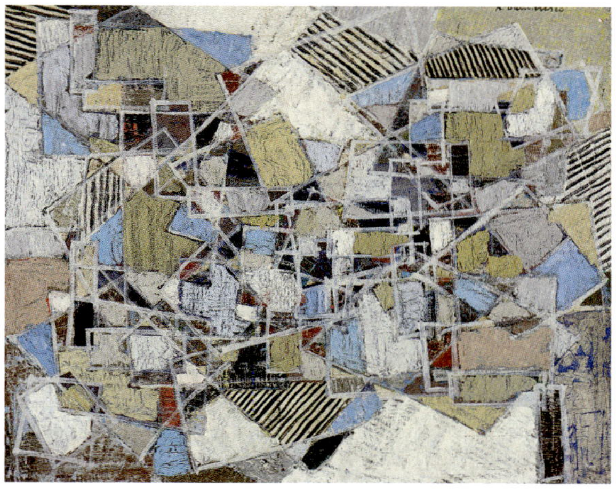

1

FIG 1 **Natalia Dumitresco**
Composition, 1952. Oil on canvas, 28¾ × 36¼ in. (73 × 92 cm). Fondation Gandur pour l'Art, Genève

In the United States, the frequent evocation of nature in the work of second-generation Abstract Expressionists was interpreted as a way out of the double bind of self-expression becoming a common language after Pollock,[16] but it was cast in a different light in France, where "non-figuration" (a word used by French critics to describe works that looked abstract but were grounded in experiences of the outside world) had been at the center of debates since the immediate postwar years.[17] Bazaine, for one, continuously emphasized this relationship between abstraction and the feeling of a remembered landscape: "The strange force of forgotten memories . . . how many times was I subject to it? A certain texture of the landscape of Lorraine (completely forgotten but linked with the memory of cold weather and fear), coming out ten years later in a painting—*Winter*—that had no intent to be figurative."[18] Even someone as adamantly opposed to any hint of figuration as painter Pierre Soulages could write in the early 1950s:

> If, through figuration, a painting introduces a relationship of precise equivalence with the world, when it isn't figurative it introduces other relations; for the viewer as for the painter, the world is no longer looked at but lived, it resides in their experience. This experience is sustained through the significations that are made and unmade on the canvas by experiencing it. Thus, this painting that does without representation is surrounded by the world and it owes its meaning to the world.[19]

Mitchell vs. Riopelle

When Mitchell returned to Paris in the summer of 1955, it was explicitly to escape—at least for a short time—not only her tormented relationship with Michael Goldberg but also the competitive atmosphere of the so-called second-generation abstract expressionist community, of which she had been an active participant at least since

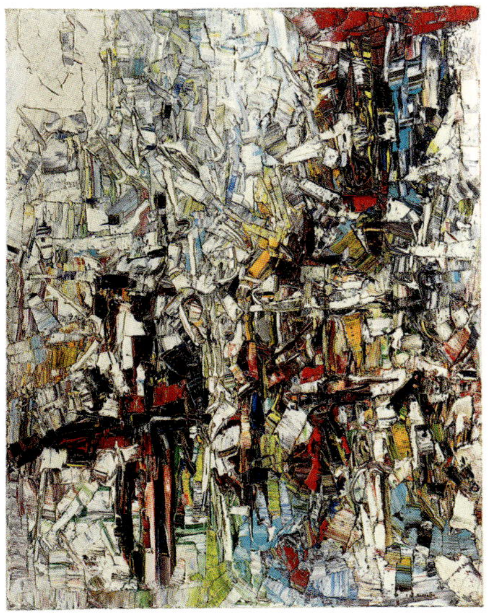

2

FIG 2 **Jean Paul Riopelle**
Plowing under Snow, ca. 1957. Oil on canvas, 63¾ × 51⅛ in. (162 × 130 cm). The Israel Museum, Jerusalem, gift of Baron Berthold and Baroness Gigi Urvater, Paris and Antwerp, in memory of Levi Eshkel

FIG 3 **Joan Mitchell**
Untitled (La Fontaine), 1957. Oil on canvas, 78½ × 66¼ in. (199.4 × 168.3 cm). Private collection

her inclusion in the 1951 Ninth Street Show, even if she didn't like the term and later preferred to refer to herself as "AEOH (Abstract Expressionist Old Hat)."[20] In Paris, she soon met Jean Paul Riopelle, then a star among all the competing abstract tendencies that were variously called *abstraction lyrique* (lyrical abstraction), *art informel,* or *art autre* (art of another kind), depending on the critic/curator who was showing his paintings.

Their mutual influences have been thoroughly studied in a recent exhibition curated by Michel Martin.[21] Yves Michaud has stated that "in the early years of their relationship Jean Paul Riopelle had a decisive influence on Joan Mitchell by enabling her to embrace a lyricism she had hitherto—probably through puritanism—rejected."[22] If one concentrates on formal issues, the reverse influence, Mitchell's on Riopelle, was initially the most important, however. Riopelle acknowledged it in 1956, when Mitchell had just gone back to New York: "I am at the studio, where I've just been trying to paint with gouache. . . . [U]ltimately these large gouaches of 3 feet by 3 resemble your paintings, my love."[23] In 1957, looking at Riopelle's *Plowing under Snow* (fig. 2), a friend exclaimed: "I've never seen anything that reminds me so much of Mitchell and her painting,"[24] while Mitchell soon produced a response with *Untitled (La Fontaine)* (fig. 3). These mutual influences endured during the first years of their relationship. Around 1958, Mitchell wrote to Riopelle, who was famous for his virtuoso use of the palette knife: "Last night I painted eight pictures on paper (sort of a very hard paper) some were grey & dark had an influence of someone I know in Paris—including a palette knife."[25] And Martin has noted that around 1964, "the similarity between their practices is most marked," specifically pointing to Mitchell's *Girolata* (fig. 5.4) and Riopelle's *Untitled* (Hirshhorn Museum and Sculpture Garden).[26]

The "Duthuit Group"

Riopelle was among the artists and writers who regrouped around art critic and art historian Georges Duthuit. They shared their views on art, in French and English (Mitchell was one of the only U.S. artists in Paris who had a thorough command of the French language), gathering in the same cafés every evening, having dinner together, sometimes visiting each other's studios and exhibitions, vacationing near Aix-en-Provence where the Duthuits had a house, and even exchanging works.

For various reasons, including being reduced to the status of Riopelle's companion through sheer misogyny, Mitchell never fully received Duthuit's anointing. She eventually broke with him in the summer of 1959, during a stormy sailing trip in the Aegean Sea aboard Riopelle's boat. She later stated: "I never felt there was a group. . . . I thought it was sort of Americans clinging to Americans."[27] But she did share some of the group's biases or principles: a professed dislike for Picasso; a strong inclination toward Matisse (Duthuit's father-in-law) and van Gogh, on whom Duthuit had written a beautiful essay in 1948; a disdain for the U.S. expatriate artists who had operated Galerie Huit between 1950 and 1954 (although they had briefly socialized and sometimes shown with them[28]), and for those connected to Galerie Arnaud and the art magazine *Cimaise,*

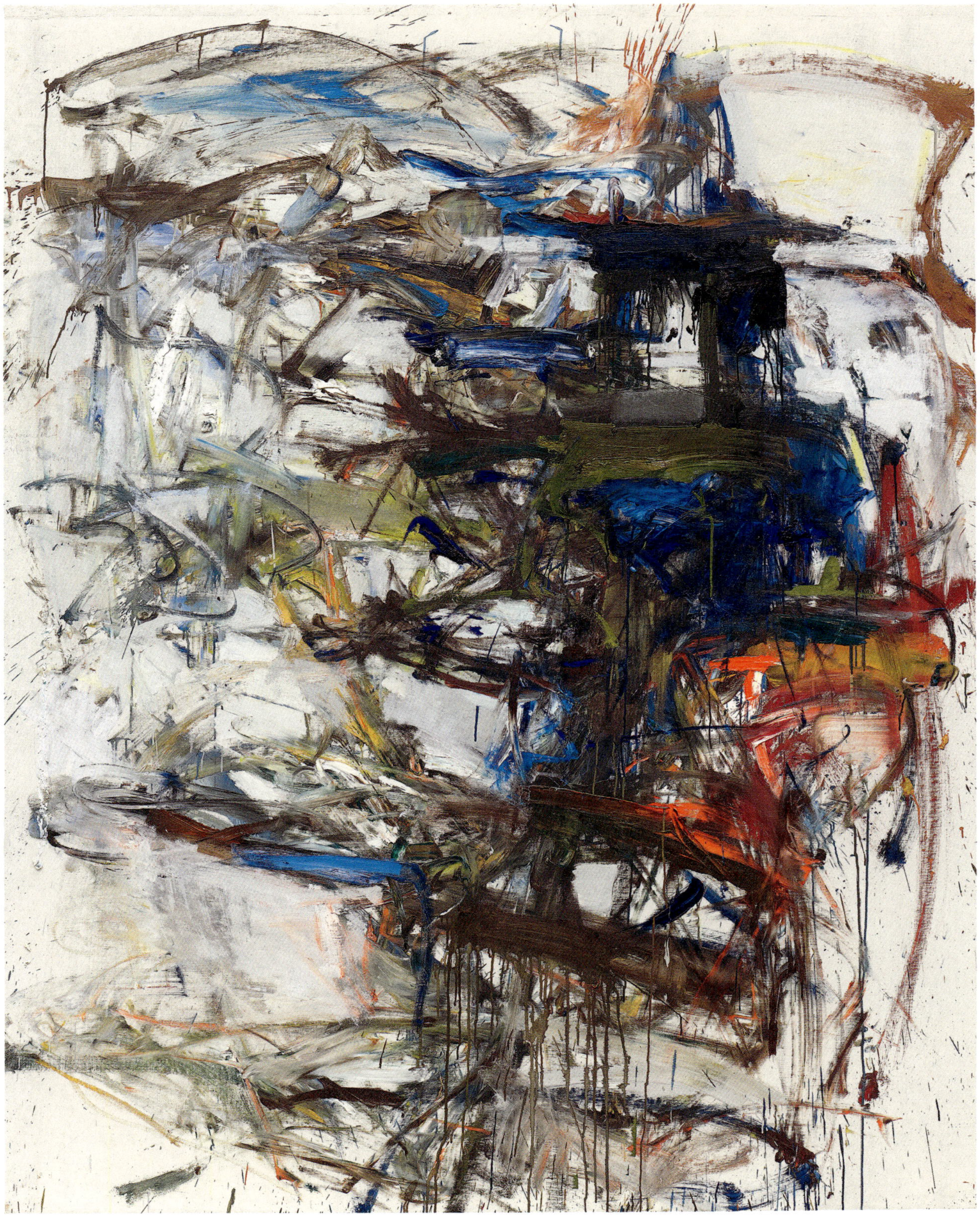

3

such as John Franklin Koenig[29]; and a rejection of the type of abstraction that was premised on creating subjective signs—heralded in particular by Georges Mathieu—in favor of coupling abstraction with experienced feeling and subject matter.

The way Duthuit wrote poetically about the paintings of Sam Francis and Riopelle, his two American champions, resonates with what Mitchell was actually doing in her Paris studio: their paintings "impose themselves like a heavy bush of undifferentiated feelings,"[30] akin to an "elementary epiphany" ("form will define itself by itself, so to speak, as if the artist were a sort of narrowing whose only role is to assume and hold in check the pressure of the stream which, through it, by it, bursts forth on the canvas, unpredictable—lyrical"[31]). And when Duthuit expressed his doubts about their achievements, speaking in the guise of the old Matisse admonishing the younger U.S. Abstract Expressionists ("I still believe that painting holds other possibilities, including helping us know things, and ourselves through things, looking into a certain heart of the world that still beats when ours has been condemned to death"[32]), wasn't Mitchell doing exactly what Duthuit wanted (but could not see in her work)—that is, redeeming the world, even without images?

Tachisme

FIG 4 **Marcelle Loubchansky**
Seabed, 1954. Oil on canvas, 45¹¹⁄₁₆ × 28¾ in. (116 × 73 cm). Private collection

Like the other members of this loose group (with the exception of Shirley Jaffe[33]), Mitchell claimed to have no interest in the current French art scene. When she arrived in June 1955, before meeting Francis and Riopelle, she had, according to one of her letters, "blistered to the Louvre—the Picasso, Pignon, Degas, Derain, shows or whatever"[34]—names of artists she did not particularly like (although she might have recognized in Pignon a similarity with her own early work). Throughout the 1950s, she considered Paris "a small town—half the Cedar running on half its fuel,"[35] and said in 1959: "Not much art here, except the kind sauces are poured over."[36] This metaphor probably referred less to French *cuisine* than to the debate in Paris around *tachisme,*[37] a tendency among local artists to use the stain as their preferred tool (albeit in a very different way than U.S. Color Field painters), identified by one of the most prominent critics of the day (Duthuit always remained in the margins of the art world): Charles Estienne. In March 1954, Estienne had gathered some of these artists, in particular Hantaï and the vivid colorist Marcelle Loubchansky (fig. 4), in a recurring exhibition called Salon d'Octobre, in the name of "a total freedom of expression" embodied by the stain.[38] Many critics violently objected to what they felt was a haphazard regrouping of very different artists.[39]

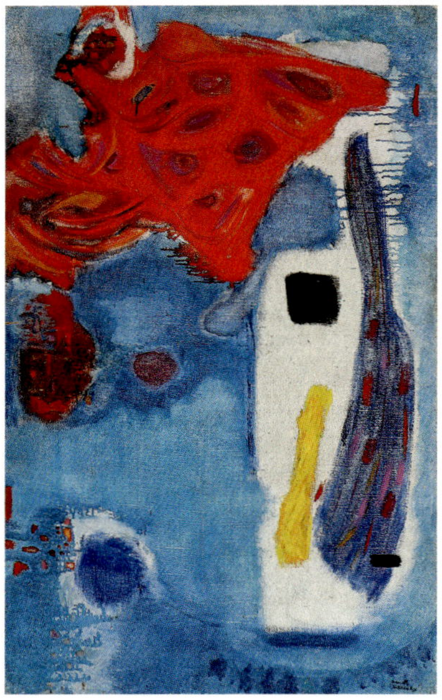
4

Even if, in 1959, she professed not to like tachisme, Mitchell showed in group exhibitions with some of the artists sponsored by Estienne, including Loubchansky, whose work Estienne thus analyzed at that time: "The colored stain is born, develops, from the work of the brush; and all this is ... lyrical tension and creation of a language."[40] But Mitchell must have felt as if the Paris painters were doing what she had been doing in the early 1950s in New York—the kind of paintings she had shown in 1952 at the New Gallery and had abandoned after 1954. Moreover, in the mid-1950s, many younger artists and critics living in Paris were very critical of the situation. Thus,

Julien Alvard, the critic who coined the term *nuagisme* (cloud painting), wrote in *Cimaise*: "As for the artistic resources, they are rather slim. Paris offers neither the best museums nor the best galleries, far from it."[41] And Alain Jouffroy, a critic who tried to revive Surrealism independent of André Breton, stated that "the situation of young painting in Paris isn't brilliant, to say the least.... All the abstract painters ... seem to aspire, with good or bad conscience, ... to an official recognition of their talent."[42]

Paris vs. New York

When she settled for good in France, in 1959, Mitchell participated in several group exhibitions, amidst a mounting rivalry between Paris and New York. Earlier in the decade, under the tutelage of critic and curator Michel Tapié in particular,[43] there had briefly been some attempts to adopt a less nationalistic viewpoint, but this effort had faded. Mitchell was clearly identified as a U.S. artist at a time when anti-Americanism became a state affair, with the Suez crisis in 1956 and President Charles de Gaulle announcing in 1966 that France was withdrawing from NATO, while, in the art world, Americanness and Frenchness were seen as completely distinct characters, to the point of caricature. In 1956, for example, in an issue of *Cimaise* devoted to U.S. art, German-born art historian Herta Wescher wrote, "If the young Americans bring to today's art a fresh vitality, and delight in an unleashed violence, the French distinguish themselves from them by their greater sensitivity for painting values, acquired through a long tradition, backed up by a distinct sense of moderation and discipline."[44]

After cultivating confrontations with U.S. artists and placing Francis or Riopelle at the center of contemporary debates, the French art scene, in a gesture of pure denegation, became vociferously disinterested in the U.S. situation (before returning to it at the time of the opening of Centre Pompidou, in the mid-1970s). In 1956, poet and art critic Michel Ragon observed: "It could be said, without chauvinism, that there is no art today but that which is made in Paris."[45] And in 1960, a French television program boasted: "Is Paris still the capital of the arts? Yes. It's even truer than ever.... If we have any doubt about it ourselves, the young foreign artists don't."[46] The program interviewed critic Pierre Restany who, just before championing *nouveau réalisme,* had published a book triumphantly called *Lyrisme et abstraction.* Restany said: "Paris isn't the city of an entire career. In Paris, you come to do an internship ... from which recognition in the national [*sic*] countries stems and which allows for an international career.... Paris is the essential city for acquiring a universal language in the arts."[47]

By 1955, when she had returned to New York after her summer in Paris, Mitchell had relinquished the heritage of "French painting" by doing away with the gridded structure ("cubistic" in essence) that had hitherto supported her brushstrokes, and by abandoning, as Pierre Schneider later noted, perspectival backgrounds (typical of French Abstract Expressionism) in favor of a more objective space (typical of New York Abstract Expressionism).[48] Her work from the late 1950s (see plate 30), done in a studio near Montparnasse, can also be seen as anti-French, as if the Paris context had fueled a certain anger against it. Paradoxically, in New York, it could be seen as the very reason she could still obtain great results from what was becoming an outmoded style. Thus, critic William Rubin wrote in his review of the exhibition *School of New York: Some Younger Artists,* which took place at the Stable Gallery from December 1959 to January 1960:

> The only really refreshing painter working in this vein [Abstract Expressionism] . . . is Joan Mitchell and it may be significant that this exception is a painter who for some years has lived in Paris. When this style was most alive . . . it was an insurgent direction, in competition with other modes of painting. The more common it became on the New York scene, the less it seemed to have to say. In Paris, I rather suspect that it has been to Mitchell's advantage. In any event, her work retains a freshness that one misses in her near counterparts in New York.[49]

From then on, Mitchell would be considered "too French" in the United States and "very American" in France. As she stated: "In France they've always said my work is violent gestural painting. In New York, they've said it's decoration. On both sides, they say it's female."[50]

Hantaï and Fournier

In a way, apart from Francis and Riopelle, the only artist in Paris whom Mitchell clearly emulated in the late 1950s—and for the rest of her life—may have been Hantaï, with reciprocity. As noted above, they had known each other since 1948–49, and this relationship deserves a close study of its own. Hantaï's widow, Zsuzsa, recently stated: "Joan Mitchell was a real friend. I saw her in Vétheuil later. And much earlier and after her falling out with Riopelle. Joan and Simon liked each other. Which was rather exceptional for them."[51] I do not know when Mitchell and Hantaï resumed their friendship, but it must have been no later than May 1957, when Mitchell helped the art dealer Jean Fournier, who had been showing Hantaï since 1955 in his Galerie Kléber, install an exhibition of large-scale paintings by Riopelle. The way Mitchell started in 1958–59 to concentrate her colored gestures in fewer and larger strokes on a more or less neutral background reflects a strong affinity with Hantaï's works shown in the exhibition *Peintures récentes: souvenir de l'Avenir* (March 1958), albeit in reverse. Hantaï veered from his Surrealist-influenced paintings by first establishing a ground and then scraping through it in negative gestures, while Mitchell built her compositions on top of the ground. Mitchell started from an experienced feeling to create an abstraction: "What makes me want to squeeze the paint in the first place, so that the brush is out, is a memory of a feeling. It might be of a dead dog, it might be of a lake, but once I start painting, I'm painting a picture."[52] Hantaï, on the

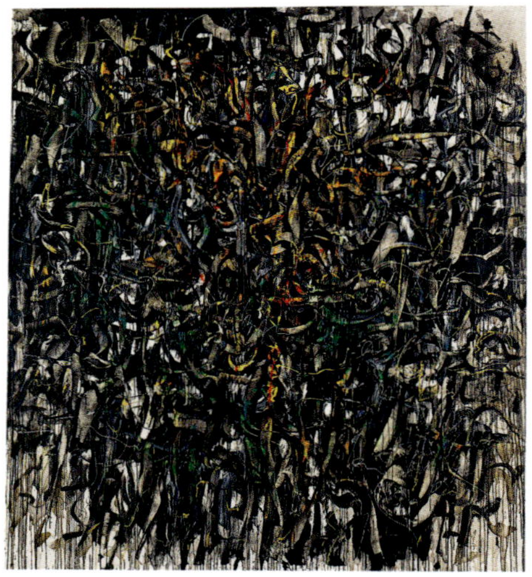

5

FIG 5 **Simon Hantaï**
Saint Francis Xavier in India, 1958. Oil on canvas, 91⅜ × 84⅝ in. (232 × 215 cm). Private collection

contrary, started from an abstract gesture to establish a feeling without referencing a specific impression—although the final result strongly evokes the feeling of teeming landscapes, as in *Saint Francis Xavier in India* (fig. 5). As he wrote in 1958: "In these conditions the indefinable instant is the meaning, hence the impossibility of prefixed meanings and the importance of notions such as absence of preconceived gestures and forms *préconçus,* velocity of execution."[53] While the subtractive method of one can be opposed to the additive process of the other, Hantaï's rambling spiritualist apologies remained utterly foreign to Mitchell. Nonetheless, both wanted their paintings to be experienced principally on painterly terms. In view of their relationship, it could be said that Hantaï's paintings of the early 1960s, especially the *Catamurons,* with their violently broken shapes on top of a more continuous ground, entertain a dialogue with Mitchell's work from the same period—and that the reverse is also true.

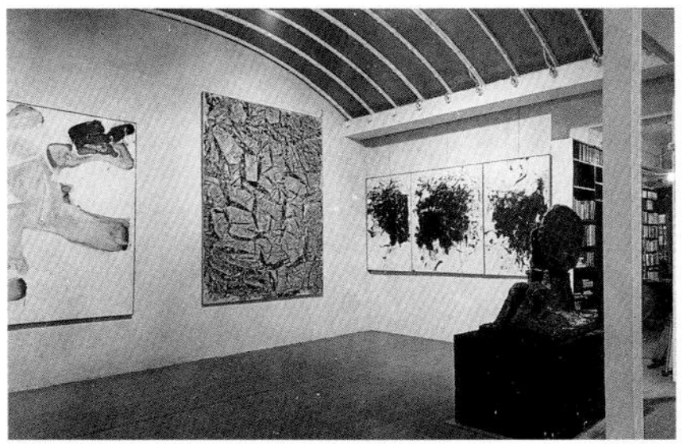

6

In the inaugural exhibition of Galerie Jean Fournier, in November 1963 (fig. 6), Mitchell's triptych *Untitled* (1963, MoMA[54]) was indeed confronted with Hantaï's *Mariale m.d.1* (1962), alongside Francis's *Blue Figure* (1960, Galerie Jean Fournier). Fournier became an essential supporter for Mitchell, and his gallery a favorable milieu for the promotion of her work in France. Already in November 1958, Fournier had included her in a group show at Galerie Kléber, the previous gallery he operated. Each of the listed artists in that exhibition, titled *À propos du baroque: Jean Degottex, Marcelle Ferron, Sam Francis, Simon Hantaï, Shirley Jaffe, Marcelle Loubchansky, Joan Mitchell, Judit Reigl, Jean-Paul Riopelle,* both French and non-French, was related, in one way or another, to her. Mitchell's work would regularly be presented by Fournier in solo exhibitions after 1967, establishing a family of artists who had their own methods and goals but—as Fournier would later say frequently[55]—were united by the question of how color cuts the space established on the canvas.[56]

FIG 6 Installation view of inaugural exhibition at Galerie Jean Fournier, Paris, 1963. Galerie Jean Fournier, Paris

A Country of Her Own

In 1967, Mitchell bought a house in Vétheuil, outside Paris. She literally cut herself out of any artistic context, becoming what she called "an outsider anyway i.e. painter & having become more so, foreigner, in a foreign country."[57] Her geographical distance from both Paris and New York effectively settled the very question of her belonging to the Paris or New York Schools, with an emphatic *neither.* When she had her first solo museum exhibition in the United States, in 1972 at the Everson Museum of Art in Syracuse, she aptly titled it *My Five Years in the Country,* playing with the double entendre of the word "country." She now belonged to a country of her own, even if she continued to have relationships with many artists, French and American, especially much younger ones who no longer cared about the rivalry between Paris and New York but just wanted, by their own means, to visit *her* country. In 1986, Mitchell could say: "I really like this house. I really like this view. I really like Paris better than New York—or not better, or equally, or differently, or something, which is quite true—instead of sitting—which I can do, I used to do—and missing the country and missing New York, or missing France."[58]

4

Frémicourt Sarah Roberts

Why from this window am I watching leaves?
Why do halls and steps seem narrower?

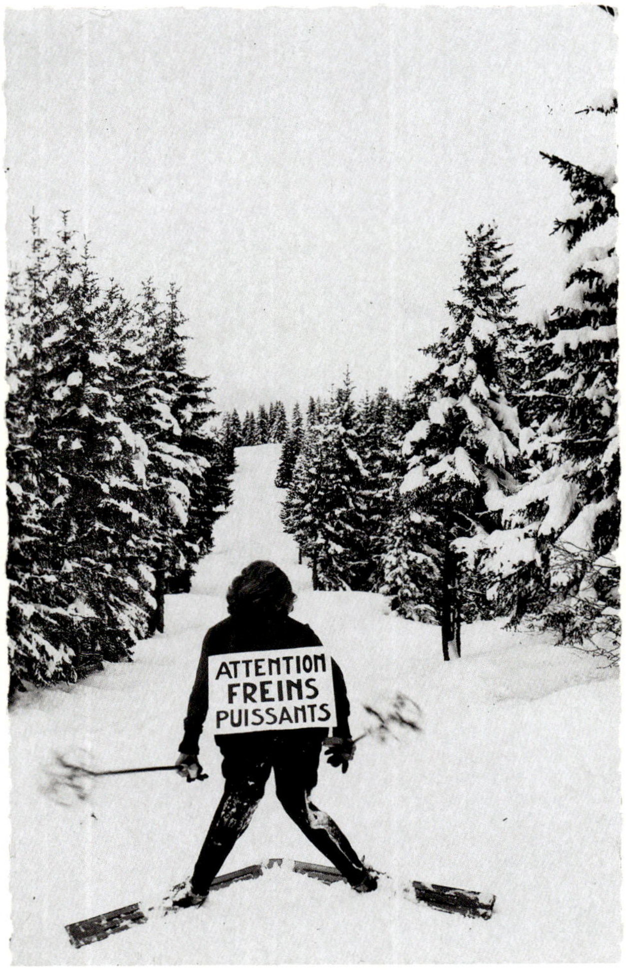

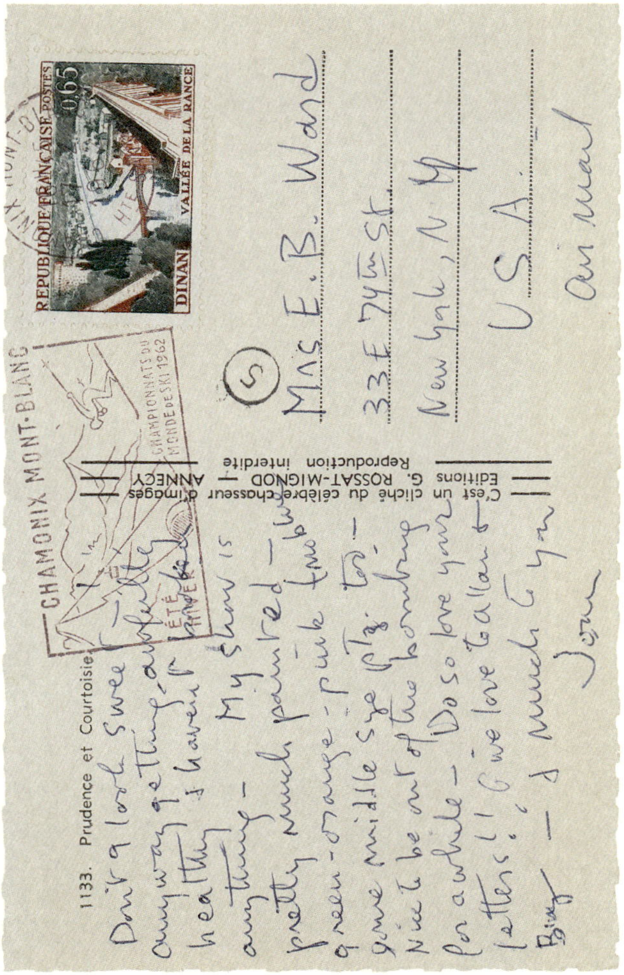

Why at this desk am I listening for the sound of the fall of color, the pitch of the wooden floor and feet going faster? —BARBARA GUEST, "THE LOCATION OF THINGS"

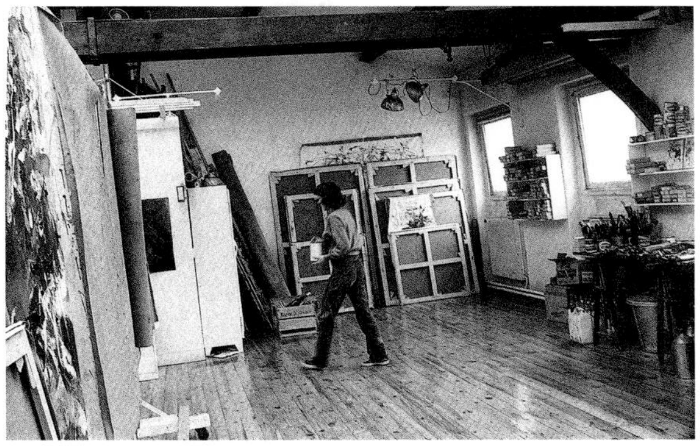

4.1

"I've found the closest thing to a loft that exists in Paris . . . give me money—please!!"[1] No more scraping paint off floors. No more rolling canvas after canvas to move from one temporary studio to another. After four years of shuttling back and forth between Paris and New York, hustling to find space each time, and dealing with the hassles of a transient life, Mitchell wrote to Eleanor Ward begging for help to lease a large studio. She finally secured this place of her own in early 1959. Her incessant travel would continue unabated—flying to New York and Chicago several weeks each year, spending summer months visiting Long Island or sailing around the Mediterranean. But 10 rue Frémicourt in the fifteenth arrondissement became her primary home and studio for the next nine years. After completing extensive renovations, she moved in the fall of 1959, along with Jean Paul Riopelle, newly separated from his wife. Mitchell began to work in the first space in Paris that she had chosen for herself, had arranged, and could leave knowing her brushes, colors, and canvases would be undisturbed upon her return. With Frémicourt, Mitchell procured stability and a place where she could easily show (or not) her work to visitors. She also gained the freedom to paint as she wished, at a considerable remove from the pressures of New York. Within a year of occupying her new studio, Mitchell would have her first solo exhibition in Paris and let loose a series of fervent experiments, testing herself and the physical properties of her medium as she fought to establish a name for herself in Paris as she had New York.

At the outset, the Frémicourt studio delivered on its promise of time and freedom and quickly led Mitchell to intensify and solidify her habit of working cyclically. The first works she made here (a subset of which would later be shown under the title *Cercando un Ago*) puzzle through a particular set of spatial, color, and compositional strategies. Photographs show multiple locations throughout the living and working space where she could tack up unstretched works, including a movable wall, as well as stacks of stretched canvases (fig. 4.1). Mitchell also began working frequently with standard-size, prestretched canvases in this time frame. The ample walls and the ease of temporarily setting aside stretchers facilitated having multiple paintings in progress at

FRONTISPIECE
Postcard (recto and verso) sent by Joan Mitchell to Eleanor Ward, February 17, 1962. Stable Gallery Records, Archives of American Art, Smithsonian Institution, Washington, D.C.

FIG 4.1 Joan Mitchell in her studio at 10 rue Frémicourt, Paris, with a movable wall for tacking up unstretched works visible at left, 1963 once, even side by side in direct dialogue. This ability to step away from works and later return to them, either for reference or to continue painting, spurred Mitchell's cyclical way of thinking, latent in her approach since the early 1950s. She knew well the cohesive painting series of her friends Franz Kline and Willem de Kooning, and also those of Claude Monet. Her new studio afforded her the opportunity to fully explore this way of working, and the suite of paintings around the *Cercando un Ago* group exhibits a shared internal logic and cohesive sensibility reflective of their unfolding in proximity, over time. Mitchell's theme-and-variation approach took strong hold in 1959–60 and would be central to her process for the rest of her career.

Her late 1950s letters to Michael Goldberg, Eleanor Ward, and Paul Jenkins mention opportunities for solo shows in Paris, and her inclusion in numerous significant group exhibitions[2] clearly had drawn the notice of dealers and other art world figures across Europe.[3] But either the one-person shows failed to materialize, or she flatly turned them down. "I have for the moment no desire to show at all—because I don't work well under pressure. . . . Many people have called—wanted to see—I say no."[4] Her first solo exhibition in Paris finally came in April 1960 at Lawrence Rubin's Galerie Neufville. An American with close ties to New York galleries, critics, and curators, including his brother William Rubin, as well as connections to gallerists throughout Europe, Lawrence Rubin was friendly with artists in Mitchell's circle including Riopelle, Sam Francis, Kimber Smith, and Norman Bluhm. Rubin had stayed for several weeks in Mitchell's Frémicourt studio while it was still being renovated in early 1959;[5] thus, the exhibition likely grew from their social connection. Three works are known to have been included—*Untitled* (ca. 1959, plate 30), *Small Mephisto* (ca. 1959), and *Cherchez l'aiguille* (Look for the Needle, later *Cercando un Ago,* 1958).[6] All build on strategies visible in works from her 1958 Stable Gallery exhibition, including latticed structures of singular, forceful brushstrokes that operate as lines as well as forms. These compositions begin to contract toward the center, with leggy right-angle marks creating a sense of spiraling or oscillation, as seen in *Untitled*. Through Rubin's efforts, the grouping was later shown at the Galleria dell'Ariete in Milan. At that point, the French title *Cherchez l'aiguille* was applied in Italian to all the works.[7] As would be the case for so many of her successive bodies of work, the series title was assigned for the exhibition, linking a finite selection of works shown, but leaving out many intimately related paintings.

The Galerie Neufville exhibition elicited Mitchell's first substantive reviews from French critics. Pierre Schneider and Pierre Restany, both significant voices with robust networks in the United States and Europe, respectively, engaged with her work and sought to place her in relation to her American contemporaries. Restany's review in *Cimaise* is particularly notable in light of his fading interest in gestural painting at that time—his 1960 book *Lyrisme et abstraction* essentially concluded that gestural painting in both France and the United States had devolved into convention, and he wrote his manifesto establishing *nouveau réalisme* as a movement the same month as Mitchell's exhibition.[8] He describes her as far outside the "anonymous crowd of New York Action painters" due to her ability to orchestrate color and harness spontaneity of gesture with a measure of control. He praises her canvases' "organic consistency and internal order rarely equaled in abstract expressionism (and entirely absent in de Kooning . . .)."[9] Restany identifies in Mitchell's work a "solution to the stalemate of action painting,"[10] yet laced throughout his review is the implication that this kind of painting has reached a dead end.

In fact, Mitchell's emergence in Paris at this moment ran counter to a growing recognition among critics, collectors, and many artists that abstract painting was on the wane.[11] In spite of the best efforts of ambitious artists and dealers, as well as the presence of numerous contemporary art salons and prestigious group exhibitions, the market for contemporary painting in Paris remained sluggish, having never fully recovered after the war. The city maintained its reputation as an elite center of the art world, prompting many U.S. artists to try to show there and U.S. galleries to try and establish business networks with Parisian peers.[12] But Paris-based dealers, including Rubin, struggled to find a collecting audience for contemporary art, and they relied on relationships with galleries in New York and European cities including Bern, Düsseldorf, London, and Milan to create momentum and generate sales for their artists.[13]

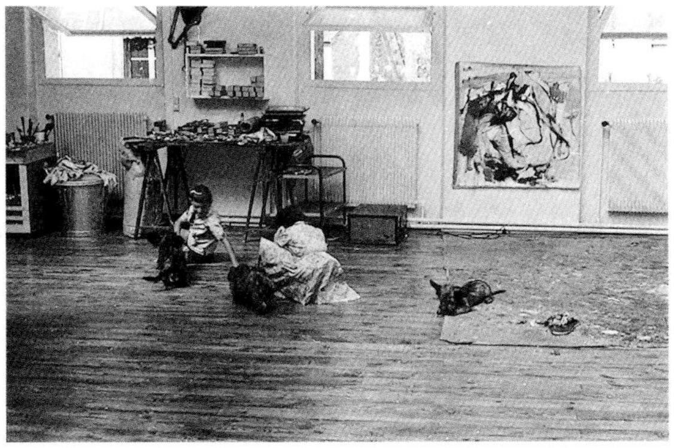

4.2

FIG 4.2 Jean Paul Riopelle's daughter Sylvie and a friend playing with Joan Mitchell's three dogs in her studio at 10 rue Frémicourt, Paris, ca. 1959. The Miriam and Ira D. Wallach Division of Art, Prints, and Photographs, New York Public Library, The Walter Silver Collection, gift of George and Carole Silver, 2000

Once she moved to Frémicourt, Mitchell, together with Riopelle, created a small center of social gravity in the Parisian art world. They hosted two or three lunches each week attended by painters, poets, critics, dealers, and friends, both local and visiting, celebrated and unknown. Regulars included artists Francis, Smith, Alberto Giacometti, Shirley Jaffe, David Budd, Marc Berlet, Mario Garcia, Zuka, John Bennett, Anne and Hugo Weber, and Zao Wou-Ki; writers Samuel Beckett, John Ashbery, and Pierre Martory; and gallerists Jacques Dubourg and Pierre Matisse, along with Schneider. Mitchell and Riopelle were "*the* couple" in Paris, whom all Americans passing through went to see.[14] They also spent long nights at the Café du Dôme in Montparnasse, often in the company of Beckett and Giacometti, drinking, talking, and fighting. Riopelle's daughters, Yseult and Sylvie, came and went (fig. 4.2), as did numerous artists and poet friends from New York. Mitchell was both drawn to and drained by the social swirl. As time passed, the lack of separation between her living and working space and the glut of visitors began to impinge on Mitchell's time and room to work, compelling her to paint later and later into the night.

Beckett became a refuge from these social pressures. Mitchell met him in 1955[15] through Barney Rosset, who published *Waiting for Godot* in the United States in 1954 and remained Beckett's publisher through the end of his life. Beckett was a literary giant already when he and Mitchell met. He was also highly regarded in the Paris art world for his serious engagement with art (first evidenced in his 1949 text *Three Dialogues,* written with Georges Duthuit) and his sustained support of painters, particularly Bram van Velde, a friend of Riopelle's. Mitchell and Beckett lunched, drank, walked Paris streets, and played billiards together casually, and then found their way into a deeper relationship and brief affair as she slipped away with Beckett both to inflame and escape Riopelle's anger. Their natures suited each other: both valued silence and long looking at paintings, both were preoccupied with death and experienced depression. Eventually, they settled into a lifelong friendship and profound mutual respect for each other's work.[16] In 1986, Mitchell reemphasized Beckett's importance to her. "He doesn't describe anything. It's like good painting. He doesn't illustrate anything. If something is green, you know it is green, but he doesn't say it's green."[17] Beckett strove for the same kind of accuracy in capturing experience in language that Mitchell sought in paint. She described him to Rosset as "remote & spiritual,"[18] a clear counterpoint to Riopelle's boisterous gregariousness and explosiveness.

Following her 1960 Paris and Milan exhibitions, Mitchell flew back to the United States, having convinced Riopelle to spend the summer on Long Island and the fall in New York and Chicago with her. While the paintings shown at Galerie Neufville in 1960 had expanded on vocabularies developed in 1956–57, those made later that year grasped at something entirely new.[19] *Water Gate* (1960, plate 32) testifies to the transition—traces of the spiraling and latticed structures in the paintings of 1957–59 are still visible, but the emphasis has turned away decisively from linear brushwork to an energetic, almost gleeful array of alternative marks. Mitchell scrubbed and smeared paint into loosely overlapping passages, wiped and dabbed at the surface with rags, and flung paint from the tips of heavily loaded brushes. The new vocabulary conveys a greater sense of impulsiveness and velocity than that of previous works, yet is equally deliberate and solidly structured.

Many observers, including Mitchell herself, have described the 1960–62 paintings as "violent" (as discussed by Amy Rahn on pages 104–5). Perhaps with works like *Mud Time* (1960, plate 34) and *Rock Bottom* (1960–61, plate 31) underway, she wrote to Francis in early 1961, "I'm getting my N.Y. show together—sort of blue & pink & très tormenté."[20] Linda Nochlin, Yves Michaud, and others have understood this violence as an expression in paint of Mitchell's personal, and specifically female, rage.[21] In addition to this psychological explanation, however, it is worth noting the unrest and violence in Paris from 1958 to 1962 arising from increased political and police repression of the Algerian independence movement. Mitchell experienced this hostility firsthand, witnessing nearby bombings and being roughed up and jailed with Riopelle after he was stopped under suspicion of being Algerian.[22] The couple's constant fighting also frequently turned physical, each provoking the other to the point of explosion. Such immediate experiences of brutality might easily have taken root in her work. But beyond violence, these paintings also express tremendous risk-taking, athleticism, and sensuality, as Mitchell experimented aggressively and developed an astonishing range of intensely physical techniques in works such as *Mud Time, La Chatière* (1960, plate 33), and *Bonhomme de bois* (1961–62, plate 35). Rather than emphasize the mark on the canvas, these works are about the materiality and behavior of paint—its body, its color, the way it moves, reacts, and obeys or does not obey the artist's direction.

A staggering array of paint applications fills the surface of *Bonhomme de bois*. Though Mitchell primarily worked with the canvas oriented vertically, drip angles, pooling, and circular drops indicate clearly that she tackled it from multiple orientations—including briefly laid flat, a rare occurrence in Mitchell's paintings. After an initial loose pass with a broad brush in watery blues, teals, and pinks, she used varying pressure in successive campaigns of brushstrokes—wide, thin, and in-between; long, short, angular, scrubbed, swirled, abrupt, and sinuous. Viscous paint mingles with the barest trace of pigment thinned to a liquid transparency. She squeezed tubes directly onto the surface to make ropes and dots with trailing tails. She also threw, flicked, and whisked paint through the air to land on the surface in bewilderingly complex threads, shreds, and droplets. One imagines the full-body sidearm throw required to create such long thin strings of paint and the wiry wrist action necessary to press bristles onto the surface, and then snap them free to discharge a spidery skein. Gestures still fill the canvas, but many issue from a brush in the air rather than one touching the surface.

To venture to place this many layers onto a canvas, this many textures, this many colors, is to risk the total collapse of the painting into a chaotic, unsightly sludge. Within four square inches one might encounter black, white, umber, deep blue-green, crimson, lemon yellow, olive, lavender, and cornflower blue. This riot should not work together, yet Mitchell's command of placement, proportion, and transparency—again, the underlying order—forces it to succeed. Some of the most intriguing paintings from this period, such as *Cous-cous* (1961–62, plate 37) and *La Chatière,* contain passages that do tip into chaos, thereby demonstrating the knife's edge that Mitchell flirted with from layer to layer. Compared to much of her earlier (and later) work, these canvases are less directly connected to her memories and the external world of landscape, people, and dogs, and are activated by a sense of play and a sensual absorption with paint. This new direction is not simply a wave of vigorous improvisation; it is a virtuosic display of Mitchell's intuitive control of effects and her sensory understanding of, and almost physical identification with, the material qualities of paint.

Perhaps this energy came from the freedom of having a place where she could throw paint and not worry about cleaning it up, or perhaps it arose from having enough psychological distance from New York to let go and pursue new directions without fear of negative responses. But Mitchell's deepened exploration of the materiality of paint also intersected with the heightened focus on process and materials of many abstract painters actively showing in Paris in the late 1950s and early 1960s (as discussed by Éric de Chassey on pages 86–95). In spite of her dismissal of much of what she saw ("people speak too much here of the 'métier'—I miss the brutality—fuck the school of Paris"), she was undoubtedly looking.[23] Within her own social network, she knew Riopelle's and Francis's work best and lived with their paintings on her walls (see the Francis painting in fig. 4.3), but she also spent time with van Velde and Simon Hantaï. Among the broader circle of artists associated with *art informel,* tachisme, and the lingering École de Paris, she frequently saw or was shown alongside works by Wols, Nicolas de Staël, Jean Fautrier, Georges Mathieu, Judit Reigl, Pierre Soulages, and Maria Helena Vieira da Silva. For Mitchell, looking was always far more meaningful than talking, and extended looking led to absorbing aspects of what she saw. The vast array of techniques that these artists employed to foreground the material nature of oil paint perhaps contributed to her own turn toward investigations of the same.

The painter whose work she knew most intimately was, of course, Riopelle. Their letters offer little insight into their dialogue about painting, touching on day-to-day frustrations but not on the nature of the work. Mitchell bemoaned, "I've been trying to paint—and it's all wrong—the red doesn't look red & the blue looks like some *affiche*—and probably it's just because I have either too much feeling or not enough or not the right kind."[24] In an earlier reply to a similarly doubting letter, Riopelle encouraged her, saying, "I am very unhappy about your pessimism on the subject of your recent painting. . . . I said to G. Duthuit . . . that you are the most important painter right now, baby, that is what I think deep down."[25] Yet some measure of dialogue in the work is inevitable for two people living together, seeing each other's work daily, and engaged in an intense rivalry. In this period, Mitchell certainly took up and made her own some of the methods of throwing and spraying paint that Riopelle had used in the early to mid-1950s. And Riopelle's works, around 1959, began to coalesce from his signature shard-like mosaics into larger patches and branch-like forms. He also selectively painted vibrant red and magenta lines over earlier layers to the same effect of Mitchell's red disruptive marks (fig. 4.4),[26] and he began using white in ways that connect with her work—pushing it in from the edges to emphasize a central form and adding brief bands to give breath to an otherwise aggressively dense surface.

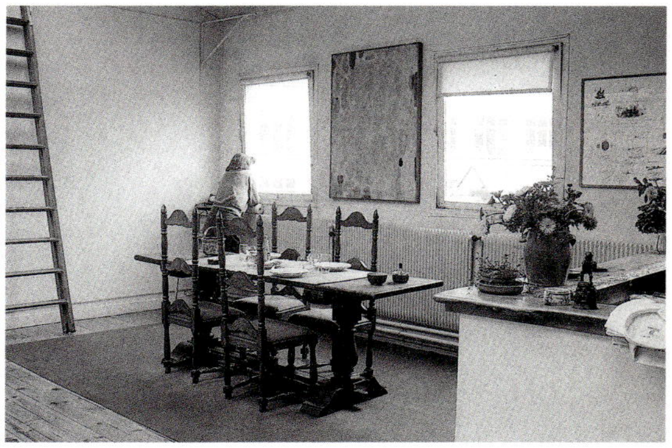

4.3

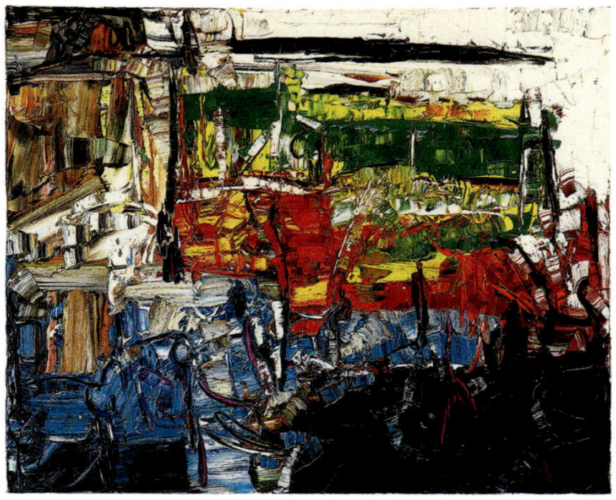

4.4

FIG 4.3 Joan Mitchell in the living area of her studio at 10 rue Frémicourt, Paris, with artworks by Sam Francis and Saul Steinberg, 1963

FIG 4.4 **Jean Paul Riopelle** *Untitled,* 1961. Oil on canvas, 51¼ x 64 in. (130.2 × 162.6 cm). Art Gallery of Hamilton, Ontario, Canada, gift of Irving Zucker, 1990

But a deeper reverberation between their works lies in their responsive use of color. Both bought their paint from Lefèbvre-Foinet. As a result, they were working with similar chromatic ranges, wrestling with the same harmonies and contrasts of hues. Both worked additively and intuitively, with paint straight from the tube. Their decisions entailed judiciously placing each color in reaction to others—an act of juxtaposition or superimposition, almost never one of blending or mixing. Even within Riopelle's knife work, he did not apply the kind of motion that would have caused true blending of two colors into a third—the streaks remain deliberately distinct and readable, their adjacencies being strategic and crucial to the finished work.[27] Mitchell's later statement describes the approach: "Give me a dead color. It's dead because of what's next to it. Then if it's not a color, then move something to make it into a color."[28]

Because of such resonances and their cohabitation, Mitchell understandably took pains to separate her work from Riopelle's and was loath to discuss any sort of correlation between them.[29] From the start of their relationship, she had coped with being seen as just another of his mistresses and as an unknown in the French art world compared to "the great Riopelle"[30]—the inverse of the situation in New York, where her stature significantly overshadowed his. This demotion surely rankled, given her competitive nature. Thus, Mitchell's vehement gamble in a new direction also might have been spurred by an intense desire to establish herself in Paris as a painter of consequence, entirely separate from—and equal to or greater than—Riopelle.

The risk reaped rewards. Concurrent, jointly organized solo shows at the respected gallery of Jacques Dubourg and at Rubin's Galerie Lawrence[31] in May 1962 brought sales and recognition. Mitchell reported on the Paris shows to Goldberg: "I gather my shows were a success. The reviews were good (odd for France) & Dubourg sold all he had . . . (poor Rubin puffing behind). Nice to make money."[32] In addition to the welcome sales, reviews appeared in *Le Monde* as well as major art publications, many applauding Mitchell for moving beyond recent trends in both New York and Paris.[33] Schneider also wrote a review for *Art News* in which he

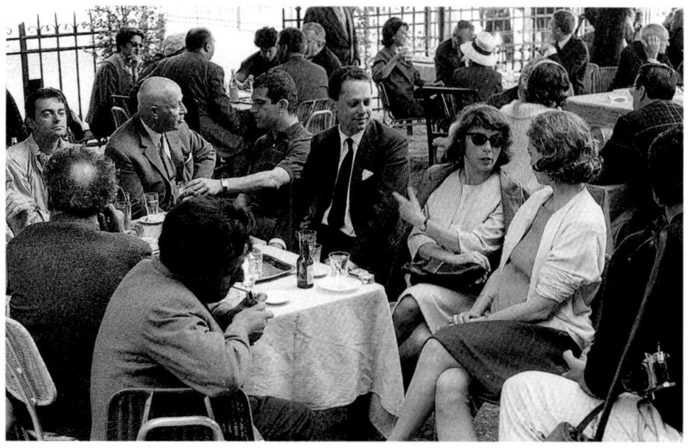

4.5

FIG 4.5 Jean Paul Riopelle, Alberto Giacometti, Joan Mitchell, and Gaby Smith at the Venice Biennale, 1962

memorably lauded Mitchell's "oscillation and mediation between beauty and disaster."[34] Ashbery noted in his review that her direction had at first been disconcerting but now seemed fully justified: "The old broad strokes and rhythmic push and pull have melted into a new iridescence, into a maelstrom of unseizable colors that are ravishing in both senses of the word."[35] At Riopelle's suggestion, Schneider handwrote a text for the catalogue that would become a cornerstone interpretation of Mitchell's work and go on to be translated into English and reprinted multiple times across her career. In it, he elaborates on the idea of her work as a carefully calibrated dialectic between order and chaos, body and spirit—an ambitious endeavor that he sees as raising her above her peers and connecting her to the grand traditions of painting.[36]

Between finishing her paintings and hanging them in the Dubourg and Galerie Lawrence exhibitions, Mitchell went sailing with a group including Riopelle and Mitchell's sister, Sally Perry, making stops in Cannes, Monaco, and Saint-Jean-Cap-Ferrat. They all returned to Paris for the opening on May 8, and Mitchell and Riopelle then departed immediately for Corsica and the Venice Biennale, where they were joined by Pierre and Patricia Matisse, Giacometti, and other friends who helped them celebrate when Riopelle won the UNESCO prize, representing Canada (fig. 4.5). Their success continued that October, when Mitchell's solo exhibition opened at Galerie Klipstein und Kornfeld in Bern, Switzerland, where *Bonhomme de bois* made its debut along with similarly imposing vertical and horizontal canvases including *Cous-cous* and *Grandes Carrières* (1961–62, plate 38). Ambitious, symphonic, and restless, these works—and all those made from 1960 to 1962—pull back from the natural world as Mitchell's attention focused firmly instead on the material dynamics of paint. Roiling with energy, commitment, and urgency, they echo the tempo and tenor of her first years on rue Frémicourt.

Mud Time, 1960
Amy Rahn

Mud Time is illustrated in full as plate 34.

FIG 4.6 List of poem titles written on the back of the 1961 Stable Gallery exhibition invitation. Joan Mitchell Foundation Archives, New York

FIG 4.7 **Joan Mitchell** *Mud Time,* 1960 (detail). Oil on canvas, 82 × 78 in. (208.3 × 198.1 cm). Private collection, courtesy McClain Gallery, Houston

In April 1961, Mitchell arrived in New York from Paris with paintings to be stretched for her upcoming exhibition at the Stable Gallery, including the painting she titled *Mud Time* (plate 34).[1] Scrawled on the back of a card for the show, a list of fourteen poem titles, among them "Two Tramps in Mud Time" by Robert Frost, suggests the source of the painting's title (fig. 4.6).[2] In the poem, the narrator (presumably Frost) splits logs during "mud time," that period in northern climates between winter and early spring. Made soon after she settled in France, Mitchell's *Mud Time* reflects her own in-between time, during which the artist, like the narrator in Frost's poem, found satisfaction in intense, even violent labor undertaken during a restless season.

At the core of Mitchell's painting, crimson red, darkened magenta, and flashes of vermillion cavort and commingle with a family of greens that range from mossy muted and somber blue-dimmed tones to assertive kelly greens (fig. 4.7). A vertical axis of cobalt blue rises like a song nearing its crescendo, around which the central mass seems to rotate as if it were a vortex inhaling color, pulling vibrancy from the looser pastel edges and sparsely painted corners. The tumultuous interior broil builds on lateral passages near the painting's bottom edge that climb the canvas, the type of vertical movement a reviewer of Mitchell's work once likened to a trellis.[3] Grays and blue-grays build from the lower left corner, mounting in a washy, open tower of marks that leap into the upper left corner as white verticals overlying mauve. Adjacent broad strokes of sage green punctuated by sorties of white and blue-green edge the turbulent center, above which an impasto stroke of deep terra-cotta red arches into wide vermillion and salmon pinks that bend toward the painting's right edge like a dancer stretching. Underneath, a few pale washes of gray drip toward a long, assertive line of black that plummets into the painting's lower right corner, which almost glows with swirls of thinned marigold yellow, white, and sage green that wind around and across the painting's bottom edge before meeting the black, ladderlike horizontals that the eye climbs up again. Throughout the composition, paint circulates, builds, and expands in every conceivable application; it is dripped, flung, brushed, clotted, smeared, slathered, pressed, and pulled away.

As the narrator splits logs in Frost's poem, two "tramps" emerge from the woods, aiming to take over the task for pay. The exchange instigates a meditation on the pleasure of a labor chosen in contrast to the waged labor the men hope to make of it.

> The time when most I loved my task
> The two must make me love it more
> By coming with what they came to ask.
> You'd think I never had felt before
> The weight of an ax-head poised aloft,
> The grip of earth on outspread feet,
> The life of muscles rocking soft
> And smooth and moist in vernal heat.[4]

Poised between seasons, the task also hovers between work as chore and work as pleasure, evoking a sense of in-betweenness that similarly characterizes Mitchell's *Mud Time,* a work made between painterly moments, as the artist transitioned from New York to Paris, and as the linear color that had vivified paintings from 1957 like *Evenings on 73rd Street* (plate 26) and *Ladybug* (plate 28) became the compressed "hive" forms of *Calvi* (1963–65). Moreover, in its almost encyclopedic variety of painterly applications, the canvas appears as a visual instantiation of Mitchell thinking and feeling both *through* and *in* the materiality of her chosen medium, a strategy she shared with others in her Parisian circle, as attested, for example, by both Jean Paul Riopelle's troweled-on paint and the pinched, attenuated bronze of Alberto Giacometti's sculpted figures.

Frost further reflects upon his wood-splitting labor as the pleasure of suppressed violence channeled toward meaningful work.

> The blows that a life of self-control
> Spares to strike for the common good
> That day, giving a loose my soul,
> I spent on the unimportant wood.[5]

In 1965, Mitchell described her Frémicourt works as her "boldest paintings" made during "a great violent period."[6] In naming one of those paintings *Mud Time,* the artist seemed also to reference Frost's unleashed blows in an act of skilled precision around which his poem rotates, reinforcing the role of expertise in channeling the more unruly intensities of feeling—even rage—to satisfying ends. Writing in 2002, a decade after the artist's death, art historian Linda Nochlin credited Mitchell with an ability to "take possession of her rage and, like a man, transform it into a rage to paint."[7]

The early 1960s, when Mitchell chose Paris but remained socially and emotionally invested in New York, were a time of division without rupture, of moving across two places like Frost's wood splitter working between seasons, between pleasure and rage. *Mud Time* delivers a storm of painterly gestures from this fertile in-between, an emanation of the artist's own skilled precision in transforming lucid feeling into ferocious virtuosity.

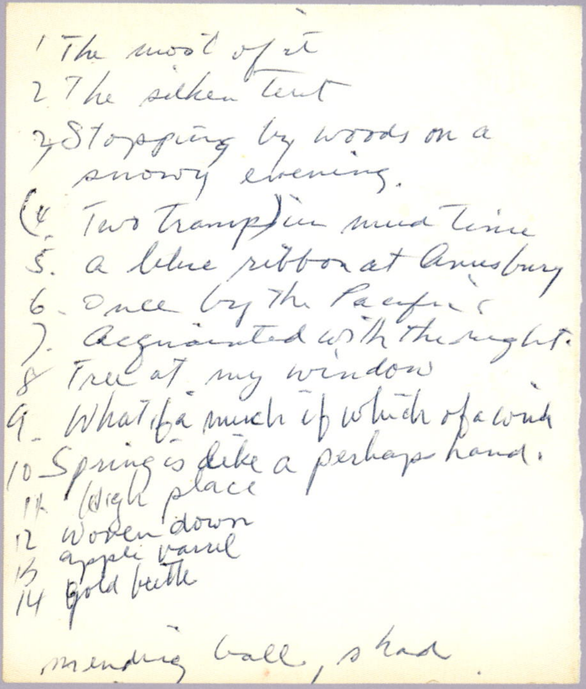
1 The most of it
2 The silken tent
3 Stopping by woods on a snowy evening.
4 Two Tramps in mud time
5. a blue ribbon at Amesbury
6. Once by the Pacific
7. Acquainted with the night.
8 Tree at my window
10 Spring is like a perhaps hand.
11 High place
12 Woven down
mending wall,

4.6

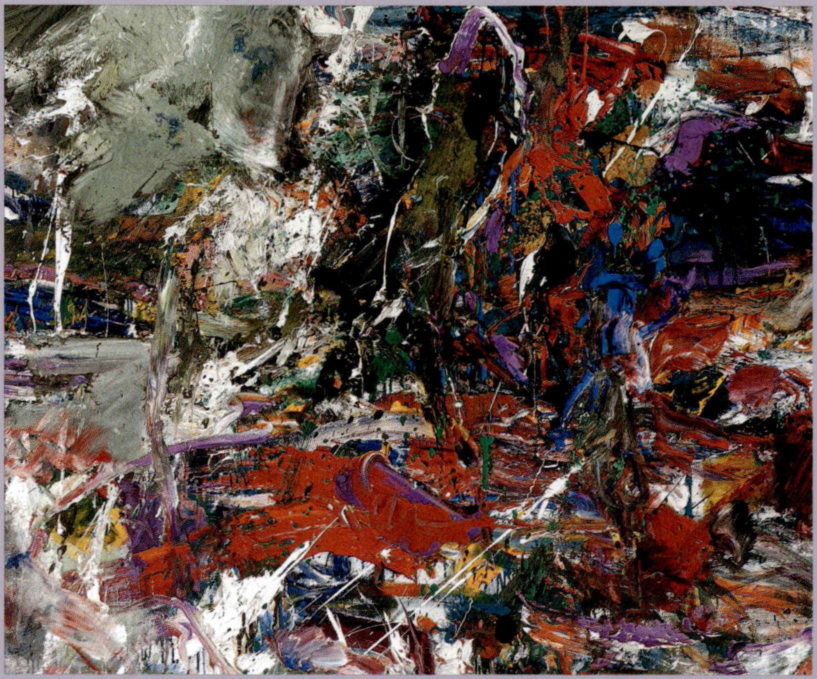

4.7

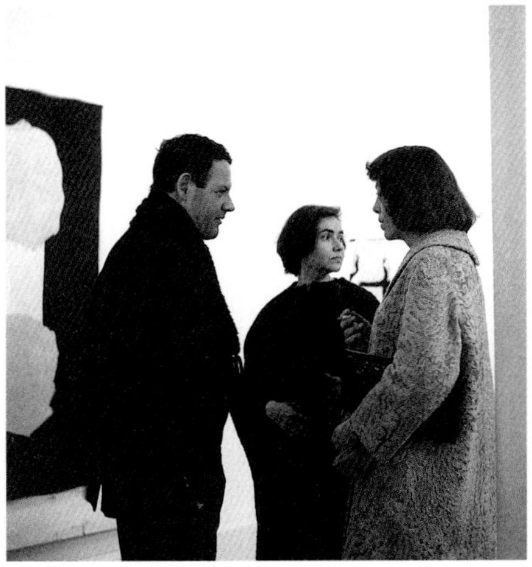

1

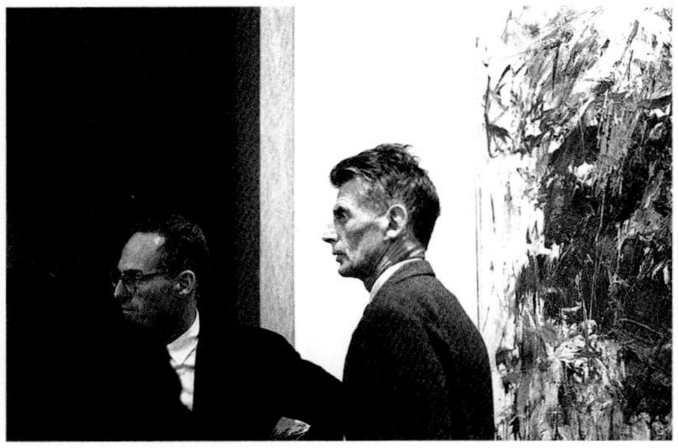

2

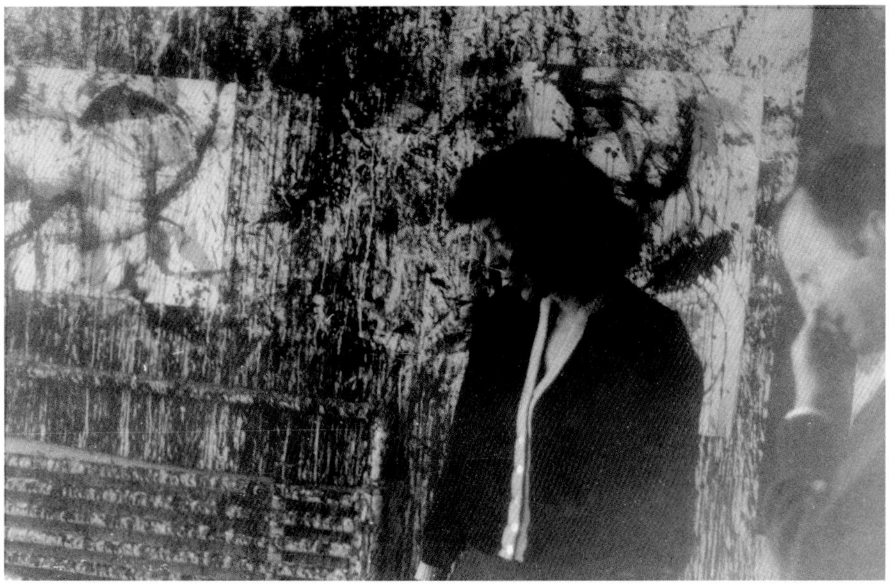

3

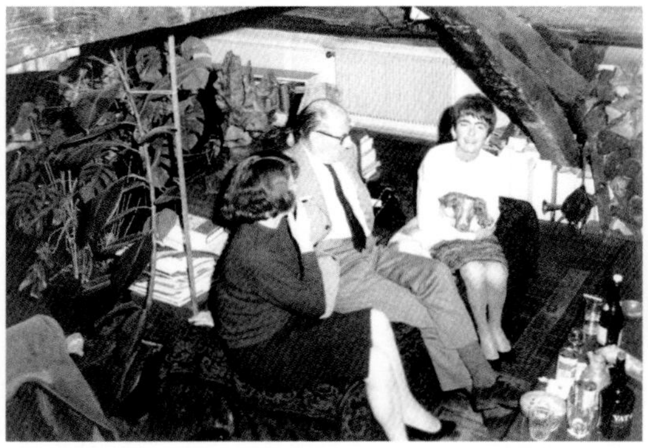

4

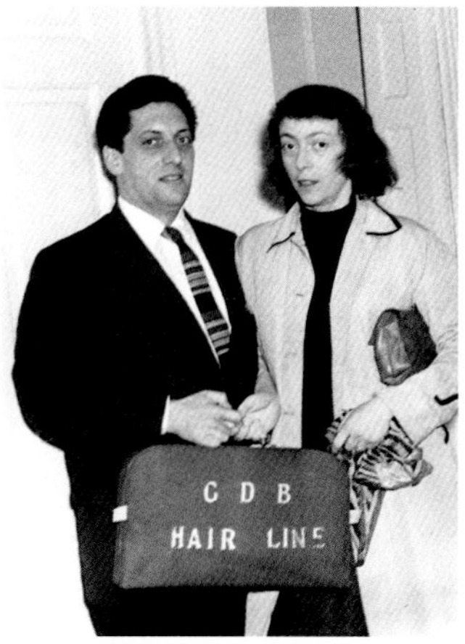

5

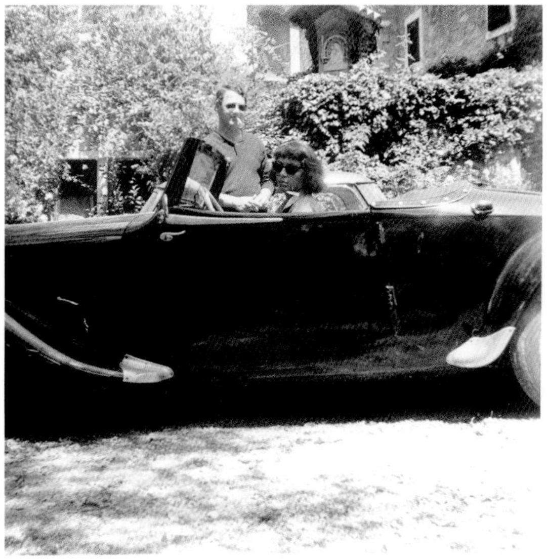

6

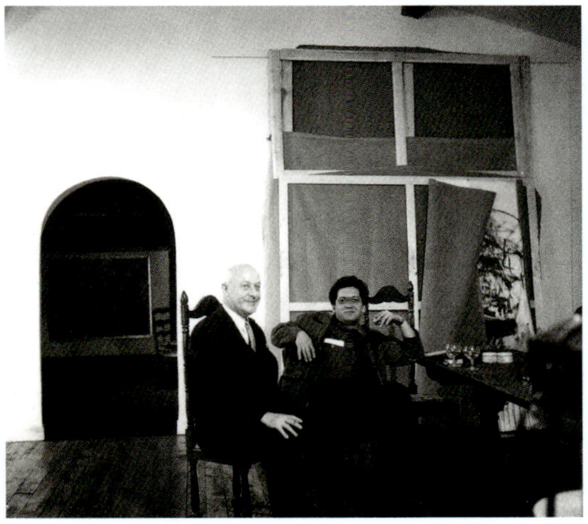

7

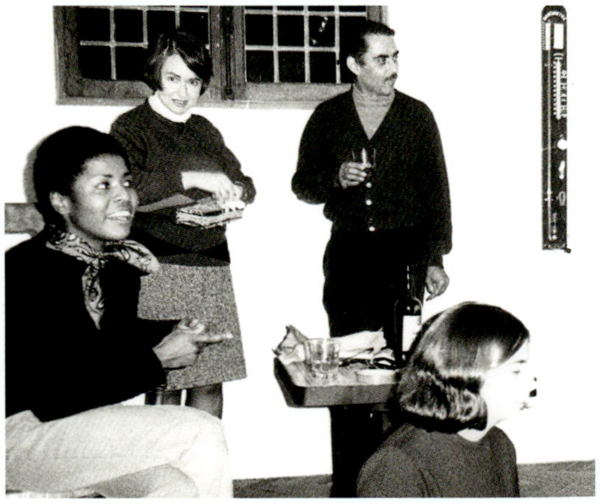

8

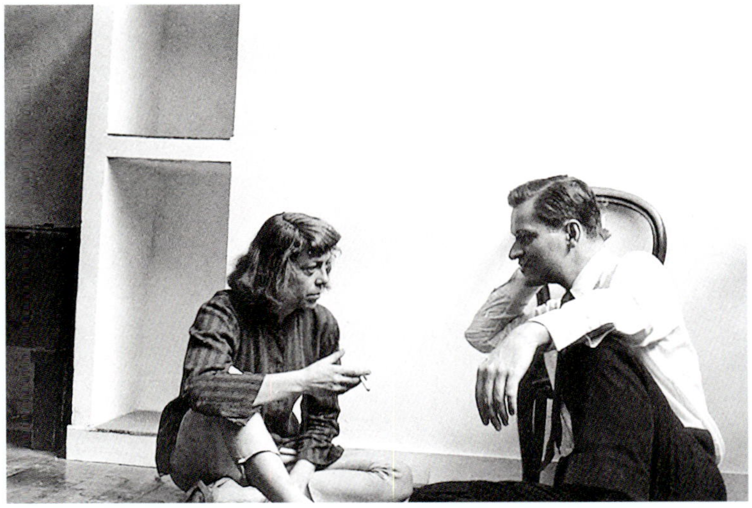

9

1 Joan Mitchell, Shirley Jaffe, and Kimber Smith at *Kimber Smith,* Galerie Lawrence, Paris, 1962

2 Barney Rosset and Samuel Beckett standing near Mitchell's *Le Chemin des écoliers* (1960) at the opening of *Joan Mitchell,* Galerie Lawrence, Paris, 1962

3 Joan Mitchell and Frank O'Hara in Norman Bluhm's studio at 333 Park Avenue South, New York, 1959. Joan Mitchell Foundation Archives, New York

4 Joan Mitchell with Pierre and Patricia Matisse at 10 rue Frémicourt, Paris, 1960s. Joan Mitchell Foundation Archives, New York

5 Jean Paul Riopelle and Joan Mitchell posing with a souvenir Air France bag, n.d. The letters "GDB" refer to *guele de bois* (a hangover), the nickname of one of Riopelle's cars. Archives of Yseult Riopelle, Montreal

6 Joan Mitchell behind the wheel of her Citroën, ca. 1965. Joan Mitchell Foundation Archives, New York

7 Jacques Dubourg and Jean Paul Riopelle at 10 rue Frémicourt, Paris, ca. 1960. Joan Mitchell Foundation Archives, New York

8 Hedy Clark, Shirley Jaffe, Ed Clark, and Sylvie Riopelle at La Tour, Vétheuil, France, 1968. Joan Mitchell Foundation Archives, New York

9 Joan Mitchell and John Ashbery at 10 rue Frémicourt, Paris, 1959. The Miriam and Ira D. Wallach Division of Art, Prints, and Photographs, New York Public Library, The Walter Silver Collection, gift of George and Carole Silver, 2000

10 Joan Mitchell posing with Wilfrid Zogbaum's *Bird in 25 Parts* (1962), Musée Rodin, Paris, 1965. Joan Mitchell Foundation Archives, New York

11 Joan Mitchell and Pierre Soulages in front of his *Peinture 162 × 114 cm, 28 décembre 1959* (1959), Paris, ca. 1967. Joan Mitchell Foundation Archives, New York

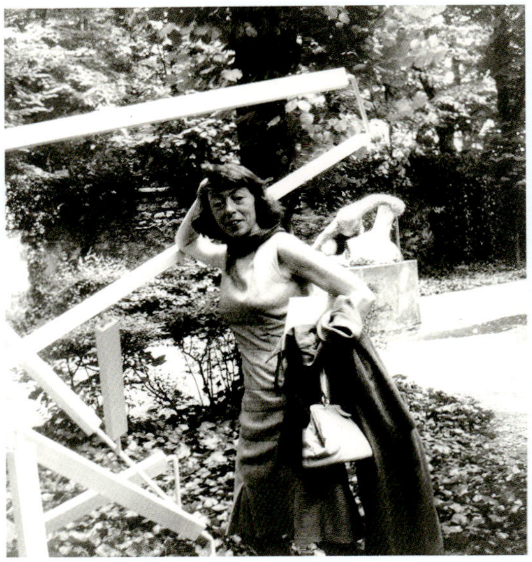

10

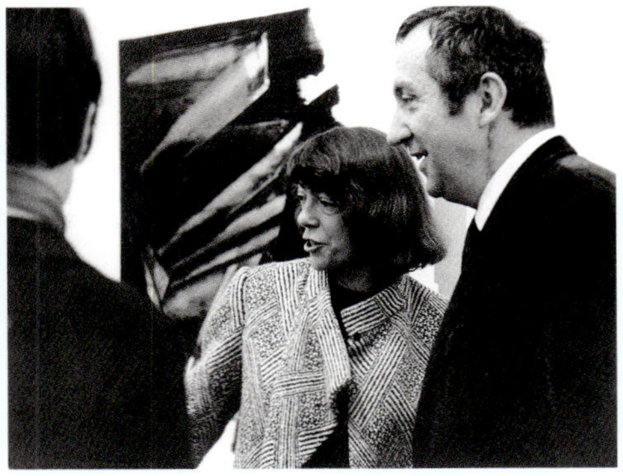

11

5
Voyages Sarah Roberts

Étonnants voyageurs! Quelles nobles histoires
Nous lisons dans vos yeux profonds comme les mers!
Montrez-nous les écrins de vos riches mémoires,
Ces bijoux merveilleux, faits d'astres et d'éthers.

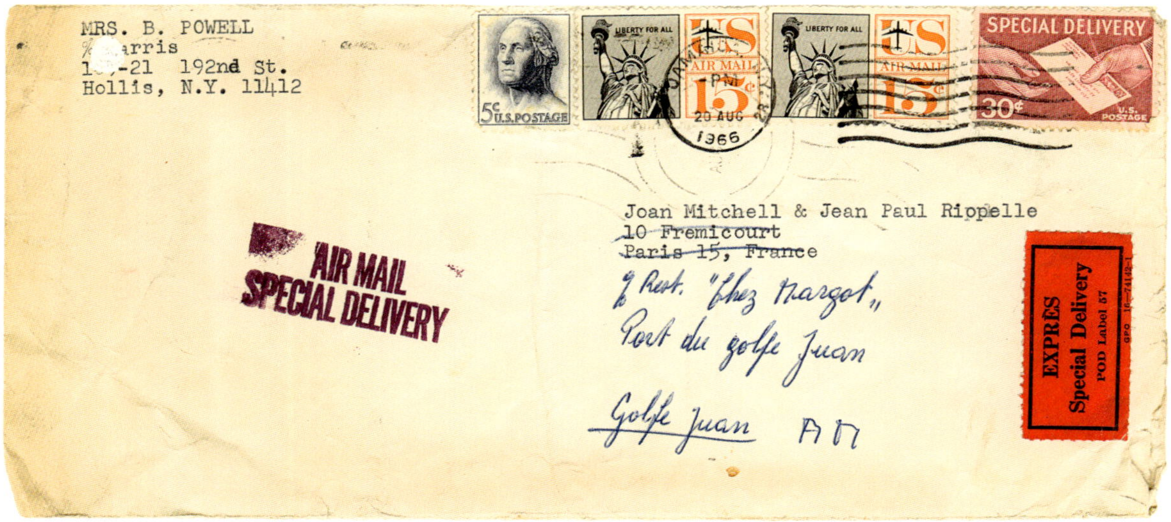

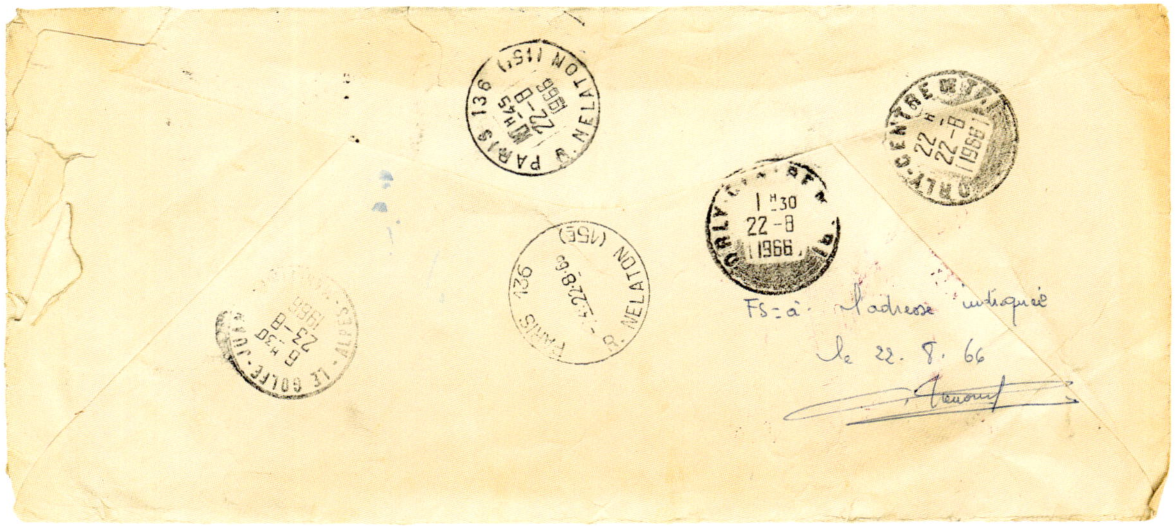

Nous voulons voyager sans vapeur et sans voile!
Faites, pour égayer l'ennui de nos prisons,
Passer sur nos esprits, tendus comme une toile,
Vos souvenirs avec leurs cadres d'horizons.

Dites, qu'avez-vous vu? —CHARLES BAUDELAIRE, FROM *FLEURS DU MAL*

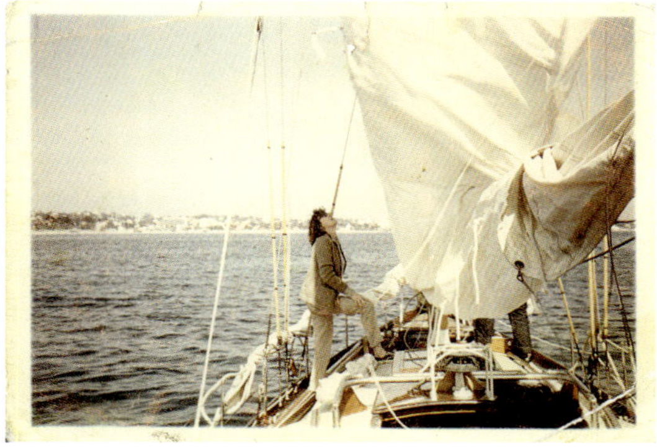

5.1

"We do go like a bat out of hell—spinnaker flying—& sweet porpoises following."[1] Mitchell and Jean Paul Riopelle began sailing together in 1958, and after he acquired his boat the *Sérica* in 1961, they spent weeks each summer and fall going from port to port along the Mediterranean coast. Based in Golfe-Juan from 1962 on, they often sailed alongside Pierre and Patricia Matisse and invited family and friends to join them for day trips or longer sails along the Côte d'Azur and to Corsica, Italy, and Greece. From 1963 to 1966, the trips added up to months spent on the Mediterranean each year, going back and forth from Paris and living on the boat or in rented apartments. Mitchell took pride in learning to sail and loved or hated it depending on the weather and to whom she was writing. "I must say the last storm I thought the mast would break & every other fucking thing. Couldn't even get the cognac down the hatch.... [Y]ou had to be attached anywhere to change the bloody sails. ... *[M]erde*.... I always thought of sailing as a summer activity—you know—getting brown & having a drink—well it ain't at all."[2] The danger, exertion, and adventure of sailing stood in sharp contrast to the leisurely Lake Forest resort summers of her youth and the carousing artist community on Long Island. The seaside villages, rocky coasts, and wide expanse of sea were unlike any landscapes she had experienced in depth before, and Mitchell's paintings from 1963 to 1966 bear witness to her voyages.

These seasons in the South of France were highly social and the most family-oriented phase of Mitchell's adult life. Riopelle's daughters, Yseult and Sylvie, and Rufus Zogbaum, son of her good friend sculptor Wilfrid Zogbaum, regularly joined them, and Mitchell genuinely liked being a mother figure (fig. 5.2). She took the children sightseeing in various ports, and as they grew she taught them Greek history and English, offered advice, and picked up the latest teen slang.[3] While in port, they always stayed in the same rented rooms, and friends knew to send mail to, and find them in person at, the café downstairs, Chez Margot (fig. 5.3). Many artists, curators, and gallery owners also summered in the area, part of a broader upsurge in Mediterranean travel in the 1950s and 1960s that brought everything from artists seeking exposure to classical culture on a modern

FRONTISPIECE
Envelope (recto and verso) addressed from Mrs. B. Powell to Joan Mitchell, 1966. Joan Mitchell Foundation Archives, New York

FIG 5.1 Joan Mitchell aboard the *Sérica*, ca. 1965. Joan Mitchell Foundation Archives, New York

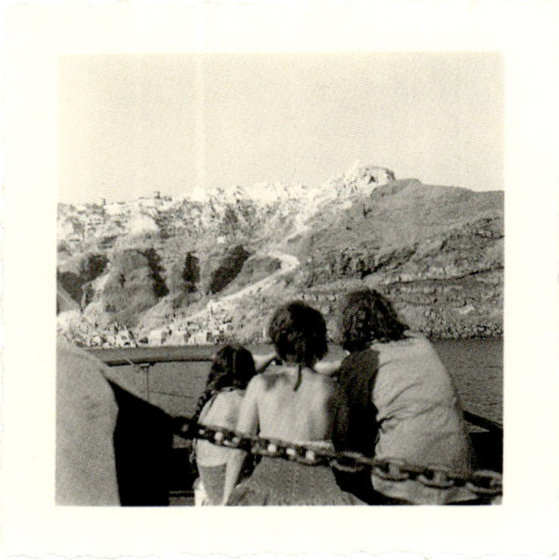

5.2

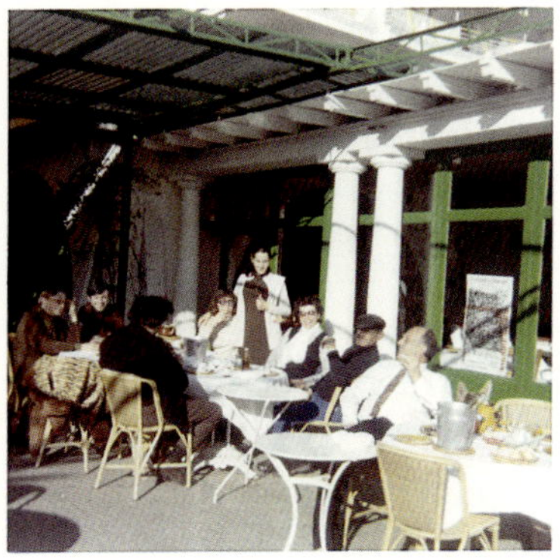

5.3

version of the grand tour, to the formation of bohemian artist colonies and the founding of upscale exhibition spaces such as the Fondation Marguerite et Aimé Maeght, which Riopelle's dealer Aimé Maeght and his wife, Marguerite, opened in 1964.[4] Riopelle mixed easily with all, and he and Mitchell passed much of their time surrounded by friends and acquaintances from Paris and beyond. "Spent chic & dull afternoon with Miró, Soby, Maeght, Matisse & I can go on name dropping—about 20 of them."[5] Others whose company Mitchell appreciated more included poet Jacques Dupin and his family; Louis le Brocquy and Anne Madden, married painters from Ireland; and composer Betsy Jolas and her husband, Gabriel Illouz, with whom Mitchell and Riopelle considered purchasing a home in Corsica. As with the ceaseless socializing in Paris, Mitchell both enjoyed this life and found it taxing. The demands of entertaining, supplying and maintaining the boat, keeping the children busy, and walking the dogs left little time to paint. Compounding the pressures on her time and energy, Mitchell's turbulent relationship with Riopelle grew increasingly dark and violent, their highs and lows noxiously amplified by alcohol.

Given the circumstances, it is not surprising that Mitchell's productivity declined from 1963 to 1966. This decrease coincided with a drop in exhibition activity, as she had both less work to show and little opportunity. After the success of her 1962 solo exhibitions and being at the center of the Venice Biennale with Riopelle, Mitchell's burst of momentum in Europe rapidly dwindled. An annual deal with Lawrence Rubin fell through, then he dropped her entirely—a matter of great consternation to Mitchell, who blamed it on Clement Greenberg, stung by his ongoing disregard for her work.[6] Jacques Dubourg's support also amounted to little; his business was waning and Mitchell never had another exhibition with him. Letters to Goldberg mention exhibition opportunities in Basel, Zurich, Germany, and London, but none came to fruition.[7] She did participate in a few group shows in Paris, including the *Salon des réalités nouvelles* (1963 and 1966) and the *Salon de mai* (1963), as well as the 1963 inaugural group exhibition of the Galerie Jean Fournier. Though this first opportunity had little impact for Mitchell, the relationship would prove to be long and sustaining—Fournier began to represent her in 1966, and he and his artists were critical to Mitchell in her later decades. On the U.S. side, her momentum also slowed. Distance grew between her and Eleanor Ward; their letters evidence gaps in communication and less familiarity with each other's activities and social circles. She doggedly pursued Riopelle's New York dealer Pierre Matisse to no avail.[8] She had no solo exhibitions from fall 1962 until her spring 1965 presentation at the Stable Gallery, which would be her last with Ward, as a dispute over money ended the relationship. Though Mitchell quickly signed with the Martha Jackson Gallery, she would not have her first show there until 1968.

In a May 1965 interview with art historian Dorothy Gees Seckler, Mitchell acknowledged that in the past, she had typically finished a painting within one month. However, for the past two years, she had worked much more slowly, a deceleration due to the amount of time she spent sailing, the lack of a show to work toward, and what she described as being "down about painting for some reason and without a feeling of a landscape."[9] Her intervals of working—turning a painting to the wall when she lost the thread and then returning to it some days or months later—lengthened due to all these factors. Of either *Calvi* (1963–65) or *Girolata* (fig. 5.4), for example,

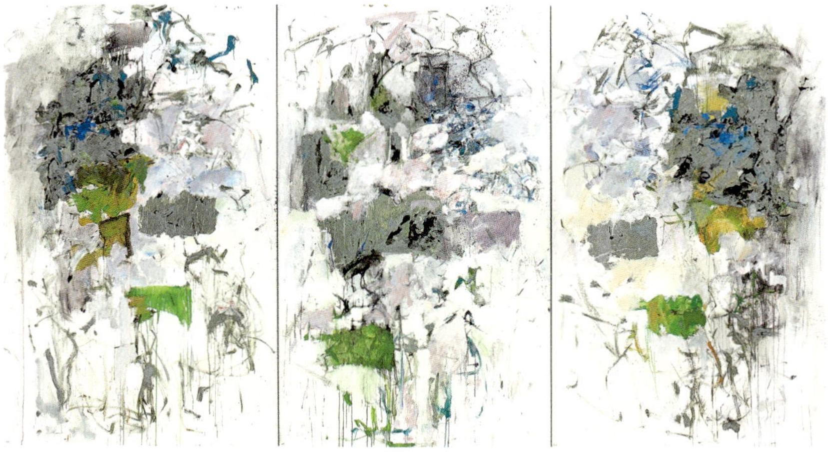

5.4

she noted that she had spent more than a year working on it: "that I did when Kennedy died [November 1963] and I was picking around on it this last January [1965]."[10] As discussed in chapter 4, this pattern of intermittent spurts likely contributed to her working in suites. It also significantly impacted her development of multipanel works by embedding an element of memory within her very process of painting. A painting halted was still present in her mind, still being puzzled through on some semiconscious level and, therefore, was in dialogue with others on which she was actively working. A panel held in memory played a role in how others developed, whether as background or an active point of reference. And panels developed separately often retained their own identities, as evidenced by the fact that Mitchell rearranged the order of some panels, and even occasionally dropped panels out of diptychs and triptychs to make them standalone works.[11]

After the anomalous 1956 *The Bridge* (plate 18) and a very small diptych made in ca. 1960, Mitchell did not produce another multipart painting until the triptychs of 1963. Up to this point, she had been working with both vertical and horizontal canvases, favoring the former but often producing one or two of the latter on a grand scale to anchor an exhibition.[12] In 1963–64, she painted wide horizontals[13] as well as her first triptychs—including *Girolata Triptych* (1963, plate 39; see the essay by Meredith George Van Dyke on pages 116–17)—simultaneously exploring these two very different approaches to capturing the feeling of a landscape. Both Riopelle and Sam Francis had painted multipanel works in the 1950s, so Mitchell had ample opportunity to consider firsthand the visual experience of adjoined verticals versus that of a standalone horizontal canvas.[14] The unified wide horizontal plane implies a static vista, a single experience of passively gazing from a fixed point into an expanse of space spreading out to the left, right, and straight ahead. French artists and critics frequently perceived this type of wide horizontal as a particularly American format. While this perception arose chiefly with reference to the paintings of Jackson Pollock, whose work was associated with the vast landscapes of the western United States,[15] it also circulated around the work of Willem de Kooning, Franz Kline, and

FIG 5.2 Left to right: Yseult Riopelle, Sylvie Riopelle, and Joan Mitchell boating in Greece, 1959. Joan Mitchell Foundation Archives, New York. Photograph by Jean Paul Riopelle

FIG 5.3 Joan Mitchell and Jean Paul Riopelle surrounded by friends at Chez Margot, Golfe-Juan, France, ca. 1965. Joan Mitchell Foundation Archives, New York

FIG 5.4 **Joan Mitchell** *Girolata,* 1964–65. Oil on canvas, 101¾ x 189⅝ in. (258.4 × 481.6 cm). Hirshhorn Museum and Sculpture Garden, Smithsonian Institution, Washington, D.C., gift of Joseph H. Hirshhorn, 1966

Clyfford Still.[16] Coupled vertical panels, in contrast, suggest the presence of an active (upright) subject, a person looking at multiple views, experiencing varying sensations or memories, and moving through a space or landscape over time. Multiple panels also introduce an element of measuring and control, parceling an idea, memory, or landscape across each component. With joined verticals, Mitchell thus distinguished herself from prevailing American painting and gained greater capacity to convey a multisensory, multifaceted experience or feeling of a landscape. She soon ceased making single-panel horizontals altogether and would not return to them for the rest of her career.

The views that Mitchell remembered and painted previously were defined by their surrounding structures, whether she was looking out through windows high above Lake Michigan, toward the Brooklyn Bridge, or over Paris rooftops, or walking among tall Manhattan buildings. Her perspective from the *Sérica* was radically different, immersed in an open expanse, without framing, exposed. In 1957, in order to emphasize that Mitchell painted from memory, critic Irving Sandler quoted her saying, "I am up against a wall looking for a view."[17] (Her studio at the time looked straight into a neighboring building, so there was no real "view" to paint directly.) But in his interview notes Sandler records her thoughts at greater length: "I'm always up against a wall looking for a view, in search of a view with some obstructions in it. I'm conscious of four walls in a city. . . . But in an open space I'd probably find four walls because this is my experience and also the experience of these New York painters."[18] Indeed, confronted with the open sea, she painted not the water but its walls—the trees at water's edge and the limestone bluffs of Corsica, sun-bleached and studded with scrub and cypresses.[19]

These works carry heavy dark forms floating off-center within mostly white fields, as if the densest sections of heaving sprawl in paintings like *Cous-cous* (1961–62, plate 37) and *Grandes Carrières* (1961–62, plate 38) have contracted into a focal mass.[20] Mitchell specified one visual experience as the germ for this suite—"The cypress tree was so black and the ochre wall was a pale, pale ochre and it moved me"—and explicitly referred to the works that followed as cypress and blue tree paintings.[21] *First Cypress* (ca. 1964, plate 40) retains some of the splatter and agitated brushwork of the previous three years but introduces thin, jittery lines and a distinct central form. Though Mitchell insisted that she was painting "the moment,"[22] not an actual tree, the leftward reach of the lines and blunted right edge of the main form in *First Cypress* suggest the windswept asymmetry characteristic of coastal cypresses around the Mediterranean and in Santa Barbara, California, where Mitchell frequently visited her sister in the 1950s. These are her first paintings to present trees as direct subject matter, with forms and titles that she acknowledged as having real points of reference in the natural world. As such, they move closer to representation than a work like *Hemlock* (1956, plate 24), which Mitchell titled retroactively, making the association to the titular tree in response to her finished canvas via the mediation of a Wallace Stevens poem.[23] The tree would soon become a recurring theme in her work, often connected to specific people and to death.

Throughout the tree paintings, the central forms rise up in layers of deep greens and blues with occasional licks of teal, violet, and umber. In contrast with the complex interpenetrating space that dominates her earlier work, these canvases set up surprisingly stable figure-ground relationships with their strong contrast between the dark masses and their surrounding fields of creamy whites and grays. Mitchell framed her decision

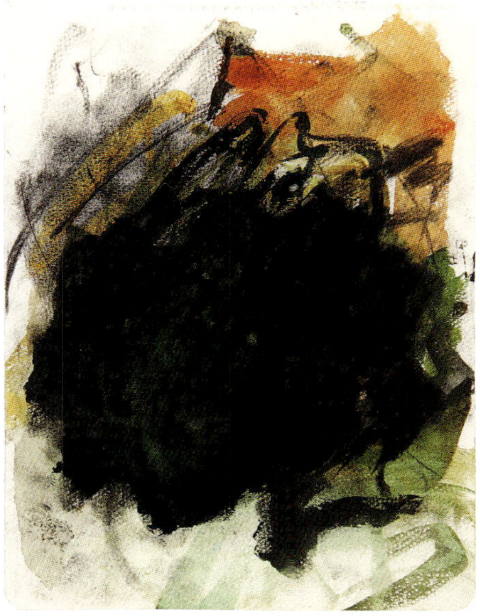

5.5

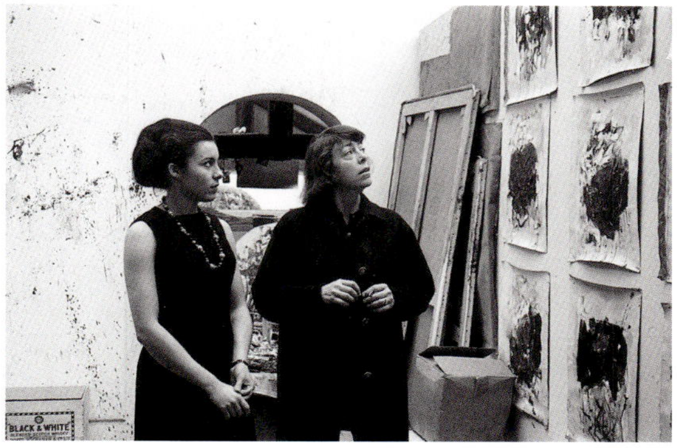

5.6

to explore this type of composition as one of defiance: "Clement Greenberg said there should never be a central image so I decided to make one."[24] The remark may have been tossed off, but the tree subject and her interest in the possibilities of a floating central figure were sustained. She explored them in closely related charcoal drawings and watercolors from 1964 to 1965, as well as a compelling group of small paintings identified on a Stable Gallery checklist as "14 Stations on Paris Subway."[25]

Related watercolors from this period play with overlays of near-black greens and blues swirled over layers of vivid color, not to obliterate but to obstruct and redirect focus (fig. 5.5). The eye's first response to the dark blot is to try and discover the colors underneath it; its second, almost immediately, is to stop and examine the subtle variations within the darkness itself. These works balance intimacy with gravitas and play with the confrontational character of their densely articulated central shapes. The charcoal drawings (such as plate 41) instead activate and break up the dominant body with erasure, smudging, and finely drawn lines that tie them more closely to the tree paintings. Still forceful, they investigate texture, from the barest dustings of the paper grain to delicate tangles of lines and dense rubbing. Sweeps of the eraser cancel earlier marks and reintroduce light and space, echoing Mitchell's characteristic late passes of white and gray paint, very much in evidence in *First Cypress* and *Blue Tree* (1964, plate 42). Together, the watercolors and charcoal drawings demonstrate Mitchell's extended attention to the possibilities of this central pulsing form.

A similar spirit of investigation inhabits the related Paris subway paintings (plates 45–49), which constitute a concentrated study of the central mass rendered at a small scale and in a generally far more colorful palette than the tree paintings from which they grew.[26] They demonstrate Mitchell's skillful experimentation with scaling down her marks, shifting the weight of the central mass up and down, left and right, while alternately compressing or opening it up with contrasting color, fine detailing, and dabs of white. Not preparatory sketches, the series appears to have been conceived as a tightly focused group, each in dialogue with the rest (fig. 5.6).

FIG 5.5 **Joan Mitchell** *Untitled,* ca. 1964. Watercolor and charcoal on paper, 10½ × 8¼ in. (26.7 × 21 cm). Collection of Jill Weinberg Adams

FIG 5.6 Yseult Riopelle and Joan Mitchell with paintings from the Paris subway suite in Mitchell's studio at 10 rue Frémicourt, Paris, ca. 1964. Joan Mitchell Foundation Archives, New York

Mitchell never directly discussed their subject matter, but this group of works might be remembered responses to individual metro stations she frequently used, their variations on a consistent form mapping her experience of moving through the city.[27] Mitchell employs essentially the same formal vocabulary for both the tree and metro paintings—perhaps the most direct example of her refusal to distinguish between urban and rural environments in her conception of landscape.

John Ashbery, who lived in Paris from 1955 to 1965 and wrote art criticism for the *New York Herald Tribune, Art International,* and *Art News* from 1960 to 1965, authored the most substantial review of Mitchell's 1965 Stable Gallery exhibition. The presentation included six tree paintings and two large triptychs, as well as a selection of the metro paintings. Ashbery dedicated his first page or more to describing Mitchell as one of a number of U.S. artists living in Paris who are "not expatriates but *apatrides*."[28] It is a curious word choice, "apatride," and one that he intended to describe not a political situation of statelessness but a psychological condition of being neither here nor there, a disinterested and slightly disgruntled state of between-ness, without investment in either the United States or France as a permanent home, let alone a mother country.[29] For Mitchell, who chose to live in France but continually considered returning to New York, the description was apt. A kind of rootlessness does characterize her life and painting in this period, particularly the 1964–66 paintings that fall outside the central suites with dark forms embedded in white backgrounds (plates 43, 44, 51). She cycles through ideas new and old, combining and recombining techniques, her palette, and compositional elements. *Untitled* (ca. 1964) revisits the heavy use of thrown paint of the 1960–62 canvases to soften and activate the expanded, thickly built-up central mass, which fills more of the picture plane than those in most other works from the period. In other paintings, such as *Untitled* (ca. 1965), the angular lines characteristic of so much work in the late 1950s return as looser, more organic tangles, with new blocklike patches of color nested within them. Much of the 1965–66 work seems unsettled, as though Mitchell is determinedly experimenting her way out of one body of work in search of the next.

Ashbery's review dwells on Mitchell's statements that she depicts her "'feeling' about a landscape,"[30] and he considers the paintings' occasional resemblance to the actual landscapes that stimulated those feelings—particularly notable, to his mind, in *Girolata* (fig. 5.4). He taps into Mitchell's slipperiness with the term "feeling," which she uses variably to mean memory, emotion, essence, and sensory experience, as well as subtle fusions of any of the above. The paintings in the exhibition, he concludes, refer to a vast range of feelings conveyed in a purely visual language: "We move in and out of these episodes, coherent or enigmatic ones, always with a sense of feeling at home with the painter's language, of understanding what she is saying even when we could not translate it."[31] Ashbery valued and regularly advocated for abstract art that was made by and for the senses, beyond the grasp of language.[32] He went so far as to state that an artist's primary concern should be "to create a work of art that a critic cannot even talk about."[33] Mitchell drew on Charles Baudelaire for her framing of painting as a struggle to transmute into visible form multisensory experiences bubbling up through memory.[34] As she would later say, "Obviously, people paint or write music because they can't express some things with words."[35] Ashbery echoes this formulation, declaring that Mitchell's paintings "*are* meaning and therefore do not have a residue of meaning which can be talked about."[36]

Mitchell shared her deep affinity for the poems of Baudelaire with many artists and writers in her circle and beyond, including Ashbery, Michael Goldberg, Frank O'Hara, Thomas B. Hess, Barbara Guest, and James Schuyler, many of whom also produced works directly informed by Baudelaire.[37] All reflected a broader cultural concentration on Baudelaire in the 1950s and 1960s, as his unflinching iconoclasm, infatuation with the city, redefinition of beauty, and conception of the act of artistic creation as a voyage served as a compelling source for a wide range of artists, writers, and musicians. Sandler's 1957 profile of Mitchell used Baudelaire as a lens, and O'Hara amiably referred to her as "ma Baudelairienne actuelle."[38] Resonances between her work and Baudelaire's have been considered thoughtfully by many previous authors, particularly Judith E. Bernstock, who notes that poet and painter both valued silence and solitude and shared an emphasis on landscape and nature as the primary source of feeling, capable of prompting intense, malleable, and commingled sensory experiences that persist in memory.[39] Baudelaire describes memory as both a wellspring of ideas and a burden, a potential cause of ennui or even depression.[40]

> More memories than if I'd lived a thousand years!
>
> A giant chest of drawers, stuffed to the full
> With balance sheets, love letters, lawsuits, verse
> Romances, locks of hair rolled in receipts,
> Hides fewer secrets than my sullen skull.
> It is a pyramid, a giant vault
> Holding more corpses than a common grave.[41]

Memory plays a similar double emotional role for Mitchell—it is both font and drain.

Voyages figure large throughout Baudelaire; voyages through city streets and across time, voyages of love, imagination, creativity, death, and deterioration. The 1963–66 black paintings have often been related to death, and indeed, Mitchell lost many good friends and family members in this half decade. Riopelle's father, Kline, Wilfrid Zogbaum, Alberto Giacometti, and O'Hara all died between 1962 and 1966, as did U.S. president John F. Kennedy, whose assassination she acknowledged as having affected her work. Closer still, Mitchell's mother had been in treatment for cancer since 1960, and her father died in 1963, the first passing in her immediate family. Mitchell's fear of death and her very real losses in these years seep into the starkness and gravity of her work in this period. But more than death, these paintings are about a life in motion, Mitchell's voyages real, remembered, and imagined, passing across canvases.

Girolata Triptych, 1963

Meredith George Van Dyke

Girolata Triptych is illustrated as plate 39.

FIG 5.7 Still from Jean Paul Riopelle, *Untitled,* n.d., showing Torra di Girolata from the *Sérica.* 16mm film. Joan Mitchell Foundation Archives, New York

FIG 5.8 **Joan Mitchell** *Untitled,* ca. 1964. Charcoal and pastel on paper, 24 × 18 in. (61 × 45.7 cm). Private collection

The Côte d'Azur was a frequent holiday locale for Mitchell. Antibes, Cannes, and the many beaches along the French Riviera acted as fashionable backdrops for socializing and relaxation, but they did not inspire her like the island of Corsica.[1] In particular, the small village of Girolata seized her imagination. There, "passing fishermen, off-beat tourists and artists, and gangsters cheating the law" were among the few to make the challenging three-mile trek (five kilometers) over dense terrain or the circuitous—but less taxing—arrival by boat.[2] Despite or perhaps because of its remoteness, Mitchell repeatedly returned to the enclave. She sought out Girolata's fresh visuals as she found respite from the demands of her life in Paris, drawn in by its rocky coast with pockets of blue-green agave, purple rock roses (*Cistus albidus*), and windswept trees (fig. 5.7). *Girolata Triptych* (plate 39), one of the artist's first three-panel paintings, captures her peripatetic lifestyle at this moment and brims with the bright essence of its namesake.

Although Mitchell briefly had studio space in 1961 at La Bergerie, an upscale holiday property in Cap d'Antibes near collectors Olga and Joseph Hirshhorn's Villa Lou Mirandou, she did not paint prodigiously there. And she did not have a dedicated studio space in the South of France thereafter. Starting in 1962, Mitchell and Jean Paul Riopelle rented a room from the owners of the restaurant Chez Margot (their de facto salon) on rue Chabrier in Golfe-Juan, where Mitchell lamented that there was "no place to work."[3] They frequently embarked on Riopelle's boat, "complete with crew of one—René," to complete half-day sails to Corsica or the small islands off Cannes.[4] On short excursions such as this, Mitchell would read or complete crossword puzzles; the boat's incessant movement and space constraints made painting impossible and left more time for looking.[5] Importantly, these expeditions offered new imagery that Mitchell would remember and reimagine in her paintings, including *Girolata Triptych,* which she likely completed in her rue Frémicourt studio in Paris. Among the many sights, she recalled that "black rubber tires under the quai looked like something Motherwell should have seen . . . also there was a mad rock that Rufus [Zogbaum] took photographs of little bits of ideas—strange light."[6] These observations underscore the way imagery seared itself into Mitchell's consciousness, providing inspiration for her later translations into paint, from *Girolata Triptych* to *Rufus's Rock* (1966).

Despite *Girolata Triptych* belonging to a body of work that Mitchell sometimes referred to as the "black paintings," little if any black is present.[7] The main craggy forms in *Girolata Triptych* appear charred, but closer inspection reveals at least three distinct greens that sprout forth. These resilient outcroppings contain flowering teals and pink-lavenders, a bright life amidst the rich, warm ground. Mitchell also mined some of her past compositional strategies, using spurts of burnt sienna on the right panel to create an almost archaeological depth that is apparent in both *La Chatière* (1960, plate 33) and *Vert galant* (1960). The painting's white passages were particularly important to Mitchell as they provide the most structure.[8] The three panels have a wide range of whites, especially in the far right panel, whose pearly passages appear wet. A few select brushstrokes punctuate the white expanses and bridge the vertical divides where the canvases abut.

This period is marked by a quest for a particular form: a dense, consolidated shape with one long straight edge whose opposite side bursts with energetic, coiling brushstrokes. The far left panel of *Girolata Triptych* features one such example, suggestive of a steadfast tree upright against the winds, with tendrils of greenery trailing to its left. Variations of the motif are found in *First Cypress* (ca. 1964, plate 40), whose mass of dark paint extends to nearly all four edges of its canvas. *Blue Tree* (1964, plate 42) is elongated, its hard edge smudged to create a softer effect. All three benefit from Mitchell's dexterous skill and practiced eye. From cords of paint straight from the tube to delicate, translucent drops of turpentine-oil mixtures, Mitchell's three-dimensional masses appear to grow from their canvases. Drawings reveal how adept Mitchell was at achieving these highly textured and articulated shapes in both media (fig. 5.8). Among gritty swaths and diaphanous passages of charcoal, fine lines and erasures show the range of textures found in the artist's paintings.

The monumental combined panels of *Girolata Triptych* echo contours of the town's sole landmark, a sixteenth-century structure called the Torra di Girolata. Repeat excursions to the tower allowed Mitchell to understand constants and changes along the island from various viewpoints. Lushly verdant during rainy seasons but a hot, dry clayscape at the peak of summer, only its rock-encrusted incline endured. Mitchell's triptych portrays these permutations through surprising color juxtapositions reminiscent of the changing flora on the island, and areas of glossy oil paint glimmer like the fleeting reflections of sunbeams on lapping waves. She captures an expanse of time, memory, and multiple viewpoints in one cohesive composition. In 1965, she commented that she was both "trying to remember what she felt about a certain cypress tree" and "trying for something more specific than movies of my everyday life: to define a feeling."[9] *Girolata Triptych* uniquely combines these two sentiments: it encapsulates aspects of a specific place, yet imparts a sensation of Mitchell's inquisitive, nomadic life.

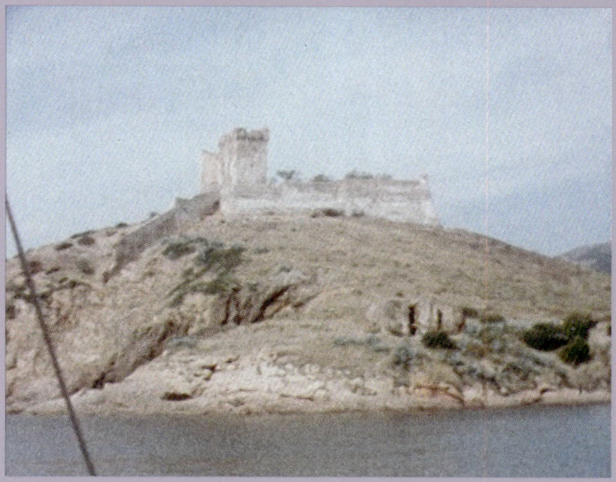

5.7

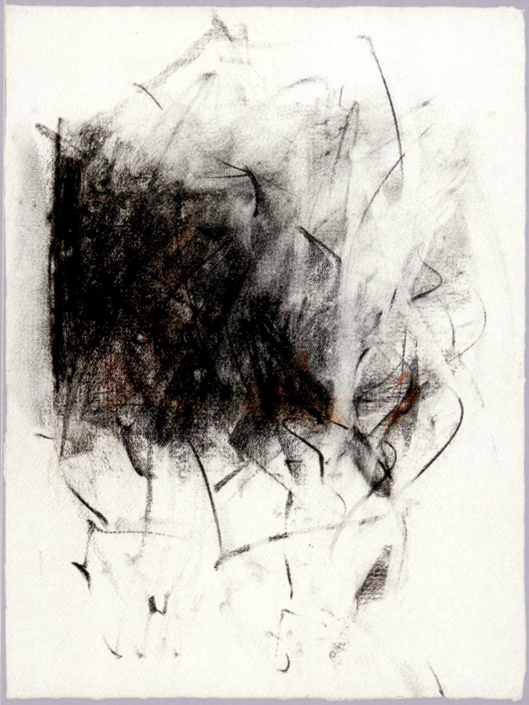

5.8

6
Vétheuil Katy Siegel

Yes, they are alive and can have those colors,
But I, in my soul, am alive too.

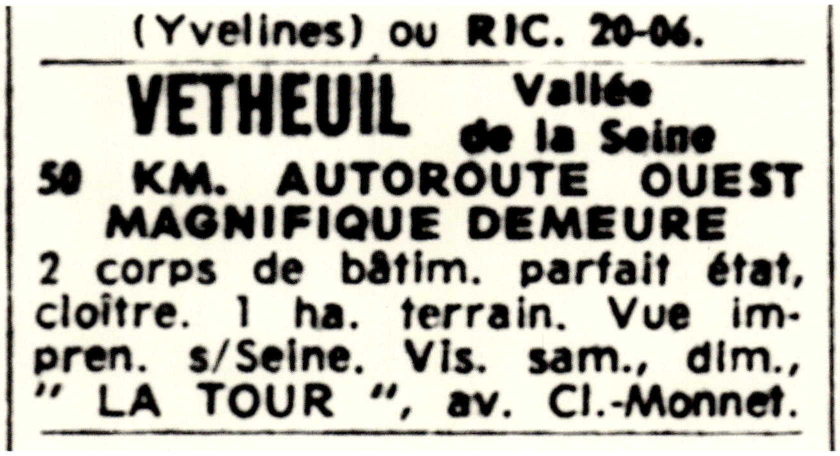

(Yvelines) ou RIC. 20-06.

VETHEUIL Vallée de la Seine

50 KM. AUTOROUTE OUEST
MAGNIFIQUE DEMEURE
2 corps de bâtim. parfait état, cloître. 1 ha. terrain. Vue impren. s/Seine. Vis. sam., dim., " LA TOUR ", av. Cl.-Monnet.

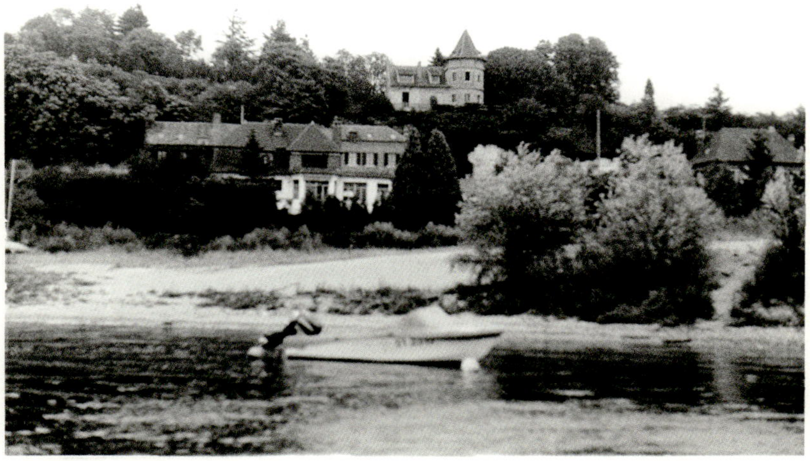

I feel I must sing and dance, to tell
Of this in a way, that knowing you may be drawn to me.

—JOHN ASHBERY, "A BLESSING IN DISGUISE"

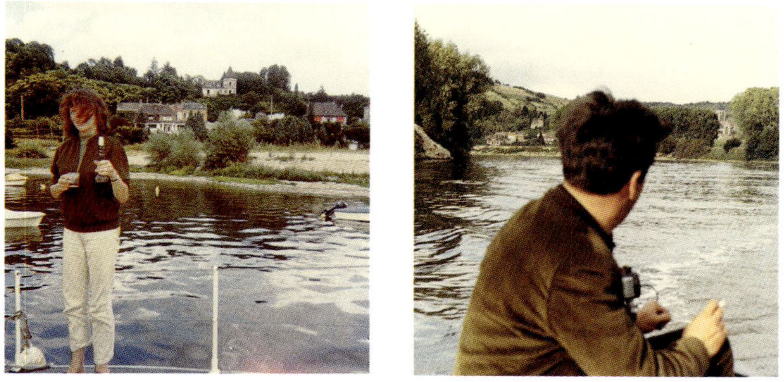

6.1

"I've never seen a place so goddamn beautiful."[1] Painter Ed Clark succinctly captures the central fact of Vétheuil, a small village about forty miles (sixty-five kilometers) northwest of Paris. Betsy Jolas's mother, who owned a home in Chérence, told her that a nearby estate was available, and in April 1967, Jolas showed Mitchell and Jean Paul Riopelle the advertisement in *Le Monde* (at left).[2] It offered "LA TOUR, av. Cl. Monnet"; if the spelling of "Monet" was off, the rest was as advertised: La Tour was a magnificent house with a magnificent direct view of the Seine (see pages 312–13). Vétheuil would feed the artist's love of color, her feelings for trees and water and sky, her affinity for elevated views that recall other views, and her investment in painting traditions going back to the nineteenth century.

Buying the estate represented a commitment to France. Mitchell's mother had died in March of 1966, leaving her the money to buy the property; Marion Strobel's death also weakened her daughter's ties to the United States, leaving less for her to return to. The embrace of the countryside was also a rejection of the city. Jolas says that by the mid-1960s, Mitchell and Riopelle had grown "bored" with their life in Paris, a restlessness not alleviated by their peripatetic summers of sailing and voyages. "Bored" stands in for a complex knot of sentiments: after more than ten years together, their relationship was often strained by alcohol and infidelity, both facilitated by late nights at the Café du Dôme. That social world was growing stale; alongside the deaths of Giacometti and other individual artists, the broader postwar ethos shaping literature and philosophy in Paris had been supplanted by the political tumult of escalating activism among anticolonialist protesters and then a nationwide uprising. This cultural shift likely left the two electric personalities feeling sidelined, even old; as Mitchell wrote Barbara Guest in June 1968, "This 'revolution' has been awful."[3] Most of all, she felt depreciated in the context of the art world, where gestural painting had been pushed aside in favor of *nouveau réalisme* and Pop, followed by other inheritors of the mantle of currency. In January 1967, more than a year before her first exhibition at the Martha Jackson Gallery in New York, Mitchell forecast that her new paintings would not suit

FRONTISPIECE
Top: Advertisement for La Tour, the estate Mitchell would purchase in Vétheuil, France, *Le Monde,* April 22, 1967. Bottom: La Tour, Vétheuil, France, ca. 1967. Joan Mitchell Foundation Archives, New York

FIG 6.1 Left: Joan Mitchell standing on the dock in front of La Tour, Vétheuil, France, ca. 1967. Right: Jean Paul Riopelle piloting a boat along the Seine, 1967. Joan Mitchell Foundation Archives, New York “the ‘young married’ collectors.”[4] In a positive sense, the familiar feeling of being out of place was matched by the will to choose that difference, as she had with her earlier move to Paris. At Vétheuil, she would later say, “Je veux être libre.”[5]

In late 1965 and into 1966, Mitchell began to move away from the masses of 1963’s *Girolata Triptych* (plate 39)—“no more dark centers alas”—unfurling them in tendrils (see plate 51), a strategy that recalls her earlier unwinding of the *City Landscapes*.[6] The new bright red, green, and blue paintings, such as *Woods/Country* (1966, plate 52), have “lots of *color*” and “‘old-fashioned’ paint quality,”[7] traits she particularly associated with Matisse.[8] The new direction debuted in spring 1967 at her first solo exhibition at Galerie Jean Fournier in Paris, perhaps not coincidentally a gallery that emphasized the legacy of Matisse (as discussed by Éric de Chassey on pages 86–95). Joining the gallery had been a complex process, anticipated and delayed, and came after Mitchell both courted and rejected other offers for exhibitions in Switzerland and London as well as in Paris, where the situation was further complicated by Riopelle’s enormous presence.[9]

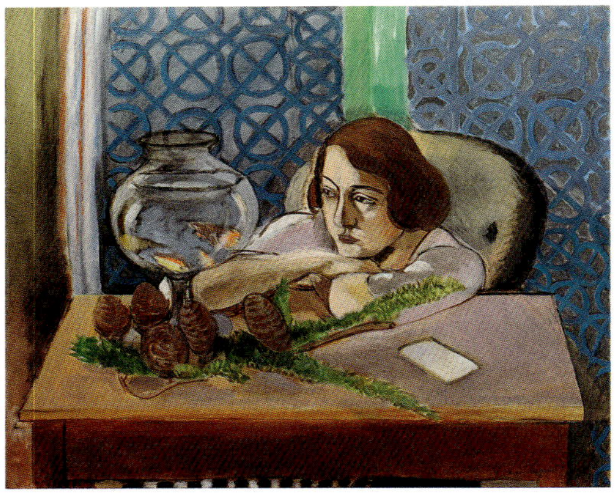

6.2

For her inaugural Fournier exhibition, alongside recent single-panel paintings, Mitchell showed a triptych and one of her first known quadriptychs—likely *Chicago* (1966–67, plate 50) and *Aquarium* (1967, plate 53), respectively—both fashioned from standard-size French canvases.[10] *Chicago* poignantly revisits Lake Michigan in the wake of her mother’s death. An expanse of white with green masses, now trailing delicate strokes, it also suggests Mitchell’s Mediterranean voyages of the 1960s. The form and title of the quadriptych *Aquarium* takes this oceanic sweep and plays on the contrast of vertical structural divisions of tanks like those at Chicago’s Shedd Aquarium. It certainly alludes to Matisse’s *Woman before an Aquarium* (fig. 6.2). Mitchell saw the painting growing up in Chicago, mentioning it to friends, and also possibly at the Museum of Modern Art (MoMA) Matisse exhibition of 1951–52.[11] The two paintings share similar green and blue palettes punctuated by orange and an occasional flash of red; Matisse’s fishbowl sits on a table against a background of circles with a diamond lattice echoed in Mitchell’s rounded patches of color and crossing paint strokes. The vertical divisions of the panels recall the fabric screen of Matisse’s painting; both paintings also suggest enclosure, an object to be peered into (or out of), as the woman in Matisse’s painting stares moodily at the fish swimming in their small, clear globe. We might ask, given Mitchell’s complaints about the lack of privacy at rue Frémicourt and on the *Sérica* (Riopelle’s boat), Did she see herself reflected in their condition: looking out, but also too much seen?

Aquarium is filled with floating ovoid pods and balls—solid and drawn, closed and open—weighted toward the top with filmy drips and tendrils extending downward. Mitchell would continue to work out these organic forms in drawings made for *In Memory of My Feelings,* a book put together for MoMA by Bill Berkson to memorialize Frank O’Hara. In Mitchell’s contribution, a lithograph composed of two drawings layered together, these pod forms, open at bottom, suggest flower heads, hanging heavy from a thicket of stems and leaves. Related charcoal drawings from the time (plates 56, 57) play with this vocabulary, sometimes in the form of a more central composition recalling the massed horizon of *City Landscape* (1955, plate 14), with the added suggestion of the tendrils found in *Chicago*.

This new vocabulary permeates the paintings of the late 1960s. Mitchell saw it as beginning with *My Landscape I* from very early 1967, a title whose significance she underlined with *My Landscape II* (1967, plate 55) and *Mon paysage* (1967).[12] Here the masses have diffused fully, the white no longer surrounding an obdurate central form but interposed amidst the brightly colored passages of paint—the light between the trees, perhaps (a favorite effect), recalling late Cézanne watercolors (a favorite influence). While one might assume that *My Landscape* refers to her new country home at Vétheuil, the title predates the ad for the property by several months. The valence is larger, resonating with Mitchell's statement of 1957 about carrying her landscape with her (as discussed in chapter 3). It also recalls the thinking of the poet Rainer Maria Rilke, one of her favorite writers, about "my landscape," contrasting his immediate surroundings with a powerful memory of earlier experiences of place (Russia, Toledo), or simply describing the inner sensation prompted by the exterior world.[13] As in the titles for the slightly earlier paintings *My Plant* (1966) and *My Other Plant* (1965)—named for her houseplants in the Frémicourt apartment—Mitchell tangled with the possibility of territory and possession.[14] Perhaps the possessive was meant to assert her right to paint the French countryside (other titles included *Gouise* in the Ardèche and the mountain village *Chamrousse*) in relation to the claims of the "J.-P. forest," which belonged to Riopelle's Quebec childhood and also his paintings. "Mine" may also acknowledge the fact that having lost both of her parents, she was now truly on her own. In any case, La Tour would certainly become hers: in late May, Mitchell used some of the family "bridge money" to pay a $10,000 deposit to its owner, L. V. Schneider, the widow of a steel magnate. She would share the enormous house and rather formal grounds with Riopelle, who relocated his own garage/studio to a hangar in a nearby village.[15]

FIG 6.2 **Henri Matisse** *Woman before an Aquarium,* 1921–23. Oil on canvas, 31¹⁵⁄₁₆ × 39⁷⁄₁₆ in. (81.2 × 100.2 cm). Art Institute of Chicago, Helen Birch Bartlett Memorial Collection, 1926

Mitchell described La Tour to friends as a country home, using it for weekends, holidays, and in the summer, although the couple still often traveled to the south coast in warmer months.[16] The idea of a country home was natural for Mitchell, the child of an upper-class family that summered in the country, and for Riopelle, who, although working-class, had grown up in the countryside and loved to fish and hunt, as well as to race cars. In light of their frequent absence from the property, Mitchell invited Clark and his wife, Hedy, to live at Vétheuil after meeting them in a café in Paris, and they stayed for fifteen months. Mitchell had seen that they had run out of money, and in her eyes Clark, a fellow graduate of the School of the Art Institute of Chicago, was a rare and welcome "real" painter; in what would become the large studio space, he would develop his oval canvases (with the help of carpenters working there), in addition to a series dedicated to Vétheuil.[17] The visits Mitchell made with Riopelle were intensely social and often festive, facilitated by Raymonde Perthuis, the housekeeper and cook, and her husband, Jean, who tended the formal gardens. Along with the Clarks, they hosted Riopelle's daughters and entertained Jolas and her husband, as well as an assortment of Paris friends including Shirley Jaffe (see fig. 6.3 and pages 106–7). Mitchell was not painting at La Tour, but she was clearly looking; by that first fall, the view from the house would become evident in paintings made at rue Frémicourt, notably in the spectacular blue and green painting titled *Vétheuil* (1967–68, plate 64).[18] As she put it, "an intelligent critic could" see the development of the work, the bright, clear color and the emergence of a new composition grounded in two blocky

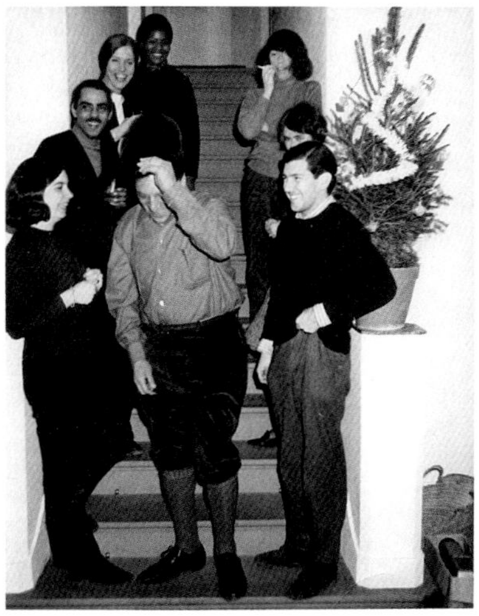

6.3

FIG 6.3 Clockwise from lower left: Sylvie Riopelle, Ed Clark, Betsy Jolas, Hedy Clark, Joan Mitchell, Shirley Jaffe, Pierre Remy, and Jean Paul Riopelle celebrating the holidays at La Tour, Vétheuil, France, 1968. Joan Mitchell Foundation Archives, New York

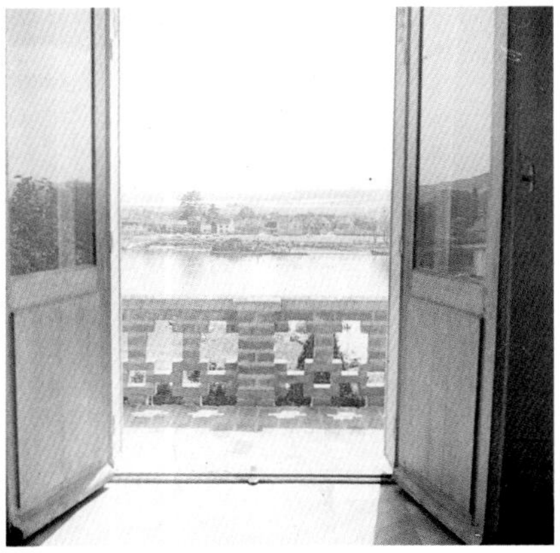

6.4

FIG 6.4 Terrace view at La Tour, Vétheuil, France, ca. 1967. Joan Mitchell Foundation Archives, New York

horizontal forms at the bottom of the painting—territory that had always given her trouble.[19] Just above these forms runs a band of white and thin gray, atop which stack two large blocky blue shapes balanced by an arc of rounded green and blue forms and a central scrum of strokes. We are looking at the Seine: its near bank, flowing water, and beyond to the trees on the distant shore. In countless photographs taken over the next twenty-five years of her life, we see Mitchell on the terrace of La Tour; sometimes talking with friends, most often looking out at the river, at the shore, at the far banks, and at the town of Lavacourt and the lake beyond, all capped with a sky (fig. 6.4). As numerous friends recall, that terrace is also where much of the social life of Vétheuil happened over the years.

While she would not paint on canvas at La Tour until late in 1968, not having nor apparently desiring a full studio setup on her country weekends, Mitchell did draw and paint on paper with watercolors, sometimes outdoors: "alone with watercolors & sun—& dogs working in a bathing suit."[20] The watercolors, some of which she sent to the Martha Jackson Gallery in advance of her first show there, in 1968, pile geometric shapes in primary and secondary colors that seem to reach back to the late 1940s. Mitchell's sketchbook drawings from ca. 1967–68 are more numerous—and more sensitive and lovely (see plates 61–63). The brilliant colors of the wax crayon open Mitchell's palette wider than ever, the layering of line and wash or crayoned mass without losing clarity perhaps a lesson derived from making the layered lithograph for *In Memory of My Feelings*. The pages feature loosely drawn yet largely recognizable natural forms: trees, tangles of thicket, gorgeous flowers, and views—both broad stretches of river and views of stacked landscapes framed by windows. In a few, the composition oscillates between forms, showing how easily river could become tree and vice versa (fig. 6.5). It seems possible that the range of colors and brightness of the sketchbooks' multiple media (including wax crayon and marker, all likely from boxed sets that spanned the spectrum) may have inspired the range of *Sans Pierre* (plate 69) and other 1969 paintings. The sketchbooks' palette, of course, also derived from the colors of the flowers and trees around La Tour, whose variety and splendor far surpassed the modest red tulips of Long Island.

Drawings of her view from La Tour represent another significant body of works on paper from the period. At her first solo exhibition at the Martha Jackson Gallery, the horizontality of the Seine seen from Mitchell's terrace was reflected in the dramatic sweep of twenty-two drawings displayed in two long rows. Perhaps having accepted being "old hat," or in sympathy with the French landscape tradition, or through her return to the medium of the sketchbook, Mitchell felt a freedom to commit herself to a more clearly representational register. The drawings were sometimes clustered in threes and fours, shifting between panoramic views of the river—with its distant and near banks, trees, and buildings—and the rhythmic repetition of related forms and images (plate 60), between representation and abstraction, view and process.

These drawings clearly fed an early quadriptych titled *La Seine* (fig. 6.6), composed of four standard-format French canvases (the use of multiple panels was originally necessitated by the size of Mitchell's Frémicourt studio and the expense of shipping large canvases by air).[21] The sketchbooks and drawings also use the vertical format to frame a window view bridging interior and exterior, as so often seen in Matisse's paintings.

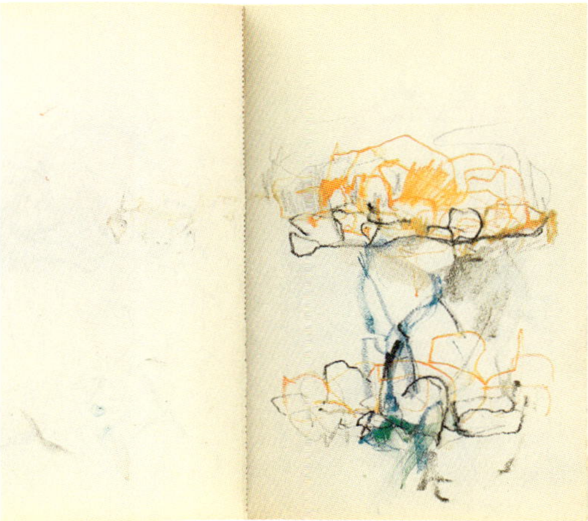

6.5

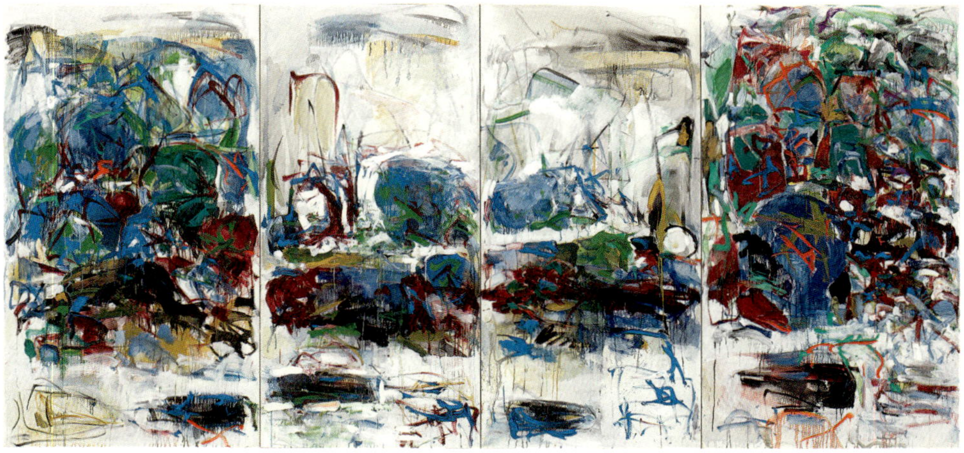

6.6

Mitchell's renderings alternate between sweeping views from the terrace and vertically framed views, looking out through the open floor-to-ceiling French doors from inside the house.[22] For Pierre Schneider, her most insightful and closest critic in these years, Monet was the reference, and he associated her vertical stacking of bands or zones with Monet's Vétheuil paintings.[23] This play between the horizontal and the vertical—river and tree, ocean and harbor, exterior and window view, panorama and individual panels—permeates the work. As Mitchell described it, "I like the up and down thing. Because I feel up and down."[24] Perhaps her feeling encompassed both a kinesthetic duality born of diving and skating and an emotional state—"ups-and-downsy," as her mother described their shared tendency.[25] Most of all, it is a visual condition where seeming opposites relate to and reflect one another.

The 1968 Jackson press release trumpeted her French connection: "From France Joan Mitchell sends fourteen new paintings for her eighth one-man exhibition. . . . This entire series was painted on the banks of the Seine in the neighborhood made famous by Claude Monet, who lived and painted closeby [*sic*]."[26] The artist herself was less sanguine about the connection. After a decade of resisting the critical association with Monet and "Abstract Impressionism," she was living on a property that included Monet's residence from 1878 to 1881, a setting to which he devoted a series and many individual works. While in these first few years she was able to acknowledge—with a touch of pride—that embedded history, her annoyance and flippancy grew over the years she owned La Tour, making it difficult to assess her true relationship to Monet's work. Here, at Vétheuil, she grappled more deeply with his precedent—to some degree, with the painterly nature of his work, but most of all with their shared relation to a specific terrain, especially as she began spending time in the country year-round, experiencing the seasons with a daily intimacy.

Despite the gallery's confidence, Mitchell was concerned that her inaugural Jackson exhibition did not present a coherent group, that it found her midstream in a rapid development.[27] Nonetheless, in the end she

FIG 6.5 **Joan Mitchell**
Sketchbook, ca. 1967. Pages 6 and 7 of 92. Water-soluble wax crayon and wash on machine-made wove paper, 7³⁄₁₆ × 10⅛ in. (18.2 × 25.6 cm). Joan Mitchell Foundation Archives, New York

FIG 6.6 **Joan Mitchell**
La Seine, 1967. Oil on canvas, 76¾ × 166½ in. (195 × 422.9 cm). Governor Nelson A. Rockefeller Empire State Plaza Art Collection, New York State, Office of General Services

made almost the same report, in French and English, to friends Jean Lamouroux and Shirley Jaffe: "L'exposition n'est pas mal—(ça veut dire qu'il me plait!!)," and "I'm pleased with the show—which is saying quite a lot for me."[28] It is worth noting that in the face of weak reviews—weak in their incomprehension and lack of interest, their reflexive insistence on the attenuation rather than the exhilaration of gestural painting—she nonetheless maintained her own pleasure and equilibrium, her confidence in the work.[29]

To Mitchell's surprise, she loved the country, enjoying the beauty and also the solitude (except when she did not) and the fact that it made Riopelle behave (except when he did not). During late 1968, they spent more and more time in Vétheuil; finally, she told Clark that after he finished the last three of his current painting group, she needed to claim La Tour to paint, which she did by November.[30] At this moment, Mitchell's practice expanded in a way that was apparent even to the usually self-critical artist, who told friends that she was painting well and feeling "lucky"; later she would say that her mother never saw her best works, which in her eyes included those painted at Vétheuil beginning in the late 1960s.[31] With her full-time move to the country, Mitchell entered another transition. She had begun a painting in response to "A Gift of Violets," a poem sent to her by former boyfriend Evans Herman, and the rather modest flower became "enormous" and expensive: "violet—(cobalt violet) costs an arm and a leg.... The violet pic turned into a sunflower—apologies to Vincent."[32]

"Vincent" and Monet were both very much present in these years. Monet had grown mammoth Russian sunflowers in Vétheuil, and Riopelle brought in the same seeds, flinging them around so that the plants sprung up all over the lawn and by Mitchell's studio, growing to remarkable heights of ten and twelve feet—"like trees"—as she excitedly wrote several friends.[33] The sunflowers thrilled Mitchell with their willful randomness, their wildness in the face of Jean Perthuis's formal French garden, as well as their beauty.[34] As in 1954, she turned to van Gogh's sunflowers, one of his great subjects, this time with joy rather than desperation, and in France rather than New York (see fig. 2.6). The place mattered because of its historical resonance, as she was seemingly experiencing what van Gogh himself once did. Vétheuil also afforded Mitchell the opportunity to work without distraction. As she complained with characteristic ambivalence, chafing at her "sunflower prison," she overheard Riopelle tell her New York dealer, "She could only paint those paintings here in the country."[35]

The new studio, in a freestanding building on the grounds, also had an effect. Although relatively narrow, the doors were large; for the first time, Mitchell didn't need to roll her large canvases to take them out of the studio, which in the past had sometimes cracked the paint or flattened the delicate topography of denser passages.[36] While the stacked organic shapes of late 1968 through 1970 are related to paintings from the previous year, the paint is much thicker; Mitchell apparently squeezed or knifed great piles onto the canvas and then smashed wet into wet—adding orange to white, for example—or simply used a clean brush to draw into the mass of paint. She was sensitive to the varying levels of viscosity and dryness of the paint, working not only wet into wet, but wet into semi-dry, and wet into/over dry. The technique resulted in a dramatic variety of textures that includes heavy impasto, peaks of paint dragged into a partially dry blob, and touches of color applied with both brush and knife that oscillate between describing the anatomy of her monumental subjects and embodying pure pigment (see fig. 6.7). She used white paint prominently to model form, often with a touch of opalescence that added shine to increase the effect of dimension; the white also works with an astonishing range of color—"all colors"—to create a searing brightness. This combination evokes Monet's paintings of winter scenes at Vétheuil; as Mitchell wrote in November 1968 (when she began the *Sunflower* series), "am painting 'very well' for me—big pics—sunflowers—but it snowed today & the whole joint looks like Monet."[37] The title of *Sans neige* ("without snow"; 1969, plate 73), a related work suffused with fluffy white, could be a summer painting, or, more wryly, another teasing of her putative connection to Monet. These paintings are cumulative: the 1950s paintings speak to Mitchell's growing bodily knowledge—her control of her own reach, touch, and motion; those of the early 1960s, to her familiarity with paint as physical material; and to all of this, her canvases from the late 1960s add a nuanced understanding of the image of an object in space.

This turn toward the object continued at her 1969 exhibition at Galerie Jean Fournier, where Mitchell showed three paintings with the title *Sunflower* (including plate 67),[38] multiple untitled works, *Sans Pierre, Sans neige,* and others, all from the first four months of that year—an extraordinarily productive period for the artist. The works at Fournier were all related, with the usual blurred line between works that formally belonged to a series and those that were related but perhaps had simply not been given the same title.[39] The gallery's use of "series" in the press release also made it clear that the concept was linked to Monet, whom Mitchell playfully referenced in her titles for the *Cercando un Ago* and Paris subway groups. If in 1965 Mitchell had used the term "series" as a neutral commonplace, by 1973, she insisted to curator Marcia Tucker that she "never painted in series. Group them by subject." She was "not a series painter but a subject painter": "series" pulls toward the painting as painting, "subject" pulls toward content in the larger world.[40]

"Subject" also returns us to O'Hara's early proposals about painting and nature. In the 1950s, it went against the predominant rhetoric of abstraction for him to emphasize content, and he did so in terms of a subjective response, praising painting that tended to be allusive rather than representational. Nearly two decades later, Mitchell returned to the landscape with a new ability to encounter nature frankly and openly, free of earlier prohibitions against representation, and free perhaps too of the need to declare herself so adamantly. Strong emotion was native to Mitchell; in the 1950s, visible aggression and ambition also countered critical labels of femininity, decorativeness, or the *retardataire* that Clement Greenberg and other critics associated with nature painting in a lyrical vein. As she observed the surrounding world at Vétheuil, the former vehemence was replaced by a growing delight in and registration of the changing atmosphere across seasons and the times of day, much like Monet before her. As described by Pierre Schneider (and later by Yves Michaud), the painters and paintings of the past were vividly present at Vétheuil; van Gogh, Cézanne, Monet, and Matisse became the peer group she had previously found in New York or Paris. Their visions of nature affirmed Mitchell's increasingly detailed and pleasurable encounters with the world and its rendering. As Schneider put it in 1968, long after the bridge connecting subject and object was washed away, she continued to try to cross that river.[41]

Untitled, 1969

Mara Hoberman

Untitled (1969) is illustrated in full as plate 70.

FIG 6.7 **Joan Mitchell** *Untitled,* 1969 (detail). Oil on canvas, 102½ × 184½ in. (260.4 × 468.6 cm). Musée de Brou, Bourg-en-Bresse, France

FIG 6.8 Joan Mitchell in the garden at La Tour, Vétheuil, France, 1972

With sunflowers growing in her garden and Vincent van Gogh's golden-hued paintings ever blooming in her mind, Mitchell began referring to some of her own works as "sunflowers" as early as 1968. Just as van Gogh's decampment in 1888 to the "yellow house" in Arles compelled him to paint "nothing but large sunflowers,"[1] Mitchell's move to Vétheuil in 1968 precipitated a pivotal *Sunflower* series. During the prolific year that followed, Mitchell painted a suite of large-format, single-panel works that she titled *Sunflower I–VI,* as well as more than a dozen other paintings of varying sizes and formats that, though not titled as such, feature the same evocative explosions of yellow and orange paint.

In contrast to Mitchell's more typical densely painted landscapes, her 1969 sunflowers are relatively stark compositions featuring isolated blossoms. Throughout these works, the artist repeats halos of golden petals surrounding roughly circular dark-red forms that represent the flowers' large, disklike centers, varying their configurations to evoke different stages of floral bloom and wilt. Deceptively spare, the paintings' distinctive pale backgrounds are, in fact, a complex blend of thick white paint subtly tinged with the same colors used to depict the sunflowers themselves, a commingling of chromatic and conceptual sophistication that gives the areas surrounding the sunflowers the appearance of being haunted by ghostly afterimages of blossoms past. Comprising buds, blooms, droops, and memories, Mitchell's still lifes flout the genre's traditional frozen perspective in favor of one that thrums with the living energy of phases and cycles.

Plate 70 is one of many untitled sunflowers that Mitchell painted in 1969 and is a rare multipanel masterpiece in this style. If the religious connotations of the painting's triptych format are heightened by its current home—a fifteenth-century French monastery (where it hangs as part of the Musée de Brou collection)—more striking still is how Mitchell uses the three panels to describe temporal and ephemeral effects.

The central panel boasts a substantial blossom whose magnificent orange-flecked yellow corona surrounds a crimson heart accented with dabs of vibrant green. The flower's gravity-defying petals seem to explode toward the edges of the canvas, their momentum given mass by Mitchell's thick impasto, which appears to strain away from the picture plane. This vibrant (and nearly three-dimensional) flower head is supported by a hearty stem, which Mitchell represents as a thicket of mostly green dabs and strokes embellished with flourishes of yellow, blue, red, and orange (fig. 6.7).

The painting's side panels are considerably less resplendent by comparison, recalling the humble kneeling patrons flanking a coronation or annunciation scene in Renaissance triptychs. Chromatically and materially less intense, the peripheral blossoms seem to be fading and falling, drifting down toward the bottom of the composition. This effect is further emphasized by Mitchell's use of thinner paints, which causes curls of familiar colors—yellows, oranges, blues, and greens—to trail long, watery drips. Writing for the French weekly *L'Express* in 1975, Pierre Schneider attributed the "miracle" of Mitchell's flowers (which he admiringly compared to Édouard Manet's peonies) to the way in which they "disintegrate into a chaos of pigments."[2] Indeed, Mitchell's ability to conflate the materiality of her medium with that of her subject is perhaps nowhere more apparent than in her early sunflowers. Modulating the heft and opacity of her paint and varying her application from punchy dabs that pull the medium away from the canvas to smooth swipes that push it into the surface,

Mitchell simulates (as opposed to merely illustrates) an evanescent life force and a tangible process of decomposition. Thick impasto suggesting magma-like eruptions of light, heat, and mass is counterbalanced by calligraphic strokes of crimson and cerulean that flutter, as if weightless, across the canvas.

Once Mitchell began painting sunflowers, she never stopped. "Sunflowers are something I feel very intensely," she said in 1986, nearly two decades after inaugurating her first *Sunflower* series. "They look so wonderful when young, and they are so very moving when they are dying. I don't like fields of sunflowers. I like them alone, or, of course, painted by van Gogh" (fig. 6.8).[3] Indeed, Mitchell would return periodically to the motif as a means of self-reflection throughout her career, inflecting each iteration with mood and season. Compared to her later sunflowers, particularly the wilting ones she painted in 1990–91 (plate 123), near the end of her life Mitchell's 1969 sunflowers are optimistic—euphoric, even—self-affirmations that helped advance her career on its own resolute and distinct path. As art historian Barbara Rose put it, Mitchell "spent the sixties and seventies literally cultivating her own garden and emerged from, if not isolation, then separation from the New York art scene as one of the strongest and most independent artists in the world."[4] Fruits of this intense period of cultivation, including *Sunflower I–VI,* were presented in the artist's first major museum exhibition, in 1972, at the Everson Museum of Art in Syracuse, New York. Reviewing this seminal show for the *New York Times,* Peter Schjeldahl lamented Mitchell's underrated status since the 1950s, describing her as "a most important victim of sixties taste," yet confidently predicted that she would ultimately be recognized "as one of the best American painters not only of the fifties, but of the sixties and seventies as well."[5] Realized at the end of a decade both tumultuous and empowering—marked by the loss of both parents; the purchase of and subsequent relocation to La Tour, her Vétheuil estate; and debut solo shows with Jean Fournier and Martha Jackson—Mitchell's glorious 1969 sunflowers reflect the artist herself in peak bloom.

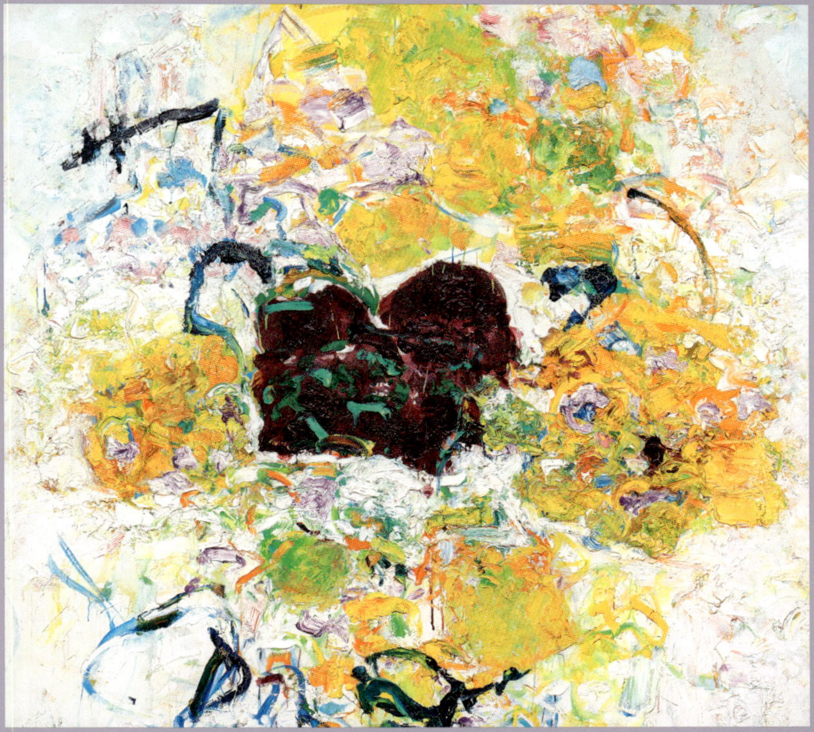

6.7

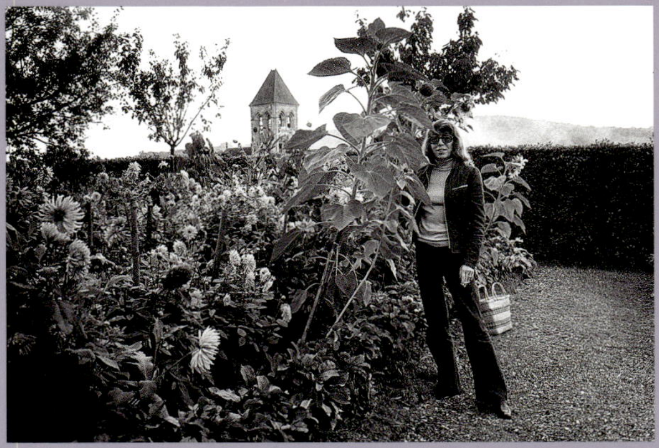

6.8

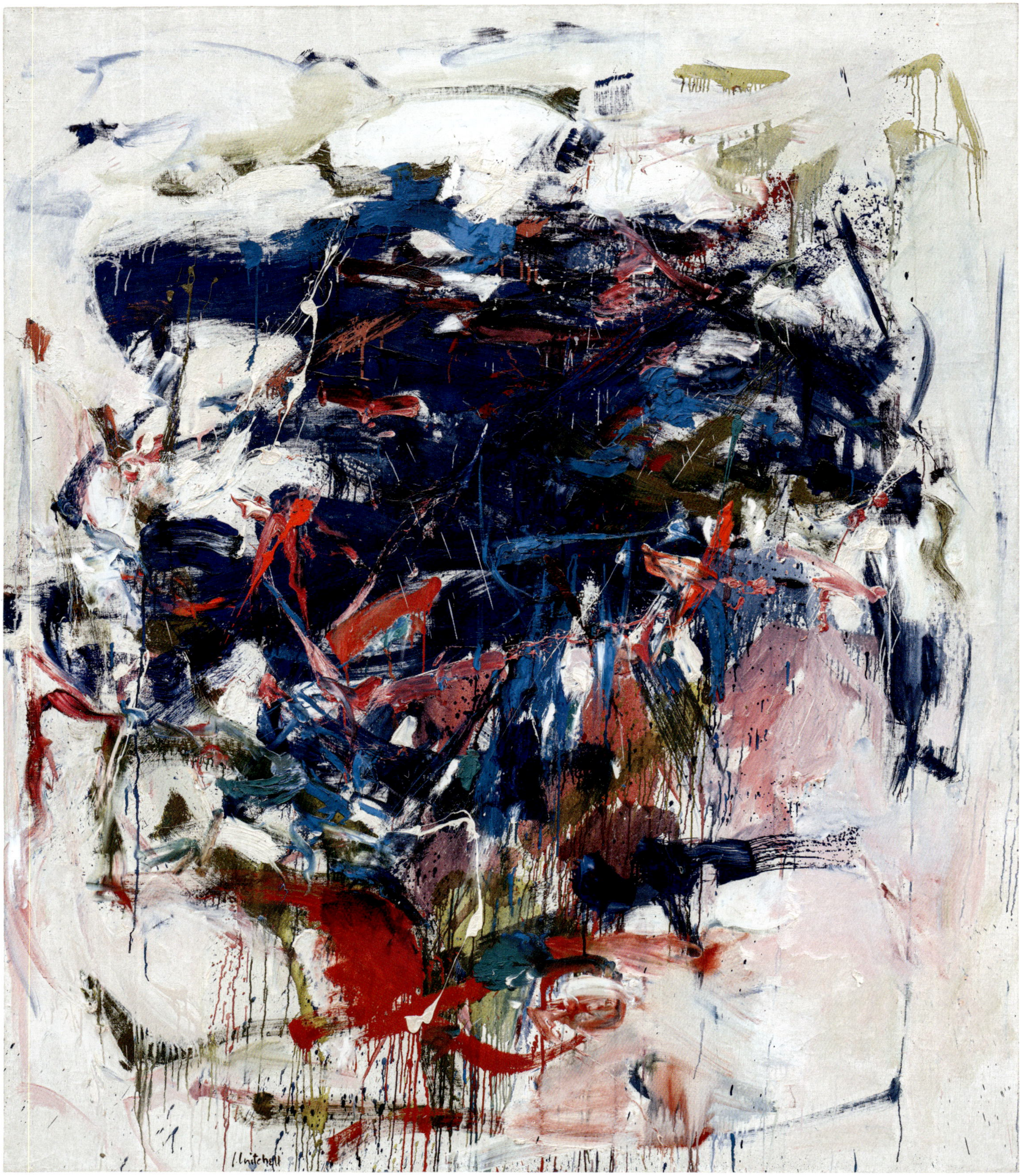

Rock Bottom, 1960–61. Oil on canvas, 78 × 68 in. (198.1 × 172.7 cm). Blanton Museum of Art, The University of Texas at Austin, gift of Mari and James A. Michener

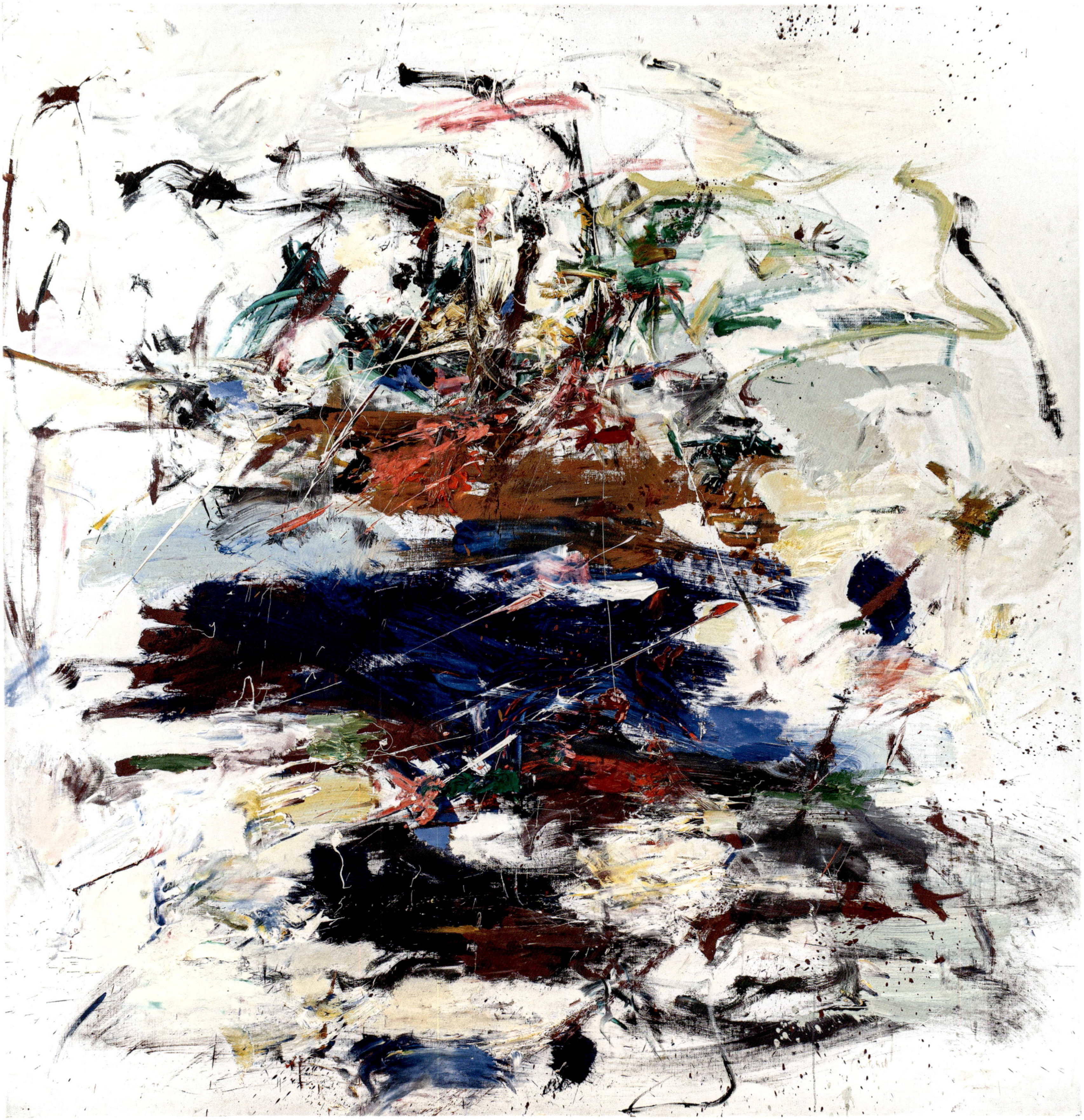

Water Gate, 1960. Oil on canvas, 86 × 84 in. (218.4 × 213.4 cm). Private collection, courtesy McClain Gallery, Houston

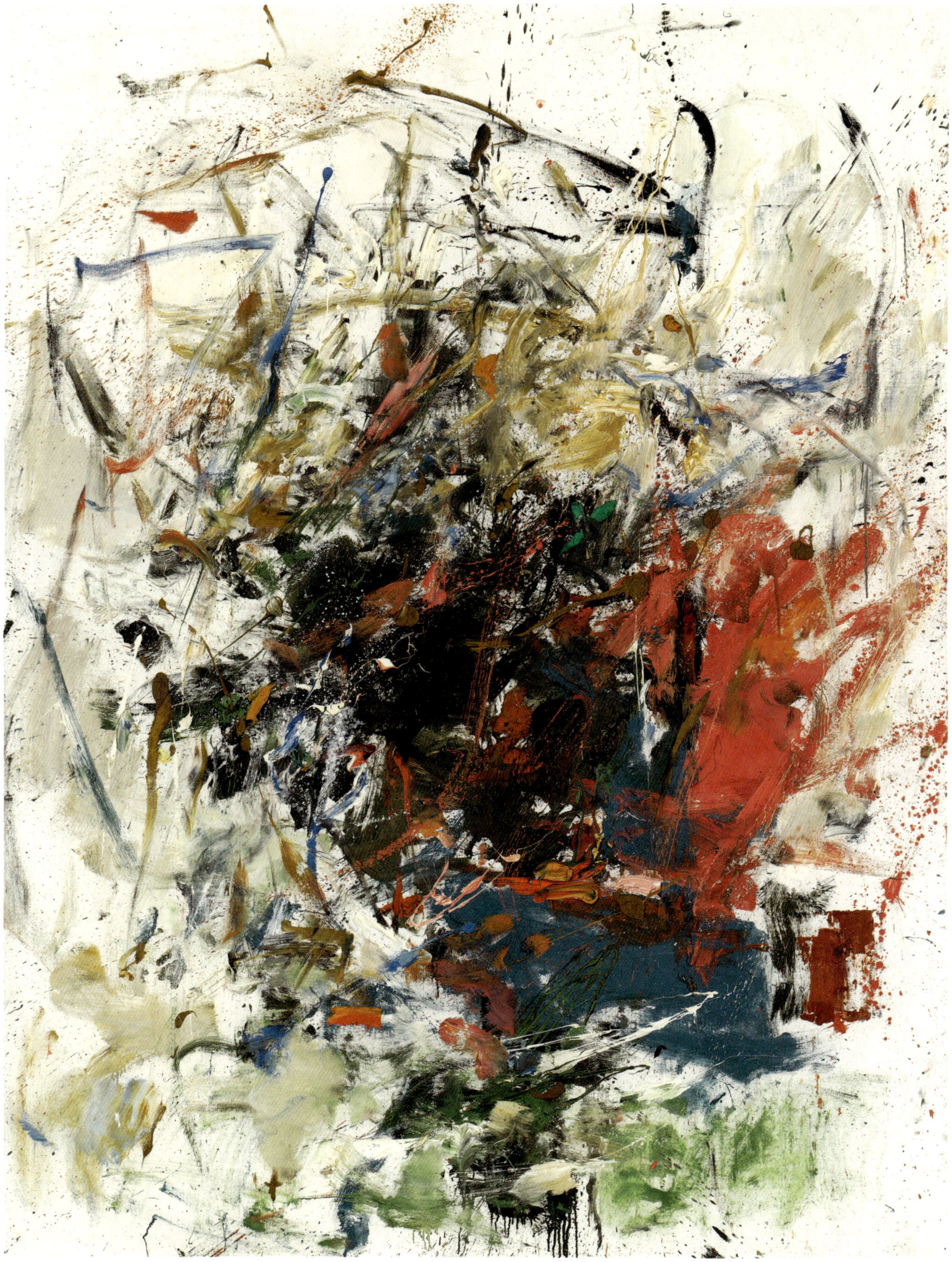

La Chatière, 1960. Oil on canvas, 76⅞ × 58 in. (195.3 × 147.3 cm). Joan Mitchell Foundation, New York

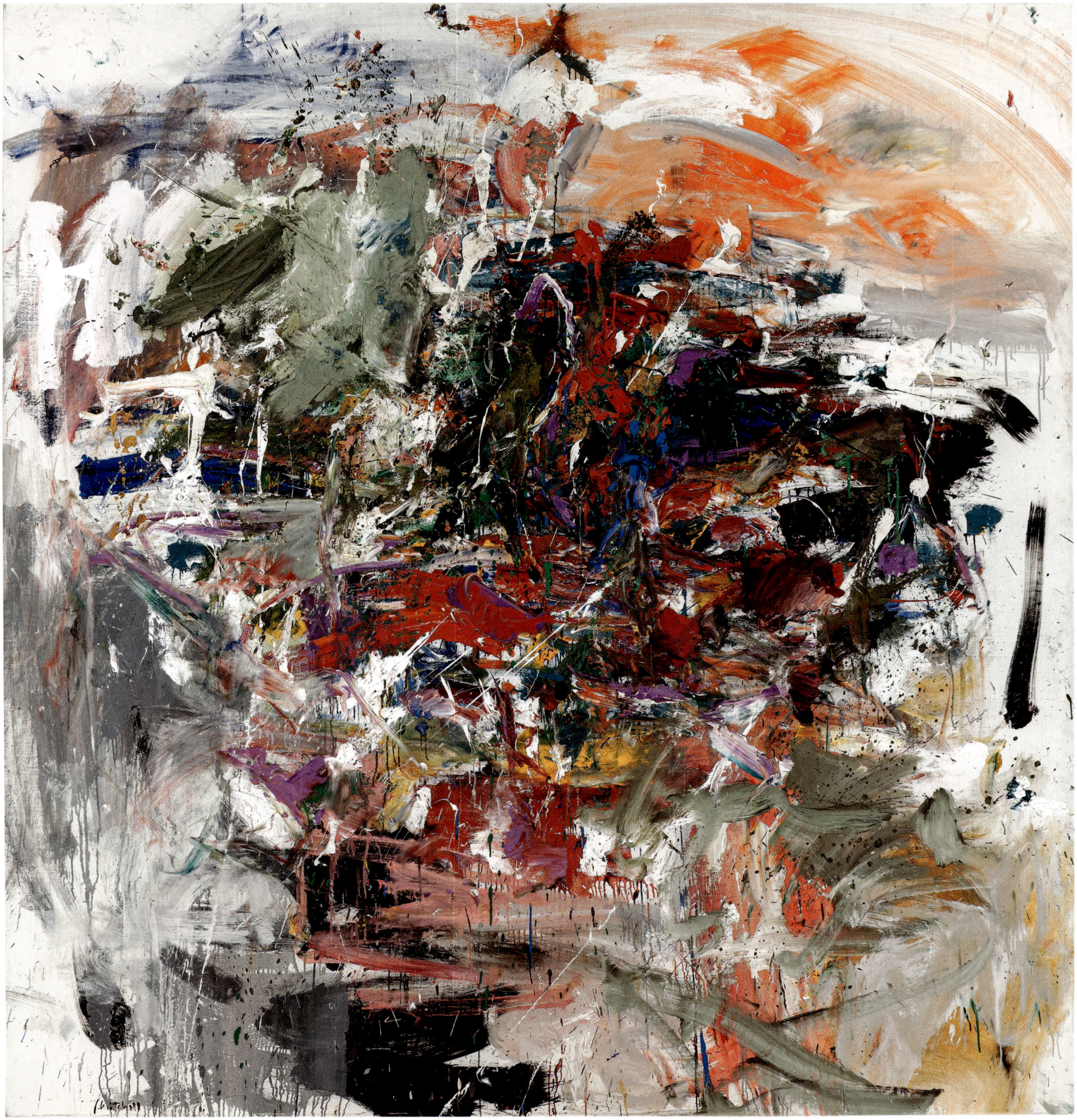

Mud Time, 1960. Oil on canvas, 82 × 78 in. (208.3 × 198.1 cm). Private collection, courtesy McClain Gallery, Houston

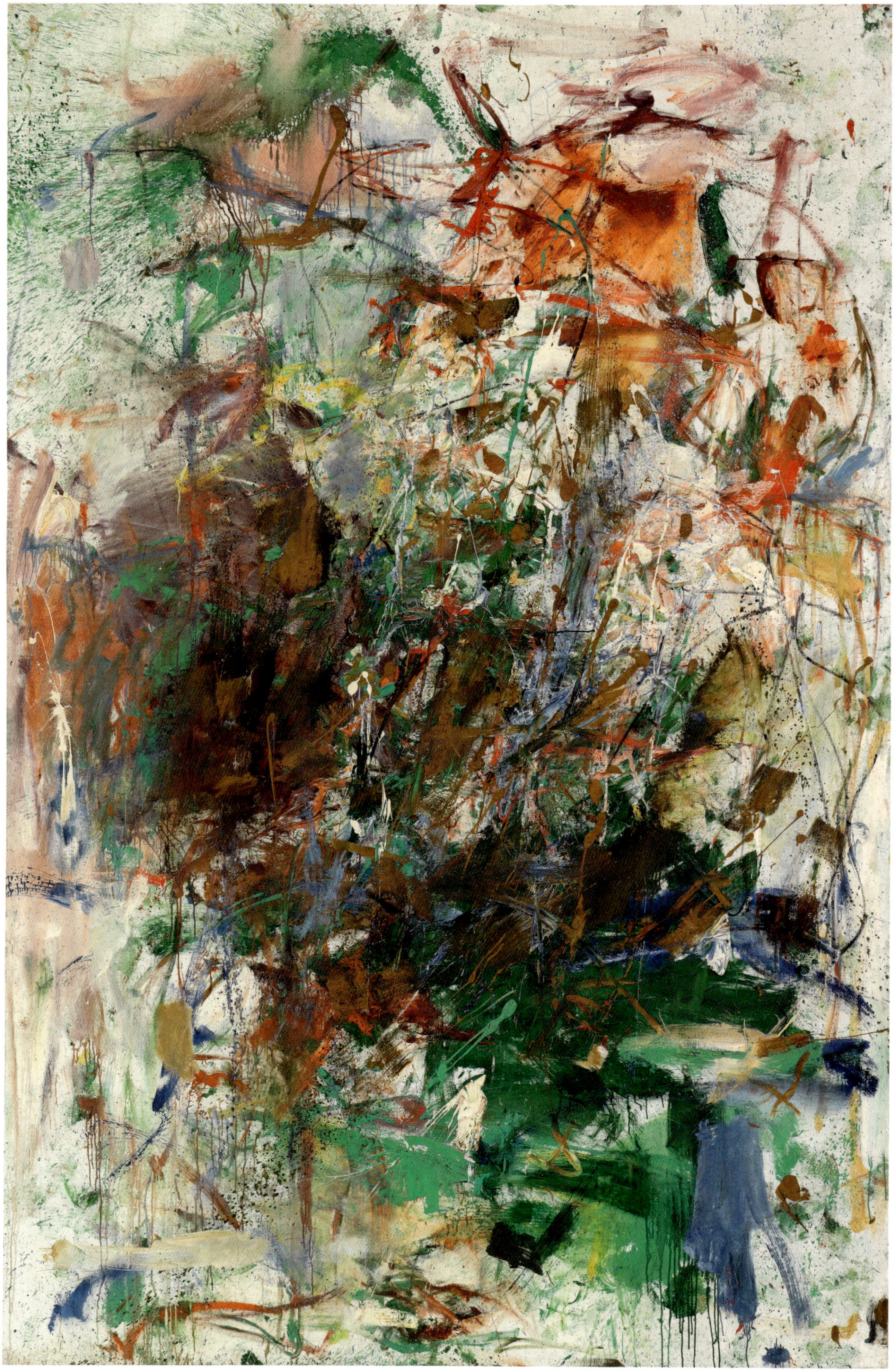

Bonhomme de bois, 1961–62. Oil on canvas, 120⅝ × 79 in. (306.4 × 200.7 cm). Private collection, courtesy Hauser & Wirth Collection Services

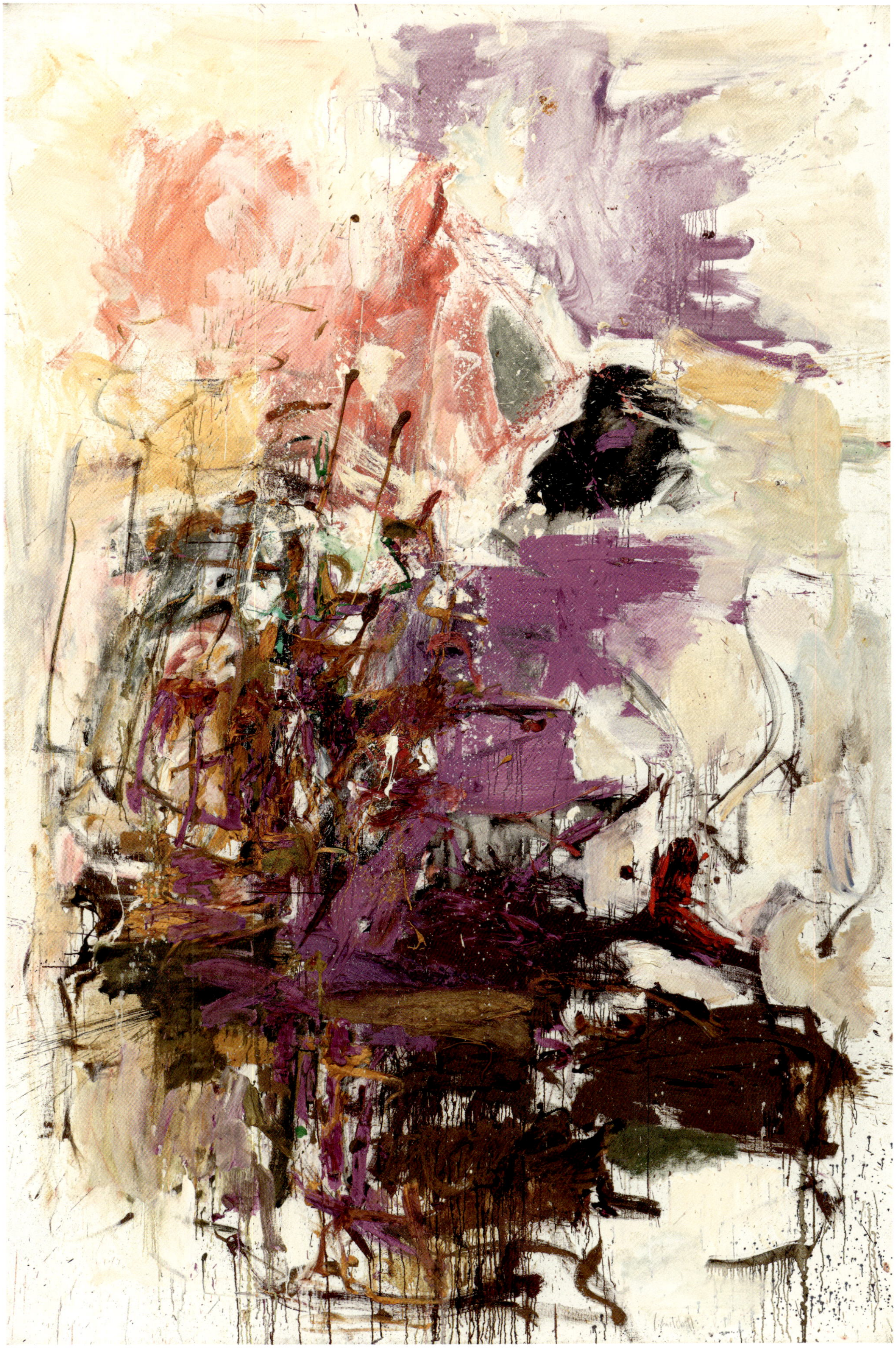

Untitled, ca. 1961. Oil on canvas, 118⅛ × 78¾ in. (300 × 200 cm). Modern Art Museum of Fort Worth, gift of Anne and John Marion

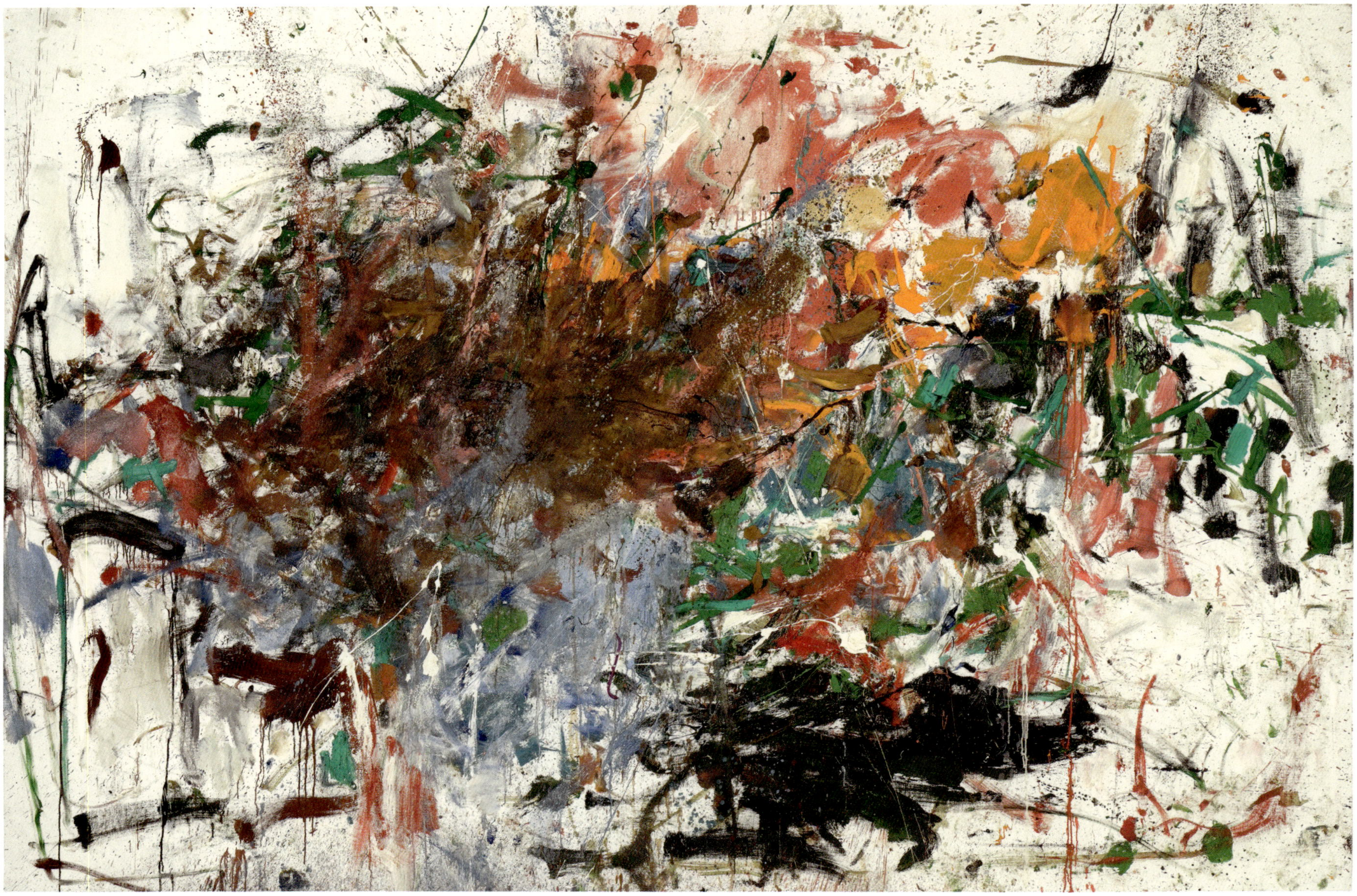

Cous-cous, 1961–62. Oil on canvas, 78¾ × 120¼ in. (200 × 305.4 cm). The Currier Museum of Art, Manchester, New Hampshire, gift of Sam and May Gruber

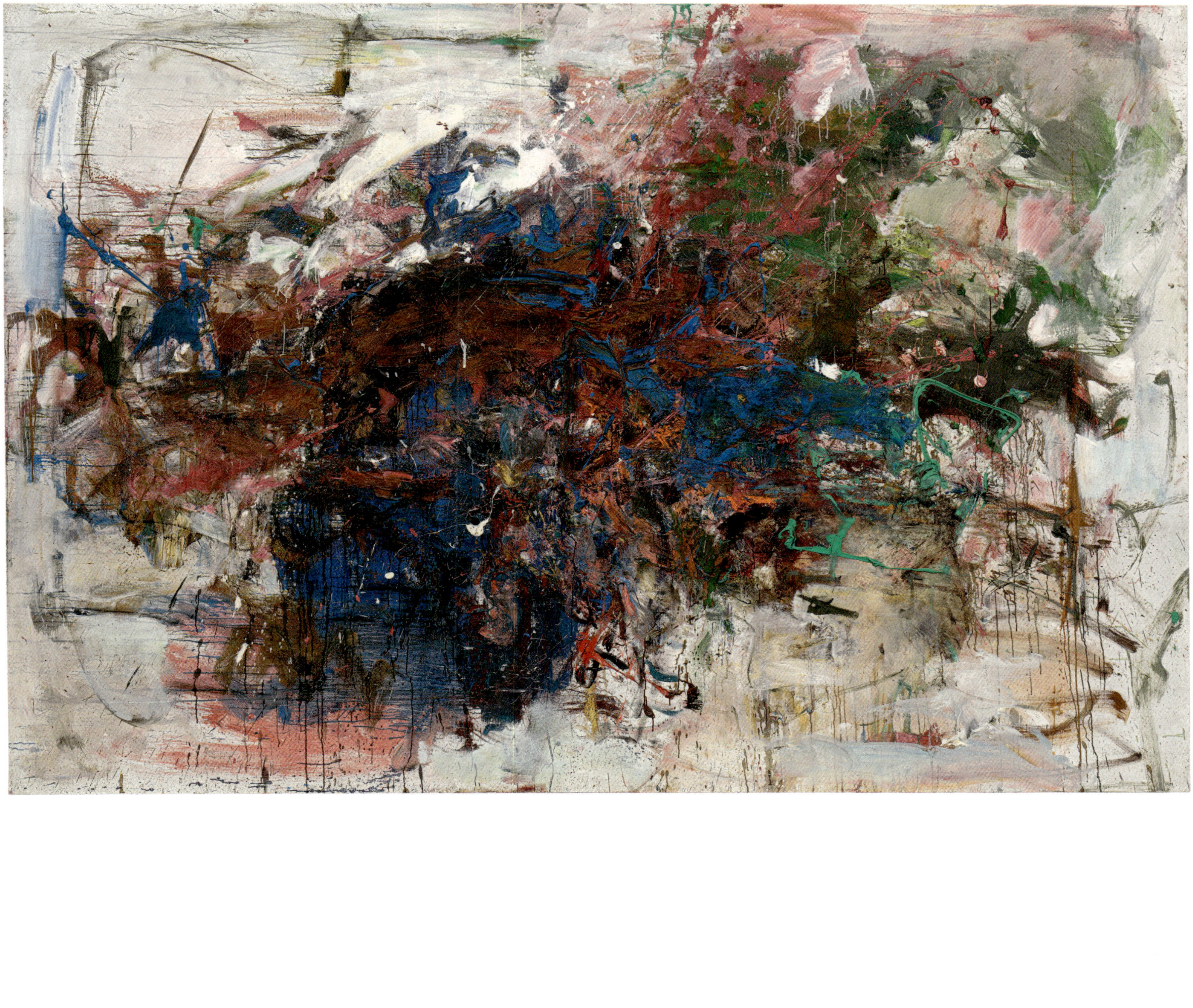

Grandes Carrières, 1961–62. Oil on canvas, 78⅜ × 118½ in. (199.1 × 301 cm). The Museum of Modern Art, New York, gift of The Estate of Joan Mitchell

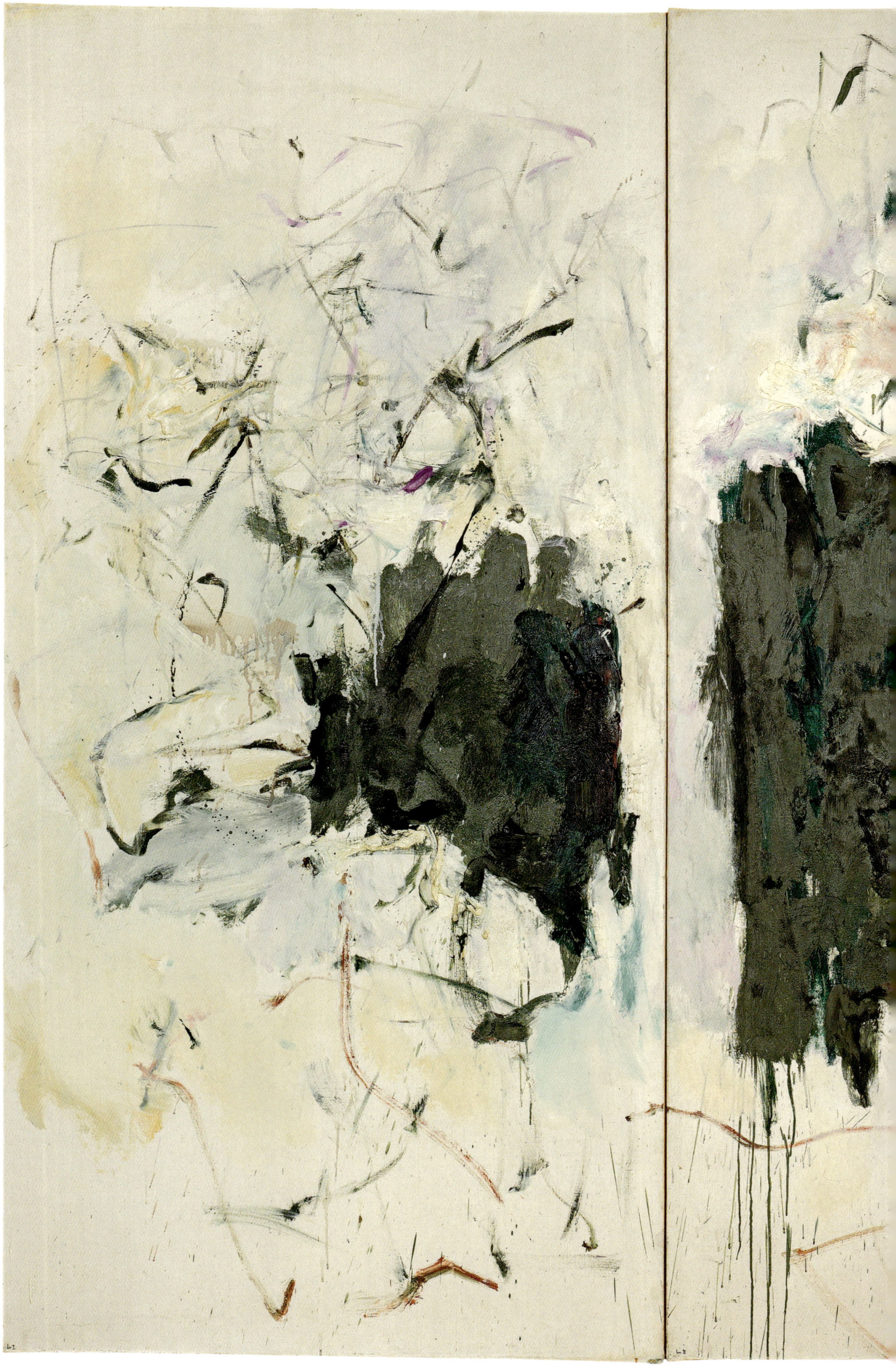

Girolata Triptych, 1963. Oil on canvas, 76⅞ × 127⅝ in. (195.3 × 324.2 cm). Private collection

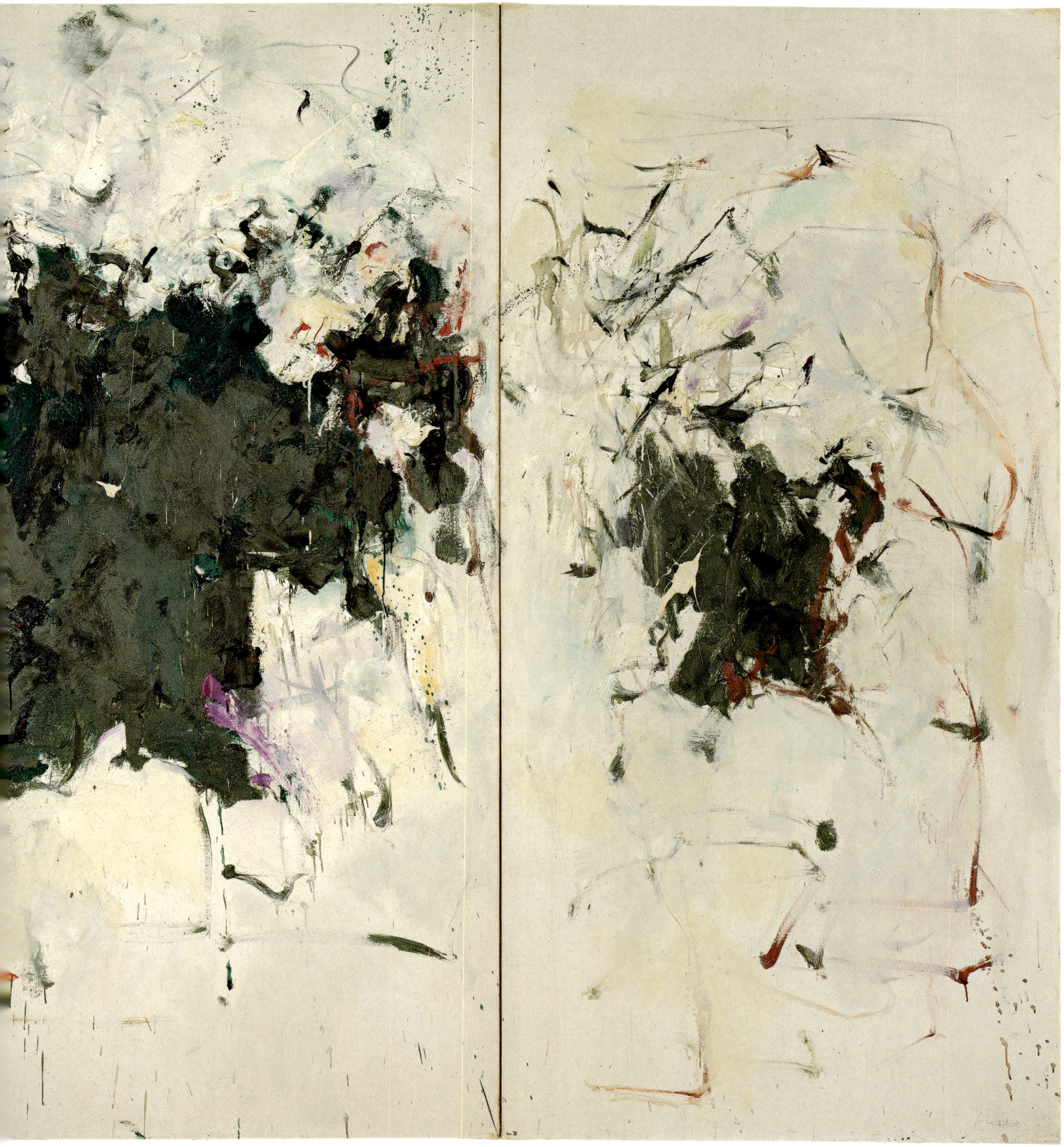

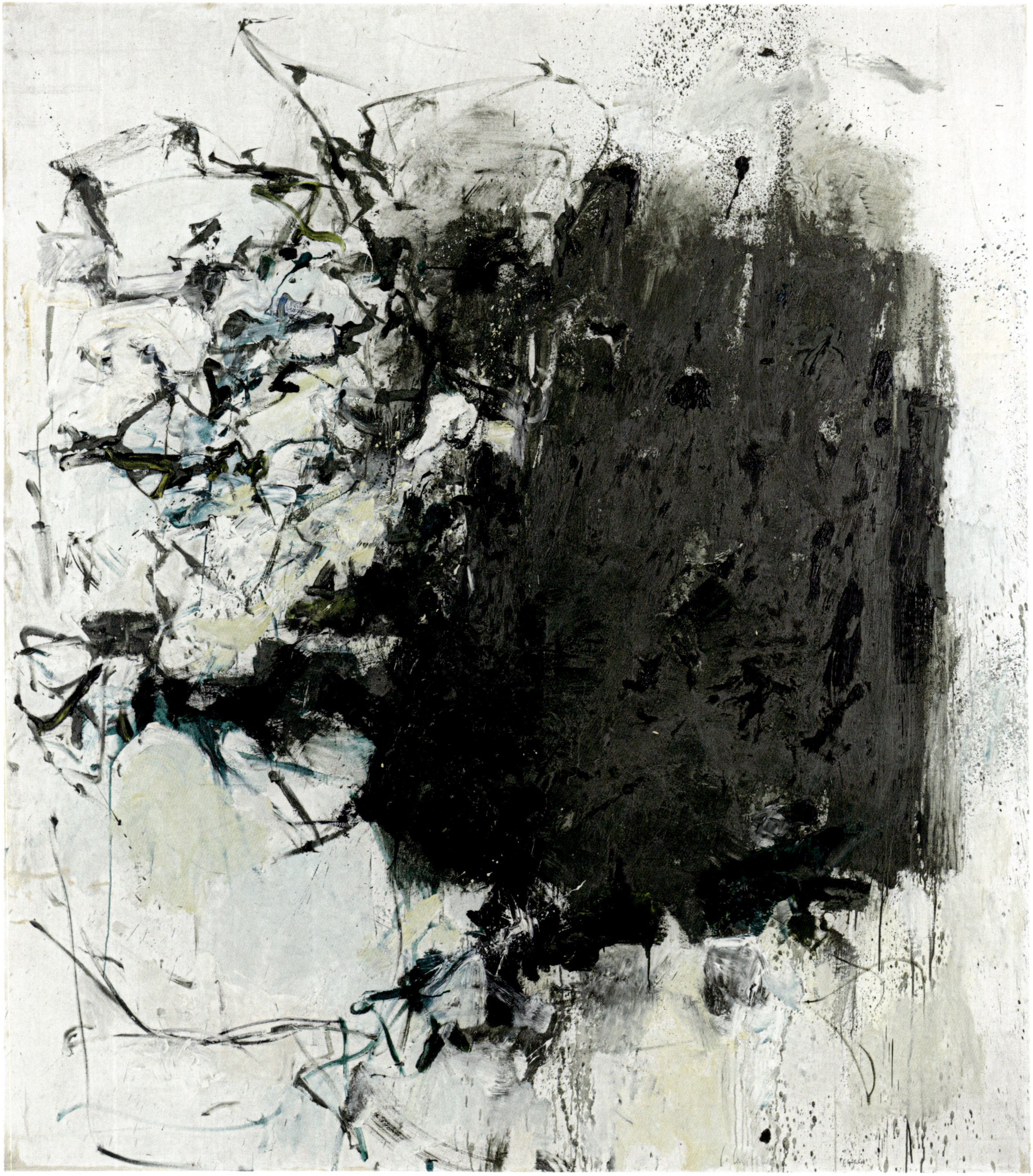

First Cypress, ca. 1964. Oil on canvas, 88¼ × 77¾ in. (224.2 × 197.5 cm). Private collection

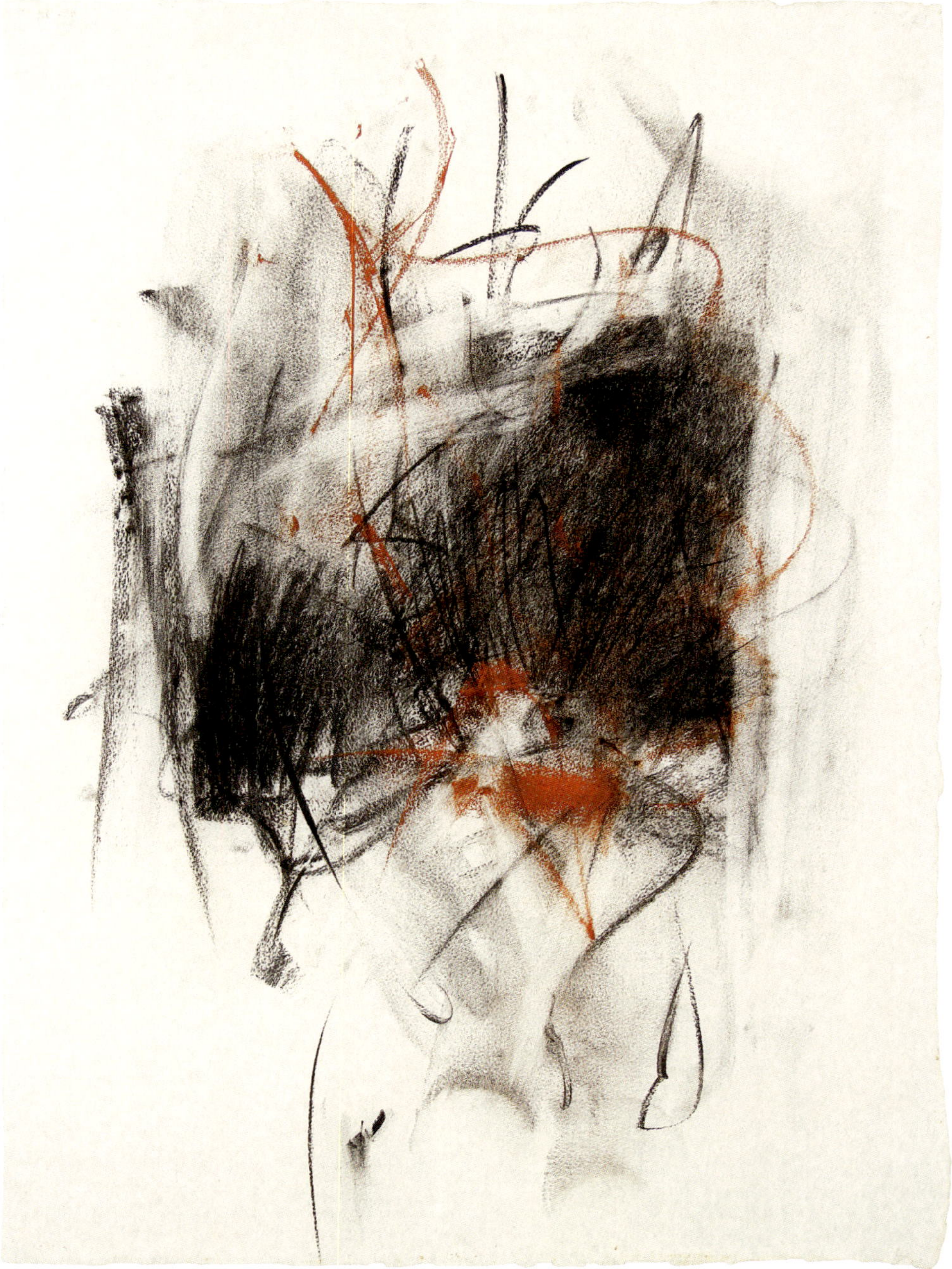

Untitled, ca. 1964. Charcoal and pastel on paper, 24 × 18 in. (61 × 45.7 cm). Private collection

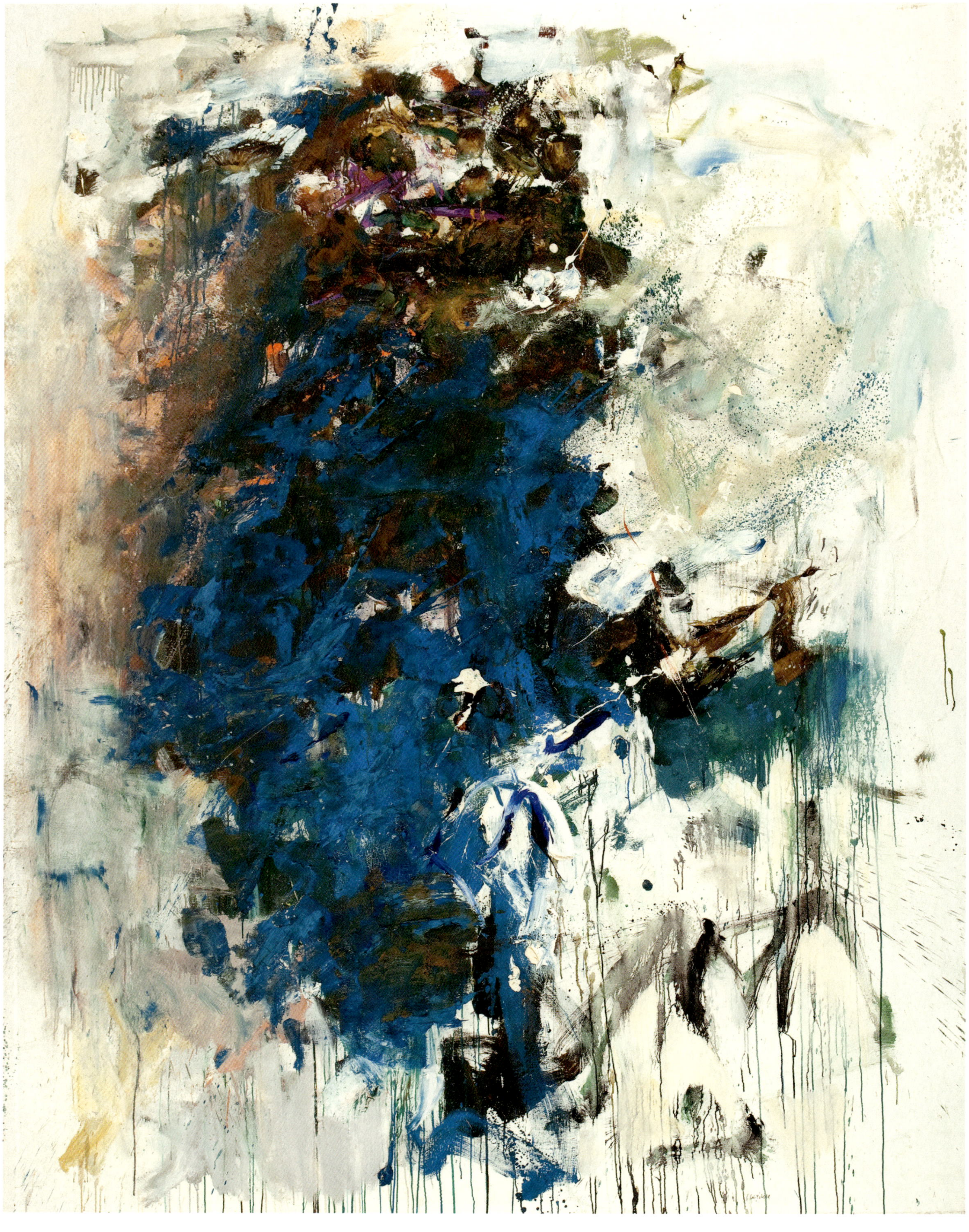

Blue Tree, 1964. Oil on canvas, 96⅝ × 78 in. (245.4 × 198.1 cm). Worcester Art Museum, Massachusetts, museum purchase

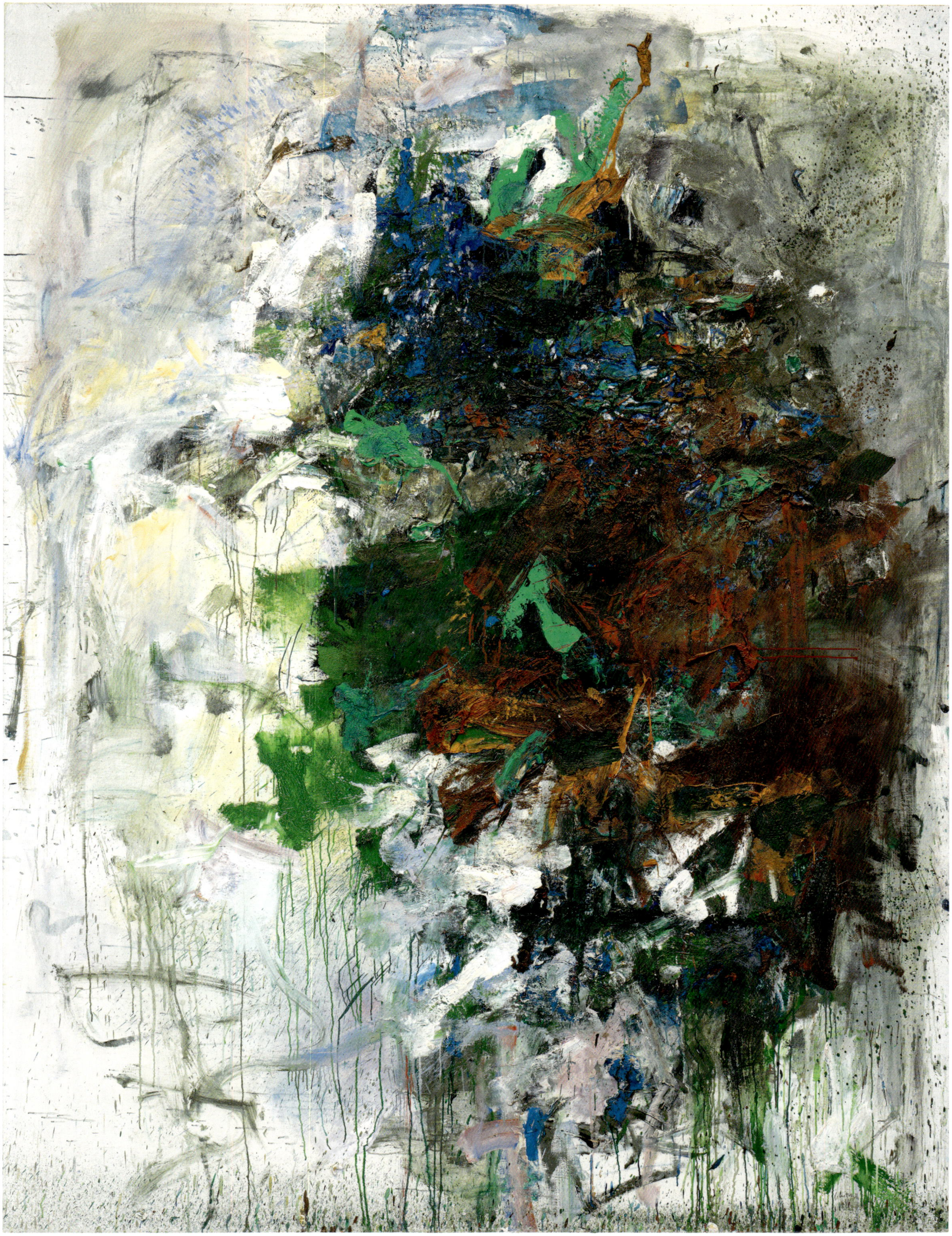

Untitled, ca. 1964. Oil on canvas, 100 × 78⅛ in. (254 × 198.4 cm). Collection of Jon Shirley

PLATE 44

Untitled, 1964. Oil on canvas, 78 × 82 in. (198.1 × 208.3 cm). Private collection

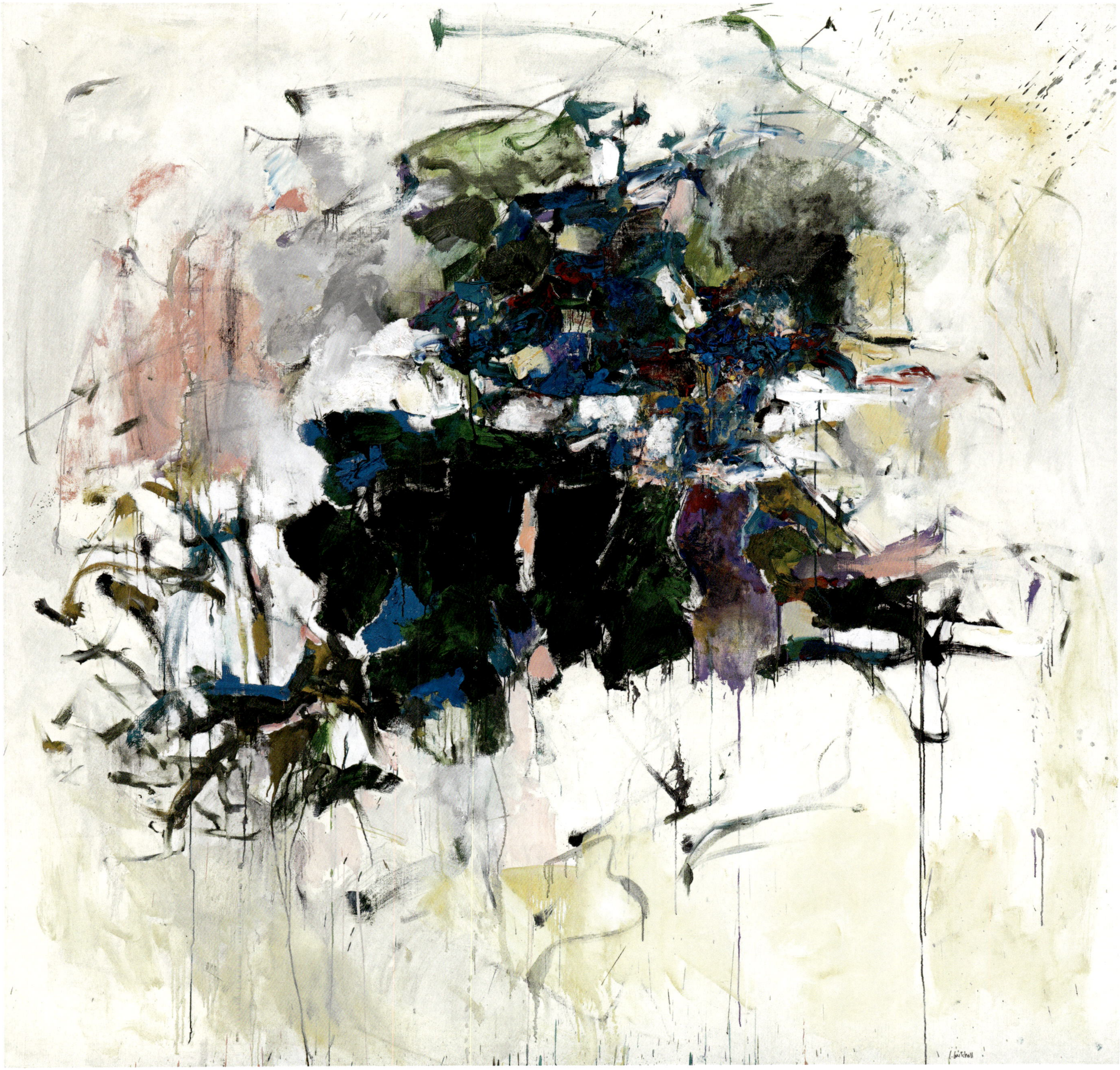

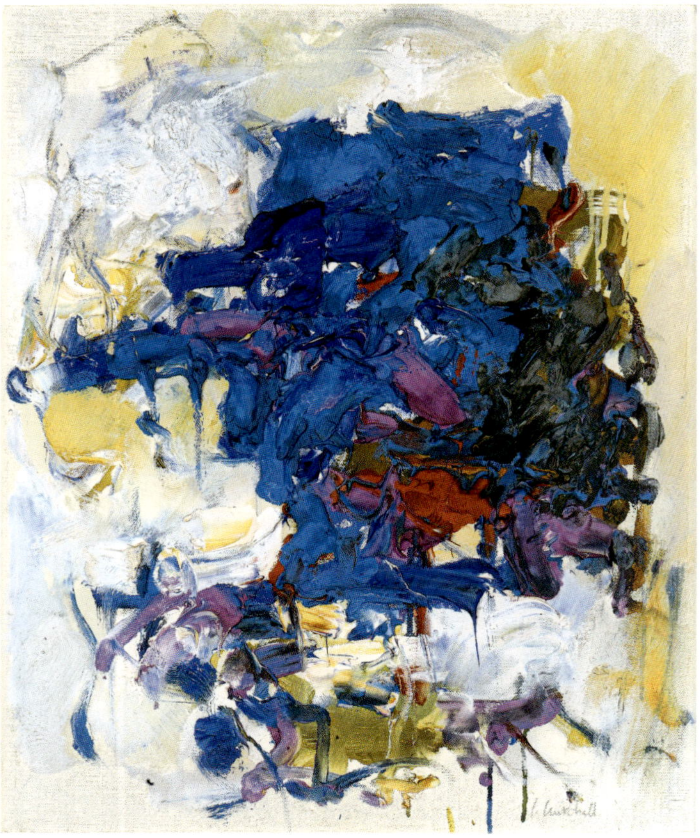

45

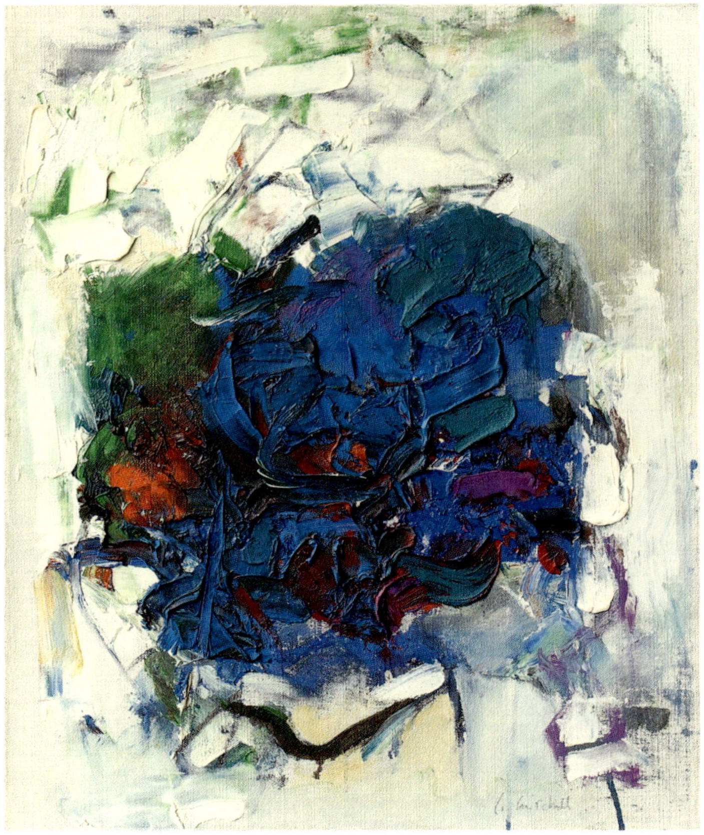

46

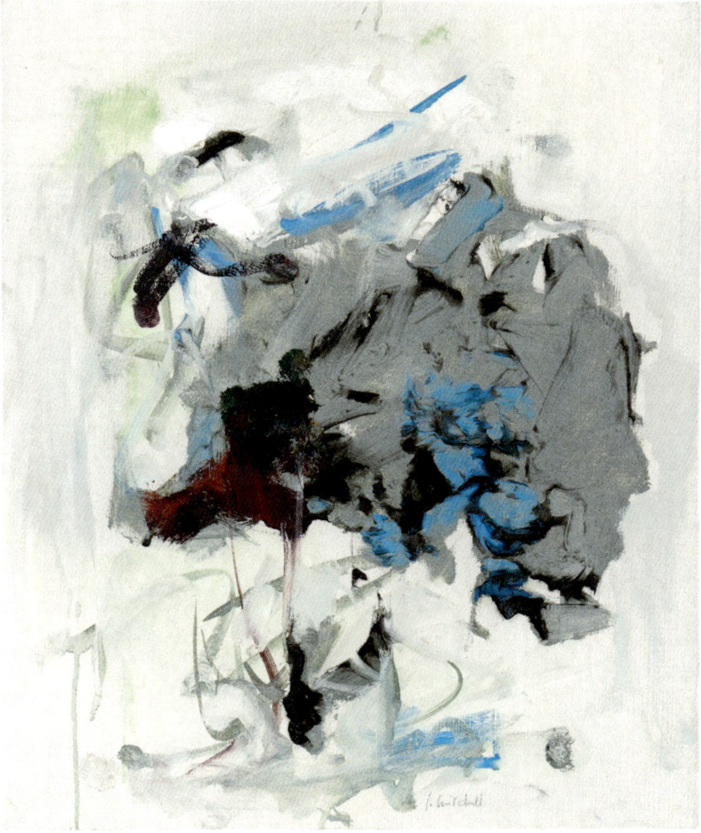

47

Untitled, ca. 1964. Oil on canvas, 20¼ × 17 in. (51.4 × 43.2 cm). The Kreeger Museum, Washington, D.C.

Metro, ca. 1964. Oil on canvas, 20 × 16⅞ in. (50.8 × 42.9 cm). Hofstra University Museum of Art, Hempstead, New York, gift of Dr. and Mrs. Milton Gardner

Untitled, ca. 1964. Oil on canvas, 20 × 17 in. (50.8 × 43.2 cm). Des Moines Art Center, gift of David Kruidenier, Jr. Estate and Elizabeth S. Kruidenier, 2002, Revocable Trust

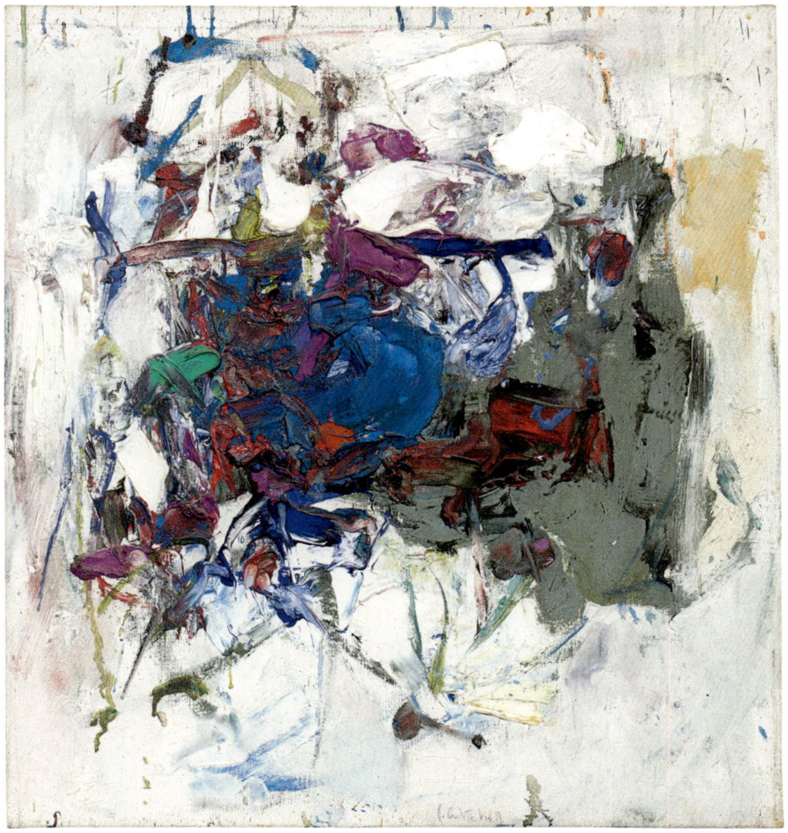

49

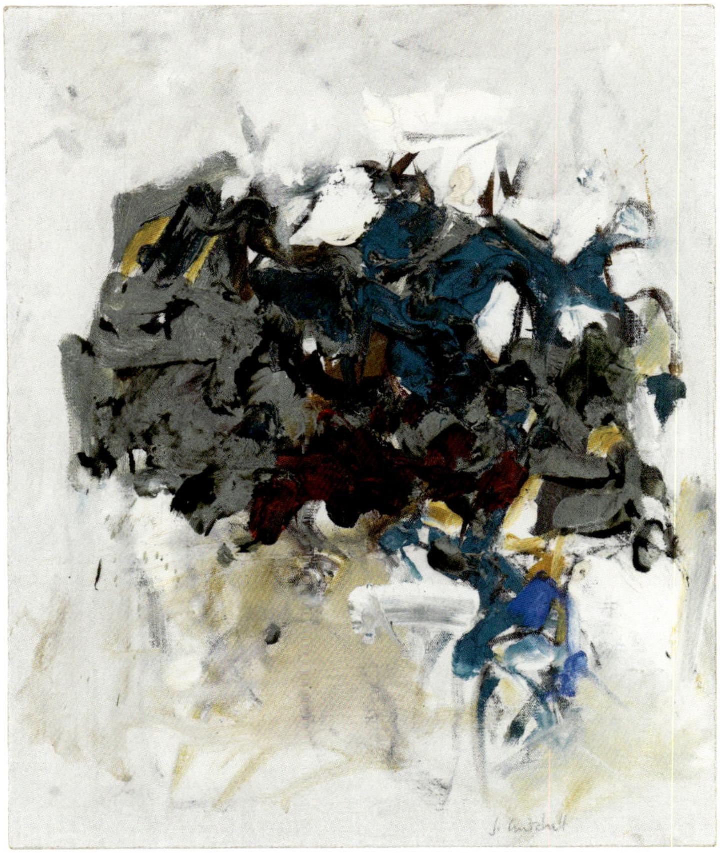

48

Untitled, ca. 1964. Oil on canvas, 19⅞ × 17 in. (50.5 × 43.2 cm). Private collection, New York

Untitled, ca. 1964. Oil on canvas, 19¼ × 18⅛ in. (48.9 × 46 cm). Private collection

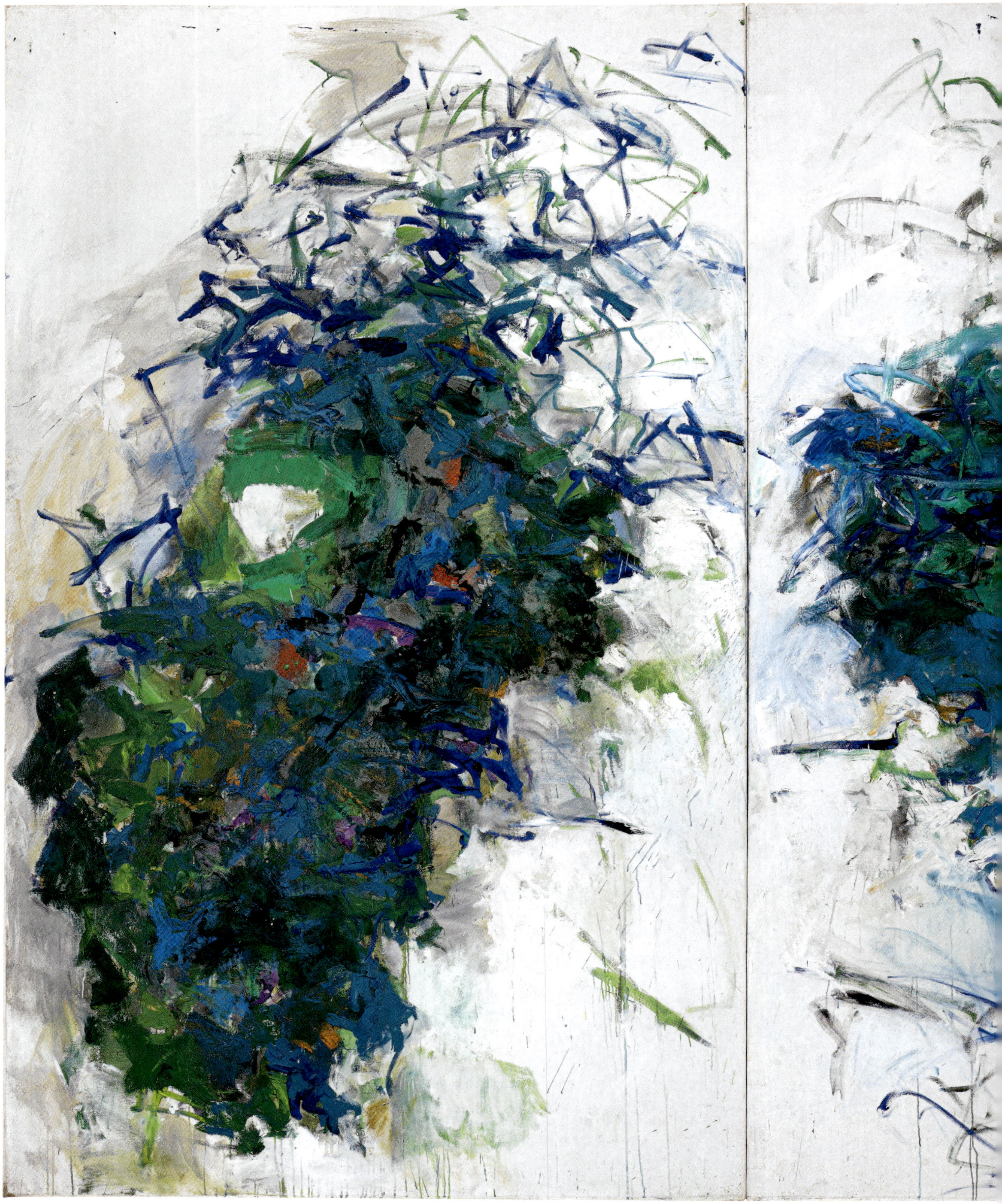

Chicago, 1966–67. Oil on canvas, 103 × 191 in. (261.6 × 485.1 cm). Collection of Gilbert and Ann Kinney

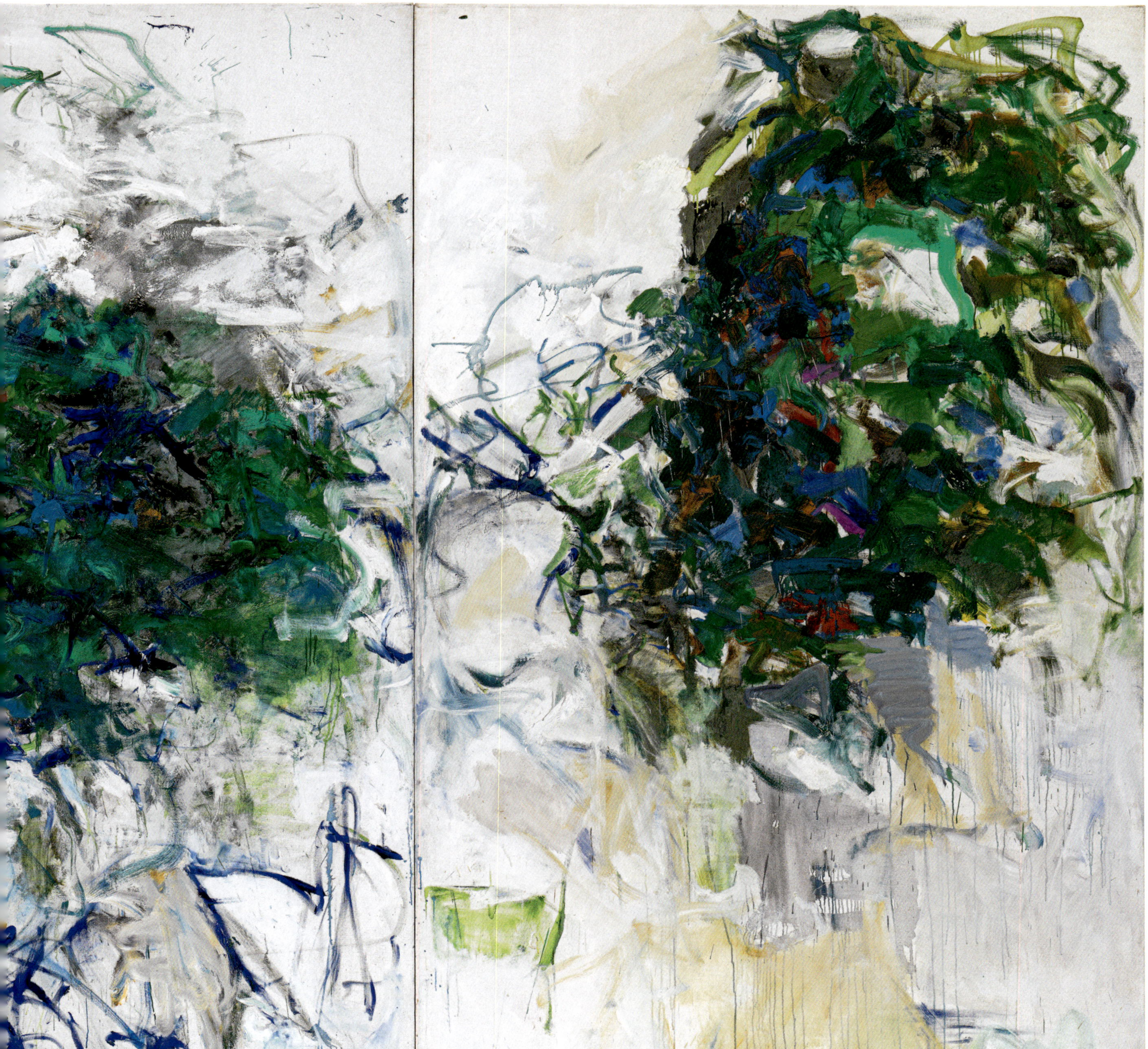

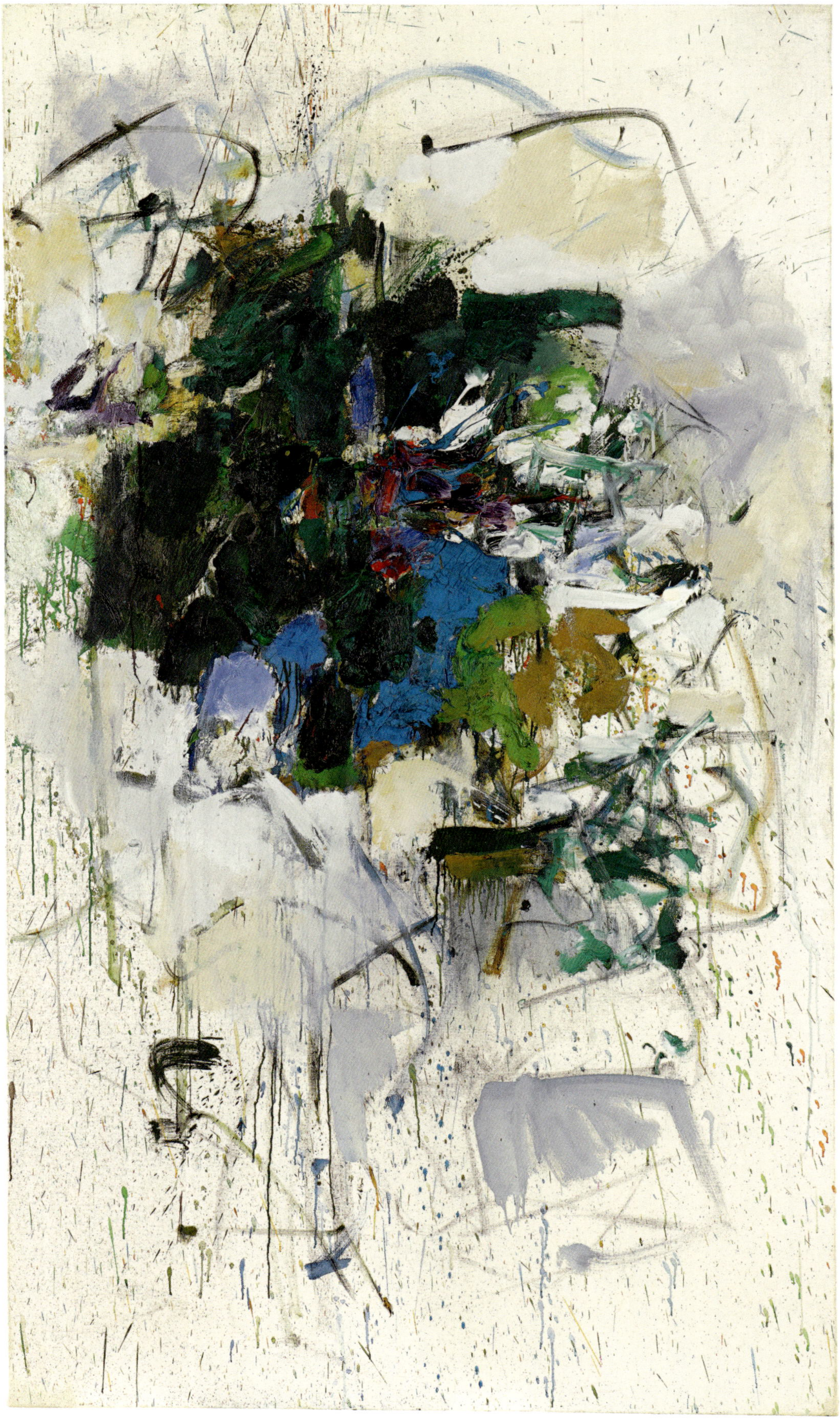

Untitled, ca. 1965. Oil on canvas, 76⅞ × 45 in. (195.3 × 114.3 cm). Collection of Josh and Suzy Tanzer

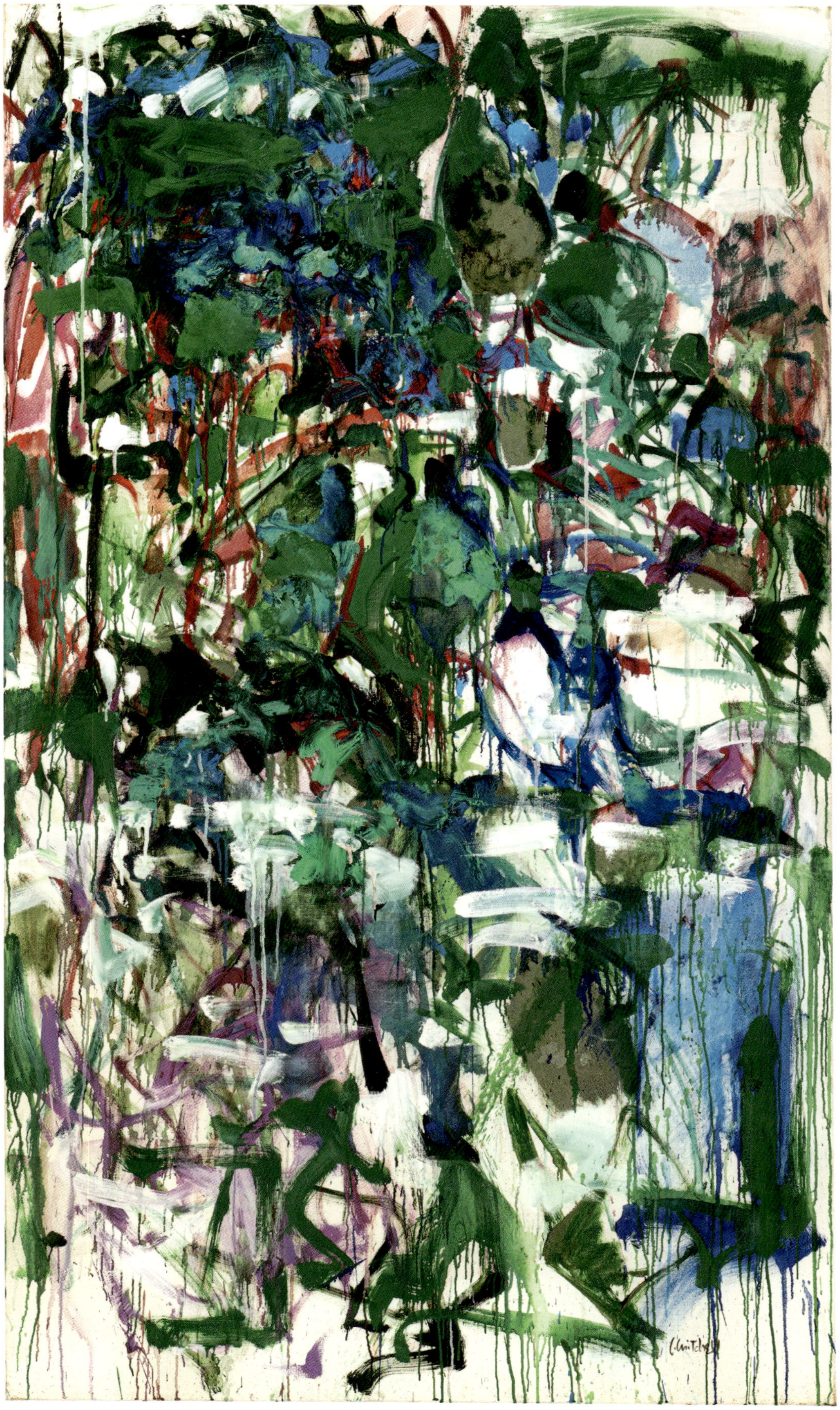

Woods/Country, 1966. Oil on canvas, 76¾ × 44¾ in. (194.9 × 113.7 cm). McNay Art Museum, San Antonio, Texas, gift of Robert L. B. Tobin

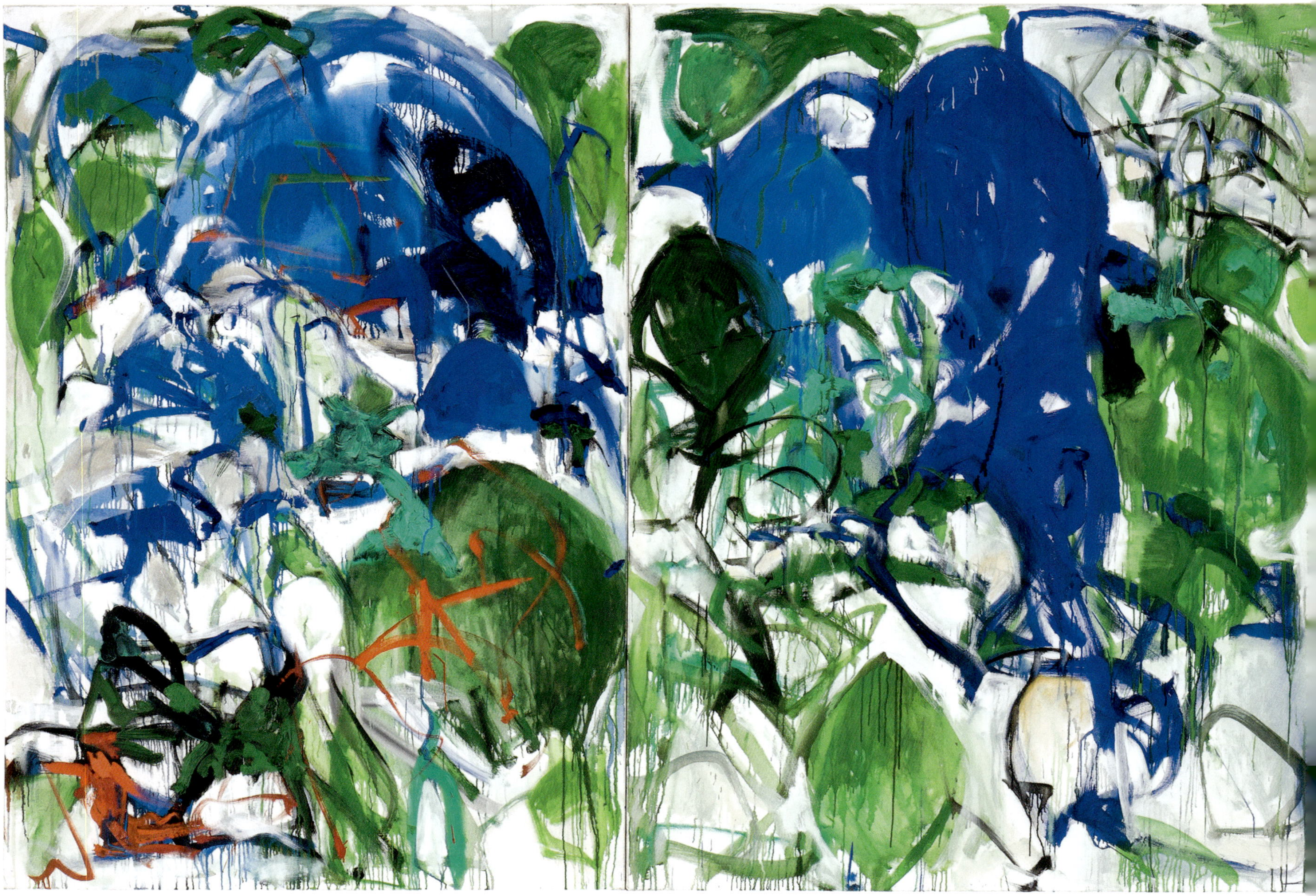

Aquarium, 1967. Oil on canvas, 63¾ × 192½ in. (161.9 × 489 cm). Private collection

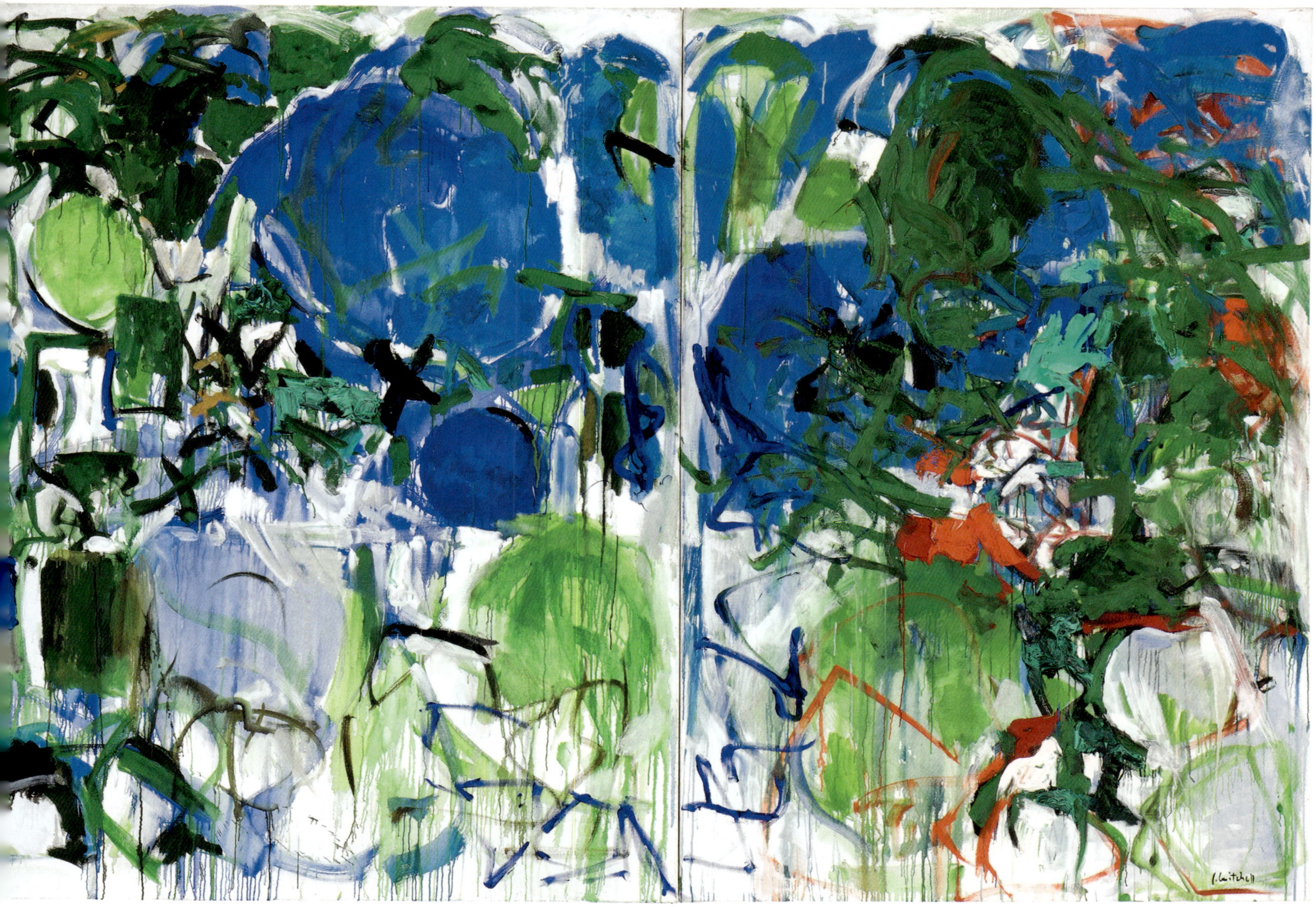
J. Mitchell

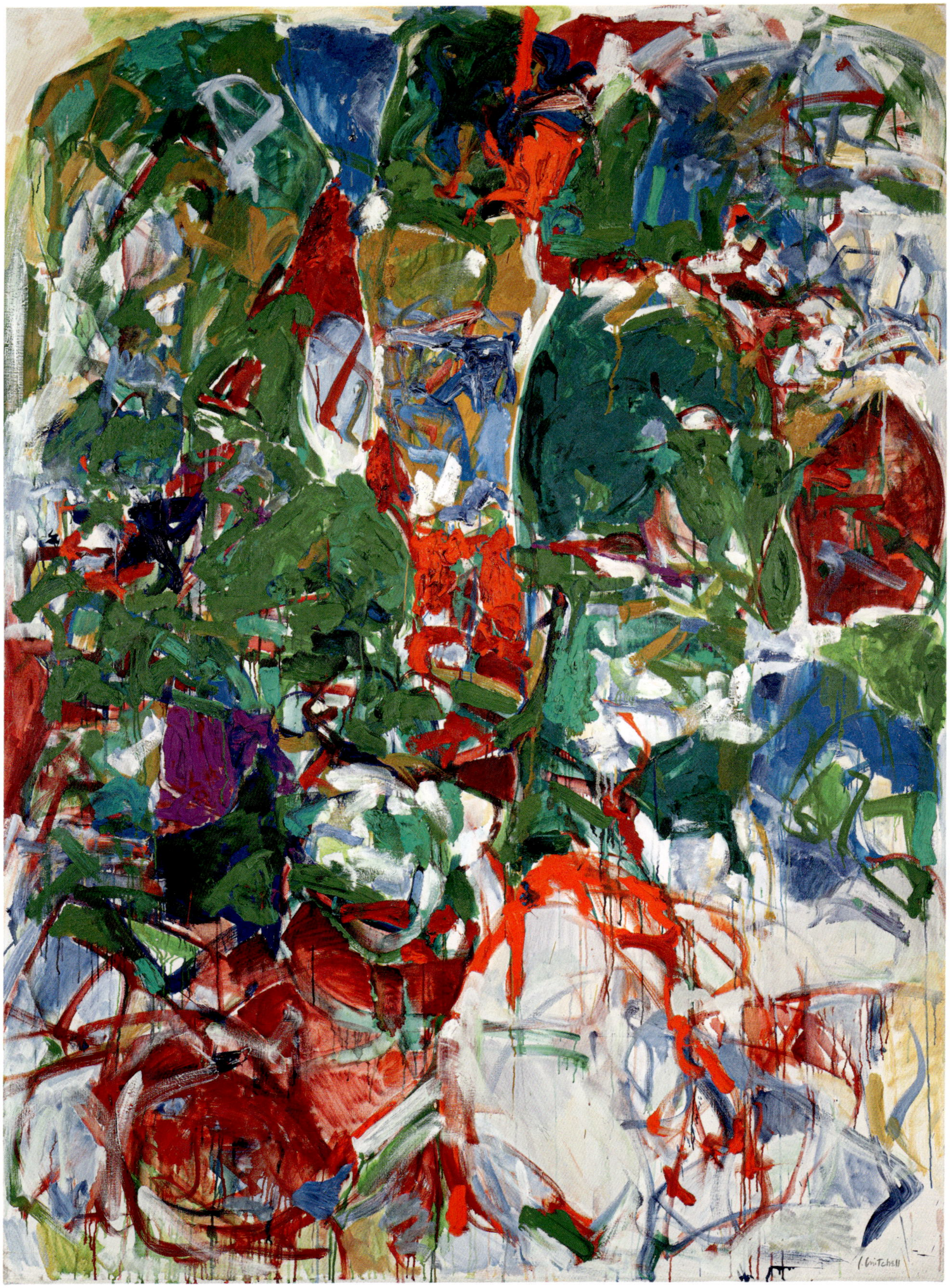

Russian Easter, 1967. Oil on canvas, 78⅞ × 58⅛ in. (200.3 × 147.6 cm). Private collection, Liechtenstein

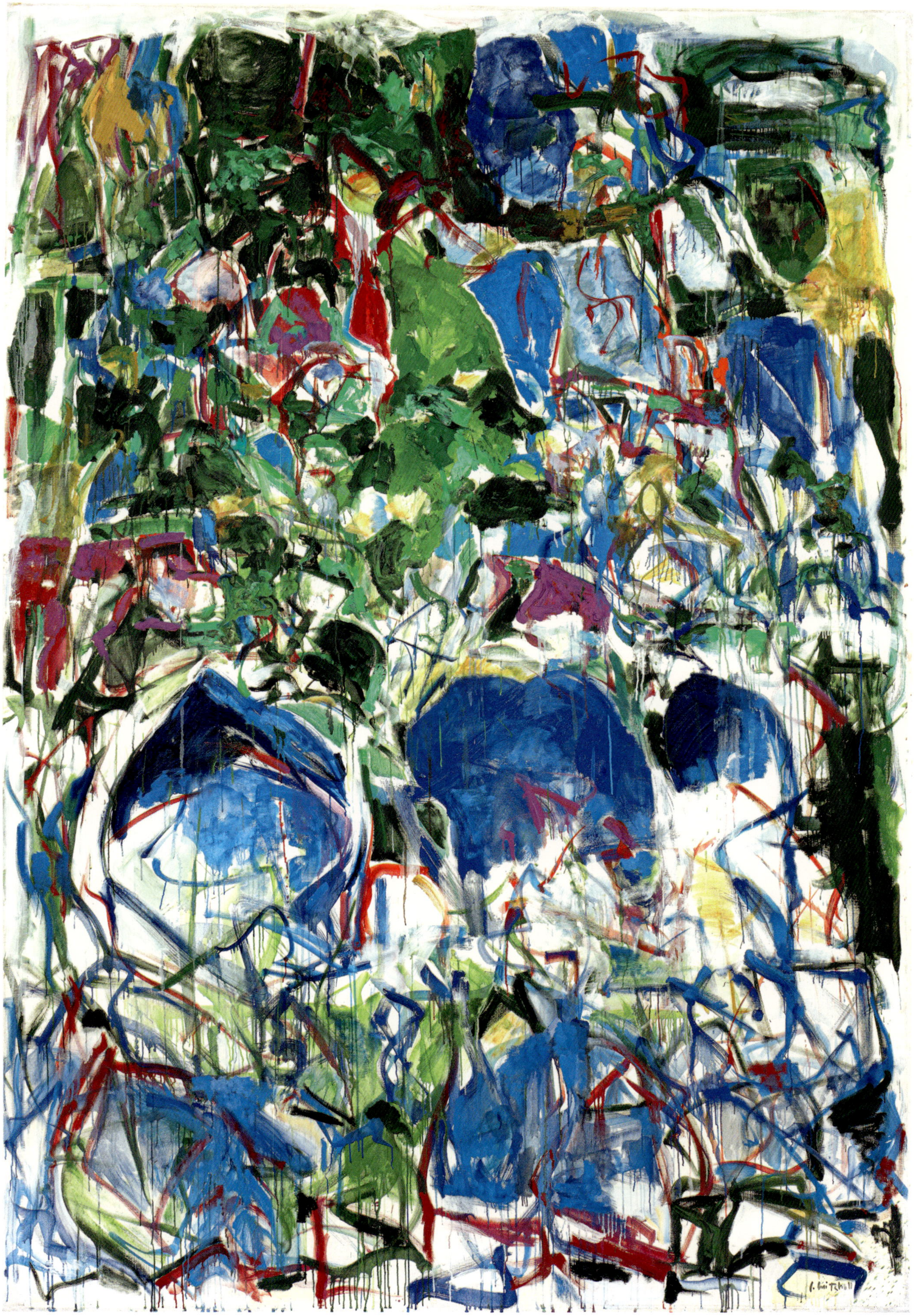

My Landscape II, 1967. Oil on canvas, 102⅞ × 71¼ in. (261.3 × 181 cm). Smithsonian American Art Museum, Washington, D.C., gift of Mr. and Mrs. David K. Anderson, Martha Jackson Memorial Collection

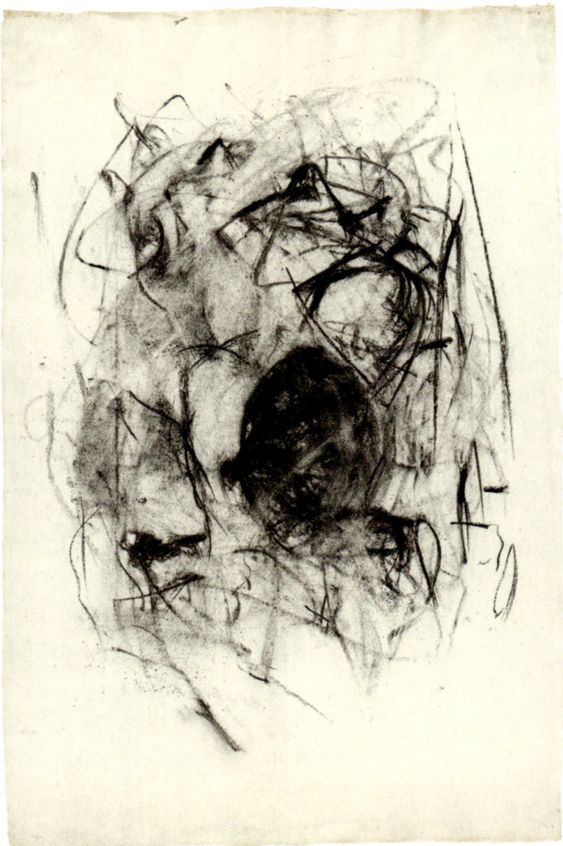

56

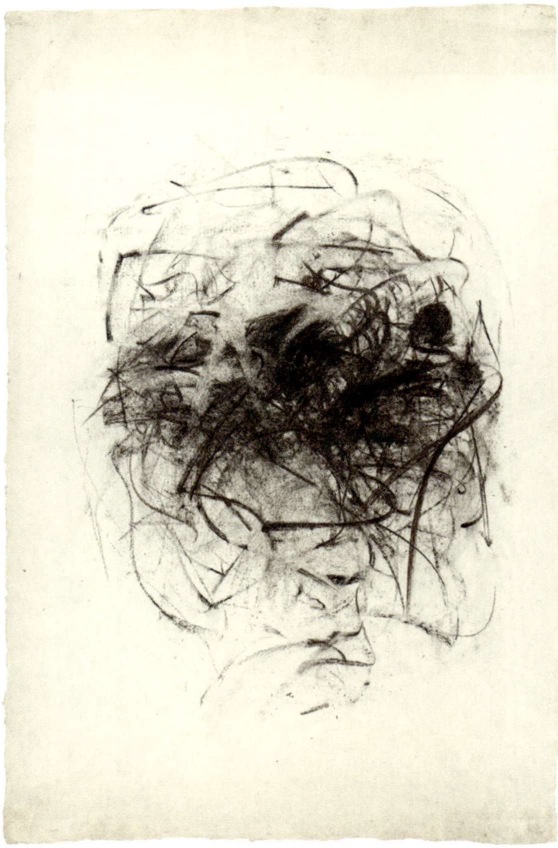

57

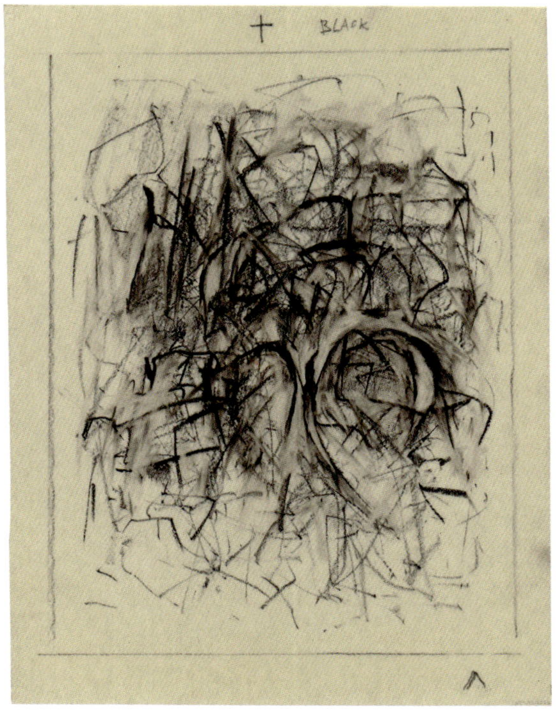

58

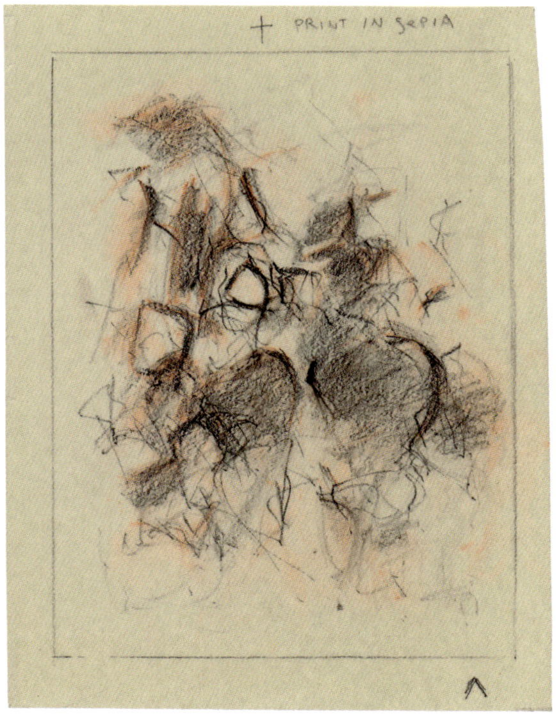

59

Untitled, 1967. Charcoal on paper, 36⅛ × 24¼ in. (91.7 × 61.5 cm). Joan Mitchell Foundation, New York

Untitled, 1967. Charcoal on paper, 36⅜ × 24 in. (92.4 × 61 cm). Joan Mitchell Foundation, New York

Preparatory drawing for *In Memory of My Feelings,* 1967. Crayon on acetate, 14 × 10⅞ in. (35.5 × 27.6 cm). The Museum of Modern Art, New York, gift of the artist

Preparatory drawing for *In Memory of My Feelings,* 1967. Crayon on acetate, 14 × 10⅞ in. (35.5 × 27.6 cm). The Museum of Modern Art, New York, gift of the artist

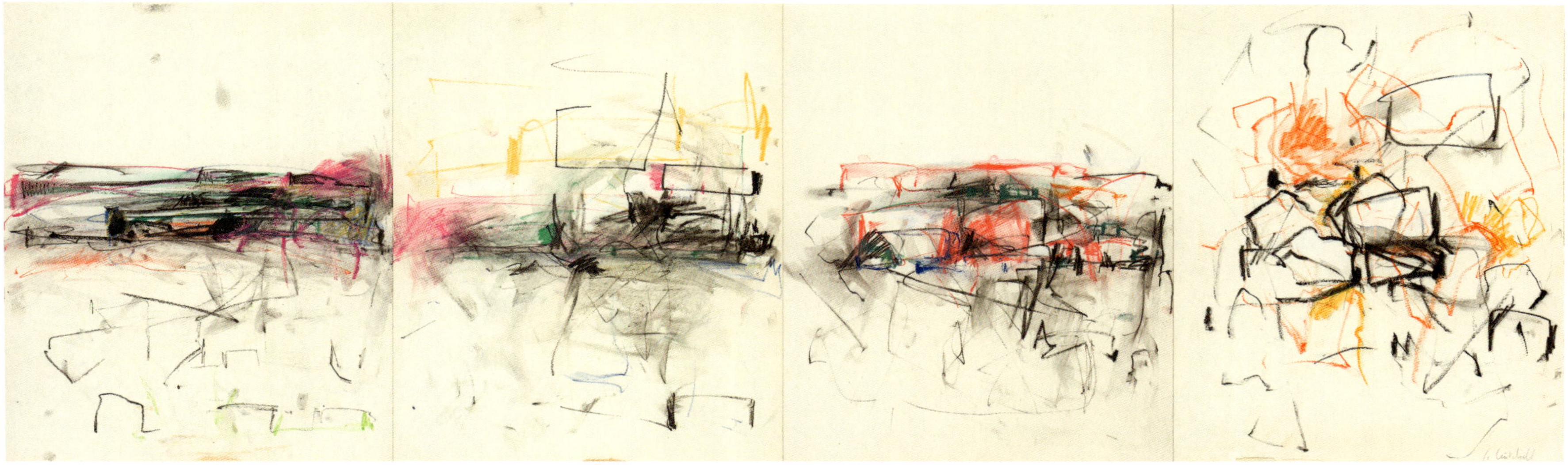

Untitled [Seine], 1967–68. Water-soluble wax crayon and wash on paper, 12⅛ × 40¾ in. (30.8 × 103.6 cm). Joan Mitchell Foundation, New York

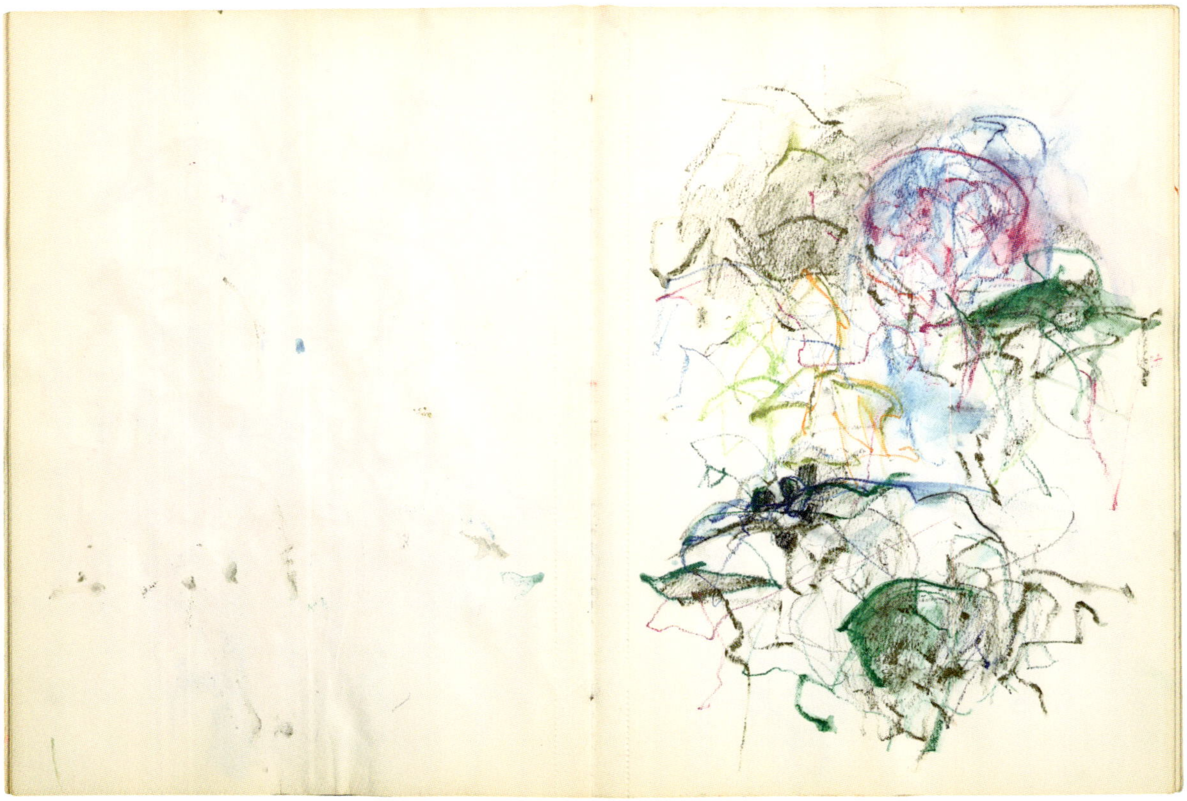

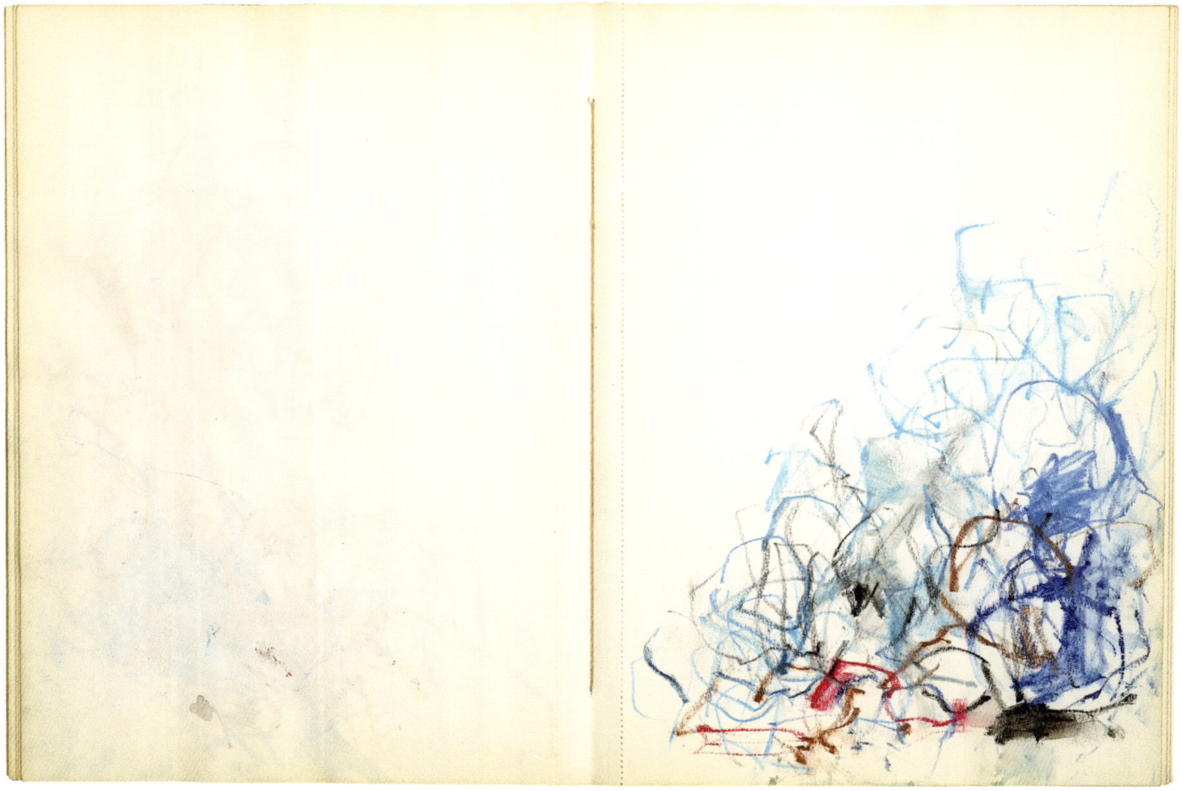

Sketchbook, 1967–68. Pages 14 and 15 of 84. Pastel, ink, and graphite on paper, each page: 9¾ × 7¼ in. (24.5 × 18.5 cm). Private collection

Sketchbook, 1967–68. Pages 30 and 31 of 84. Pastel, ink, and graphite on paper, each page: 9¾ × 7¼ in. (24.5 × 18.5 cm). Private collection

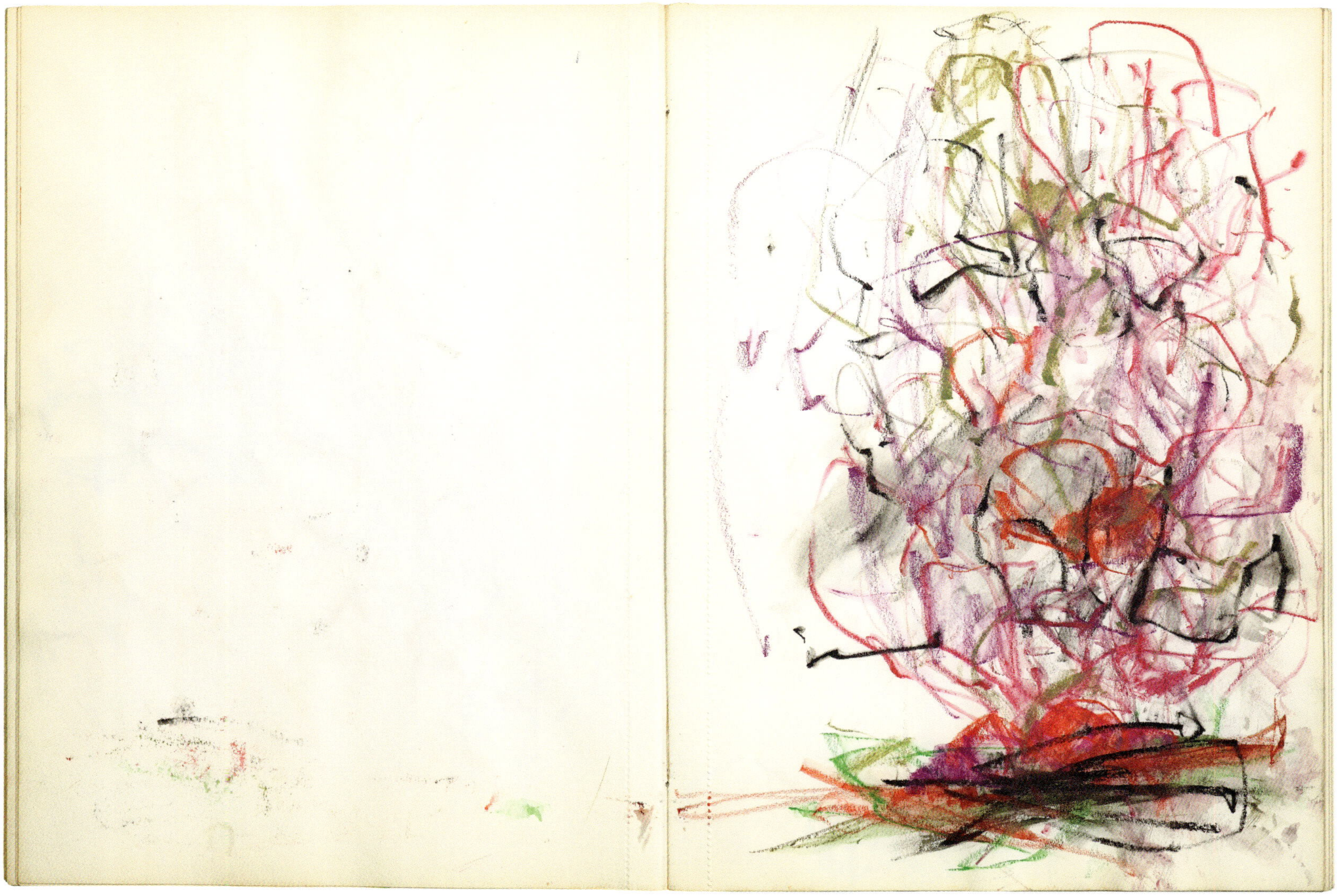

Sketchbook, 1967–68. Pages 24 and 25 of 84. Pastel, ink, and graphite on paper, each page: 9¾ × 7¼ in. (24.5 × 18.5 cm). Private collection

PLATE 64

Vétheuil, 1967–68. Oil on canvas, 76¾ × 49⅞ in. (194.9 × 126.7 cm). Private collection, New York

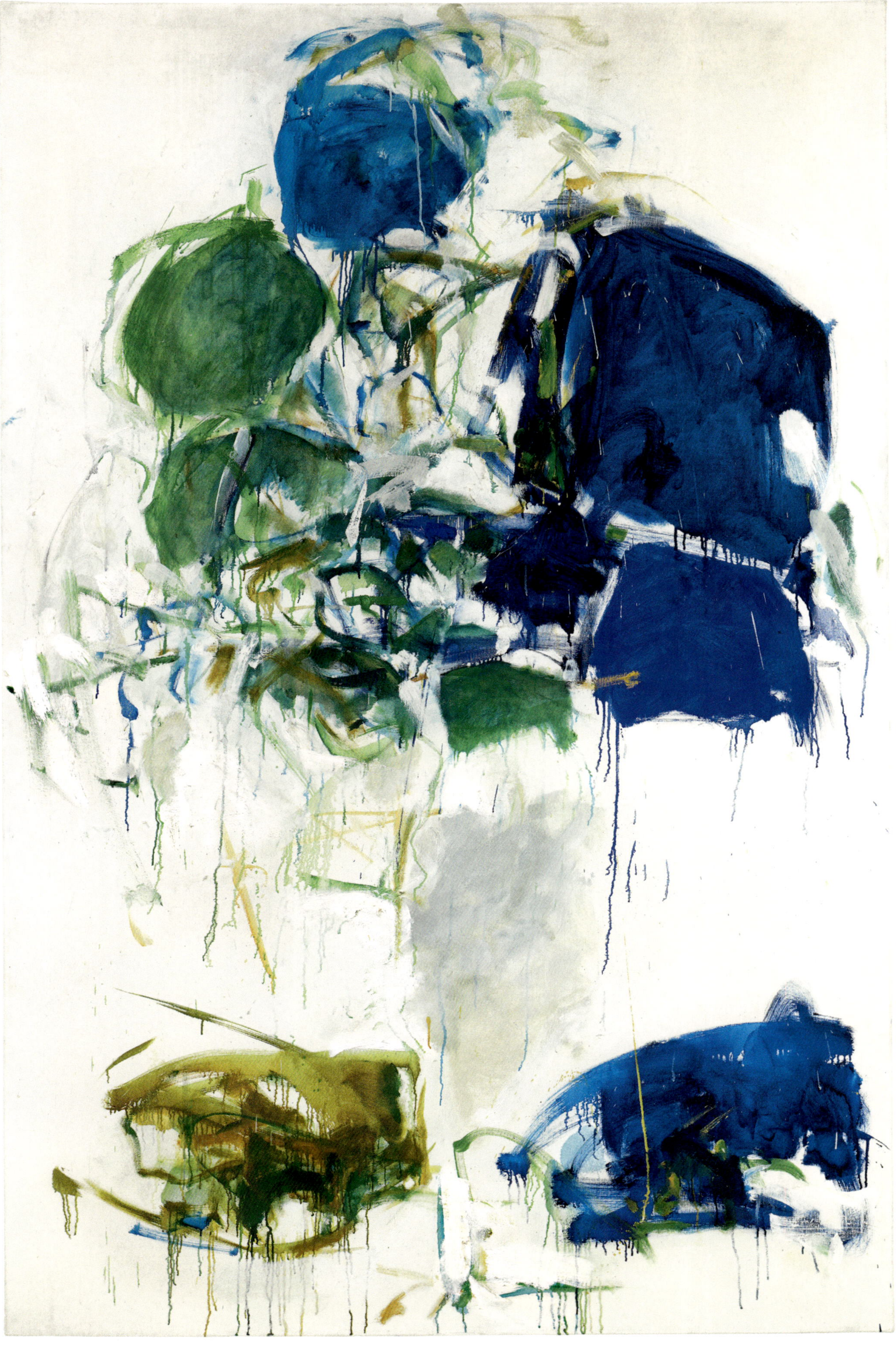

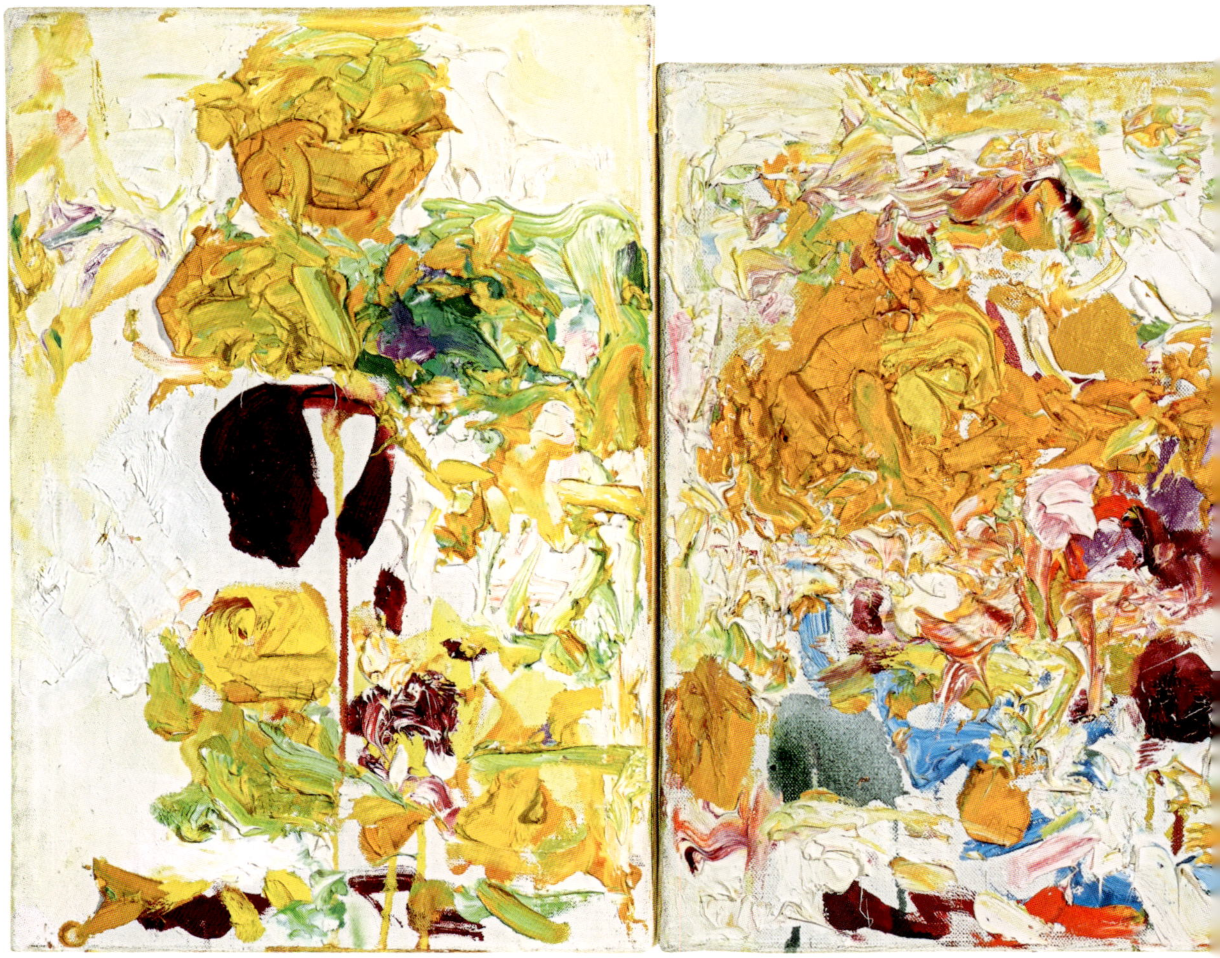

Little Trip, 1969. Oil on canvas, 13⅞ × 45⅜ in. (35.2 × 115.3 cm). Private collection

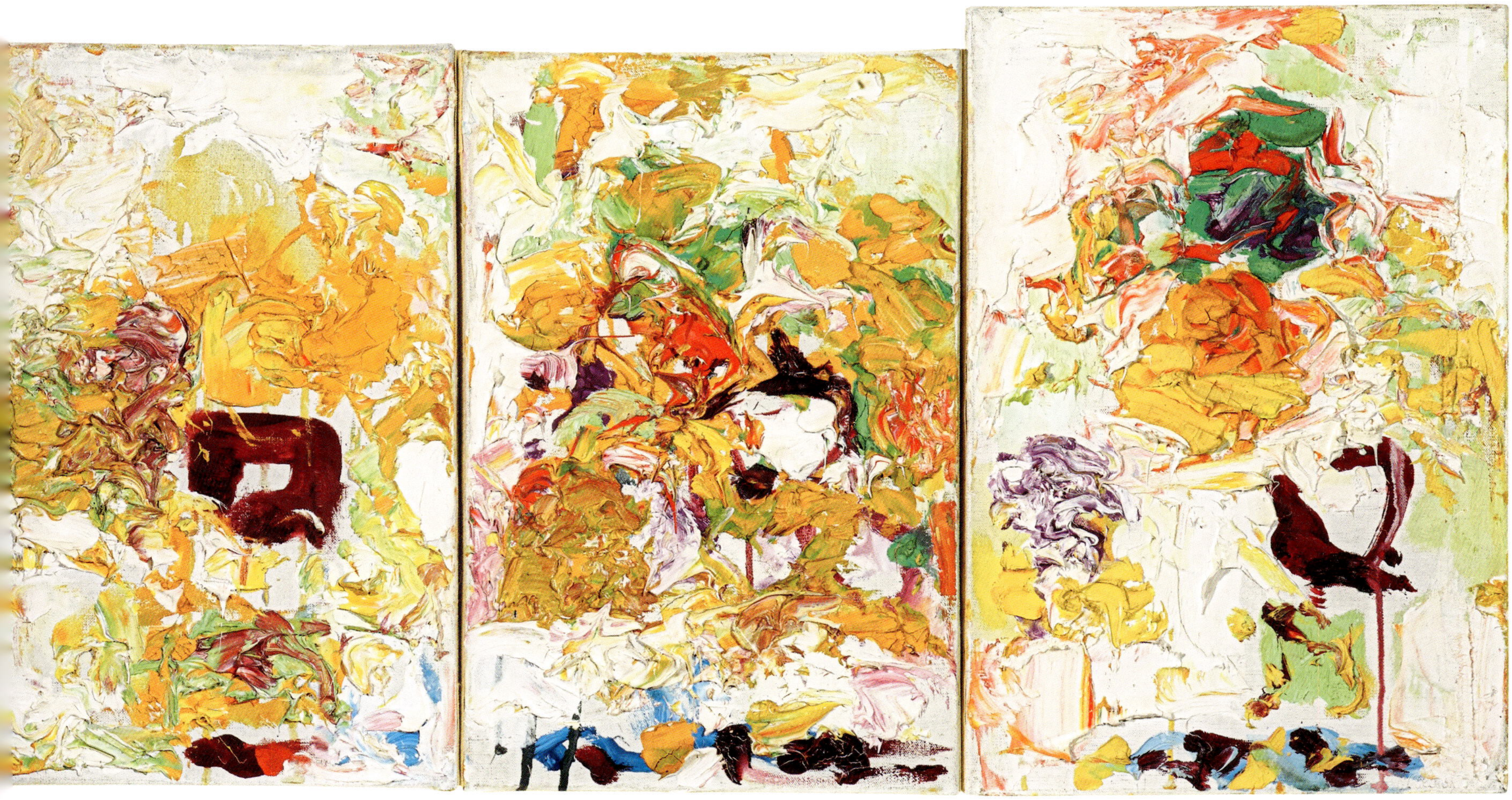

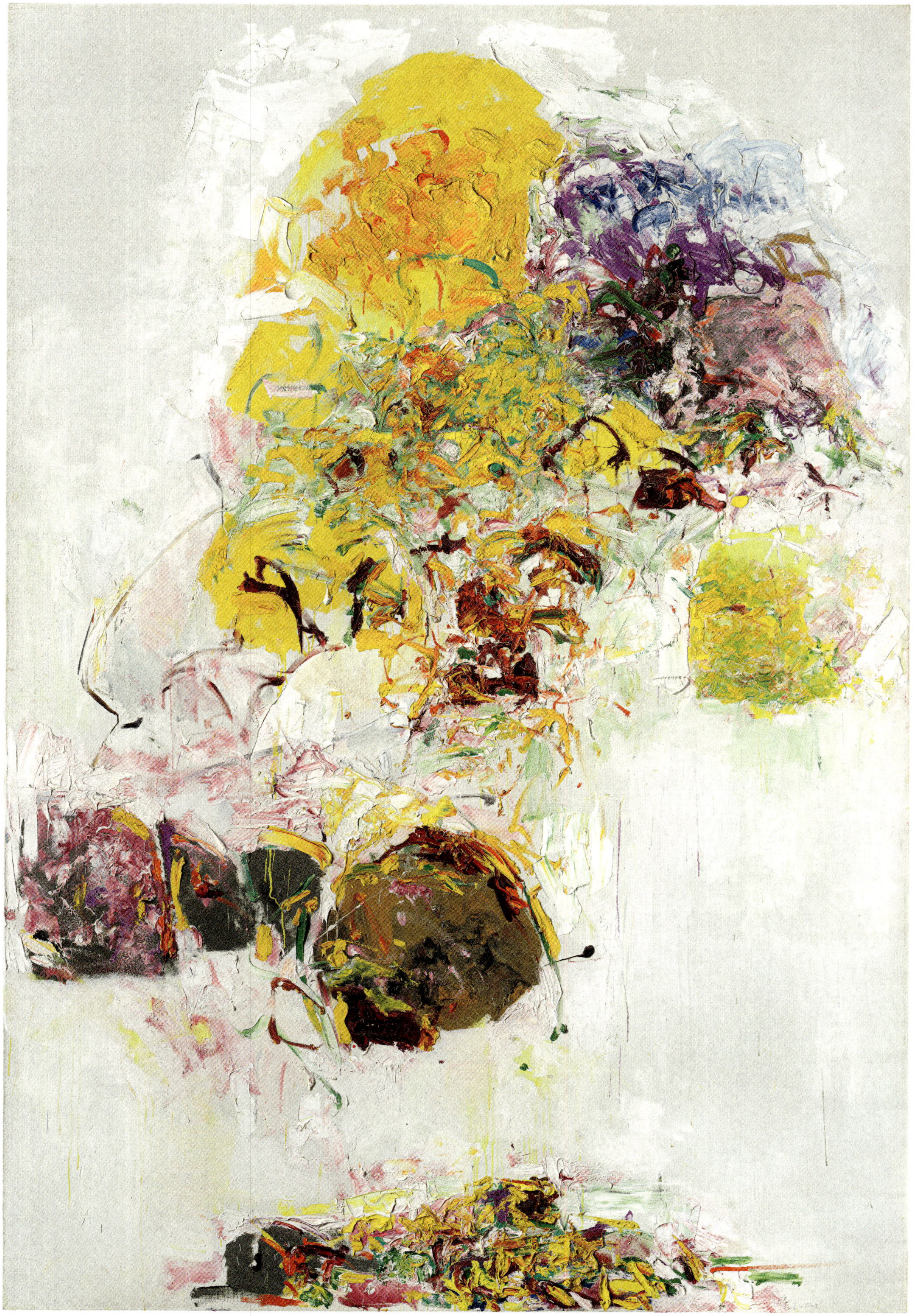

Sunflower, 1969. Oil on canvas, 102 × 70½ in. (259.1 × 179.1 cm). The Metropolitan Museum of Art, New York, gift of Pierre Matisse

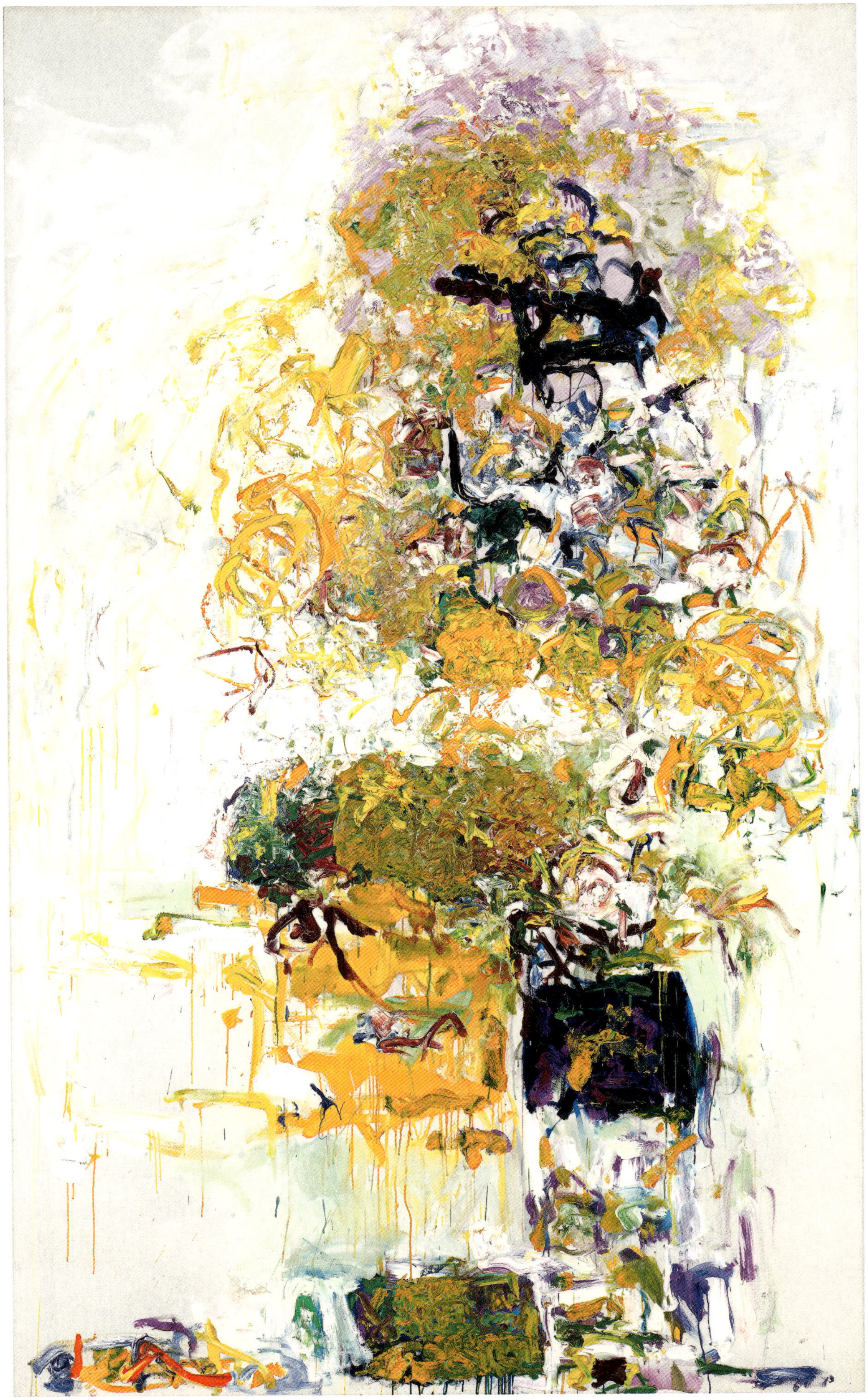

Sunflower VI, 1969. O l on canvas, 102¼ × 63 in. (259.7 × 160 cm). Williams College Museum of Art, Williamstown, Massachusetts, anonymous gift, in tribute to L nda Shearer and her late husband Hartley Shearer

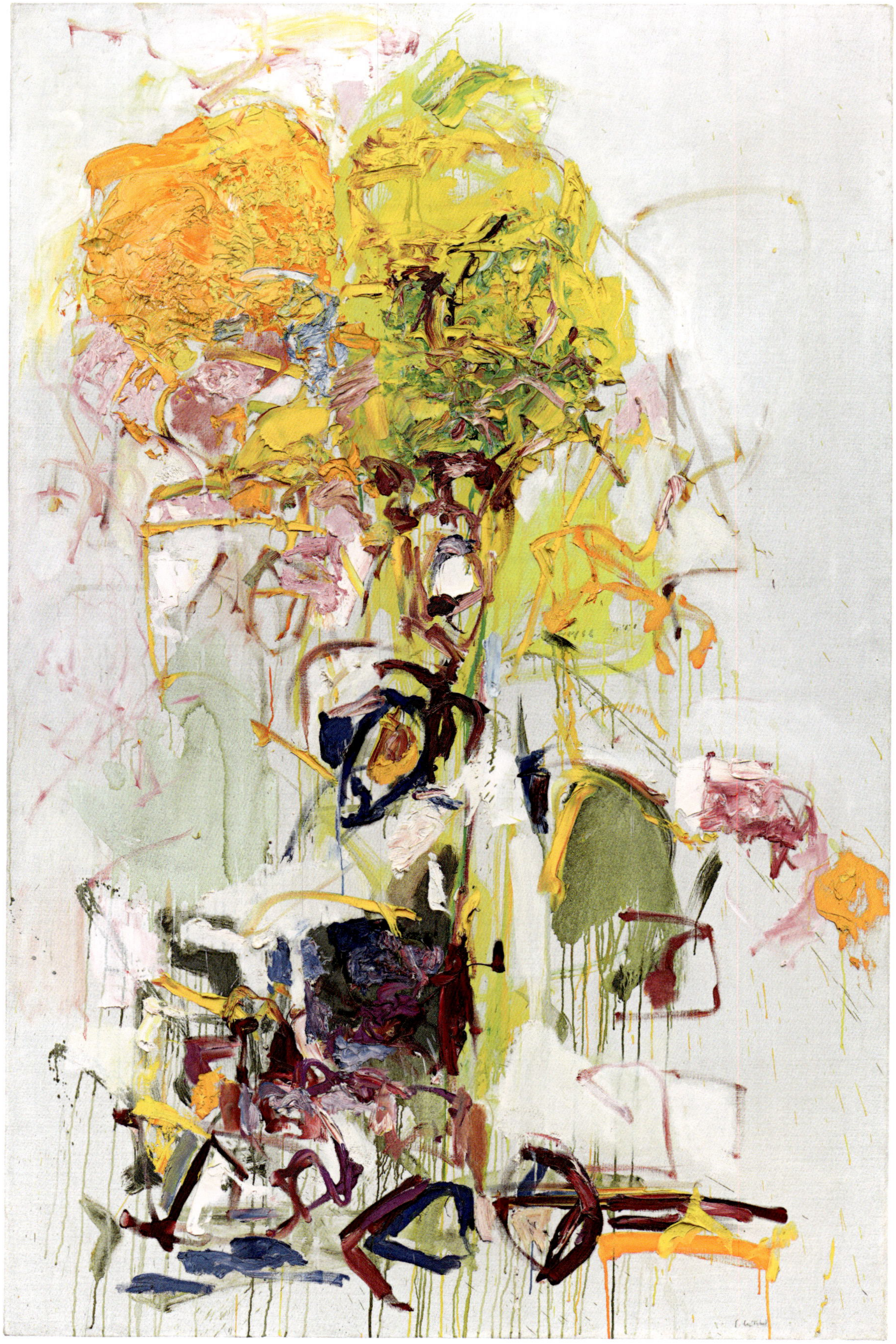

Composition, 1969. Oil on canvas, 76⅝ × 51¼ in. (194.6 × 130.2 cm). Private collection, courtesy Hauser & Wirth Collection Services

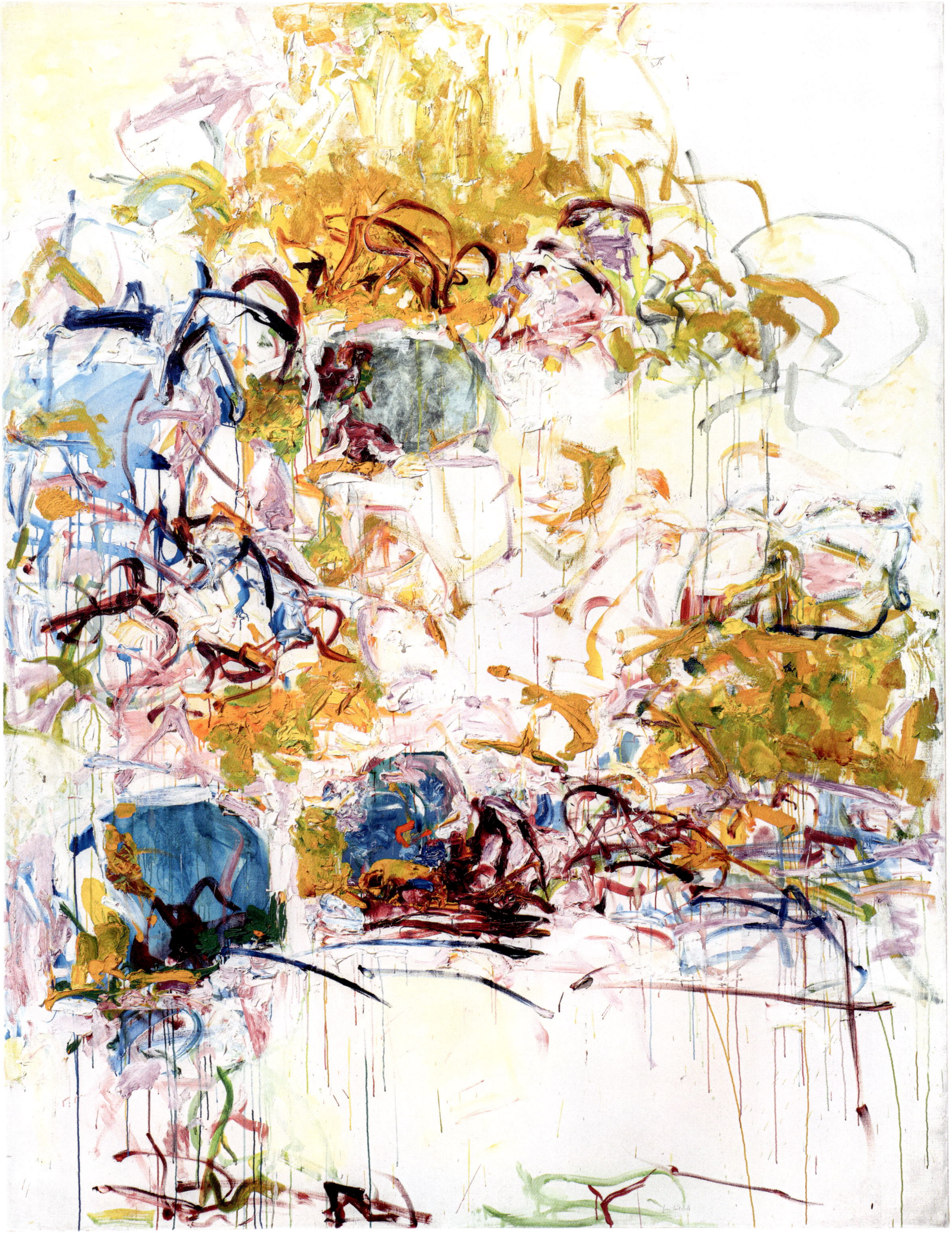

Sans Pierre, 1969. Oil on canvas, 102½ × 78½ in. (260.4 × 199.4 cm). Collection of The Long View Legacy LLC

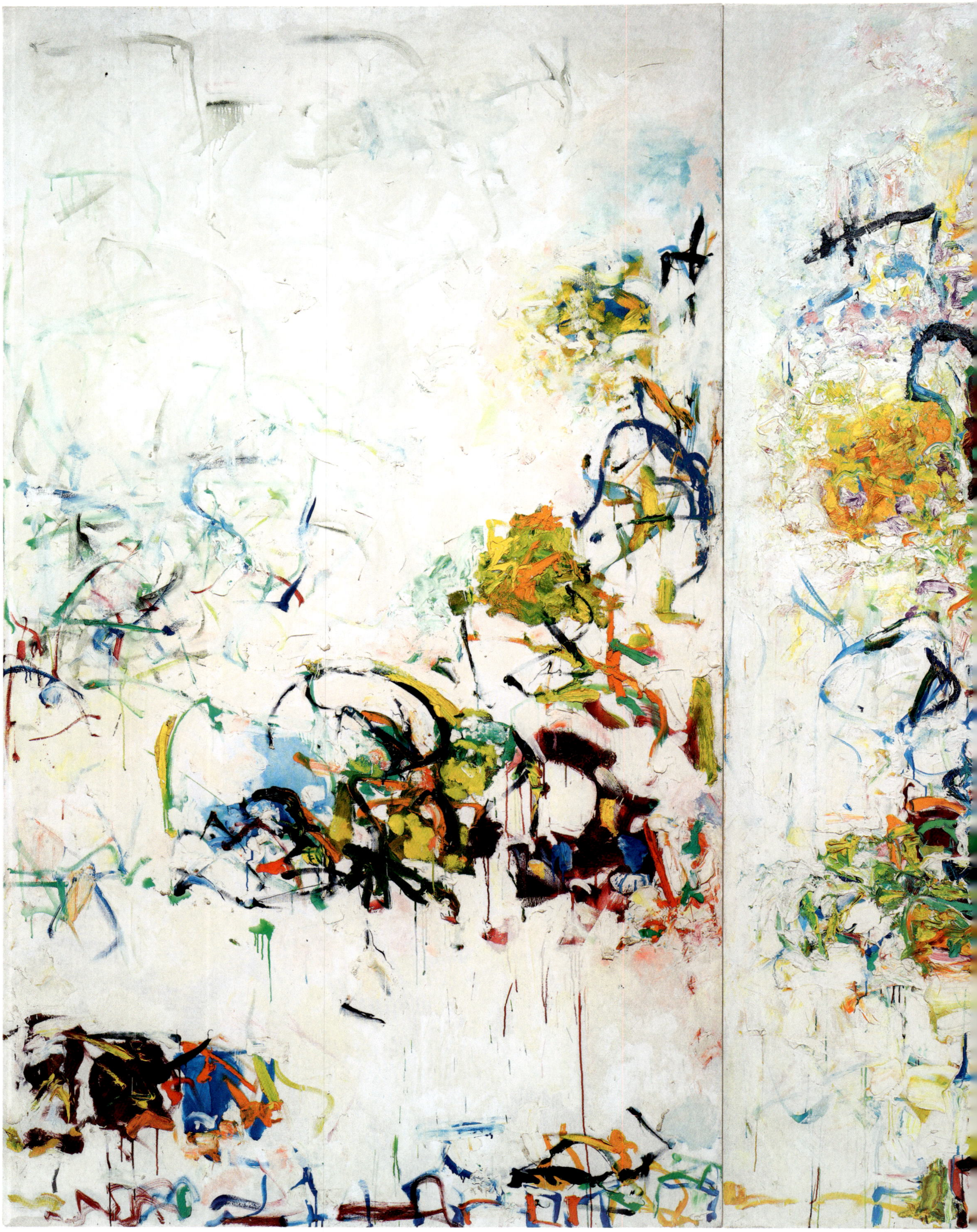

Untitled, 1969. Oil on canvas, 102½ × 184½ in. (260.4 × 468.6 cm). Musée de Brou, Bourg-en-Bresse, France

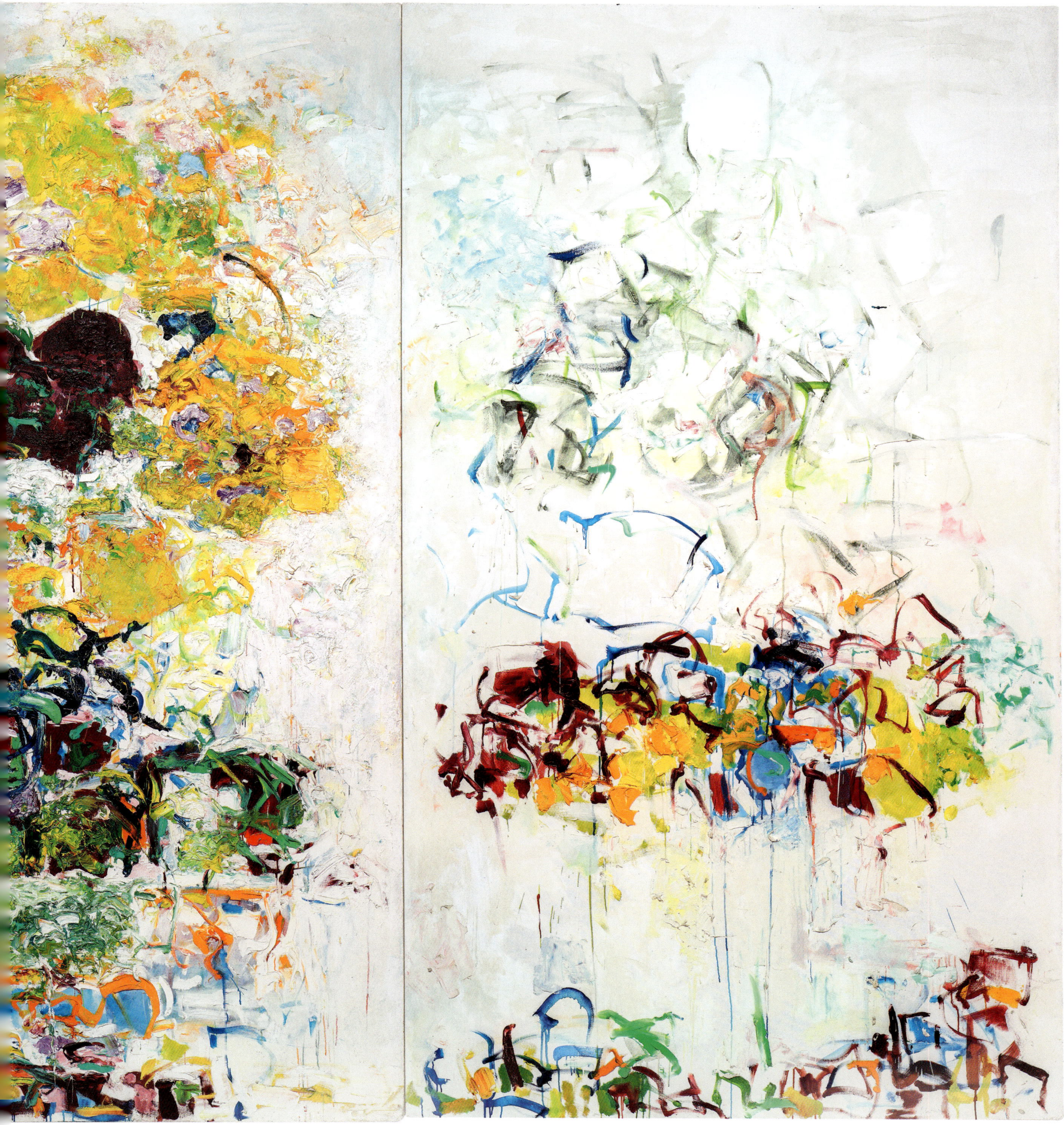

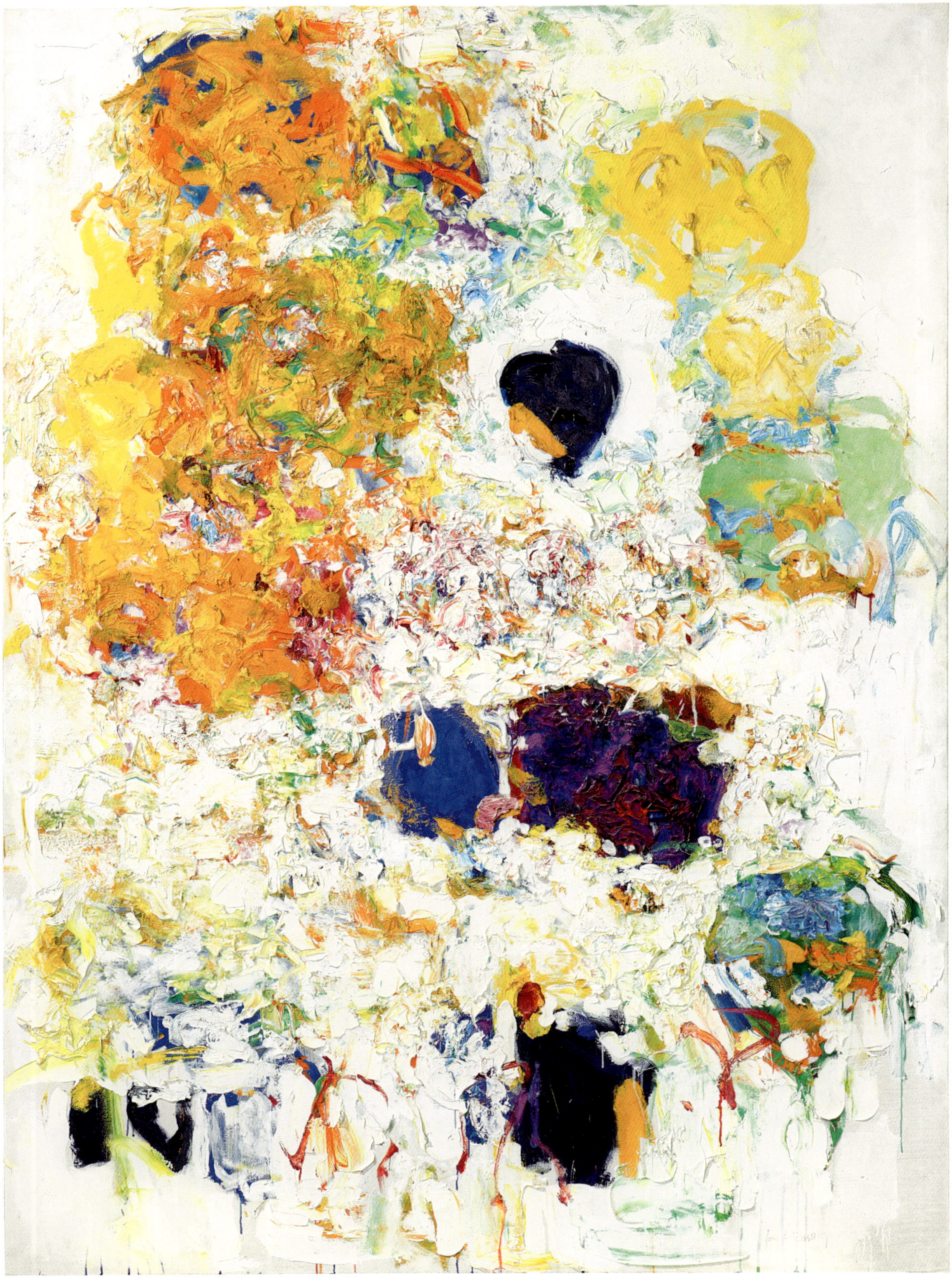

Blueberry, 1969–70. Oil on canvas, 78⅞ × 59 in. (200.3 × 149.9 cm). Private collection, Florida

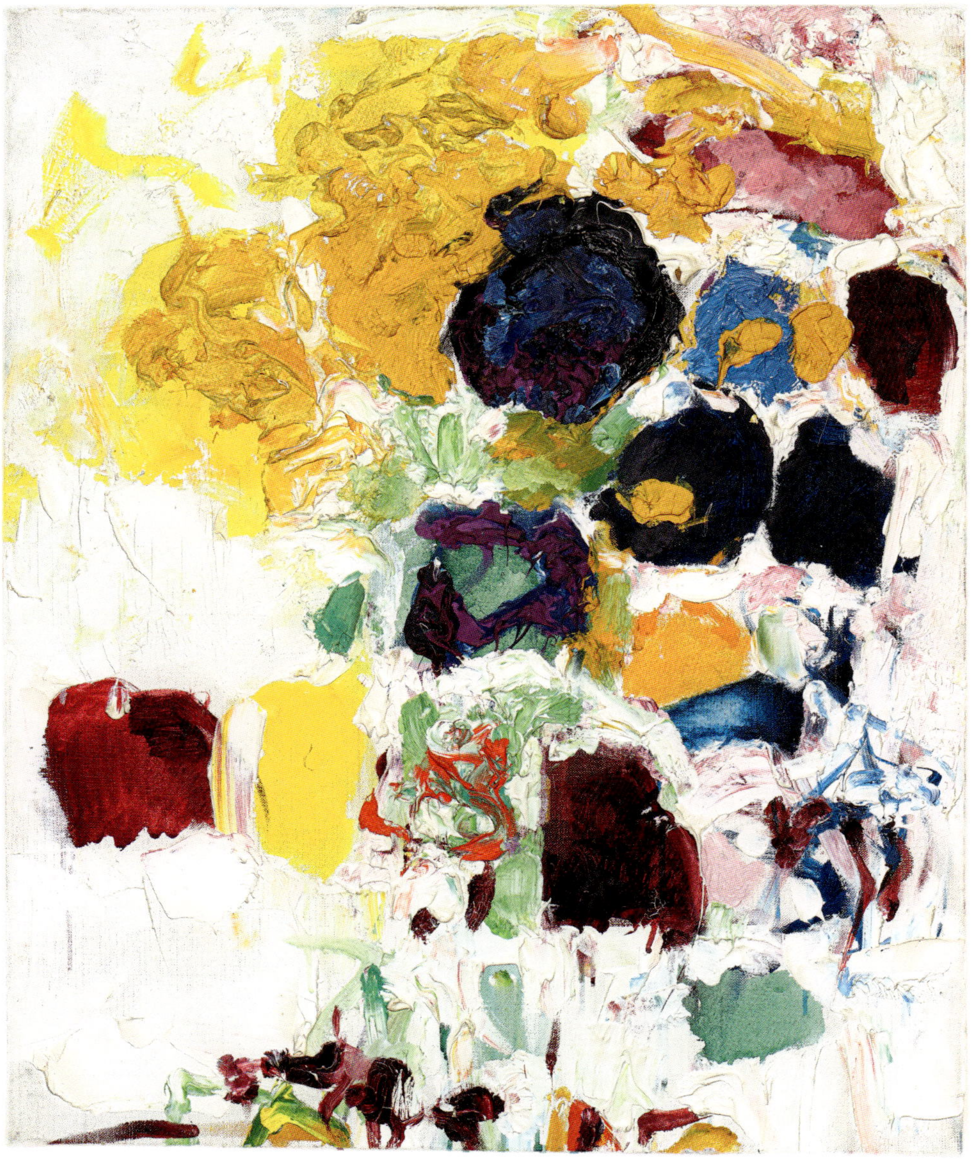

Also Returned, 1969. Oil on canvas, 25⅝ × 21⅛ in. (65.1 × 53.7 cm). Private collection

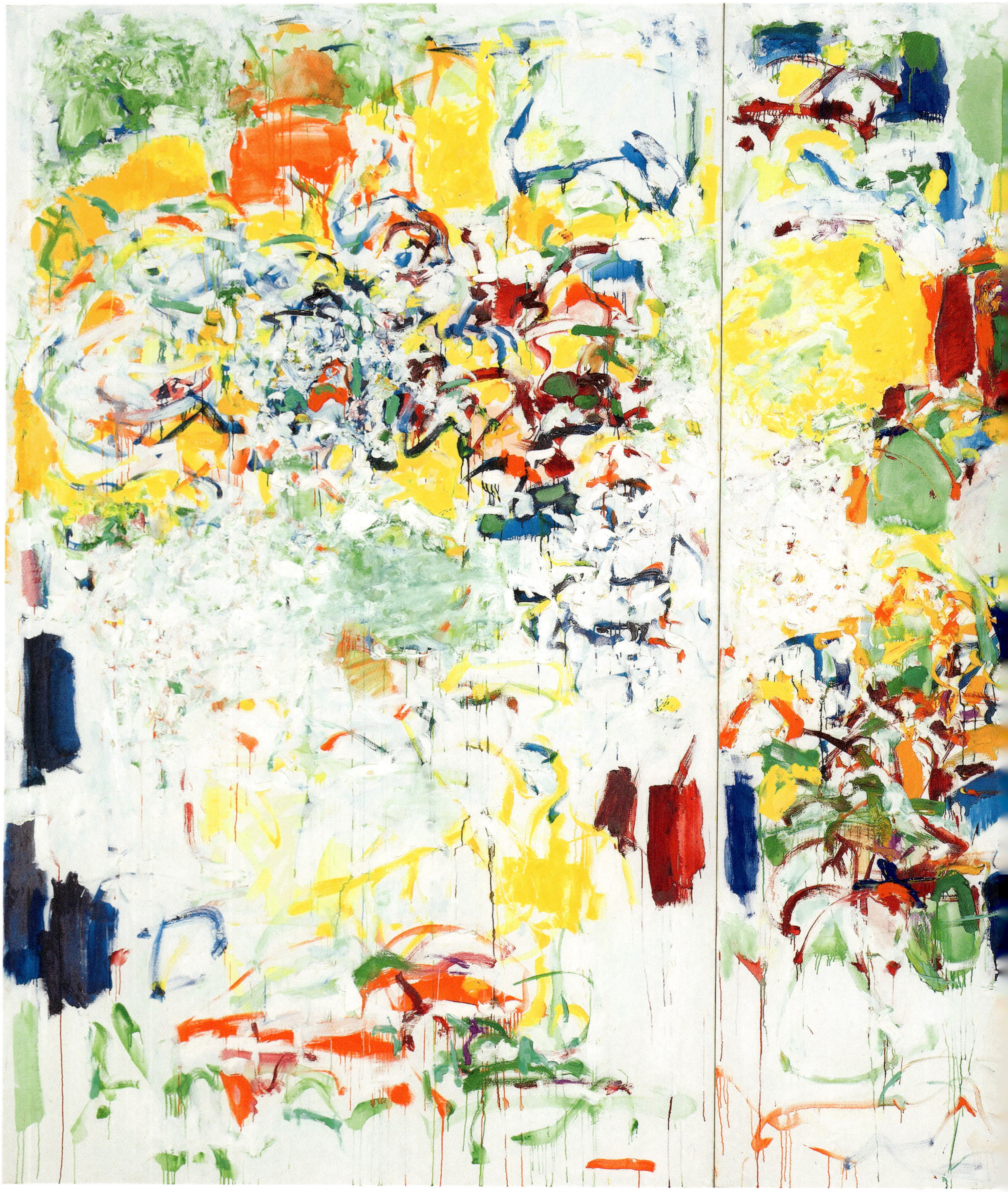

Sans neige, 1969. Oil on canvas, 102 × 198¼ in. (259.1 × 503.6 cm). Carnegie Museum of Art, Pittsburgh, gift of the Hillman Foundation

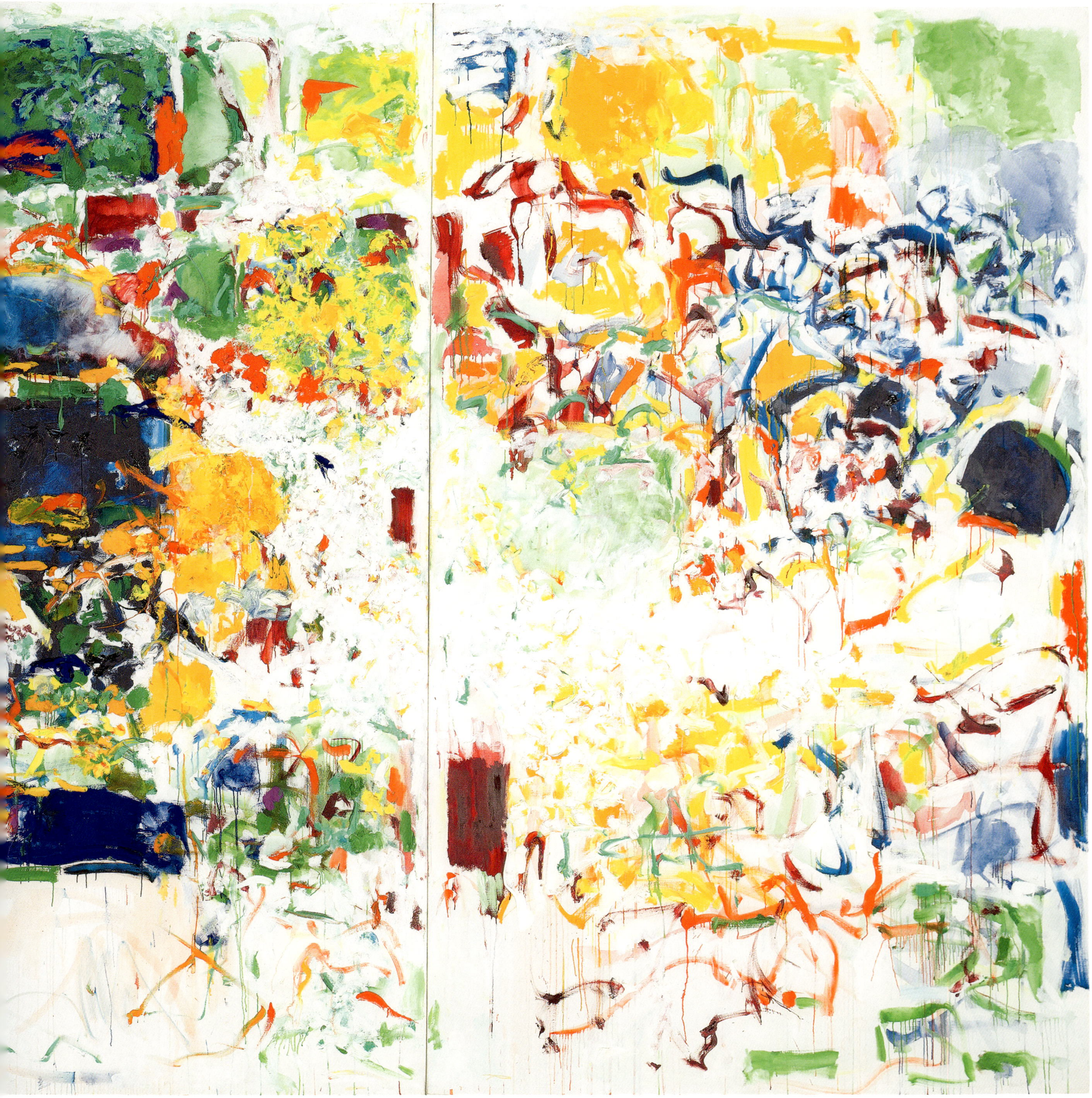

PLATE 74

La Ligne de la rupture, 1970–71. Oil on canvas, 112 × 79 in. (284.5 × 200.7 cm). Private collection

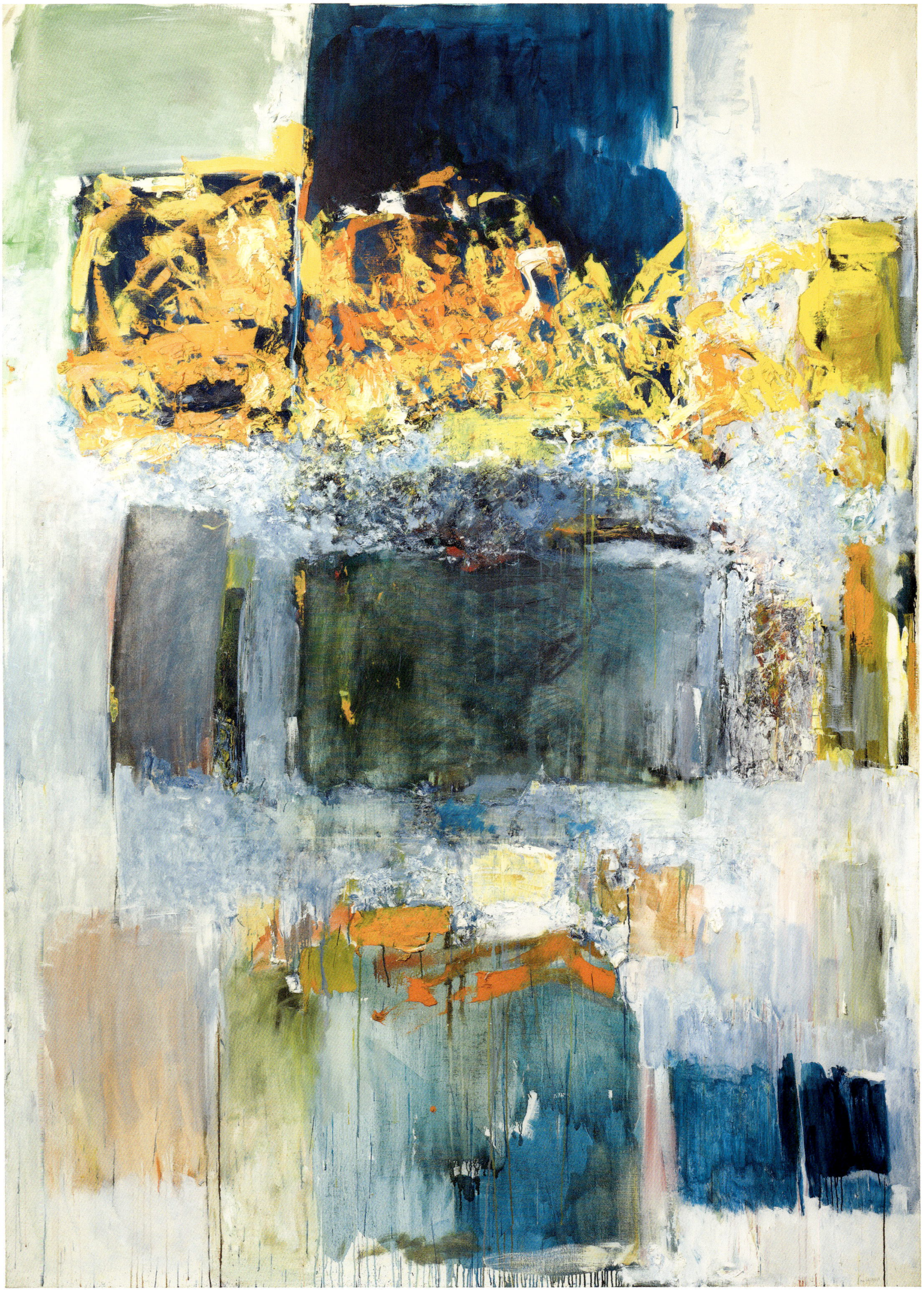

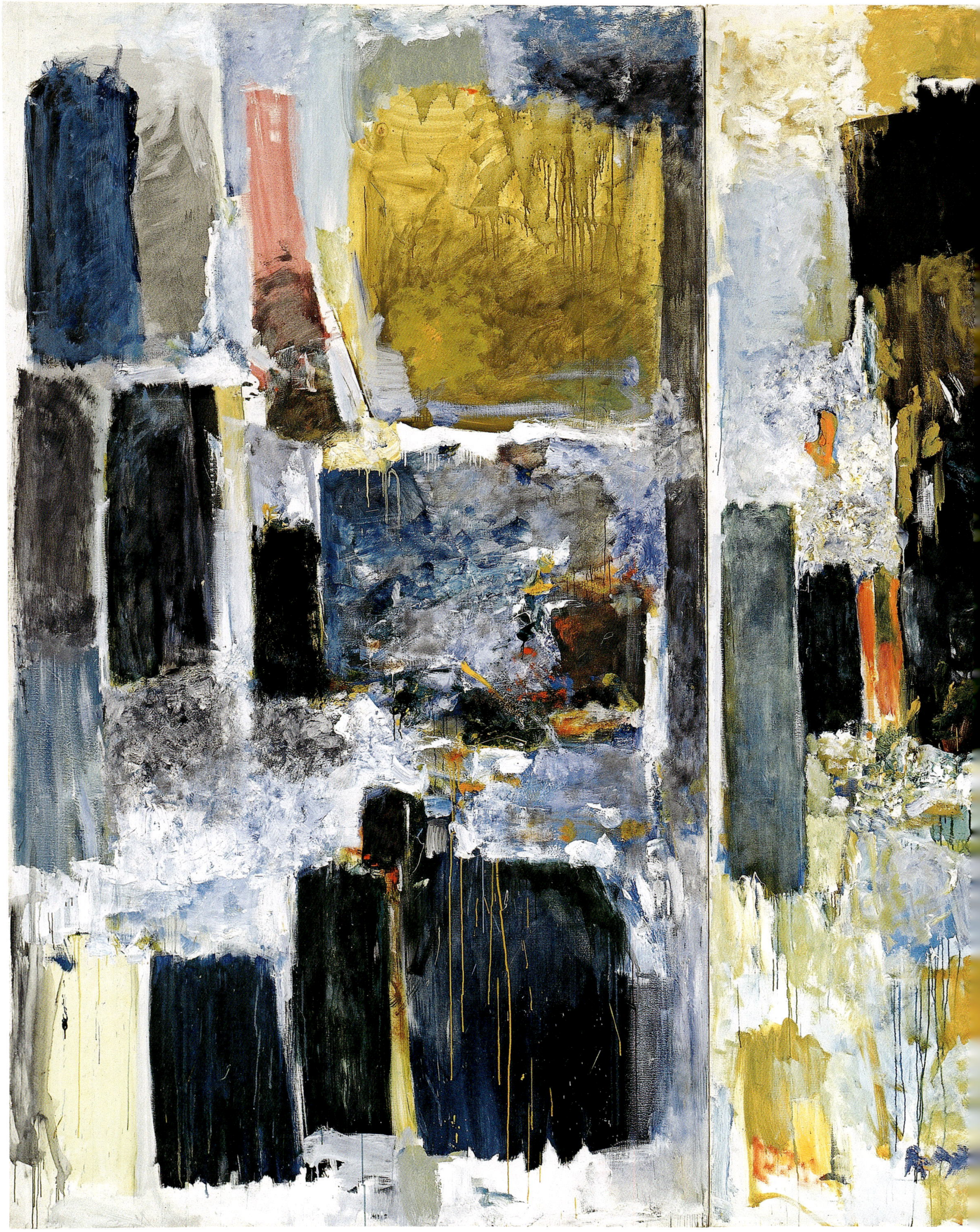

Ode to Joy (A Poem by Frank O'Hara), 1970–71. Oil on canvas, 110½ × 197¼ in. (280.7 × 501 cm). University at Buffalo Art Galleries, gift of Rebecca Anderson

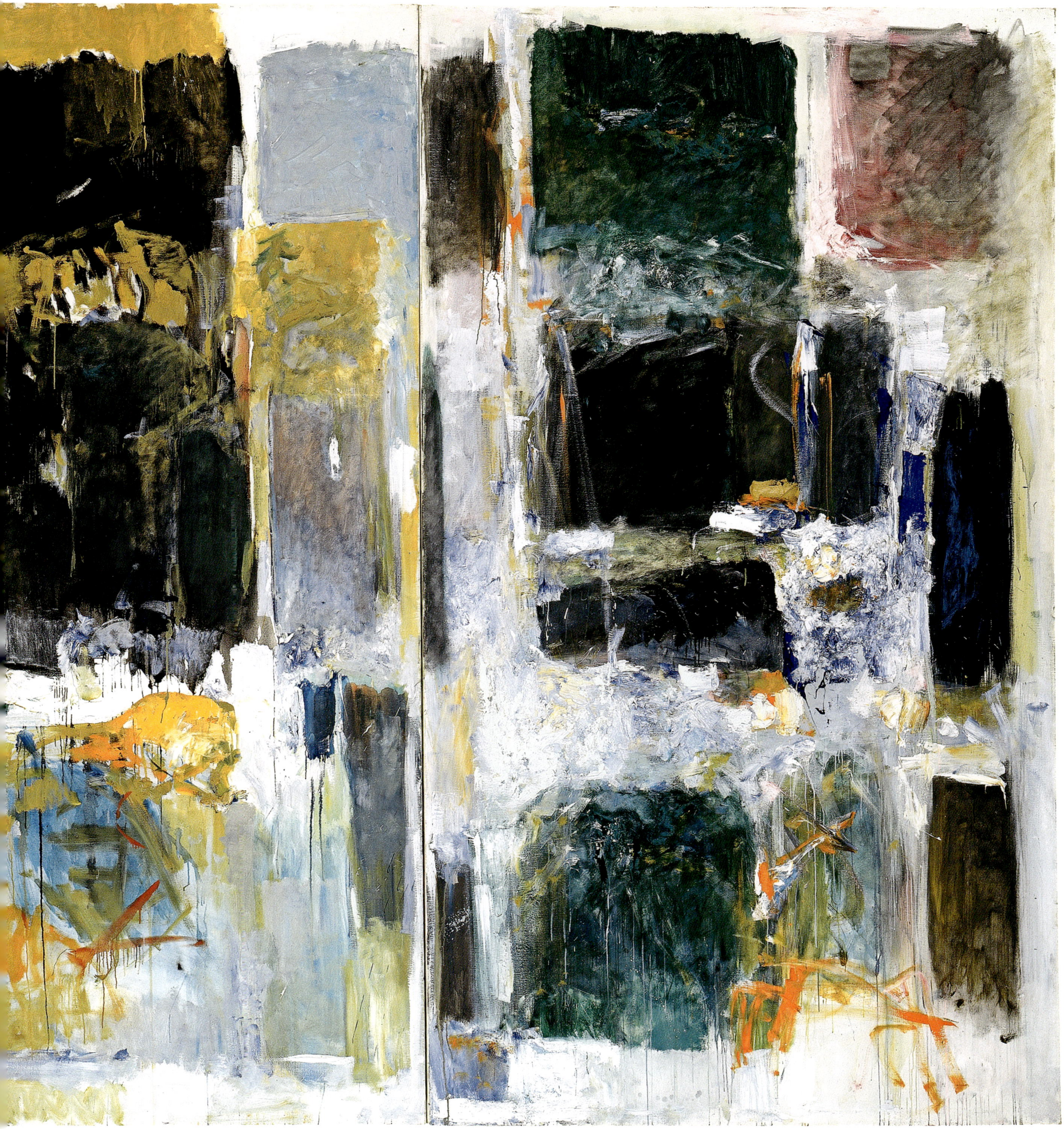

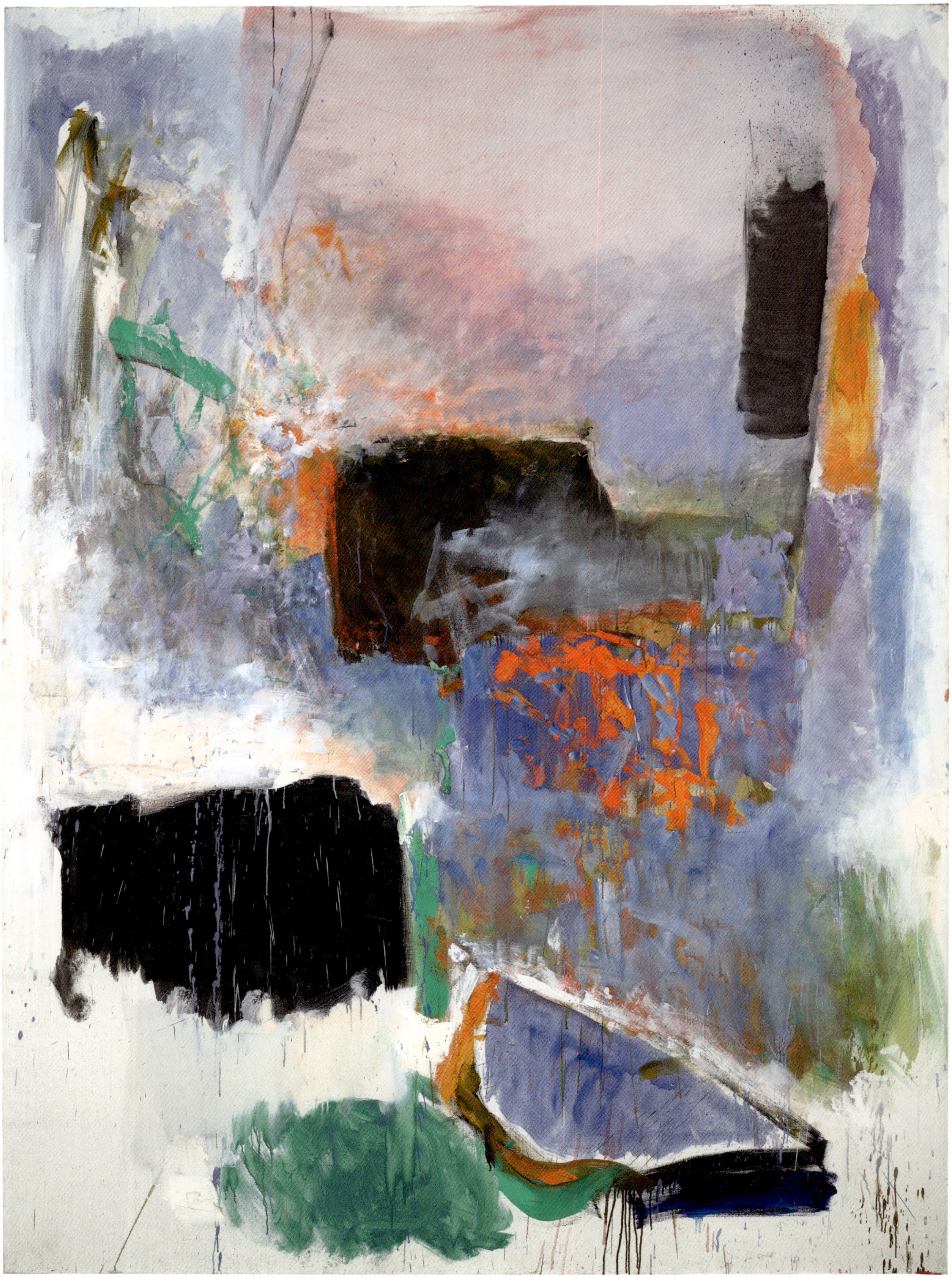

Mooring, 1971. Oil on canvas, 94½ × 70¾ in. (240 × 179.7 cm). Museum of Art, Rhode Island School of Design, Providence, gift of Bayard and Harriet K. Ewing

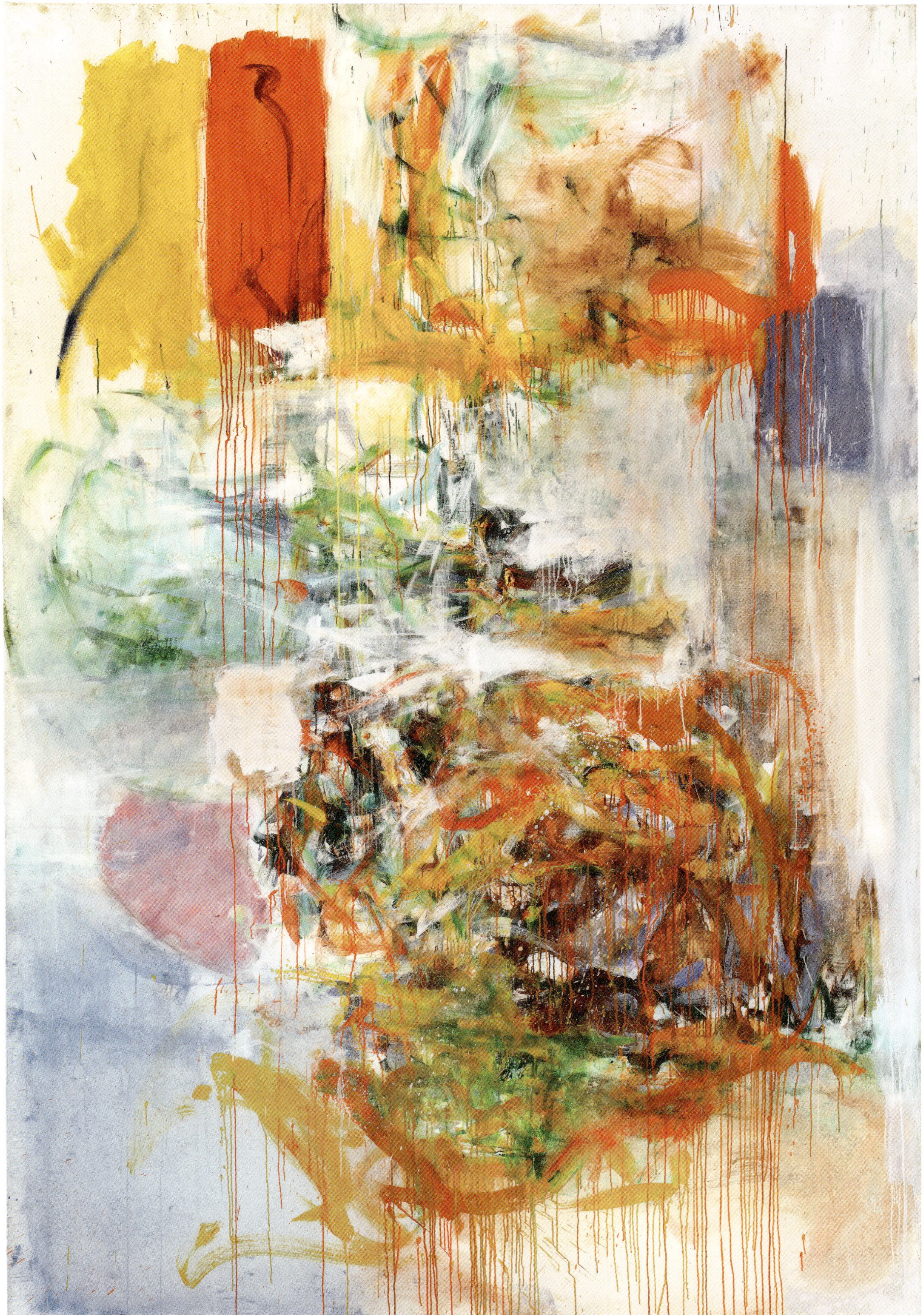

Belle Bête, 1973. Oil on canvas, 102¼ × 71 in. (259.7 × 180.3 cm). Collection of Richard and Mary Jo Kovacevich, San Francisco

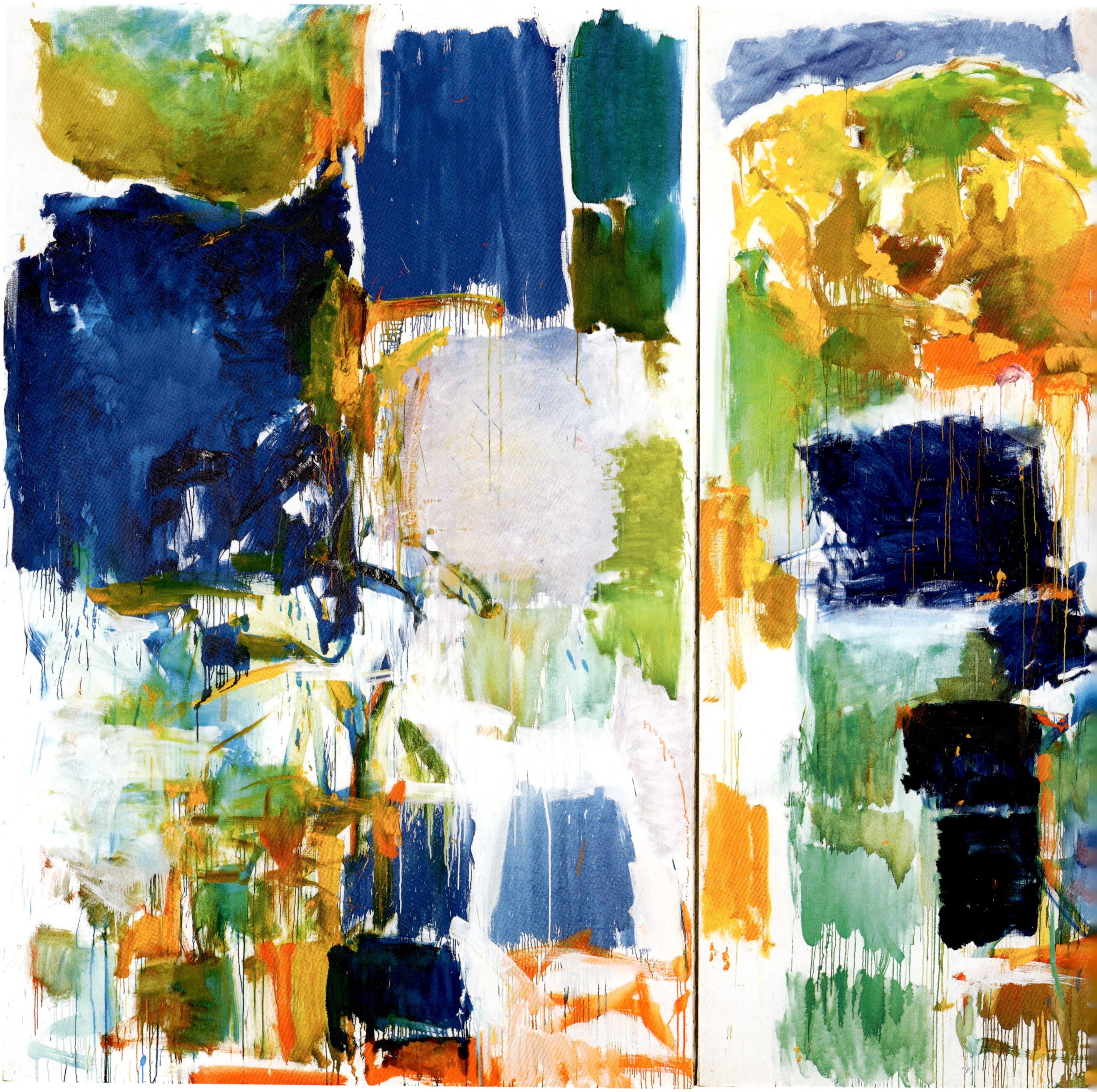

Bonjour Julie, 1971. Oil on canvas, 110½ × 230 in. (280.7 × 584.2 cm). Collection of the Art Fund, Inc. at the Birmingham Museum of Art, purchase with funds provided by the Merton Brown Estate and the Thelma Brown Trust

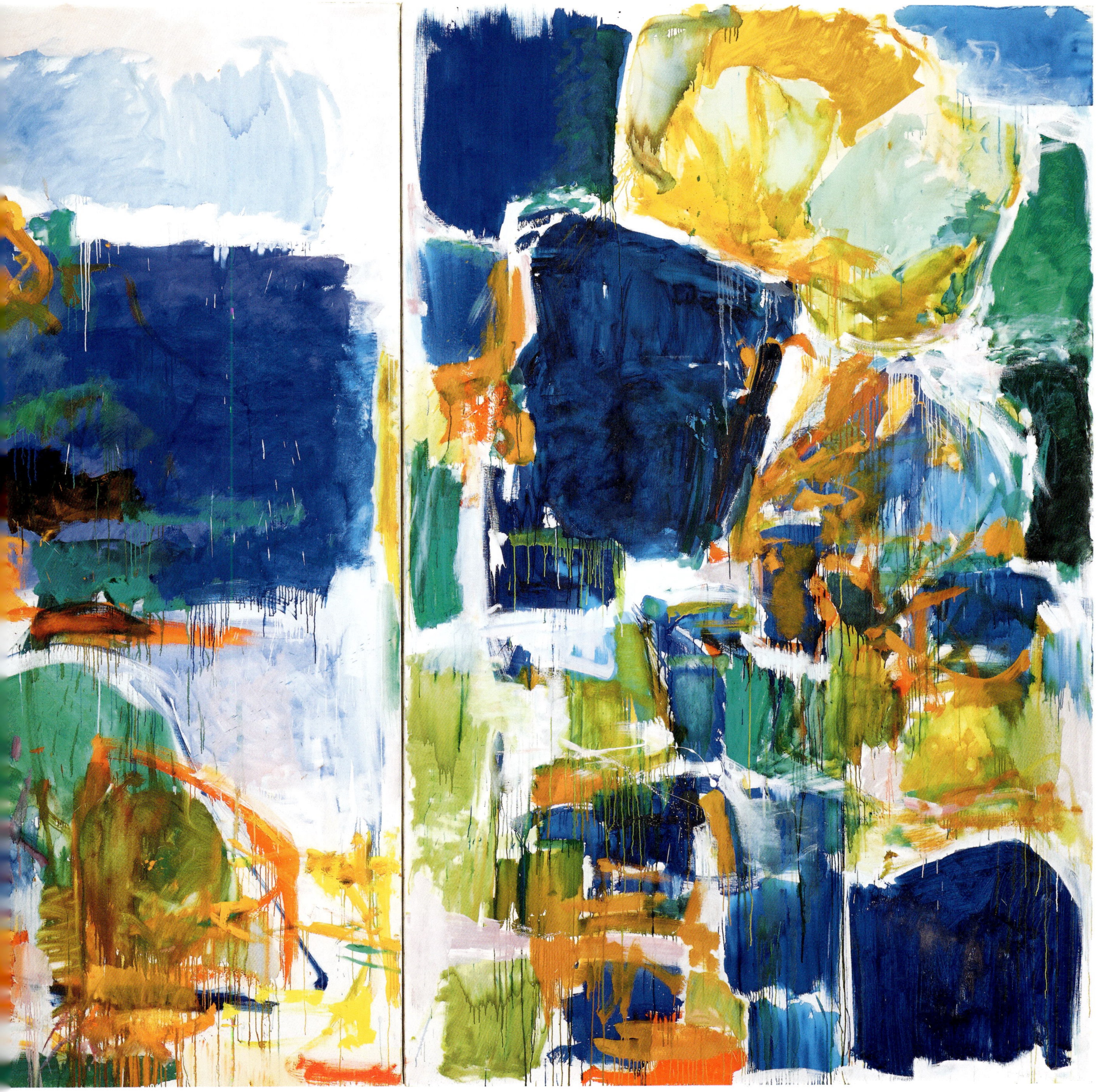

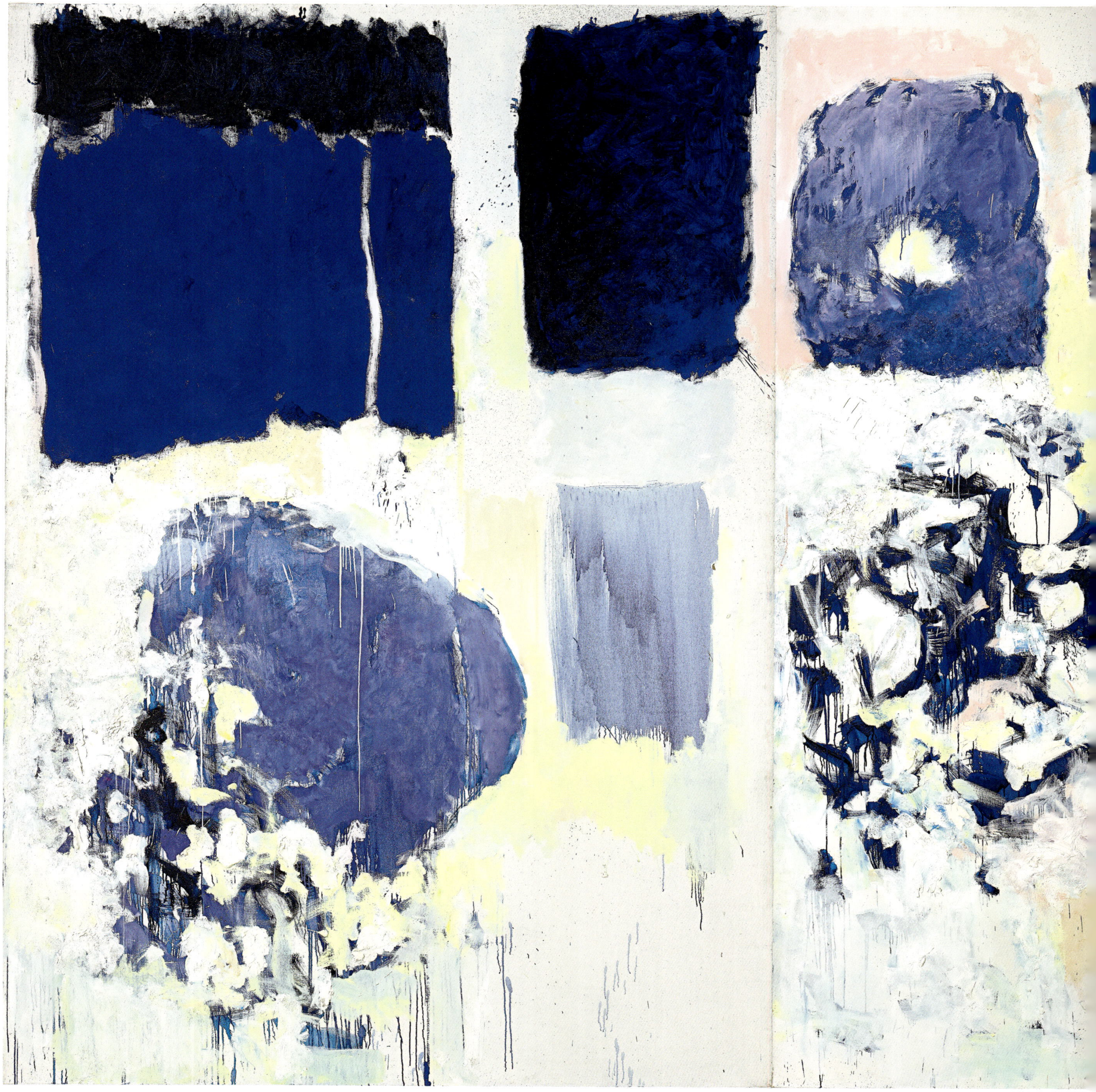

Les Bleuets, 1973. Oil on canvas, 110⅜ × 229½ in. (280.4 × 582.9 cm). Centre Pompidou, Paris, on deposit at the Musée d'Arts, Nantes, France

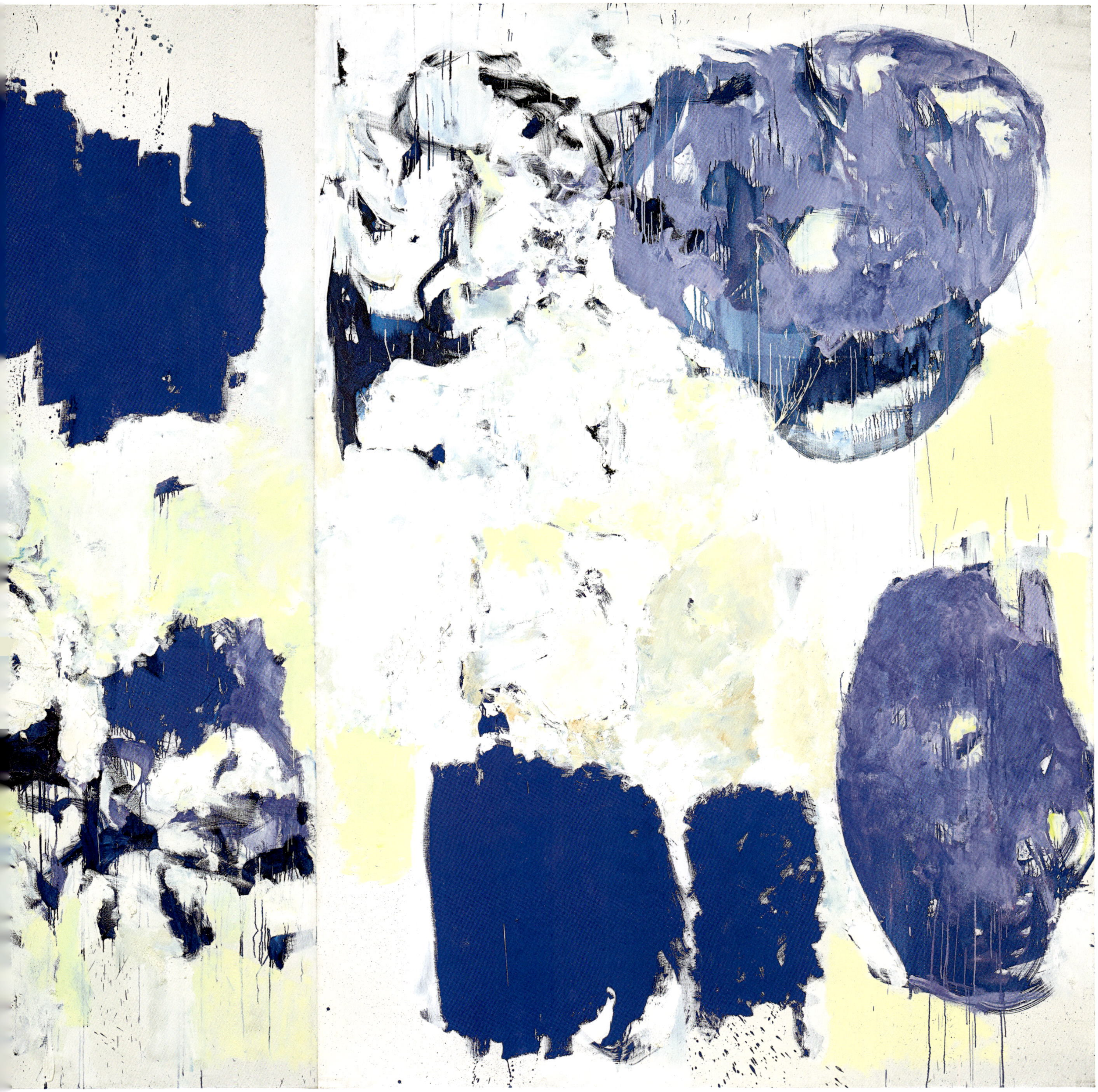

Daylight, poem pastel with James Schuyler, ca. 1975. Pastel and typewriter ink on paper, 14 × 9 in. (35.6 × 22.9 cm). Collection of Nathan Kernan

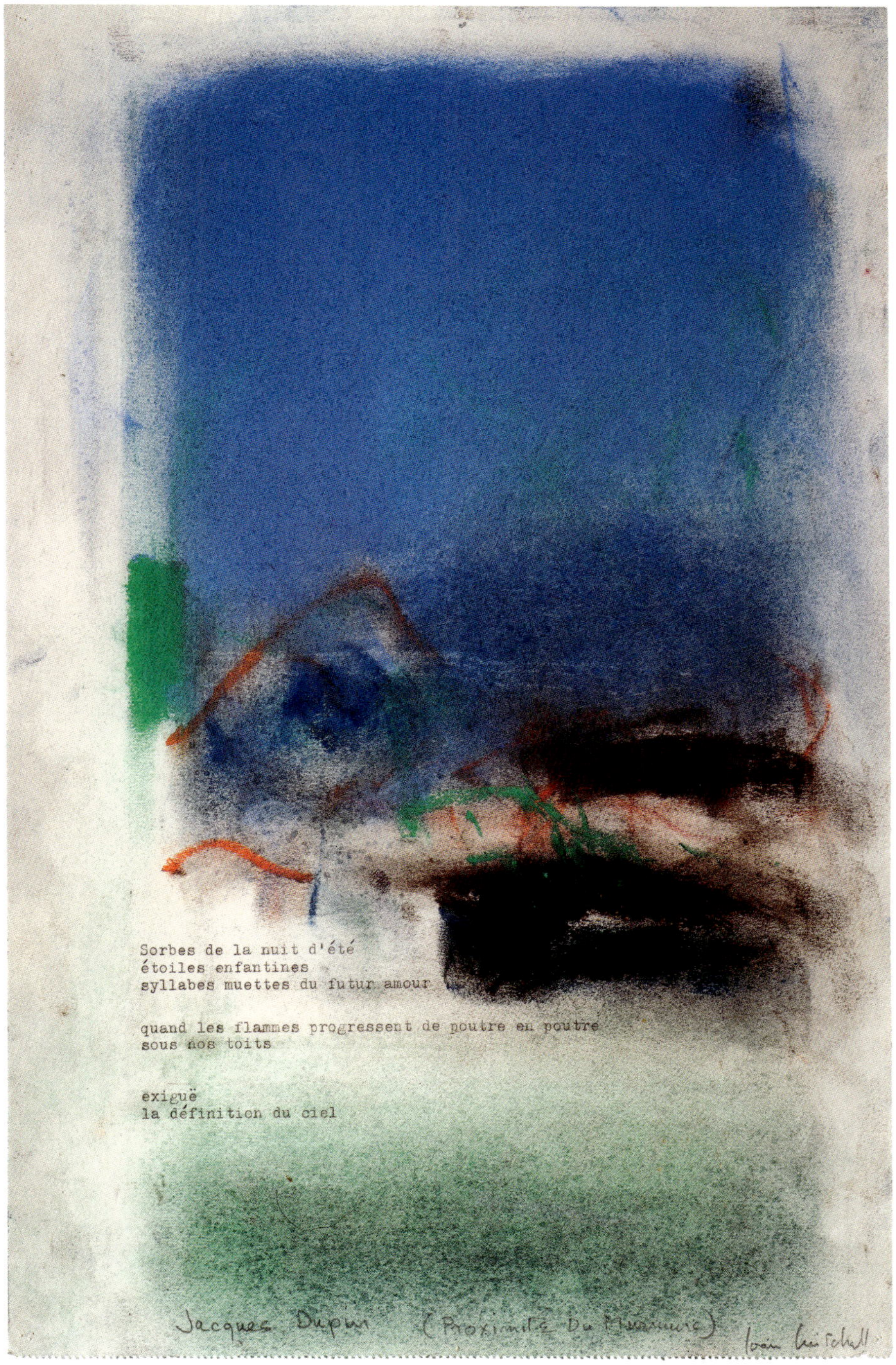

Sorbes de la nuit d'été, poem pastel with Jacques Dupin, ca. 1975. Pastel and typewriter ink on paper, 13¾ × 9⅛ in. (35 × 23 cm). Private collection

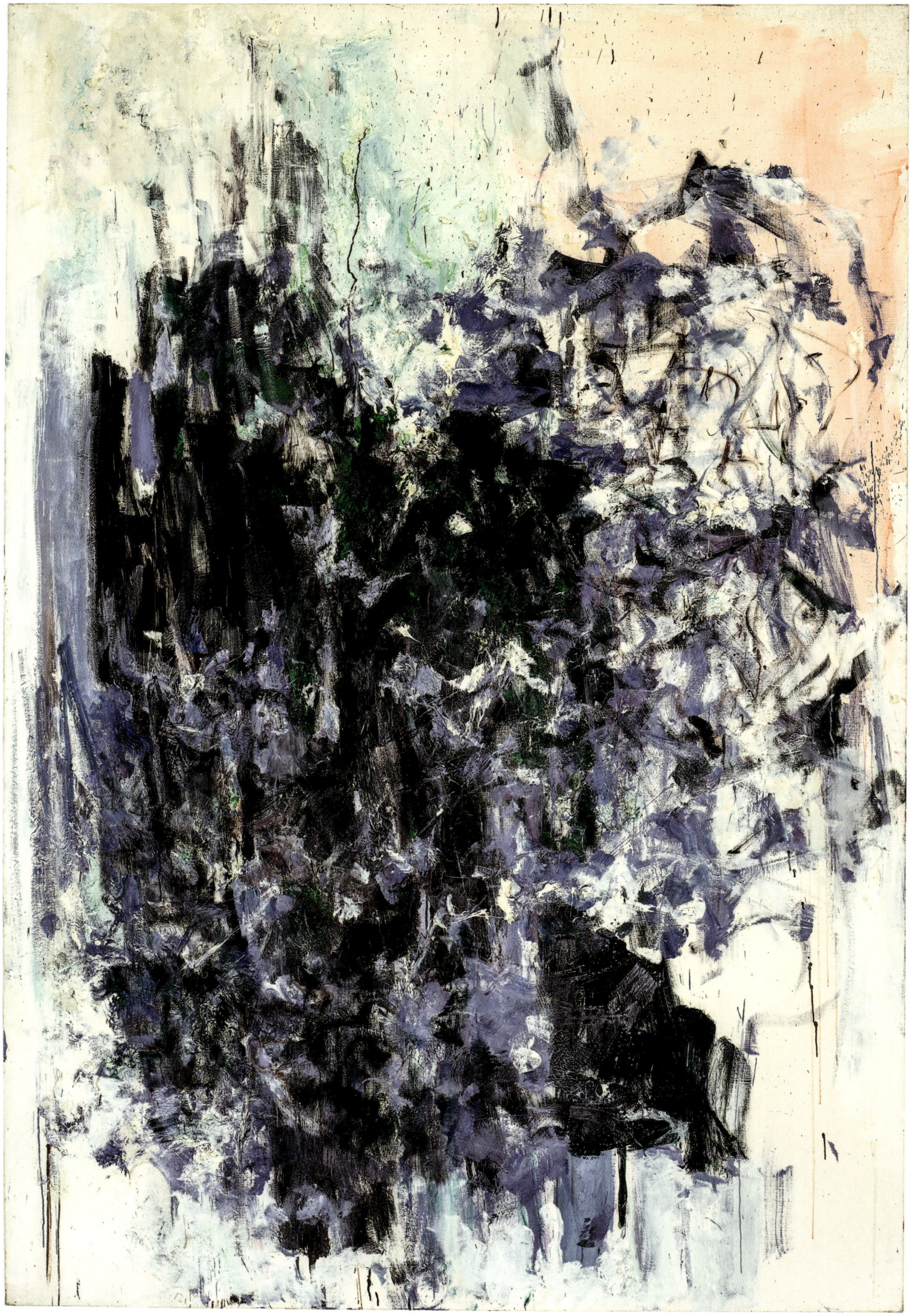

Chris's Dead Tree, 1975. Oil on canvas, 102½ × 71 in. (260.4 × 180.3 cm). Private collection

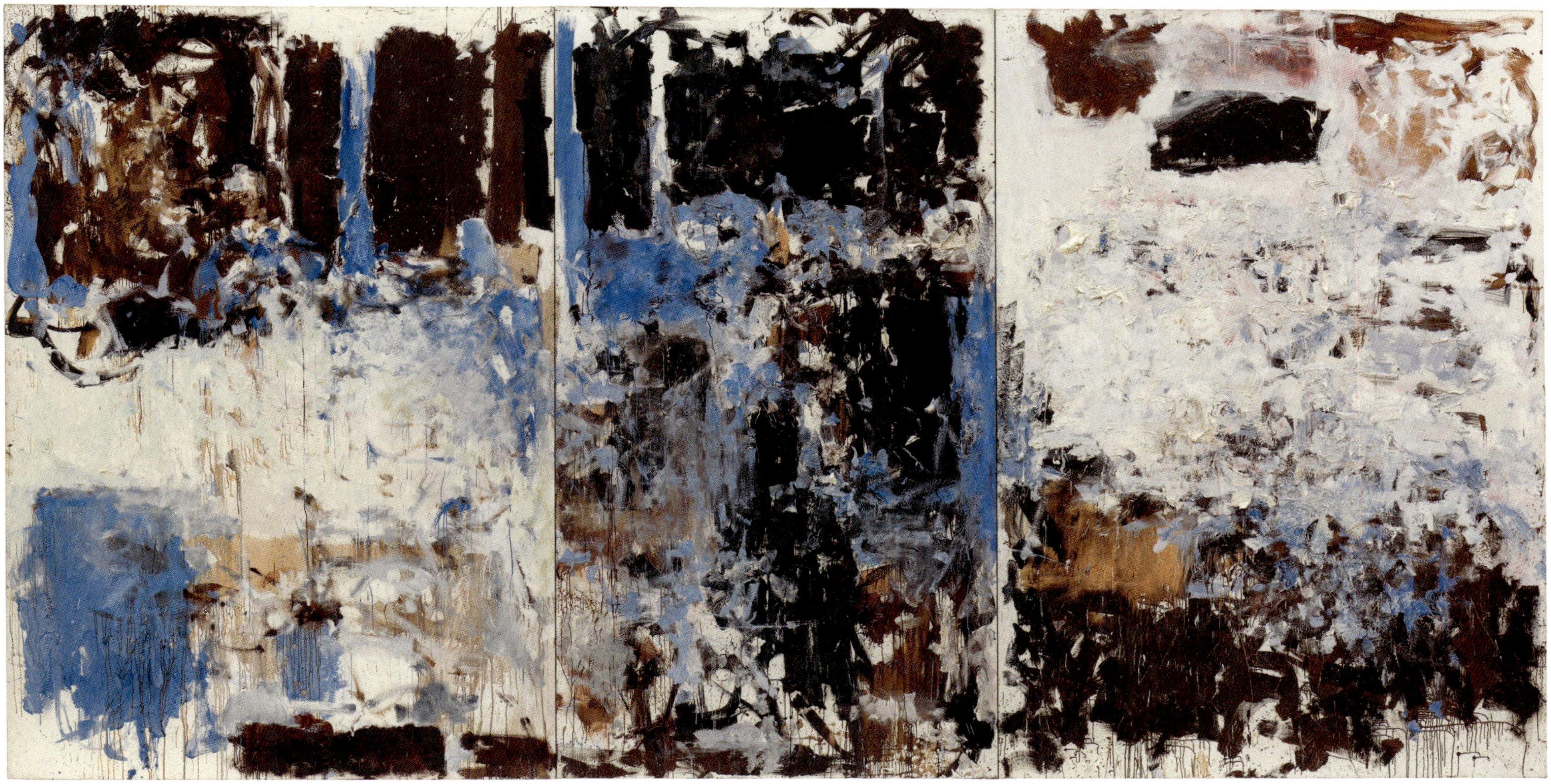

Canada I, 1975. Oil on canvas, 110½ × 220⅝ in. (280.7 × 560.4 cm). Solomon R. Guggenheim Museum, New York, anonymous gift

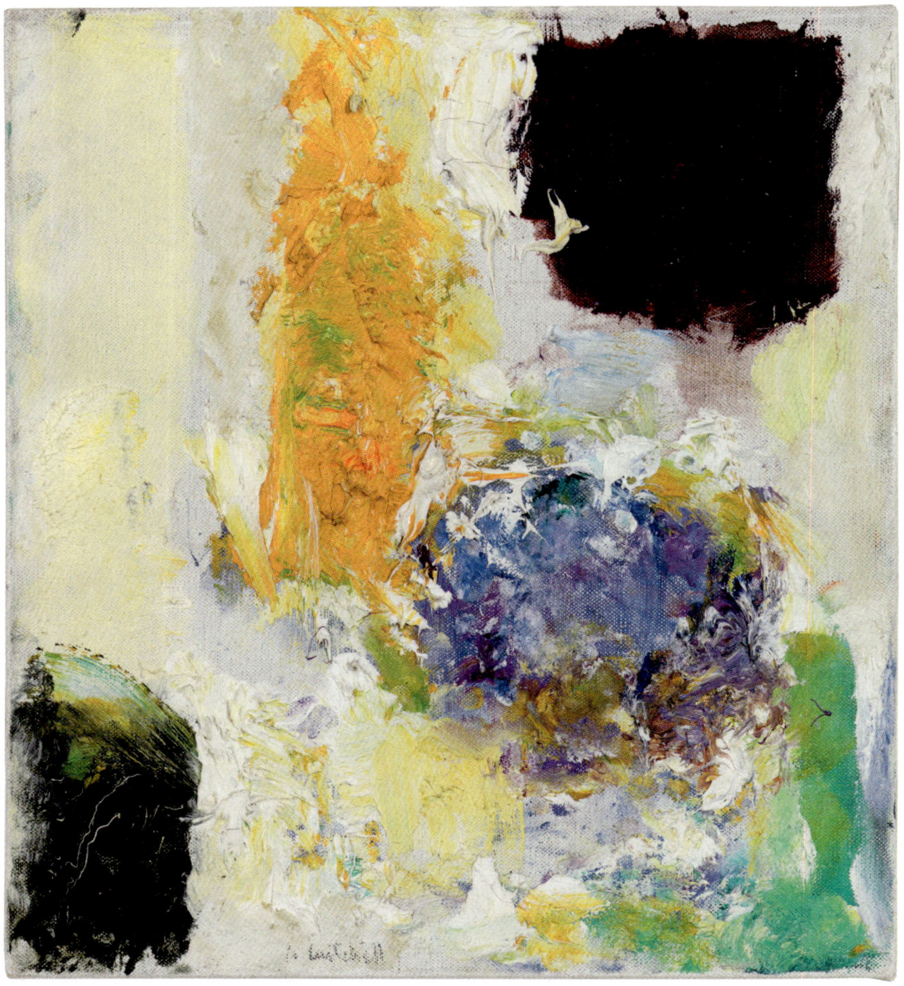

Untitled, 1973. Oil on canvas, 13¼ × 11⅞ in. (33.7 × 30.2 cm). Private collection, New York

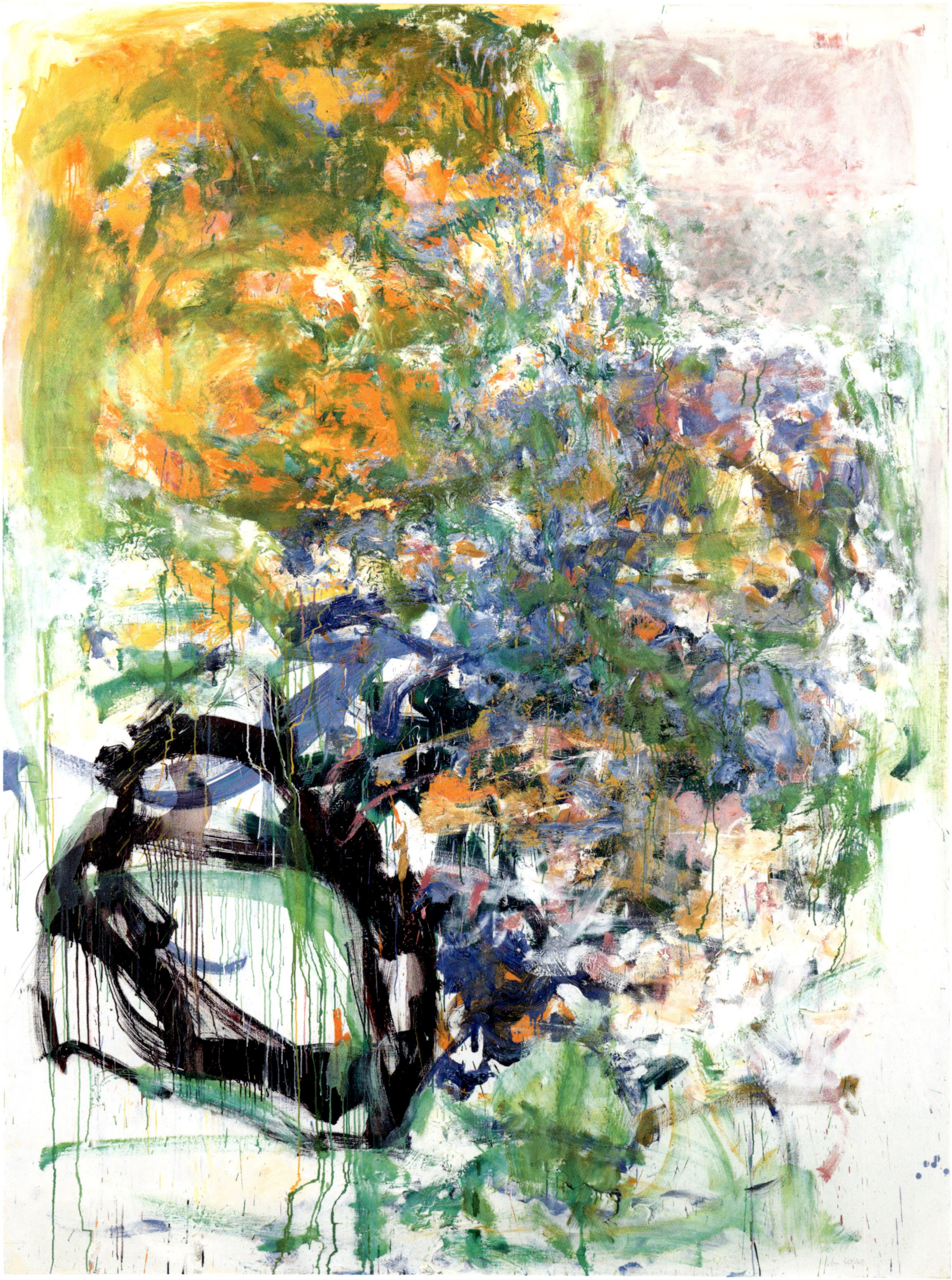

Untitled, 1975. Oil on canvas, 94½ × 71 in. (240 × 180.3 cm). Private collection, New York

“Love Is the Condition of Arriving at Infinity”:

Joan Mitchell and Poetry

Jenni Quilter

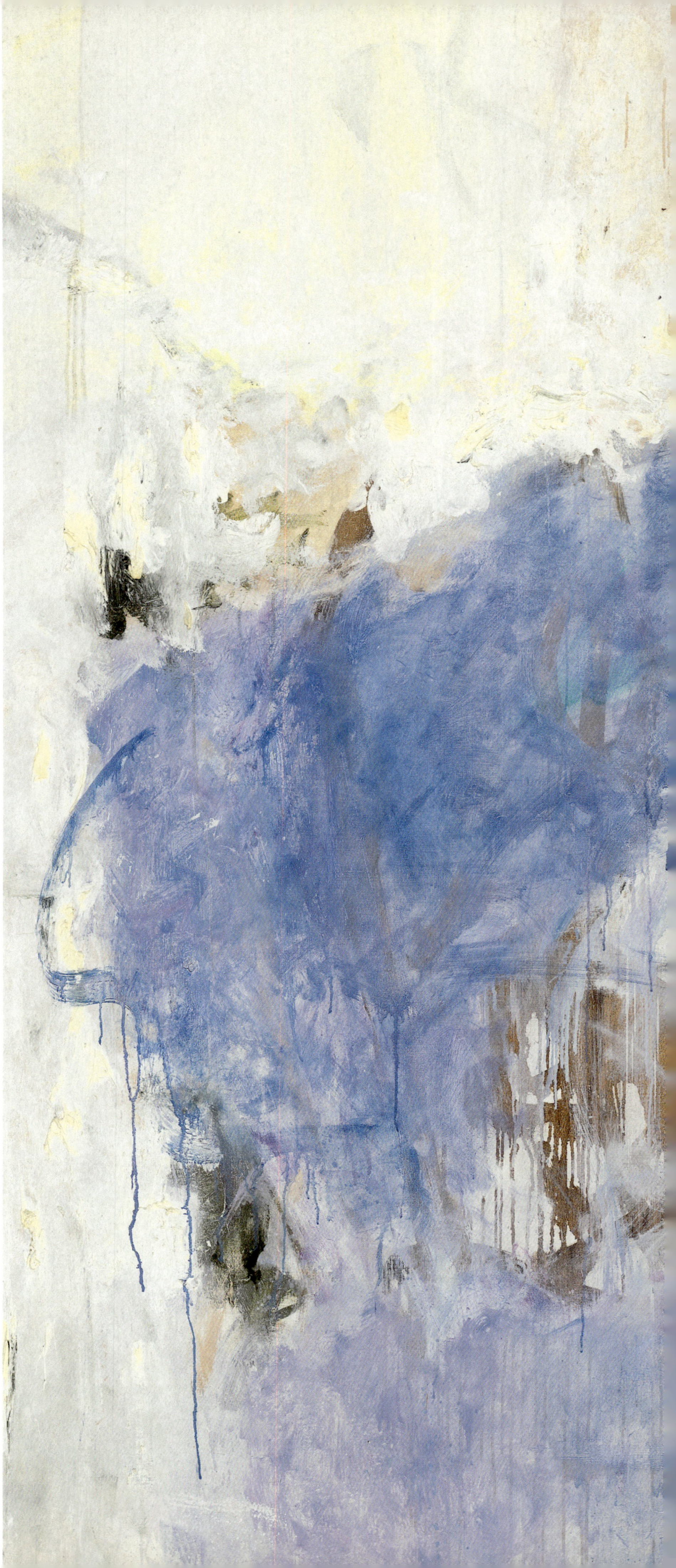

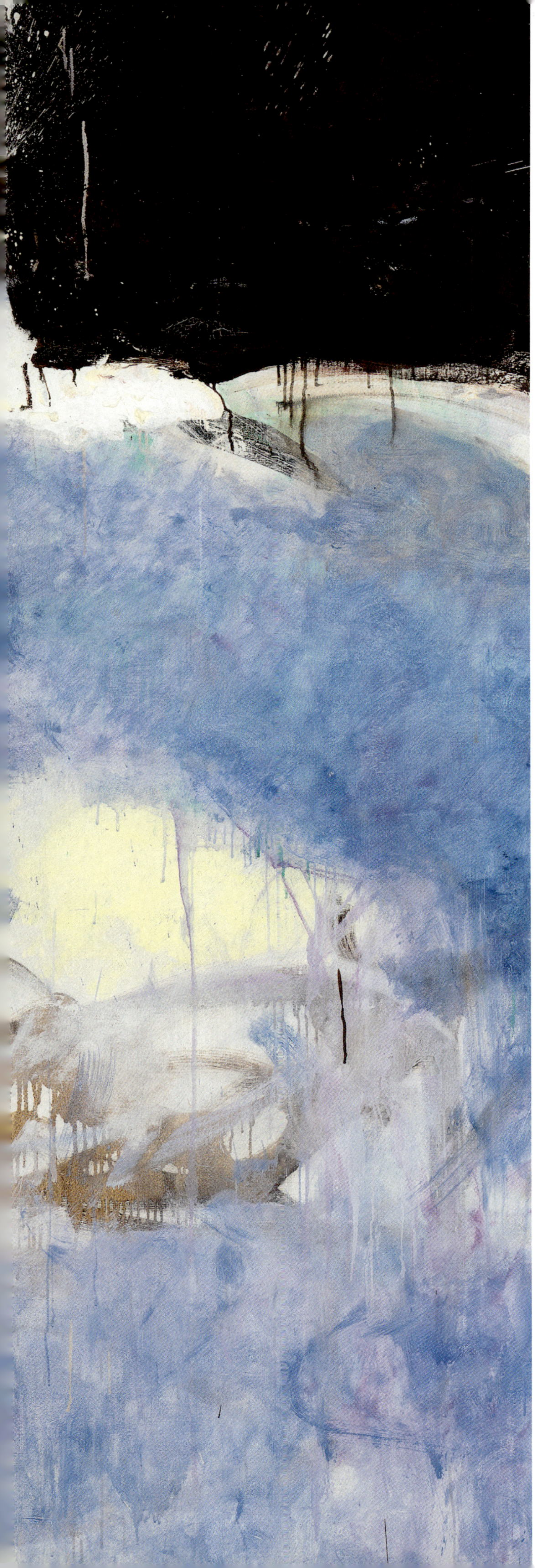

The first full monograph on Joan Mitchell was written when she was in her early sixties. In preparatory interviews with the curator Judith Bernstock, which stretched over seven days at the artist's home in Vétheuil, Mitchell time and again returned to poetry as a foundational force in her work. Indeed, the first sentence of the monograph considers the two arts as equals: "Inspired by her parents as a child growing up in Chicago, Joan Mitchell developed a love for poetry and painting." Her mother, Marion Strobel, was a notable figure among Chicago's literati, publishing poetry, novels, and reviews, and was an associate editor of *Poetry* magazine from 1920 to 1925. Mitchell grew up with poets regularly visiting the apartment on Chicago's North Side. When Mitchell wrote a precociously restrained poem at the age of nine, it seemed entirely logical that Strobel would submit it to *Poetry*'s editor, Harriet Monroe, for consideration. Mitchell could still remember the poem's last line more than half a century later, and recited it to Bernstock: "And bleakness comes through the trees without sound." She liked it, she noted, for the line's "feeling for sound and silence."[1] Strobel was partially deaf, so Mitchell associated poetry—perhaps surprisingly—with silence. For all her mother's socializing, it was the *look* of poetry on the page that moved Mitchell, as did the sight of her mother at her desk, deeply absorbed in her work.[2]

Joan Mitchell
Clearing, 1973 (detail). See fig. 2.

Beyond a few newspaper reviews at the time of publication, little critical attention has been paid to Strobel's work. She published two volumes of poetry when Mitchell was very small—*Once in a Blue Moon* (1925) and *Lost City* (1928)—both of which contained sections devoted to her children and motherhood. As the jacket to *Once in a Blue Moon* rather patronizingly put it, the poems capture "all the moods

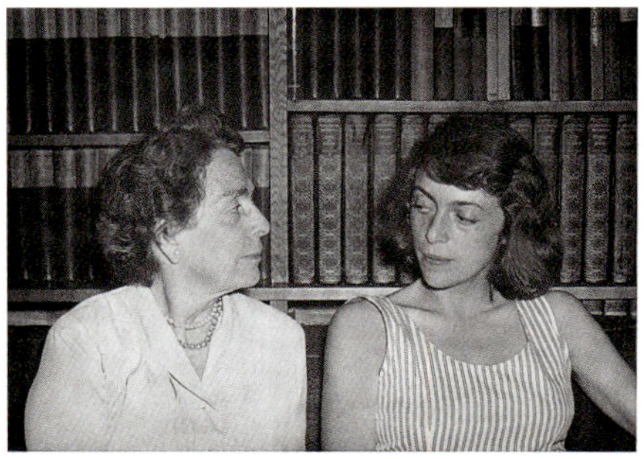

1

FIG 1 Marion Strobel and Joan Mitchell, Chicago, 1955. Joan Mitchell Foundation Archives, New York of young womanhood—moods that are in turn gay, tender, capricious, pathetic and defiant—in transparent verses that are as musical and direct as bird songs."[3] They were also lyric poems through and through: short, intensely rhyming, and often focused on an experience of love so strong that it felt like loss. Lyric was a meditation designed to evoke feeling, as opposed to the rationalizations of prose. It created a psychological interiority, a perceiving eye. Though it had been the dominant mode in the Western European tradition since Greek antiquity (suffering a slight decline in England and France in the eighteenth century but enjoying a revival in the nineteenth century with Romantic poetry), it had recently fallen out of favor, dismissed by early twentieth-century poets like William Carlos Williams as emphasizing melodious language rather than a complexity of thought.[4] The characterization was a little unfair—lyric poetry can evoke complex emotion—but lyric does often rely on a sentimentality that confirms rather than extends the reader's emotional vocabulary. While Strobel was quick to sense this sentimentality as an editor, traces of it appear in her poetry. For example, the last poem of *Lost City,* "A Cloak for Joan," turns on a series of self-abnegations. The speaker gifts the child a beautiful cloak and almost immediately anticipates her throwing it away. The protection she has to offer—even the words in the poem—will not hold the child, and the speaker cannot do anything other than end with a facile compliment: the fabric looks "pretty with your hair."[5]

Within lyric poetry, this attentiveness to the queasy pleasures of diminishment was (and is) nothing unusual; as Laura Quinney has pointed out, "a disproportionate number of lyric and meditative poems concern disappointment—not just those that address individual disappointments, as for example, disappointments in love, but those that plumb the generalized, chronic condition."[6] Critiquing Strobel's poetry, one could argue that the leap from the individual to the generalized sometimes falters in her verse, remaining within a very particular understanding of love (well-to-do, heteronormative, feminized) that assumes it is more universal than it is. The same criticism could be made of Strobel's novels, which all deal with the private scandals of women of means on Chicago's North Side—namely, with whom they fall in love, and what they decide to do about it.[7] A character at the climax of *Fellow Mortals* (1935) claims, "Every woman's intent is love"—and is not corrected.[8]

Mitchell's allegiance to lyric poetry was not to her mother's writing but to the promises lyric poetry made as a genre about the self in relation to the world. Lyric poetry was a way to think and access grand ideas, unrepentant in their scale: a love that stretched outward, to encompass nature and the infinite. In her final term paper on the Romantics at Smith College, Mitchell sliced and diced her way through the pantheon of nineteenth-century greats (Percy Bysshe Shelley, Thomas Carlyle, Charles Lamb, Thomas De Quincey, William Hazlitt, Lord Byron, John Keats, and even Charles Dickens), categorizing each of their stances on transcendentalism ("whether the source of faith be in the mind or sense") with a series of confident, though somewhat impenetrable, declarations. She treated them as philosophers rather than poets, noting their position, but paying little attention to the formal qualities of their poetry. Yet out of nowhere, toward the end of her second paragraph in the essay, she offered a seeming non sequitur: "Love is the condition of arriving at infinity."[9]

The sentence is out of place in Mitchell's essay, flashing out from the page like a lighthouse on a distant point—there is no call for it in the context of what she is actually discussing—but it is entirely at home in the context of Mitchell's painting career. Her paintings are often engulfing in scale and color and texture; they stretch utterance in the way that poetry stretches past prose, elliptically harnessing the world. Poetry contained a fullness of thought that resisted explanation, and which accessed emotion more directly than prose. To Irving Sandler, she noted that the feelings she strove to express in her painting were "the qualities that differentiate a line of poetry from a line of prose."[10] To Bernstock, Mitchell said that she had never looked for *a* meaning in a poem: "It seemed perfectly clear. If it's not spelled out, it doesn't matter. That's how I feel about my painting."[11] In lyric poetry, absolutes are often treated like directions without limit: an arrow flying, never hitting. Rainer Maria Rilke, who was one of Mitchell's favorite poets, is a particularly good example; in his poems, even his memories appear to stand outside time, charged with the platonic potential of each object. He is interested in transformation rather than causality.[12] Mitchell's paintings also aimed at revelation rather than just realization, a swiftness of comprehension. She paid close attention to how lyric poets charted the paradoxes of intuition, of knowledge lagging, then leaping. William Wordsworth defined poetry as "the spontaneous overflow of powerful feelings: it takes its origin from emotion recollected in tranquility."[13] Comfortable with the quiet contradictions undergirding this definition (Spontaneity *and* reflection? Overflow *and* tranquility?), Mitchell hewed close to these terms when describing the subjects of her own painting. Her often-quoted remark that she painted from "remembered landscapes that I carry with me—and remembered feelings of them, which of course become transformed" is remarkably precise in echoing Wordsworth, even though the comment was made more than a decade after she had graduated college.[14]

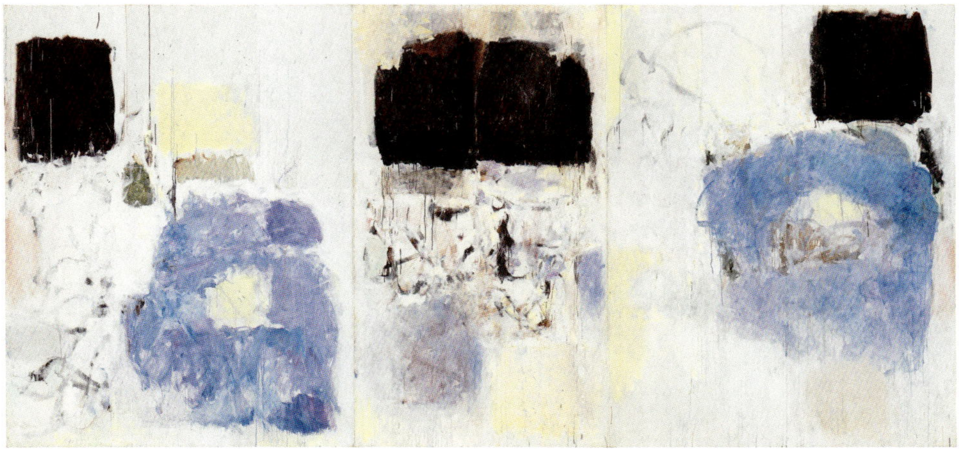

2

FIG 2 **Joan Mitchell**
Clearing, 1973. Oil on linen, 110¼ × 236 in. (280 × 599.4 cm). Whitney Museum of American Art, New York, purchase, with funds from Susan Morse Hilles in honor of John I. H. Baur

By the time Bernstock visited Mitchell in Vétheuil, it is obvious that Mitchell *had* absorbed certain formal elements of poetry—namely, the genre's ability to move rather than persuade. The space that poetry often gives to words encourages the reader to consider them more closely. Shades of pause (line breaks, indents, stanza breaks) make us better interpreters of what is generally understood as silence. White space both slows and speeds up the reader, and so the constant gauging of distance and intimacy is more pronounced. It seems no accident that Mitchell used white paint as distinctively as she did, creating space and light in ways comparable to a poet's positioning of a line break. (*Hemlock* [1956, plate 24], named after "Domination of Black" by Wallace Stevens, is a particularly good and early example of this.) As she noted, painting was a process of perception, the continual observation of the relationships emerging on the picture plane: "The way to do it is relationship, relationship."[15] Multipanel works like *Clearing* (fig. 2) or *Ode to Joy (A Poem by Frank O'Hara)* (1970–71, plate 75) could even be paintings of poems about landscapes rather than paintings of landscapes. The panels operate like pages; within each, a series of rectangular or square blocks of color echo one another just as verses do in an open book of poetry held at a distance, the verses aligning and drifting away from one another.

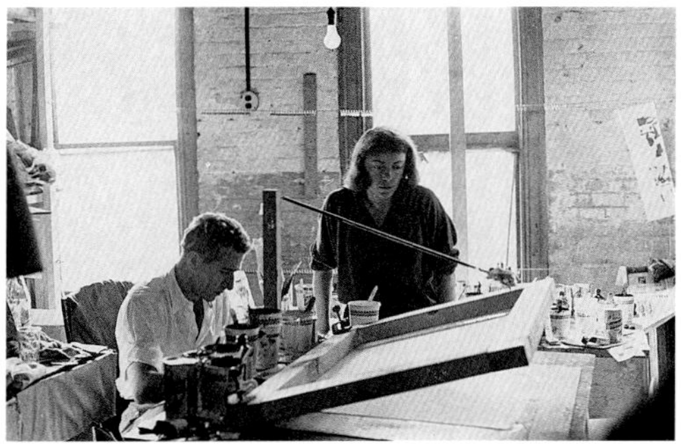

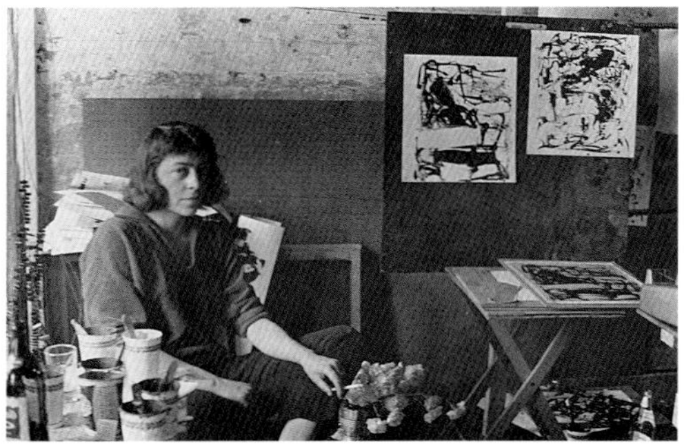

3

These formal echoes are slight, and it is easy to overinterpret them. To those who know Mitchell mainly for her time in New York in the 1950s, when she was part of a sprawling social circle centered around the downtown abstract art world, it might come as a surprise that Bernstock's catalogue devotes limited attention to this period. Mitchell emphasized the painters she encountered (Jackson Pollock, Willem de Kooning, Franz Kline, Arshile Gorky) and her membership in The Club (launched by a number of first-generation abstractionists in 1948), and she noted her association with other female painters around her age, like Grace Hartigan and Helen Frankenthaler. However, Mitchell obviously did not consider the title "second-generation Abstract Expressionist" to be particularly meaningful, nor did she reflect on the collaborative esprit de corps that characterized the scene.

Most New York painters and poets agreed with Baudelaire's maxim that various art forms might "lend one another new energies," and one of the first organized discussions at The Club concerned the relationship between painting and poetry. (Other panel topics that year included the relationship between art and architecture and the painter as editor.) It was expected that an artist be well-read in areas other than visual art. Given Mitchell's upbringing, this would have suited her just fine, but she did not see the need to speculate on what the arts gave each other. To Bernstock, she did not emphasize her collaboration with John Ashbery for *The Poems,* one of four limited-edition books issued by the Tiber Press.[16] These were large, self-consciously beautiful objects, typeset by hand and printed on fine paper, and obviously recalled the tradition of European *livres d'artistes,* making a case for a shared set of sensibilities between artists and poets. The painter Fairfield Porter, reviewing all four books for *Art News,* thought the most successful collaboration was Ashbery and Mitchell's, commenting, "she seems to treat her poet with sensitive understanding and respect. They are both abstract, and her graphic illustrations combine into page designs in which the illustration looks like writing, with Ashbery's lightness of touch."[17] Mitchell would have likely shared Porter's skepticism of a collaborative rationale that considered one art form as reducible or directly proportionate to another. Elsewhere, Porter wrote dismissively of Wyndham Lewis's writing on Pablo Picasso, observing that Lewis "looks at paintings through the spectacles of words and without those spectacles would be blind. He does not know the difference between the pictures and his talk about them."[18] A distinction between forms had to be preserved and respected; without this distinction, any emotion would be flattened, turned into an archetypal paste of creativity that connected artworks by equalizing them. It was significant that Porter noticed—and praised—the ways in which Mitchell respected the self-sufficiency of Ashbery's verse.

Mitchell also did not recall to Bernstock her collaborative discussion with Frank O'Hara, Elaine de Kooning, Norman Bluhm, and Michael Goldberg, which was recorded over three nights, condensed, and published as "5 Participants in a Hearsay Panel" in *It Is* (1959). This purported transcript of comments made during an evening at The Club began:

> JOAN: We'll open with a question. Is style hearsay?
>
> FRANK: Well, Pavia says, nowadays everyone talks about you behind your back in front of your face.
>
> ELAINE: Yes, Philip Guston told Andrew Wyeth that Louis B. Mayer told John Huston: Well, if you don't like it here, go back to Greenwich Village and starve on a hundred dollars a week.[19]

The obvious joke was that everyone was always quoting someone else. In this emergent scene, a slippery triangulation of authority emerged from aestheticizing gossip. But in the text, Mitchell's presence was limited: her comments were brief, and often referee-like (for example, "Now, possibly, the panel will discuss the question of craftsmanship"). The social scene in New York caused Mitchell a great deal of anxiety, and she later observed that her relationship with the art world "is distant, and occurs mainly through individuals"—no triangulation necessary.[20] It was probably her close friendship with O'Hara that prompted Mitchell's participation in "5 Participants."

As the artist Larry Rivers noted at O'Hara's funeral in 1966, "There are at least sixty people in New York who thought Frank O'Hara was their best friend."[21] Reading O'Hara's letters to Mitchell, you can see why. He had a wonderful habit of imagining—in type—what the other was thinking, conducting a conversation on the page well in advance of the reader. This habit of imaginative projection structured his poetry, which made no bones about its epistolic roots. In 1959, for example, he began a letter to Mitchell by noting that he had just come from lunch with Bluhm—and with it, he included a poem ("Adieu to Norman, Bon Jour to Joan and Jean-Paul") that had obviously been written just *before* lunch with Bluhm.[22] Both letter and poem began by covering the same ground: O'Hara's forthcoming weekend trip to Southampton, the book of poems he was working on (and how helpful Mitchell's studio on St. Mark's Place had been in providing some peace and quiet). In his letter to Mitchell, he imagined her days in Paris, and in the poem, he also wished he were "reeling around Paris/ instead of reeling around New York." As he noted in his looping cursive at the top of the page, both poem and letter were written under the cloud of a hangover. It was an extraordinary performance. To be invited, so swiftly and gracefully, onto the stage of another's art making—to witness his regard for her settle into a poem—must have been just as beguiling to Mitchell as it was to the numerous others that O'Hara mentioned in his poetry.

O'Hara is best known for his "I do this, I do that" poems, which (at least in their beginnings) recall the artist Joe Brainard's description of O'Hara's walk: "Light and sassy. With a slight twist and a slight bounce. It was a beautiful walk. Confident. 'I don't care,' and sometimes, 'I know you are looking.'"[23] Yet O'Hara's eye for exhilaration made it easy to overlook the elegiac undertows in his poetry—but Mitchell, raised on a diet of lyric poetry, would have noticed. Consider "Poem Read at Joan Mitchell's" (1957), written for a celebration of Jane Freilicher and Joe Hazan's marriage at Mitchell's. Midway through the poem, O'Hara pauses, considers the avalanche of details he began with, the coordinates of that moment in time and space (the date, the time, even the weather), then shifts tone: "This poem goes on too long because our friendship has been long. . . . / and I

FIG 3 Top: Michael Goldberg and Joan Mitchell. Bottom: Joan Mitchell, Tiber Press, New York, ca. 1958. The Miriam and Ira D. Wallach Division of Art, Prints, and Photographs, New York Public Library, The Walter Silver Collection, gift of George and Carole Silver, 2000

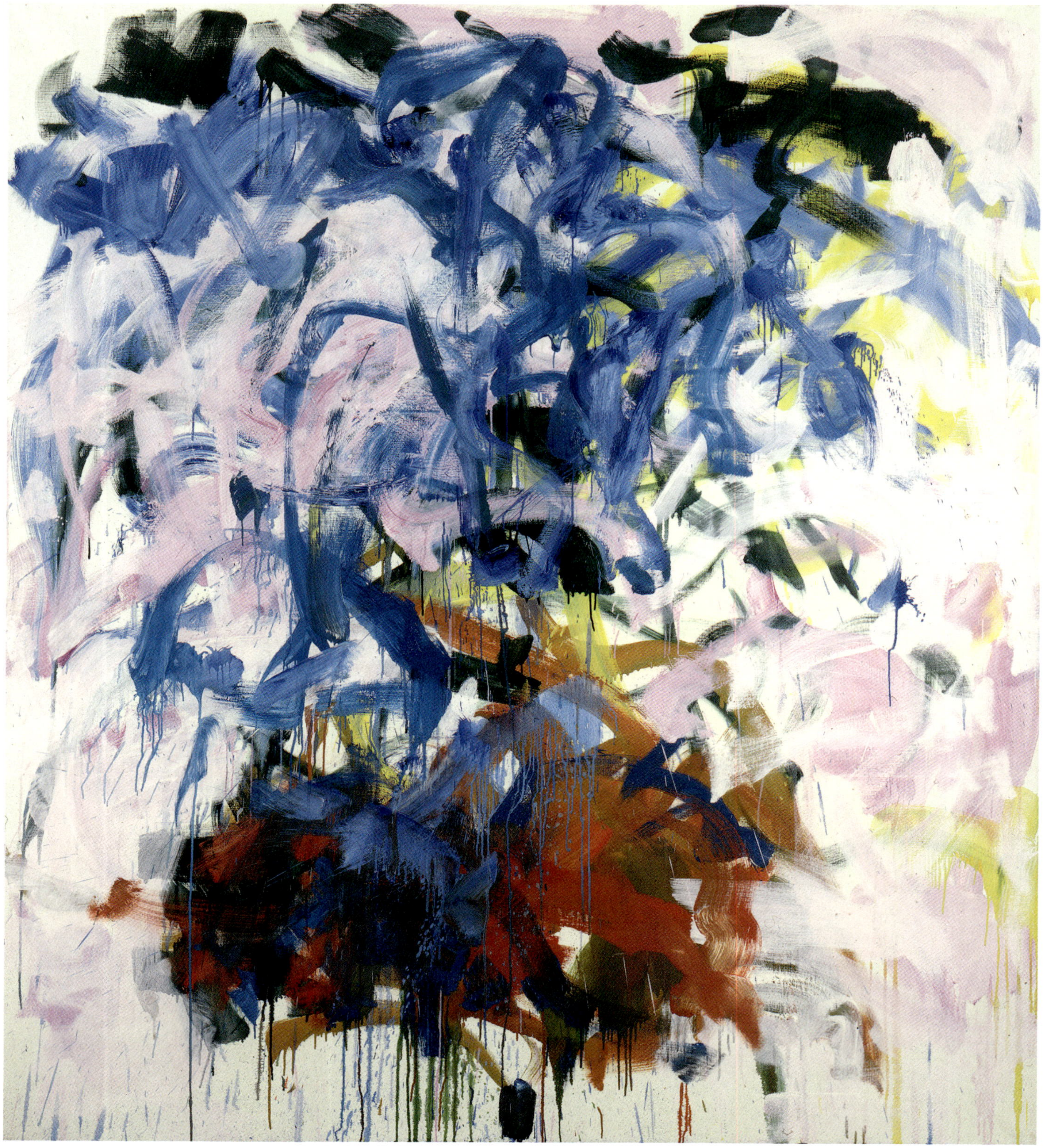

4

would make it as long as I hope our friendship lasts if I could make poems that long." It is an impossible wish—for both friendship and poetry—and he knows it. The most he can hope for is that Freilicher and Hazan's happiness is a "sign that we will be happy too."[24] Similarly, the climax of "Adieu to Norman, Bon Jour to Joan and Jean-Paul" (1964) also operates as a charm to ward off loss: "the only thing to do is simply continue/ is that simple/ yes, it is simple because it is the only thing to do." But O'Hara does not end here. The last stanza is a list of all things that O'Hara, on faith, assumes are continuing: in Paris, "the Seine continues," "the Bar Américain continues to be French," and "Jane Hazan continues to be Jane Freilicher (I think!)." He asks fellow poets "René Char, Pierre Reverdy, Samuel Beckett it is possible isn't it." (He had met Beckett while visiting Mitchell and Ashbery in Paris the year before.) The final line concludes: "I love Reverdy for saying yes, though I don't believe it."[25] The poem is so celebratory that it is easy to overlook O'Hara's refusal, tucked in at the very end.

In an optimistic reading of the disappointments recounted in lyric poetry, one may lose the girl or the boy or one's self-regard, but that loss is compensated by new self-knowledge.[26] O'Hara hewed to this trade-off, or at the very least, to the sense that there was a set of scales to be balanced. Less so did Ashbery, which is perhaps why Mitchell never thoroughly warmed to his poetry, even though they overlapped for almost a decade in Paris, from 1955 to 1965, when they lunched together almost weekly, and although Ashbery sensitively reviewed her work for *Art News*. In his poetry, Ashbery persistently thwarts the reader's expectations of an easily legible emotional arc resolving then questioning, admitting then sidestepping; in general, he was a little suspicious of the swift or singular grace of revelation.[27] On a visit to Paris with O'Hara in 1961, the poet Bill Berkson recalled Mitchell reading the page proofs of Ashbery's experimental long poem "Europe" and remarking, "God! How I worked over that poem!" To her, it was about the "death of culture."[28] More than twenty years later, Mitchell directed Berkson to "early, lyrical" poems of Ashbery's for them to discuss.[29]

FIG 4 **Joan Mitchell**
A Few Days II (After James Schuyler), 1985. Oil on canvas, 86⅝ × 78¾ in. (220 × 200 cm). Private collection

By then, Mitchell had been painting in earnest for forty years, and had lived in Vétheuil for twenty. She had settled into a working routine in relative isolation, close to nature, with a domestic life populated by the same pleasures that James Schuyler celebrated in his poetry. His long poem "A Few Days"—after which Mitchell titled two paintings (fig. 4)—catalogs many of them ("a Remington Rand, my Olivetti, the ashtray and the coffee cup") and darts into side valleys of memory, occasionally stepping back, noticing the views beyond: "And there was goldenrod and tattered Queen Anne's lace and the noble Hudson/ on which just one sailboat sailed, billowing, on a weekday afternoon."[30] These are remembered landscapes as much as Mitchell's paintings are, the line breaks like well-placed oar strokes moving the reader through the poem at unhurried and elegant speed. The details of these days appear ahistorical, as does Mitchell's painting in its unwavering intensity of light and color. For Mitchell, this was never a problem. To Bernstock she noted that "lyric" was "now [generally considered] a dirty word," as was "nature."[31] It is always tempting to understand Mitchell's painting and Schuyler's poetry as more universal than they actually are: their sense of scale was far greater than, say, Strobel's, though it was always bounded by class and a very particular canon. Neither was particularly interested in acknowledging those larger limits; it just did not seem that interesting or profitable. It seemed better to explore "pure" paradoxes of sensation and consciousness as a condition of being rather than to interrogate the historical and political assumptions that undergirded them.

To Mitchell, it was little more than historical accident and art gallery whim that meant Schuyler, O'Hara, Ashbery, Kenneth Koch, and Barbara Guest were conclusively grouped together as the New York School poets. John Bernard "Johnny" Myers, cofounder of the Tibor de Nagy Gallery, coined the phrase in a piece for *Nomad* magazine in 1962, more than a decade after the poets had met and started collaborating with one another and their artist friends, many of whom were represented by de Nagy. Myers had instigated a number of these collaborative projects, and the poets themselves saw the label as a marketing convenience rather than an aesthetically meaningful title. Mitchell was already skeptical of Myers (painfully, the gallery had not chosen to represent her when she was starting out in New York), but she was also more aware (than many U.S. readers) of other traditions in which she situated her friends' work. She knew, for example, how important French poets like Char, Reverdy, and Paul Verlaine were to O'Hara (to Koch, O'Hara wrote, "I'd rather be dead than not have France around my neck like a rhinestone dog-collar"[32]), or how the well-established French tradition of antitraditional poetry could rejuvenate poetry written in English. (The fact that both Ezra Pound and T. S. Eliot had suggested as much in print in the early twentieth century, entirely independently from each other, suggests how unfamiliar contemporary French poetry was to the general reader of poetry in the United States.[33]) Mitchell also saw how English poetry tended to emphasize the concrete, and French poetry the conceptual. Paul Auster clarified the difference when he noted Yves Bonnefoy's observation that English poetry operated like a mirror, and French poetry like a sphere: "the one Aristotelian in its acceptance of the given, the other platonic in its readiness to hypothesize a 'different reality, a different realm.'"[34] Even before she moved to France, Mitchell was predisposed to be interested in spheres as well as mirrors, in platonic realities rather than Aristotelian ones. (In at least one studio, she kept a long-distance mirror so she could take in the overall effect of a painting all at once, rather than in parts. The reflective effect of a sphere is the same.) Mitchell would have been able to sympathize with her friend Beckett ("everything Beckett has ever done" was important to her art, she told Bernstock[35]) and his frustrations translating *Endgame* from French to English. In the play, Clov addresses Hamm and says, "Il n'y a plus de roues de bicyclette"; Beckett complained to a correspondent that the English equivalent "There are no more bicycle wheels" did not convey the much larger problem that the line in French did: that bicycle wheels *as a category* had ceased to exist.[36] Mitchell understood these transatlantic crosscurrents: what it might mean, for example, for O'Hara to write in "Flag Day," "It seems that everything's merely a token/ of some vast inexplicable feeling." She understood the value of the inexplicable, in honoring the categorical rather than the specific.

Mitchell's interest in lyric poetry—sustained over a lifetime—gave her a frame large enough to exist independently of her friends, and distinct enough for her to be particular in her reading (fig. 5). When Bernstock asked about her favorite poets, Mitchell replied, "John Donne, shall we start from there?"[37] She saw the value in Parnassus, a crowded hill of poets: Rilke to her left, O'Hara and Jean Genet to her right, Wordsworth chatting to Stéphane Mallarmé, and Baudelaire just beyond. And in 1975, she also embarked on a number of what she termed "color abstracts," selecting short poems and fragments from longer ones, then framing or overlaying the words with atmospheric washes and lines of pastel, working with texts by Jacques Dupin, J. J. Mitchell, Schuyler, Pierre Schneider, and Chris

FIG 5 Joan Mitchell's study at La Tour, Vétheuil, France, 1983. Joan Mitchell Foundation Archives, New York

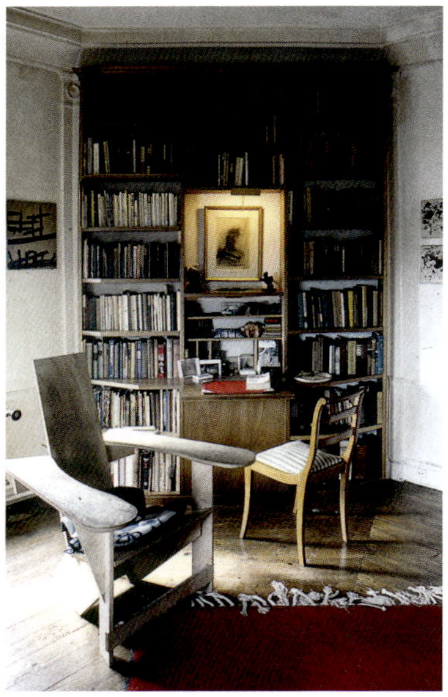

5

Larson—all young friends, or close friends of close friends.[38] Her choices were remarkably reminiscent of her mother's verse half a century before: just as brief and emotional, just as attentive to loss and love. The most well-known of these poem-pastels, for example, reproduces Schuyler's "Daylight" (plate 80): "And when I thought,/ 'Our love might end'/ the sun/ went right on shining." She selected poems that recalled the epistolic as well, choosing a poem by J. J. Mitchell (that began "Dear/ Joan"), which was titled "Frank O'Hara's Birthday." More than a few were exercises in intimacy; in the pastel *Sally Up My Alley,* Mitchell listed nicknames for her family members ("Mitchie/ Poondie/ Newtie/ Joanie/ Jimmy")—though it was J. J. (no relation) who had written the source poem, rather than Joan Mitchell herself. In retyping their words (sometimes meant for her, sometimes not, but always for a particular *other*), she deflected and reflected the lyric outward, inviting the unknown viewer to listen in on a party-line phone call.

Intimacy functions like a skipping stone in these collaborations, the frames of address widening but never losing focus. In this sense, love *could* aspire to infinity. O'Hara's presence is clear, even a decade after his death. In his mock manifesto "Personism"—written in 1959 in an hour, and which retains the sharp improvisatory edge of something written in a rush—O'Hara suggested that one of Personism's aspects "is to address itself to one person (other than the poet himself), thus evoking overtones of love without destroying love's life-giving vulgarity, and sustaining the poet's feelings towards the poem while preventing love from distracting him into feelings about the person."[39] For O'Hara, affection could act as a kind of creative catalyst, but it shouldn't be a smooth trade. Your love (for anyone and anything) could—and should—direct the focus of your own art without collapsing into sentimentality. The person and the art were related—even mutually sustaining—but never the same. It was a distinction that Mitchell, who had spent so much of her life working from feeling, would have appreciated. For Mitchell, poetry was a call across water, a model for hailing one another. It gave her a form in which to feel the world.

7
Territories Sarah Roberts

l'attente pas trop lente les regrets
pas trop longs l'absence
au service de la présence

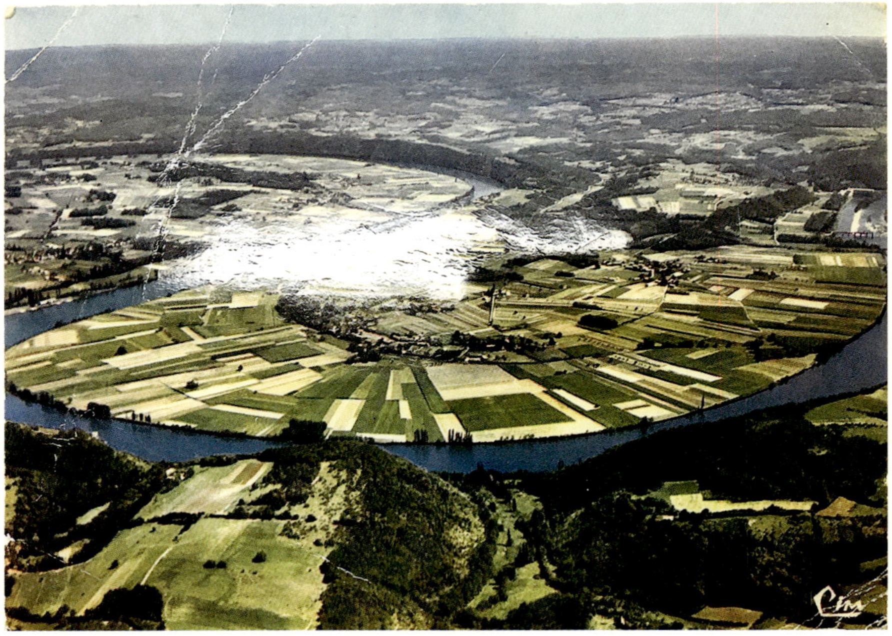

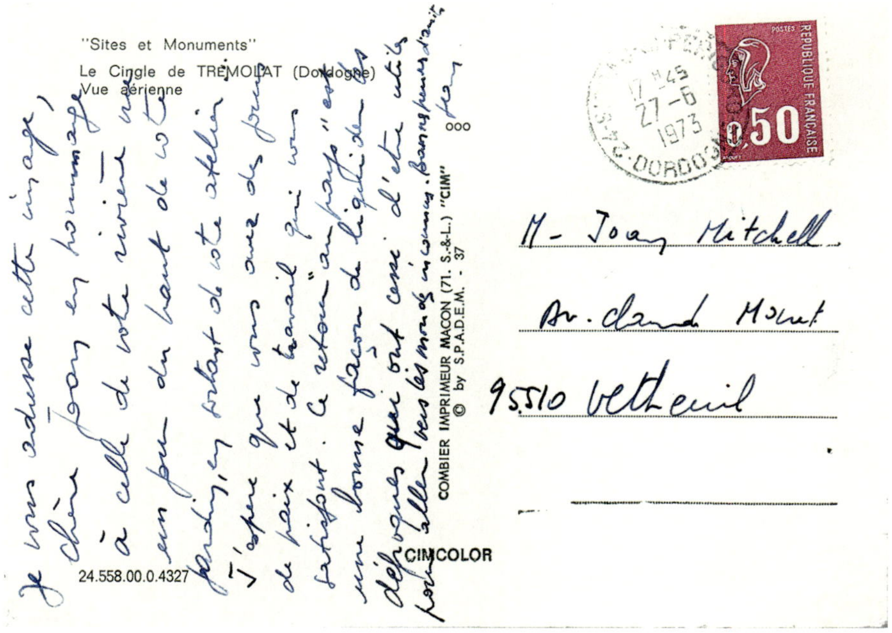

les quelques haillons d'azur dans la tête les points enfin morts au coeur —SAMUEL BECKETT, "À ELLE L'ACTE CALME"

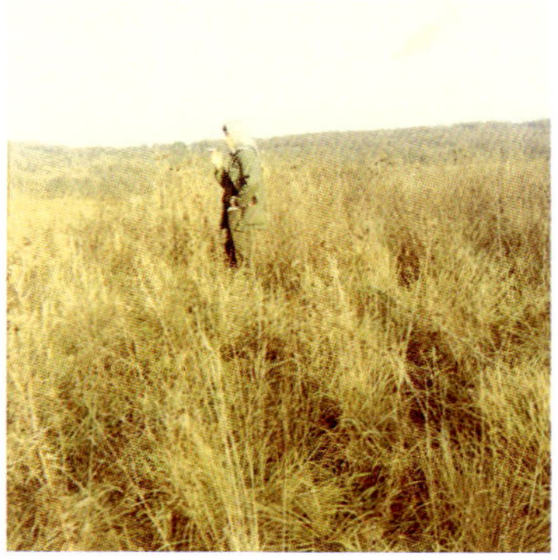

7.1

"Still don't want to live in New York—love walking through the mud and fields."[1] As the novelty of living in the beautiful landscape of Vétheuil stretched into a lasting, relatively isolated existence in the countryside, Mitchell negotiated and renegotiated with herself the terms of her life there (fig. 7.1). Her relationship with Jean Paul Riopelle continued to disintegrate, and she waffled between wanting him to move out and wishing he would not spend so much time away. "We don't do 'togetherness.'"[2] Restless and angry, she considered leaving but wrote to friends of not knowing where else to go.[3] She coped by focusing on her work, her dogs, and her friends, and by inviting young artists and writers to live with her for extended periods. Increasingly, she turned to poetry and music to generate feeling and propel her creativity. Within this unstable personal terrain, she remained assured in her studio, and she took her work in a bold direction at a grandly ambitious scale. In the 1970–74 paintings, she grappled with capturing the panoramic landscape around her as well as its particularities, claiming certain elements, ignoring others, and inscribing them within the bounds of her canvases. She also found herself and her work being deliberated in new contexts, as curators and critics in the United States reassessed the relationship of her painting to the New York School and considered her connections to the artists and concerns emerging in the 1970s.

Mitchell sustained the momentum and productivity of 1969 into the subsequent two years even as she pivoted away from the relatively clear figure/ground relationships established in the *Sunflower* series, and away from compositions dominated by circular clusters and showers of individual linear brush marks. The deep blue and green orbs and blocks that provide underlying structure for works like *Sans neige* (1969, plate 73) and *Blueberry* (1969–70, plate 71) emerged as a key subject of exploration. The horizontality implied in the central panels of *Sans neige* and *Untitled* (1969, plate 70) transmuted into loose strata and relaxed grids in 1970–71 works like *La Ligne de la rupture* (plate 74) and *Ode to Joy (A Poem by Frank O'Hara)* (plate 75). These canvases swell edge to edge with broad swaths of color, emphasizing patches and blocks of paint rather than the

FRONTISPIECE
Postcard (recto and verso) showing aerial view of Dordogne, France, sent by Jean Fournier to Joan Mitchell, August 27, 1973. Joan Mitchell Foundation Archives, New York

FIG 7.1 Joan Mitchell, n.d. Joan Mitchell Foundation Archives, New York individual strokes that dominated the previous paintings. The luminous, relatively pure chroma of the *Sunflower* suite shifted toward an earthier and more dissonant palette. And, whereas the surfaces of the 1969 paintings revel in luscious effects of wet-into-wet paint strokes, those of the following years bear rich textures and visual complexities wrought from patient layering of wet over dry.

This new direction was first shown at Galerie Jean Fournier in May 1971, an exhibition that Mitchell referred to as her "'blue' show."[4] The reviews were mixed and attention scant, though Pierre Schneider's substantial essay originally written for the Galerie Dubourg catalogue of 1962 was published for a third time, in the major journal *XXe siècle*.[5] Marcelin Pleynet's tepid response labeled her a second-generation action painter (meaning American and implying second-rate) and suggested that although Mitchell showed great facility with juxtaposing broad fields with fine touches of color, she would benefit from being more daring and moving closer to the teaching of Hans Hofmann.

The only works confirmed as having been shown, *Three Seasons* (1970–71) and *La Ligne de la rupture,* both reference poems, an indication of Mitchell's turn in this period to poetry as a fresh source of ideas and creative energy.[6] The centerpiece of the exhibition, *La Ligne de la rupture,* was titled after a poem by her close friend Jacques Dupin,[7] and its surface embodies a disrupted continuity that closely parallels the linguistic strategies at play in Dupin's poem (see the text by Paul Auster on page 318). As a director of Galerie Maeght, Dupin had been in Mitchell's orbit since at least the early 1960s, when he wrote major essays on Joan Miró and Alberto Giacometti (the latter translated into English by John Ashbery). Dupin's poetry from this period has been described as a confrontation between written language and lived experience, which by definition cannot be adequately conveyed in words—an analogue to Mitchell's efforts to visually capture verbally inexpressible felt experience. Purposely abstruse, his work departs decidedly from the lyric poetry to which she was typically drawn. His syntax and arrangement of words on the page deliberately upset continuity in order to express the inherent uncertainty of existence, a modus operandi directly referred to in the title of this poem.[8] Synergistically, a strong sense of interruption and reinitiation defines Mitchell's painting. The canvas comprises three distinct horizontal passages separated by turbulent dappling and fine-tipped brushwork streaked with contrasting hues. Other than a final thatching in vivid yellow and orange, each of the many paint layers shows evidence of intervention after the initial pass, whether washed with turpentine, knifed away, submerged, or overlaid with delicate finishing marks. Feral and elegant, *La Ligne de la rupture* pulses with tensions arising from these disruptions of surface and internal contrasts of color, scale, translucency, and texture.

After a dearth of exhibitions in the 1960s outside of her primary galleries, significant institutional support for Mitchell's work suddenly returned. Not long after the Fournier show, she began preparing for her first major museum exhibition in the United States, *My Five Years in the Country: An Exhibition of Forty-Nine Paintings by Joan Mitchell,* presented at the Everson Museum of Art in Syracuse, New York, in March and April of 1972, and then at the Martha Jackson Gallery, as two sequential shows. A selection of these works went on to the Carnegie Museum of Art for *Fresh Air School,* a group exhibition with Sam Francis and Walasse Ting that traveled to four other cities. And curator Marcia Tucker's invitation for a major exhibition at the Whitney Museum of American Art arrived in June 1972, just as Mitchell returned to France following the Jackson openings.

Having the Everson and Jackson exhibitions on the horizon had prodded her to work. In late 1971, she wrote to painter and friend Jon Schueler, "I'm painting my ass off . . . fields—(flat Normandy fields—bit of sky above, natch—) quadriptychs—horizontals."[9] Mitchell's daily visual experience included these flat fields, as Vétheuil is about six miles (less than ten kilometers) from the Normandy region and shares its terrain and agricultural activity. The road Mitchell traveled by taxi to Mantes-la-Jolie to catch the Paris train, sometimes several times weekly, winds through abutting fields of wheat, barley, and rapeseed marked by dramatic seasonal color changes, particularly when the rapeseed blooms vivid yellow. A postcard with an aerial view of the Dordogne river sent to Mitchell by Jean Fournier pays homage to the significance for her of the surrounding landscape (see page 198).[10] The raised view from her hillside offered another perspective on the patchwork terrain:

> There's always this three-part division of what you see. There's the ground right in front of you, that rooftop of Monet's with those tiles and then the river. And then, there's a little region of the river with some houses in the center . . . that's where things happen. . . . And then the sun will come . . . as it does along the Seine here, making patches of yellow-white on the grass or on the straw. And then by the border of the river there's a ridge of yellow sand. And the river runs blue or green or black or white and far in the distance are the blue mountains.[11]

The works made in preparation for the Everson presentation manifest Mitchell's shift to a pulled-back, panoramic impression of this environment of divided fields and layered slices of land and river.

The catalogue for *My Five Years in the Country* separated works into concise series named La Seine, River and Tree, Sunflower, Sans neige, Blue, and Territories, categorizations advocated for by David Anderson of the Martha Jackson Gallery.[12] *Bonjour Julie* (1971, plate 78), *Mooring* (1971, plate 76), and *Little Fields* (fig. 7.2) were all listed as Fields their vastly different sizes, palettes, and compositions demonstrating the tenuousness of these groupings, as well as the striking diversity of work coming out of the studio from 1971 to 1972. Active, densely arrayed rectangular patches in the lower region of *Bonjour Julie* open into upper expanses of cobalt and cerulean blue of varying densities, with select areas of blended pale blue and blush pink punctuated by tangles of orange, green, and ocher. The center panel releases at the top into thinly washed blue surrounded by white, perhaps her "bit of sky." The composition marries the recession of landscape into the distance with a view from above—not an aerial perspective but one from a height, like her view from La Tour overlooking the Seine. Nearly twenty feet wide, the three panels together immerse the viewer in color, but the vertical lines between panels underscore Mitchell's ordering of visual experience. "I want them to hold one image, despite all the activity. It's a kind of plumb line that dancers have; they have to be perfectly balanced, the

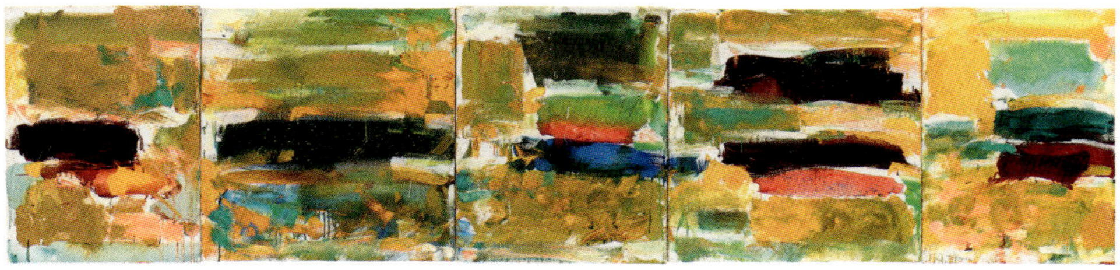

7.2

FIG 7.2 **Joan Mitchell**
Little Fields, 1972. Oil on canvas, 24 × 103¾ in. (61 × 263.5 cm). McNay Art Museum, San Antonio, Texas, museum purchase with funds from the Tobin Foundation

more frenetic the activity is."[13] The triptych structure brackets the action across the surface, creating cohesion through subdivision.

In further describing her "three-part view," Mitchell called out the level of detail within the panorama: "In this beautiful French banks of the Seine atmosphere, so clear air [*sic*], each tree has its own marked, defined kind of leaf form almost like in that Chinese Art of Painting book, so that you can pick out from such a distance the pear tree, the locust tree, the pine tree, the willow tree."[14] A marriage of the overall with the specific is characteristic of both the large-scale multipanel works from this period and many of the single-panel paintings—they simultaneously push us back to take in the overall view and pull us in to roam the surface section by section, detail by detail. *Mooring,* one of the most unabashedly beautiful and lyrical works of Mitchell's career, balances sweeping sheets of color and precisely calibrated minute finishes that draw, then halt the eye. Carter Ratcliff observed: "Mitchell's vision seems joined by her own vigorous physicality. Looking blends in with walking. There often appears to be an equation of looking and pointing, looking and gesturing."[15] Mitchell stated that she was more at ease making big works because of her far-sightedness, and that she frequently stepped back as far as she could in her studio to look at works in progress from a distance because she was unable to see them well when close.[16] The habit of alternately pulling back and zooming in may also explain Mitchell's extraordinary ability to make very small works, such as *Untitled* (1973, plate 84), as powerful as her grandest.

The distinct horizontal levels of *Little Fields* echo Mitchell's divisions of land and river described above—dabbed brushwork at the bottom suggests Monet's roof tiles; the bands of river run carmine, black, and blue across the center; the distant hills and mountain take the form of the widest, haziest block near the top. The five panels of *Little Fields* recall Mitchell's lining up of drawings on her studio wall to create a collective viewing experience of independently drawn but intimately related sheets. Further dividing an already segmented panorama, the multipanel format in this period represents an exertion of control over the view and the landscape, an imposition of edges and boundaries, and a pictorial claim of territory that differs from both the multivalent perspective of the 1963–65 triptychs and the serial views of the Seine in the 1967–68 drawings.

The Everson and Jackson shows received relatively little attention from major outlets,[17] the exception being an extraordinary review by critic Peter Schjeldahl in the *New York Times* proclaiming the Syracuse presentation to be "almost awesomely beautiful" and proof enough that Mitchell was not only one of the best painters of the 1950s but also one of the best of every decade since.[18] Schjeldahl, also a poet, was close to the New York School circle and steeped in Frank O'Hara, Ashbery, and Charles Baudelaire—all of which likely contributed to his openness to Mitchell's work and by extension to much of the new painting emerging in the early 1970s. He makes a case for Mitchell's relevance in the present, a notable deviation from other reviewers' insistence on casting her as a holdover Abstract Expressionist. In doing so, he hints at the contested "is it dead or alive?" state of painting in the United States generally at that moment. This debate would deeply color the reception that Mitchell's Whitney exhibition received two years later.

The Whitney survey included roughly two dozen paintings made between 1969 and 1973, with about half of them having appeared in the Everson exhibition, and half newly made in 1973. Some of the 1973 works continued with the loose, blocky vocabulary of *Bonjour Julie* and *Little Fields*; others softened and pared it back to quieter, more atmospheric terms, such as in *Les Bleuets* (1973, plate 79). As noted in chapter 6, Mitchell flatly rejected the use of the word "series" in conversation with Tucker, likely a reaction against the rigid categories wedged into place for the Everson show. In an effort to underscore instead the fluidity and connections among these intimately related bodies of works, Tucker avoids such fixed classification. In her discussion of the work, she identifies parallels between formal aspects of the paintings, the physical nature of Mitchell's subject matter, and the psychological profile of the artist. Rather than repeating the usual statements about Mitchell capturing a feeling about a landscape on canvas, Tucker expands on the idea: "The canvas itself can and does become an active, immediate modification of her physical and emotional environment. It is characteristic of the human organism to create 'sanctuaries and structures of physical security and psychic identity' by marking off an area to occupy."[19] The act of making a painting is an act of creating new territory—a new physical place within the confines of the canvas, but also a psychological space for Mitchell herself. Mitchell later identified Tucker as one of two writers about her work whom she particularly liked, noting the psychological framework of her approach.[20]

Echoing Pleynet's assessment of her 1971 Fournier exhibition, reviewers of the 1974 Whitney show for *Art International,* the *New York Times,* the *Village Voice,* and *New York Magazine* all deemed Mitchell a "second-generation Abstract Expressionist," typically to imply obsolescence and lesser achievement. The Whitney's press release and the catalogue essay also apply the term.[21] Tucker's handwritten note "Yes 2 second generation A-E" from her 1973 conversations with Mitchell suggests that she asked the direct question and Mitchell approved the designation.[22] Though she knew it made her "old hat," as she said, on some level it still resonated and connected her to de Kooning and Kline, a lineage of which she was proud. As reviewers cast about for other art historical anchors, two names surfaced again and again—Hofmann and Monet. The Hofmann references were inevitable given both artists' emphasis on vivid color and the superficial resemblance of their overlapping colored rectangles; most left the obvious at that. Harold Rosenberg's ostensibly complimentary *New Yorker* review takes pains to frame Mitchell's enterprise as picking up Hofmann's crumbs (and Pollock's, and Guston's, and Rothko's). He invokes Hofmann to underscore her second-generation status—which for him meant second-tier—noting that with works like *La Ligne de la rupture,* she "approaches the Master himself in variety and lyricism,"[23] a stunningly concise model of a sexist, backhanded compliment. The only substantive discussion of Mitchell's and Hofmann's convergence or divergence comes in April Kingsley's column in *Art International*. She distinguishes Mitchell's use of pale hues and whites to cause richer colors to "shine" from Hofmann's use of similar shades to neutralize or tone down his stronger colors, and she contrasts Hofmann's receding space with Mitchell's vibrating sense of motion in front of the picture plane.[24] Indeed, Mitchell's use of color is far subtler than Hofmann's—she calibrates and places her hues to complicate and enliven one another and to create a pictorial space that is fluid and interwoven, in contrast to Hofmann's rigidly tripartite conception of space, which he described as in front of the object, in the object, and behind the object.[25]

Similarly, reviewers linked Mitchell's paintings to Monet's due to their beauty, size, and wide horizontal orientation, and of course, because of the Vétheuil connection.[26] Rosalind Krauss equated Mitchell and Monet for the way their respective paint marks "declare and then transcend" their inert physical nature, and for the artists' shared ability to make us recognize the limitations of human capacity to describe or imitate the scale and luminosity of nature.[27] In a note to Michael Goldberg, Mitchell indicated her approval of Krauss's review and resignation to the Hofmann references (which Krauss did not make): "Art Forum [*sic*] was lovely with 'towels on the beach'—oh well why not—or a Hofmann rectangle—They 'got' to fit it (rectangle) in somewhere."[28]

Though Mitchell ultimately endorsed Tucker's approach to her painting, she antagonized the curator at the start of their work together and suspected her motives.[29] Writing of herself in the third person to her sister, Mitchell reported, "Joan feels Miss Whitney is using her for Women's Liberation. Shirley and Zuka figure, 'Fuck 'em all and get the pics on the wall.'"[30] The remark captures Mitchell's complex response to the rise of the women's movement in the 1970s, and the resulting inclusion of her work in exhibitions such as *The Permanent Collection: Women Artists* at the Whitney and *Contemporary Women Artists* at the Hathorn Gallery of Skidmore College, both in 1970;[31] *Women Choose Women,* organized by Lucy Lippard for the New York Cultural Center in 1973; and *Woman's Work: American Art 1974* at the Museum of the Philadelphia Civic Center. Tucker's forceful advocacy for women artists and artists of color set her apart from other curators at the time, and her fiery and well-publicized political activism made Mitchell wary. As discussed in the following chapter, Mitchell would eventually absorb feminist ideas, but because all forms of categorization and clubbiness had been anathema to her since her youth, her initial instinct was to recoil, even if she did decide to "get the pics on the wall."

FIG 7.3 Left: Joan Mitchell in Jean Paul Riopelle's home and studio at Sainte-Marguerite-du-Lac-Masson, Canada, 1974. Right: Views from the studio. Joan Mitchell Foundation Archives, New York

FIG 7.4 **Joan Mitchell** *Returned* (originally known as *Canada*), 1975. Oil on canvas, 19¾ × 88 in. (50.2 × 223.5 cm). Private collection

Mitchell's unstable life at Vétheuil formed a dark backdrop to this surge in exhibition activity. She contemplated leaving and returning to the United States: "He [Riopelle] won't get out so I will—oh masochism—I'm sorry Mother's books are here & not there—frontiers & customs & shit—& I wish I didn't have the pics—size etc to cart about."[32] Ultimately, the problem of moving all her belongings felt insurmountable; Mitchell persisted in Vétheuil. She turned back to music, especially opera, and poetry to spur creative energy, and surrounded herself largely with painters and poets, both French and American, many of them gay men. She remained close to O'Hara's circle, particularly Ashbery, Joe LeSueur, and Hal Fondren, inviting them to visit and relying on them to report the latest goings-on in New York. Among writers in France, she still saw Samuel Beckett occasionally as well as Dupin. As drawn as she was to these long-established intellectual figures, she also took an interest in younger, emerging authors, including American writers Paul Auster and Lydia Davis, to whom Mitchell was introduced by Dupin, whose work Auster translated.

Young writers often received invitations to stay for a day, weeks, or months. Success and publication were not required, just a commitment to writing and one's creative life, such as that Mitchell and her generation had made in the 1950s. If such dedication was seen to be lagging, Mitchell applied pressure, both cajoling and whip cracking. She met poet Karen Edwards through Goldberg, and the two carried on a long correspondence, with Mitchell sending encouragement and urging Edwards to send new work that Mitchell could "push" for her.[33] She did the same for poet Chris Larson, who lived in Vétheuil for several months in 1973. Larson testified to her effectiveness: "I'm writing a lot these days—all day yesterday as a matter of fact. First time in years. Can't be helped. Some weird lady painter put me up to it, dared me, shamed me to try. I love her for it."[34] Another young poet, J. J. Mitchell (no relation, and hereafter referred to as J. J. for clarity), lived with Mitchell to help with the dogs and keep her company from summer 1974 through the end of 1975. A former partner of O'Hara's, J. J. wrote light, crisp poems that often directly address Mitchell and her dogs, like affectionate notes to a friend. Together J. J.'s poems and Larson's letters open a window on days at Vétheuil. From Paris, Larson wrote Mitchell: "I imagine you in your studio wearing a sweater with holes in the sleeves, wondering whether the upper right area of your latest canvas needs something or works as is; singing along with rambunctious Verdi who thumbs his nose at the Abyss and fills it with music; squeezing innumerable tubes of paint, making squiggly turds of color in pie-tins . . . and maybe, if today is a good day, you'll lose all track of time."[35]

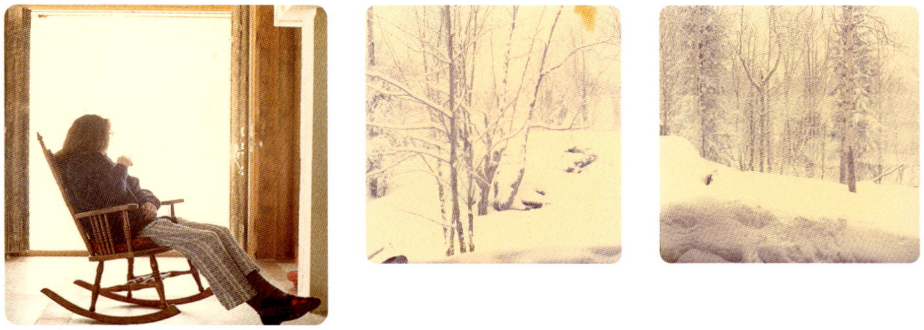

7.3

In 1974, days when Mitchell was painting so well that she lost track of time became scarce as she experienced a post-exhibition depression, and her life grew more unsettled. Riopelle had begun building a new house and studio north of Montreal, a further, greater separation. She had split with Martha Jackson Gallery in late 1973, and though she was thrilled to have been taken on by Fourcade, Droll, the gallery that represented de Kooning, she and Fourcade did not make plans for an exhibition in 1974 or 1975. Instead, he focused on selling works already in New York for the Whitney exhibition and facilitating her 1974 exhibition at the Arts Club of Chicago. Her first solo show there since a small presentation at the Holland-Goldowsky Gallery in 1961, it could have been a triumphant homecoming, yet she did not attend, sending Fourcade in her stead. She also was invited to represent France in the Venice Biennale, but hesitated.[36] Ultimately, the exhibition went unrealized as the entire Biennale was given over to Chile in protest of Pinochet's dictatorship. Finding it impossible to paint, Mitchell collaborated with J. J. on a group of poem pastels, drawing on sheets of paper around poems that he typed out on her mother's typewriter, a prized possession shipped from Chicago (see Erin Kimmel's discussion of the pastels on pages 206–7). Mitchell later credited these collaborations with pushing her back into painting: "Working with other people's feelings—i.e. their poems has helped a lot."[37]

7.4

In August, she found a direction, writing to Fourcade, "Am doing 'snow scenes' smallish probably because the house is full of plaster as they are redoing the electricity. Oh merde. Anyway I'm trying."[38] A few months later, she traveled to Riopelle's home in Canada. Snapshots show thick drifts and trees laden with snow seen through windows in a Spartan wood interior (fig. 7.3). Back in the studio, Mitchell continued her snow scenes into 1975, tumbling loss, anger, and memories of the plaster and frozen landscape into a suite of works that is by turns soft, elegiac, bleak, and gritty (fig. 7.4 and plate 83). Claiming the word and its associations for herself, and bringing it all into her territory—her studio—for transformation, she called the series *Canada.*

Poem pastels

Erin Kimmel

Poem pastels, including *Daylight,* are illustrated as plates 80–81.

FIG 7.5 **Joan Mitchell** *What Makes This,* poem pastel with J. J. Mitchell, ca. 1975. Pastel and typewriter ink on paper, 14 × 9¼ in. (35.6 × 23.5 cm). Private collection, courtesy Mark Borghi

FIG 7.6 **Joan Mitchell** *Daylight,* poem pastel with James Schuyler, ca. 1975 (detail). See plate 80.

Mitchell often compared her paintings to poems, and throughout her career she referred, somewhat hazily, to the quality of a painter's light as a measure of meaningful painting. So it was fitting when, around 1975, she chose to "pastel up" a trio of James Schuyler poems, each of which abides in the flickering light of a passing day.[1] Mitchell selected three short poems—"Sunday," "Daylight," and "Sunset"—from Schuyler's collection published that same year, *Hymn to Life,* a dedicated and signed copy of which sat in her library until her death. In the three "poem pastels," each on a sheet of roughly fourteen-by-nine-inch paper, Mitchell meets Schuyler's poetic command of atmosphere by rendering quiescent layers of cornflower blue, marigold, or lilac in rectangular masses that appear to hover alongside the typewritten text. Swift, confetti-like flourishes of green and black interrupt, accent, or frame these passages of color, establishing the figure/ground relationships that are reminiscent of both her paintings and the landscapes that inspired them. Mitchell's elaborations of Schuyler's poems are part of a larger body of similar work that the artist began earlier in 1974 when she was struggling to paint. Accustomed to switching modes when stuck, she asked J. J. Mitchell (hearafter J. J., for clarity), a young writer who was moonlighting as her dog walker, confidant, and secretary of sorts, to use her mother's Hermes typewriter to type up some of the poems he had written while staying at La Tour in Vétheuil. She took the pages and added pastel. Pleased with the result, she expanded the collection to include works that feature the poetry of other poet-friends, including Jacques Dupin, Pierre Schneider, and Chris Larson, as well as Schuyler. Mitchell later objected to describing these works as collaborations. "I just took the poems," she said.[2]

A younger member of the New York School, J. J. deftly chronicled daily life at La Tour in his poems, moving seamlessly between comedy and pathos. From the fits and starts of Mitchell's creative process to the comings and goings of Jean Paul Riopelle to the wisdom of Mitchell's cherished German shepherd, Iva, they track the entire reality of Mitchell's newly consolidated life in the country, including the dark, alcohol-drenched intimacy she shared with J. J. *Untitled (What Makes This)* (fig. 7.5) asks, "what/ makes/ this/ fine/ line/ bleed/ hurt/ like/ a/ paper/ cut?" Mitchell, who directed the placement of the poem on the paper, mirrors the searing column of text with two vertical streaks of color: a rich slab of blue and a comparatively thin smudge of rust. In a letter to Xavier Fourcade, Mitchell referred to these as "color abstracts" that respond to the "shape of the poem itself," implicating the formal dimension of the poem as well as the feeling of pain stemming from the in-betweenness of indecision that it evokes.[3]

The quickness and darkness of these two muddy slashes, and Mitchell's illustrations of J. J.'s poems as a whole, differ from the radiance and studied deliberation that characterize the Schuyler cycle. Frank O'Hara had introduced Mitchell and Schuyler in 1952; all three were members of a brood of young painters and poets full of rowdy, hopeful erudition rollicking around New York. Though Mitchell and Schuyler never became particularly close, they maintained an enduring reverence for each other's work. After she moved to France, their relationship was primarily mediated by writers with whom she was closer, including O'Hara, Joe LeSueur, John Ashbery, and Nathan Kernan. At the end of a 1957 letter celebrating Irving Sandler's article about Mitchell in *Art News,* O'Hara writes, "Many people have praised it, particularly your ardent admirer Jimmy Schuyler."[4] Peppered throughout LeSueur and Mitchell's long correspondence are affectionate updates on Schuyler's mental health. "Jimmy Schuyler, who loved your show, was sorry he didn't have a chance to see you," LeSueur writes in 1977. "He is (after all) both our favorite poet and schizophrenic."[5] More than a decade later, Mitchell learned of Schuyler's death from Kernan. At the poet's funeral in the Church of the Incarnation in Manhattan, just a year before her own death, she sat in the lyric distance the two had long shared.

Their connection was perhaps rooted in certain mutual affinities. Schuyler was a poet of the view at hand—elucidating the "literal/ and unsymbolic/ day."[6] Like Mitchell, who rejected metaphor in painting, Schuyler described the subject matter of his poems as feelings rather than symbols. "I do begin more from a feeling or something seen or a word," he once explained.[7] In "Daylight," a jolt of anticipation interrupts the pleasant casualness of a daydream. Beginning slowly, mid-contemplation, with "And when I thought," the poem is quickly interrupted by the idea "'our love might end.'" But just as soon, the sadness and fear evoked by the thought are swept up in the reality presented in the poem's next and final lines: "the sun/ went right on shining."[8] Neither triumphant nor cloying, and in heartbreakingly clarion terms, the poem contrasts the transitory nature of emotion to the enduring intimacy and indifference of the sun. This sting is softened by its sureness—dissolving thought into atmosphere and becoming feeling.

With pastel, Mitchell literalizes the relationship by rendering a radiant block with rich layers of orange and yellow. Both a scoured sun and a wall of light dominate the page, and, like Schuyler, she merges feeling and object. Below, a few drags and skitters of blue and green suggest a shallow foreground that reinforces the largeness and immediacy of the feeling (fig. 7.6). Mitchell's loss of her rue Frémicourt studio only a few months earlier and the growing absence of Riopelle meant the consolidation of her life in and around Vétheuil. During a difficult period, it seems, Schuyler's poems streamlined the tangled swells and swerves of emotion that account for the breadth of her paintings, offering instead an immediate warmth in a singular, resonant form.

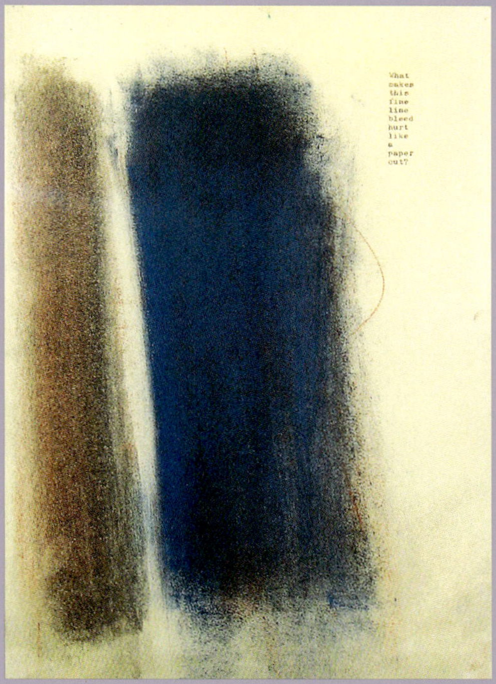

7.5

7.6

8

Green Katy Siegel

An expanse of green, in bedded surface, but which also slowly gushes, on all sides, in anonymous appeal (unanimous, anonymous) or response to the rain.

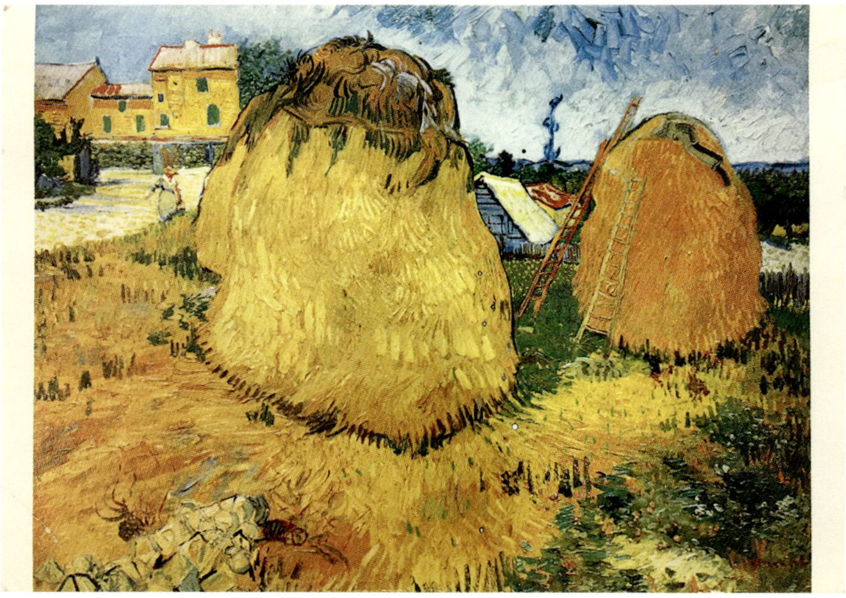

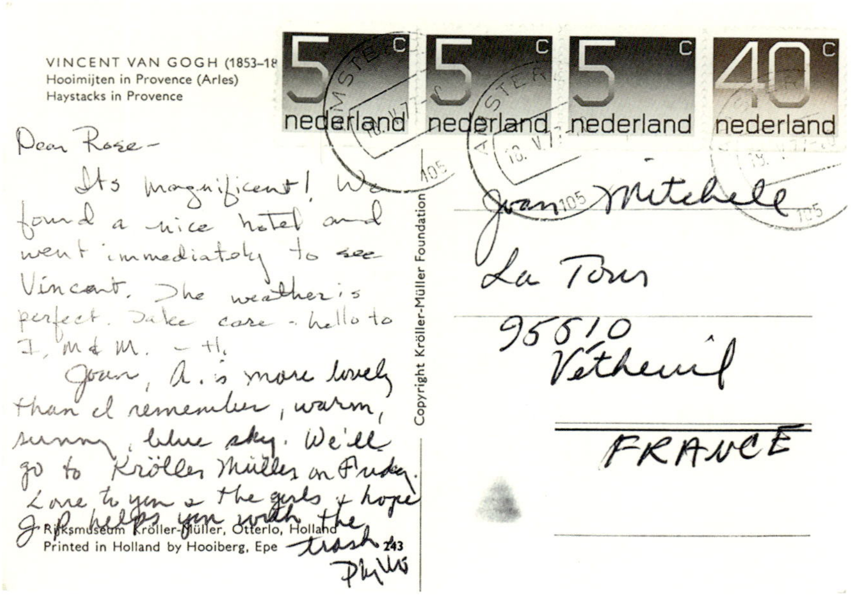
VINCENT VAN GOGH (1853–18
Hooimijten in Provence (Arles)
Haystacks in Provence

Dear Rose–
Its magnificent! We found a nice hotel and went immediately to see Vincent. The weather is perfect. Take care – hello to J, M & M. – H.
Joan, A. is more lovely than I remember, warm, sunny, blue sky. We'll go to Kröller Müller on Friday. Love to you & the girls & hope J.P. helps you with the trash.
Phyllis

Rijksmuseum Kröller-Müller, Otterlo, Holland
Printed in Holland by Hooiberg, Epe 243

Copyright Kröller-Müller Foundation

5c nederland 5c nederland 5c nederland 40c nederland

Joan Mitchell
La Tour
95510
Vétheuil
FRANCE

Green incarnation of rain, jet of sap upright in response to the rain. —FRANCIS PONGE, *LA FABRIQUE DU PRÉ*

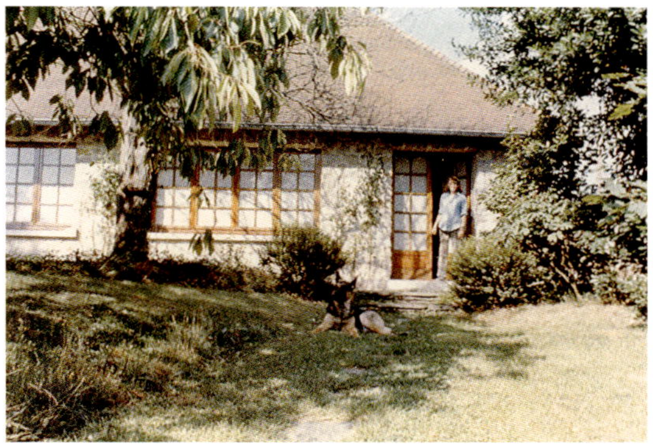

8.1

"I'm working so hard I can't see straight."[1] And also, Mitchell added in her reply to Patricia Molloy, she could not see, or rather read, the letter she had just received—it had finally rained in Vétheuil, and the downpour had drowned the paper and dissolved the ink. Mitchell's relentless studio practice of the late 1970s was doubtless inspired by a growing awareness of painting's renewed energy in both Paris and New York. The awareness came on the heels of her 1974 Whitney exhibition, in anticipation of her first New York gallery show in four years, and also amidst a string of group shows that put her recent paintings on the wall next to those by younger artists—women artists in particular—in full contact with new ideas about painting. If a single quality could characterize these artists and ideas of the 1970s, it was direct and transparent physical process. For Mitchell, this contemporary approach unexpectedly intersected with the immediacy of Vincent van Gogh's technique, and with her own experience of trees, gardens, meadows, grass, and woods.

In a year of fewer works but several major paintings, she began to move away from the elevated view and stacked compositions of the early 1970s. Mitchell painted *Garden for Audrey* (1975, plate 86) to memorialize Thomas B. Hess's wife, Audrey, who had died suddenly, less than a month after a lovely lunch at La Tour with Annalee Newman, widow of painter Barnett Newman, in summer 1974. Audrey had given Mitchell a flowering tree;[2] the diptych centers on its vibrant presence in the garden. Audrey's gift was one of many meaningful trees throughout Mitchell's life, like the cypresses of the mid-1960s, and was also one of many works and actual gardens, trees, and plants or flowers dedicated to friends. Greens dominate, set off by lilac and red-orange, feathered by white, alternating local color in thinly stroked forms and marks with multihued, dappled texture, and perhaps Mitchell's most dramatic use of drips, with the upper left and lower right corners weeping green. The painting, like *Chris's Dead Tree* (1975, plate 82) and *Aires pour Marion* (1975–76, plate 88), emerged from what continued to be a difficult period personally: Kimber Smith visited during the course of his radiation treatment for throat cancer, and in March 1975 came "the fucking demolition of Frémicourt, moving moving," amidst the

FRONTISPIECE
Postcard (recto and verso) showing Vincent van Gogh's *Wheat Stacks in Provence* (1888), sent by Hollis Jeffcoat and Phyllis Hailey to Joan Mitchell, May 20, 1977. Joan Mitchell Foundation Archives, New York

FIG 8.1 Joan Mitchell with her dog Iva outside her studio at La Tour, Vétheuil, France, 1975. Joan Mitchell Foundation Archives, New York conviction that Mitchell and Jean Paul Riopelle were also reaching an end composed in equal parts of violence and indifference.[3] Poet Chris Larson committed suicide in January 1976, a misery Mitchell contrasted with the joyful birth of her German shepherd Iva's puppies.

The "key" painting declaring the new direction of 1976–78 was an enormous quadriptych inspired by the musical composition *Quatuor II* by her friend Betsy Jolas.[4] The quartet replaces the traditional first violin with a coloratura soprano, who, rather than voicing a traditional narrative, makes abstract sounds until the very last, when she sings *point* (period, conclusion). Mitchell's *Quatuor II for Betsy Jolas* (1976, plate 87) is similarly strange and gorgeous, an enormous painting that took her over a year. The artist admired Jolas's music and was surprisingly knowledgeable about her lyrical, "personal" style in relation to that of new music peers such as Earle Brown. Mitchell likely also noted the two women's parallel career struggles.[5] As a 1976 *New York Times* article pointed out, Jolas was building a reputation despite her bent toward tradition in an avant-garde context; Mitchell would also have related to her dual French/American status and, above all, to her being a woman in a male field.[6] In the mid-1970s, both Mitchell and Jolas reached not only new levels of accomplishment but also public recognition for their mastery.

The seed for *Quatuor II* was a small drawing Mitchell made while waiting for Riopelle in his nearby rural studio, struck by the view from his window: "The greens are trees. Trees rather than lakes or fields. Marvelous trees. And that was the beginning."[7] The drawing's making shines a light on the role that drawing in direct response to her everyday surroundings played in Mitchell's artistic life. She was moved to reorient her work, both drawing closer to her subject and also emphasizing its verticality amidst the horizontal expanse of multipanel canvases, continuing her play of "ups and downs."[8] The left center panel of *Quatuor II* offers a green tree, its composition of mass above trunk barely distinct from a full ground. Together, the four panels offer a wide view, stacking distant trees and thickets of green that shifted as she moved the panels around and marshalled a glossary of marks and effects—most strikingly, the atmospheric white veiling the deep colors of the far right panel.[9] The white, together with pale blue and lavender expanses, plays on the light and sky between branches; the effect was a motif, even a metaphysical injunction: over the years, Mitchell told friends that these "space feelings," these glimpses, were necessary to nature and to her work.[10] Such feelings are stark, unmediated, in the deeply colored naked branches and white ground of *Red Tree* (1976, plate 93).

Mitchell's *Quatuor II* was the centerpiece of her summer 1976 exhibition at Fournier's Paris gallery: "a mixed bag of puppies, trees & suicides—really smashing."[11] The show was almost all large paintings, including *Sylvie's Sunday* (named for Riopelle's daughter; see page 218, no. 2), Mitchell's first work to be purchased by the Musée national d'art moderne (the Centre Pompidou), Paris, a landmark event for any artist.[12] Xavier Fourcade came to see Fournier's show and praised the new direction, encouraging Mitchell, who was painting furiously in anticipation of her late 1976 exhibition with his gallery in New York.[13]

In these paintings, the segmented stations of the fields and the elevated, distant view give way to flow and passage between spaces. Mitchell moved daily through "her" landscape, walking through green grass, gardens, even the woods at Vétheuil; behind and around the property was an enormous meadow that belonged to adjoining conservation land. Walking between the kitchen and the studio every morning, every afternoon, every

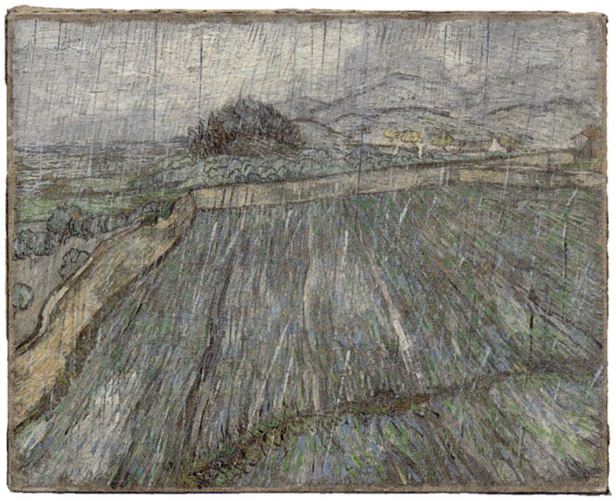

8.2

FIG 8.2 **Vincent van Gogh**
Rain, 1889. Oil on canvas,
28⅞ × 36⅜ in. (73.3 × 92.4 cm).
Philadelphia Museum of Art,
The Henry P. McIlhenny Collection
in memory of Frances P. McIlhenny,
1986

night, she looked at these greens, emerging around 5 a.m. to witness the "blue dawns."[14] When she left the house to get the train to Paris, she would pass through the flower gardens, past the red maple tree, down the stairs by the vegetable plot (territory of gardener Jean Perthuis) surrounded by chestnut trees, along the path leading to the blue gate where her taxi waited. A massive linden tree stood outside the house's front door, and outside the studio, an *allée* of smaller *tilleuls*. Her intimacy with these greens—moving amidst, not viewing from above—produced paintings that bring us close to what we see. And what we see is, largely, colored marks. The landscape in these years is external and experienced; at the same time, the paintings have the feel of the studio, with their considered use of restricted and specific materials and marks.[15]

Mitchell clearly felt her new direction was important, announcing it with her image selection for the catalogue cover, noted in the handwritten checklist she sent to Fourcade that October.[16] *No Rain* (1976, plate 89) telegraphs what would become the fully realized style of the suite of works painted in 1976–77: largely done in an array of greens, and in what for Mitchell was a strikingly consistent register of marks. (For a discussion of *Weeds* [1976, plate 92], an outlier in palette, see Cecilia Wichmann's focus essay on pages 216–17.) The dominant brushstroke is vertical, relatively short, blunt, and wide, likely done with a two-inch brush—all unusual for an artist who was sensitive to tools and enjoyed working with a wide array of brushes. She applied paint directly, with relatively little layering or variation of viscosity, and fewer of the detailed textural touches that had characterized so much of her work. As Mitchell herself pointed out, even the small and medium-size paintings could hold the scale of the large multipanel works.[17] The slight variation of the marks in works like *No Rain* and *Posted* (1977, plate 91) also suggests a shallow depth of field relating broadly to van Gogh's drawings, in which particular marks correspond to foreground, middle ground, and background.[18] *No Rain,* in fact, has a striking visual relationship to van Gogh's similarly vertical painting *Rain* (fig. 8.2). Mitchell's title may play on van Gogh's, as well as refer to the return of green to Vétheuil after a summer with little rain in France.[19]

In any case, van Gogh was a renewed presence for Mitchell in these years (although at no time did he disappear completely).[20] In addition to the complete volumes of his letters, which include the related sketches, she owned the catalogue of the collection of the Van Gogh Museum in Amsterdam exhibited at the Musée de l'Orangerie in Paris in late 1971–72, and certainly saw the enormous exhibition.[21] In early 1976, Fourcade asked Mitchell to go to Amsterdam to represent him and Willem de Kooning at an opening; we don't know whether she went, but the following year, Mitchell paid for two younger friends to visit the Van Gogh Museum.[22] If van Gogh's intensity appealed in the 1950s, and the stippled texture and unabashed color of his sunflowers in the 1960s, it was his simplicity and directness that resonated with her in the 1970s. Both artists celebrated the ordinary/extraordinary quality of their surroundings, of gardens, trees, and plants, as they described their daily routines (and occasional bouts of being shaken from them by mental and emotional unrest).[23] They wrote about marking time—hours, days, and seasons—as it occurs in nature and in the process of painting; Mitchell noted the dawns and noons and evenings, the fall and spring "pics," the feel of sun, rain, cooling temperatures, dormancy, and bloom.

Discipline and structure overcame romanticism in these years as Mitchell continued—the repeated refrain—"*working, working,*" even after she shipped her paintings to Fourcade that October.[24] The marks themselves, in their seriality, have a regular rhythm, as van Gogh observed regarding his own productivity, "The brush strokes go like a machine."[25] "Direct" was a word used to describe both van Gogh and Mitchell, and two decades earlier she had remarked on the "quality of intimacy and removal . . . immediacy of technique itself" in notes from a 1951 art history class on van Gogh.[26] In the context of 1970s painting, that fresh, immediate technique, unmasked and unfussy, was particularly visible and appealing. Even as Mitchell reanimated van Gogh, her own work had newfound appeal among younger artists; one review of the Whitney Biennial positioned her large triptych *Bonjour Julie* (1971, plate 78), with its bare canvas and unguarded strokes, as a beacon for "younger disciples" such as Joan Snyder.[27] Many painters emerging in both Paris and New York in the late 1960s and 1970s made their marks or chose their colors, as Claude Viallat put it, without regard for expression or preference, guided by conditions of support or structure such as the grid.[28] There are hints in Mitchell's 1977 interview with Eleanor Munro of this kind of indexical thinking about her work; in a lighter vein, speaking with painter Emily Cheng, Mitchell humorously referred to her brushstrokes as "paw marks."[29]

Mitchell had noticed that "painting painting" was back.[30] Little is known precisely of Mitchell's thoughts about the newer artists and their ideas about painting, but she subscribed to *Artforum* beginning in 1971 and *Art in America* in 1975, and occasionally mentioned names like Lynda Benglis, Brice Marden, and Jennifer Bartlett, alternating approval and withering sarcasm.[31] Mitchell's work appeared for the first time at Fourcade's gallery (then called Fourcade, Droll) in a group show together with Pat Steir in July 1975. During Mitchell's visits to New York in 1974, 1976, and 1977, the city was filled with process-based painting: Marcia Tucker's Whitney shows of artists like Jack Whitten and Ree Morton; painters whose names Mitchell may have known from group shows and reviews that tied them to her, like Elizabeth Murray; and exhibitions of Mitchell's peers Jasper Johns, Ed Clark, and Cy Twombly, who had also successfully unmoored themselves from the 1950s. Similar conditions prevailed in Paris. Galerie Jean Fournier represented Viallat, who participated in the Supports/Surfaces group

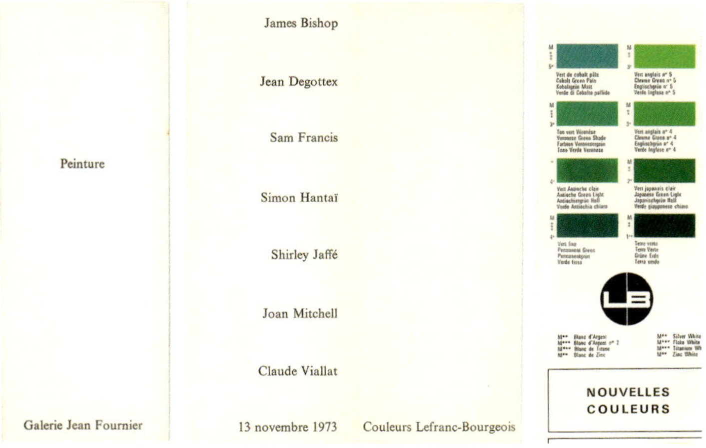

8.3

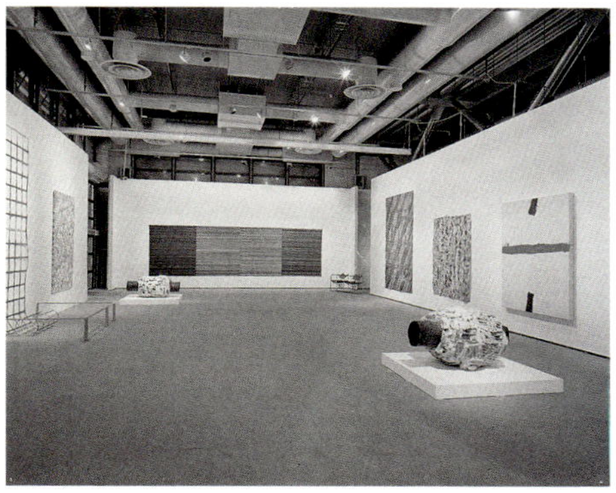

8.4

of experimental French painters, and in late 1973 showed him together with Mitchell and other longtime gallery painters. The announcement features a grid of green paint samples, the colors registering as arbitrary and automatic rather than as a depictive paean to nature (fig. 8.3).[32] At the newly opened Centre Pompidou (fig. 8.4), the increasing interest in Mitchell's work was situated amidst the aggressive acquisition and exhibition of postminimalist, material painting from both the United States (David Reed, Alan Shields) and France (Pierre Buraglio, Daniel Dezeuze).[33]

Fourcade and Fournier were not alone in framing Mitchell within this new context. Mitchell had her own eye on the possibility of renewed relevance, and in a letter to Fourcade suggesting invitees to her 1976 post-opening dinner—along with Pierre Matisse, her sister, Sally, and old friends Newman and Elaine de Kooning—she ticks off figures from the changing art scene: Tucker; Peter Schjeldahl, the poet who had reviewed her Everson show; and Lucy Lippard, Linda Nochlin, and Elizabeth Baker, who had included her work in the 1973 *Women Choose Women* exhibition at the New York Cultural Center.[34] These younger curators and critics placed Mitchell not as a lone holdout waving the Abstract Expressionist flag, as older critics Harold Rosenberg and Paul Brach positioned her, but as a significant contemporary voice.[35] Mitchell certainly valued the emerging sense of herself as independent, no longer "second" to older New York painters or the postwar Paris crowd. Even as she groused, she declared a new sense of self, of value: "Then, in the '70s they had to dig up someone new. So they came and dug up my, quote, little oil paintings. But the funny thing was I hadn't quit. . . . I was going to do my own thing no matter what happened. You have a certain sense of being sure of yourself, that you'll go on."[36]

Some of this attention recognized Mitchell as a precedent for younger female artists; the first Whitney Biennial of 1973 had shown Mitchell alongside Murray, Snyder, and Louise Fishman, and at the same time her work was featured in *Women Choose Women*. The next few years would see her work in many shows of women

FIG 8.3 Exhibition brochure for *Peinture, couleurs LeFranc-Bourgeois,* Galerie Jean Fournier, November 13, 1973

FIG 8.4 Installation view of *Accrochage II,* Musée national d'art moderne (the Centre Pompidou), Paris, 1979. Works by Daniel Dezeuze, François Rouan, Jean-Michel Meurice, Vivien Isnard, Pierre Buraglio, Jean-Pierre Péricaud, and Bernard Pagès are visible.

artists, including several in France.[37] She had appeared in the *Feminist Art Journal* in 1974, and in the same year Kate Horsfield and Lyn Blumenthal interviewed her for a project focusing on underrecognized women artists.[38] Although Mitchell's generational suspicion of labels flared early on with regard to being a "woman painter," it seems that she increasingly saw the merit of the case, both as it changed the appraisal of her own work and, more broadly, as it applied to a sexist society. Beginning in 1975, she was seeing feminist historian Linda Nochlin (see page 219), who traveled regularly to France for her research on nineteenth-century painting and was also close to Zuka and Shirley Jaffe (fig. 8.5).[39] Nochlin visited Vétheuil in November 1977 amidst the enormous success of her traveling exhibition *Women Artists: 1550–1950,* and Mitchell recalled that they spoke about the subject at length: "Women couldn't paint and women didn't paint and all that sort of thing. I'm always called Rosa Malheur, Jean Paul calls me Rosa Malheur."[40] During her discussion with Mitchell of the exhibition's appearance at the Brooklyn Museum, interviewer Munro noted to herself, "[Mitchell] talks a great deal about how women only find themselves in relation to men . . . how her mother was sort of only an amateur poet because she got into the mother business and how all women at all time [*sic*] only define themselves in relation to men."[41] In 1976, Mitchell had added another new subscription to her list of art magazines: *Women Artists Newsletter*.[42] Her slightly delayed absorption of feminism happened in mutual relation to changes in her domestic life—as she grew distant from Riopelle and increasingly made significant friendships with younger women, with whom she alternated between the roles of playful peer, mother figure, and teacher.[43] Among the first was the charming and adventurous Karen Edwards, who spent time with Mitchell in Vétheuil and New York, and in letters acted as a confidant for the older artist as she essayed an early vision of herself as an independent, even single, woman.[44]

Not surprisingly, Mitchell's invitation list for Fourcade also included younger female artists: "The 3 'lady painters' I am inviting are extremely talented—not arriviste."[45] Mitchell was referring to Phyllis Hailey, Hollis Jeffcoat, and Carol Engelson. Mitchell had met Hailey and then Jeffcoat, as well as Cheng, through Elaine de Kooning, who was teaching in the Paris summer program of the New York Studio School, where Mitchell was listed as visiting faculty in the summers of 1975 and 1977 (fig. 8.6). Elaine came to see her in Vétheuil in these years (see page 218), sometimes accompanied by students.[46] Among the young women who visited and helped/worked for Mitchell, Jeffcoat quickly emerged as the favorite, coming to live at La Tour in fall 1977, where she became a fixture of the household: "Hollis is the best 'live in' I've had—she's Gertrude (I'm Mildred)—paints very well—dog feeds with me—serves the 'master' & he adores her—no fights."[47] A van Gogh postcard sent by Hailey and Jeffcoat as they traveled in Holland (a trip subsidized by Mitchell) is addressed to "Rose," casting Mitchell as Rosa Bonheur (see page 208); she also played "Thea" (female version of van Gogh's brother Theo) to Jeffcoat's "Vinnie."[48] Hailey signs off, "Love to you & the girls," for the dogs, too, were female, and Iva and her puppies Marion and Madeleine were, like the young women, occupying an increasingly central place in Mitchell's daily and emotional life—and keeping her company in the studio.[49]

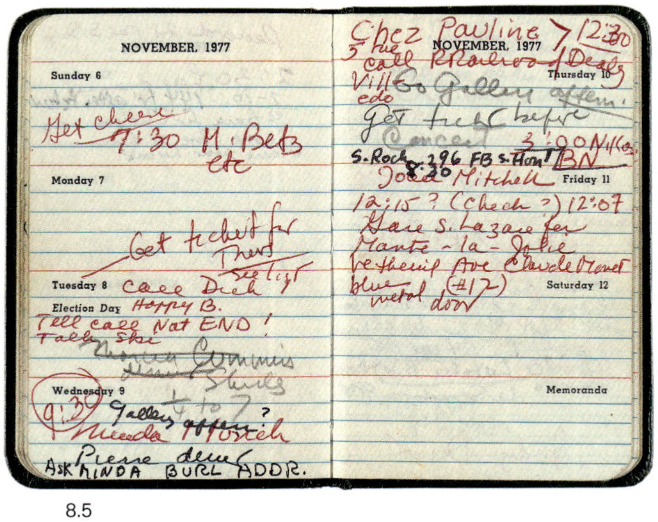

8.5

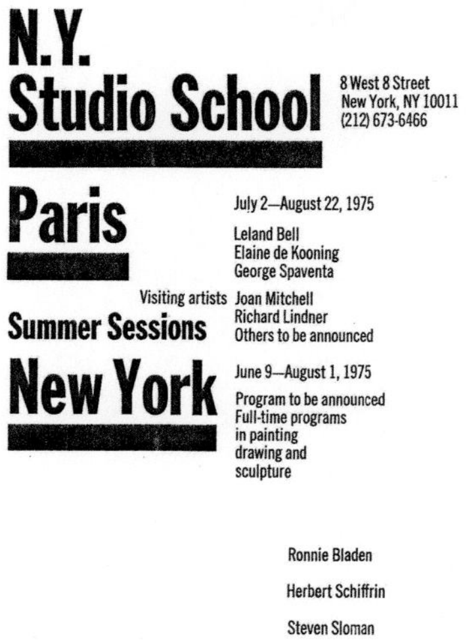

8.6

As Mitchell maintained her pace after shipping the paintings for her 1976 show with Fourcade, what came next, in works like *Posted,* was "the field reappearing . . . a different space but there's a field with a sky and—and homage to Vincent perhaps."[50] Through the next year she continued the stroke paintings, adding a range of yellow and oranges and also darker tones in works like *Sarrians* (1977, plate 94). The "ups and downs" of the 1970s ended with another tree: the linden on the terrace outside Mitchell's home, where she had lunched with Audrey and Thomas B. Hess, who, in the summer of 1978, had died suddenly, as his wife had done four years before. Mitchell saw the tree every day when she opened her door (see page 312, no. 5).[51] The *Tilleuls* (Lindens) are the most extreme of the process-heavy paintings: strong vertical strokes, largely in black, painted into a wet white ground, with touches of bright blue or teal (see plate 98). The subject also inspired dense pastels in related colors, employing relentless repetition that sometimes overtakes and obliterates the image (plate 97). The touchstone of the everyday was essential amidst the emotional chaos of the time: Riopelle told Mitchell that he and Jeffcoat had begun a romantic relationship, a wrenching betrayal and protracted double-parting that occupied much of fall/winter 1978 into the next year. Some report that the *Tilleuls* were the first works Mitchell undertook upon hearing the news.[52] The everyday constancy of making those marks structured her time, and the solid, unwavering fact of the linden gave her something outside herself to hold onto. As Mitchell paraphrased van Gogh, "I give gratitude to trees because they exist."[53]

FIG 8.5 Linda Nochlin's datebook noting a meeting with Joan Mitchell, November 11, 1977. Linda Nochlin Papers, Archives of American Art, Smithsonian Institution, Washington, D.C.

FIG 8.6 New York Studio School advertisement, 1975. The New York Studio School of Drawing, Painting, and Sculpture

Weeds, 1976

Cecilia Wichmann

Weeds is illustrated in full as plate 92.

FIG 8.7 Xavier Fourcade with *Weeds* (1976) in Joan Mitchell's studio at La Tour, Vétheuil, France, ca. June 1976. Joan Mitchell Foundation Archives, New York

FIG 8.8 **Joan Mitchell** *Weeds I,* 1992. Etching and aquatint, 22¾ × 33¼ in. (57.8 × 84.5 cm), ed. 25. Printed and published by Tyler Graphics Ltd., Mount Kisco, New York

When Xavier Fourcade visited Mitchell at La Tour in June 1976 to lay the groundwork for her first exhibition at his New York gallery that fall, *Weeds* (plate 92) was well underway but not quite finished, as a photograph of Fourcade in Mitchell's studio attests: the painting leans against the wall behind him, its two panels pushed together (fig. 8.7).

Compare *Weeds* as it appears in the photograph to the completed work. The left panel was already covered top and bottom with vertical strokes—"those seductive pawmarks," one critic would call them at Fourcade—though a rosy clearing near the panel's center would soon be worked over.[1] Search for this patch of pink in the completed painting and find it glowing beneath a diagonal procession of arcing blue forms—trusses, branches, legs with feet—tunneling in nearly linear perspective. Traipsing down and to the right, the color blue leaps the boundary between panels and pools underneath an orange triangle. These adjustments, made between Fourcade's visit and the work's completion, built momentum, a lateral choreography that propels the composition from left to right.

Yet Mitchell also worked to disrupt this trajectory, calibrating tension at the interstice where the two panels meet. Orange vertical marks alternate on either side of the gap. Some she laid down before the photograph was taken, but others she added, tightening their relation to one another. Notice a wide orange mark at bottom right, parallel to the floating triangle, and a knife-thin one at center left. They firm up the boundary between the two panels, reinforcing their separateness while at the same time making an event of their proximity. The right panel compresses toward its side of this shimmering gap with roiling, centripetal energy. Instead of traversing over and across, as on the left, this view presses down and in.

By October, "the blue and orange diptych" was finished and shipped to New York ahead of the November opening.[2] The title *Weeds* first appears in Mitchell's list for the show's catalogue, along with *Straw* and *Clinging Vine,* titles that corroborated critics' observations that the artist's new body of work burgeoned with plantlike energy, "the effect of leaves and stems, of something growing."[3] *Weeds* was characteristic of this quality, even if it was more "frenetic" than the other works, an outlier for its blazing blue and orange palette.[4] The painting would be acquired out of the Fourcade show by Joseph Hirshhorn for the newly opened Hirshhorn Museum and Sculpture Garden in Washington, D.C.

The title *Weeds* does not delimit Mitchell's subject so much as spur associations that work together with the visual experience to elicit a feeling. Weeds are wayward plants, bursting from the earth and spreading out with hardy indifference to human plans. Keeping weeds in check is a disciplined practice, a job that is never done. Yet gardeners recognize it as necessary and constructive, since weeds can hinder desired plants and break apart pathways and steps. To weed is to impose limits, to constrain some elements such that others may flourish.

What counts as a weed, however, is all about context and preference. Many of Mitchell's favorite trees and flowers were weedlike: wild oaks, honeysuckle, daisies. Sunflowers became a recurring subject in her work after their "seeds flew around" and astonished her gardener by springing up "in unexpected places."[5] It is easy to imagine Mitchell admiring, even identifying with such resilient forms of life—beautiful in their toughness, untethered by discriminative social categories that would dictate where and how they should root themselves in the world.

With multiple gardens surrounding her home and studio, weeding was a routine part of life at La Tour. Notes left by Mitchell for visitors in these years, often written over nights of painting, frequently enlisted them to help with various chores, including caring for the garden. "Got your weeds through the gate," she wrote early one summer morning in 1976 to Patricia Molloy, who was visiting from New York. "Could you not 'dead head' roses."[6]

Like painting on a large scale, weeding is full-bodied work. Plants are yanked from the ground and piled up. Stems, leaves, and roots tangle, their linear forms clinging into a volume. Wrap your arms around this bundle and smell the wet heat of decomposition already underway. Allowed to live, weeds luxuriate—they thicken and spring forth, always finding new ways to grow. Like paint, weeds drip; Mitchell's close friend the composer Gisèle Barreau described *Weeds* as "herbes jaillissantes" (gushing weeds), capturing this shared liquidity.[7] Reviewing the Fourcade show, critic Ann Sargent Wooster recognized such tactile proximity as the viewpoint of Mitchell's new paintings, "as if one were not observing nature but pressing one's face into it."[8]

The struggle with weeding, as with painting, is to determine what is vibrant, desirable, and what must be brought under control. In *Weeds,* Mitchell explored the potential benefits of rigorously observed constraints. She restricted her palette to complementary blue and orange, with pink and green in a secondary role; these colors intensify when paired. She controlled her brushwork; vertical strokes demarcate oval areas that pulsate with petallike dabs. She reinforced the parameters of each panel, drawing out a dueling, oppositional dynamic in the diptych format while using color and line to span the whole. By compounding constraints—keeping color, mark, and format in check—Mitchell heightened the impact of each, resulting in a painting that bursts with weedlike energy, as if unconstrained by its own spatial boundaries.

Mitchell would reprise the theme of weeds in several print series completed at Tyler Graphics in the final month of her life (fig. 8.8). These prints distill the mechanics of *Weeds* on a much smaller scale and with graphic clarity, this time by means of a three-color layering process. Here again, Mitchell shows the discipline it takes to keep the visual field alive. Out of a tangled mass, a wayward line approaches a boundary and leaps the gap to another sheet.

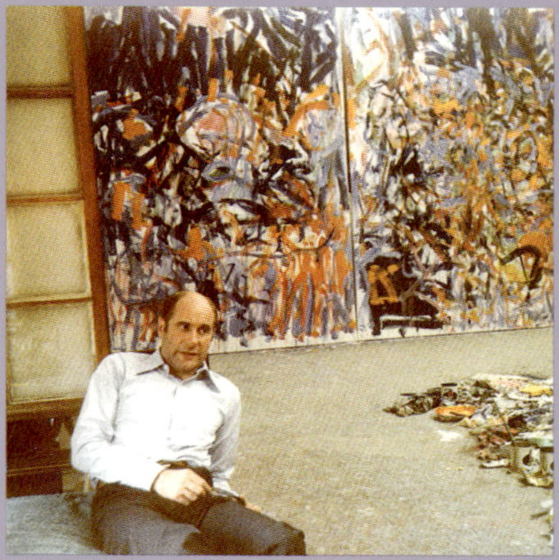

8.7

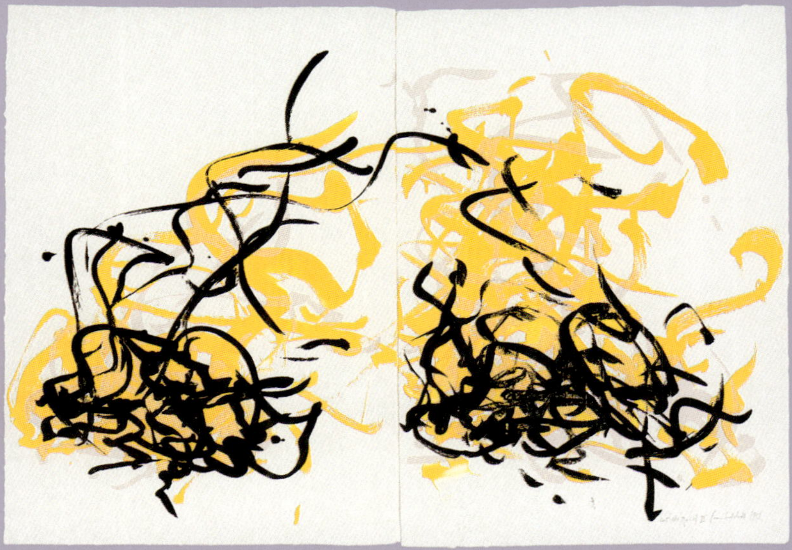

8.8

SHIFTING FRAMEWORKS 1974–79

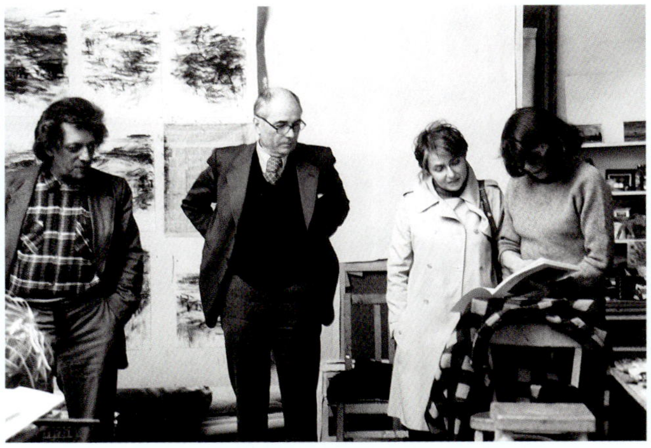

1

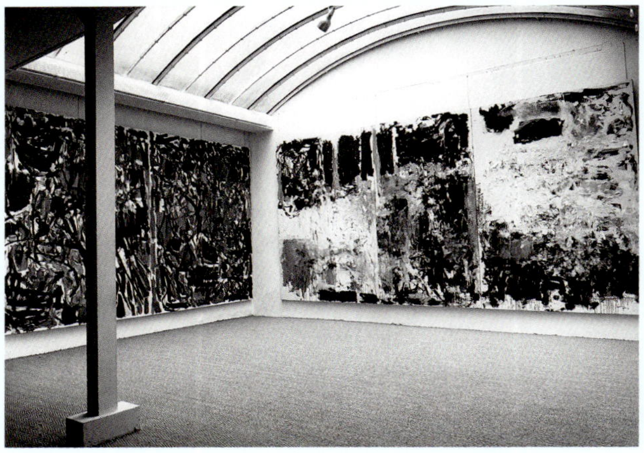

2

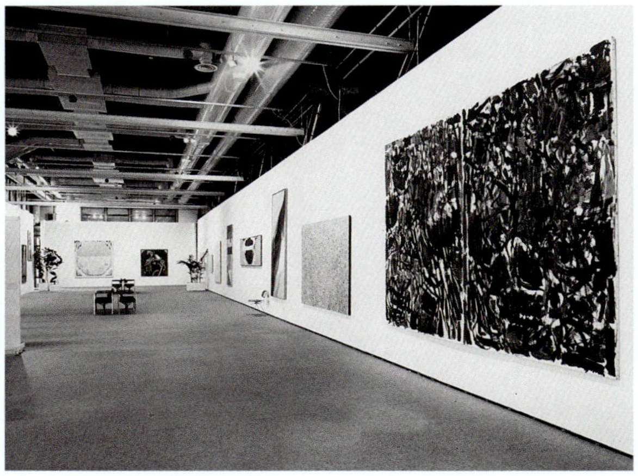

3

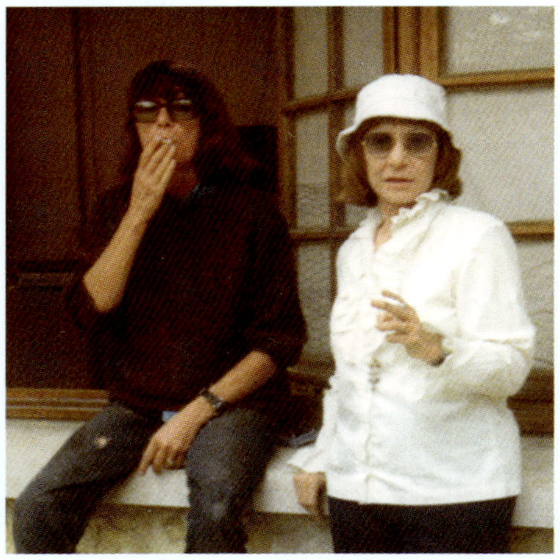

4

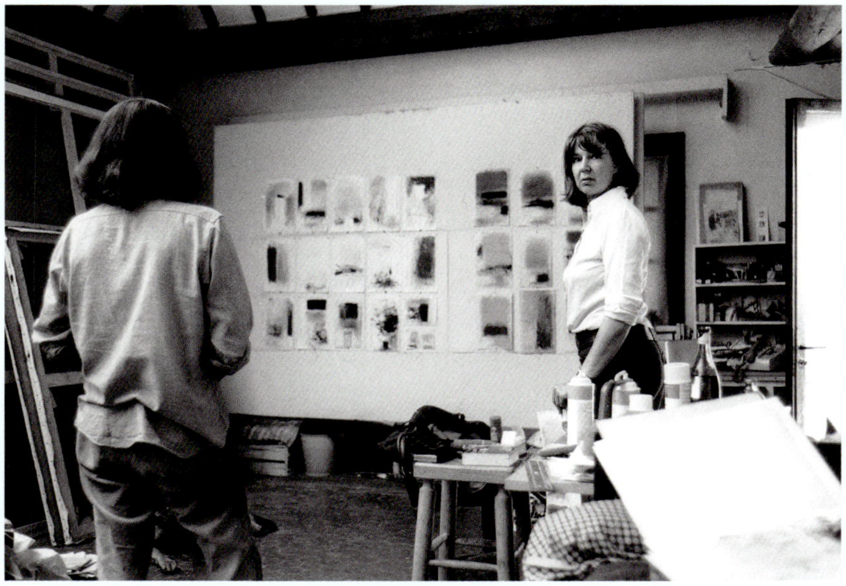

5

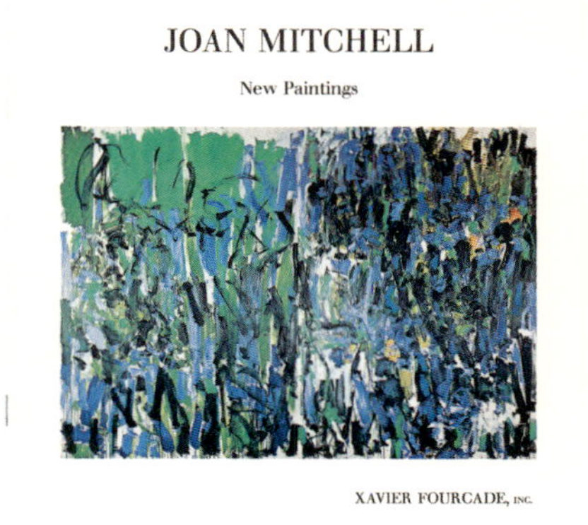

8

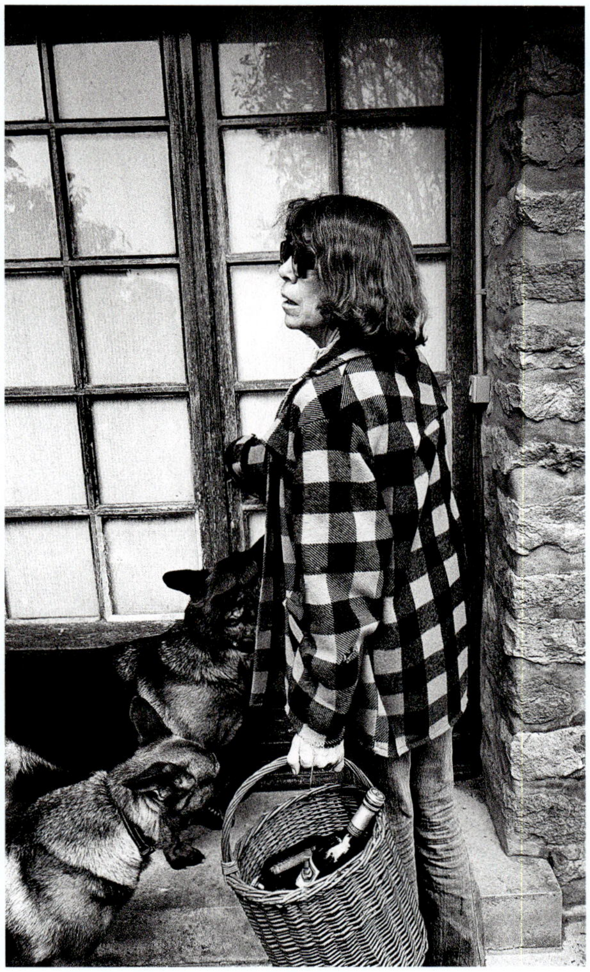

6

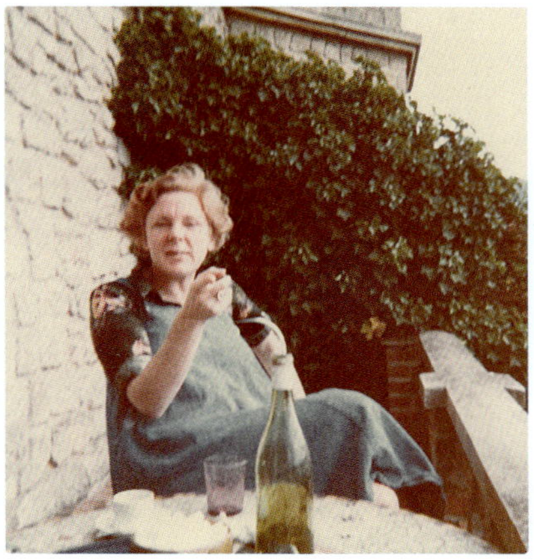

7

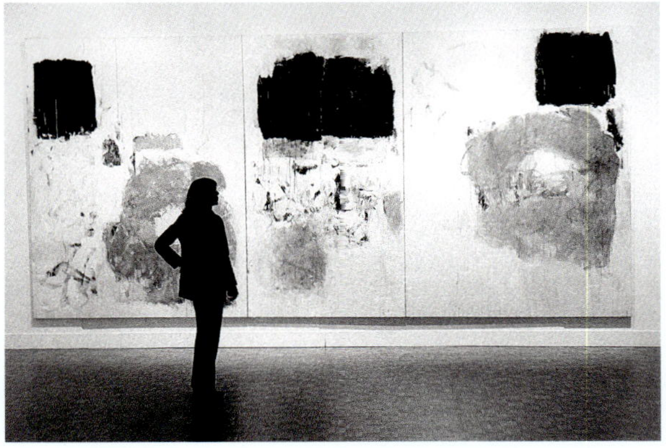

9

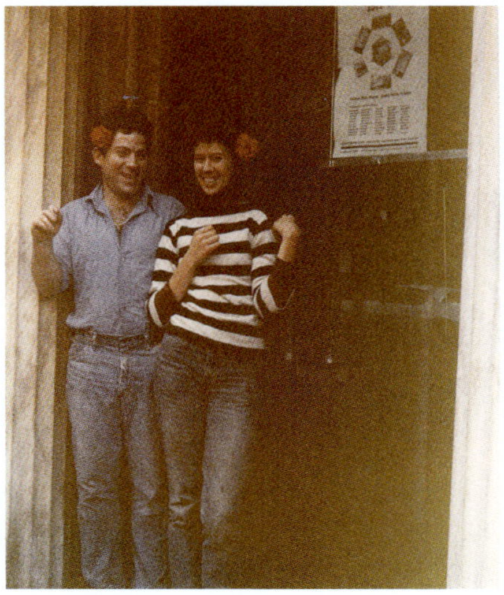

10

1 Jean Paul Riopelle, Jean Fournier, Shirley Jaffe, and Joan Mitchell in Mitchell's studio at La Tour, Vétheuil, France, 1978. Sam Francis Papers, Getty Research Institute, Los Angeles

2 *Sylvie's Sunday* (1976) and *Canada I* (1975) in *Joan Mitchell* at Galerie Jean Fournier, Paris, 1976. Galerie Jean Fournier, Paris

3 Installation view of *Quelques peintres américains à Paris,* Musée national d'art moderne, Paris, 1977. Works by Joan Mitchell, Sam Francis, Paul Jenkins, and Shirley Jaffe are visible.

4 Joan Mitchell and Elaine de Kooning outside Mitchell's studio at La Tour, Vétheuil, France, 1976 (detail). Joan Mitchell Foundation Archives, New York

5 Joan Mitchell and Zuka Mitelberg in Mitchell's studio at La Tour, Vétheuil, France, ca. 1975. Joan Mitchell Foundation Archives, New York

6 Joan Mitchell outside her studio at La Tour, Vétheuil, France, 1979

7 Linda Nochlin on the terrace at La Tour, Vétheuil, France, 1975. Linda Nochlin Papers, Archives of American Art, Smithsonian Institution, Washington, D.C.

8 *No Rain* (1976) on the cover of *Joan Mitchell: New Paintings* (New York: Xavier Fourcade, 1976)

9 Joan Mitchell at *Joan Mitchell,* Whitney Museum of American Art, New York, 1974

10 Carl Plansky and Hollis Jeffcoat outside the New York Studio School, 1978. Joan Mitchell Foundation Archives, New York

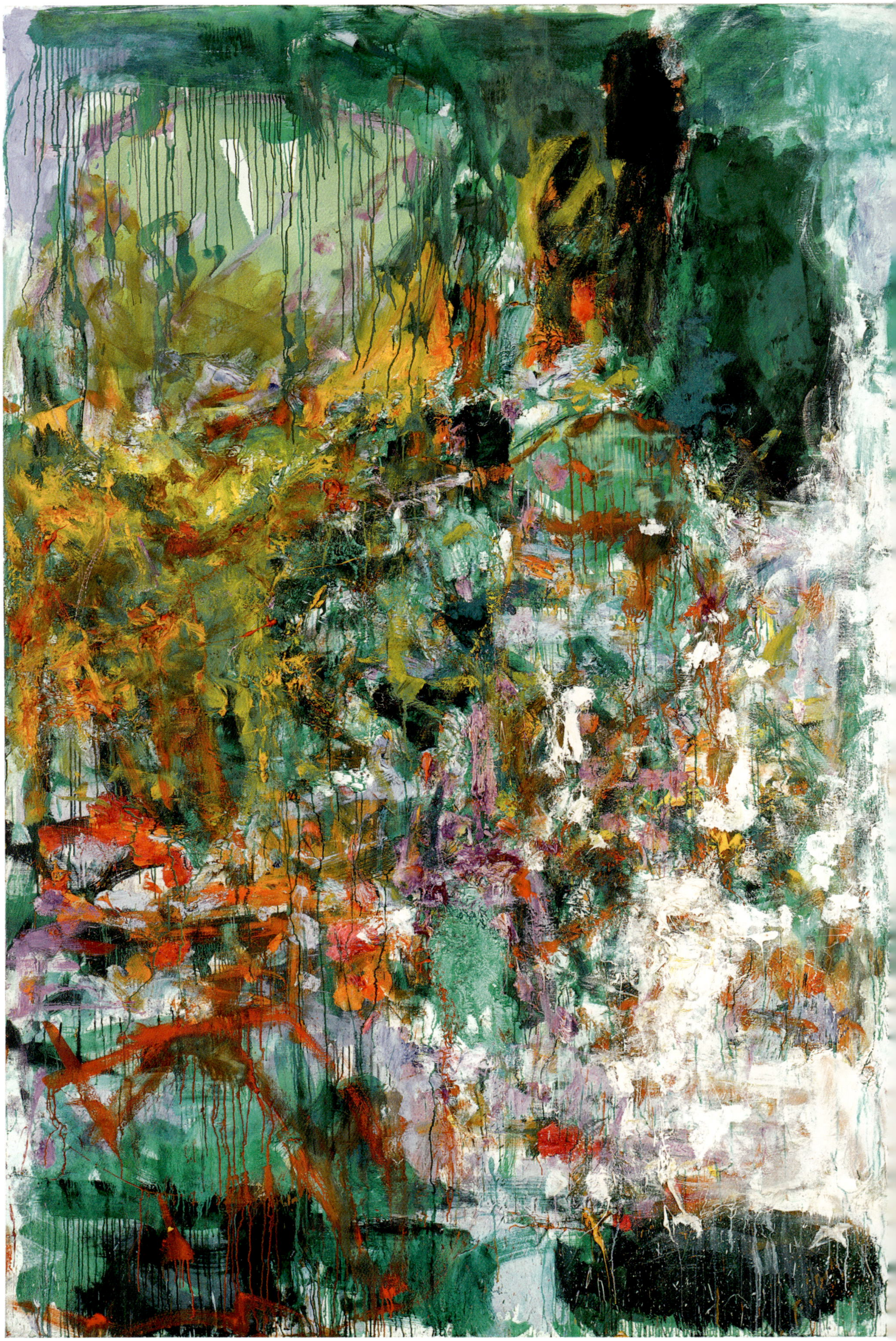

Garden for Audrey, 1975. Oil on canvas, 99½ × 141¾ in. (252.7 × 360 cm). Private collection

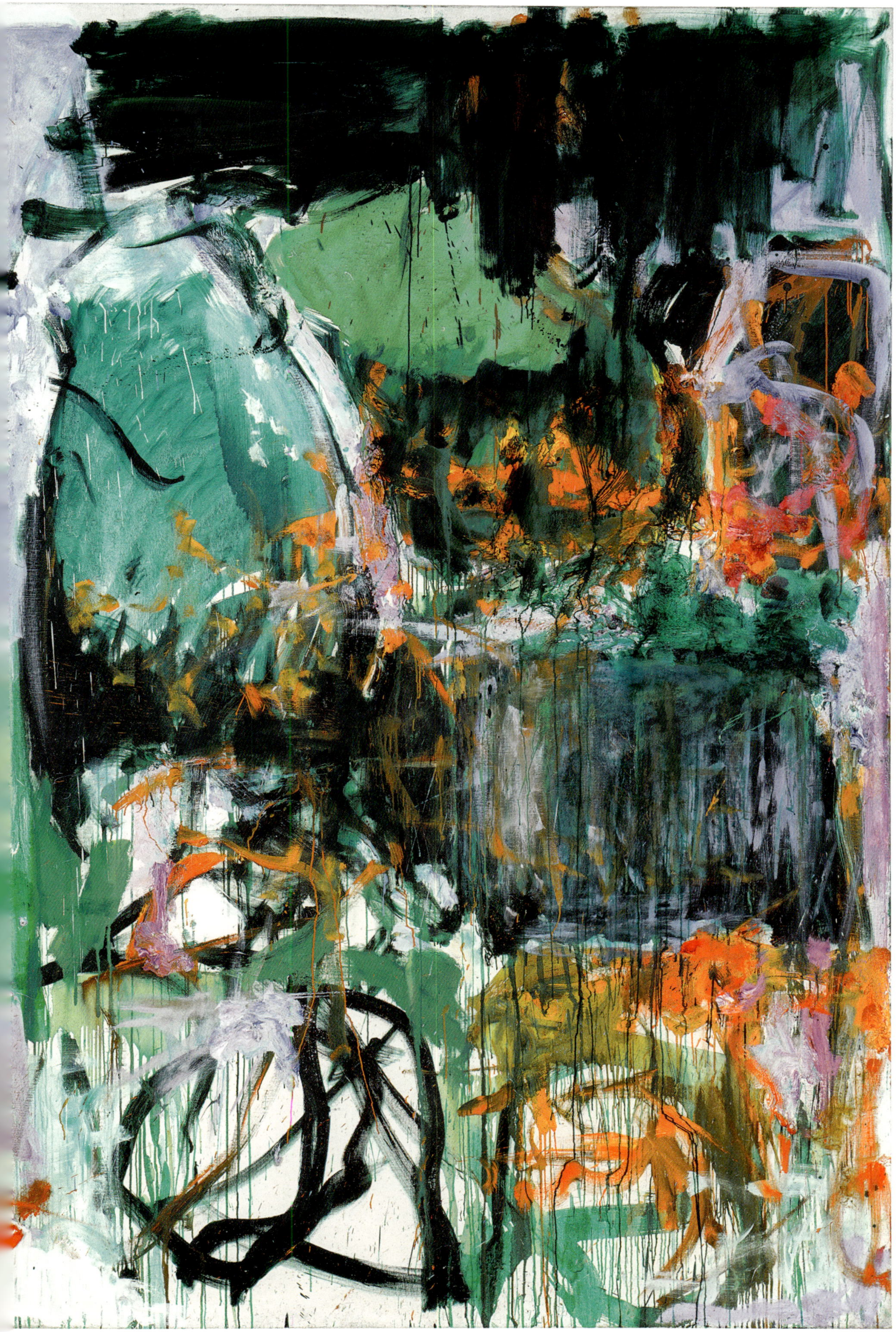

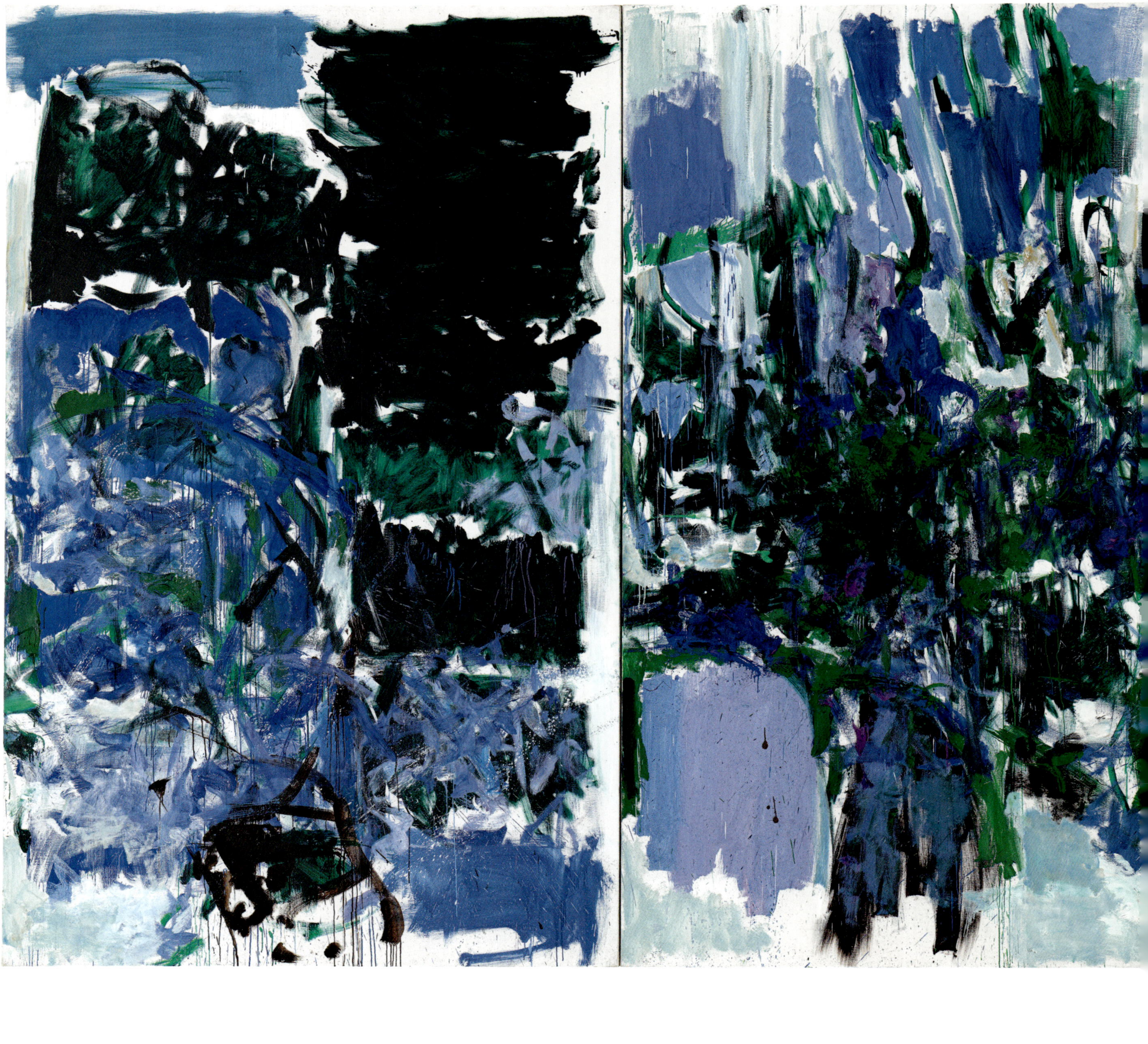

Quatuor II for Betsy Jolas, 1976. Oil on canvas, 110 × 268 in. (279.4 × 680.7 cm). Centre Pompidou, Paris, on deposit at the Musée de Peinture et de Sculpture, Grenoble, France

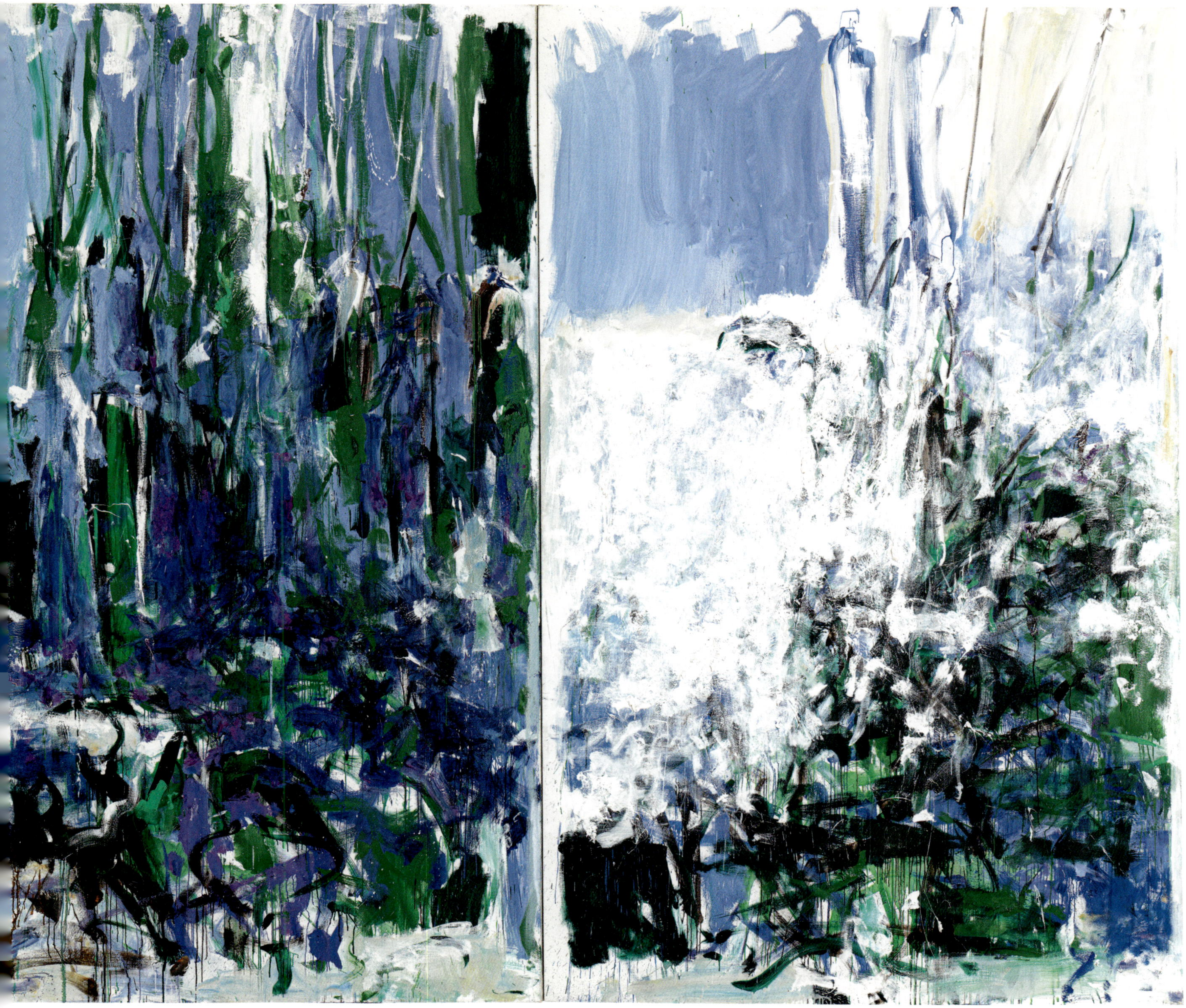

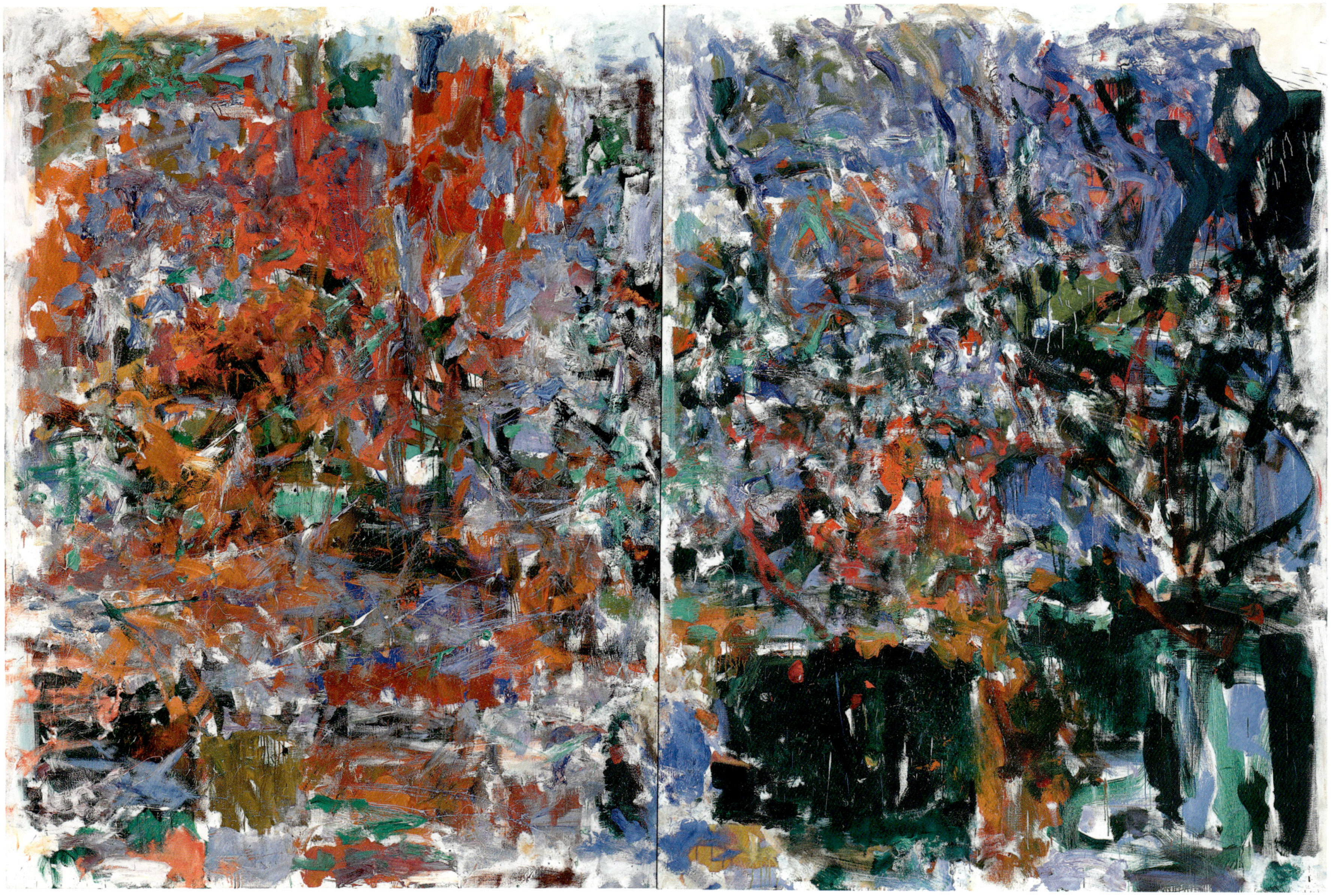

Aires pour Marion, 1975–76. Oil on canvas, 94¼ × 142⅜ in. (239.4 × 361.6 cm). Collection of Joan and Preston Haskell

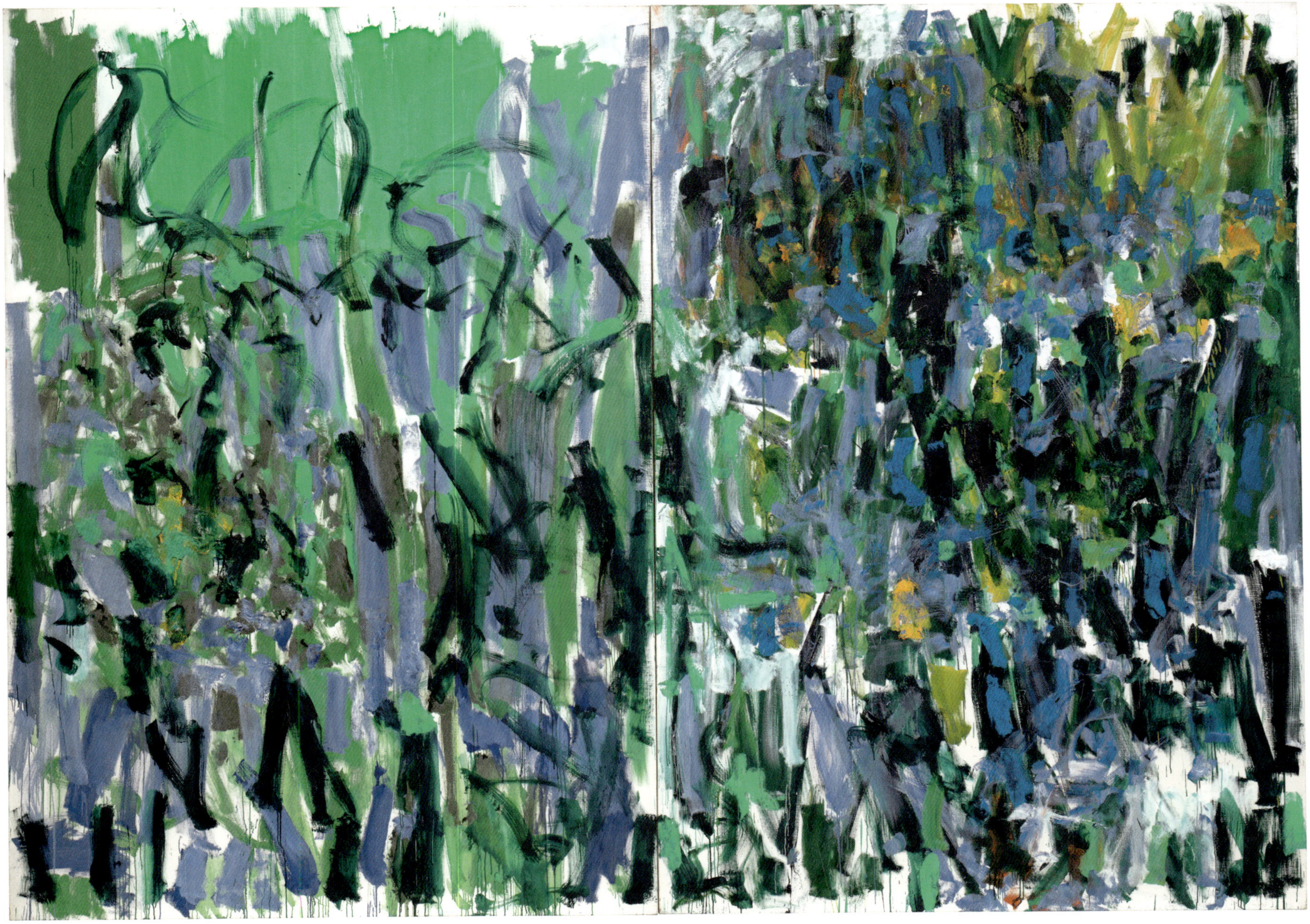

No Rain, 1976. Oil on canvas, 110 × 158 in. (279.4 × 401.3 cm). The Museum of Modern Art, New York, gift of The Estate of Joan Mitchell

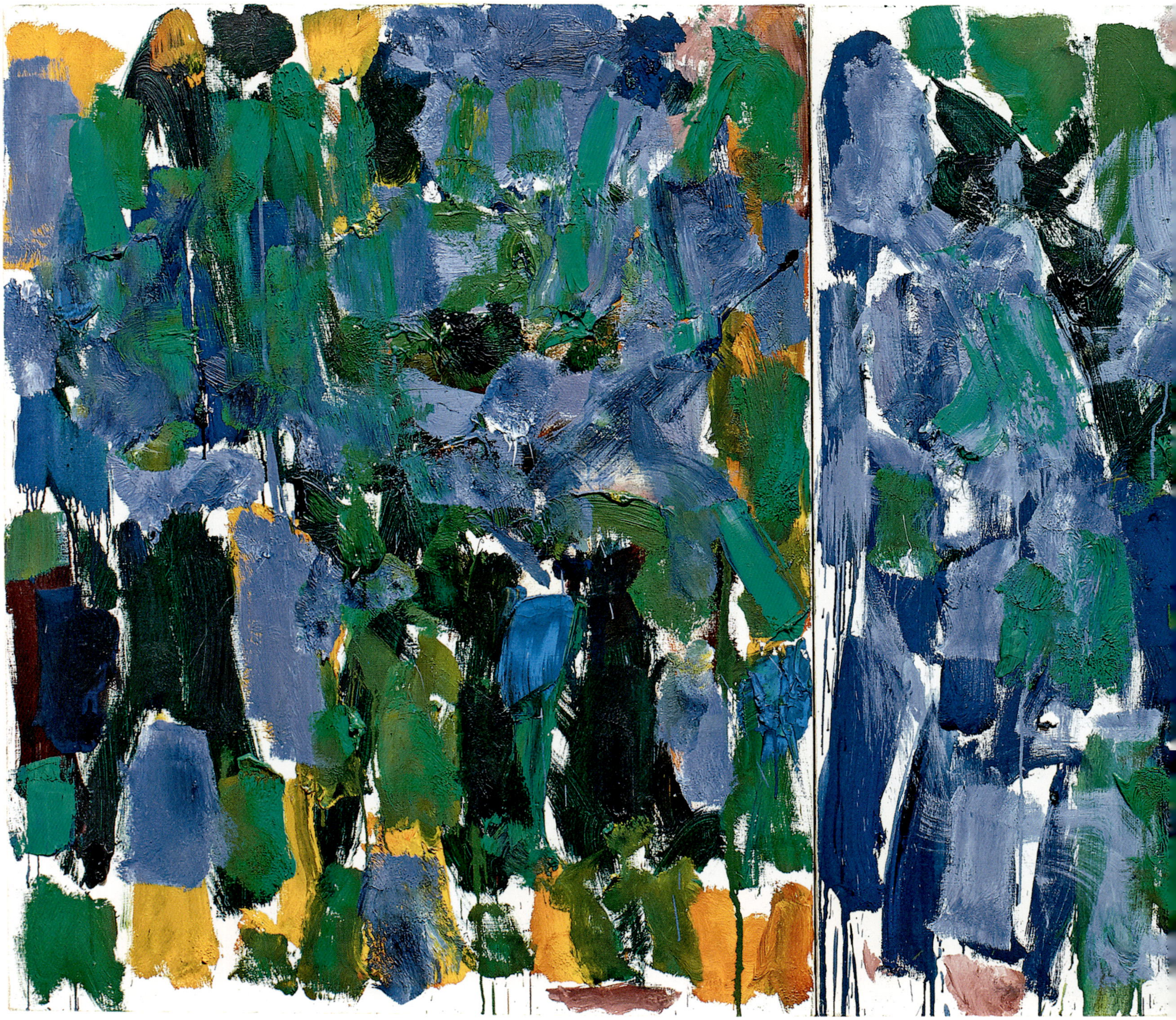

Parasol, 1977. Oil on canvas, 39⅜ × 96⅛ in. (100 × 244.2 cm). Collection of Robert J. Buford

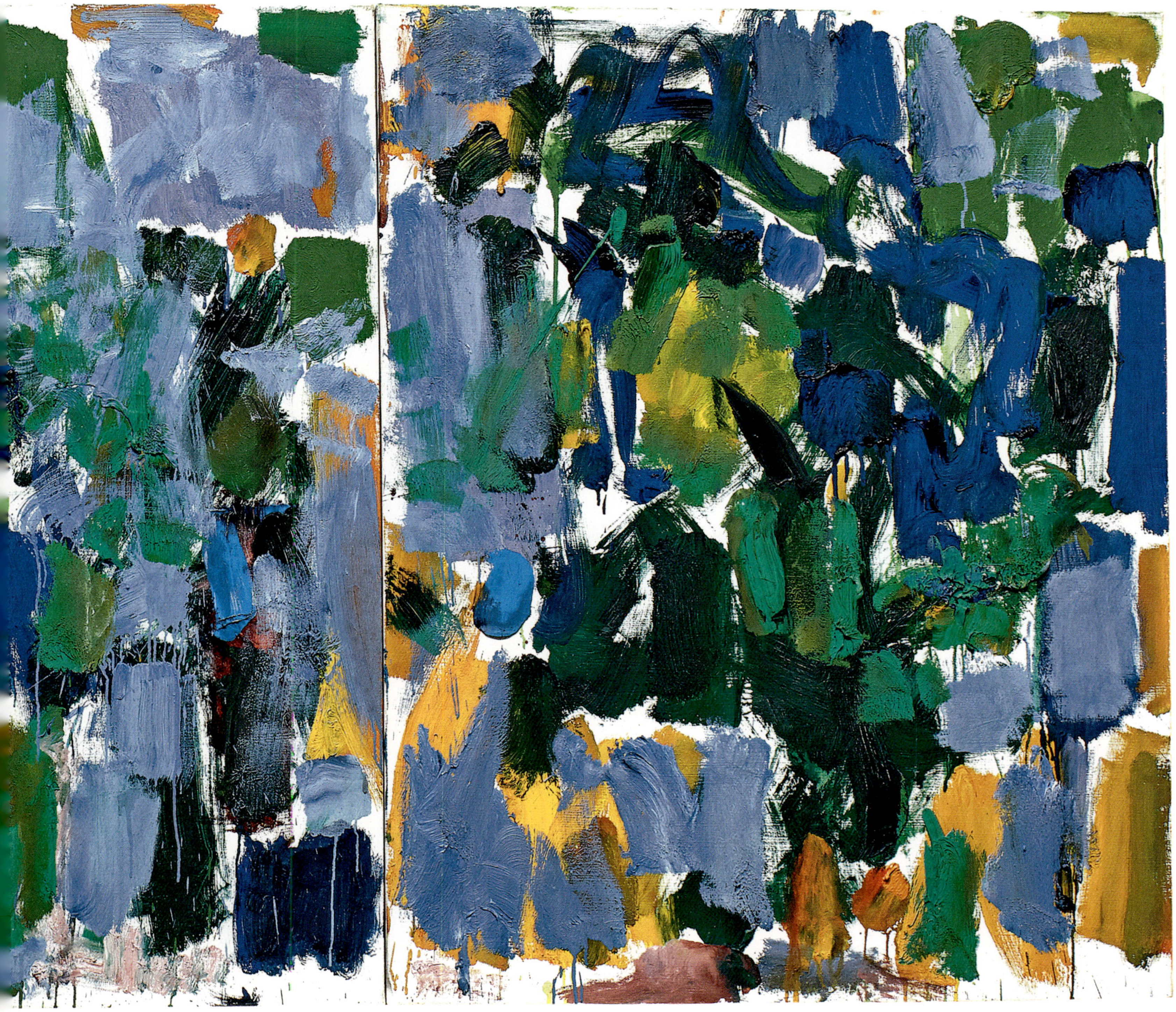

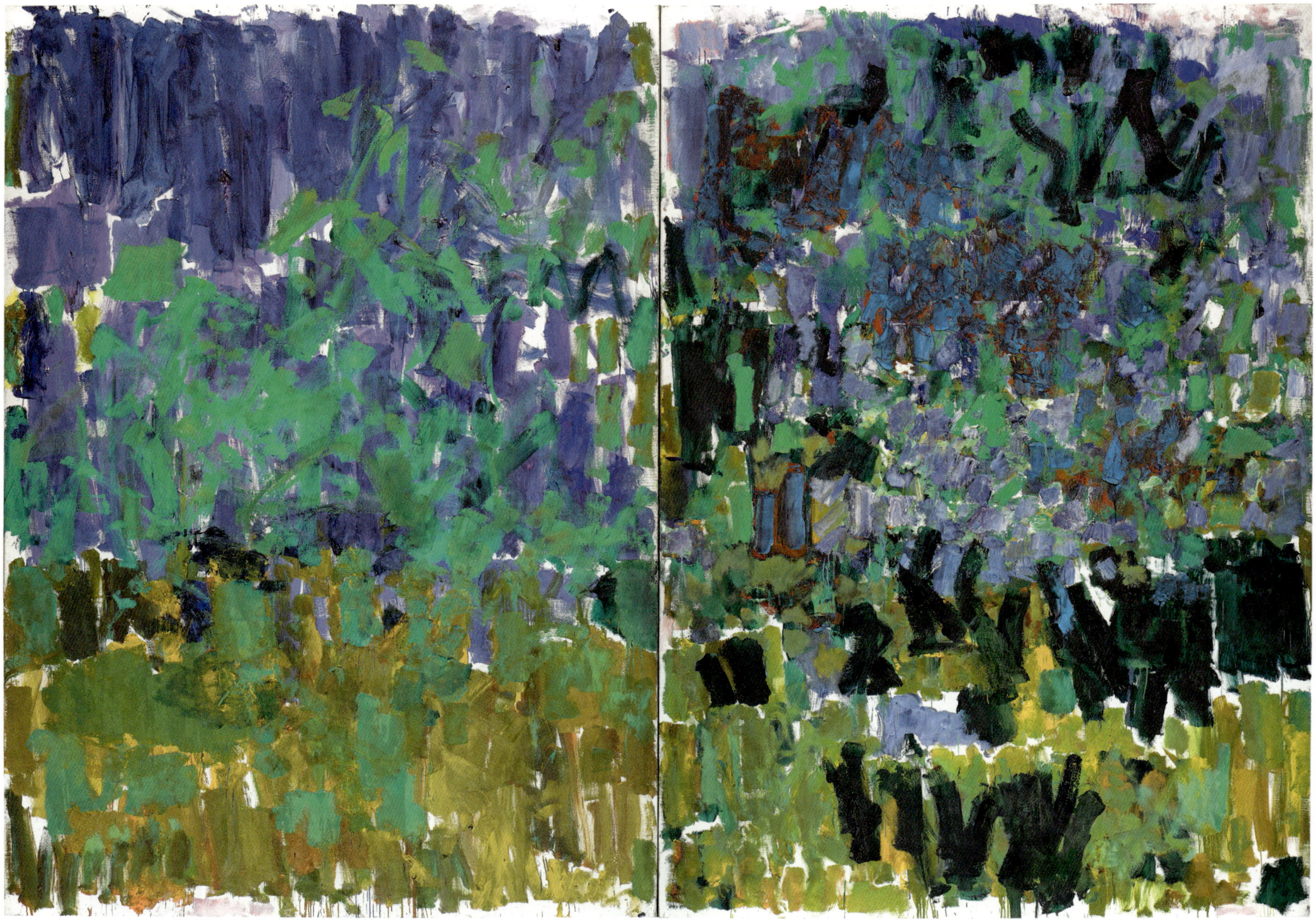

Posted, 1977. Oil on canvas, 110¾ × 157⅞ in. (281.3 × 401 cm). Walker Art Center, Minneapolis, gift of Joanne and Philip Von Blon

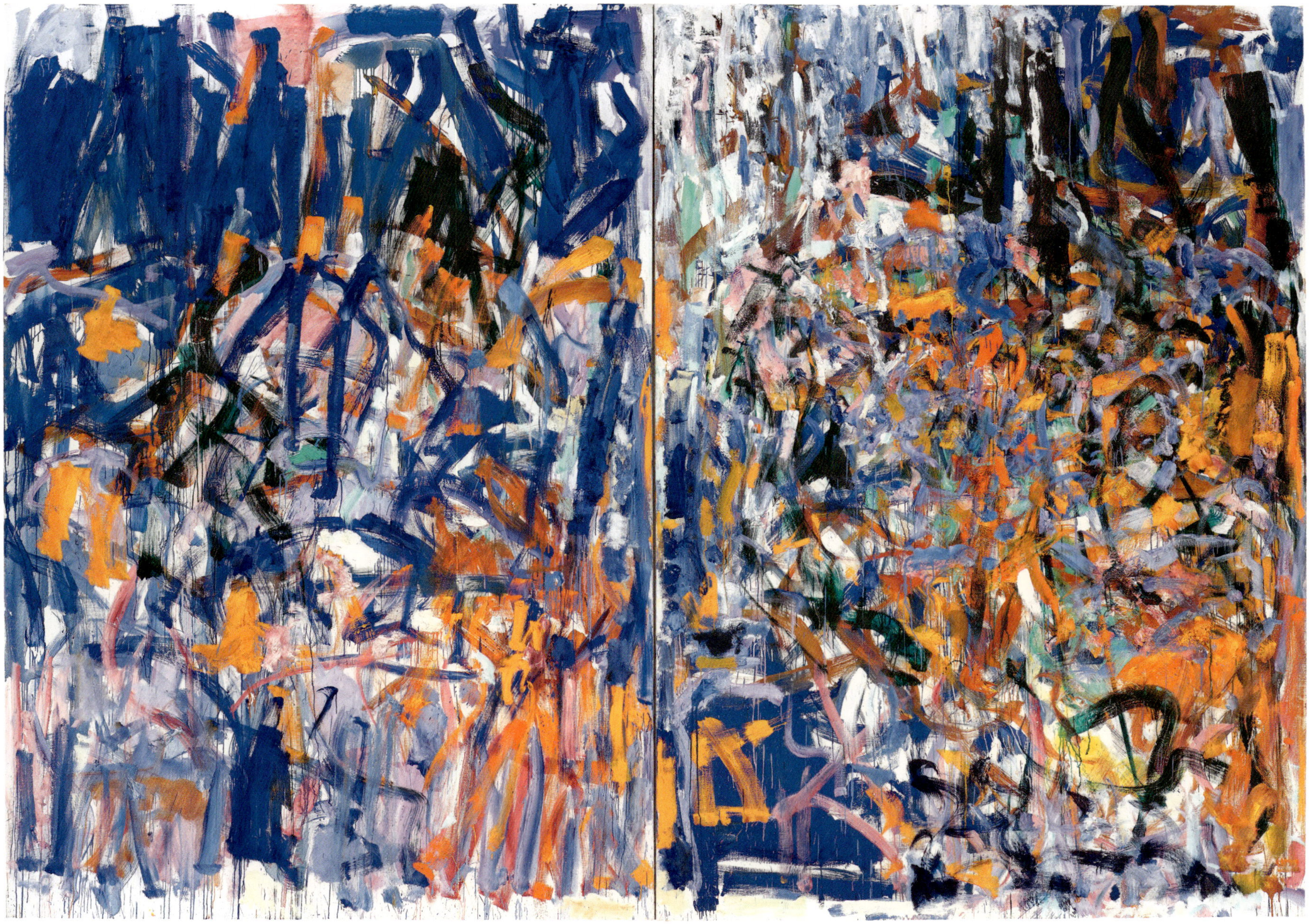

Weeds, 1976. Oil on canvas, 110½ × 157½ in. (280.7 × 400.1 cm). Hirshhorn Museum and Sculpture Garden, Smithsonian Institution, Washington, D.C., gift of Joseph H. Hirshhorn

PLATE 93

Red Tree, 1976. Oil on canvas, 110 × 63 in. (279.4 × 160 cm). Fondation Louis Vuitton, Paris

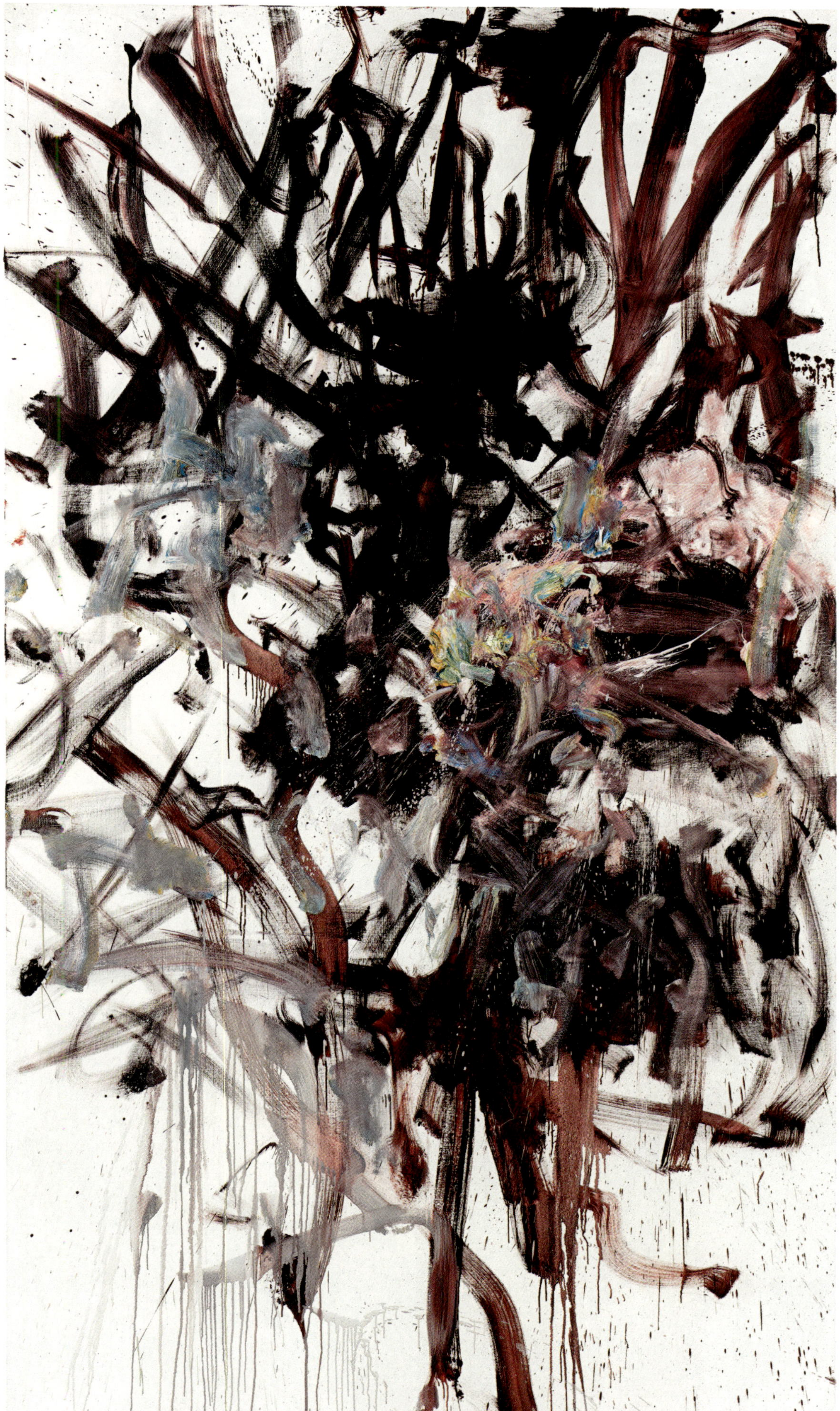

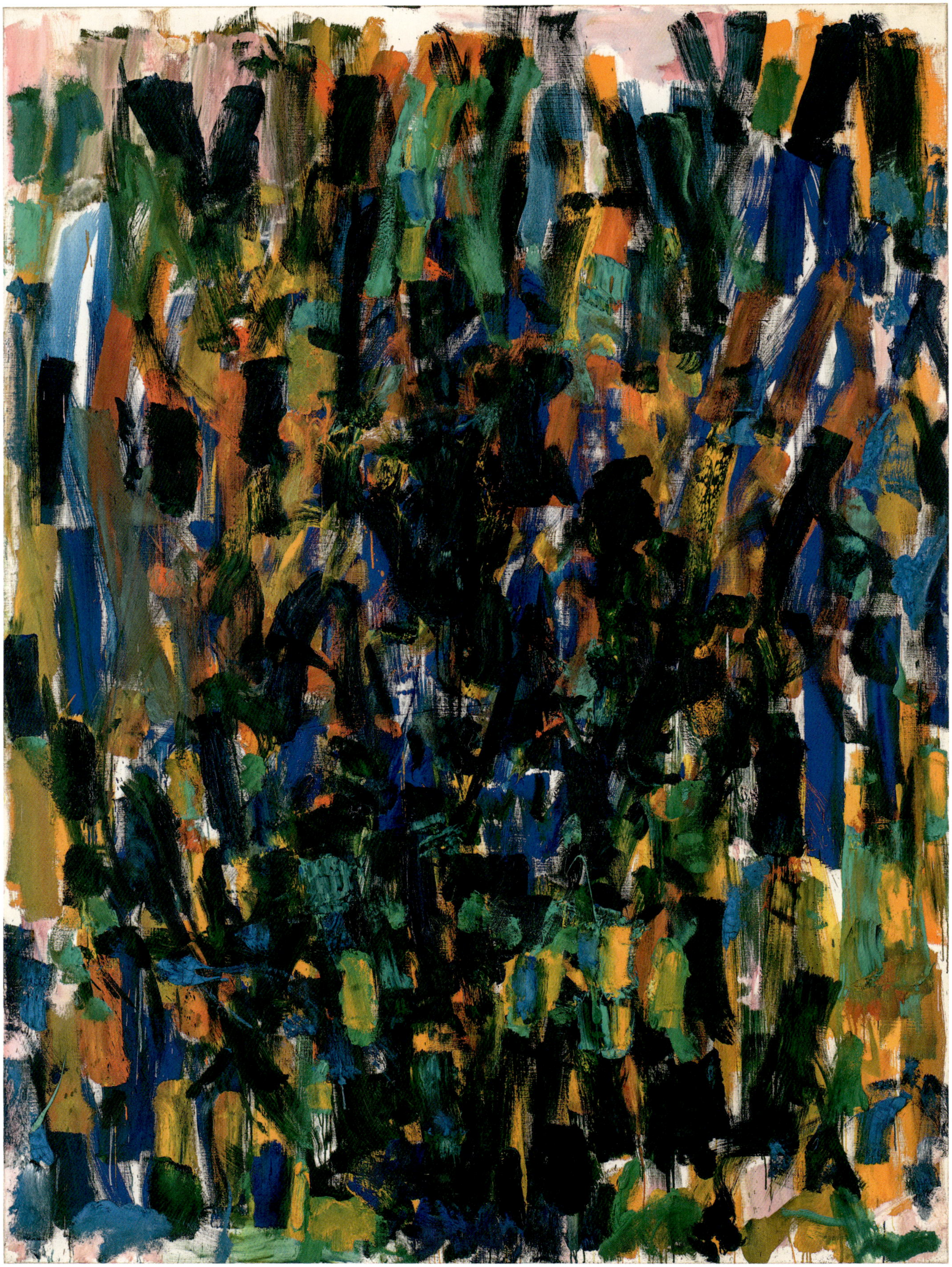

Sarrians, 1977. Oil on canvas, 94¼ × 71 in. (239.4 × 180.3 cm). Private collection

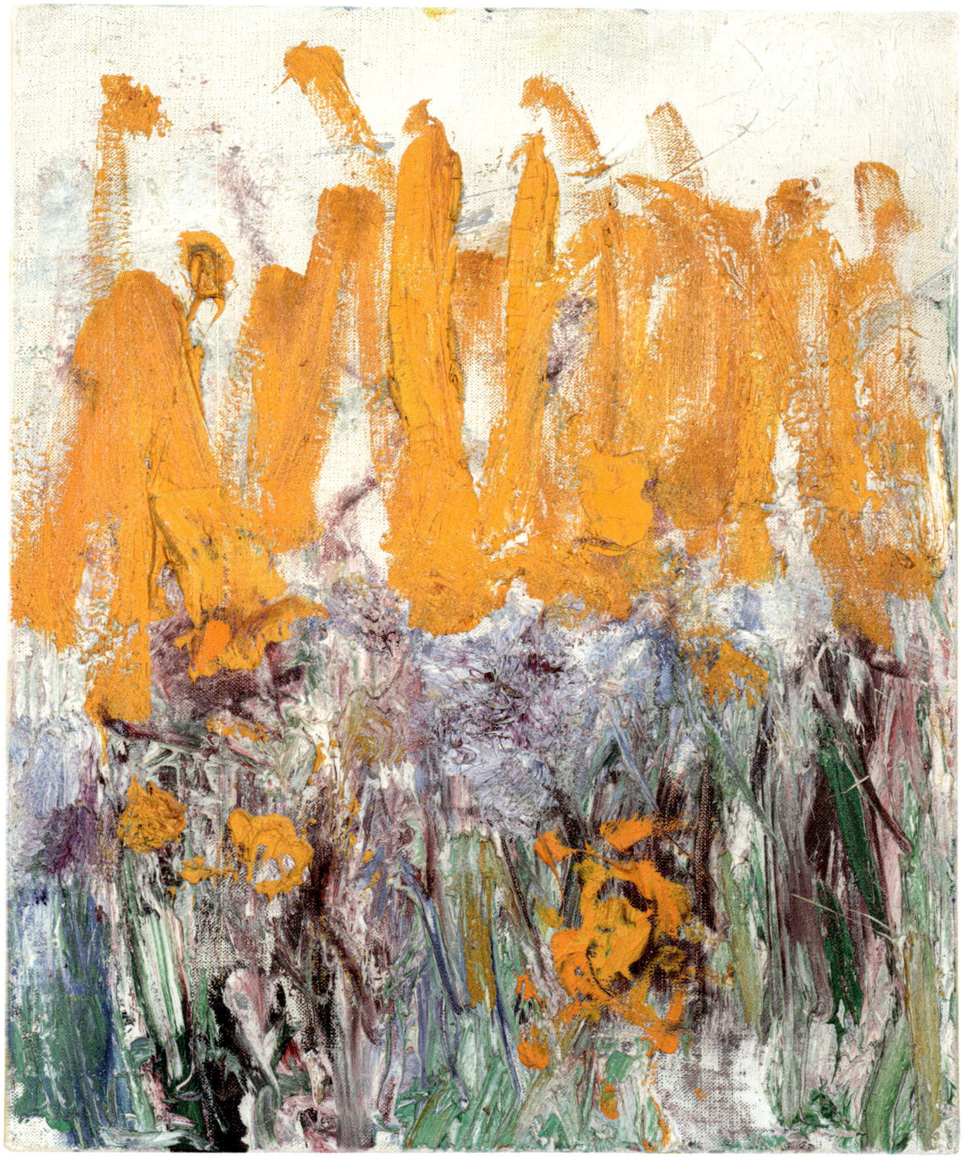

La Lande, 1977. Oil on canvas, 18¼ × 15⅛ in. (46.4 × 38.4 cm). Private collection

Untitled, 1978. Pastel on paper, 22⅞ × 15⅜ in. (55.1 × 39.1 cm). Joan Mitchell Foundation, New York

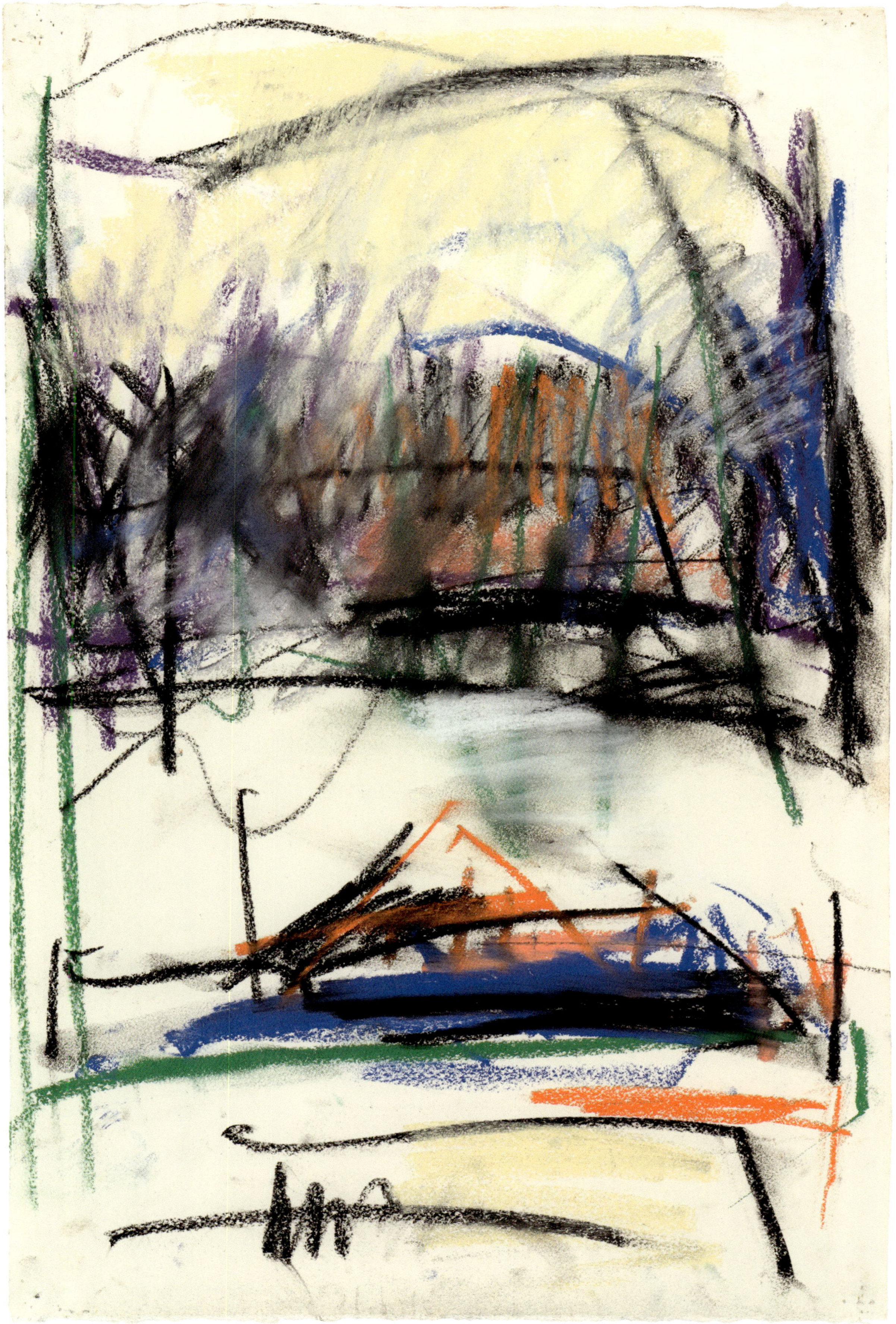

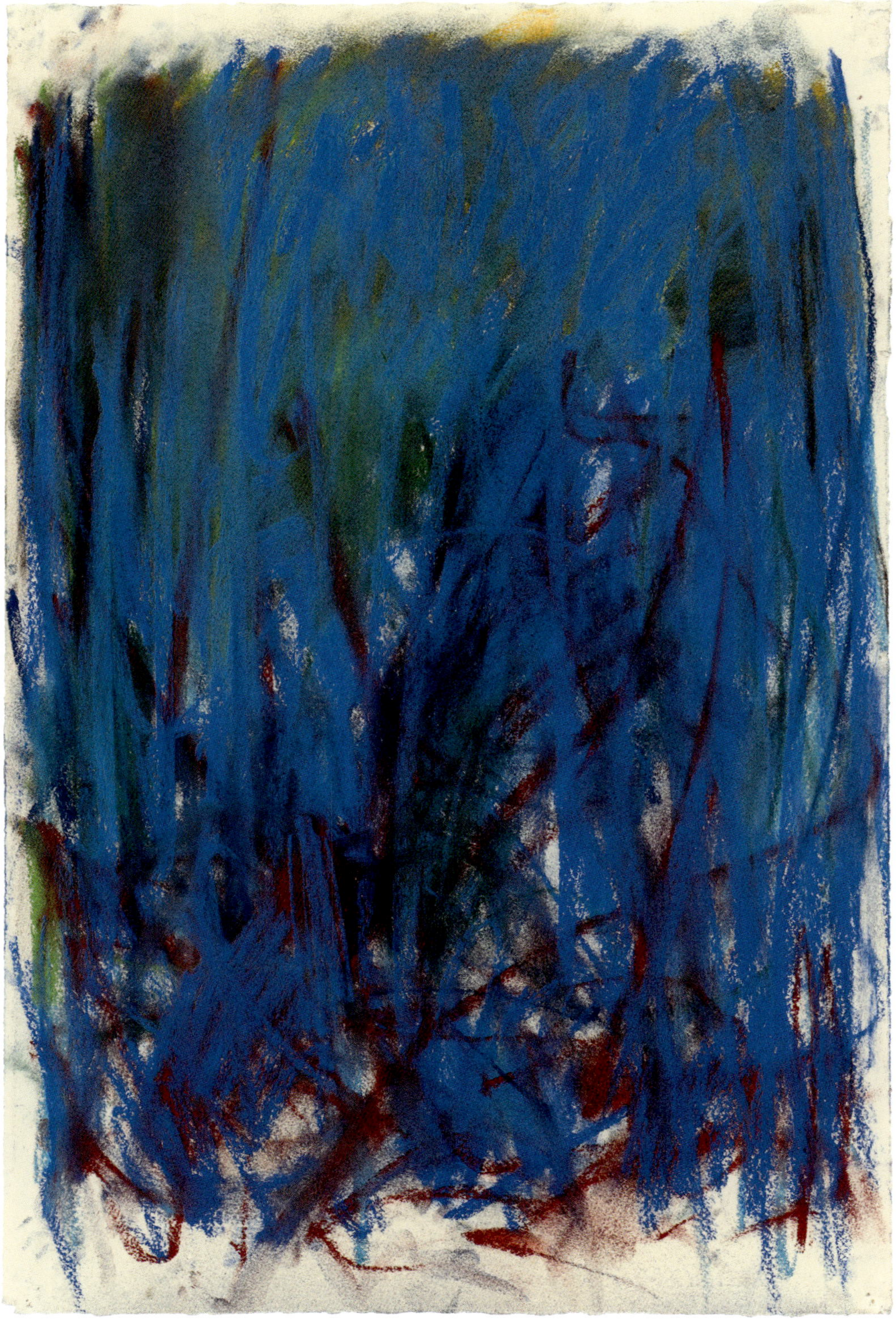

Untitled, 1977. Pastel and charcoal on paper, 22⅞ × 15½ in. (58.1 × 39.4 cm). Joan Mitchell Foundation, New York

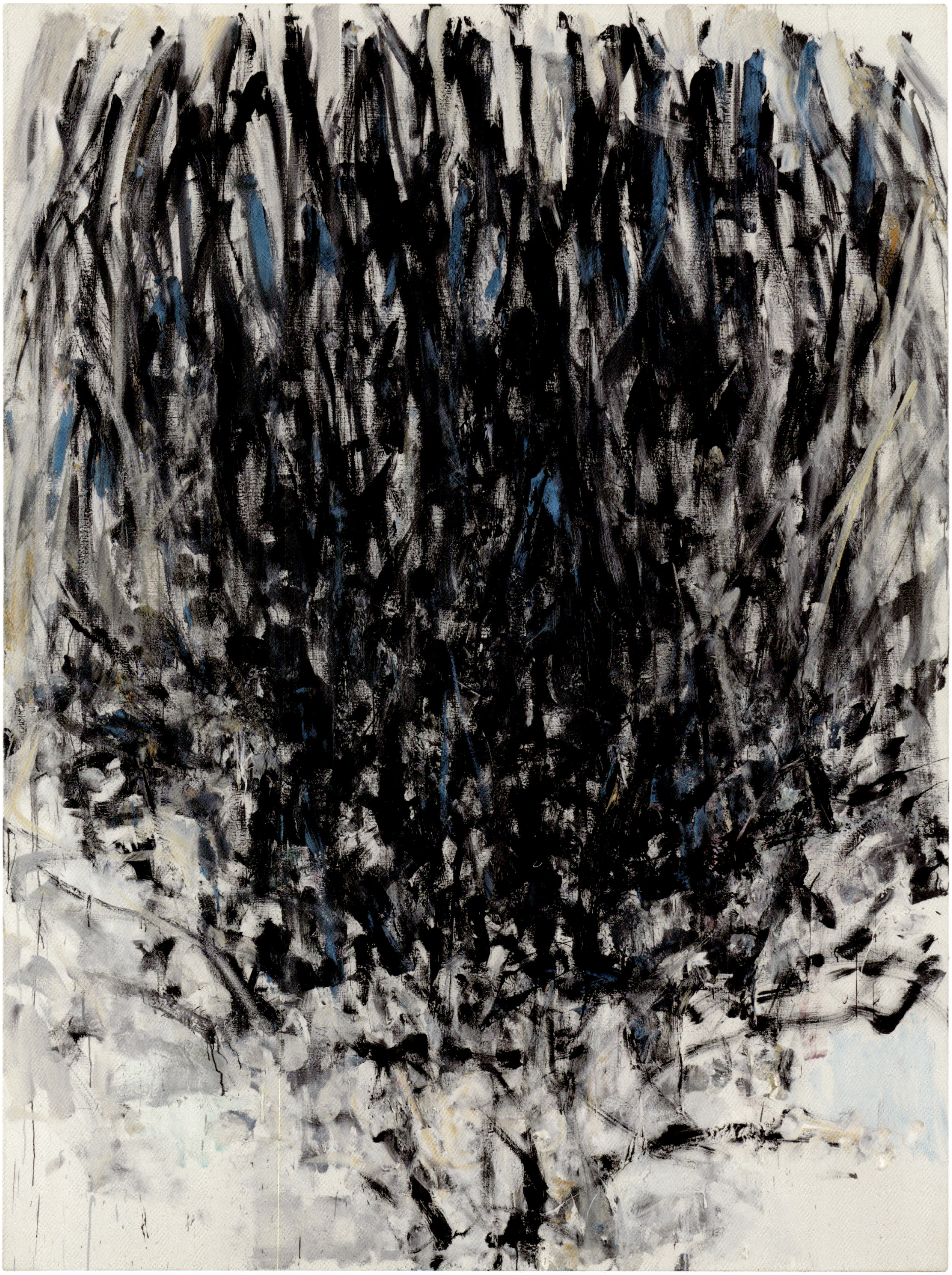

Tilleul, 1978. Oil on canvas, 94½ × 70¾ in. (240 × 179.7 cm). Fondation Louis Vuitton, Paris

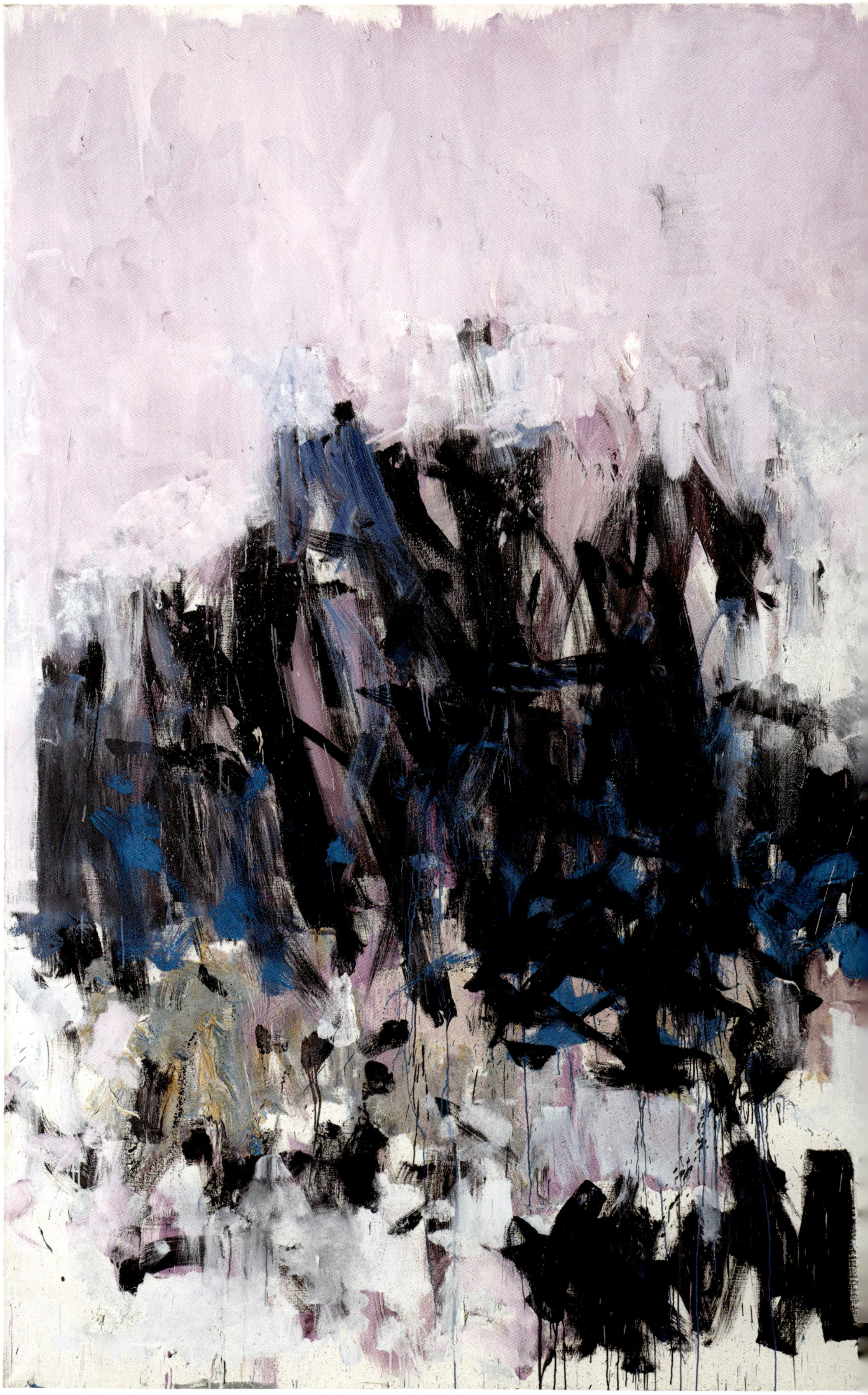

La Vie en rose, 1979. Oil on canvas, 110⅜ × 268¼ in. (280.4 × 681.4 cm). The Metropolitan Museum of Art, New York, anonymous gift and purchase, George A. Hearn Fund, by exchange

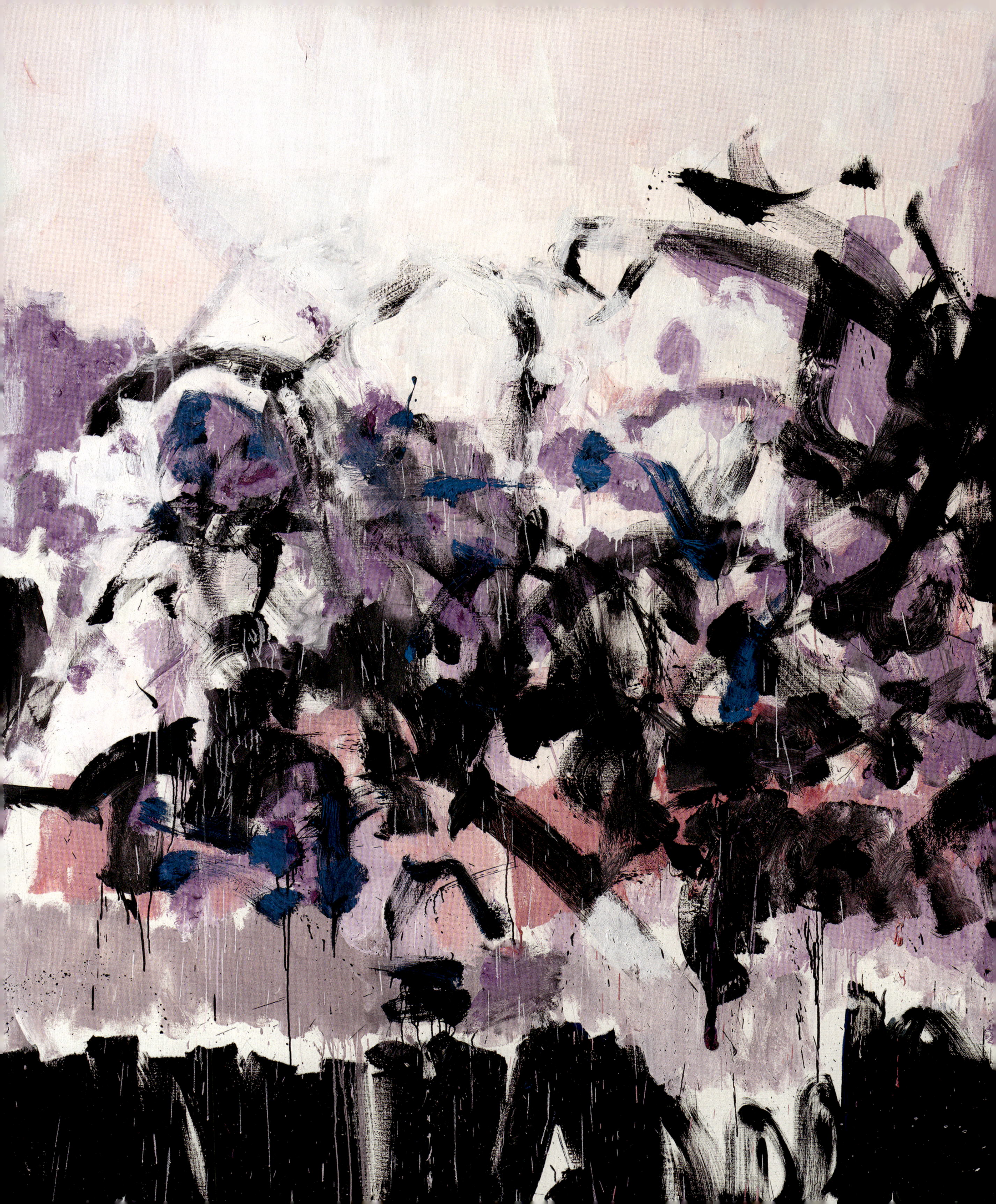

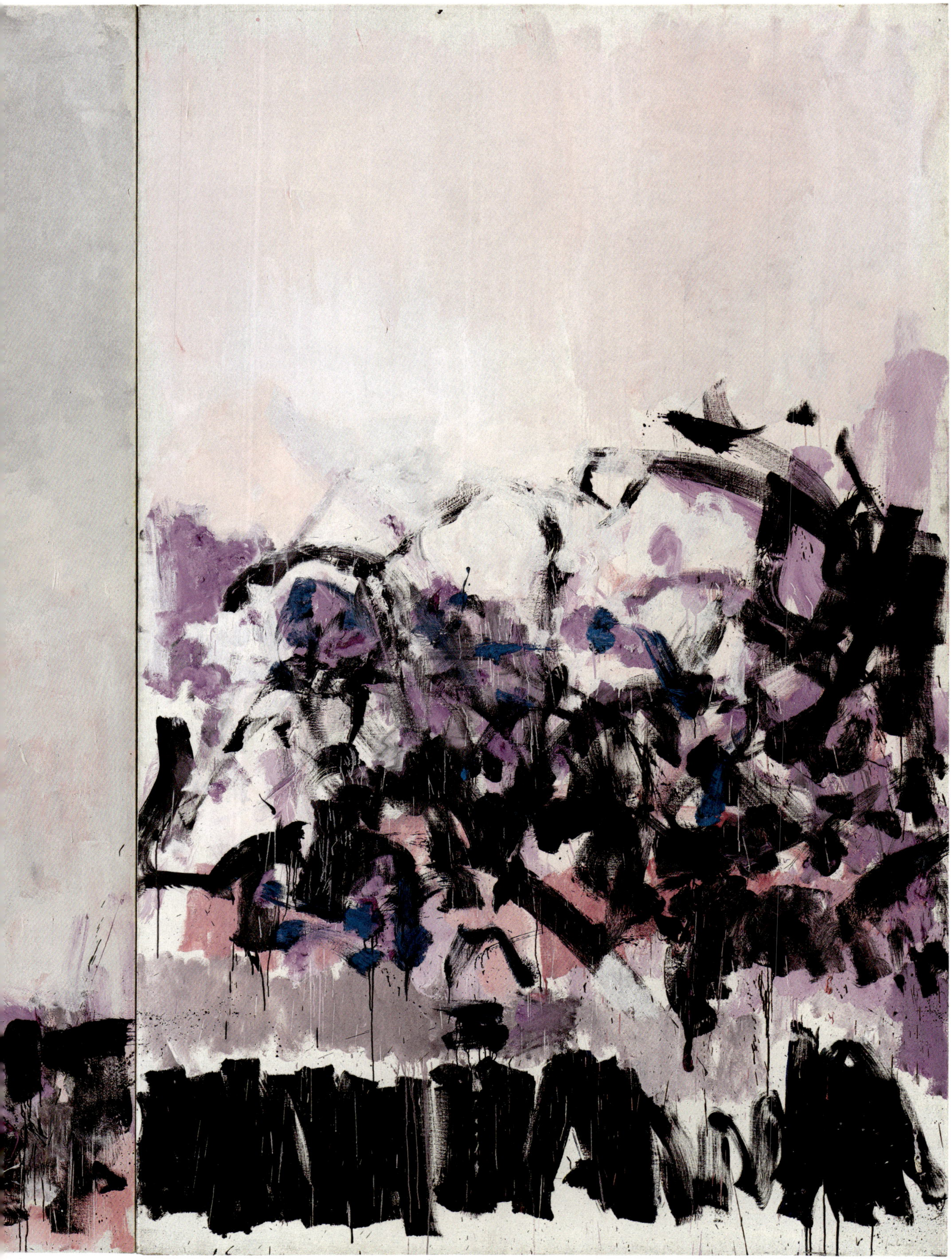

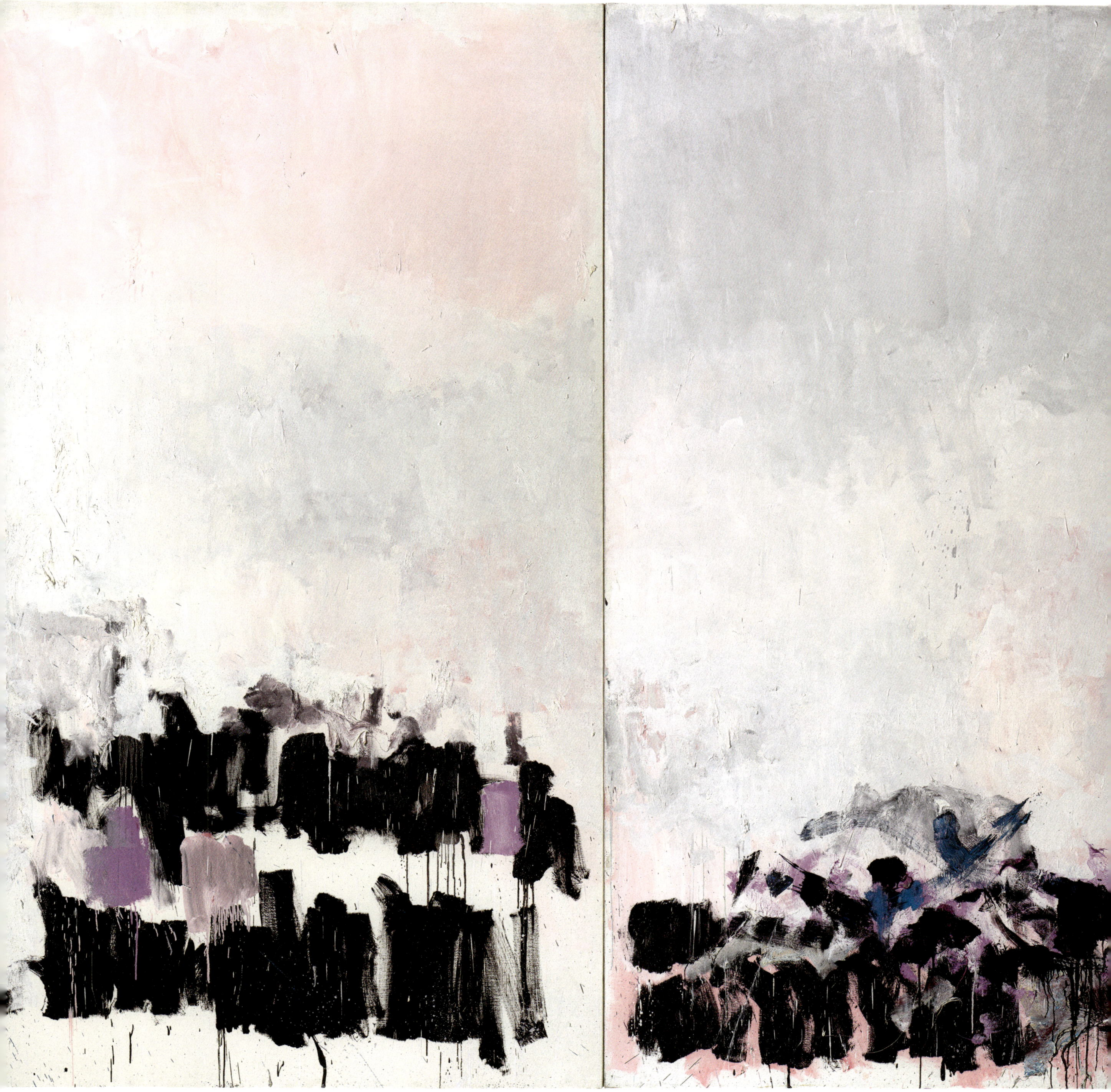

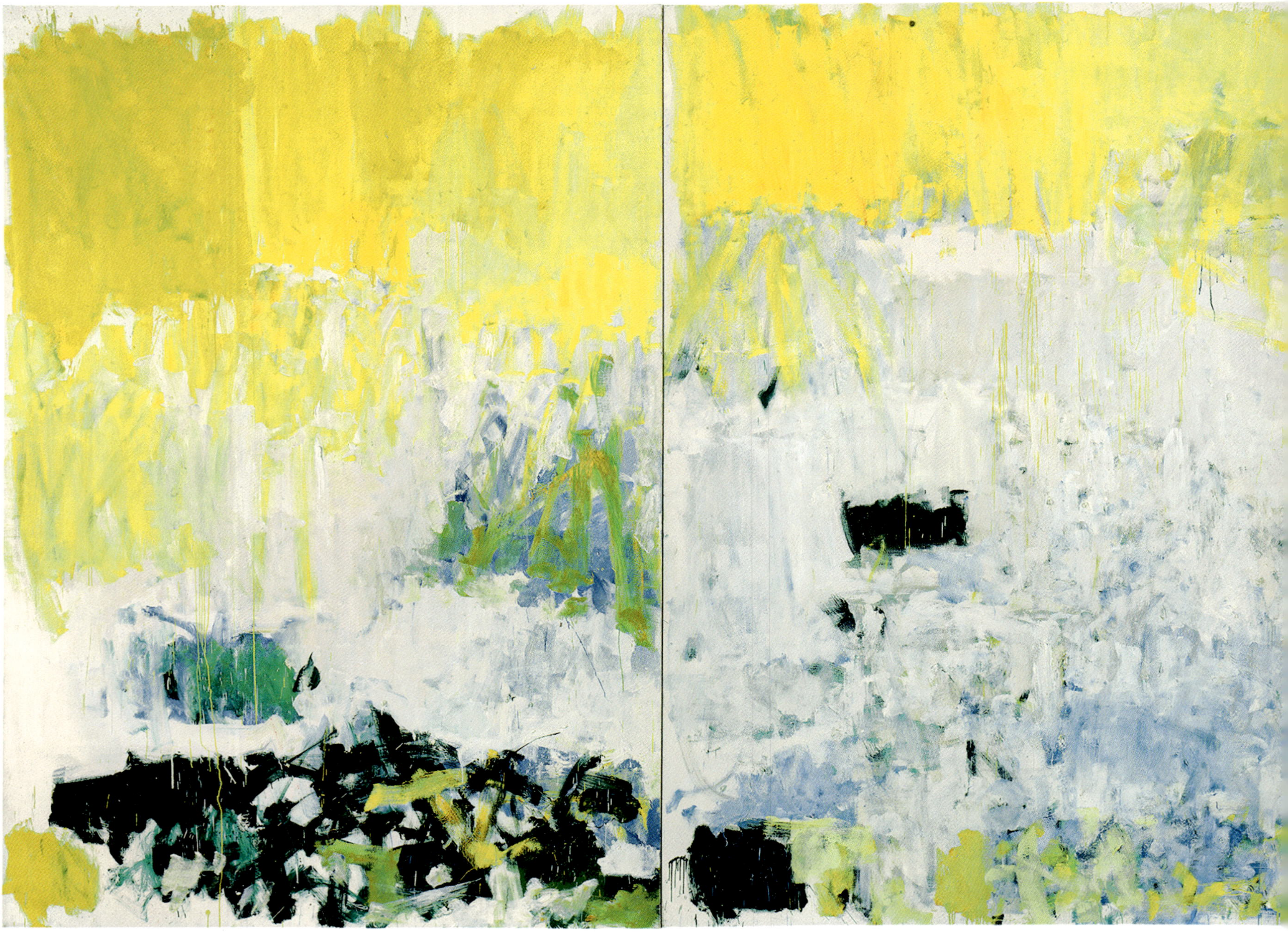

Salut Tom, 1979. Oil on canvas, 110½ × 316 in. (280.7 × 802.6 cm). National Gallery of Art, Washington, D.C., Corcoran Collection, gift of the Women's Committee of the Corcoran Gallery of Art, and Museum Purchase with the aid of funds from the National Endowment for the Arts

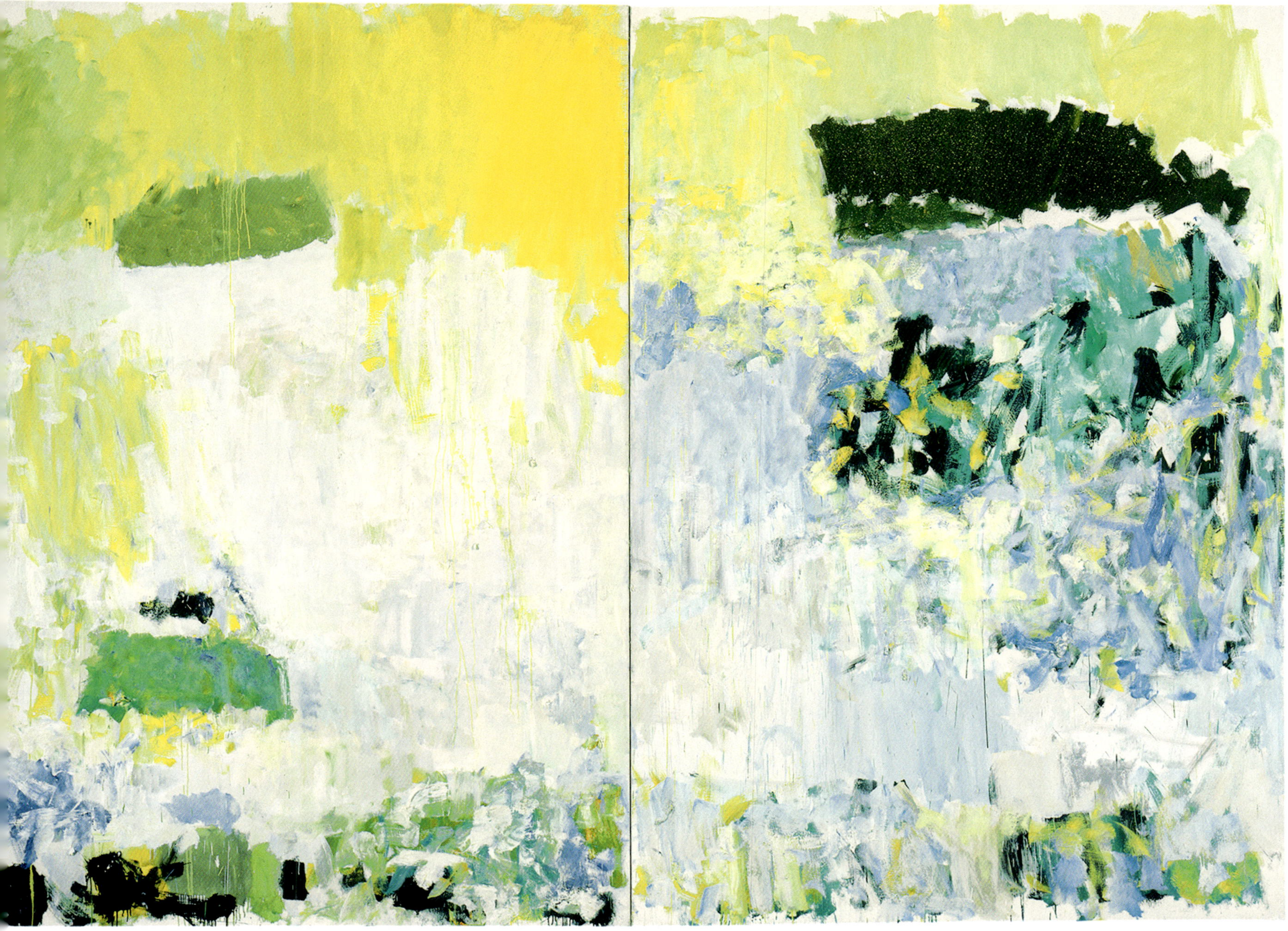

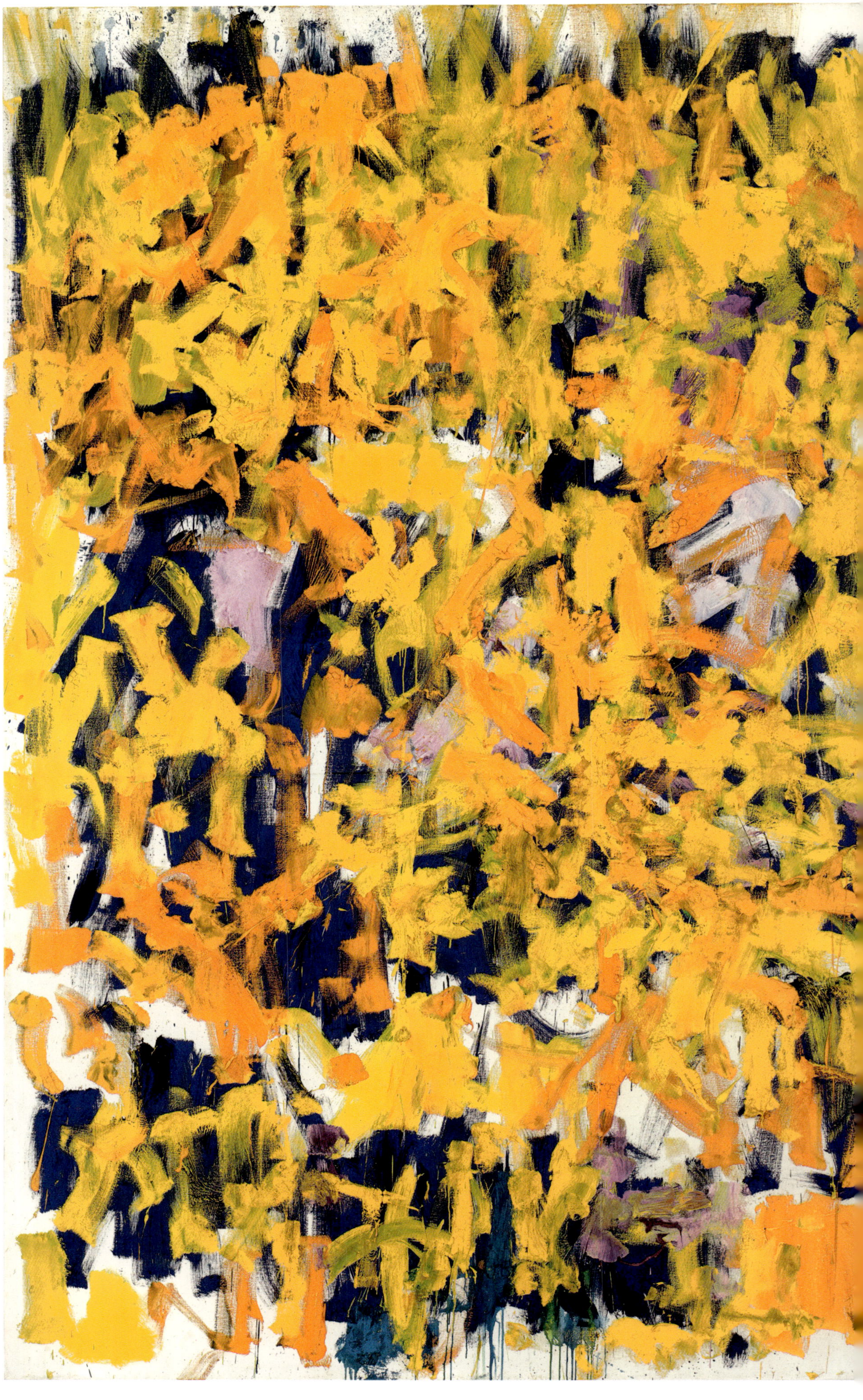

Two Pianos, 1980. Oil on canvas, 110 × 142 in. (279.4 × 360.7 cm). Private collection

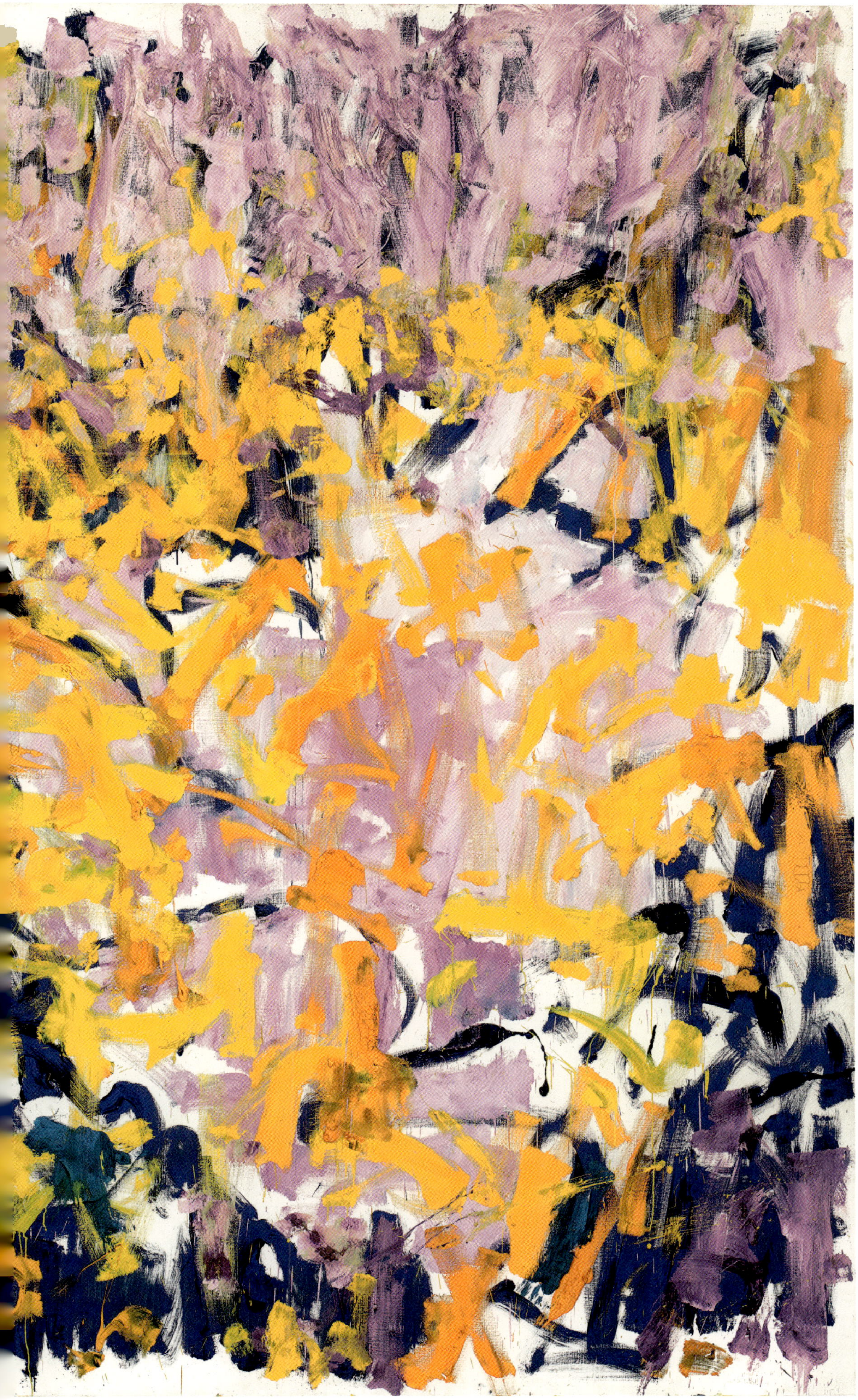

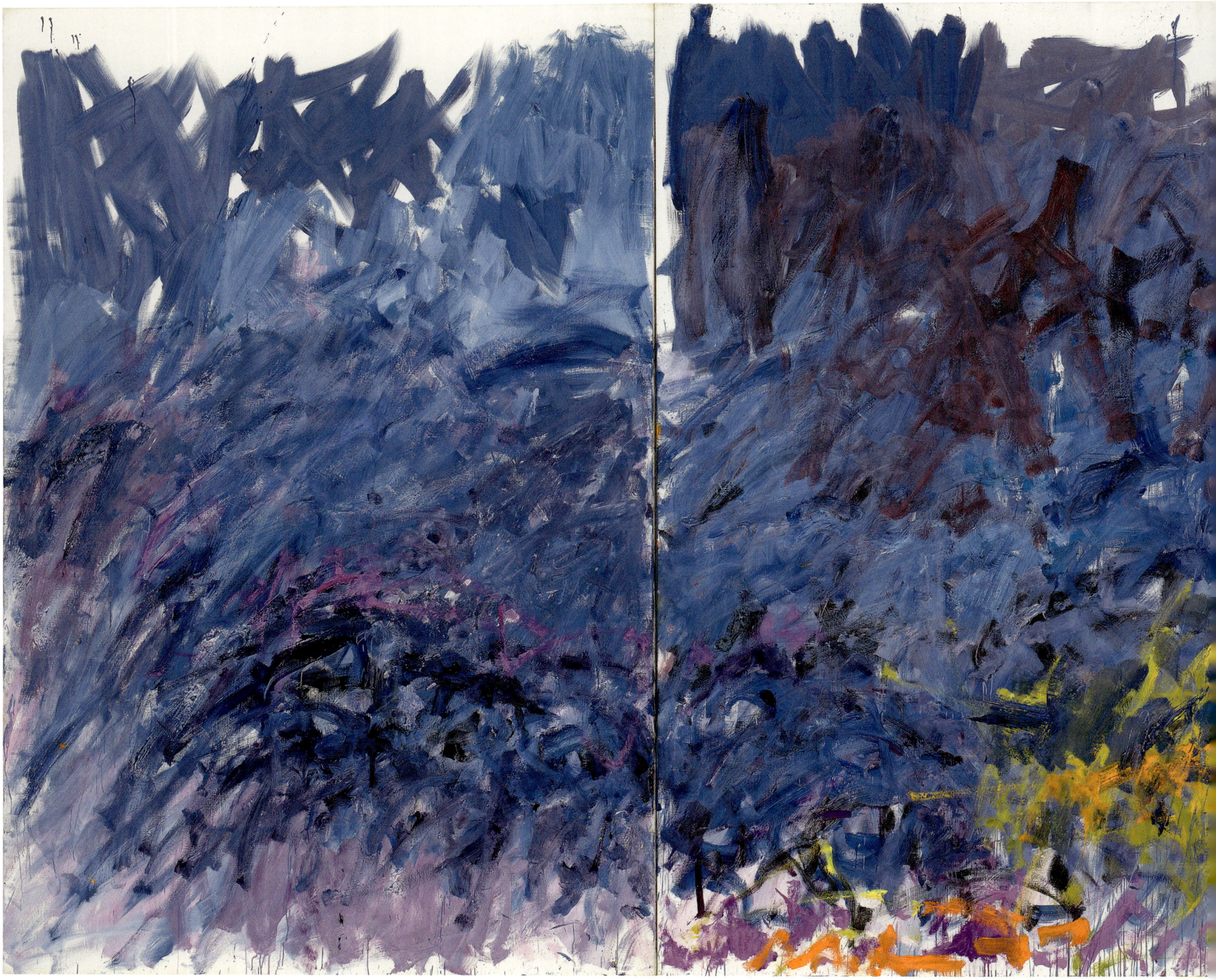

Edrita Fried, 1981. Oil on canvas, 116¼ × 299½ in. (295.3 × 760.7 cm). Joan Mitchell Foundation, New York

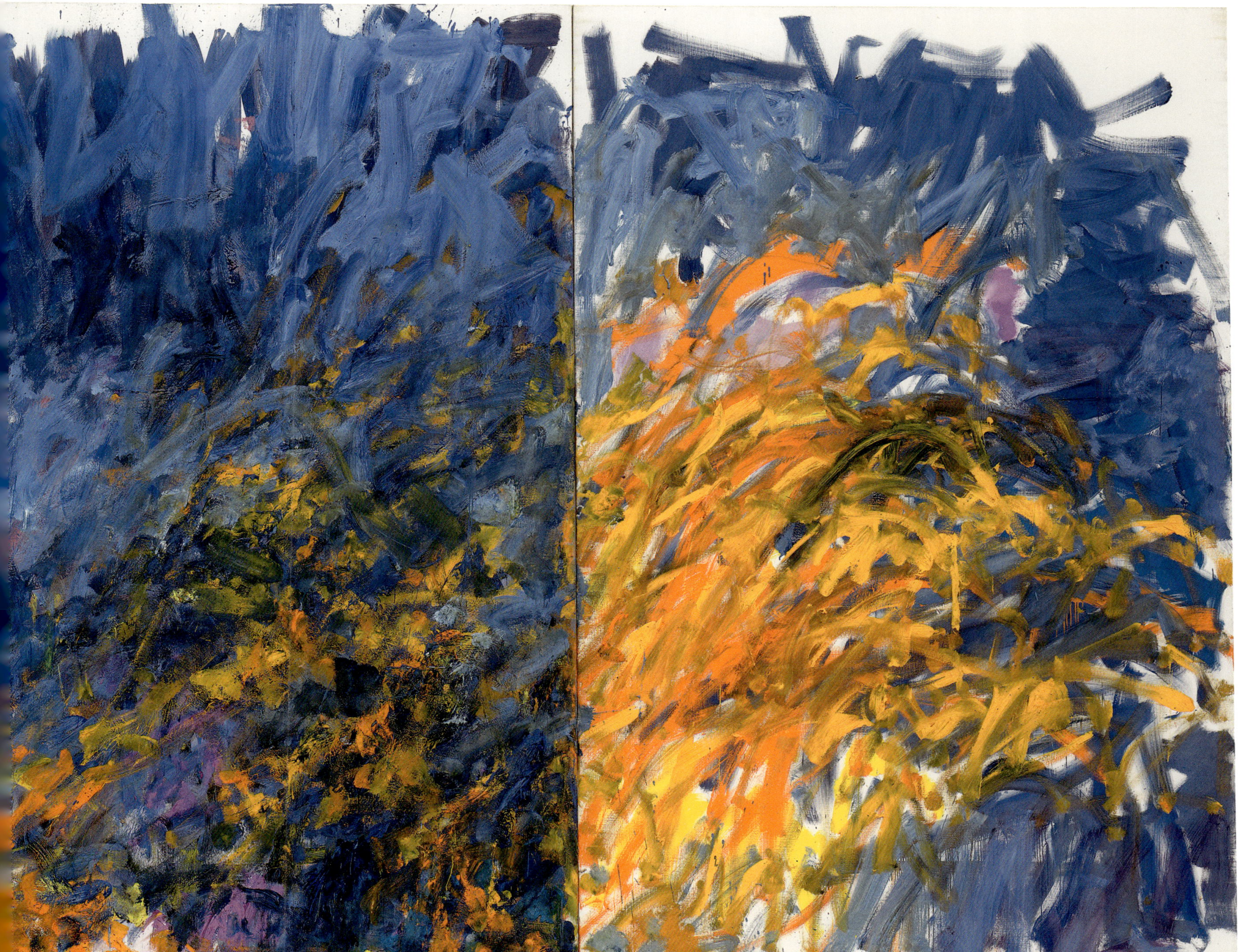

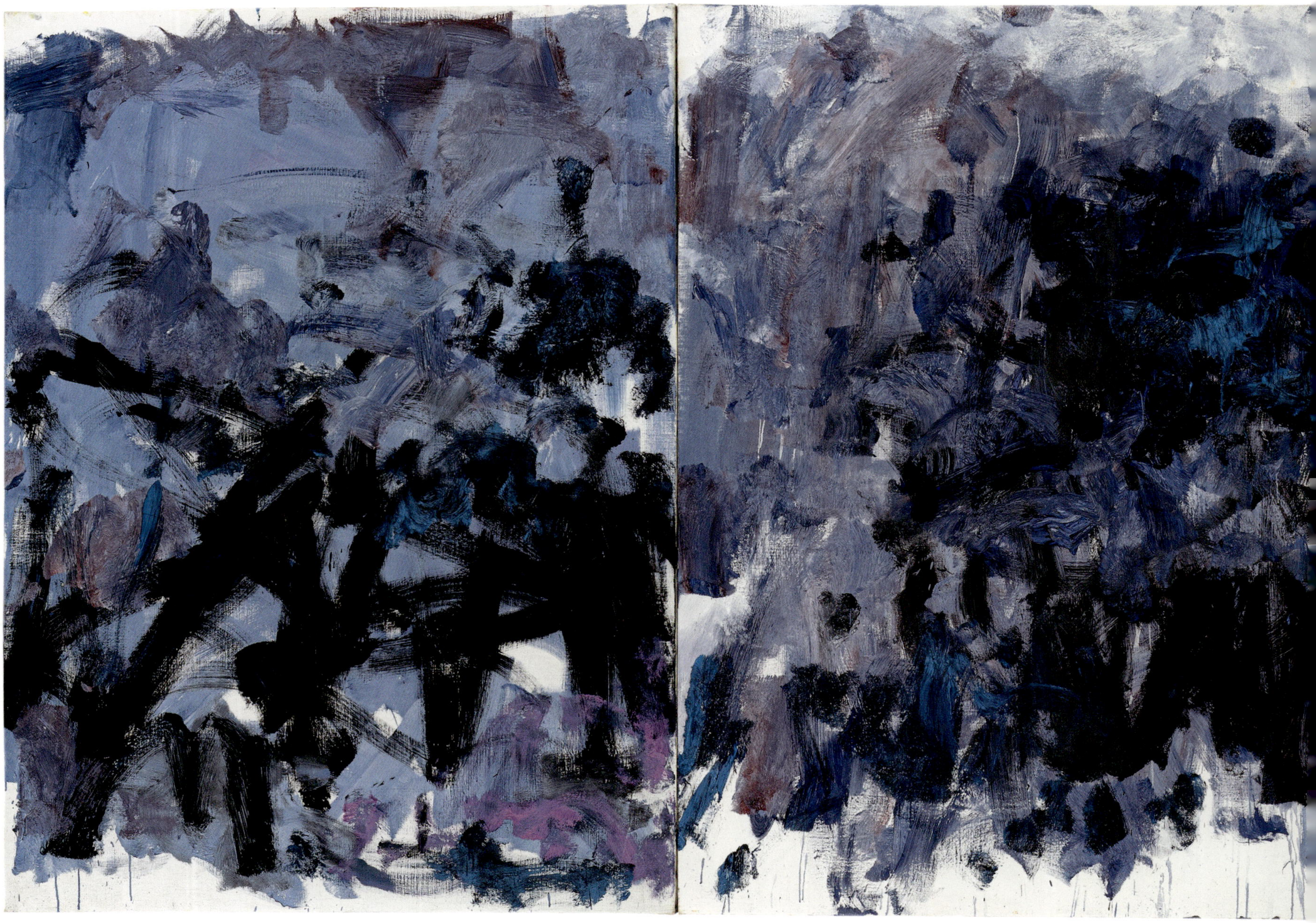

The Lake, 1981. Oil on canvas, 51 × 153 in. (129.5 × 388.6 cm). Private collection

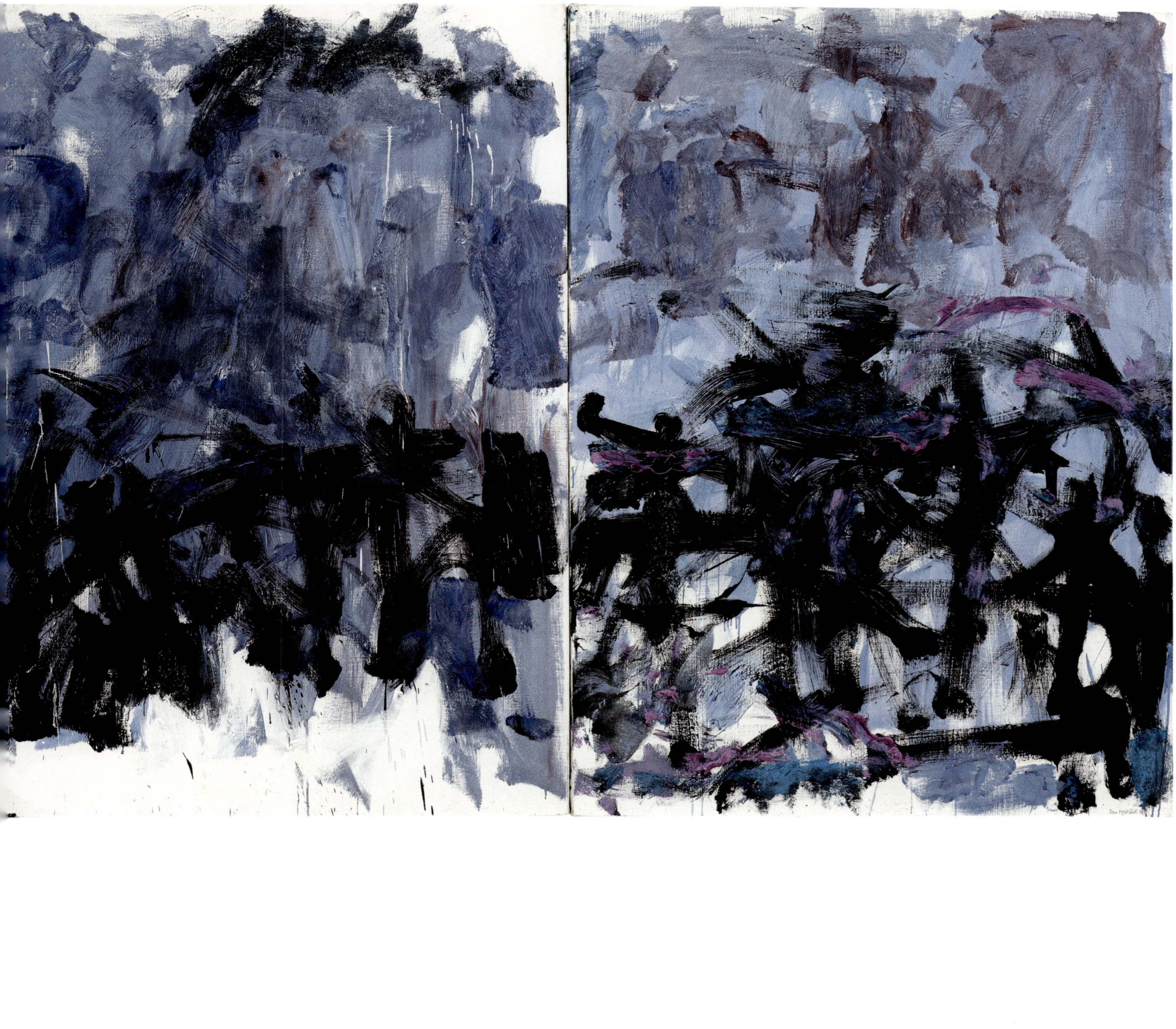

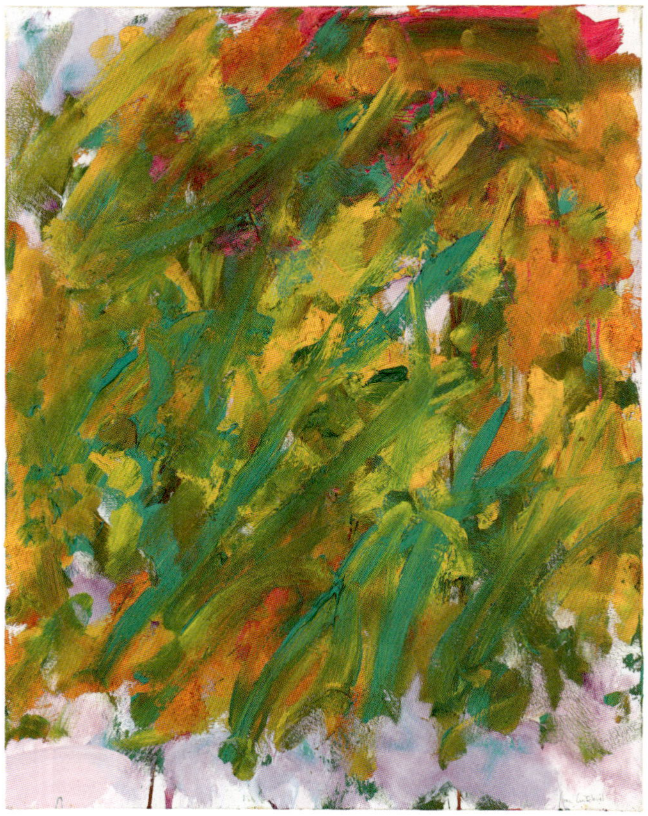

104

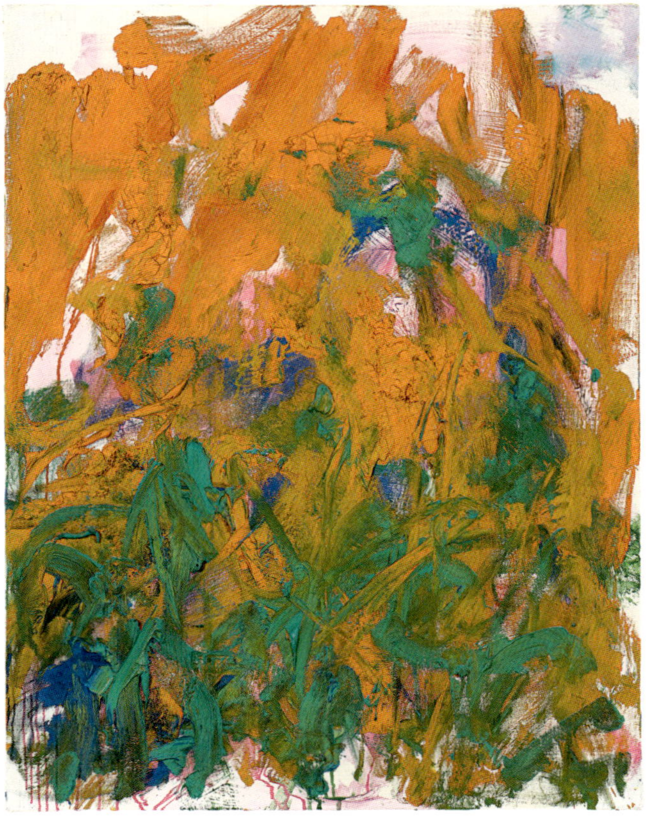

105

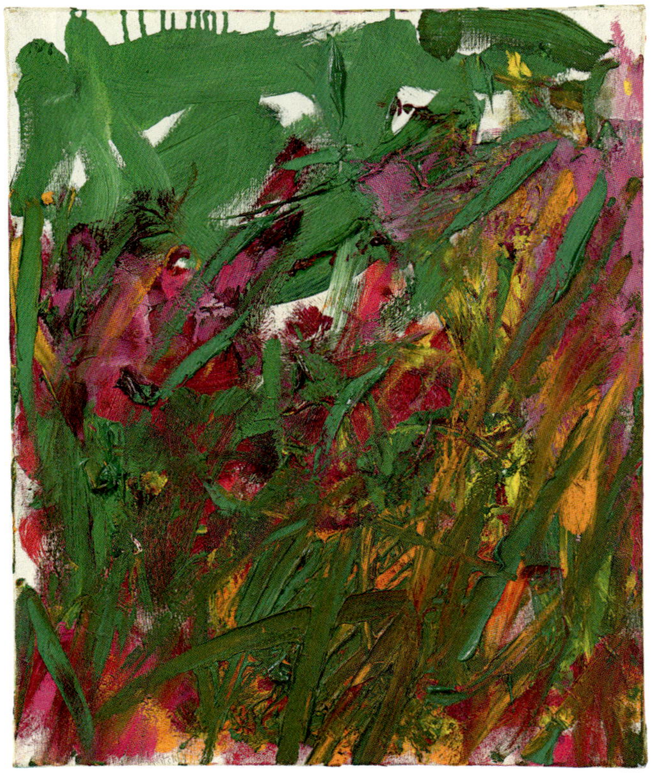

106

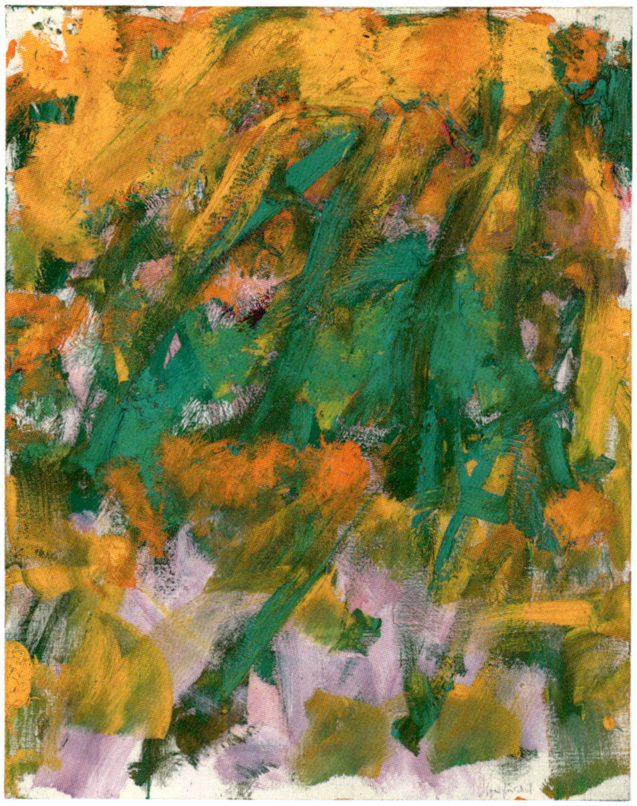

107

Merrily, 1982. Oil on canvas, 36¼ × 28⅞ in. (92.1 × 73.3 cm). Private collection

Merrily, 1982. Oil on canvas, 36⅛ × 28¾ in. (91.8 × 73 cm). Private collection

Gently, 1982. Oil on canvas, 21½ × 18⅛ in. (54.6 × 46 cm). Private collection

Merrily, 1982. Oil on canvas, 36½ × 29 in. (92.7 × 73.7 cm). Private collection

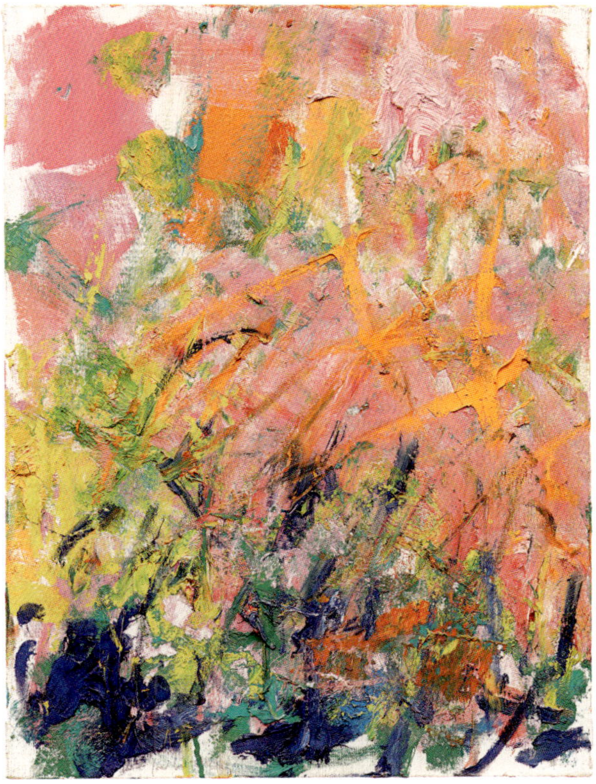

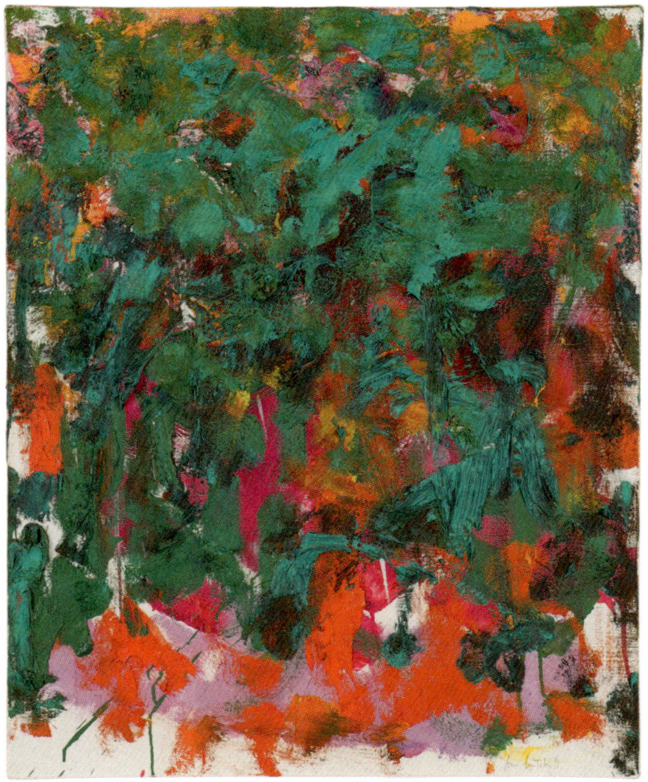

Petit Matin, 1982. Oil on canvas, 24 × 18 in. (61 × 45.7 cm). Private collection, Toronto

Petit Matin, 1982. Oil on canvas, 29 × 24 in. (73.7 × 61 cm). Private collection, Amagansett, New York

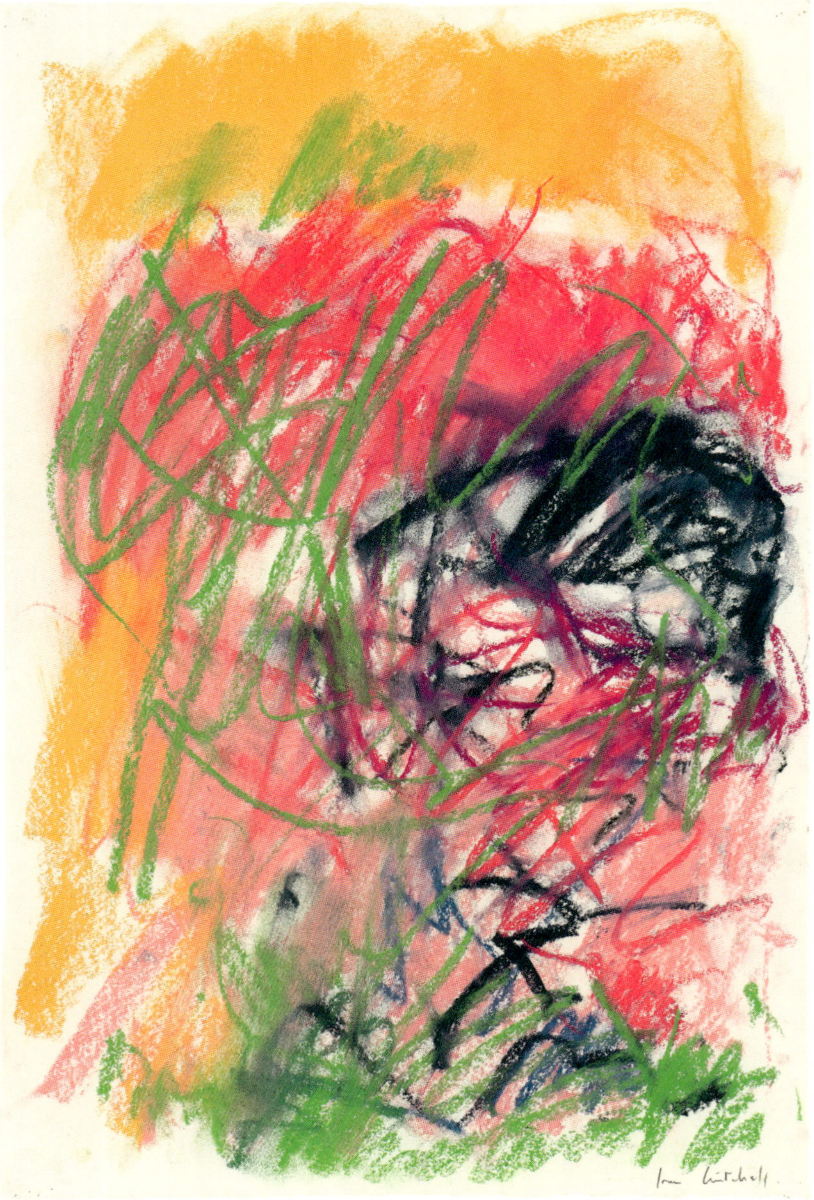

Untitled, 1980. Pastel on paper, 22⅞ × 15½ in. (58.1 × 39.4 cm). Joan Mitchell Foundation, New York

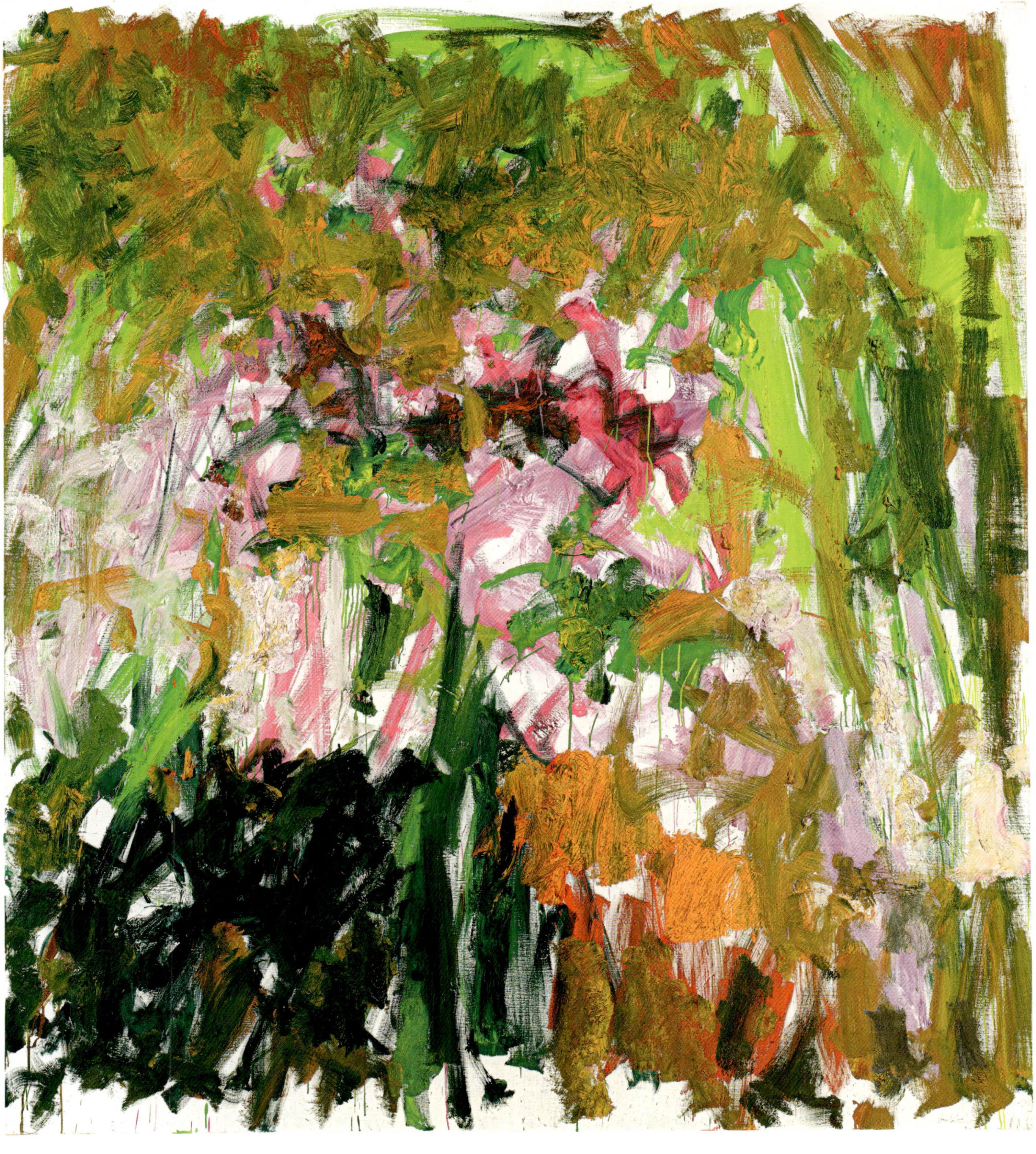

La Grande Vallée II (Amaryllis), 1983. Oil on canvas, 86½ × 78⅝ in. (219.7 × 199.7 cm). Private collection, courtesy Guggenheim, Asher Associates, New York

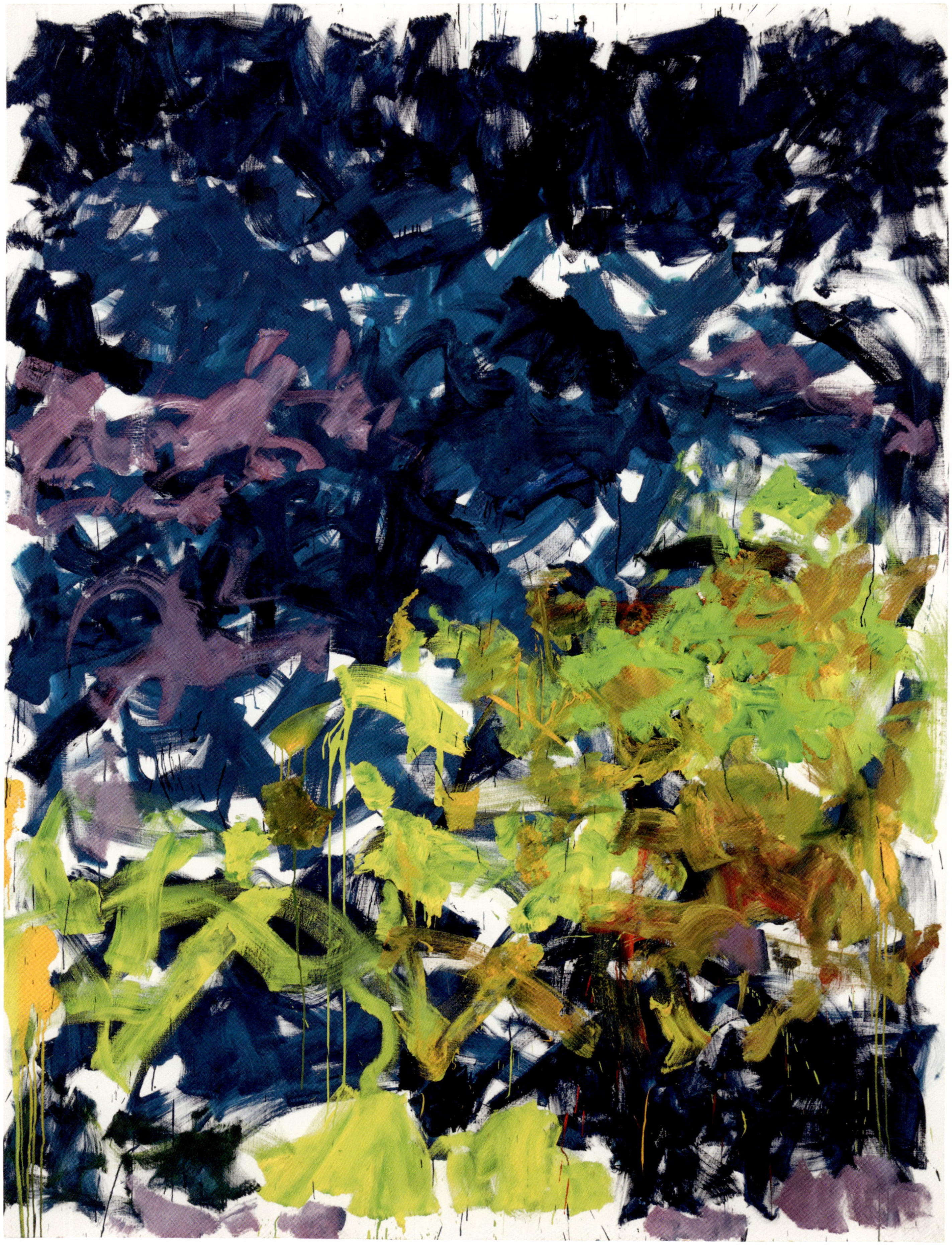

La Grande Vallée XVI, pour Iva, 1983. Oil on canvas, 102¼ × 78¾ in. (259.7 × 200 cm). Joan Mitchell Foundation, New York

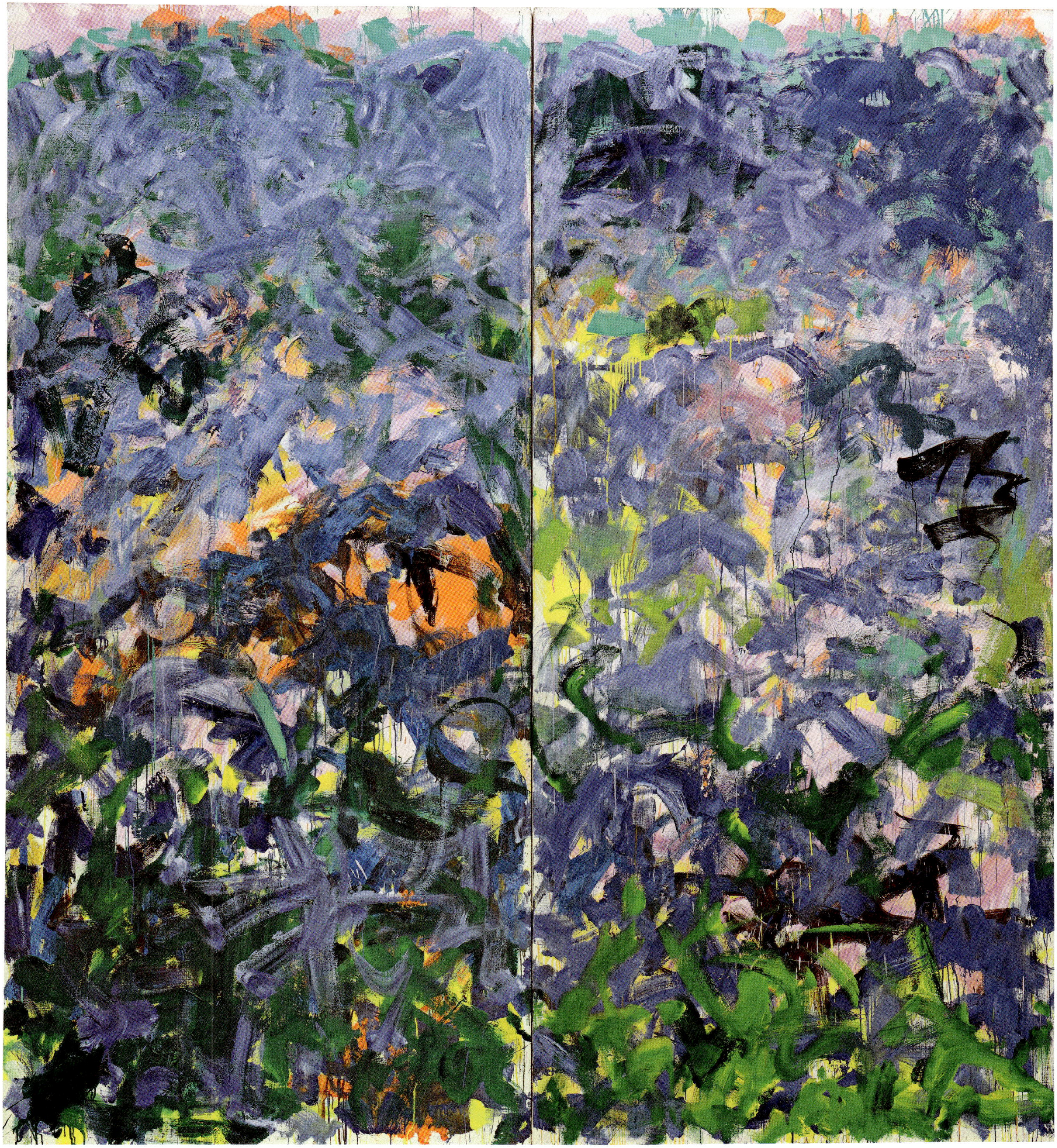

La Grande Vallée XVII, Carl, 1984. Oil on canvas, 110¼ × 102⅜ in. (280 × 260 cm). Fonds Régional d'Art Contemporain Provence-Alpes-Côte d'Azur, Marseille, France

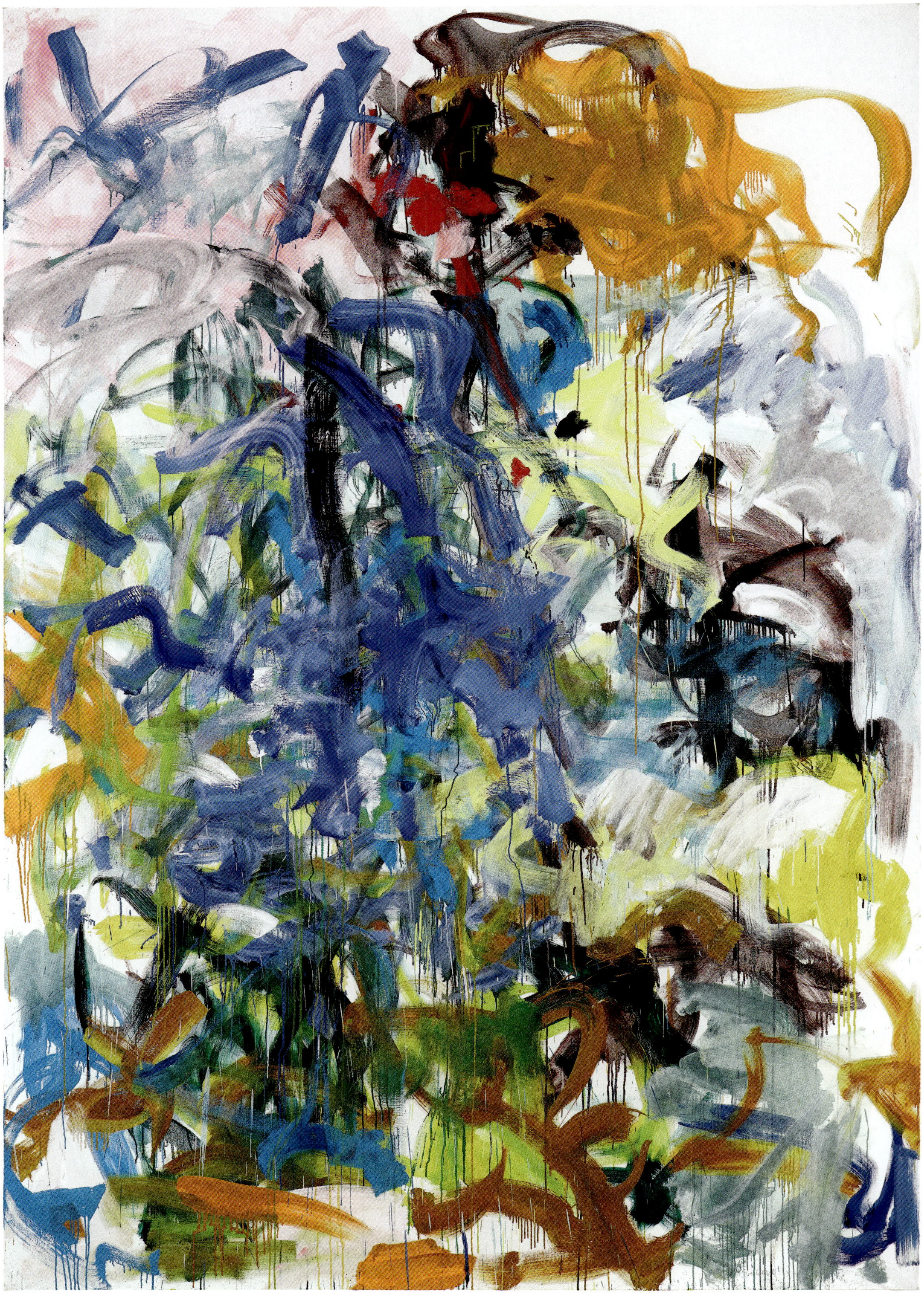

Before, Again IV, 1985. Oil on canvas, 110¼ × 78¾ in. (280 × 200 cm). Anderson Collection at Stanford University, California, gift of Harry W. and Mary Margaret Anderson, and Mary Patricia Anderson Pence

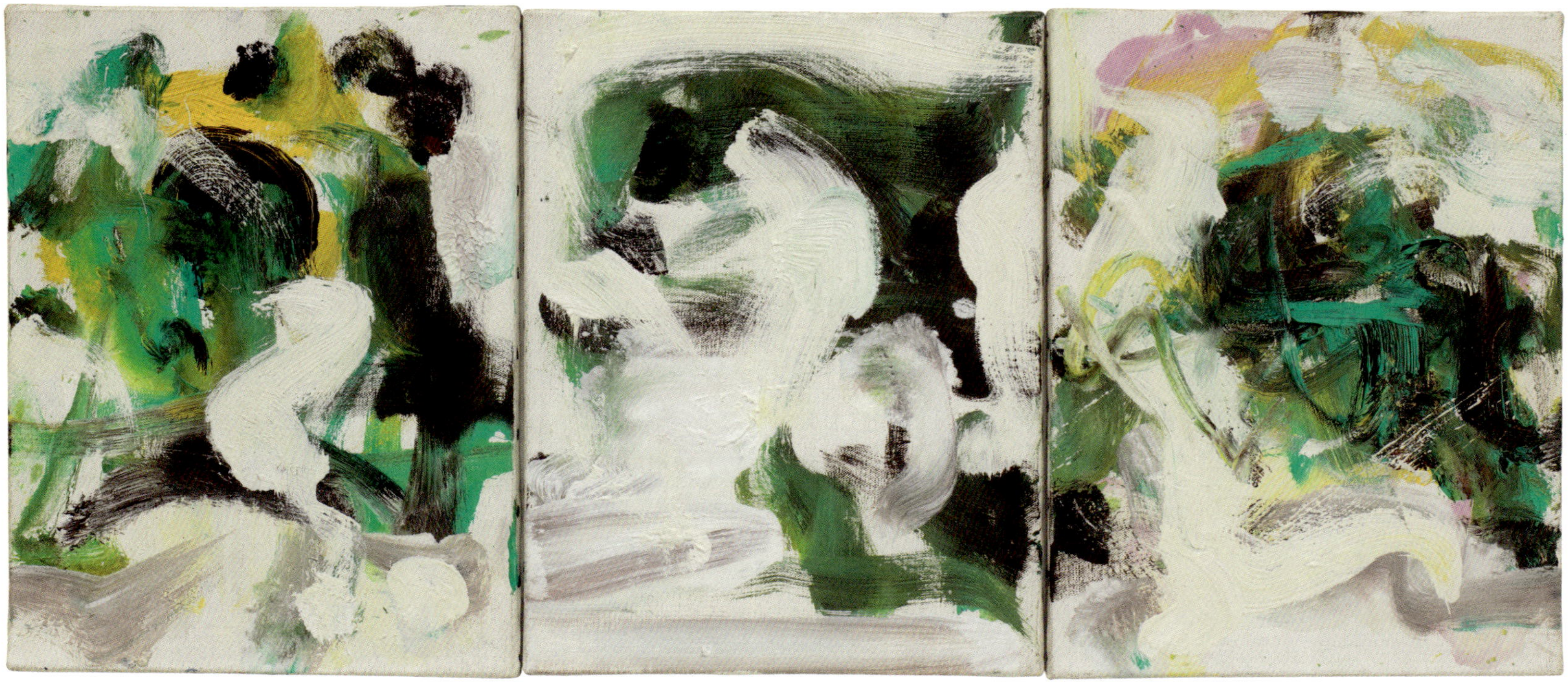

Untitled, 1985. Oil on canvas, 13¾ × 32¼ in. (34.9 × 81.9 cm). Private collection

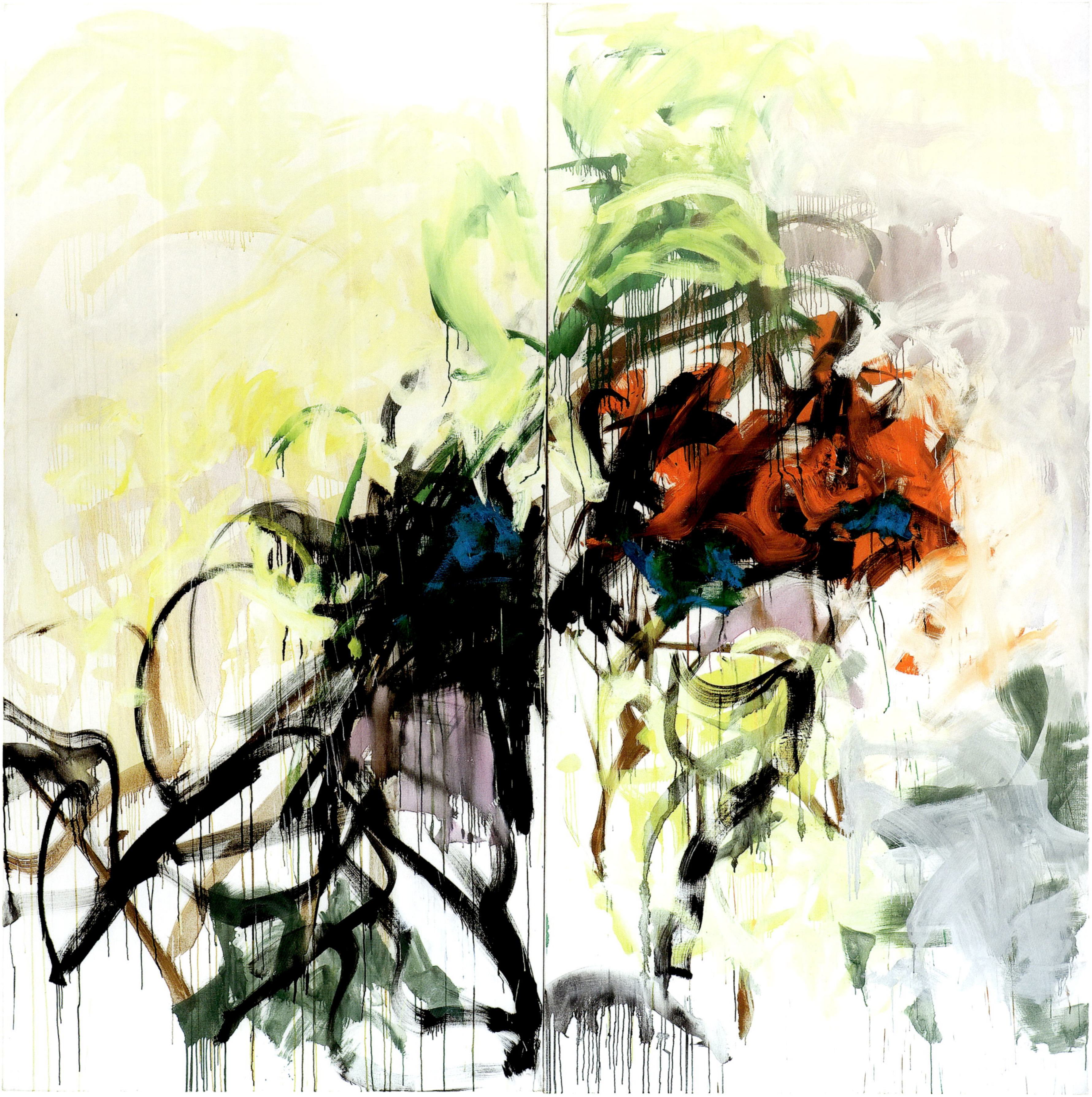

Faded Air I, 1985. Oil on canvas, 102 × 102 in. (259.1 × 259.1 cm). Private collection

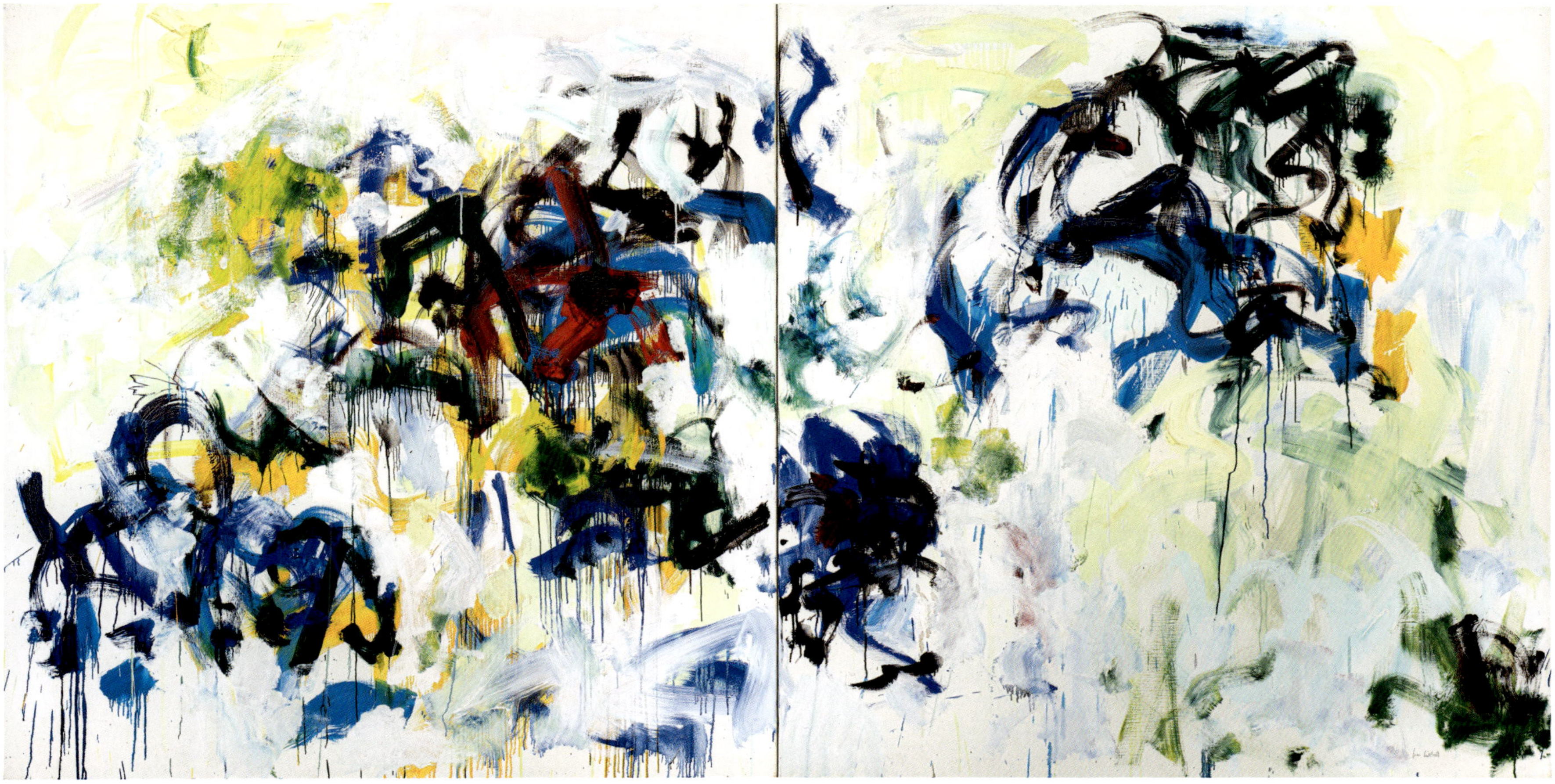

River II, 1986. Oil on canvas, 59 × 117⅞ in. (149.9 × 299.4 cm). Private collection

PLATE 118

No Birds, 1987–88. Oil on canvas, 86¾ × 156¼ in. (220.3 × 396.9 cm). Private collection

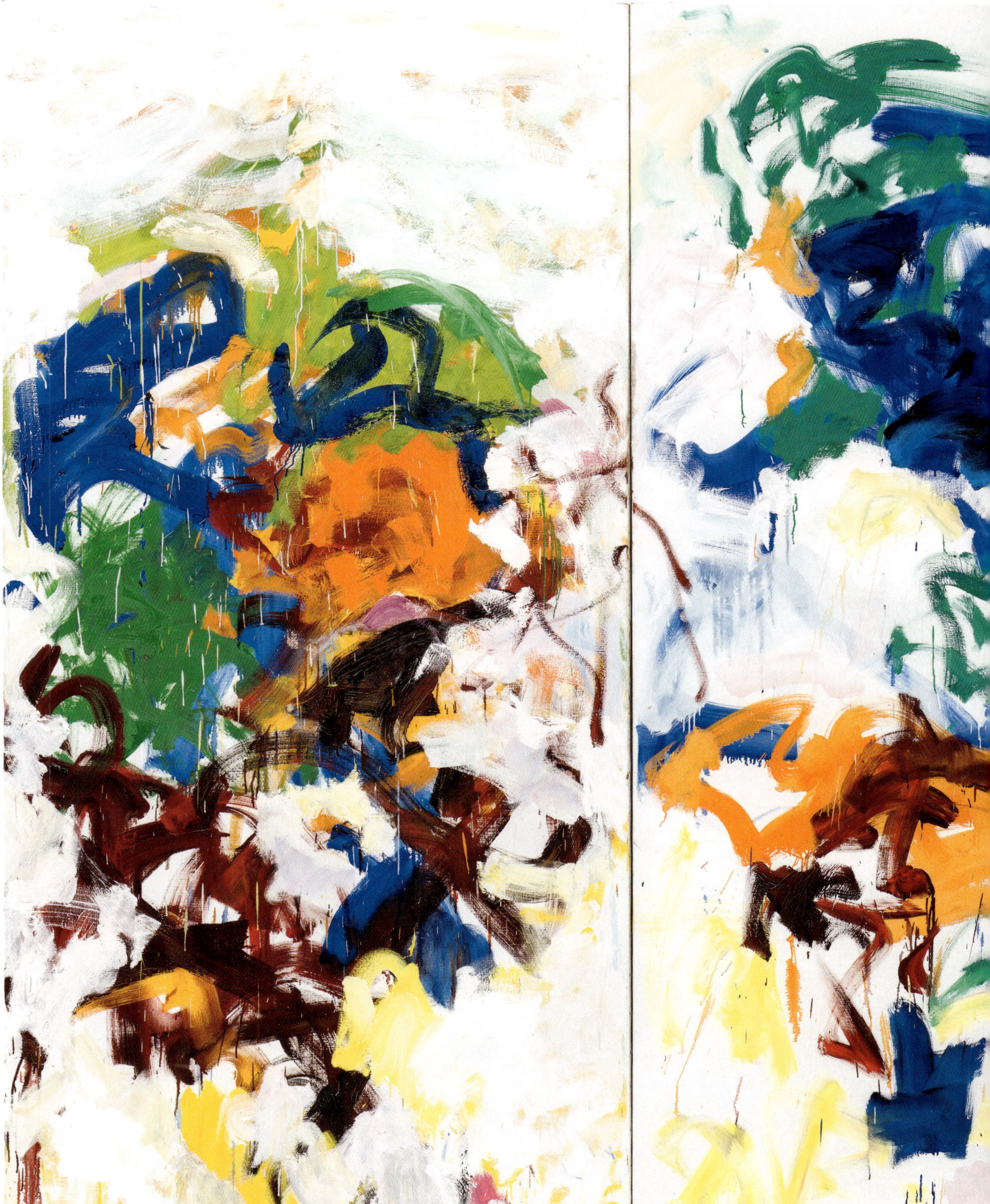

Bracket, 1989. Oil on canvas, 102½ × 181⅞ in. (260.4 × 462 cm). The Doris and Donald Fisher Collection at the San Francisco Museum of Modern Art

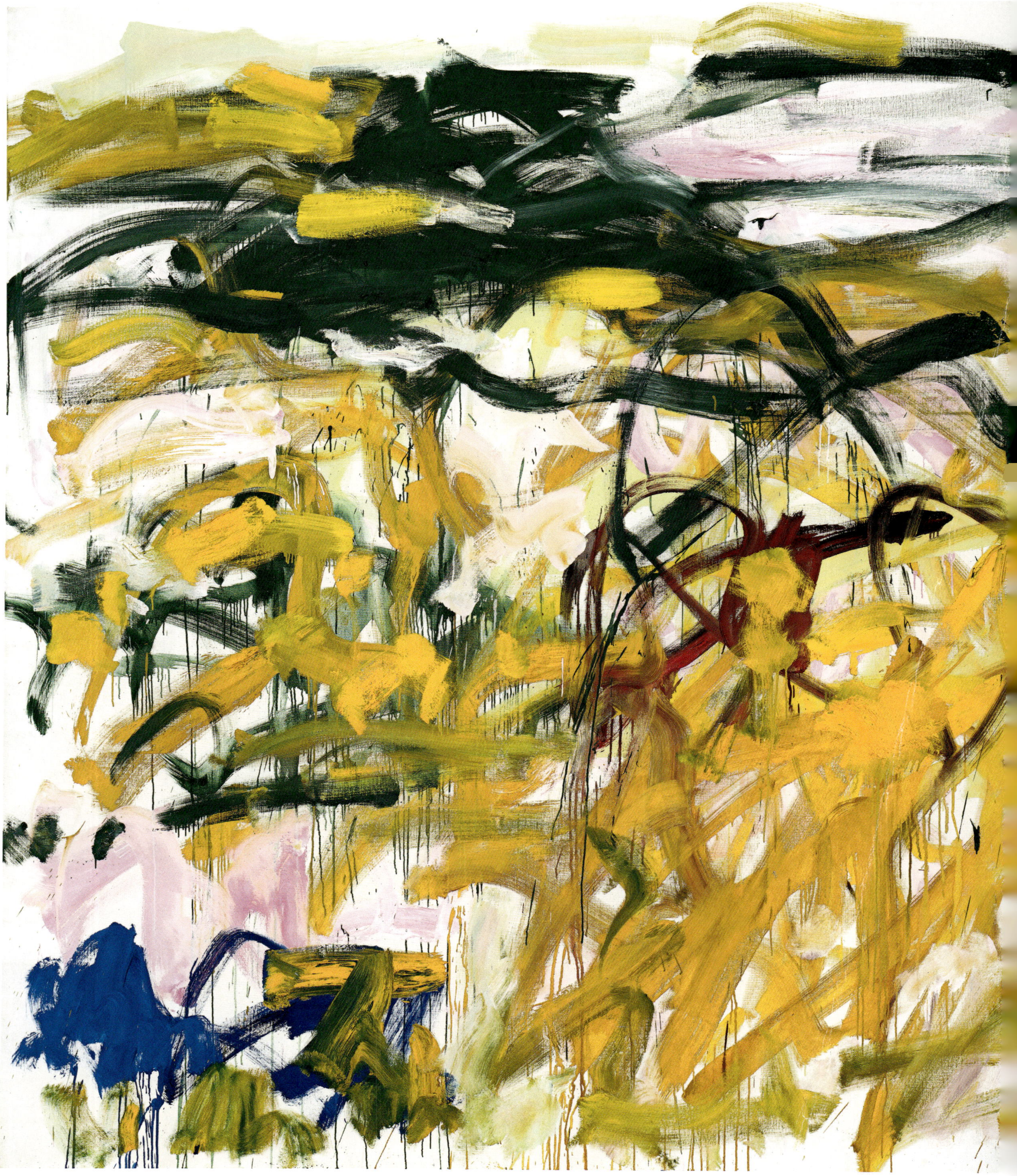

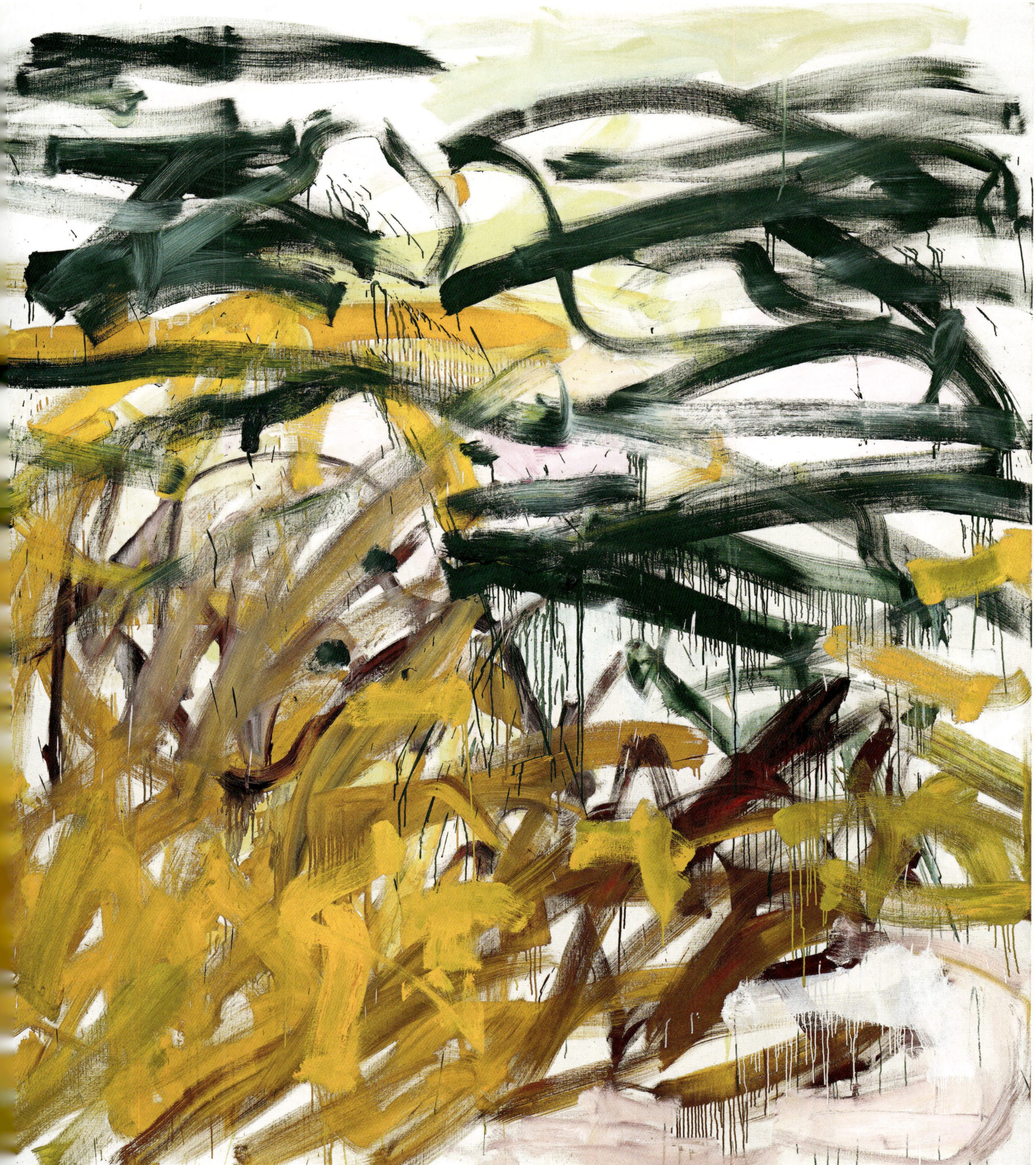

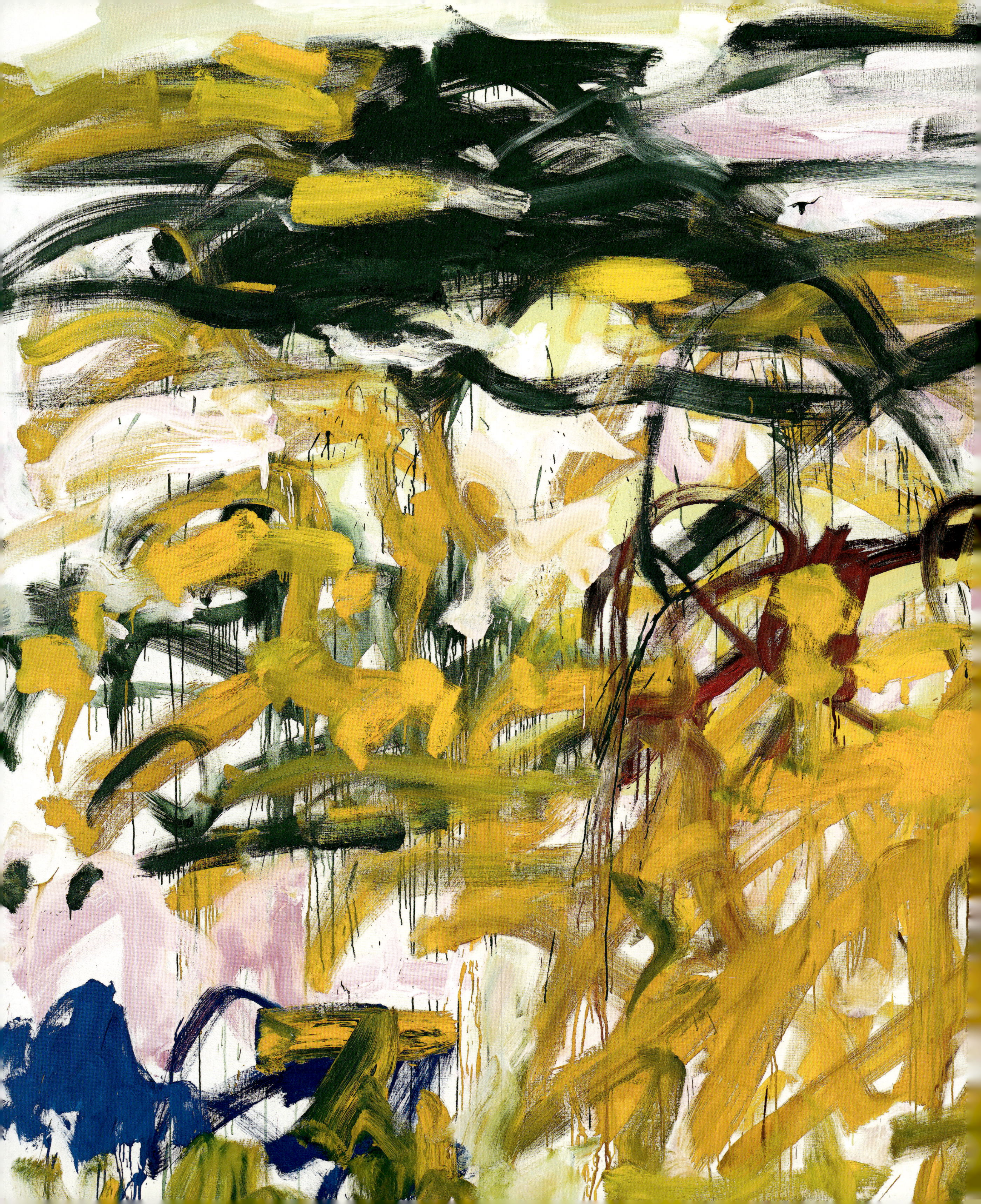

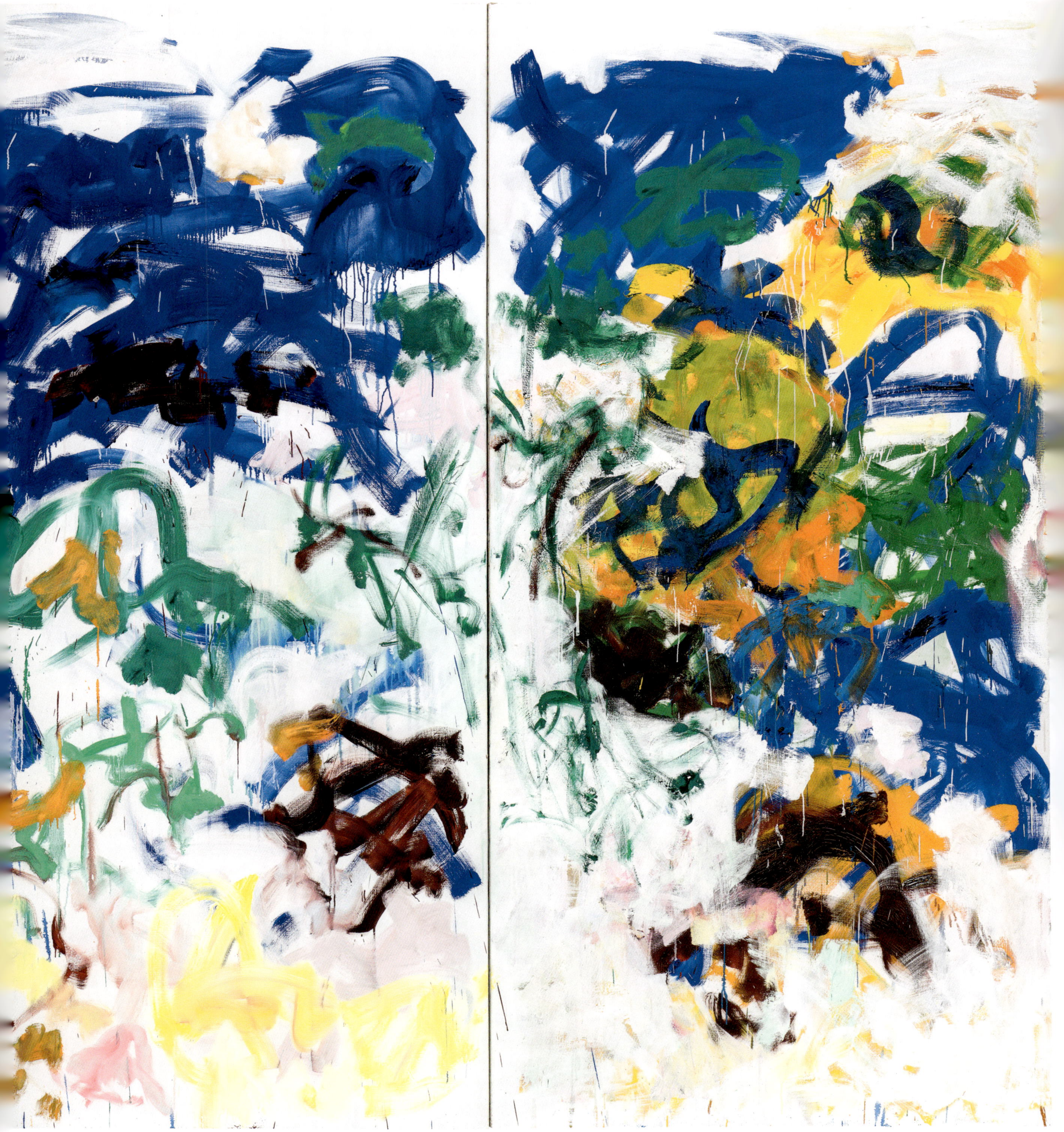

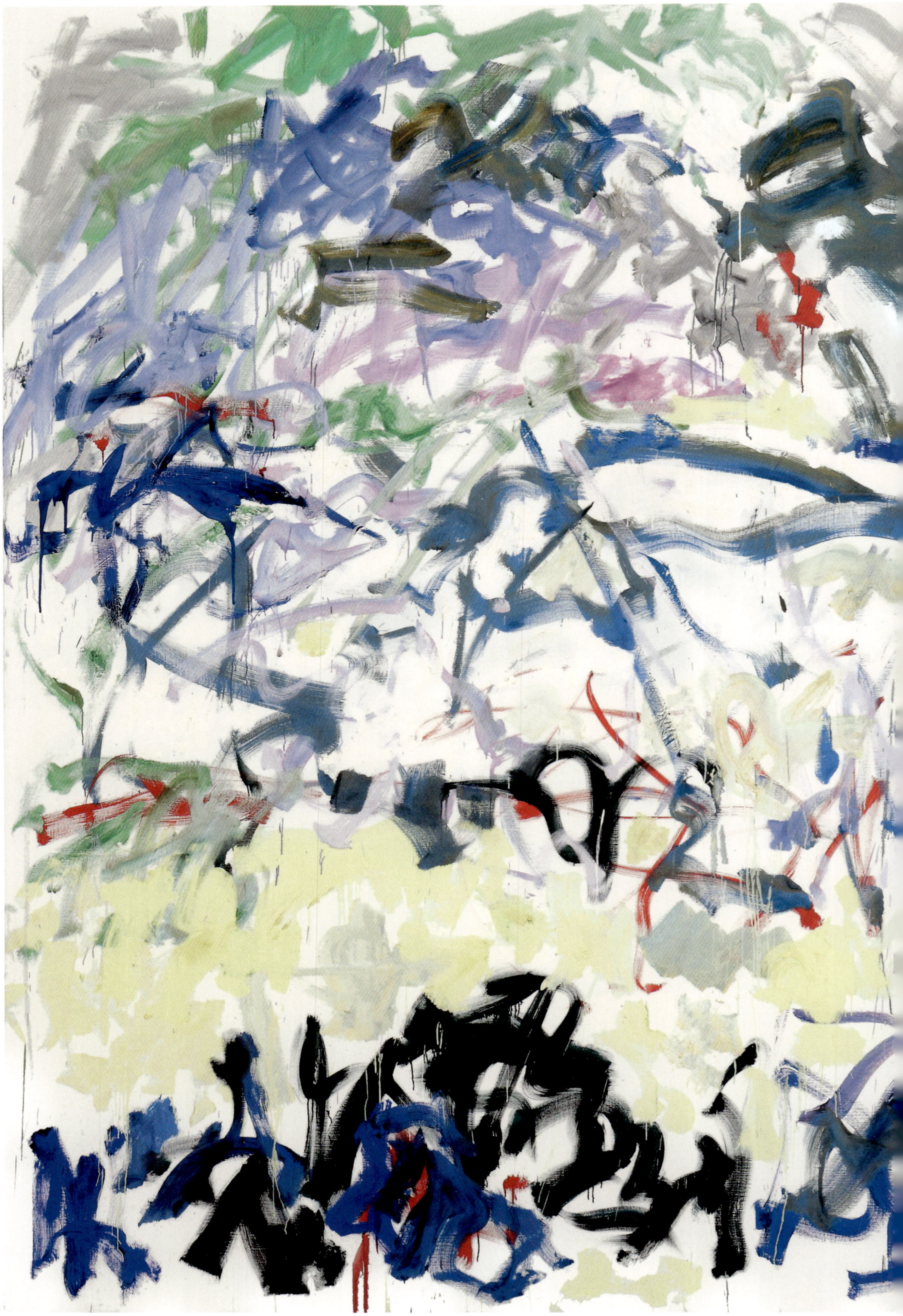

River, 1989. Oil on canvas, 110⅜ × 157⅜ in. (280.4 × 399.7 cm). Fondation Louis Vuitton, Paris

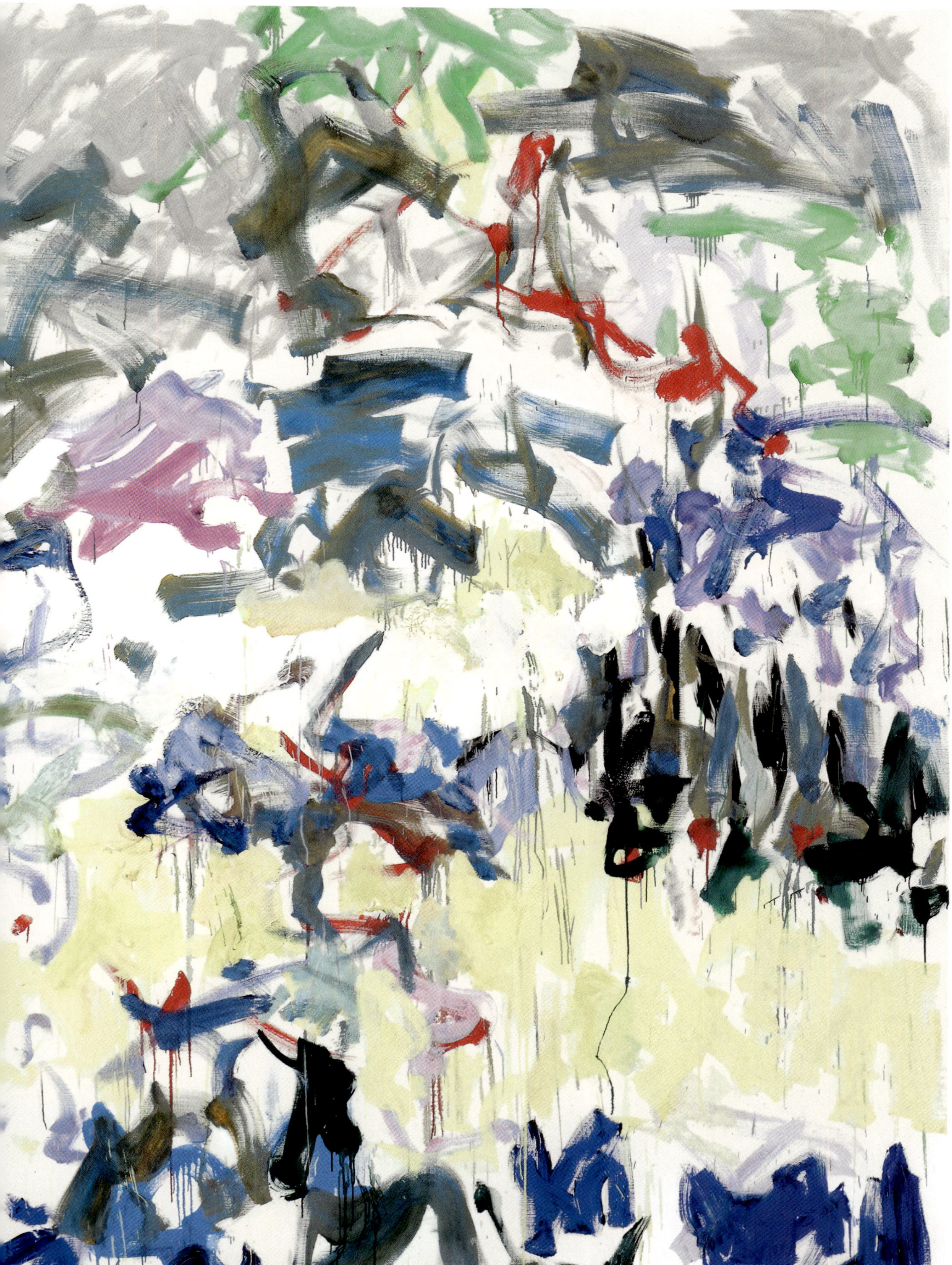

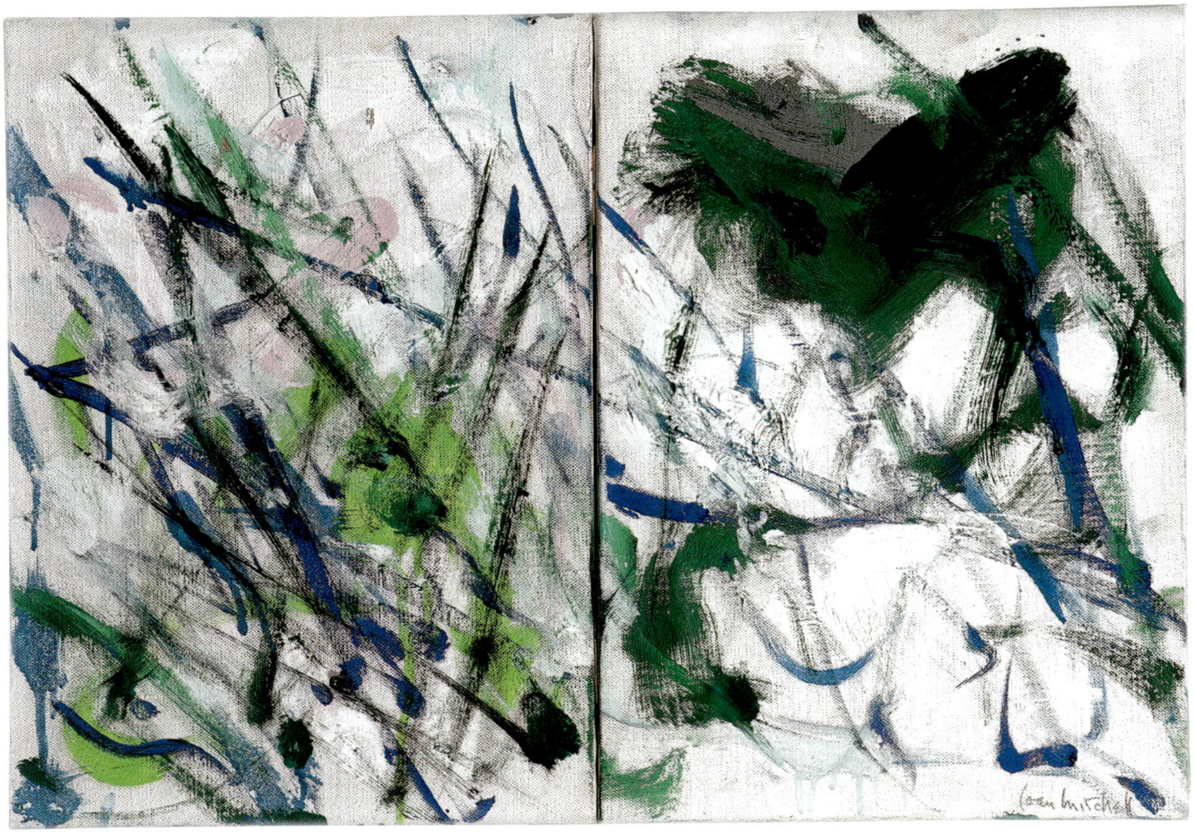

Little Rain, 1989. Oil on canvas, 13 × 19 in. (33 × 48.3 cm). Private collection

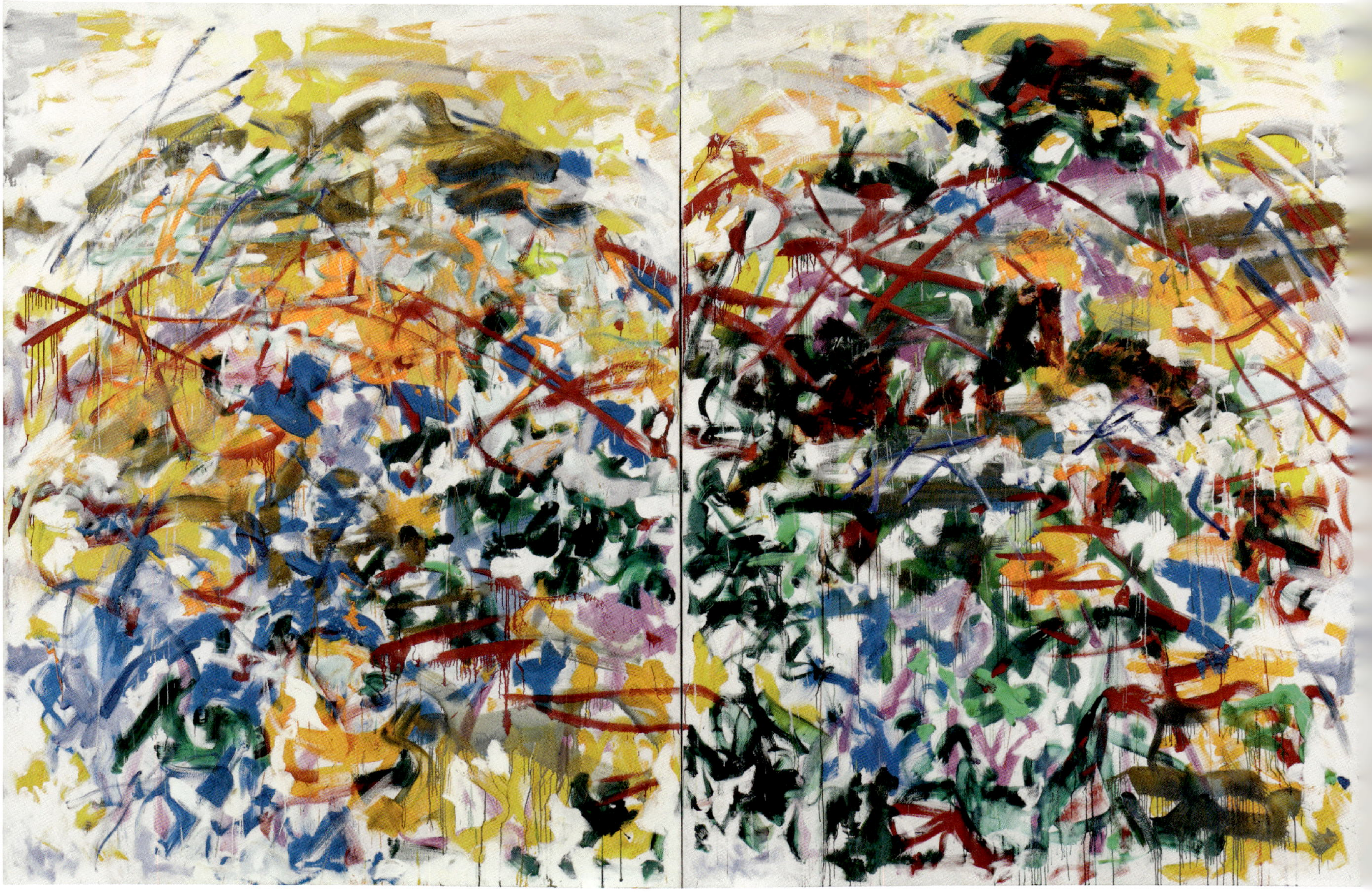

South, 1989. Oil on canvas, 102½ × 157½ in. (260.4 × 400.1 cm). Fondation Louis Vuitton, Paris

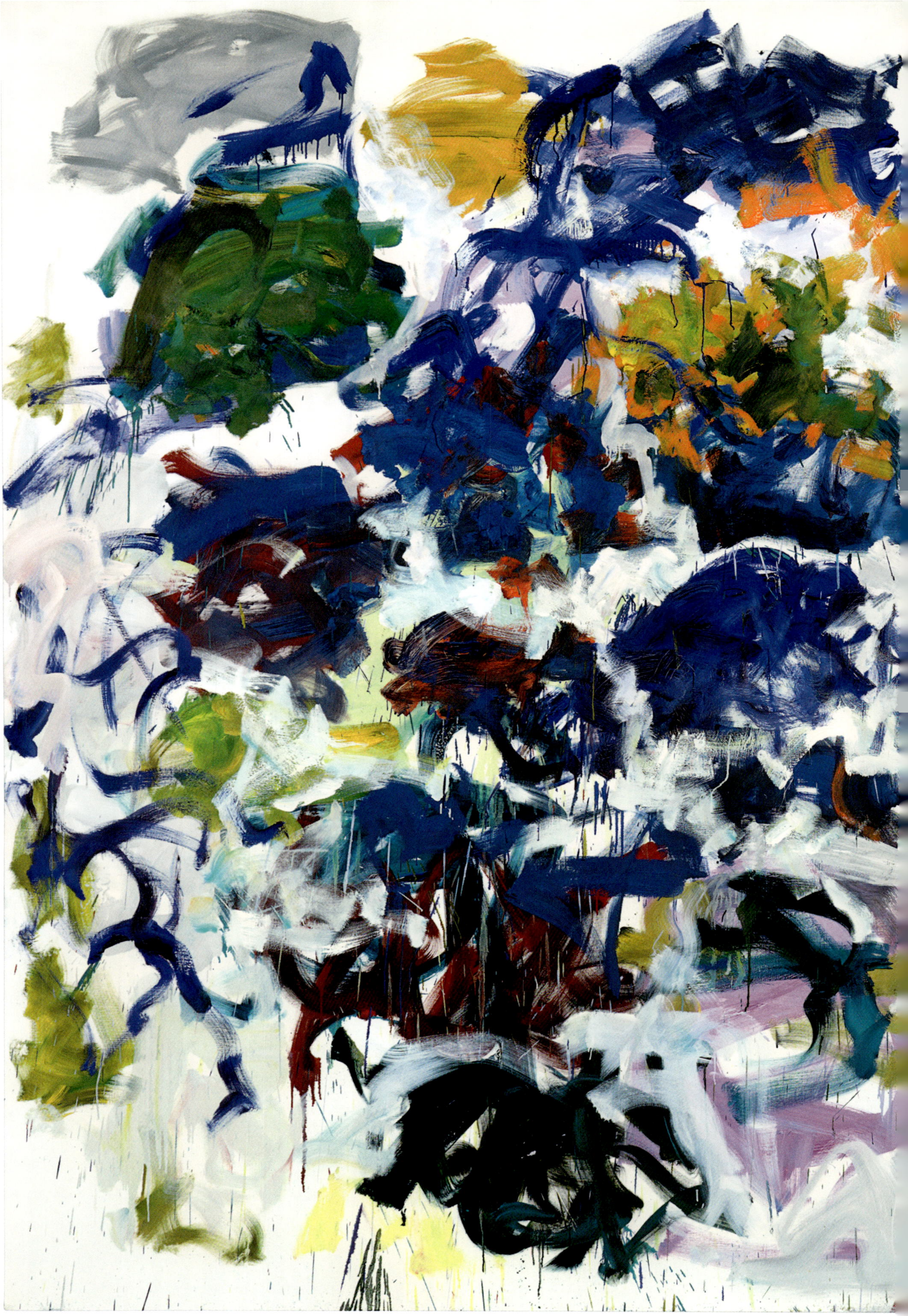

Sunflowers, 1990–91. Oil on canvas, 110¼ × 157½ in. (280 × 400.1 cm). Collection of John Cheim

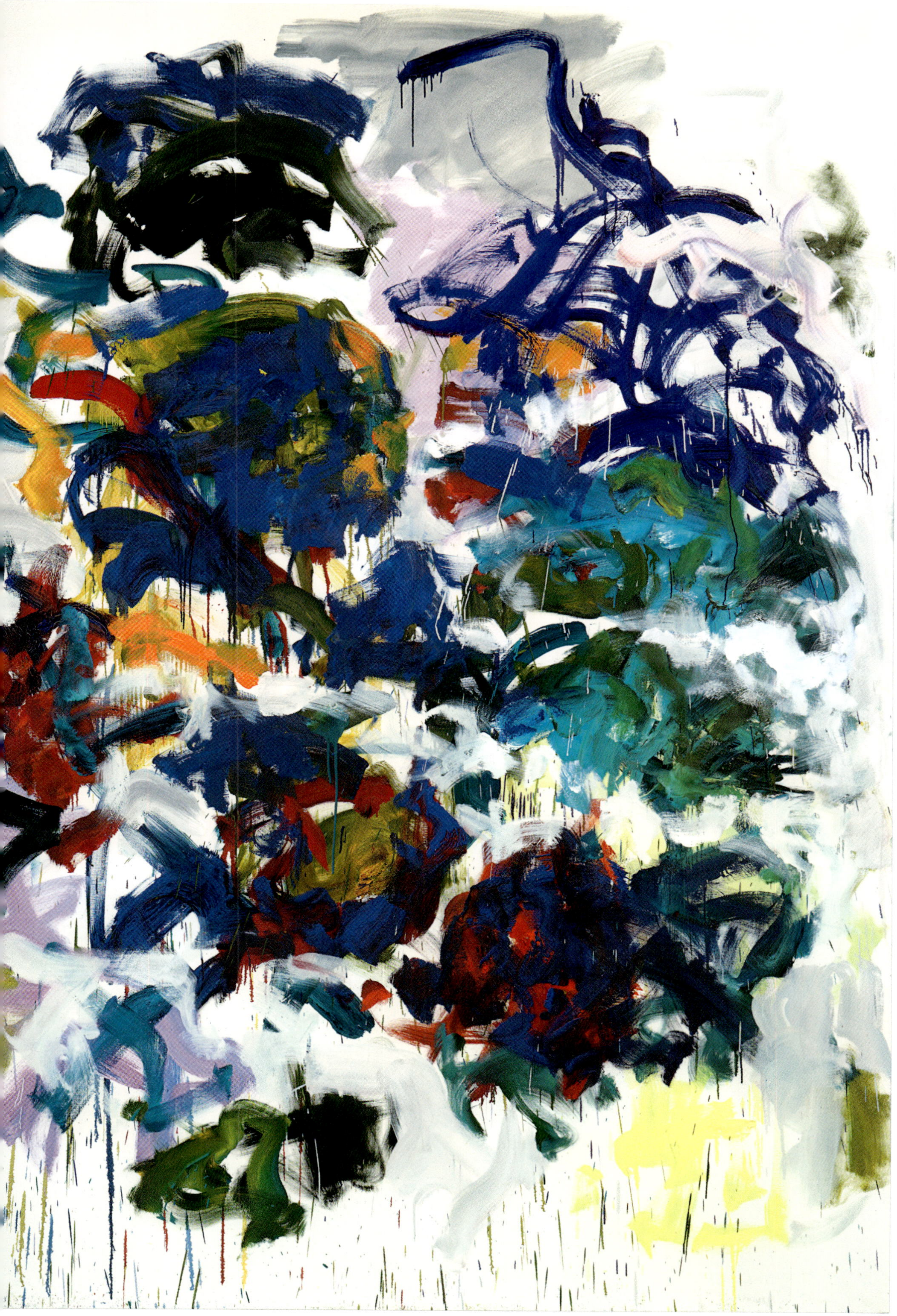

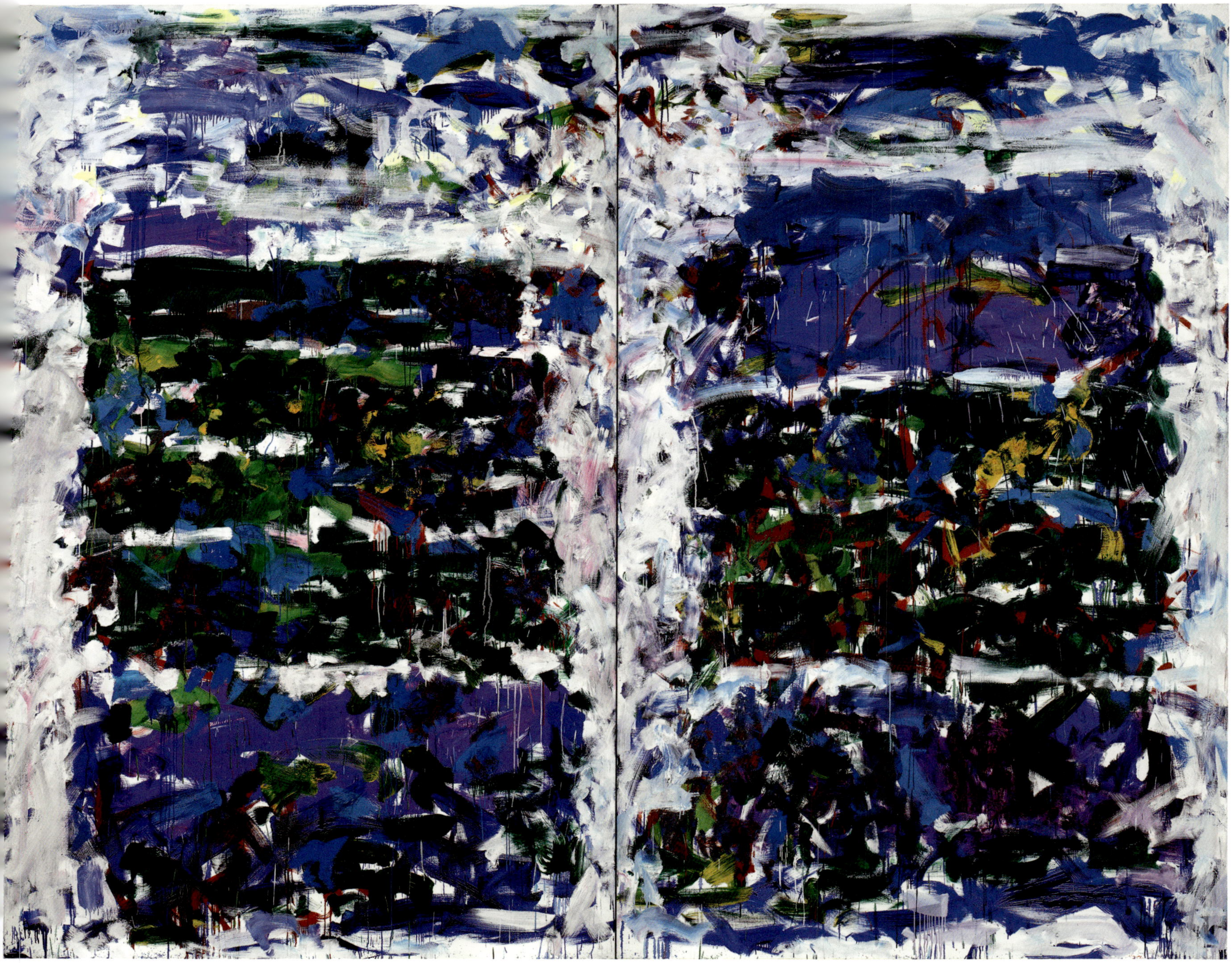

Champs, 1990. Oil on canvas, 110¼ × 141¾ in. (280 × 360 cm). Private collection

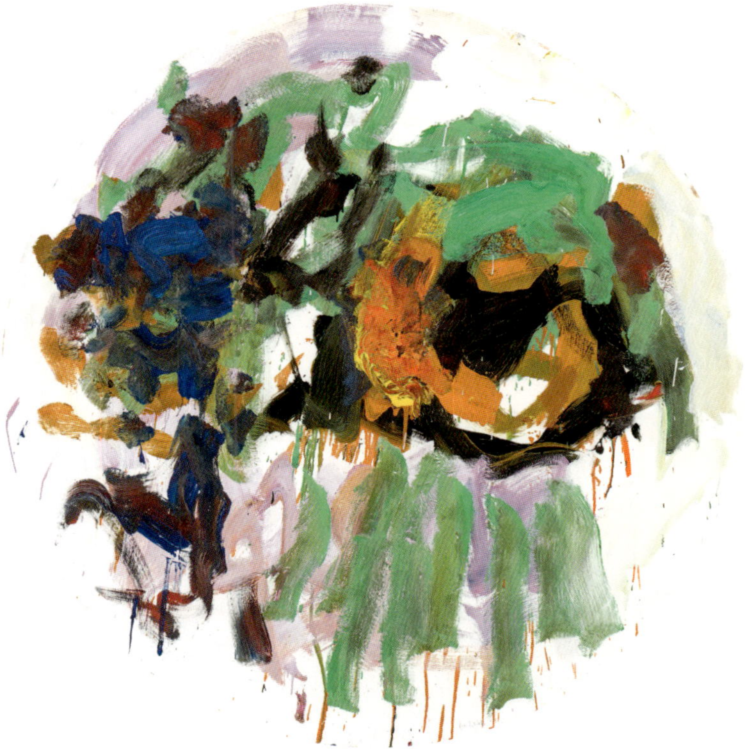

125

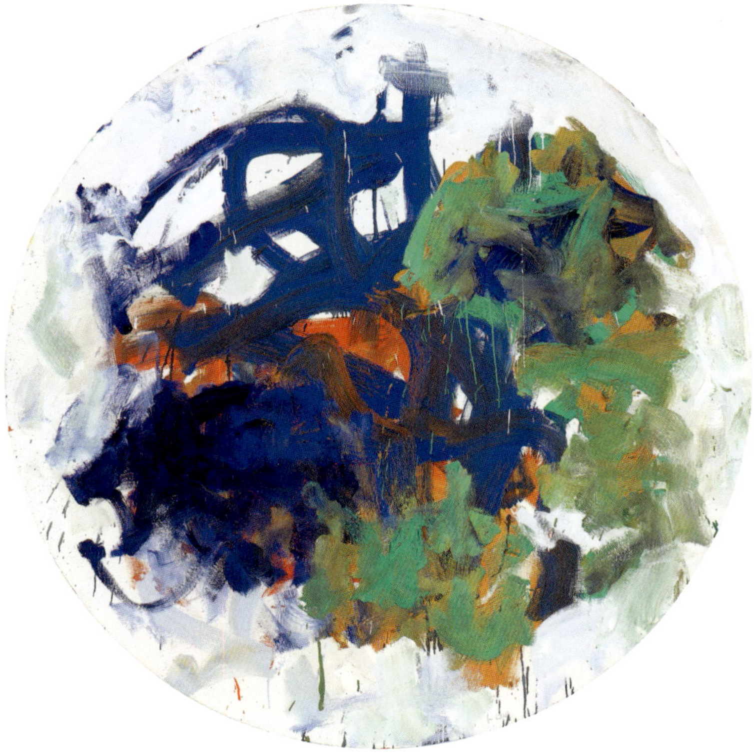

126

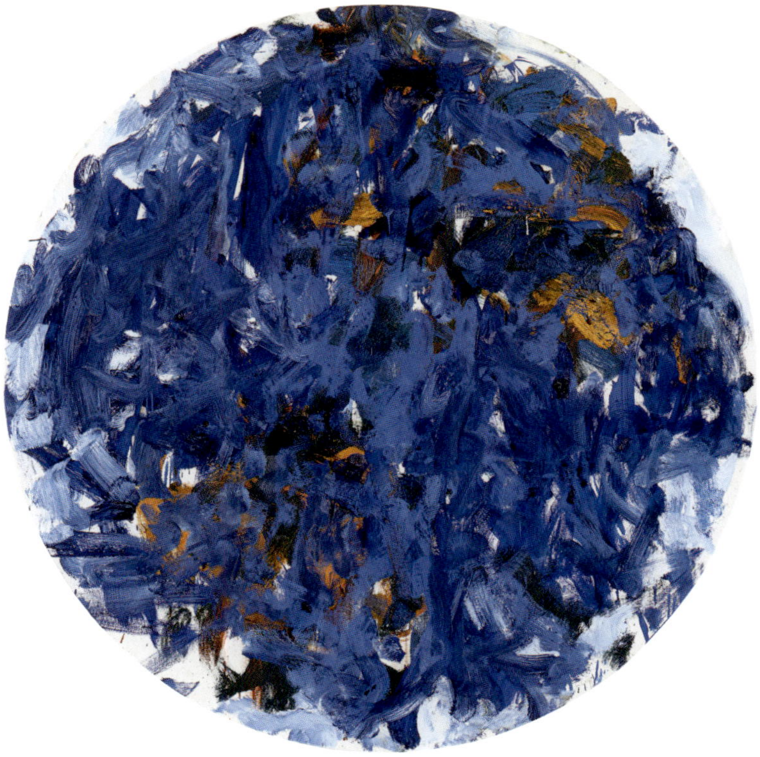

127

Tondo, 1991. Oil on canvas, 59 × 59 in. (149.9 × 149.9 cm). Joan Mitchell Foundation, New York

Tondo, 1991. Oil on canvas, 59 × 59 in. (149.9 × 149.9 cm). Private collection

Tondo, 1991. Oil on canvas, 59 × 59 in. (149.9 × 149.9 cm). Private collection

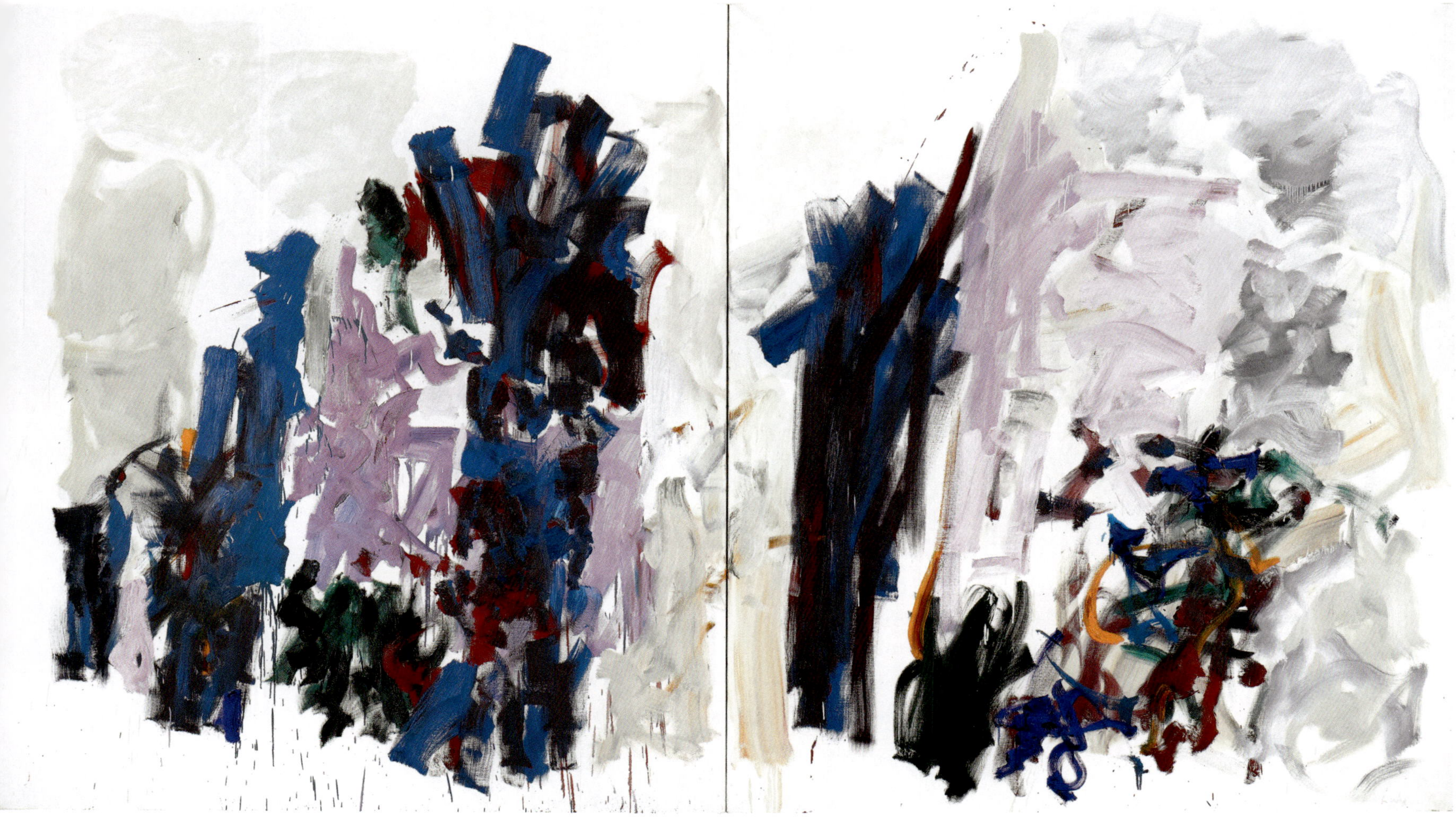

Trees, 1990. Oil on canvas, 78⅞ × 142 in. (200.3 × 360.7 cm). Walker Art Center, Minneapolis, gift of Joanne and Philip Von Blon

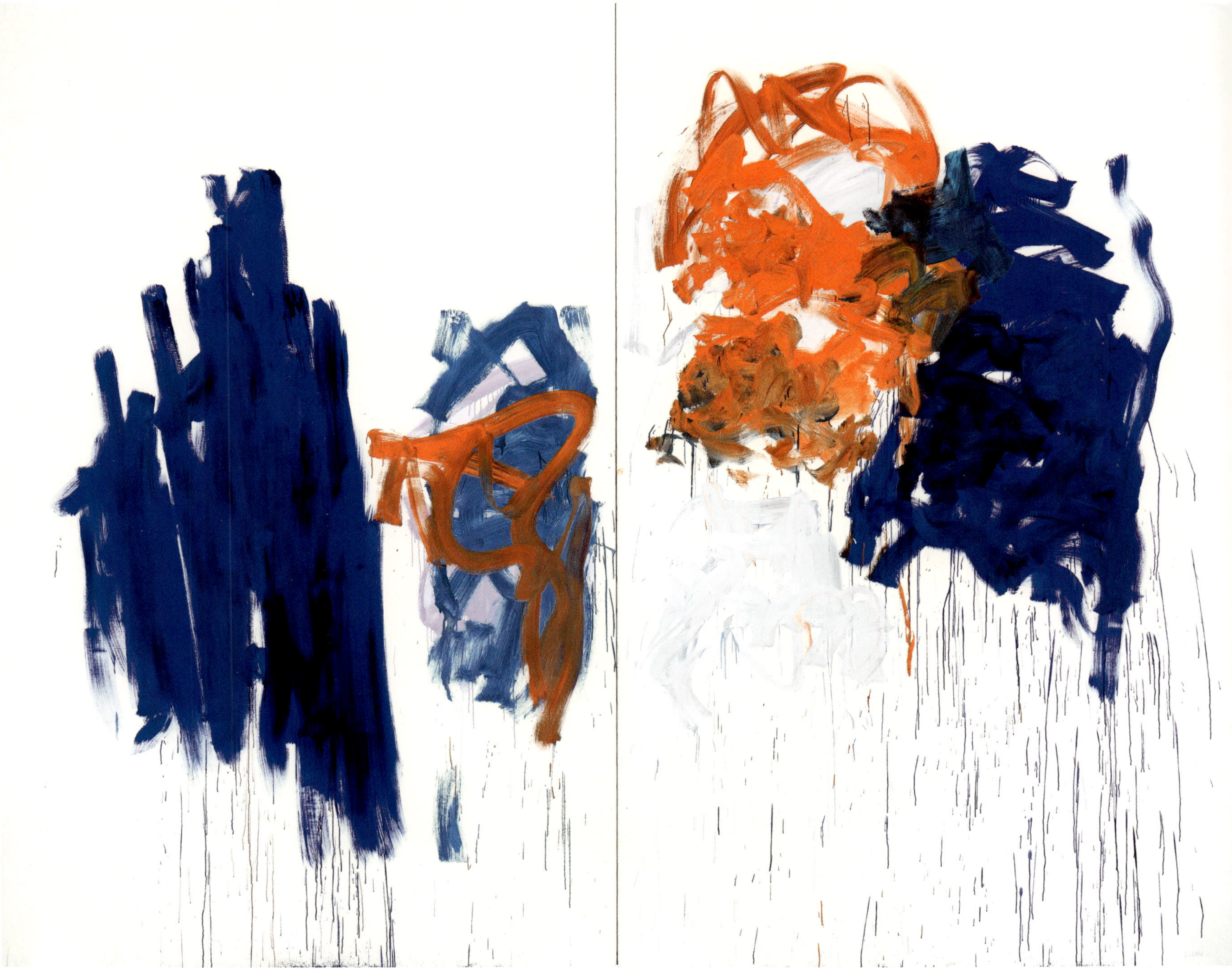

Merci, 1992. Oil on canvas, 110¼ × 141½ in. (280 × 359.4 cm). Joan Mitchell Foundation, New York

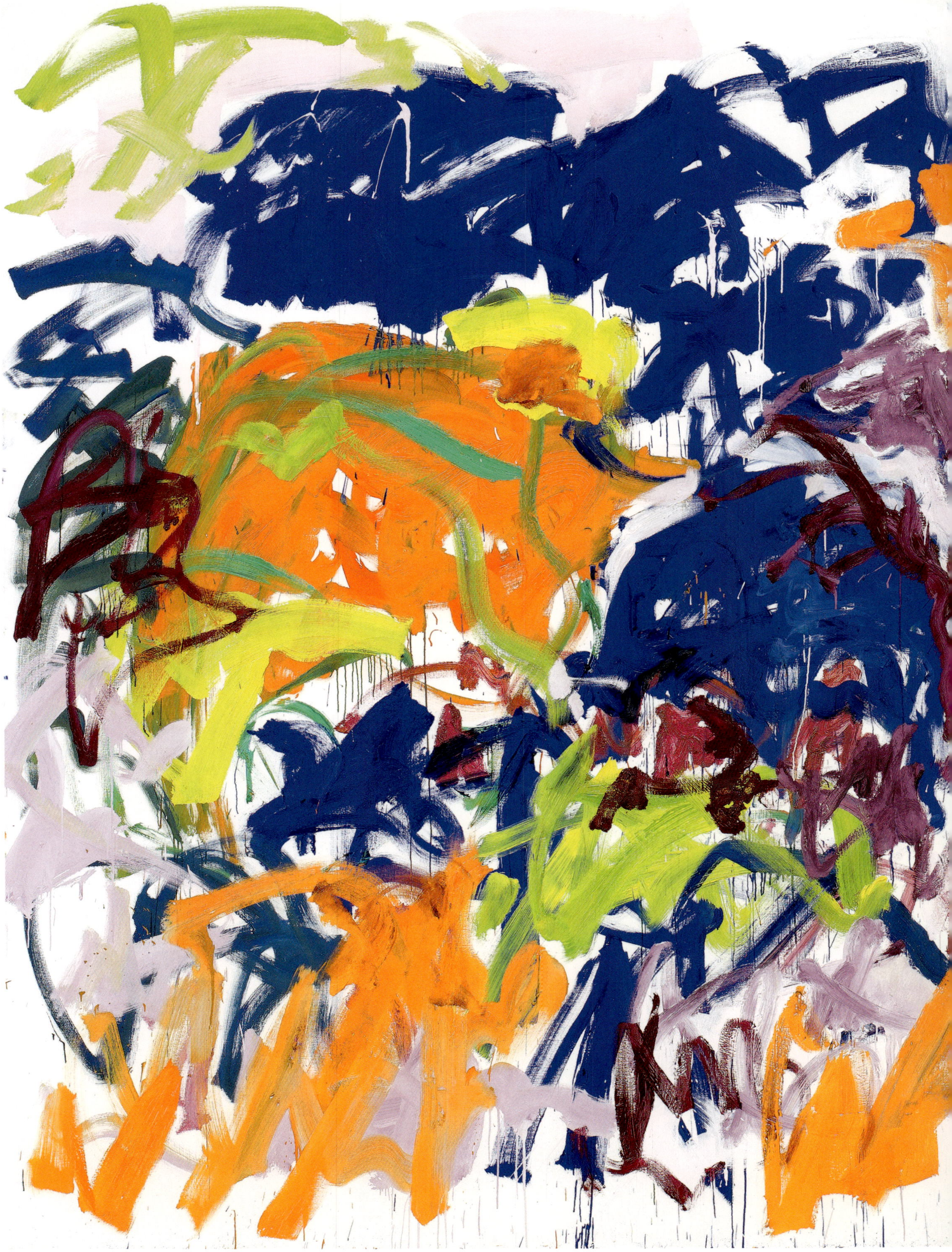

Ici, 1992. Oil on canvas, 102⅜ × 157½ in. (260 × 400.1 cm). Saint Louis Art Museum, funds given by the Shoenberg Foundation, Inc.

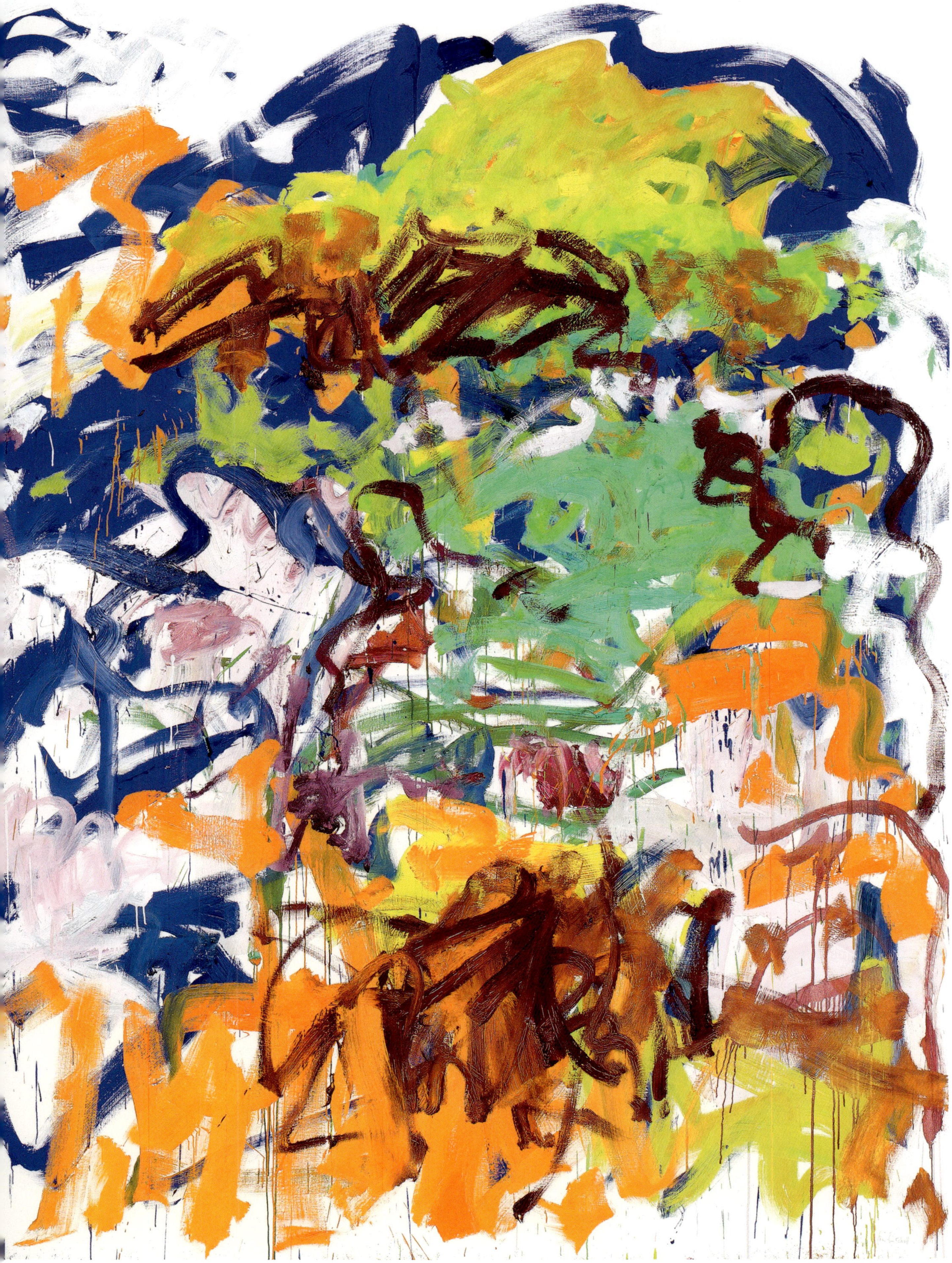

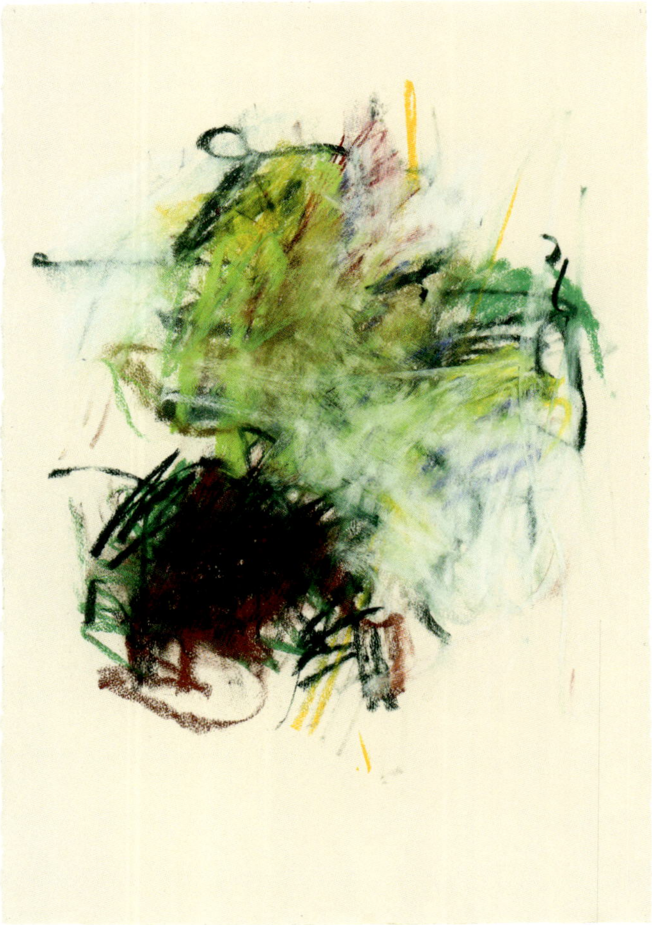

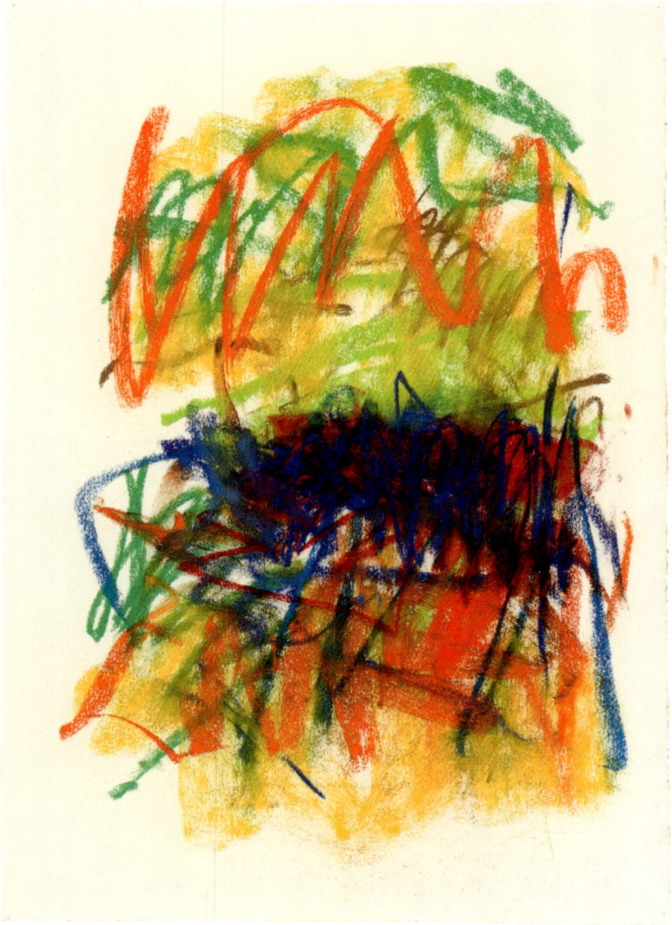

Untitled, 1992. Pastel on paper, 29⅝ × 20⅞ in. (75.3 × 53 cm). Joan Mitchell Foundation, New York

Untitled, 1992. Pastel on paper, 24⅞ × 17⅞ in. (63.2 × 45.4 cm). Joan Mitchell Foundation, New York

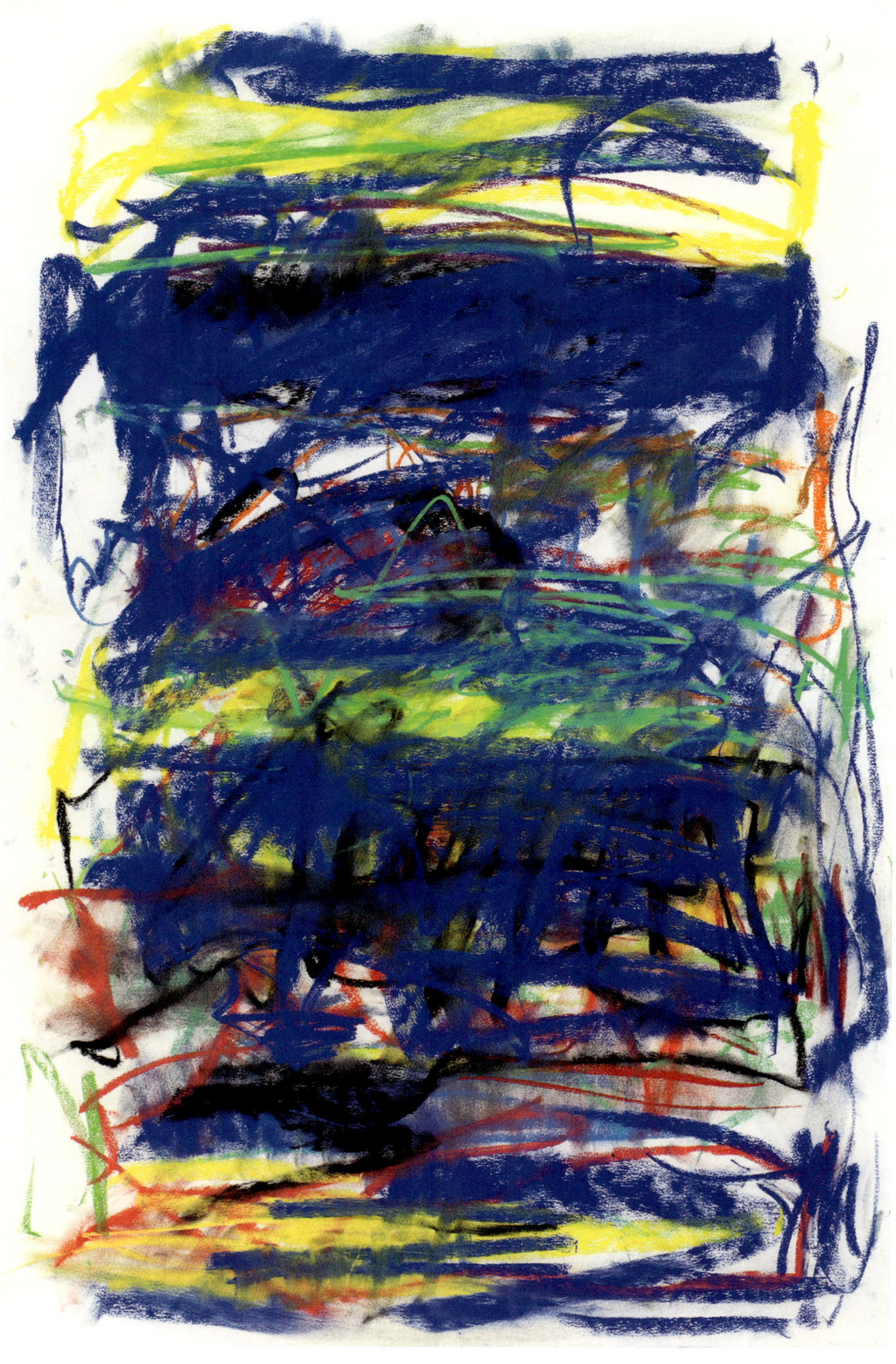

Untitled, 1991. Pastel on paper, 48 × 31½ in. (121.9 × 80 cm). Private collection, courtesy David Zwirner

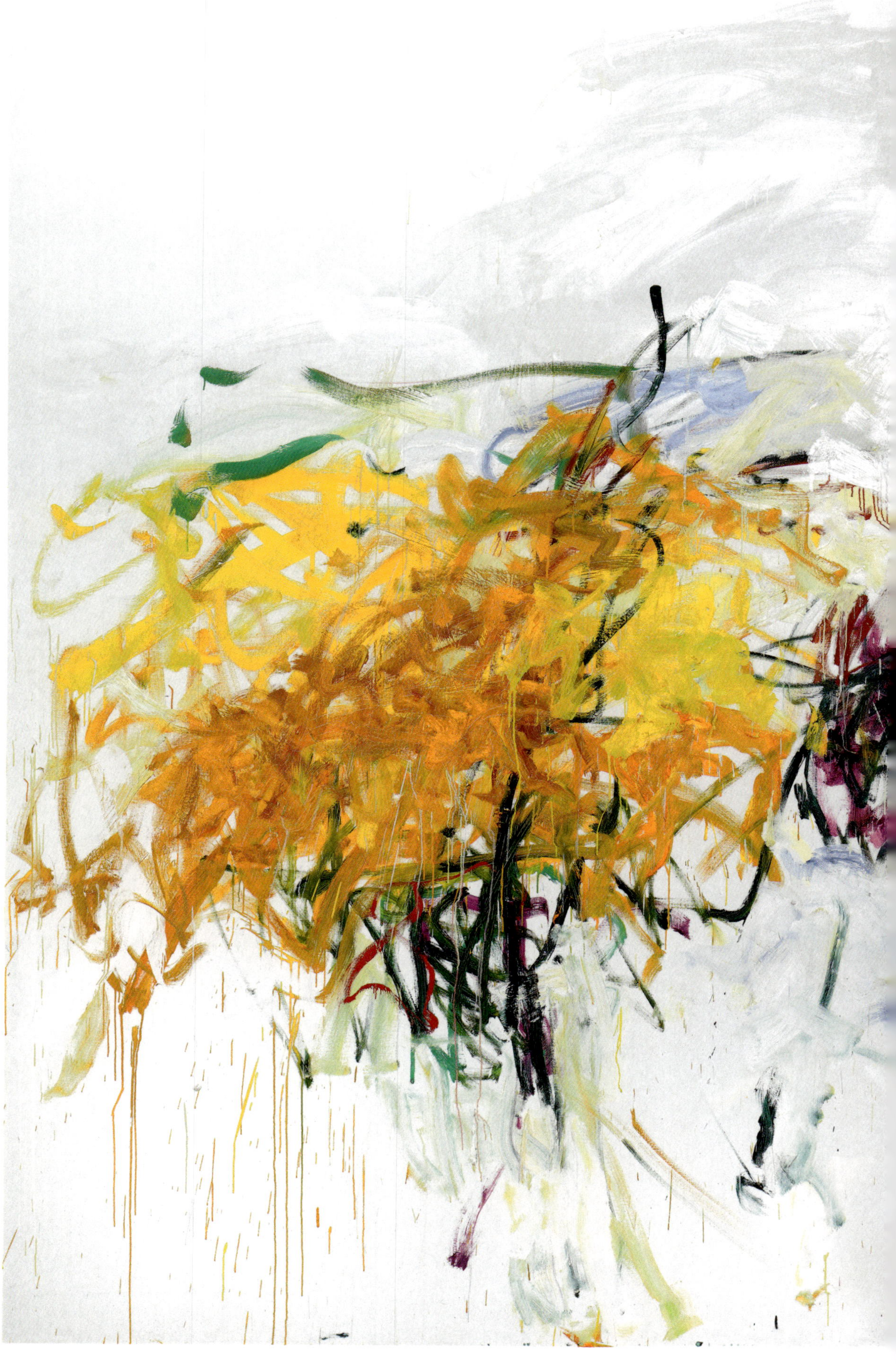

Untitled, 1992. Oil on canvas, 110¼ × 142 in. (280 × 360.7 cm). Komal Shah and Gaurav Garg Collection

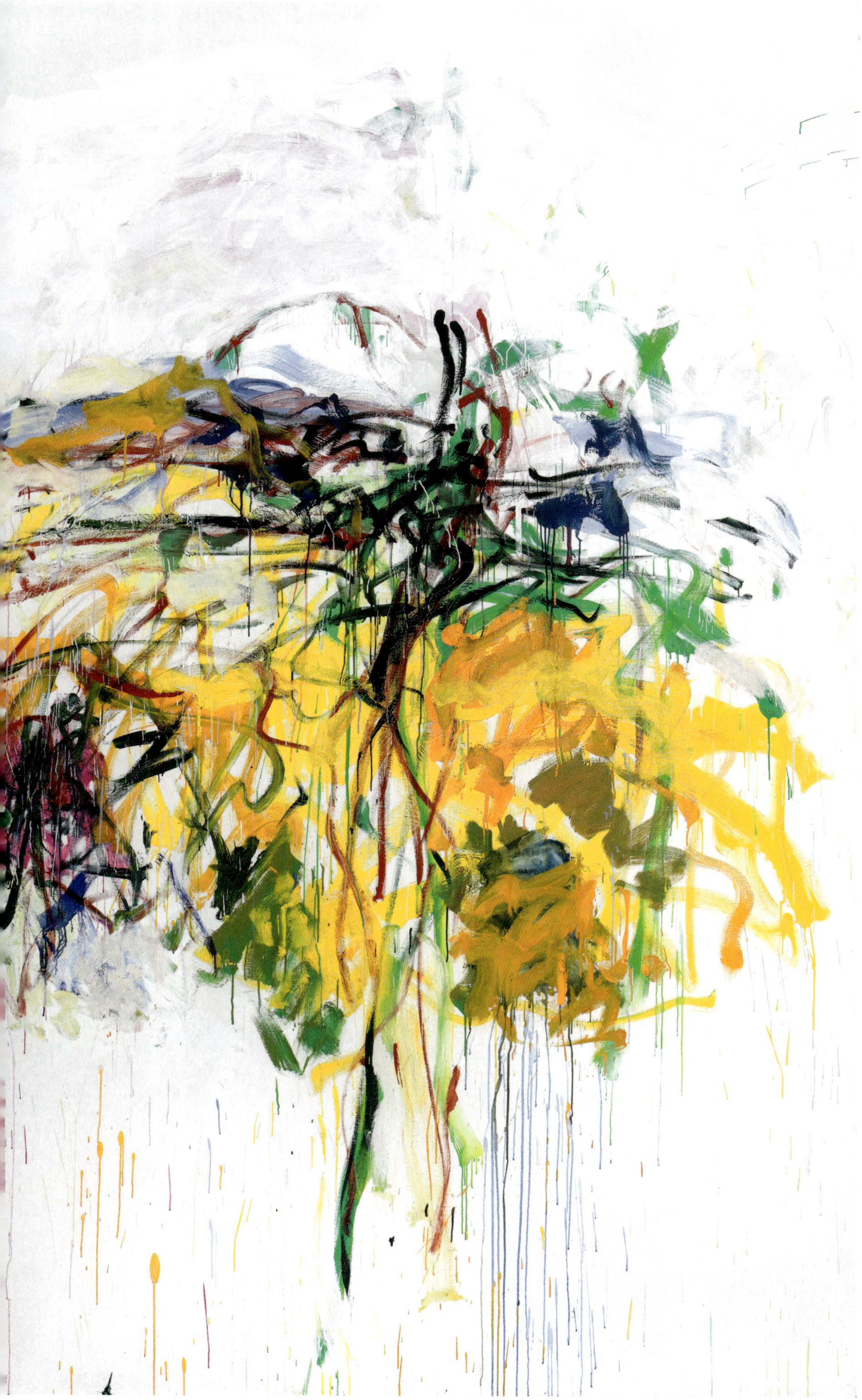

Add Red, or Not

Richard Shiff

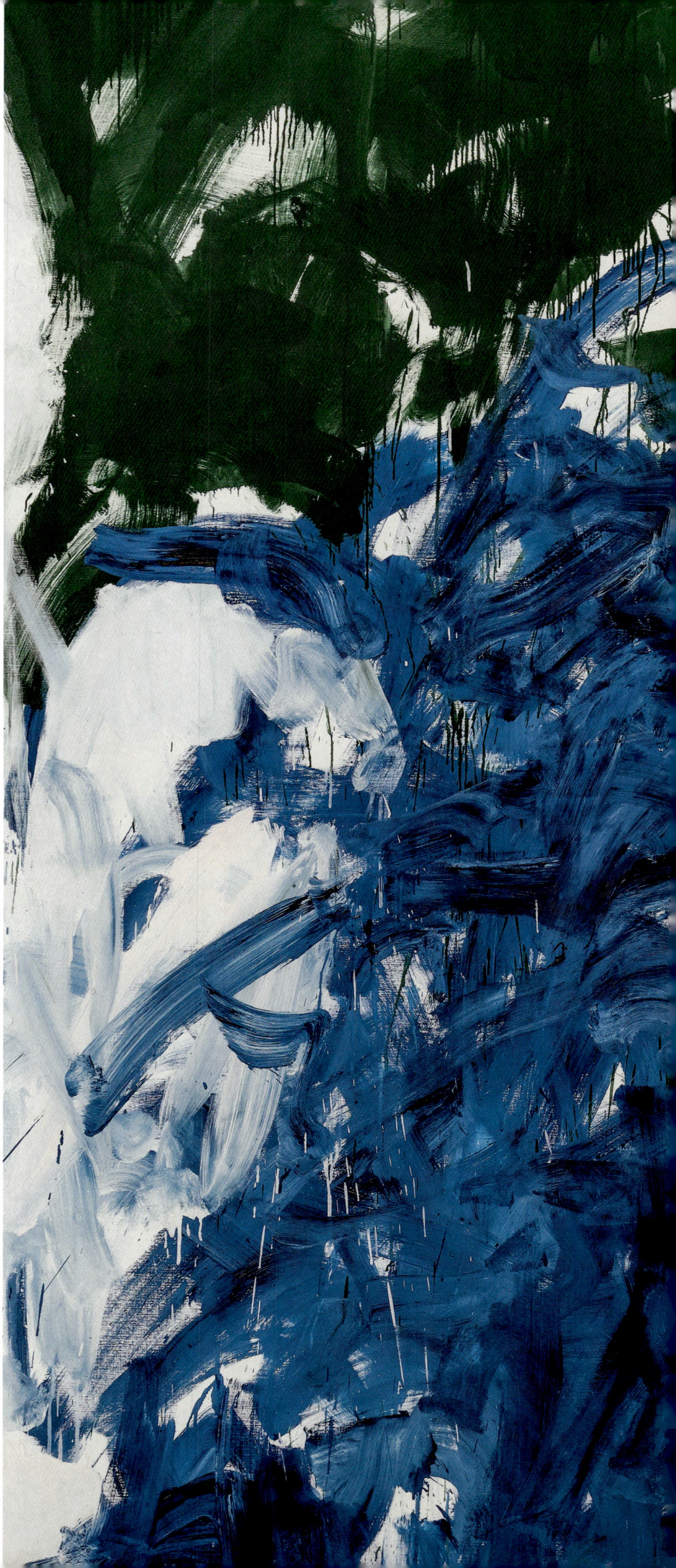

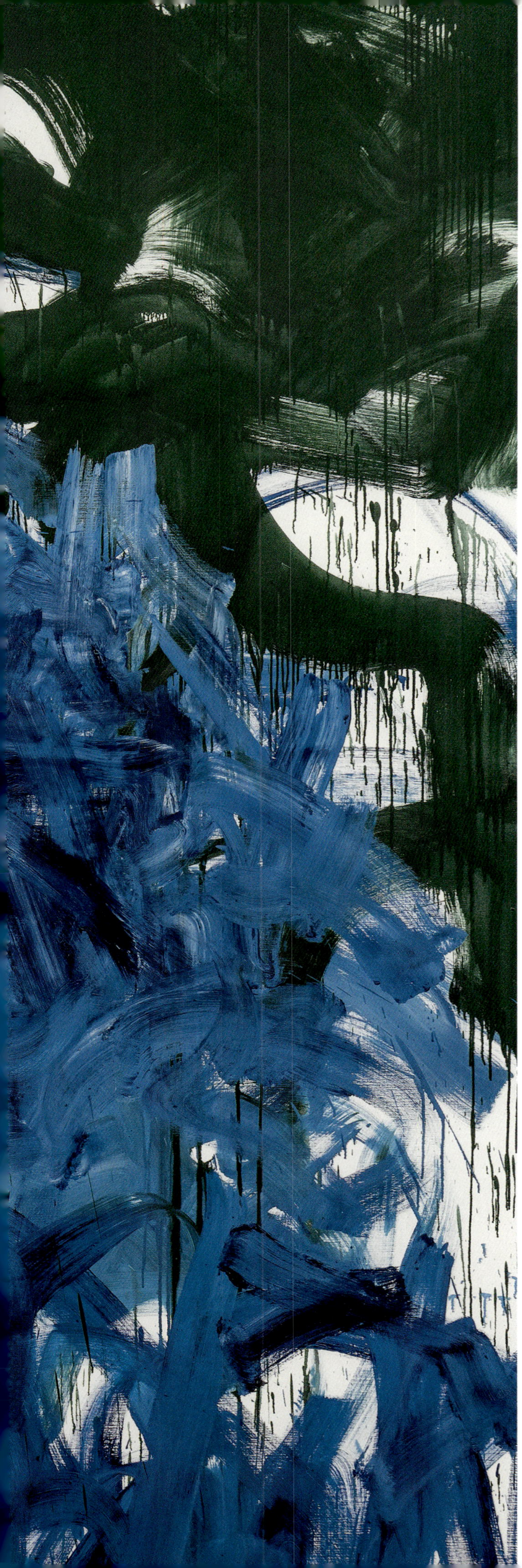

Those invigorated by the natural environment—enamored of sunsets, elevations, and vistas—might identify as "romantic." Invoking this term colloquially reflects our memory of the Romantics of the nineteenth century—poets, composers, painters—who turned to the wonders of nature, even to its commonplaces, for aesthetic inspiration. When encountered directly, nature presented an alternative to models canonized as classical Western art. Allowing no precedent to intercede, Romantics believed they could remove institutional restraint from sensory experience.

This essay associates Joan Mitchell's art with the Romantic attitude of the nineteenth-century painters she most admired. Whenever she marveled at Lake Michigan from her parents' tenth-floor Chicago apartment, she was relishing a Romantic moment.[1] This communion with nature infused her abstract art with twentieth-century Romanticism.

Joan Mitchell
Then, Last Time IV, 1985 (detail).
See fig. 5.

Feeling

Like many painters, Mitchell appreciated literature and poetry yet had limited faith in verbalization. Words are signs that refer by generalizing, and imprecision accompanies their use. In contrast, marks of color are specific. When sensed directly—like words perceived solely as shape, sound, or meter—colors hardly operate as signs at all. Whether linear and flowing or blunt and stubby, Mitchell's marks convey color self-sufficiently, neither tracing mimetic contours nor evoking familiar gestures of the human body. Her marks, far more practiced than schooled, reflect only the materiality of brushes, the viscosity of oil paints, and the fluidity of solvents.

In a late interview, Mitchell addressed the essence of her art, using the least language possible: "Forms have feeling. But what makes them have feeling, I don't know."[2] Implication: a feeling arises spontaneously, like a love of nature. In this respect, Mitchell shared the sentiments of Romantically inclined poets of her generation. Interviewed a few years later, Yves Bonnefoy provided a wordier justification for Mitchell's position:

> There is nothing before language, for there is no consciousness, and therefore no world, without a system of signs. In fact, it is the speaking-being that has created this universe, even if language excludes him from it. . . . We need poetry, not to regain [Edenic] intimacy, which is impossible, but to remember that we miss it and to prove to ourselves the value of those moments when we are able to encounter other people, or trees, or anything, *beyond words,* in silence.[3]

In another late interview, Mitchell alluded to such thoughts of sensory bliss: "Many people . . . see only learned clichés. For them apple means A.P.P.L.E., round R.E.D. things. They are always in the word stuff. . . . When I was sick, they moved me to a [hospital] room with a window. . . . I could see the pine trees, and I felt I could paint."[4] The pines were not G.R.E.E.N. but the unique chromatic array of an intimate vision. Seeing was Mitchell's Romantic mode of living—living "*beyond words,* in silence," the poet says.

An Existential Red

In 1965, Mitchell spent much of the summer with her lover Jean Paul Riopelle and a group of friends, sailing the French Mediterranean. Their home port was Golfe-Juan, below Vallauris and just to the west of the beaches of Antibes and Juan-les-Pins. It should have been idyllic. As part of a continuing correspondence with painter Michael Goldberg, located in New York, Mitchell reported her mixed emotions at the time: "On a boat they're concerned with keeping it afloat until you start wondering what you're doing on it in the first place. Painting isn't so different . . . even if you don't know what or why you're seeing it through—like why put red on or why not."[5] Not so different: painting, like sailing, lacks ultimate justification. Yet Mitchell seems to have been thinking, "I'd rather be painting." To keep an image afloat, add red. Or not.

In Mitchell's experience, no theory—no wordy concepts, no moral order—would resolve the existential course of painting. The artist's situation calls only for extending the experiential condition. When asked what a painting means, she replied: "I can't say it but the painting makes it clear."[6] The validity of each tenuous decision—red or not red—would be determined only after its results had been assessed. Her material technique was reactively additive: "The painting takes over. . . . It arrives at [its effect]. I sort of add on . . . I don't subtract, look back."[7]

To preserve the full existential history of a work kept it true to what Mitchell called "living," as opposed to merely "existing": "Feeling, existing, living. I think it's all the same, except for quality. Existing is survival. . . . *Feeling* your existence [is] not just survival. Painting is a means of feeling 'living.' . . . What matters is where that blue is in relation to that red."[8] Mitchell sometimes spoke as if her painting generated itself. Or, as she stated with utter conviction, yet to many listeners, maddeningly: "I don't think when I paint." To which she added: "Is that OK to say?"[9] Her position was insupportable, unthinkable, unsayable. Nor did Mitchell "feel" with respect to a directed, self-conscious touch that would instruct her hands: "Painting is a way of forgetting oneself.... I call that state 'no-hands.' I am in it. I am not there any more."[10]

Despite resisting any conceptualization of her practice, Mitchell was better at explaining herself than some interviewers claimed, as they judged her "inarticulate."[11] She understood the ironies of language and could deploy them. A statement published in 1958, concerning the role of nature in her painting, is an exercise—part philosophical, part poetic—in getting words to work. One passage has often been cited: "My paintings are titled after they are finished. I paint from remembered landscapes that I carry with me—and remembered feelings of them, which of course become transformed."[12] A second passage, the more challenging, has largely been ignored: "All art is subjective, is it not? I like to look out a window or first walk in it—nature—and then I paint, which is making something—an 'object' and a rather 'objective' activity."[13] Mitchell shifts from "all art is subjective" to her "rather 'objective' activity," which undermines the dualism. At work in her studio, she generated a material object, her painting in process. It became an objective source of sensation—"objective" because fully apparent, like the view from a window. Her painting would present her experience of both nature and painting itself ("telling me what to do"), and this nominally subjective image would become objective, occupying her entire consciousness.[14]

"I don't think when I paint." Red or no red is a feeling, not a thought. As Mitchell developed *To the Harbormaster* (1957, plate 27), at some point she wove a web of red into the whole, reinforcing the rhythms of strokes that had preceded.[15] The reds respond to the flow of dominant blues. Mitchell was engaged in an existential decision. Many of the prominent reds appear as definitive chromatic gestures, but others have been reset by overlays of the initial blue. An added red remains subject to whatever emerges in consequence. The red in such a work signals neither a compositional strategy nor pursuit of a theory of color. It registers a feeling exercised as the painting evolves, as if it were fulfilling itself, materially manifesting itself. Critic Clement Greenberg dismissed Mitchell as a "gestural horror," perhaps responding to inconsistencies in her idiosyncratic practice.[16] But she never sought to reason her way to stylistic coherence. Feelings assume no order.

Horizon Denied

In a Parisian studio in 1991, Mitchell worked with pastels while convalescing from hip surgery. The medium reveals her visual feeling or felt vision at an intimate scale conducive to analysis, though analysis seems—feels—anti-Mitchell. In one example (in the collection of the Joan Mitchell Foundation, New York), superimposed strokes of red draw an upper register of blue forward, as if integrating all on a single optical plane, ensuring that the chromatic differentiation develops no naturalistic composition of illusionistic space. Her colors hold "together on a flat surface," true to the materiality of painting.[17]

Interviewed in August 1989, Mitchell referred to "red lines" added to a work to be exhibited that year in New York at Robert Miller Gallery; with the red, she had intended to "return the picture to the surface and put

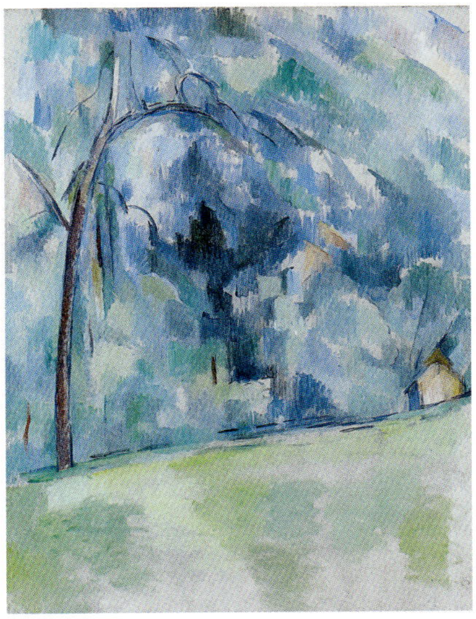

1

FIG 1 **Paul Cézanne**
Morning in Provence, ca. 1900–1906. Oil on canvas, 32 × 24⅞ in. (81.3 × 63.2 cm). Albright-Knox Art Gallery, Buffalo, New York, gift of Mr. and Mrs. Charles A. Ribbel through the Frank E. Ribbel Bequest, 1936

another dimension in the space." Stating her rationale to a greater degree than was typical, she nevertheless stopped short of a lucid explanation: "People . . . always look for the horizon. I want to hold a surface in a space. I deny the horizon."[18] She distinguishes the world of her aesthetic creation and poetic fantasy from the world of her prosaic observation. Mimesis should play no part in representing a feeling provoked by an observed scene. Horizons have a natural place in our experience of land but not on canvas or screen, where they become conceptual constructions, interfering with the direct presence of juxtaposed colors on the planar surface—a painter's alternative optics.[19]

Among the works exhibited at Robert Miller, *South* (1989, plate 122) is one of several that clearly fulfill Mitchell's interest in orienting optical energy to a frontal plane. Its linear array of superimposed red strokes appears as a screen that, rather than masking what lies behind, projects it forward. She brought her colors into equilibrium through mutual chromatic enforcement, guided by intuition, no traditional devices of composition required. If a color appears dead, she said, find the right color to set beside it, reviving it.[20] She would "mak[e] the background equal to the subject in weight." She added: "I'm not at all interested in composition. I don't mind having all the weight in the middle or on one side."[21] The two-panel configuration of *South* is symmetrical enough to provide left-right balance, even though the relative spareness of the uppermost register of each panel evokes "sky"—implying either a lapse into mimesis or a compositional conceit, an asymmetrical play against the greater density of the areas below.

South may allude to Mitchell's longstanding interest in Paul Cézanne. In September 1988, a year before her Robert Miller show, she visited the Albright-Knox Art Gallery in Buffalo to install a version of *The Paintings of Joan Mitchell: Thirty-Six Years of Natural Expressionism*.[22] While there, she was especially attracted to Cézanne's *Morning in Provence* (fig. 1), a work that resembles hers in presenting a continuous plane of colors with little hint of spatial recession.[23] "You can't enter a Cézanne because it pushes you back," she commented in 1992. "The eye is pushed back to the surface right away. That's why I like him."[24] Many of Cézanne's paintings have no obvious horizon, at times because he represented dense forest interiors, but more systemically because the aggressiveness of his marks interferes with conventional pictorial perspective. Perhaps inadvertently, his technique generated more of a surface than a scene, a condition noted by critics of his era. It caused some in the first decade of the twentieth century to apply the term "abstract": "The more he works, the more his work removes itself from the external view [and] the more he abstracts the picture."[25] Cézanne's novel aesthetic entailed "expression by means of the work itself and not the represented subject."[26]

Enhanced expressive feeling accompanied Cézanne's "abstraction" of the nominal subject, as if his painting were expressing *its* character rather than referring to externals, whether the natural environment, the cultural order, or the psychology of the artist. His art presented "all the remainder, which is nothing but painting itself."[27] To repeat one of Mitchell's thoughts: "I get feelings from the outside and I get moved by their colors together on a flat surface."[28] Her statement introduces a transformation with a history in Cézanne. As the "flat surface" (her abstraction) advances to her full attention, the "outside" (her stimulus and would-be reference) recedes from her imaginative view. Manifested in her painting, the feeling becomes both an abstraction and a comprehensive reality, an all-consuming romance with the colored plane. When Cézanne's immediate followers experienced this condition for themselves, it liberated their feel for optical color and tactile materiality from centuries of mimetic restriction that divided artist from art, subject from object. In 1906, the year of Cézanne's death, André Derain wrote to Henri Matisse of their good fortune, as the first generation of painters for whom the sensory presence of art assumed "a life of its own, independent of what one makes it represent."[29] The affect or emotionality of their art need no longer accord with the cultural identity of the depicted model and all it might connote. A more compelling emotion derived from the material basis of the artist's process. Derain and Matisse anticipated Mitchell's "feeling," though with more of a link to decipherable subject matter than she would allow.

I fantasize that Cézanne, representing his Provençal landscape, created a Mitchell abstraction of feeling; he offered an anachronistic gift that inspired hers in return. The vaguely pyramidal mass of *South,* doubled, evokes a twinned Mont Sainte-Victoire, though the famed mountain never appears so schematically in Cézanne's art. We would be unlikely to think of Sainte-Victoire, were we not already familiar with Mitchell's travels in meridional France and her interest in Cézanne. She had seen his mountain. Yet, if a critic were to attribute a mood to *South,* perhaps an expression of elation because of the hint of rise in the accumulation of Mitchell's marks, such descent into pathetic fallacy would have appalled her. "Raining therefore sadness," she said derisively, citing an example of the interpretive pitfall.[30] Moods are like the names given to emotions. Because only so many names exist, yet so many more emotions, naming becomes an exercise in approximation and reduction. Like her colors, Mitchell's feelings were entirely specific, resistant to generalized verbal description. Nor would her colors themselves describe a feeling. The colors *were* feeling—feeling in its singularity.

Mitchell often spoke of her parallel experience with the specifics of synesthesia. She perceived the letters of words as colors: "S is red, K is blue grey, and Y is yellow ochre.... Sky is mixed up of those colors." By additive optical mixture, "sky," the word, appeared "fairly white."[31] The sky above might be bright blue or dull gray or silvery, but the word was white. In stark contrast, the word "concept," Mitchell stated, "is to me C.O.N.C.E.P.T. There is no image."[32] Presumably, "horizon," a pictorial concept, presented the same problem. Such words relate ideas but convey no color, sensation, or visual feeling. "When I read," Mitchell said, "I'm seeing too, except of course for conceptual philosophy."[33]

"You will feel what I mean"

By the late 1960s, academically oriented critics had introduced "conceptual philosophy" with a vengeance, gradually marginalizing Mitchell's concern for "feeling," as well as her commitment to painting as a medium.[34] In 1965, she confessed that she "enjoyed looking, and I know that's not very profound to some people."[35] "I'm very old-fashioned," she told curator Marcia Tucker in 1974. "My paintings aren't about art issues. They're about a feeling."[36] In 1986, she lamented that "feeling" remained "a dirty word."[37]

As critical attention turned to Pop and Conceptual art, to both vernacular culture and academic theory, Mitchell maintained her romance with nature. Her art was "from [and] about landscape," she said, "not about me."[38] Psychology and mood became far less relevant to her results as her practice evolved in the 1970s and later.[39] She benefited from a long relationship with a psychoanalyst, yet kept her emotional states apart from the feelings of landscape motivating her paintings. This compartmentalization followed from her desire to lose her quotidian self in blissful immersion in her medium. I have nonetheless been implying that Mitchell's aesthetic practice entails abandoning the habitual binary of subject and object. The celebrated Modernists she most admired—not only Matisse, but those preceding him, Cézanne and Vincent van Gogh—had already discounted this conceptual dichotomy. The practice of nineteenth-century art, especially landscape, demonstrated how deceptive the division of subject from object could be.

The techniques of Cézanne and van Gogh were especially direct. To their contemporaries, they represented the "coarse or rough" end of Impressionist practice.[40] Their art extended a Romantic tradition of depicting nature as immediate sensory experience—sensation with an emotional aspect to it, with *feeling*. Instructive in this regard are the mid-nineteenth-century writings of critic-historian Théophile Thoré, a radical republican who promoted individual experience as antidote to institutionalized doctrine. Reviewing the Paris Salon of 1847, Thoré noted the diminutive bronze serpent that Auguste Clésinger added to his highly sexualized sculpture in marble, *Woman Bitten by a Snake*; it would placate the exhibition jury by invoking the historical conceit of a Cleopatra. No matter, Thoré countered, for "in the arts, the subject means little." He recalled that the precise themes of the majority of antique and Renaissance masterworks were unknown. Titles attributed only generic identities: Venus for typical female figures, Apollo for male. Conceptualization of the imagery remained arbitrary: "Their beauty suffices and always entails in itself its meaning."[41] Sensuously sculpted surfaces and the jewellike colors of painting would impress viewers with "the value of art itself."[42]

Thoré's reasoning justifies Mitchell's "I don't think when I paint." He suggested that a painter remains absorbed in "an unreflective process, not obligated to be cognizant of its rationale"—a Romantic notion.[43] Social meaning emerges through the linguistic generalizations of critical commentary but should not limit aesthetic practice. Thoré's notion that the collective significance of a work arises outside the conscious intention of the artist has long been a tenet of modern art theory. Discursive meaning becomes the province of a liberated public response, evading prescriptive norms that reflect the ideological values of the dominant authorities (in Thoré's era, church and state). Such public "meaning" nevertheless remains incommensurate with sensory experience, an imperfect translation. Interpretation is "historical," following identifiable trends that extend causal traces, while felt experience leaves no coherent record, only a diaristic chronicle. The transformative *social* politics of Thoré's "value of art itself"—intended to resist the class-oriented dictates of traditional academic theory—had become by Mitchell's time "old hat."[44] Yet her "feeling" was no less felt, no less real, unencumbered by history.

Mitchell's feeling was also, paradoxically, not Mitchell's (not "about me"). Here, too, nineteenth-century critical thinking anticipates her position. Paul Mantz, an admirer of Thoré, claimed that the most concerted attempts at objective representation often led to thoroughly subjective results, defying what would otherwise be expected from efforts at direct transcription. Every artist, he noted, exists in an emotional state; a landscapist shares this emotion with the natural environment, as if it too had feelings. Disposed in a certain mood, whether "exhilarated or depressed, . . . it seems that something of oneself is left suspended in the hushed thickets and . . . mute trees."[45] To render nature as it is, Mantz implies, is tantamount to representing intimate feelings without intending it, nature having assimilated human emotion spontaneously. The landscape is pathetic; it feels a human presence. But this is no pathetic fallacy.

In 1965, Mitchell recounted a generative experience: "I saw this cypress tree against an ochre wall . . . [it] was so black and the ochre wall was a pale, pale ochre and it moved me, so whatever that means." However intense, the feeling did not translate to "meaning": "I was caught by it . . . moved by this particular very dark thing and this pale wall. . . . It wasn't the image of the tree, it was the moment."[46] The experience led to a series of abstractions dominated by blackish greens (*Girolata Triptych* [1963, plate 39]; *First Cypress* [ca. 1964, plate 40]). Mitchell sometimes created the darkness by mixing chromatic opposites; at other times, she included a true black among her greens.[47] She was not matching a color to nature but generating a flow of feeling—a certain greenness, a certain darkness, a certain illumination.

"Not the image . . . the moment": van Gogh's moments had been similar; his cypresses formed a "dark patch in a sun-drenched landscape."[48] His accounts rely on the French verb *sentir,* which corresponds to Mitchell's *feel.* In February 1890, he responded to praise from critic Albert Aurier, volunteering that much of the credit should be directed elsewhere: "If you will please go and see a particular bouquet by [Adolphe] Monticelli, then you will feel [*sentirez*] what I mean" (fig. 2).[49] It had to be seen to be felt. Van Gogh's French, *ce que je veux dire,* "what I mean," might be translated un-idiomatically as "what I want to say" or "what I'm trying to say," as if a verbal description of the look of Monticelli's art were impossible to articulate adequately: "You will see what I would like to be able to say (but cannot)." This is Mitchell's thought as well: she cannot say it, but people will see it. Art fosters insight and intuition, the individual's safeguard against cultural dogma, which is said, not felt.

Aurier was prolix, perceiving few limitations to language. Van Gogh paid him a painter's compliment, ironic in view of what we know of Mitchell: "You create colors with your words."[50] The critic embedded his characterization of van Gogh's cypresses within a continuous sentence occupying forty-one lines of journal text: "cypresses rising in nightmarish silhouette, like darkening flames of black."[51] In turn, van Gogh offered Aurier the gift of *Cypresses with Two Figures* (fig. 3). He had painted it in the strong mistral wind: "It is therefore the note of a certain blackness [of the trees] enveloped in blue moving in great circulating currents of air."[52] He animated his blue and white sky with swirls of impasto. Its texture is as accentuated as that of the cypresses—light sky against dark trees—virtually eliminating perspectival recession and a sense of

FIG 2 **Adolphe Monticelli**
Bouquet, ca. 1875. Oil on wood panel, 27¼ × 19⅜ in. (69.2 × 49.2 cm). The Phillips Collection, Washington, D.C., 1961

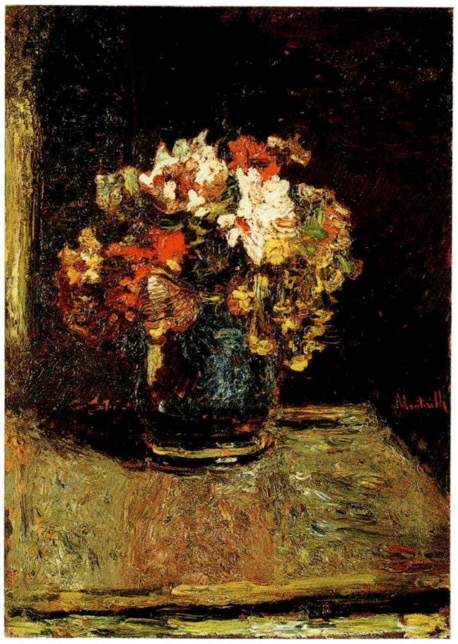

2

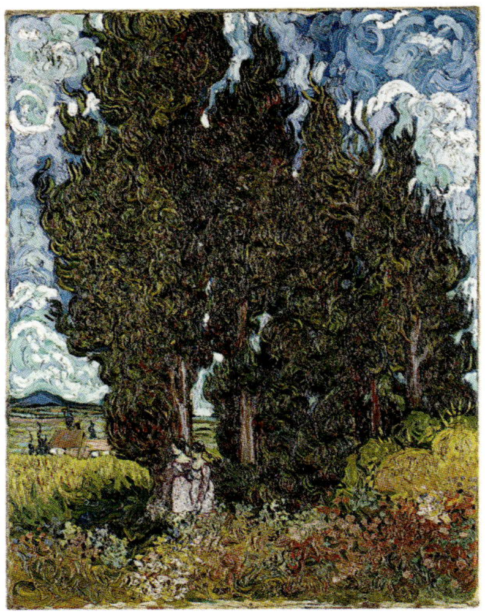

3

"horizon" (gone also from Cézanne). We recall Mitchell's "feeling": "I saw this cypress tree against an ochre wall . . ." For her, the lightness of wall-ocher was as forward and planar an element as the darkness of cypress-green. Similarly, when she added strokes of white to a work in progress, they were color, not erasure—positive elements, not blankness—analogous to her existential reds.[53]

Quality

"There's a little van Gogh over there, blue sky and green grass—no birds."[54] Filmed in her Paris studio, Mitchell was pointing to one of the pastels of 1991. Her somewhat facetious "no birds" alluded to van Gogh's famous *Wheatfield with Crows* (see fig. 10.2) as well as to her loose reference to its convergent structure, her diptych *No Birds* (1987–88, plate 118). With laconic irony, Mitchell's title relates what her painted poetry of silence does not: van Gogh's crows are superfluous to his play of color, whereas her analogous form is all color, all feeling. She appreciated Antonin Artaud's physicalized description of *Wheatfield with Crows,* which equated earth to sea: "It is as a liquid sea that van Gogh traces the earth like a series of jerks of the hoe."[55] Artaud might have added that the sky, too, becomes at once sealike and landlike; all is materially accentuated in waves, resulting in a no-horizon effect for a landscape with obvious horizon.

This is why Mitchell's pastel is a "van Gogh." Although displaying blue (as if sky) above green (as if fields), its facture of strokes is so insistent, especially in the blue, that no area visually recedes; if this pastel is a "landscape," it offers the feeling devoid of perspectival illusion. A comparable van Gogh is *Wheatfield under Thunderclouds* (fig. 4), "blue sky and green grass," as it were. As in *Cypresses with Two Figures,* its textured sky advances. When every element asserts itself equally on a plane, undermining hierarchical order, the gravitational position of an evocative color, top or bottom, hardly matters. For *Then, Last Time IV* (fig. 5), Mitchell set green above blue. In her experience of feeling-as-abstraction, as opposed to feeling-as-representation, green above blue was just as much a "van Gogh" as blue above green: "You put on blue and then you put on green and then the green says 'put on more blue,' or whatever. . . . That's what makes the painting to me, which is visual. It is not because these colors make me sad or something."[56] The upper areas of the triptych *Bracket* (1989, plate 119) show evidence of such chromatic equilibration—visual intuition rather than "mood."

Along with van Gogh's renderings of sunflowers, a lasting inspiration, Mitchell was attracted to the material boldness of his *Rain* (see fig. 8.2), which pictured the enclosed field outside his Saint-Rémy asylum.[57] By giving rain a distinctive physical presence as diagonal streaks across the canvas, van Gogh suppressed the inherent perspective of

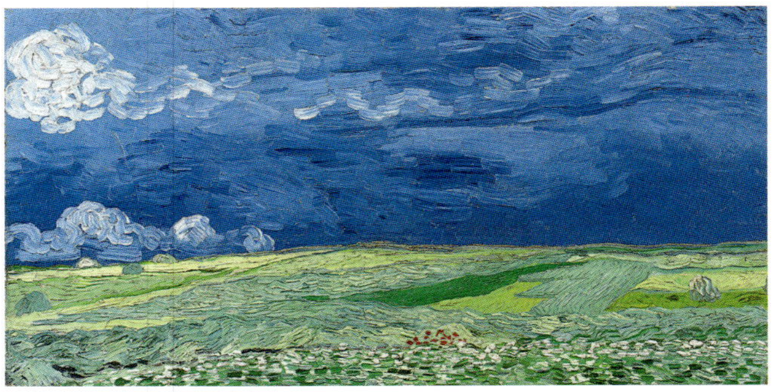

4

FIG 3 **Vincent van Gogh** *Cypresses with Two Figures,* June 1889–February 1890. Oil on canvas, 36 × 28½ in. (91.6 × 72.4 cm). Kröller-Müller Museum, Otterlo, The Netherlands

FIG 4 **Vincent van Gogh** *Wheatfield under Thunderclouds,* 1890. Oil on canvas, 19¹³⁄₁₆ × 39⅞ in. (50.4 × 101.3 cm). Van Gogh Museum, Amsterdam (Vincent van Gogh Foundation)

FIG 5 **Joan Mitchell** *Then, Last Time IV,* 1985. Oil on canvas, 102¼ x 78¾ in. (259.7 × 200 cm). Joan Mitchell Foundation, New York

FIG 6 **Joan Mitchell** *Rain,* 1989. Oil on canvas, 94½ × 157½ in. (240 × 400 cm). Private collection his landscape composition. Mitchell's diptych *Rain* (fig. 6) eliminates the pretense of landscape, leaving only the diagonals—a rain-feeling neither of rain nor of Mitchell.

Whenever confined to his room, van Gogh resorted to rendering scenes like *Rain* from his window. Analogous views had long given Mitchell sensory pleasure: "I love looking out my window" (memories of Lake Michigan).[58] Late in her career, she too had periods of hospitalization. A window allowed her to escape into feeling, as van Gogh had done. "I could see the pine trees," she said, "and I felt I could paint."[59] As we know from remarks already quoted, her sensations had "quality": "Feeling, existing, living. I think it's all the same, except for quality."[60] Like "feeling," "quality" became a "dirty word" during the course of Mitchell's career; it suggested an order of values, tantamount to an aesthetic class system, privileging the few who knew what counted as quality over the many who did not.[61] But for Mitchell, "quality" signified what it had for nineteenth-century Romantics like Thoré and those who followed: the Naturalist Mantz, the "crude" Impressionists Cézanne and van Gogh. Quality was the personal intensity of feeling that rendered theoretical precepts anodyne. As Mitchell noted, such feeling was "feeling your existence."[62]

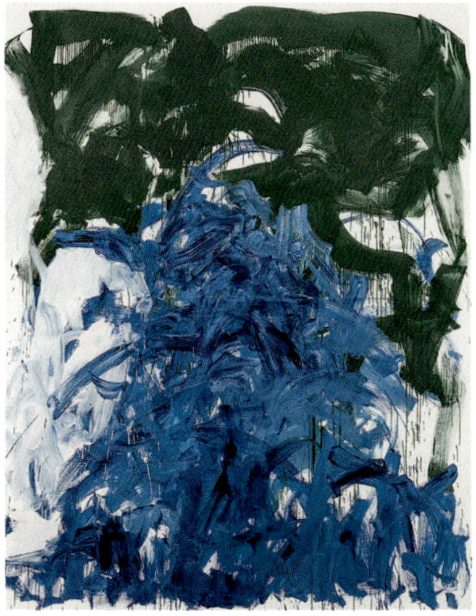

5

Whichever side of the unequal equation one favors—whether theories account for feelings or feelings acquire theories—the one never matches the other. Saying it is not seeing it. This realization may have led Mitchell back to exemplary nineteenth-century painting. Or, her lifelong attraction to this art may have sensitized her to feel that much more.

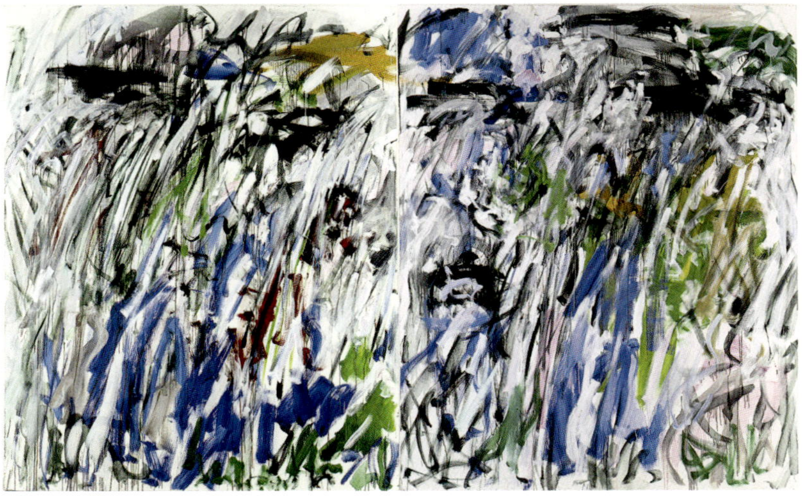

6

9

La Vie en rose Katy Siegel

Through want and joy we have walked hand in hand:
we are both resting from our travels now,

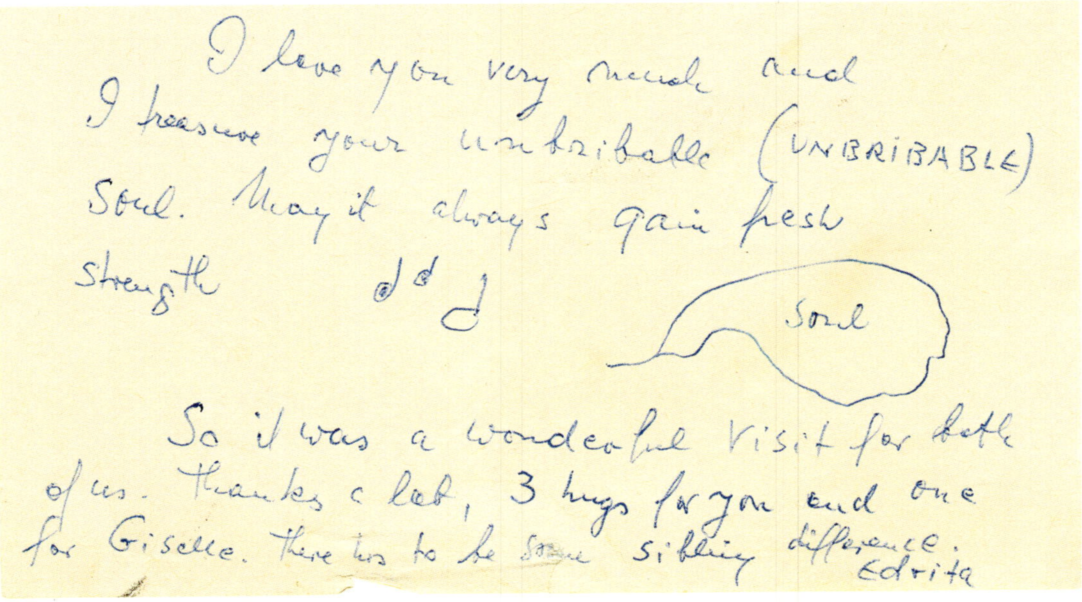
I love you very much and
I treasure your unbribable (UNBRIBABLE)
Soul. May it always gain fresh
strength

Soul

So it was a wonderful visit for both
of us. Thanks a lot, 3 hugs for you and one
for Giselle. There has to be some sibling difference.
Edrita

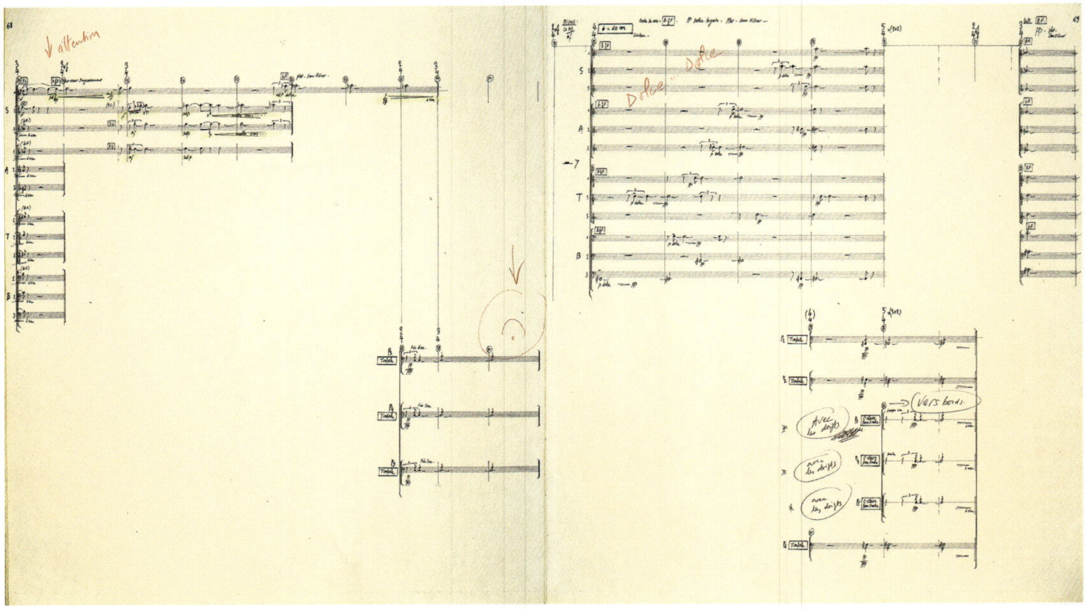

the quiet countryside below us. —RICHARD STRAUSS, "TWILIGHT," FROM *FOUR LAST SONGS*

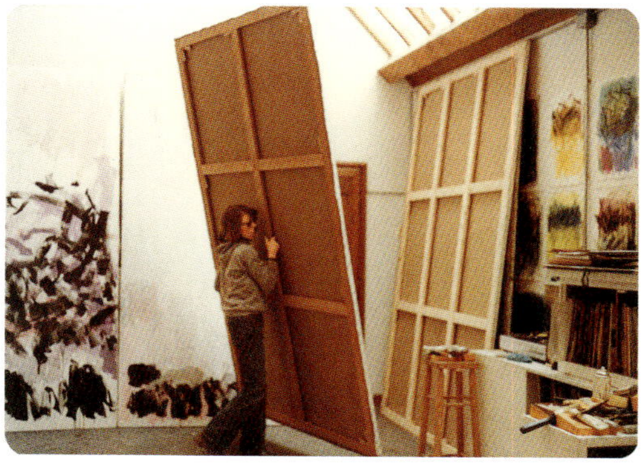

9.1

"I love you very much and I treasure your unbribable (UNBRIBABLE) soul."[1] Mitchell's beloved Edrita Fried wrote her after a visit to Vétheuil around 1980, adding a drawing of Mitchell's twinned music and spirit (at left). The years 1979 to 1986 swelled with ambition—for art, not career—and the achievement in her work manifested a metaphysical depth born of a life surveyed, prompted, but not determined, by loss and death. These years were shaped as well by her friendship with an electric younger artist, already a true peer, the composer Gisèle Barreau. Their intimacy and mutual support deepened Mitchell's relationship to music and also to nature, as Barreau's pleasure and skill with plants forged a more authentic connection to the gardens of La Tour. Mitchell's paintings reached a new expanse, even as she grew more present in and anchored to the concrete details of her life.

In early 1979, Mitchell flew to New York in the wake of the betrayal by Jean Paul Riopelle and Hollis Jeffcoat, for a "crash-shrink program" with Fried.[2] When she returned to Vétheuil in April, she found that Lefèbvre-Foinet had delivered canvas and also cleaned the studio. She reworked and began new pastels, playing her favorite painting music, wanting to want to paint.[3] Spring came late that year; "the lilacs just bloomed" in May when Mitchell herself came back to life and began to paint on a daily basis, beginning the enormous quadriptych *La Vie en rose* (1979, plate 99), whose muted pinks and lavenders play on the "rose" of the title, and perhaps the lilacs as well.[4] In the dozens of photos of the panels in progress, one can see that the early version of what would become the far left panel was much more of a *Tilleul* stroke, vertical and black, and tiered, to be later complicated with blue, masked with white and lilac/gray, and dappled with shorter touches, all of which made it more massed centrally (fig. 9.1). The photos show Mitchell trying out different sequences—in the end, she arrives at what now seems inevitable and would become characteristic: two narrow central panels flanked by slightly wider "side" panels. The painting's title ironically echoes Mitchell's long-ago declaration that upon arriving in Paris, "la vie en rose begins"; it also conjures the defiant,

FRONTISPIECE
Top: Letter from Edrita Fried to Joan Mitchell, n.d. (detail). Joan Mitchell Foundation Archives, New York. Bottom: Gisèle Barreau, score for *Aires pour Marion,* 1980. Courtesy Gisèle Barreau

FIG 9.1 Joan Mitchell with *La Vie en rose* (1979) in her studio at La Tour, Vétheuil, France, 1979. Joan Mitchell Foundation Archives, New York

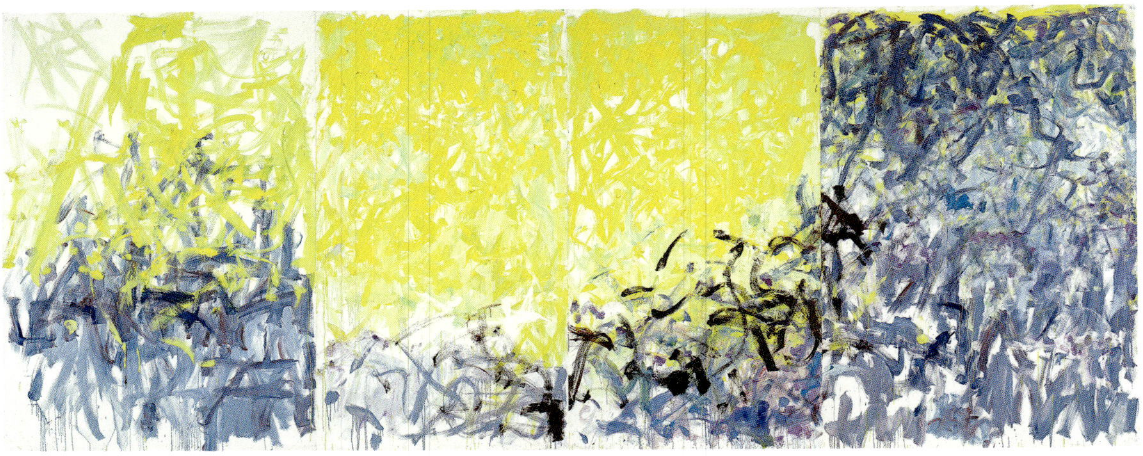

9.2

tragic image of Édith Piaf—tiny, swathed in black and starkly spotlighted on a grand stage—as Mitchell had seen her perform at Carnegie Hall.[5]

La Vie en rose was the first painting Barreau saw when she arrived in Vétheuil in late May of 1979—it seems that Mitchell had blazed through the quadriptych in just a few weeks.[6] Betsy Jolas had suggested that Barreau—who, like herself, had been a student of Olivier Messiaen at the Paris Conservatory[7]—come to help Mitchell and take care of her dogs. Mitchell had interviewed her in New York and described her in a letter to her sister, Sally Perry: "a very talented young lady composer . . . she's *frighteningly* serious but interesting."[8] Barreau had won many prizes—at the conservatory, in France, and in the United States—and was widely regarded as brilliant and intense; Mitchell responded immediately to the kind of artistic and ethical rigor she had earlier attributed to Samuel Beckett.[9] In her music, Barreau, like Mitchell, construed the lyric as color, meaning timbre and the range of effects possible with different instruments; she also welcomed experimentation, taking a diploma in electroacoustic music the same year she graduated from the conservatory.[10] Scores like *Aires pour Marion* and *Sterne* (see pages 292 and 321) are enormous and complex, with many divided parts, and use drawings to specify the spatial positions of musicians, conductor, and audience in order to create particular sonic effects. *Sterne* made an overall impression of a "very massive sound—very moving," as Mitchell noted on the program for the concert, where it was performed alongside works by Arnold Schoenberg and Gilbert Amy.[11]

The seven large quadriptychs Mitchell made between 1979 and 1982 match the immense scale of Barreau's compositions—as the composer wrote to Joyce Pensato and Carl Plansky in the fall of 1980 (the text in a spiral to form the heart of the sunflower she drew), she and Mitchell "had a bet" about their respective works, due in January, pressing each other onward.[12] By late 1980, Mitchell had been invited to have a solo exhibition at the Musée d'art moderne de la ville de Paris, a high-profile promise that also spurred her on; she would eventually show six of these enormous paintings at the museum in her summer 1982 exhibition.[13] The first large

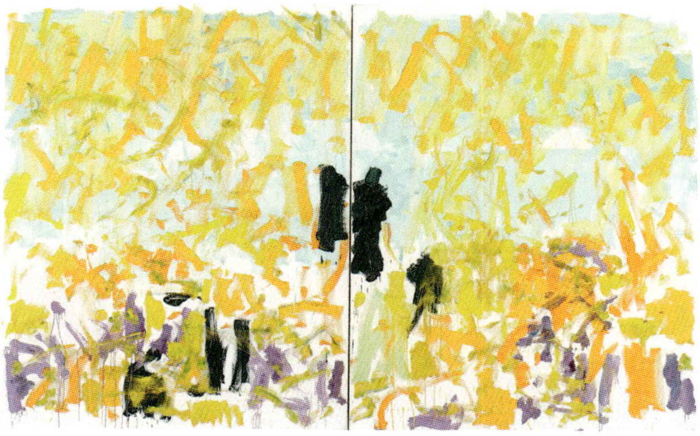

9.3

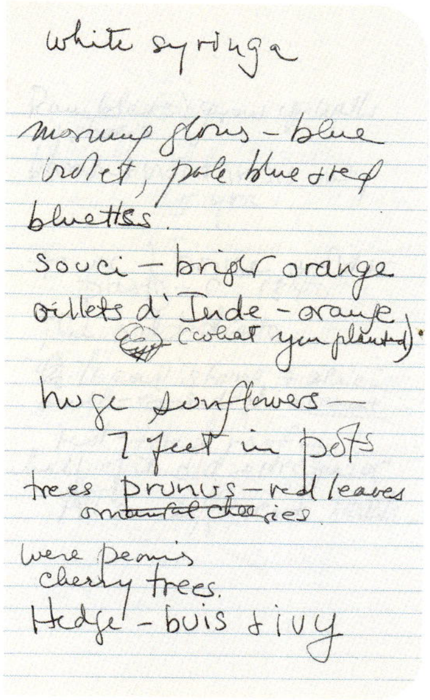

white syringa
morning glories – blue violet, pale blue & red
bluettes.
souci – bright orange
oillets d'Inde – orange (what you planted).
huge sunflowers – 7 feet in pots
trees prunus – red leaves ornamental cherries.
were peonies cherry trees.
Hedge – buis & ivy

9.4

paintings, *La Vie en rose* and *Salut Tom* (1979, plate 100), begin from the broad view of the Seine and the compositional gambits of the late 1960s, but she opened the composition with white and continued the percussive rendering of the late 1970s. Those paintings were a touchstone; as Mitchell complained, "*Part* of my problem is to make a single *pic* & I have only really succeeded with 'Barge' & the Linden trees before in years."[14] Since the mid-1960s, her single panels had all been vertical: they did not have the sweeping landscape feeling of the quadriptychs, which sometimes began as diptychs to which Mitchell added "side" panels whose more vertical, fuller compositions framed a central image.[15] In the diptychs she felt a "twoness," manifested in subtle relationships between the panels: symmetry, continuity, repetition, and difference.[16] One striking instance is *Cypress* (fig. 9.3), in which the motif of doubling takes the very deliberate form of two marks placed on either side of the diptych's divide. She had different versions of twoness; in *Two Pianos* (1980, plate 101), made in response to Barreau's composition *Piano Piano,* Mitchell did not knit together the divide through repetition or a crossing stroke—the two panels harmonize and respond to each other in counterpoint. The undergirding of deep blue resurfaces across the whole, veiled by lavender and yellow-orange. The two colors are laid on with similar short vertical strokes across the tops of both canvases, but the colors are kept separate; in the center, there is more mixing of the colors, with orange-yellow used to accent the lavender, and vice versa, but the strokes vary—dense on the left, open and broad on the right. The diptych is bound externally rather than internally, with a few late additions of long orange marks on the far edges. Each panel has its own logic, its autonomy, while working in relation to the other.

These relations became more complex and various, even as Mitchell simplified the paintings in other ways. One new vision for the larger works was a diagonal swell that crescendoed from left to right. Less familiar than the river views of *La Seine* and *Salut Tom,* this compositional approach had a source in nature: the Vétheuil garden Barreau had taken over. It was "small" in scale and also in the personal, unruly selection of plants made in defiance of Jean Perthuis's ordered landscaping, with climbing plants, daisies, and other flowers that, like

FIG 9.2 **Joan Mitchell** *A Small Garden,* 1980. Oil on canvas, 110¼ × 283½ in. (280 × 720.1 cm). Centre Pompidou, Paris

FIG 9.3 **Joan Mitchell** *Cypress,* 1980. Oil on canvas, 86¾ × 142⅛ in. (220.4 × 361 cm). Fondation Louis Vuitton, Paris

FIG 9.4 List of plants at La Tour, Vétheuil, France, as noted by Linda Nochlin, 1984. Linda Nochlin Papers, Archives of American Art, Smithsonian Institution, Washington, D.C.

wildflowers and weeds, did not register as valuable in the hierarchy of formal gardening.[17] Mitchell delighted in the irony of making this intimate place into a "mural"-scale quadriptych: "She's redoing 'her garden' & it looks beautiful. I titled my big pic for Washington 'a small garden.'"[18] The painting features the colors of flowers Barreau planted in the small garden Mitchell passed on the daily walk to her atelier—white, yellow, the blue of bleuets, the morning glories climbing the edges of the fence—to which Mitchell added black tulips (fig. 9.2).[19] The younger woman brought Mitchell into her own grounds, made her feel the gardens did, in fact, belong to her (see page 313), and while Mitchell never worked in the garden to the extent that Barreau did, the artist discovered a litany of specific flowers that she loved: begonias, asters, peonies, roses (fig. 9.4).[20] Mitchell learned to attend to the color and feel of types of plants, even the life cycles of individual flowers—a drooping aster, the symbolic rebirth of the amaryllis every year (plate 111). Barreau and Mitchell planted a pumpkin, a plant with a fast life cycle, right outside Mitchell's studio door so she could see and measure the daily change.

It was only fitting that when Fried died unexpectedly in November of 1981, Mitchell conjured her continued presence in a painting (plate 102) and, with Barreau, in a dedicated garden (see page 312). "She's certainly alive," Mitchell wrote to her sister.[21] During Mitchell's absence the following spring, Barreau wrote, "Edrita's garden will be very pretty in one month—Her peonies are working okay—We had a cup of iced tea together—nice time, *près de la petite table de méditation*—I would have preferred a Coca-Cola, but so."[22] Mitchell was visiting Perry in Santa Barbara after many years; her sister's diagnosis of advanced cancer shadowed her all through 1982, even as she was comforted by daily pleasures—a conundrum emphasized in the titles of works, from *A Small Garden* to the *Petits matins* (both 1982, plates 108 and 109). Mitchell painted these exquisite small canvases, among the most sheerly beautiful of her career, as she struggled with Perry's impending death, traveling back and forth to Santa Barbara in fact and in letters, calls, and her thoughts, while also working through the complications around her exhibition at the Musée d'art moderne de la ville de Paris. As she wrote to Plansky and Pensato while installing in the summer of 1982, "Hope you'll like my late 'terminal pics'—I didn't title them that [but] rather 'Petit matin' which is when the dawn rises. Guess the show has to do with *my life*."[23]

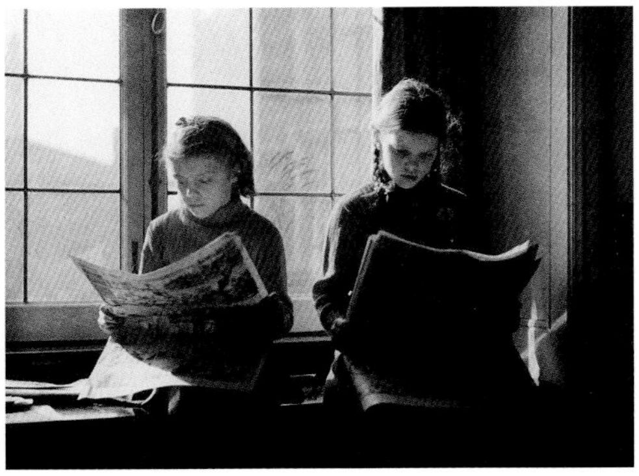
9.5

She was reflecting back on the entirety of her life with her sister as a vast landscape of familial romance—"moitié cachée, moitié pardonée"—and also in great detail: "I can resurrect 190 E. Chestnut in its entirety (recall)—the furniture etc. etc.—& all the walks to the playground . . . Barbara McClurgh's BD parties & chicken à la king—looking over lake . . . it's (recall) nice to have in my—imaginary—valise because I can go back to 190 or wherever when I want to" (fig. 9.5).[24] The barrage of letters exchanged by the sisters shifts seamlessly between past and present, the latter mostly in the form of highly detailed tales of dogs, particularly Perry's Malinois, to whom Joan reported she was dedicating a painting, *Pour ses Malinois* (1981).[25] Perry died in the summer of 1982, and among the first works Mitchell painted after her death was a series of nine paintings whose titles, taken from the tune "Row, Row, Row Your Boat," recall childhood, the metaphor of "going down the stream," and also life as a *round,* starting over and over (plates 104–7). At almost the same moment, Mitchell's exhibition opened at the Musée d'art moderne de la ville de Paris with paintings from her last twelve years, a third of which had never before been shown, including two for her sister. If most reviewers fell back on invoking Monet and Abstract Expressionism, longtime interlocutor Pierre Schneider raised the stakes, asking whether Mitchell was "la dernière héritière de la grande tradition?"[26]

Even if the tradition was "grande," it was the *petit* that inspired: "Moments of euphoria—epiphany—a poem—a flower—a pic—are so acute."[27] And these moments also comforted. As Barreau typically exhorted Mitchell as the composer was departing for one of her many absences for fellowships, concerts, and teaching, "les reine-marguerites vont être superbes, plus toutes les tulipes a venir, plus narcisses—Go inside and have a look at my primevères—2 sont fleuries—très discrètes—Full of everything—Pick some walnuts—You are not alone."[28] What Fried had called "the artist's penchant for identifications," a kind of "pantheism" directed at natural objects, meant something very different from losing oneself in the vastness of water or field: it meant caring deeply for something as small as a flower, which gives back to the caregiver.[29] Together with Barreau, Pensato, Plansky, and other friends, Mitchell staged photo sessions in the gardens, treating each sunflower and squash as a model. In a passionate letter to Pensato—somewhat lost herself at the time—Mitchell urged her to put aside the mirror and turn to something "outside yourself."[30] She was warning against not only the self-regarding gaze of the young artist, but also the current revival of German Expressionist painting, contrasting its harsh black-and-white palette and self-aggrandizement with the colors and external gaze of French painting.[31] As an antidote to harsh grandiosity, Mitchell exhorted friends to read Hugo von Hofmannsthal: "He does that spiritual thing with things."[32] She was also reading and rereading Rainer Maria Rilke for his sympathetic view of objects, which transcended the separate entities of nature and self to touch the eternal.[33] As he wrote, "External world and vision everywhere coincided as it were in the object; in each a whole inner world was displayed, as though an angel who embraces space were blind and gazing into himself."[34]

FIG 9.5 Joan and Sally Mitchell reading comics, ca. 1931. Courtesy Sally Perry

These years saw Mitchell more open to the spiritual than at any other point in her life. As Barreau saw it, seventeenth-century metaphysicians understood a human's inner workings long before Sigmund Freud, and her own lyricism had a mystical vein. The libretto for Barreau's *Aires pour Marion,* a volcanic composition for chorus and percussion, borrows from the mystical poem *Vents* ("Winds") by Saint-John Perse, sung and whispered by the voices. Mitchell was also spending time with Philippe le Thomas, a young doctor in the process of becoming a monk. Recalling a late-night studio visit spent viewing *Chez ma soeur* (1981–82), a quadriptych dedicated to Perry, the newly ordained Frère Luc wrote:

> And then the wondrous, transcendent moment, mesmerized by reality and the divine emanating from your studio, transported, thrilled by the intensity of the emotion, eyes flowering with color, the gold and the pink veil, and the frisson and the dance, the duet from the Bach cantata. . . . And you spoke of your sister and I spoke of death, God, life, love and . . . ecstasy.[35]

He was referring to the duet in Bach's *Cantata no. 78,* an expression of gratitude for the liberation from sin brought by Christ's self-sacrifice, which had spurred their intense discussions.[36] Mitchell had lost her sister;

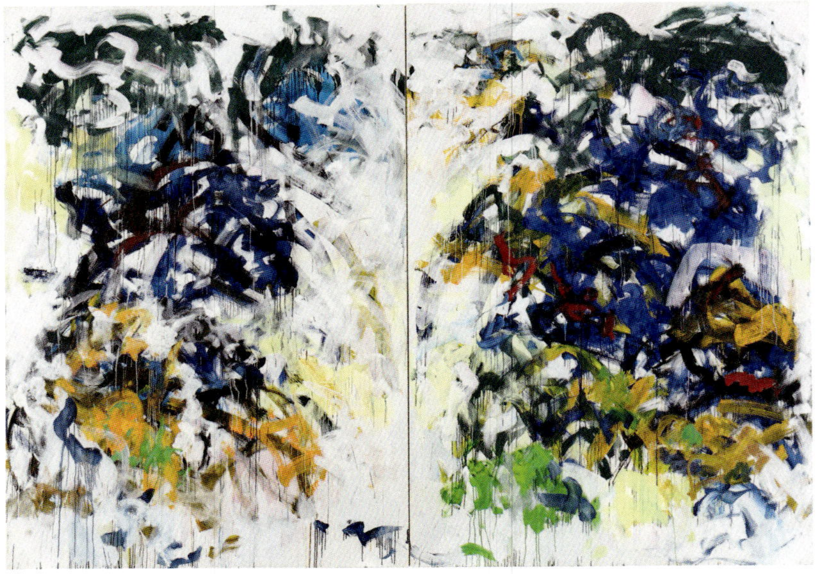

9.6

FIG 9.6 **Joan Mitchell**
Beauvais, 1986. Oil on canvas, 110⅛ × 157⅝ in. (279.7 × 400.4 cm). Fondation Louis Vuitton, Paris

1983 was also the year she began the cycle of *La Grande Vallée* paintings (as discussed by David Max Horowitz on pages 300–301). Inspired by the longing of a young cousin of Barreau's to revisit, before his death, the valley that had been their secret place, the cycle (see plates 111, 112, 113) brings together the light-hearted paradise Barreau and Mitchell imagined for Edrita Fried (wined and dined, tended to by two adoring young men) and a powerful vision of eternal life.[37] Several of the twenty-one paintings of the cycle were dedicated to friends—Plansky, Frère Luc, Iva (Mitchell's German shepherd)—human and animal.

In the summer of 1984, Mitchell was diagnosed with jaw cancer and underwent radiation, like her sister and mother before her; the following year she required hip surgery. The titles of the suites she made in the following years note the recurrence of illness and weakness, both in her own life and in more distant memory: *Before, Again IV* (1985, plate 114) and *Between, Then, Last Time*.[38] *Faded Air I* (1985, plate 116) takes a dying sunflower as its subject, lightly, fluidly painted across two panels, combining the single vertical subject with the diagonal composition of *A Small Garden* and *Edrita Fried* (1981, plate 102) to create the sensation of droop and drop, a gentle succumbing to gravity.[39] Her strokes become longer, curving, calligraphic, a habit of hand that would continue throughout the mid-1980s. The year 1985 was difficult; between the February declaration that she was cancer-free and hip surgery in December, she painted very little, although beautifully. Her mood of reflection, including invocations of Marcel Proust and Rilke (themselves touchstones from earlier moments), was colored by a vivid awareness of the cycle of life and the certainty of endings.[40] Mitchell was listening to Richard Strauss's *Four Last Songs,* whose texts by Hermann Hesse and Joseph von Eichendorff, underlined by a musical quotation from Strauss's early "Death and Transfiguration," evoke intense experience of nature and gardens in an accepting awareness of death: "We are resting from our travels/ now, in the quiet countryside."[41]

In 1986 and 1987, Mitchell returned from her illnesses to paint three significant suites, titled *River, Lille,* and *Chord,* amidst ongoing sadness. Iva, "the mother" and her most beloved dog, died in September 1986 after a long, full life. Much more difficult was the knowledge that Xavier Fourcade had AIDS; she may have known in 1985, when she titled a tall, narrow work *Xavier,* and she certainly knew by the spring of 1986, when she visited New York. As Mitchell described her time in the city, AIDS was "a shadow in the garden"; she was relieved to return to Vétheuil, where "I do cling to the garden to somehow chase away all those horror images I experienced in N.Y."[42] She sought escape, quoting Frank O'Hara's *Ode to Joy*: "And there shall be no more dying in the supper clubs."[43] Though the cycle of *River* paintings returns to a favorite subject, we no longer survey the Seine from a familiar viewpoint, but dive into the rushing waters, evoked by rippling strokes and turpentine-thinned drips that flow across the canvas to create a new kind of space (plate 117). During this grim time, it is easy to imagine that Mitchell was alluding to the sensation of drowning; one painting from this period was titled *Ready for the River,* and she had long used the fight to keep one's head above water as a metaphor for emotional and physical threat.[44] That fall she spent time with Fourcade in Paris, where he sought treatment; in December they traveled to Lille to see the Henri Matisse exhibition from the Hermitage Museum, which inspired her *Lille* works. On the way, they stopped to visit the Cathedral of Saint-Pierre in Beauvais, commemorated in the soaring *Beauvais* (fig. 9.6).[45] These paintings, and the *Chord* suite that followed, are jewel-toned and white lit, moving between density and openness with ease, evidencing intensity but not struggle. Fourcade died in April 1987.

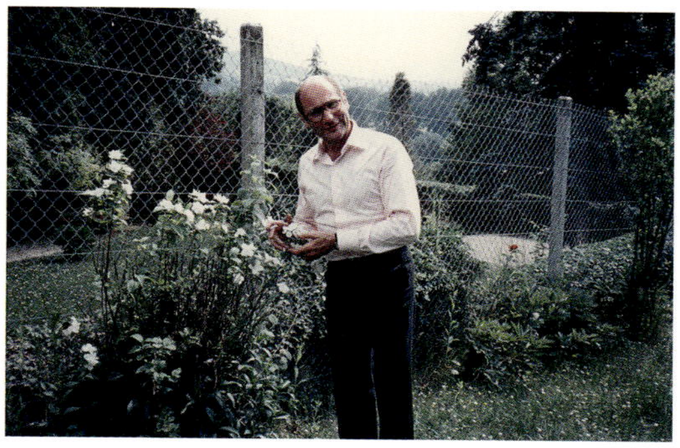

9.7

FIG 9.7 Xavier Fourcade in the garden at La Tour, Vétheuil, France, ca. 1986. Joan Mitchell Foundation Archives, New York

As always, painting gave Mitchell more than a place to put her feelings. Barreau describes her composition *Piano, Piano* as embodying the idea of "un monde dans lequel le temps est annulé";[46] Mitchell had always seen painting's special capacity to elude time, and this quality grew more important to her in the face of so much mortality, her own included. Speaking with Yves Michaud, she told him that in her head she was snapping his picture, a still image that would keep him eternally alive. That she would "frame" him, as she framed her paintings, at first by limning their edges with brushstrokes, and then, later, using side panels to bracket one or two canvases.[47] Mitchell put all of this into a late-night note, wisecracking and serious, left for Linda Nochlin to read in the morning at Vétheuil: "I want to see the 'altar' piece—honey I ain't religious—but Catholics think I am—a good pic—held—(not Al Held)—Silent—beautiful—ie—nothing to do with life—death—time—only it's [*sic*] edges—frames—still—ie quiet, not Clifford [*sic*]—lousy painter—existing always—all great pics do this."[48]

La Grande Vallée XVI, pour Iva, 1983

David Max Horowitz

La Grande Vallée XVI, pour Iva is illustrated as plate 112.

FIG 9.8 Left to right: *La Grande Vallée XIV (For a Little While)* (1983) and *La Grande Vallée XVI, pour Iva* (1983) in Galerie Jean Fournier's presentation at Foire Internationale d'art contemporain (FIAC), Paris, 1984. Galerie Jean Fournier, Paris

FIG 9.9 Joan Mitchell and Iva at La Tour, Vétheuil, France, 1973. Joan Mitchell Foundation Archives, New York

In July of 1982, Mitchell's sister, Sally Perry, died of cancer. Mired in the emotional fallout of the loss, Mitchell found herself at an artistic impasse, unsure of what to paint.[1] She was not alone in her mourning, however. One of her close friends, the composer Gisèle Barreau, had lost her cousin Jean-Philippe Halgand just days before Perry's death. Ultimately, Barreau played a crucial role in Mitchell's return to painting, most centrally by offering a recollection that resonated deeply with the artist. As a child growing up near Nantes, France, Barreau would visit a secluded, bucolic valley called "la grande vallée." Halgand, who was six years Barreau's junior, was the only person she would bring with her to this refuge.[2] During his decline, Halgand expressed to Barreau his wish to return to the pastoral setting of their youth, saying—according to Mitchell's recounting—"If we could only return to the Grande Vallée once again."[3] This tale, with its conjuring of an innocent, idyllic past and its poignant charge of irrevocable loss, offered Mitchell a way to reapproach painting while contending with her sister's death.

Alongside the emotional and narrative weight provided by this backstory, Mitchell introduced new layers of significance late in her work on the twenty-one *La Grande Vallée* paintings. She appended five titles with the names of individuals important to her: painter Carl Plansky, monk Frère Luc (né Philippe le Thomas), philosopher and art critic Yves Michaud, gallerist Jean Fournier, and Iva, Mitchell's beloved German shepherd.[4] Conspicuously, these figures do not rest easily within the suite's basic framing. Each was still alive, and none played a direct part in either Perry's life or the Grande Vallée story. These semantic frictions are especially notable given the degree to which the paintings in the group otherwise cohere, especially on a visual register (fig. 9.8).

This is not to say that those named were irrelevant as Mitchell grappled with Perry's death. In the case of *La Grande Vallée XVI, pour Iva* (plate 112), the painting's canine namesake was surely a buttressing emotional presence during this period.[5] She was also a consistent companion—along with her two adult pups—as Mitchell painted, an activity the artist found cathartic.[6] Moreover, there was some link between Perry and Iva; Perry was a professional dog breeder and trainer who had advised Mitchell on her many dogs.[7] Nonetheless, it is difficult to insert Iva into the fictive world that the suite seems to construct, named individuals notwithstanding. Her presence works against the primary readings of the paintings as tributes to Perry and Halgand or as envisioning an otherworldly paradise for the dead.[8]

This narrative split fits with Mitchell's broad feelings about her work's content. She professed being as disinterested in chronicling events as she was in representing subjects mimetically. As Mitchell put it, "My painting is not an allegory or a story. It is more like a poem."[9] In this case, though, the move away from diegetic coherence is not just a point of ideological consistency; it holds specific thematic resonance with the *Grande Vallée* paintings. During their shared mourning, Mitchell and Barreau went to the 1983 Manet exhibition at the Galeries nationales du Grand Palais.[10] Mitchell recounted the experience, in this "terrible" moment, saying, "Seeing all these paintings ... with all that silence and no time involved, no terminations was wonderful. There was no sadness, no death. It was still."[11] This description relates a negation of temporality with the evasion of a morbid focus on mortality. Similarly, Mitchell used titles to disrupt the unity and continuity of the story that initially accrued around the *Grande Vallée* suite. In doing so, she avoided constructing a trajectory with an inevitable end. She instead turned the viewer's attention to disparate moments containing separate subjects, some centered on life's joys and intimacies—in the case of *La Grande Vallée XVI, pour Iva,* those of the canine variety.[12]

The suspension of time does not only occur in the splintered focus offered by the painting's title. It also takes place on the work's surface. Mitchell claimed of her approach, "I'm trying to stop time, or frame it."[13] While gestural abstraction, by its nature, conveys duration and progression by foregrounding the process of creation, Mitchell had long challenged the standard temporality of this style, both in how she carefully built her compositions part by part and in her predilection for reintroducing colors at various stages in a work's completion. Related strategies appear with notable density in *La Grande Vallée XVI, pour Iva*. Multiple campaigns of deep blue confuse when certain strokes were applied relative to the introduction of other colors. This is most pronounced in the upper reaches of the acerbic greens and yellows. These strokes lie on top of passages of crepuscular blue, which itself seems to be of a piece with the two-toned dusky expanse that covers much of the canvas's top half. However, drips of that same underlying blue extend down from those upper reaches, passing over the mingled yellows and greens. That mixture of bright, terrestrial hues raises its own questions, its inconsistent blending obscuring whether the paints came together on the canvas or were mixed imperfectly on the artist's palette. Perhaps most curiously, two lengths of yellow apparently squeezed from the tube are thin at both ends, a quality freeing them of directionality.[14]

The way *La Grande Vallée XVI, pour Iva* suspends and confounds time, through both its divergent subjects and its intermittently inscrutable facture, puts the painting outside the flow of time that Mitchell associated with mortality. It also prevents the work from being reducible to an elegy. Instead, it is what Michaud, in his essay on the suite, characterized as "a network of sensations and effects, of attachments."[15] The painting, like many poems, is a cluster of associations, centered on Perry's passing, while remaining open to a web of other possibilities, including those associated with the experience of life rather than the remembrance of death.

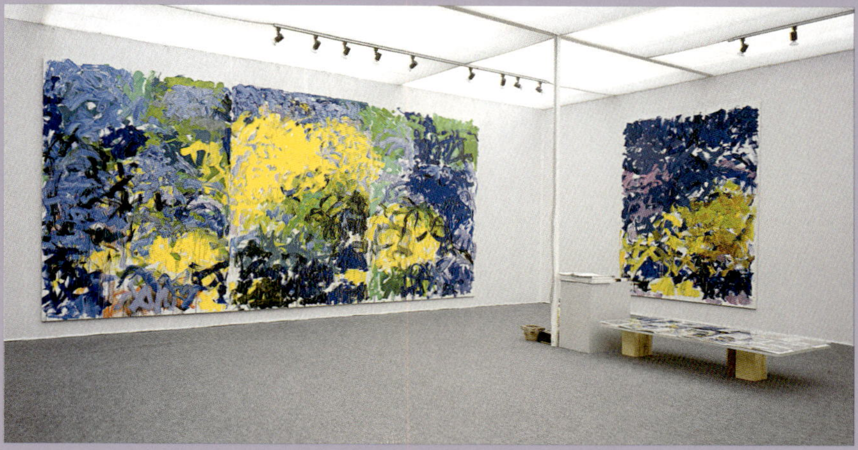

9.8

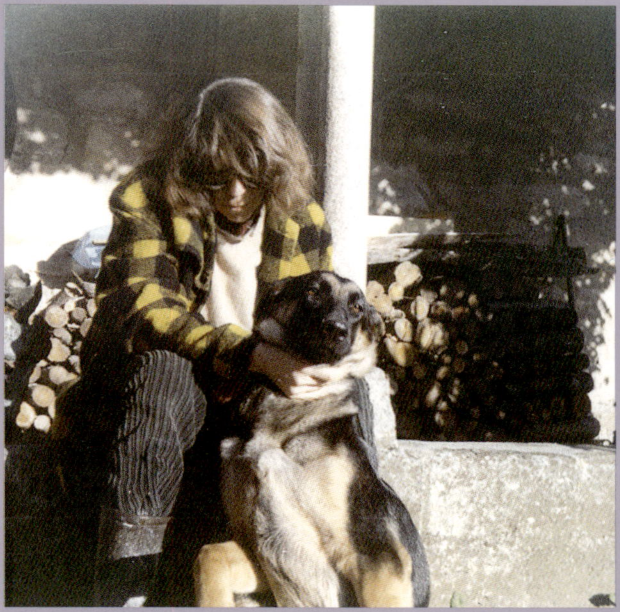

9.9

10
Painting Sarah Roberts

This is the ultimate hour
When life is justified.
The seas of experience

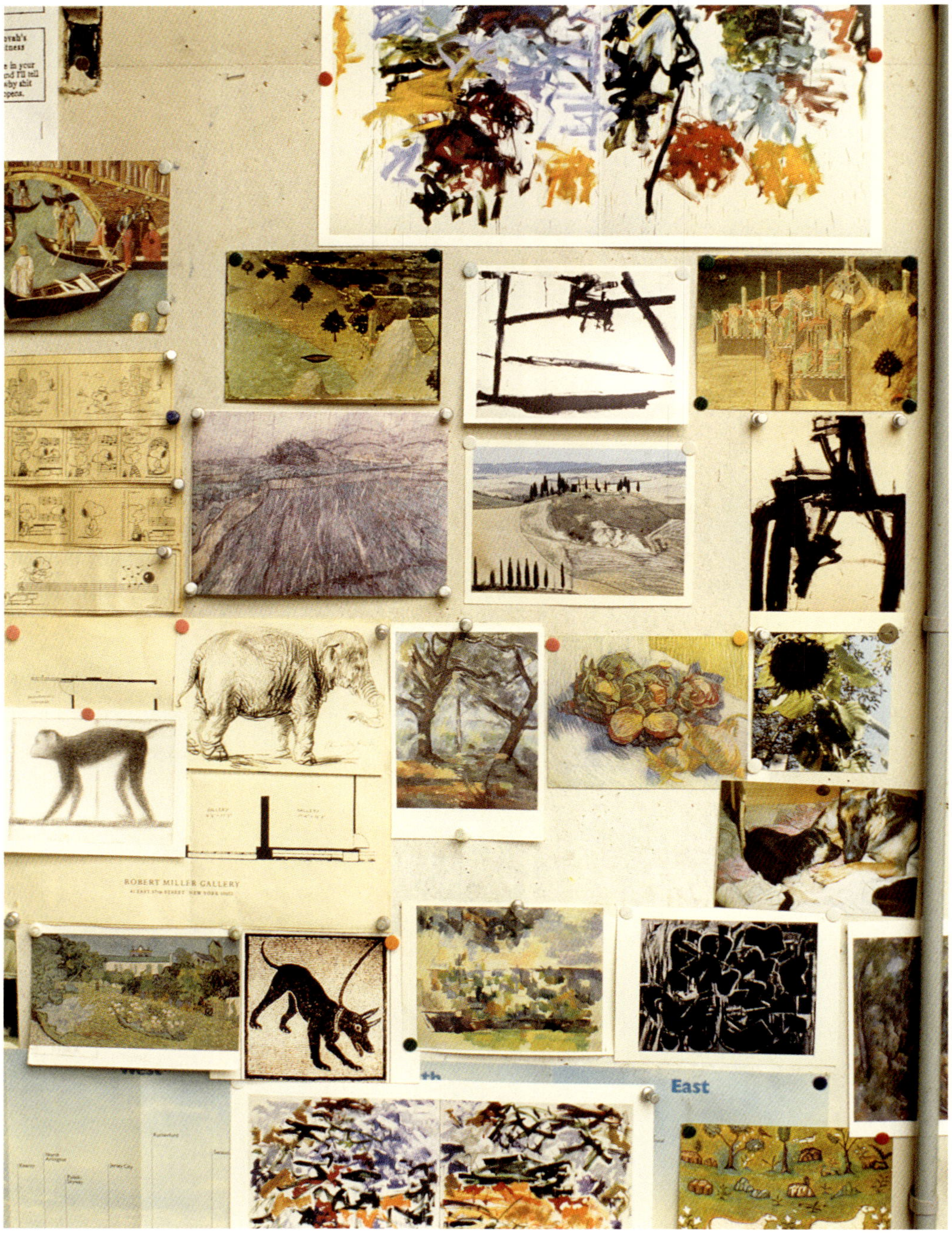

That were so broad and deep,
So immediate and steep,
Are suddenly still. —T. S. ELIOT, "SILENCE"

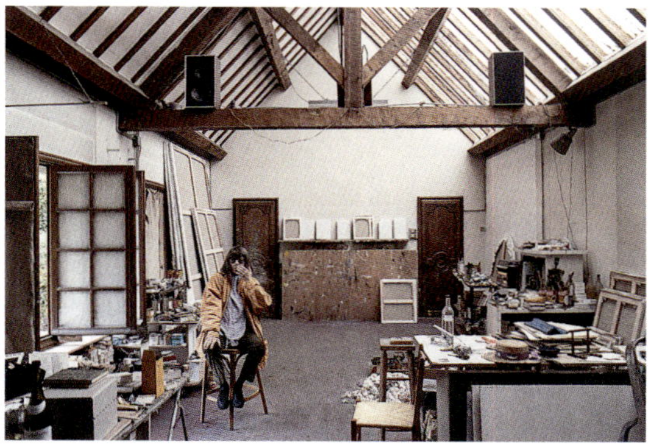

10.1

"I feel time is very short, and I have done nothing."[1] Increasingly attuned to her own mortality after a half century of dedication to her art, Mitchell reached for painting with ferocity in her last years. She countered illness, pain, depression, and fear that time was running out with a grinding determination to mount the hill to her studio and paint. The final years of her work evidence an artist looking back across history, her own and that of other painters she revered, not to reminisce or recycle, but to ignite. The paintings made near the end of her life roar with the intensity of an artist determined to push herself and her medium and committed to remaining fiercely in the present, every day to her last.

On the cusp of her 1988–89 retrospective organized by the Herbert F. Johnson Museum of Art, Mitchell painted *No Birds* (1987–88, plate 118), a work that foretold where she would direct her attention and energies in the last years of her life. *No Birds* takes up a frank dialogue with Vincent van Gogh's *Wheatfield with Crows* (fig. 10.2), which she had seen recently in an exhibition at the Metropolitan Museum of Art, New York.[2] Mitchell had spoken from the start of her career about her absorption with van Gogh's paintings, and she created work in the mid-1970s that adapted the immediacy of his mark making to her own ends (as discussed in chapter 8). The one-to-one engagement of *No Birds* with *Wheatfield with Crows,* however, represents an extraordinarily direct visual response to van Gogh—an act of homage, to be sure, but also a challenge to herself. In taking on van Gogh so openly, she risked being criticized for betraying pure abstraction and rehashing his ideas, and worse, she risked falling short. With *No Birds* Mitchell offered her work as equal to van Gogh's.

Mitchell's painting demonstrates what drew her attention. Her V-shaped composition echoes van Gogh's and is similarly built on an overall rhythm of brushstrokes that angle up from left to right. She forgoes his deep blue sky in favor of densely placed horizontal marks of viridian, so dark they are nearly black. These strokes slash across the top two-thirds of the canvas, compressing the space, much as the sharp black cuts of the birds spanning the field and sky flatten van Gogh's landscape. Whereas he left glimpses of a blue underlayer

FRONTISPIECE
Postcards and illustrations pinned to Joan Mitchell's studio wall at La Tour, Vétheuil, France, 1989

FIG 10.1 Joan Mitchell in her studio at La Tour, Vétheuil, France, 1991 between, and streaks of pale blue and white within some primary strokes to activate the autumnal mix of golden yellow, ocher, and sienna, she swept in lavender pink, positioned and proportioned with a sureness acquired over decades of such exacting calibrations of color. With its distinct upper and lower registers (sky/land) and detailed treatment of the lower corners (foreground), Mitchell's painting is also one of her most clearly readable as landscape. In that, it represented another risk ventured. She had taken pains at times throughout her life to separate her work from any idea of representation of the external, natural world—she painted the feeling of a landscape, not the landscape itself. She also denied any symbolic or psychological significance within her work. To acknowledge direct exterior referents or metaphorical meaning would have exposed her to being seen as retrograde. Such defenses now seemed superfluous. As she admitted to an audience at the New York Studio School in 1988, "But alright so I paint a sunflower, whether that's isolation, or death, or vanity, or whatever."[3] In brief flashes such as this, Mitchell increasingly acknowledged representational content in her paintings that went beyond generalized feeling or memory.

Although her primary response to van Gogh was visual (as ever), Mitchell also related to the depth of his psychological and emotional connection to the natural world: "I can't quote van Gogh but it's in . . . one of his so many beautiful letters, where he says he gives gratitude to the sunflower because it exists. And I give gratitude to trees because they exist and that's all my painting is about."[4] Notably Mitchell knew well and admired Antonin Artaud's 1947 essay "Van Gogh: The Man Suicided by Society,"[5] a text that was widely read and referenced by many artists in the late 1940s and early 1950s, but was particularly significant for Jean Paul Riopelle, who regularly spent time with Artaud at the moment of its writing.[6] The essay dwells on *Wheatfield with Crows* as a crystallization of Artaud's belief in van Gogh as a singular mind persecuted by a society that could not accommodate his individual vision. Artaud (taking up the theory that it was van Gogh's last painting) sees *Wheatfield with Crows* as a culmination of van Gogh's ability to imbue nature with unprecedented passion, a painting redolent with his imminent death at the hands of an evil society that failed to recognize or even countenance his genius. This is not to say that Mitchell saw herself as persecuted as Artaud did van Gogh; rather, Artaud's emphases on van Gogh's irretrievable isolation and on the piercing presence of death in *Wheatfield with Crows* perhaps struck her deeply at this moment, as her lifelong fear of death[7] collided with realities that confronted her with its actual approach. She painted his wheat field, but also his themes of death and isolation.

Mitchell's 1988–89 retrospective—the exercise of looking back over her life's work and having it exposed to judgment—caused her deep anxiety, as such shows do for many artists. She entered a period of depression. "Ça sent le sapin," she grumbled to friends—it smelled like death.[8] Faced with this survey of her achievement and this heightened awareness of mortality, Mitchell all but stopped painting. Current documentation suggests that she completed just ten paintings in 1988, many of them modest in size and ambition.[9] Though some of the slowdown was surely due to the practical considerations of preparations and travel for her retrospective, she acknowledged, "For a time I didn't work and then I did a lot of pastels which in a way freed me. Some of them inspired me to do a different, I don't know if it is called subject matter or whatever you call it to paint pictures."[10] As she had in 1974 following her Whitney Museum of American Art exhibition, she found her way back to the studio through the seductive immediacy and color of drawing with pastel and crayon.[11]

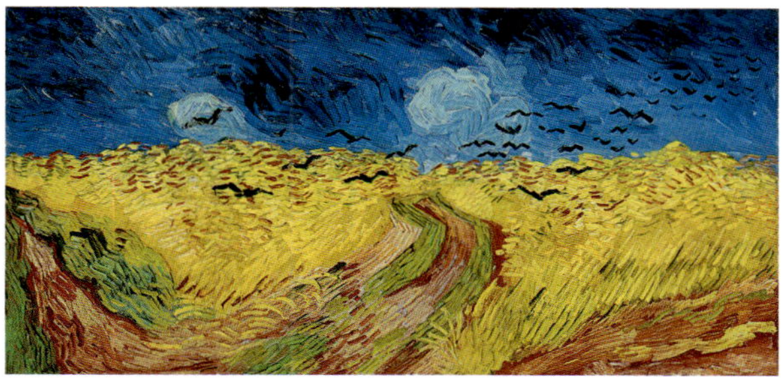

10.2

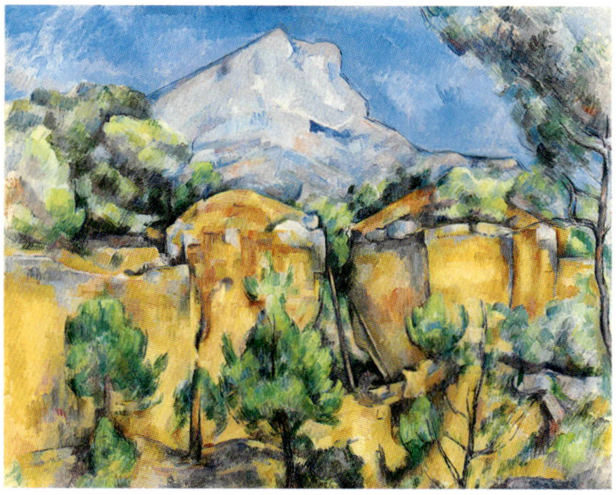

10.3

The medium held such importance for her that, with Jean Fournier's assistance, she rented a separate small studio on rue Campagne-Première in Montparnasse and kept it secret from all but a few close friends so she could draw in complete privacy.

The drawings from this era evidence her deft manipulation of the edges and flat surfaces of her pastel stick and precision control of her line. Mitchell reveled in the flexibility and textures of the medium, playing with the nap of the paper and the pressure of her hand to summon complexities, from the barest of skimmings to luxuriant velvet torrents and sprightly dancing dashes. The bold, saturated colors of her pastel box found their way into the paintings, which blaze with concentrated hues and incorporate a far greater range and number of colors than she used in any earlier period in her work. Her mark making also informed her brushwork. Paintings like *Bracket* and *River* (both 1989, plates 119 and 120) pick up the tangled, rhythmic brushstrokes of the 1986–87 *River, Chord,* and *Lille* suites but deploy them more loosely, leaving more air between marks as she often left white paper between pastel strokes. She also experimented with many more brush sizes and a wider range of paint densities than in paintings made earlier in the decade. *South* (1989, plate 122), for example, plays with translucent washes, broad and medium-width opaque strokes, and final flourishes of fine red lines, a motif that appears throughout the paintings and drawings of 1989–91. These signal red strokes appeared in her work as early as the 1950s and became a signature by the 1970s (as discussed by Richard Shiff on pages 284–85);[12] here they are reconceived, freshly informed by drawing.

Just as *No Birds* openly spoke to van Gogh's *Wheatfield with Crows, South* engaged with Paul Cézanne's paintings of Mont Sainte-Victoire (fig. 10.3), as again Mitchell acknowledged in her work an artist whose paintings she had long studied and esteemed. Unlike the construction of *No Birds,* in which the side-by-side canvases allow a single composition to stretch wide, the two panels in *South* double the rising form of the mountain, offering two glimpses of it within the conjoined span. Why two mountains? It is a peculiar choice, and these two

FIG 10.2 **Vincent van Gogh** *Wheatfield with Crows,* 1890. Oil on canvas, 19⅞ × 40½ in. (50.5 × 102.9 cm). Van Gogh Museum, Amsterdam (Vincent van Gogh Foundation)

FIG 10.3 **Paul Cézanne** *Mont Sainte-Victoire Seen from the Bibémus Quarry,* ca. 1897. Oil on canvas, 25⅝ × 32 in. (65.1 × 81.3 cm). Baltimore Museum of Art, The Cone Collection, formed by Dr. Claribel Cone and Miss Etta Cone of Baltimore, Maryland

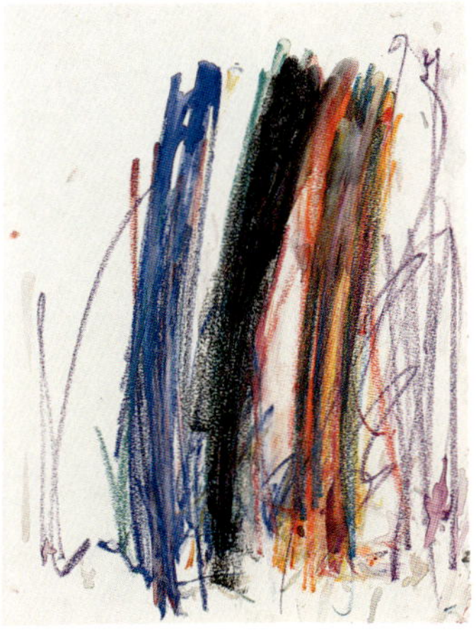

10.4

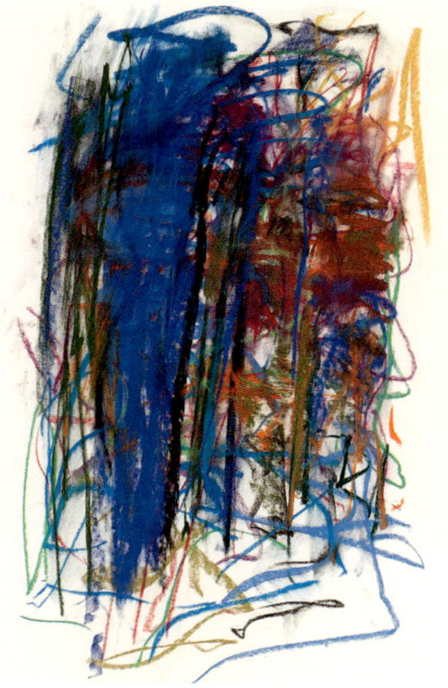

10.5

FIG 10.4 **Joan Mitchell**
Untitled, 1989. Water-soluble wax crayon and wash on paper, 15¾ × 11⅞ in. (40 × 30.2 cm). Joan Mitchell Foundation, New York

FIG 10.5 **Joan Mitchell**
Untitled, 1991. Pastel on paper, 47¾ × 31⁹⁄₁₆ in. (121.3 × 80.2 cm). Whitney Museum of American Art, New York, gift of Robert Miller, John Cheim, and Jean Fournier

panels operate more separately than those in any of Mitchell's previous multipanel works. Speaking about her predilection for diptychs, she stated that she liked the vertical interruptions between canvases as a countermeasure to the reading of the horizontal plane as a landscape.[13] In most of her multipanel paintings, the vertical line acts as a beat dropped into the visual flow to complicate the act of viewing and force us into a sequential form of looking—first at the whole, then at each unit, and then at the dialogues among the units. The panels of *South* dwell on the latter, the visual interchange between the two. This doubling echoes Mitchell's multivalent takes on a particular view or memory (as discussed in chapter 5). But the pairing in *South* more specifically reflects Mitchell's own internal dialogue about painting. The two canvases wear their own process of being made as reflections of each other, as Mitchell alternated painting on one and then on the other, working through different ideas and solutions on each. Nearly bilaterally symmetrical in composition, the two sides fold out from the centerline like pages of a book. She weighted the left panel with warm colors on the left, cool on the right, but reversed this order on the other panel. Mitchell told Philippe Dagen in 1992, "You can't enter a Cézanne because it pushes you back. The eye is pushed back to the surface right away. That is why I love it."[14] As if speaking directly to this point, she pushed cadmium yellow into cerulean blue of equal saturation on *South*'s left panel to create a compressed tension across the surface; alizarin crimson and viridian green do the same work on the right panel, keeping the eye at the surface right away. Back and forth, Mitchell worked through painting problems, using different solutions on each. The individual canvases could stand alone.[15] But in the end, she briskly stitched them together with two red lines across the center seam, one of her last touches on the surface, pronouncing the two to be one. The complexity of the relationship between *South*'s two panels underscores the centrality of "twoness" to Mitchell's way of working, visible in everything from the one-to-one mirroring that appears starting in the 1950s single canvases to the compound dialogues among multipanel works from the mid-1960s forward. Exchange and reflection among elements inform almost every painting she composed.

The tree paintings of 1990–91, such as *Trees* (plate 128) and *Taillade* (fig. 10.6), emerged from a group of 1989 drawings that concentrated on bundles of vigorously stroked vertical lines. The subject, extreme verticality of the composition, and force of Mitchell's line connect these drawings to her 1977 *Tilleul* pastels, but the voluminous mass of the latter is here replaced by individual bands sensitively placed in duets and trios. Slightly arched and narrower at the bottom, these stalklike forms often appear capped or stubbed at the top, either by brief perpendicular lines or by the blunt thickness of the vertical lines themselves, which generally start at the top of the sheet and diminish as they descend. In a 1989 untitled drawing (fig. 10.4), Mitchell further emphasized this stubbing by brushing the top of the forms with either water or crayon medium dissolved in water. Mitchell was fascinated and somewhat horrified by the French horticultural practice of pollarding—a drastic pruning of trees, sometimes down to the trunk, common in Normandy and Bretagne, which she saw as unnecessarily brutal.[16] The title *Taillade* refers directly to this practice (*taillade* means "gash"; *tailler,* "to prune"). These drawings and the related paintings (figs. 10.5 and 10.6) amplify the harshness and vulnerability of the lopped forms, which sit starkly on the sheet or canvas, like van Gogh's powerfully poignant cypress trees silhouetted against the sky or his own paintings and drawings of pollarded trees (see page 290, fig. 3, and fig. 10.7).[17] Mitchell identified these slashed trees with her physical deterioration, loss of agility, and waning strength,[18] and she continued to draw and paint her own stalk forms to the end her life.

Looking to her history, loosening up and conjuring fresh painting techniques through drawing, and allowing herself to inhabit and make her own what she had long admired in the work of van Gogh and Cézanne: it was a potent mix and one that propelled her to unleash the formidable and majestic paintings of her final years, even as she declined physically and became more isolated psychologically. By 1990, Mitchell had been diagnosed with esophageal cancer, adding certainty that time was short and compounding her ongoing pain, difficulty walking, and the ill effects from treatment for jaw cancer several years earlier. The losses of centering figures in her life—first her sister, then Edrita Fried and Xavier Fourcade, and then the last two of her beloved German shepherds—had inflamed her lifelong fear of abandonment as well as her anxiety about death. With Gisèle Barreau no longer living full time at La Tour, Mitchell had no one in her daily life who was her equal. She isolated herself further by alienating friends, and avoided future goodbyes by abruptly cutting people out and causing even Zuka and Barney Rosset to finally break with her. She did continue to go to Paris, generally twice weekly, to see her analyst, have lunch with Jean Fournier, and see what he had on view at the gallery. By giving her a place to rest and even spend the night, the rue Campagne-Première studio aided her in maintaining this routine and her Paris connections. She carried on having younger artists live with her, relying on them for companionship, for assistance in the studio and around the house, and to preserve some sense of life at La Tour. She also maintained a closeness to a small number of young painters and drew satisfaction from mentoring them in their work. Yet she was increasingly volatile, erratic, and unable to summon her gentler side. Any shred of energy that might be put toward social graces was channeled instead into the studio, and what she needed from looking at paintings, she now drew entirely from her own.

As her good days became fewer, she made some small adjustments to her materials and routines. When Klaus Kertess invited her in 1991 to show her pastels at the Whitney, she chose to make the new drawings back

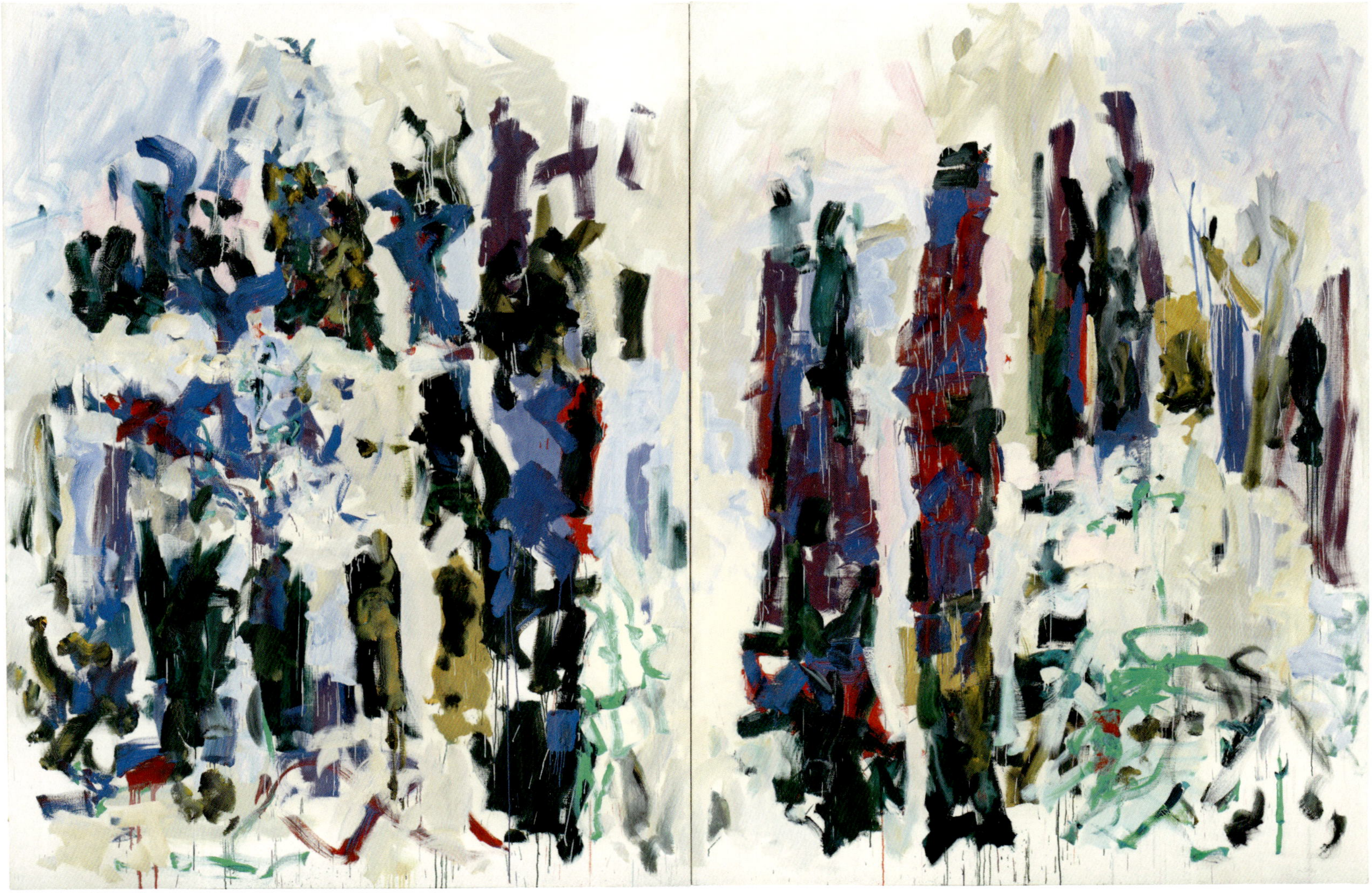

10.6

in Vétheuil, so she could work every day that she had the strength and so that people visiting and living with her could assist with pinning the large, forty-eight-inch sheets of paper to the wall. Adam, the firm she increasingly relied on for stretched canvases as Lefèbvre-Foinet reduced its operations, began constructing them from lighter-weight wood so she could move panels around more easily.[19] But painting was painting. Necessary. "I just got up on that fucking ladder and told myself, 'This stroke has to work.'"[20] The vehement ambition embodied in the paintings made in the last year of Mitchell's life attests to the fact that her most crucial tools were her drive to paint and the accuracy of her mark: making each stroke and every color count.

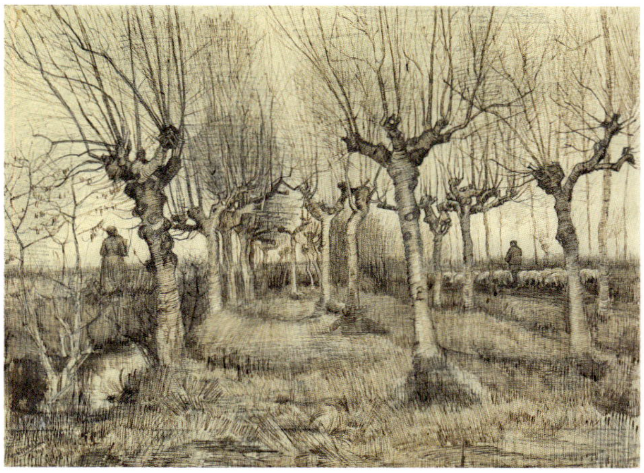

10.7

Painting and her life in the studio became all that really mattered. "The solitude that I find in my studio is one of plenitude. I am enough for myself. I live fully there."[21] As she distilled every day into a vital push to work above all else, she reflected on painting itself and let rip the kind of canvases that can only be made after decades of concentrated looking at, thinking about, and making paintings. The last works sway between explosive experimentation and raw elegy. Operatic in scale and spirit, *Champs* (1990, plate 124), *Sunflowers* (1990–91, plate 123), and *Ici* (1992, plate 130) wrest improbable yet majestic harmonies from dissonant ranges of hues. The *Champs* suite's horizontal strata feel only minimally tied to the layered landscape as seen from the house in Vétheuil, less about the memory or feeling of a specific view and more about memories of so many paintings of views. The surface of *Sunflowers* offers an odyssey of color, a pinnacle of Mitchell's masterful orchestration of intensity, placement, and proportion. The flamboyant *Ici* and spare *Merci* (1992, plate 129) differ radically in composition and complexity, yet both are charged by a heated raggedness and audacious willingness to let strokes feel unhinged or unfinished in order to bridge exuberance and pathos. Connecting all Mitchell's late works is her virtuosity and fearlessness with color. She pushed the intensity of contrast to the edge of what the eye can take in, and in paintings like *South* and *Sunflowers,* she layered in literally dozens of colors, as if she were determined to touch every tube and can of paint available in her studio. These works embrace contradiction, flout convention, and elevate lack of finish to a degree unprecedented in her work.

In the last paintings she would make, Mitchell pared down sunflower and tree figures and placed them eloquently in fields of white canvas. No longer memories of views or captured feelings of the natural world in her grandeur, they are declarations of identity. Achingly beautiful, *Untitled* (1992, plate 134) carries the weight of Joan Mitchell's life as a painter as she closed off to all but herself, alone with painting. With the sparest of means, these paintings crystallize her central concerns at the end of her life. They are about her, but they do not reveal her; they are about sunflowers, van Gogh, beauty, and death, but convey far more. Singular and uncategorizable, they are neither abstraction nor representation, but beyond both.

FIG 10.6 **Joan Mitchell**
Taillade, 1990. Oil on canvas, 102¼ × 158 in. (259.7 × 401.3 cm). The Museum of Modern Art, New York, gift of Galerie Jean Fournier, Enid A. Haupt Fund, and Helen Acheson Bequest (by exchange)

FIG 10.7 **Vincent van Gogh**
Pollard Birches, 1884. Graphite, ink, and watercolor on paper, 15½ × 21$\frac{5}{16}$ in. (39.5 × 54.2 cm). Van Gogh Museum, Amsterdam (Vincent van Gogh Foundation)

Late pastels

Rachel Mochon

Pastels from this period are illustrated as plates 131–33.

FIG 10.8 Joan Mitchell's studio at La Tour, Vétheuil, France, 1980

FIG 10.9 Joan Mitchell's studio at 23 rue Campagne-Première, Paris, ca. 1992. Galerie Jean Fournier, Paris

In her drawings from the 1960s, Mitchell used brightly colored, water-soluble wax crayons and wash to explore shape and line in her compositions. In the 1970s, she began to actively use pastels on large sheets to create swaths of rich, saturated color in broad strokes, effects that could not be achieved with the waxy surface quality and narrower width of crayons. After creating a series of atmospheric pastel drawings to accompany printed poems by contemporaries such as J. J. Mitchell and James Schuyler (see plate 80 and figs. 7.5 and 7.6), she wrote in a 1975 letter to Xavier Fourcade that she "would like to do some more pastels without poems—the medium is seductive—perhaps too much so—Anyway back in oils now."[1] Allowing herself to be seduced, she soon took advantage of pastel's powdery nature and lack of resistance on paper to capture her gestures.

Because the pastel dust would cover her Vétheuil studio (fig. 10.8), Mitchell did not work on oil paintings and pastel drawings concurrently.[2] Instead, she often worked on drawings between cycles of painting for shows at Galerie Jean Fournier in Paris and Xavier Fourcade in New York.[3] Many of the drawings share the distinctive quality of her work on canvas, yet her works on paper are not preparatory sketches for larger paintings but independent, finished works. By 1986, Mitchell had a second studio space (fig. 10.9) on rue Campagne-Première in Montparnasse, where she could devote herself to working in pastels.[4]

Pastel is a dry drawing medium in stick form that consists of fine pigment or colorant, additives, and a small amount of binder, which may include drying oils, resins, waxes, gums, or proteins.[5] Like Mitchell's predominant medium, oil paint, pastels were available in a range of colors far more vibrant than the soft palettes of eighteenth-century pastelists. The velvety strokes of dry, compressed pigment provided rich, saturated hues on white or cream papers and appealed to her sense of color and light. Colors could be superimposed in discrete layers of pigment or softly blended into one another. Additionally, with minimal binder, pastel sticks were receptive to frequent changes in the pressure and direction of the artist's hand. As such, the medium's consistency and visual properties lent themselves well to Mitchell's assertive gesture and painterly handling.

In an untitled drawing from 1992 (plate 132), Mitchell exhibits a range of mark-making techniques in pastel that together achieve something akin to the fluidity of her traditional paint medium. Her gesture on paper creates a sense of expression similar to that in paintings such as *River* (1989, plate 120). The narrowness of the lines and their jagged turns exaggerate the concentration of red and blue pastel in the center of the drawing. The sharp tails at the ends of the lines record her quick flick of the pastel stick, an assertive mark made with relative rapidity that can be compared to the end of an emphatic brushstroke.

In pastel, Mitchell predominantly combines color through the juxtaposition and superimposition of layers. In the center of the 1992 drawing, she applied at least three shades of blue and three shades of red with substantial pressure in discrete layers, establishing a distinct zone of the composition. The juxtaposition of the two colors shifts the hue of the mass to violet. This approach to constructing color in layers, which preserves the crisp edges of the lines, can also be seen in many of her paintings, such as *Two Pianos* (1980, plate 101). To achieve a different effect, she veiled thin layers of pastel over an underlying color, often by "graining"—that is, drawing with the side of the pastel stick. For example, the graining of yellow pastel over the blues and greens in the lower left of the drawing shifts the colors to reflect the warmer hues seen in the upper portion. This technique creates a blended appearance through superimposition as well as through minor smudging. In some drawings, such as an untitled pastel from 1980 (plate 110), Mitchell blended pastel with her fingers, significantly softening the line. However, she limited such extensive blending to particular zones of her compositions and avoided the risk of muddying the colors in subsequent layers. Through these methods of combining color, she strikes a balance between hard and soft edges that not only resembles certain paintings but also speaks to the sense of confidence and specificity in the mark making.

Mitchell utilized mark-making and layering techniques to build succinct compositions. Far from representational, many of her pastel drawings are reminiscent of the "remembered landscapes" that inspired her paintings.[6] The drawings are often composed of distinct blocks or bands distinguished by color and by groupings of energetic, curving lines. These areas of density may recall a horizon line, a body of water, or foliage, and look back to her multipanel paintings of the 1960s. The 1992 drawing comprises three horizontal bands, yet their stacked structure, the predominance of emphatic up-and-down marks within each, and the orientation of the paper create a wholly vertical composition. In this way, she preserves the sense of movement in the lines while creating directionality and space that could be viewed as a landscape.

Pastel has a complex history, experiencing periods of popularity, disfavor, even lack of use altogether.[7] However, American artists in the nineteenth and early twentieth centuries, such as Arthur Dove and Max Weber, embraced pastel as a medium for abstraction.[8] Mitchell furthered the reinvention of pastel in the mid to late twentieth century, using pastel sticks as if they were paintbrushes, making big, bold, confident strokes. Her complex, layered structures of gestural marks and controlled use of blending reflect the artist's signature style at the same time that they uniquely celebrate the color, texture, and working properties of pastel.

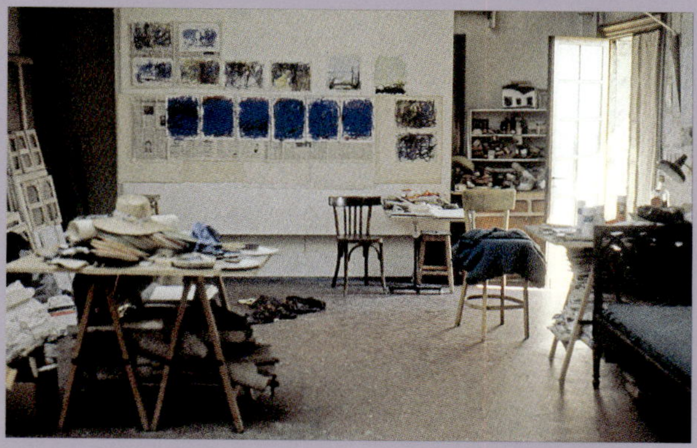

10.8

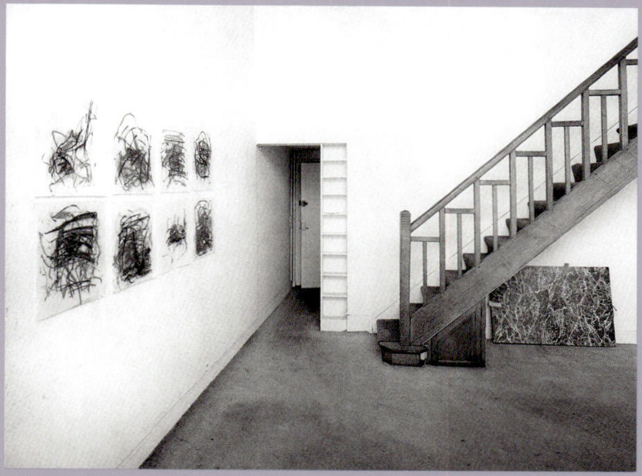

10.9

LANDSCAPES 1980–92

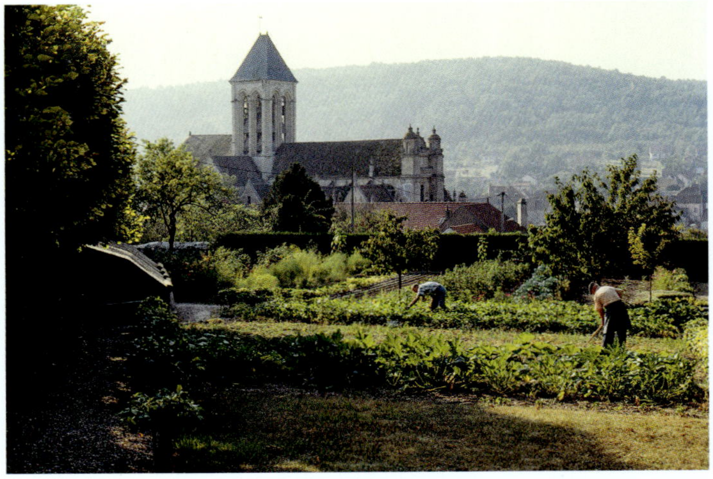

1

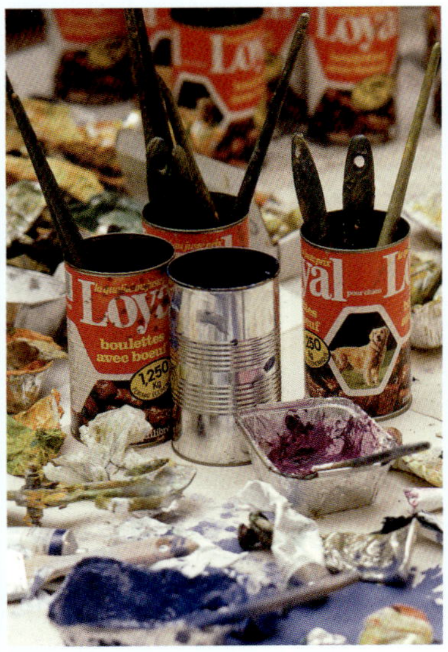

2

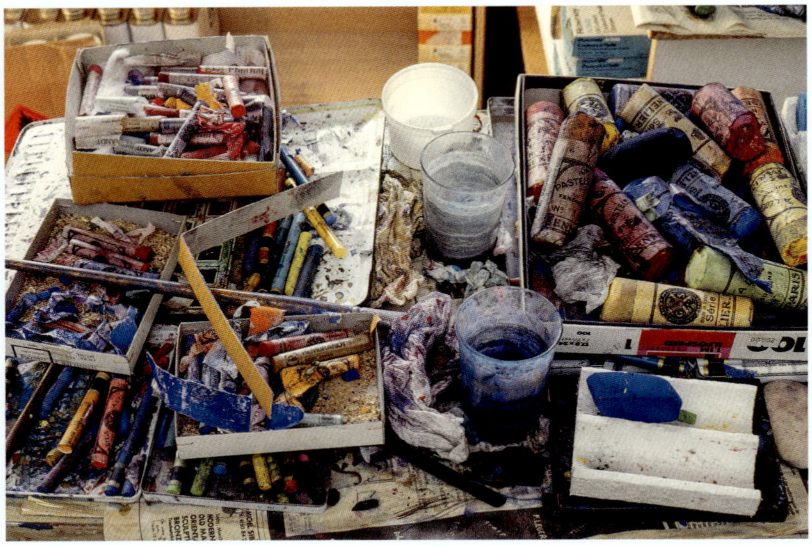

3

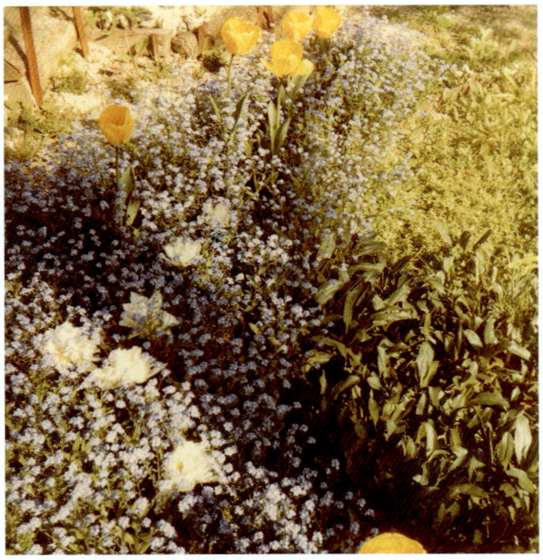

4

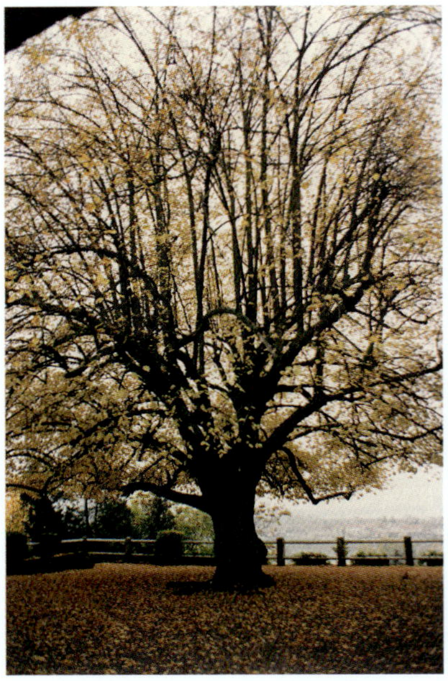

5

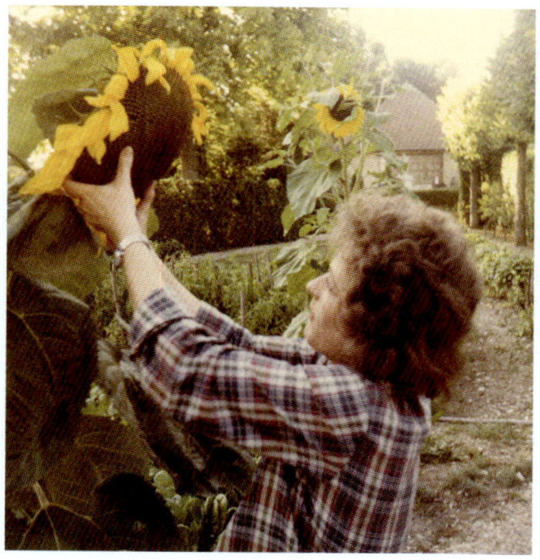

6

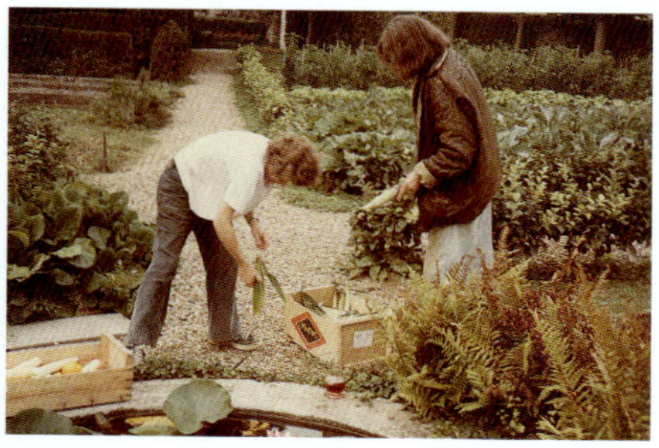

7

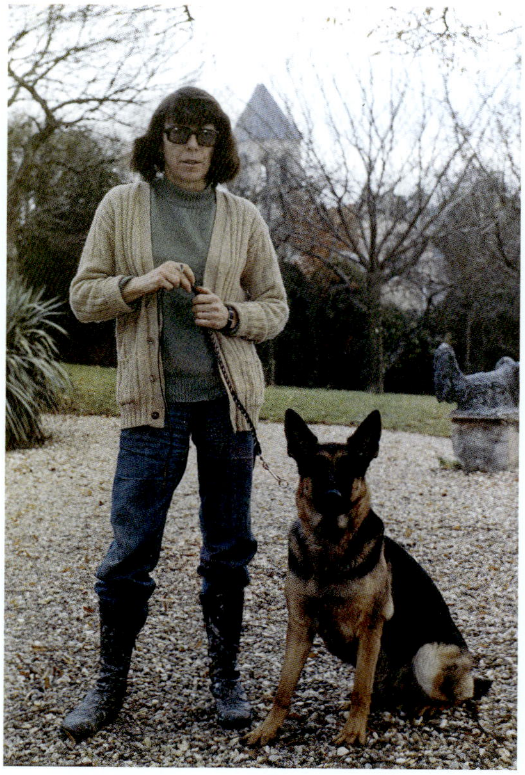

8

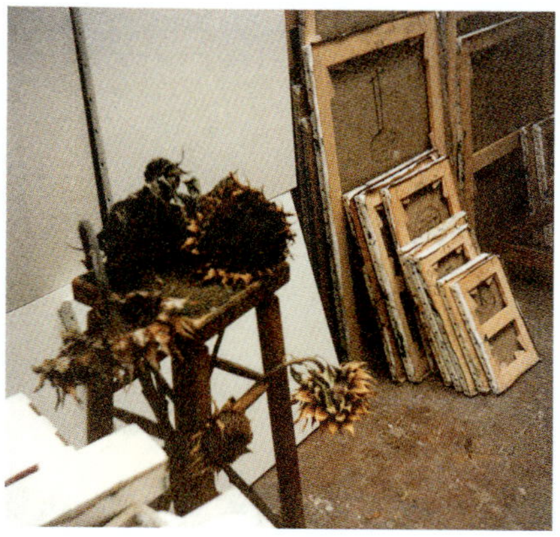

9

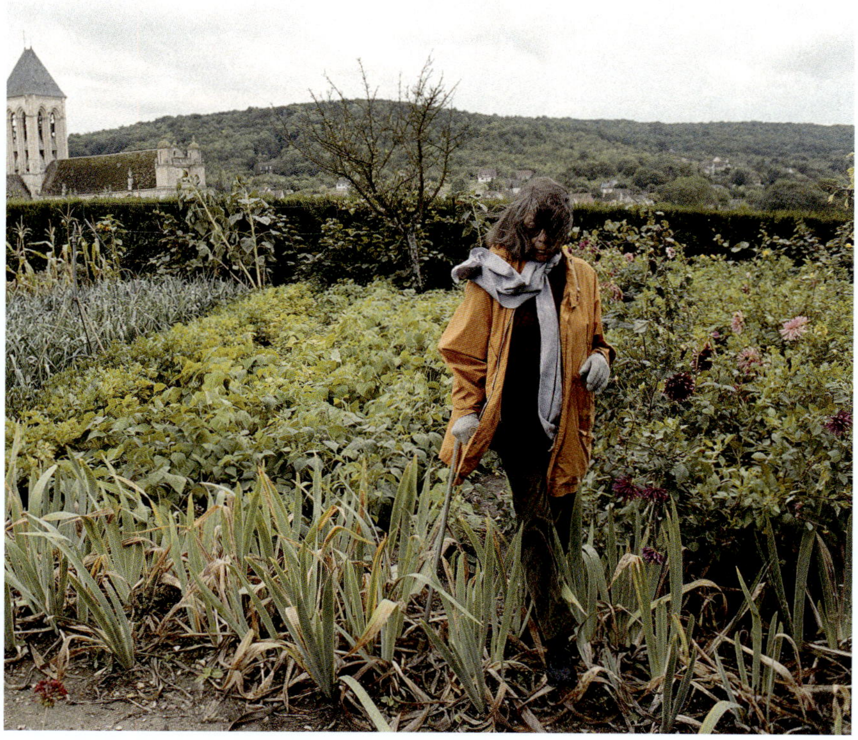

10

1 Jean Perthuis (far right) working in Joan Mitchell's garden at La Tour, Vétheuil, France, 1991

2 Painting materials in Joan Mitchell's studio at La Tour, Vétheuil, France, 1983. Joan Mitchell Foundation Archives, New York

3 Pastels in Joan Mitchell's studio at La Tour, Vétheuil, France, 1991

4 Garden dedicated to Edrita Fried at La Tour, Vétheuil, France, 1982. Joan Mitchell Foundation Archives, New York

5 Tilleul, or linden tree, at La Tour, Vétheuil, France, 1989

6 Gisèle Barreau with a sunflower at La Tour, Vétheuil, France, 1980. Joan Mitchell Foundation Archives, New York

7 Gisèle Barreau and Joan Mitchell picking corn in the garden at La Tour, Vétheuil, France, ca. 1982. Courtesy the Estate of Joyce Pensato. Photograph by Joyce Pensato

8 Joan Mitchell with one of her German shepherds at La Tour, Vétheuil, France, n.d. Joan Mitchell Foundation Archives, New York

9 Sunflowers in Joan Mitchell's studio at La Tour, Vétheuil, France, ca. 1980. Courtesy Gisèle Barreau

10 Joan Mitchell in the garden at La Tour, Vétheuil, France, 1991

Joan Mitchell's *Harbor December*

Jennifer Hickey and David Reed

FIG 1 **Joan Mitchell**
Harbor December, 1956. Oil on canvas, 80 × 80 in. (203.2 × 203.2 cm). Private collection, New York. See plate 20.

The following text is excerpted from a series of conversations that took place during and after viewings of the painting in fall 2019.

Structure

JENNIFER HICKEY: In the mid-1950s Mitchell typically began with an unstretched canvas that had been prepared with a homogenous layer of white paint and tacked to the wall. This white field would determine the rough dimensions within which she'd work.

DAVID REED: It is a confrontational setup. Facing the canvas, Mitchell was challenged to assert her presence.

2

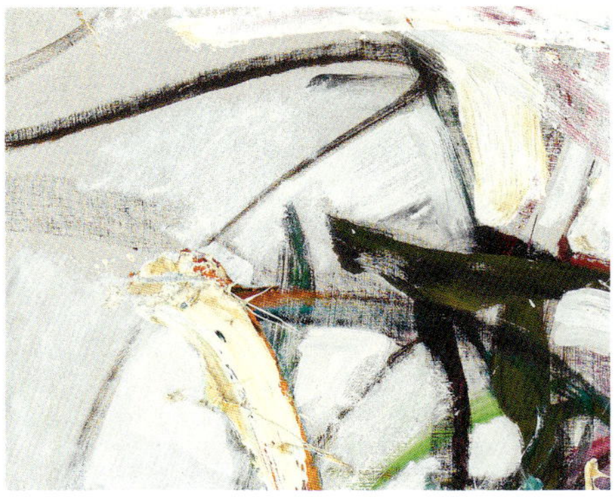

JH: Here, one can see the early brushstrokes laid in, primarily in greens and plums (fig. 2). Horizontal marks radiate from a central vertical axis, setting up a loose bilateral symmetry that one associates with the body in both scale and structure. They served as a sort of skeletal armature for the work as it developed.

DR: There could have been a balance and symmetry based on the bilateral symmetry of her body, but she tested this by going off-balance.

JH: The bottom passage of the work, for example, simultaneously anchors and destabilizes the composition. The passages of blue and viridian echo across the left and right, expanding toward the sides and bottom of the work, and they assert forward visually as well. This multidimensional expansion of color creates, in some sense, a "base" for the work. But Mitchell subverted any full grounding by punctuating the diagonal on which these blues are set with a string of orange marks. And she obliterated the blue brushwork at left, likely using a rag to blur the paint strokes and render the passage thin and ethereal in contrast to the defined strokes at right. The result is a weightiness that is off-kilter, in motion. Again, there's this tension.

DR: I wouldn't call this a compositional choice because it comes through the body and the feel of the body in active motion.

JH: Good point. "Composition" is misleading in suggesting that she is working from a preconceived image of what the painting will be. Rather, these marks were something to push against.

DR: Each new mark transformed the tension between Mitchell and the work, and she responded.

JH: I read a confidence and freedom in these early marks that I don't find in subsequent layers. Perhaps because the stakes felt low to Mitchell at this point—there was ample room to construct and change. These marks have a calligraphic quality to them.

DR: They have a wonderful freedom. But I don't think that they are calligraphic in the sense of being well drawn, precisely controlled, or following a prescribed form.

JH: Yes, I was thinking "calligraphic" in terms of their fluidity and that confident elegance achieved when one gives over to muscle memory. She was merely relying on gestures that she knew bodily as an efficient way to break the tension between herself and the canvas.

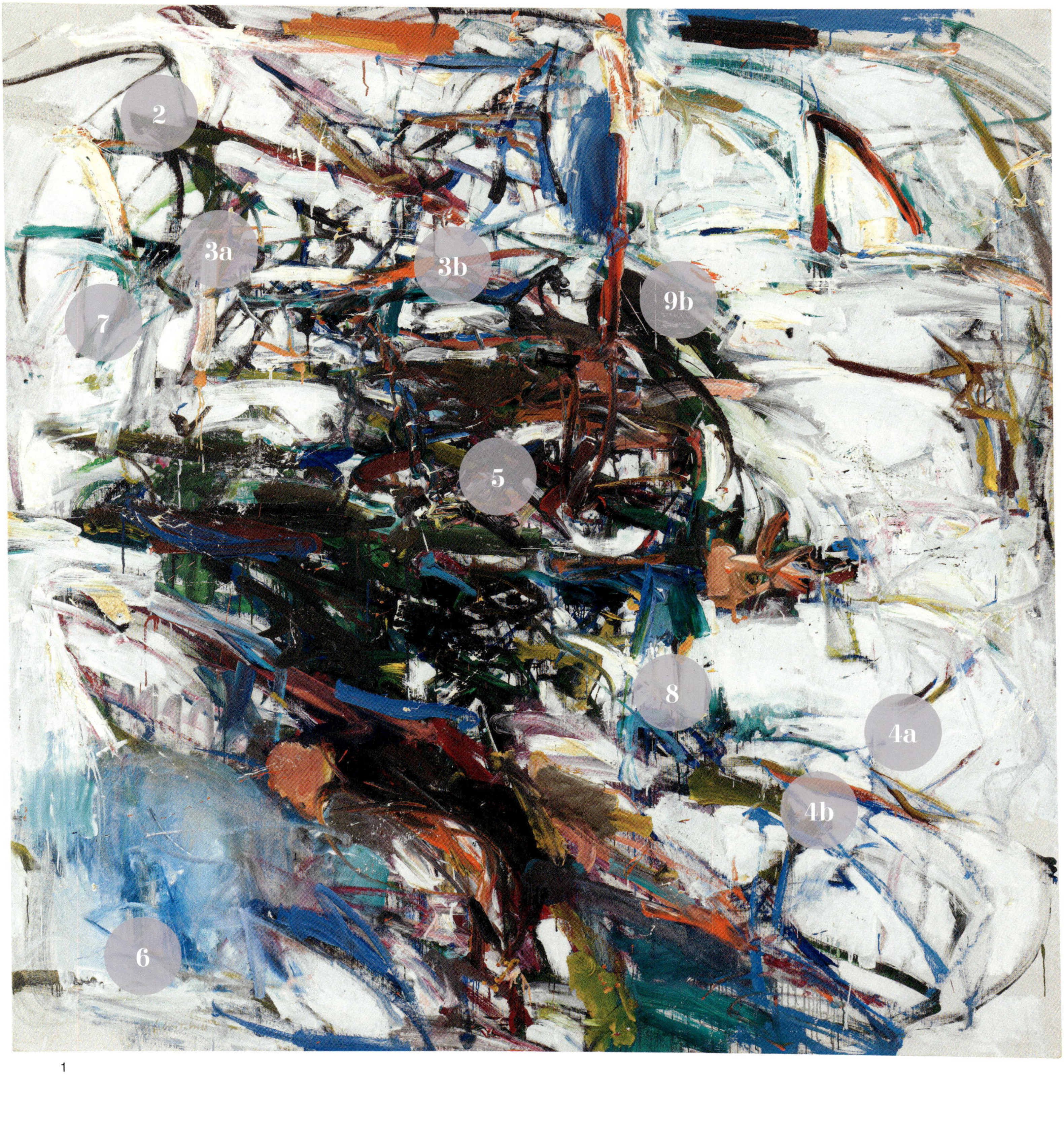

1

DR: I'm especially attracted to the "switchback" or "whiplash" marks in which the sudden change of direction causes a kind of disruption.

JH: I see these marks as wholly constructive—there is a flow to the change in direction that naturally completes the stroke. They seem to serve as shorthand for "painting" in order to break the pristine space and begin to organize it. The later mark making—I am inclined to agree with you—tends to have the aggressive aspect of canceling or disrupting.

DR: I see even these first marks as a kind of disruption. I think this painting is all attack.

Editing Strategies

DR: As Mitchell built subsequent paint layers, continual disruption was how new marks related to existing ones. One sees again and again an incisive "doubling"—the reinforcing of a mark with a similar mark. Or sometimes a mark is transformed when it is doubled in a different color. And there is another kind of doubling in which a mark is crossed over with a perpendicular mark as if it is being canceled.

JH: Yes, one sees individual strokes that Mitchell has reinforced a second or sometimes a third time (fig. 3a). (I'm tempted to describe them as "traced"; this implies too tentative a gesture, but that's roughly the effect.) The underlying layers are rarely completely masked. They remain as a record of her decision-making. (For example, the brick-red horizontal stroke at top center that Mitchell "extends" with the very late orange stroke—as in fig. 3b.) These marks reveal a cerebral appraisal of the developing layers, as well as a severity of self-criticism, especially in the vicious energy with which she cancels her work. But now I am armchair psychoanalyzing.

DR: I agree, her willingness to destroy what went before gives this painting remarkable tension and energy.

3

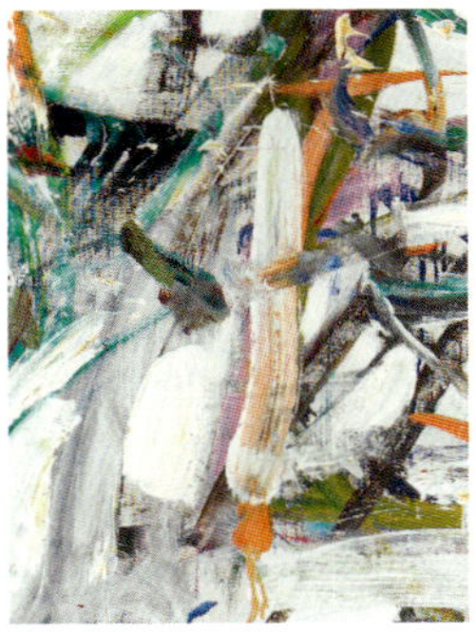

a

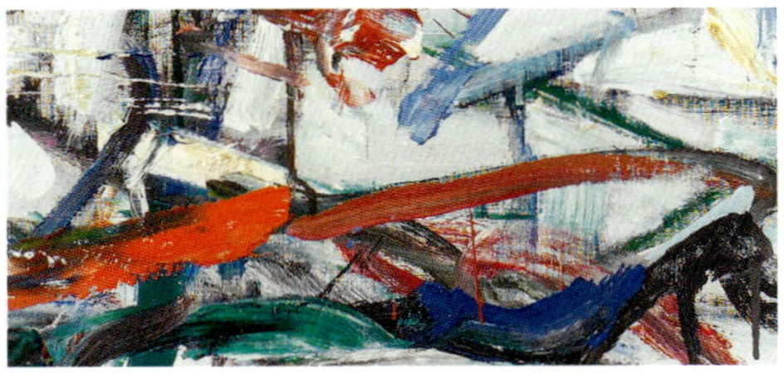

b

JH: We've been describing Mitchell's building of subsequent paint layers as "editing." This term seems to appropriately point to the analytical aspect in her painting. These marks reveal a deliberateness that counterbalances the more immediate, intuitive aspect of her technique. That these processes play out very much in concert is key to synthesis in Mitchell's work.

4

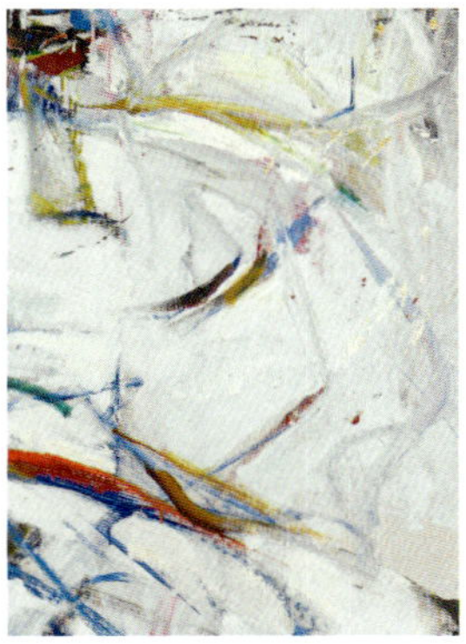

a

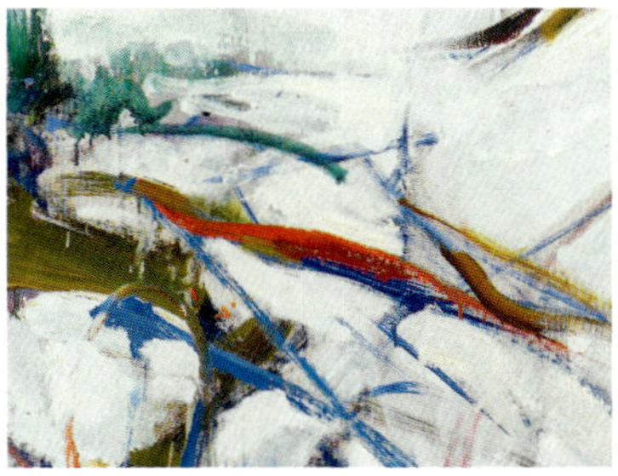

b

DR: Mitchell was continually redefining with white in extremely nuanced ways. From a distance these marks create an openness.

JH: Here she picked up color from the underlying layer, mixing on the canvas to create subtle tints (fig. 4a). In other cases Mitchell would apply a pale translucent wash that allows dry underlying colors to partially assert themselves. One sees Mitchell using white to hone space (fig. 4b) from the early 1950s, and she really developed a virtuosic understanding of its possibilities over time. Alternatively, we see passages where she doubled down on density, working with thickly applied colors, wet-into-wet, in aggressive passages of obliteration.

DR: I find these dense, wet-into-wet areas (fig. 5) especially compelling. One doesn't see them at first, and then when one does, they have tremendous depth, detail, and concentration—like paintings within the painting. One can get lost in them.

5

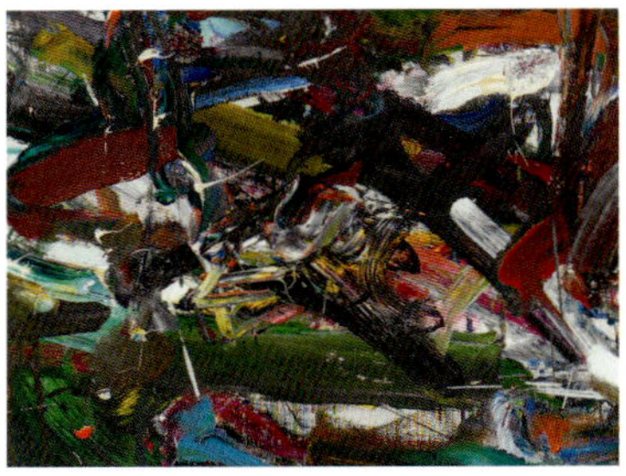

JH: She worked back and forth between broad and single-stroke edits, as opposed to "progressing" from broader to finer edits, as one might assume.

DR: Yes. The editing with white, especially, continues through all the layers. She could do this kind of editing any time as she did with other kinds of editing: blurring edges with a rag or with her fingers (figs. 6 and 7), or overpainting with complementary hues (fig. 8).

JH: The precision and variety with which these marks were executed speak to an intense consideration. There was a complex rhythm to Mitchell's process. While the brushwork is confident and energetic, this reveals a grounding in the body rather than a relenting of control or giving over to accident.

6

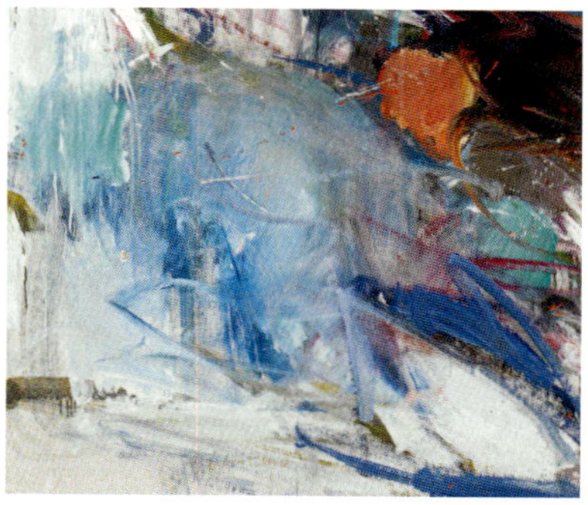

7

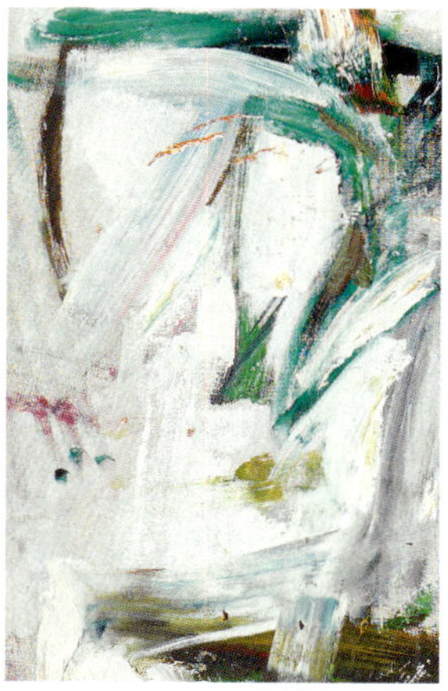

8

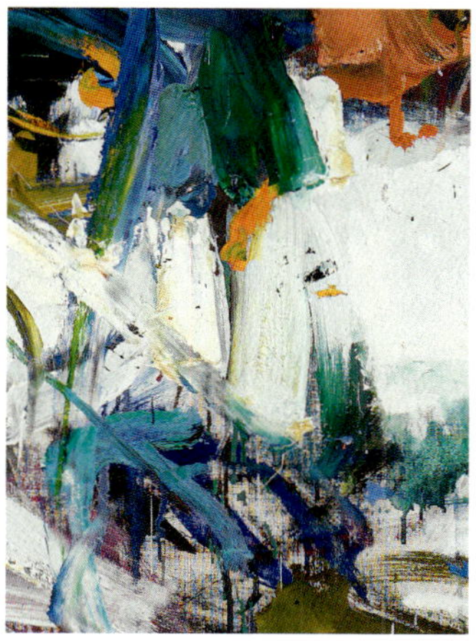

9

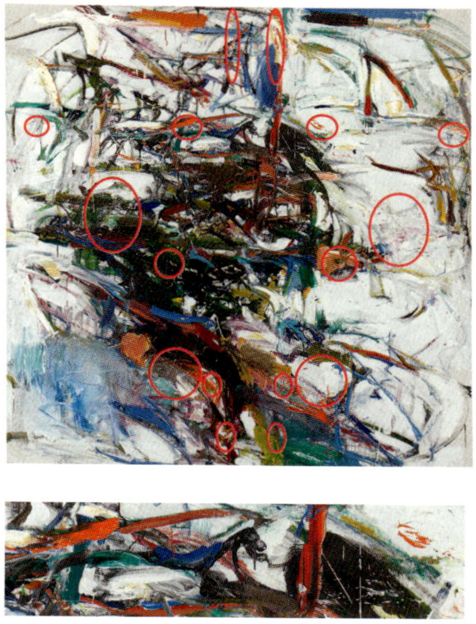

a

b

Final Marks

DR: You observed amazing evidence of another kind of giving over to the painting. You discovered a set of paint transfers, almost Rorschach-mark-like, that suggest that the painting had been folded (fig. 9a).

JH: Yes, Mitchell likely had to fold the painting before it was completely dry in order to transport it from her studio.

DR: So she did this for practical reasons, but I find the matter-of-fact directness to be very revealing. The painting was folded vertically just off center to the right.

JH: Yes, one can make out orange and white residues that mirror areas of thickly applied paint in reference to that vertical axis (fig. 9b).

DR: Cadmium orange is a slow-drying color, so it makes sense that this was the color that was still wet when the painting was folded.

JH: And, in comparing areas of heavy impasto that weren't disturbed by the fold, it's clear that these transferred strokes were added late in the game.

DR: I find the way the fold follows the bilateral symmetry of a body in front of the painting to be evidence that she was naturally thinking of the painting in this way.

JH: Good point. Her choice reinforces a symmetry—unarticulated, but certainly inherent to the work.

DR: Have you been able to find evidence of her repainting after the fold? Did she clean up? Make use of the Rorschach marks?

JH: The transfers retain that puckered texture of having been pulled clean away. Mitchell doesn't appear to have worked back into those areas. She must have accepted them. Maybe she liked them.

DR: You must have guessed that I'm still looking for the elusive final mark. That's what started off our discussions when we first looked at Mitchell's work together. I had the idea of searching for the final mark in each painting. There are some works in which the final marks are possible to determine, but in Mitchell's paintings it's a challenge.

JH: That's right—chasing the mythic mark that resolves everything. As an exercise in close and curious looking, it suits my conservator nature.

DR: Another way to think of it is that the last mark could be one that keeps a painting forever open, unresolved. In the end, finding this last mark is a much more difficult task than I imagined.

JH: The precision of Mitchell's mark making makes identifying the final stroke seem tantalizingly possible, but I think in this case the work's complexity means that ambiguity wins out.

La ligne de rupture

Paul Auster

FIG 1 Detail views of a manuscript copy of Jacques Dupin's "La Ligne de rupture," ca. 1971. Joan Mitchell Foundation Archives, New York. An inscription from Dupin to Joan Mitchell, dated August 17, 1971, is visible at the bottom of the image at far right.

I first became aware of Jacques Dupin in 1967. I was a student at Columbia University, and there was a good bookstore on campus where I discovered a little anthology of contemporary French poetry. It had three or four of his poems in it, and they made a deep impression on me. A short time later, I went to Paris to study and found *Gravir* (1963) and his first book, *Cendrier du voyage* (1950). There was something about his tone, the power of his syntax—a sort of acceleration—that knocked me off my feet. Very young, I was attracted to the latent violence in his poems. I found it invigorating, like a scream, like a declaration of war against the conventions of poetry, thought, philosophy, politics.

For me, Jacques was first and foremost a poet. I was unaware that he worked for a gallery or that he was writing essays about artists. When I met him, it was as a poet, and what struck me at that first dinner was his kindness, his intelligence, and his forthright, direct way of speaking. After about ten minutes, he said, "Okay, we can dispense with all the formalities now. Call me by my first name." I got the impression—and I think he felt the same—that we were embarking on a true friendship that evening. It was through Jacques that I met Joan Mitchell, at her rue Frémicourt studio. Not long after, I visited her in Vétheuil. There I saw her paintings of the 1970s, among them *La Ligne de la rupture* (1970–71, plate 74). This is my favorite period of her work; it was also when she was most involved with French poetry, and it has been largely overlooked.

There was a little den in Joan's house that had a shelf filled with books by friends, including Dupin (and Samuel Beckett). Her French was good—she was fluent, although she had a strong American accent. Joan liked the line "La ligne de rupture"—it spoke to her. Jacques had a startling gift for the pungent phrase. And as his work evolved, he continued to develop his experiments with language. He had been writing for a long time, since the 1940s, but he wasn't yet old, he was in the middle of his life. In "La ligne de rupture," traditional sentences have become fragments. Breaking up the poem into discrete lines is something he never would have done earlier. There's a burst, and then a silence, and then another burst. Often there are no verbs—statements hang in the air, linked by a mental or physical connection.

"La ligne de rupture" is a difficult poem. But Joan didn't like smooth, easy things. She liked knotty things. "C'est la peau du dehors qui se retourne et nous absorbe" (the skin of the exterior turns inside out and absorbs us) sounds as if the body is being drawn into the surround. It has the force of a collage. Any one of these fragments alone would be interesting, but the poem—like the painting—is about the interaction in space of the different elements and how they change in relation to one another.

This text was developed in collaboration with Katy Siegel. Portions of it are adapted from Victor Martinez, "Comme un frère: entretien avec Paul Auster," *Europe: revue littéraire mensuelle* 90, no. 998–99 (June–July 2012): 8–22.

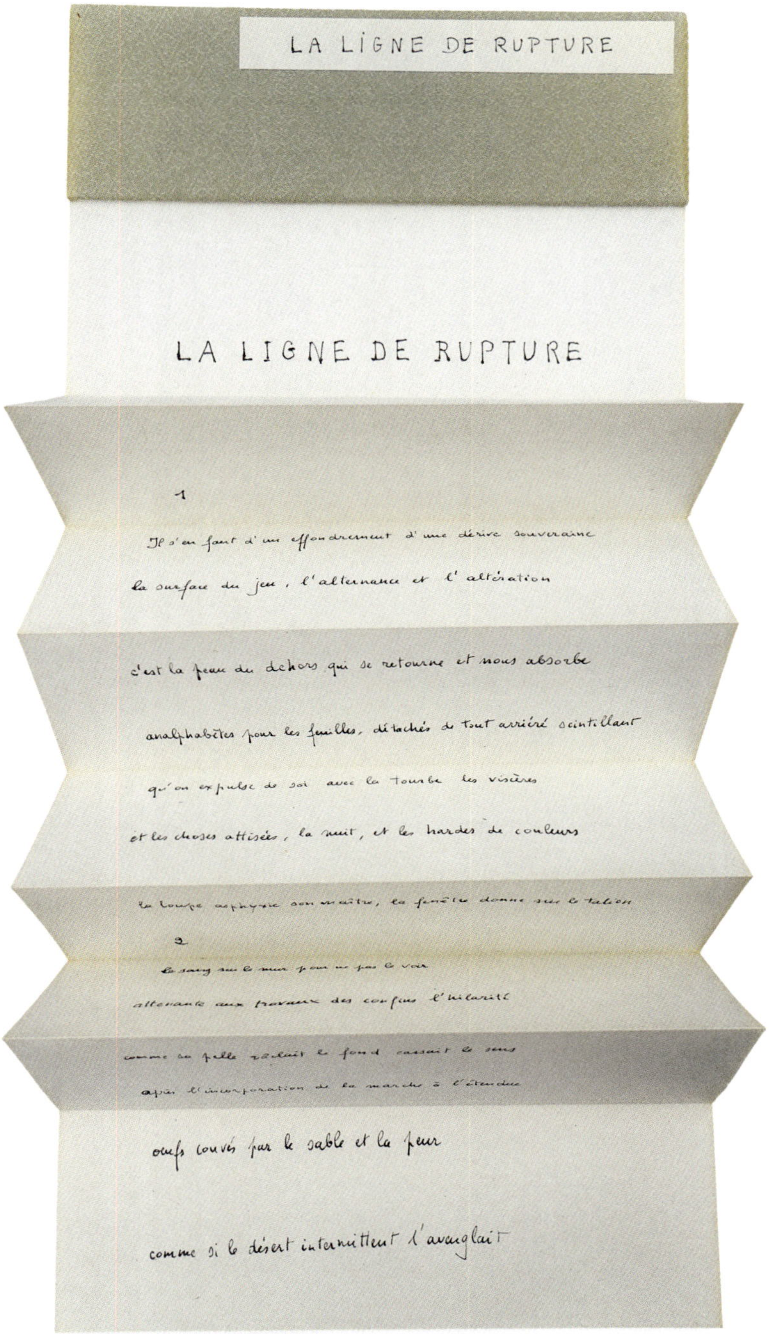
LA LIGNE DE RUPTURE
LA LIGNE DE RUPTURE
1
Il s'en faut d'un effondrement d'une dérive souveraine
la surface du jeu, l'alternance et l'altération
c'est la peau du dehors qui se retourne et nous absorbe
analphabètes pour les feuilles, détachés de tout arriéré scintillant
qu'on expulse de soi avec la tourbe les viscères
et les choses attisées, la nuit, et les hardes de couleurs
2
oeufs couvés par le sable et la peur
comme si le désert intermittent l'aveuglait

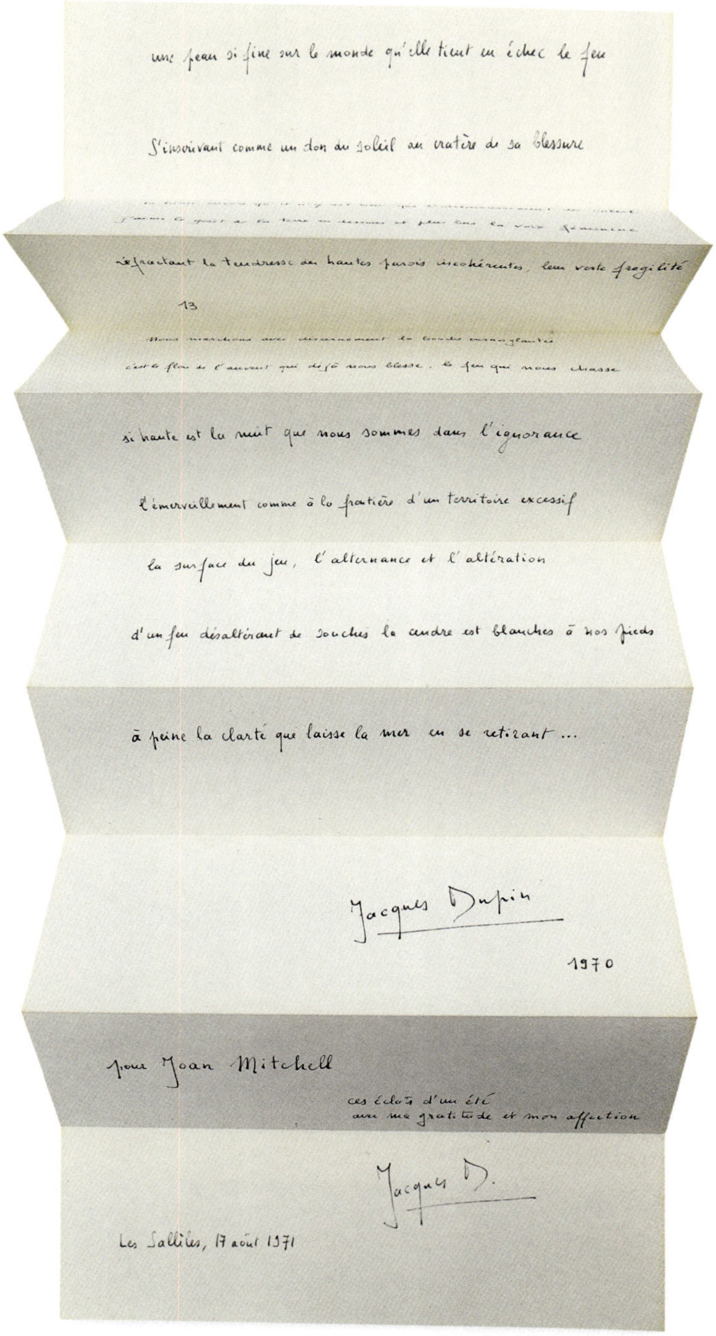
une peau si fine sur le monde qu'elle tient en échec le feu
s'inscrivant comme un don du soleil au cratère de sa blessure
13
si haute est la nuit que nous sommes dans l'ignorance
l'émerveillement comme à la frontière d'un territoire excessif
la surface du jeu, l'alternance et l'altération
d'un feu désaltérant de souches la cendre est blanche à nos pieds
à peine la clarté que laisse la mer en se retirant ...
Jacques Dupin
1970
pour Joan Mitchell
ces éclats d'un été
avec ma gratitude et mon affection
Jacques D.
Les Sallèles, 17 août 1971

1

Joan and “la musique à peindre”

Gisèle Barreau

FIG 1 **Gisèle Barreau**
Score for *Sterne,* 1983.
Courtesy Gisèle Barreau

“Piano, piano!” cried Antonio. Maybe that was his name.

Slow down, slow down! Rome, the Villa Medici... pines, boxwood, those greens, an incredible blue, the smells, the sounds, a magic villa, a sizzling city. Rome is burning, consumed by its fountains of love, its ghosts of long-gone heroes, armed no longer.

Antonio smiled dreamily, his eyes on the first Prix de Rome check clutched in my hands. “Piano, piano!” he repeated obstinately. I must be wise. And so was born the title of the work I was composing for an orchestra and two pianos, with certain sounds amplified.

Joan loved this story; she had fun coming up with titles. *Wood, Wind, No Tubas* is another example. In Vétheuil we had evenings devoted to this game.

She painted works that can be heard—radiant, lyrical, a perfect vibration. I paint in sounds, framing the music—gestures, energy, a color field expressed in a musical score that can be seen: music for the soul.

Piano-Piano.[1] The music surges and then disappears, no end and no beginning. That's the idea: a world where time no longer exists. Whites are important. Here they are composed of snare drums with pale sounds—*timbre retiré*—mixed with voices, mouths closed. There's a twirling of fingers, from the edges of the skin toward the center, very gently, a certain shade of white—a white of grief.

Joan also worked with whites. She created them constantly, sometimes allowing a particular space on the canvas to reveal a simple shade—white ground. She explained that for her, yellow and orange often evoked a feeling of sadness, sometimes to the surprise of the viewer. The choice of colors for a canvas depended on what one was feeling. Depression and grief are close. Cobalt violet—a recurring theme. Blazing blues, the flames never quenched.

I envy the painter, for there is no page to turn. The whole canvas is there—exposed and immediately perceived. As a composer, I must condense. I seize the sound matter at my disposal. I enclose it in an invisible frame in order to feel it, out of time, out of context, and then finally to reveal it. For the rest—exaltation, movements in space, speeds, colors crude and composite, lines in counterpoint, masses, underground rivers reawakened, waves in series—the painter and the musician share the same world.

Piano-Piano, Two Pianos (1980, plate 101).[2] Note against note, mass against mass, touch against touch—a thousand details are woven thread by thread, producing powerful and resonant landscapes. A painter makes her mark directly on the canvas. As a composer, I require more time to make a gesture using other signs, incomplete notation, and a necessary mediating language. Ultimately the work will be interpreted by a performer who will be the bearer, the hand, the breath, the heart, the revelation, the lover—or maybe, inadvertently, the betrayer.

Joan was fascinated by the notes in musical scores and their translation into sound: “I hear your work, I listen to it, I am affected by it. But I also approach your score visually, as if it were a painting. I can't help myself” (fig. 1). So the concert took place, *Piano-Piano* traveling the airwaves, France Musique, a journey that was nonstop, Rome—Vétheuil, direct flight.

Respect, complicity. Joan listened. She said she loved the work.

Then came a surprise: an invitation to the studio. Suddenly I was face-to-face with a new diptych, which she had mischievously titled *Two Pianos*! Sound and image interwoven in a brilliant production revealing secret paths, creating different patterns of hearing and listening. Her wonderful painting is percussive, vocal and flamboyant. It amplifies, it transcends.

Memories of a happy dream: Seated in the dining room next to *La Lande* (1977, plate 95),[3] I tell Joan about a vision of a canvas painted in blues, stirring, with a feeling of euphoria. She asks me to describe it in detail, and I do. The following day I go with the painter to her studio to look at her works and move some of them. And then another surprise: “Here is your picture.” Our relationship also functioned in language, words inseparable from colors and sounds because everything is vibration; we breathed the same air.

The poets took their repose in the library, like dormant seeds, but traveled often from the kitchen to the studio. Rilke never left the painter's side. I fed on Saint-John Perse. Verlaine set up residence in the dining room. Joan smiled and said: “Le ciel est par-dessus le toit, si bleu si calme.”[4] I replied immediately, an unavoidable ritual: “Il pleure dans mon coeur comme il pleut sur la ville.”[5] Smiles. And so the day began before we departed

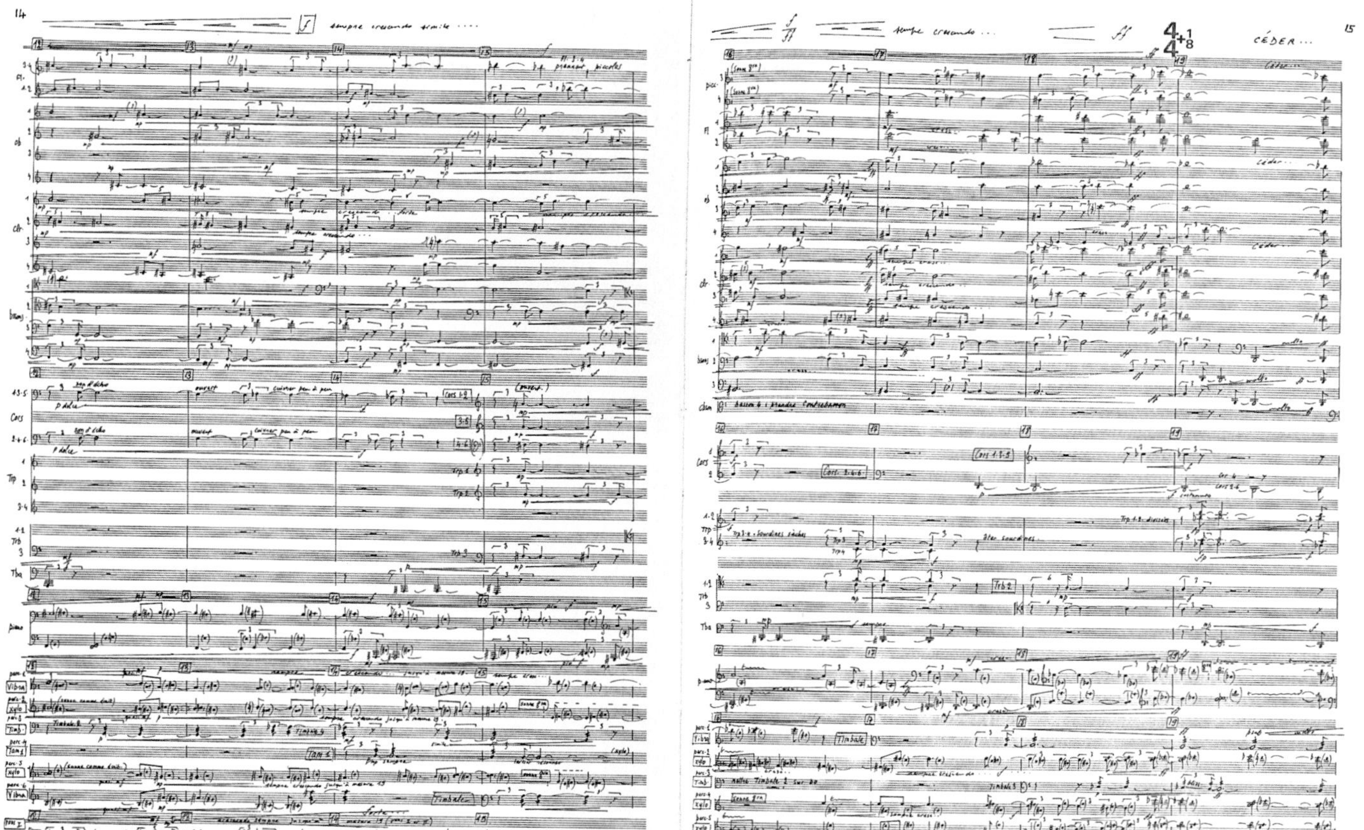

1

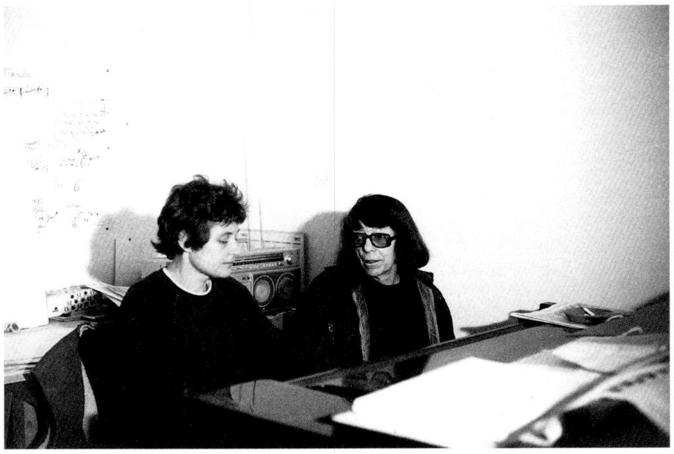

2

FIG 2 Gisèle Barreau and Joan Mitchell at the piano in Chez Belle Bête, Barreau's studio at La Tour, Vétheuil, France, 1982. Courtesy Gisèle Barreau

to our studios—Joan in the company of her "musique à peindre."

My studio, Chez Belle Bête, was at the other end of the house. Both studios faced south, looking out onto the Seine and the lake and trees and fields. A last word from the painter, not without humor, addressed daily to "the girls": "On y va qui mal y pense!"[6] There was a concert of barking—a prelude to looking at the pictures in light of day. The three German shepherds rushed up the thirteen stairs leading to the studio, all intense looks and waiting. Joan rose from her chair, and the barking stopped abruptly. In three brilliant glissandos the she-wolves evoked the alarm sirens of a Varèse. Their tails wagged furiously, like metronomes, ready to brush against the bottom of one of the still-wet canvases. A future picture restorer will delight in this: "I have found a hair in the paint!" In fact it was always a team effort—Joan was never separated from the dogs when she worked.

Another concert would follow later. Maybe an opera. Her "musique à peindre"—played often at night, sometimes during the day. Music for Joan, for us, or perhaps for some passing visitor, but also for the dead, as the graveyard was close, and even those sleeping forever will awake to hear Callas.

Tosca, dear *Tosca*! Callas the divine!

At maximum volume, two imposing mounted speakers poured out music in unison. The ceiling beam quivered. The dead of the village rejoiced! They were not abandoned. Berlioz, the *Requiem*—the work we most often listened to was dedicated to them. Handel too, the *Messiah*. Joan sang at the top of her voice, smiling broadly, marching up and down the studio: "Hallelujah! Hallelujah!" This meant that the winds were fair and the night would be creative. Work until dawn, then "L'heure des bleus."

It was in the studio that I discovered *La Vie en rose,* in 1979 (plate 99). It was my first shocking encounter with the painter's work. I heard strings in abundance then; long, slender sounds, no vibrato, using mutes, sometimes a slight tremolo on the easel, horns, brasses with a soft tone, *sans attaque.* Snare drums, the wires off, metallic sounds in the low tones, a double bass tuba. Spleen.

Just as I evoked *La Vie en rose,* Joan talked about *Tlaloc,* the first of my works she was exposed to.[7] Only drums, woods, metals. A color felt by the musician—red, orange and fire, to Life, to Death, strange *Tlaloc.* Nobody knows, perhaps it's a lightning bolt? Or perhaps a sower, or the trickling of water? Then it was a *Petit Matin* (see plates 108 and 109).[8] We visited Jean Fournier and his gallery in France. Jean was a very erudite bookseller, a specialist in old books. Another surprise awaited me: "Choose your book!"

Complicity again. I selected a book about the Aztecs, of course.

We shared a meal afterward at Le Grand Venise to celebrate life, rebirth. And finally we returned to Vétheuil after these glorious adventures. We visited each other's studios, we gazed at the landscape from Chez Belle Bête, with its full southern exposure. Joan looked at the three-legged piano I brought from Rome (fig. 2). Nostalgia. She gently stroked the Brittany spaniel she had inherited from Jean Paul Riopelle's hunting days. Belle Bête, who preferred to hunt butterflies, was stretched out next to the piano. Joan has always wanted to play this instrument but, according to her, it had been intended, since childhood, for her sister Sally.[9]

She looked at the display of percussion instruments on the wall, the ongoing *Aires pour Marion,* with its chorus sometimes amplified—a tribute to her great diptych.[10] Total almighty fire. I hear percussion in her volcanic painting, amplified voices with harmonic sounds inspired by sacred Tibetan music, voices using song, screams, the spoken word, whispers. All of this was inspired by the stormy depths expressed in the writings of Saint-John Perse, the great swell.

And once again the pleasure of titles: *Aires* (the territory), a *Chasse interdite* (no hunting allowed!), *Fields,* many *Champs* to come, the poet's gaze.[11] Then the Ayre, its phonetic resonance, magnetic, the song—a heart that beats. Then Marion, the beloved mother, because it is all about her: the sickness, the death. Then Marion once more, one of Joan's German shepherds, and the most fiery.

I drew up a list of the six percussionists on the wall, separating them geographically because there are many instruments. Joan wondered about them. I explained that one had to consider the time the musicians needed to move, to change drumsticks. Their hands must constantly be ready to smother a Tam, a cymbal. So much necessary preparation before performing. I dreamt of making a simple brushstroke on the canvas, imposing the color or defining the territory, not having to deal with the practicalities of producing music. Joan, greedy for knowledge, wanted to learn and share.

Her knowledge of music was stupendous. Beginning with the Middle Ages and, among many others, Machaut's *Messe de Notre Dame,* she traveled the centuries up to contemporary works. She played Boulez for me and his *Marteau sans maître,* one of many records in her studio. I added my own.

Her exposure to music began in early childhood. Her mother, a poet, often invited artists of all disciplines to their home. Her father, a doctor and a lover of drawing, used to take her to concerts and talk to her about Debussy. One piece Joan loved is Betsy Jolas's *Quatuor II.* She and Betsy were friends, and Joan paid tribute to her in her great multipanel painting *Quatuor II for Betsy Jolas* (1976, plate 87).

Joan was American and rooted in the culture of jazz, gospel music, and the blues. She listened to Charlie Parker. She was intimately attached to voices. Among her favorites were Bessie Smith, Ella Fitzgerald, and Nina Simone. But she particularly loved Billie Holiday. The two women seemed to share an intensity, an inner tragedy, a sense of solitude, an unsatisfied need for love. She spoke of Piaf, of attending a concert in New York, of her emotion, her admiration. She discussed the song "La Vie en rose" and its implicit message. And I in turn responded, "Allez venez, Milord."[12] After all, one has to smile.

Bursts of laughter, complicity.

It was good in the studio, with its lingering smell of turpentine. Joan would say: "Homey, isn't it?" Yes, it was the home of the heart, or maybe the heart of the home, filled with her "musique à peindre," as she called it. She would explain, almost blushing: "You know, opera, orchestra, voices, emotion, Pavarotti, Callas, Domingo, all the others. Verdi, Puccini. You understand?"

I can't list everything she listened to. Monteverdi, Purcell, then Bach and Handel, suites, concertos, operas, oratorios, cantatas. Among her favorites were Bach's *Cantata no. 78* and, in particular, the duet Cantata BWV 78, "Allein zu dir." She was passionate about the operas of Mozart—especially *Don Giovanni,* but also *The Magic Flute*. I nicknamed her "La Reine de la Nuit."[13]

She listened to Haydn's *The Creation,* Beethoven, the symphonies, quartets, sonatas. Then she moved on to the nineteenth century: Schubert; Schumann; Brahms, with Fischer-Dieskau interpreting; the lied to deep love, tragedy in miniature, piano and voice. And also the orchestra, with the great Berlioz and his *Cleopatra*; Mahler's *Kindertotenlieder*; Strauss's last lieder and his operas. And let's not forget Italy! Orchestra again, solo voices and choirs, Bellini, Donizetti, Verdi—Joan knew all of his operas. Puccini's *Madame Butterfly* and *Turandot,* not to mention Bartók's *Bluebeard's Castle* and his quartets, Berg's *Wozzeck,* and so many others...

The needle on the old record player in the studio constantly needed to be changed. It labored ceaselessly, developing for the oldest of the albums a totally locked groove, the famous *sillon fermé* of a Pierre Schaeffer who would have adored it. How fabulous then, when a romantic duet is stuck on one word for eternity—or, better yet, when the death song of a heroine contemplating suicide never concludes, instead repeating endlessly. What a perfect warm-up for a painter who then works in a trancelike state.

In the main house, for the *salon de musique*—Joan's words—I bought an upright piano after returning from Italy, a Grotrian-Steinweg. I loved its generous sound—its amber color. Joan asked me sometimes to sit and play. "Improvise if you want."

So I did. And she listened, silent, gazing toward the Seine and the lake. She was already at work; she fed on the intermingling of the sounds and colors. Her chin rested on one of her hands. She had a faraway look and listened in a somewhat detached way, *écoute flottante*.

We talked about music. Webern, occasionally—his Bagatelles—*oeuvre atomique*. Or maybe a concerto grosso of Handel, creating its own life with a micro-cell in the last movement. Or Varèse with his *Amériques* and *Déserts*. We discussed electroacoustic music, white noise, filtering sounds, loops, textures, weaving, ranges in space, mixing, clusters—a language shared between the painter and the musician.

Technique always yields and gives way to the inner music—emotion—with this word dear to the painter: "Feeling." Joan often said, "I can only paint with a feeling of love." A shared expression. And so the song of the soul arises from the infinity of sound, as with the indomitable Beethoven in his *Pastoral Symphony*—his hymn to nature, "The Storm."

I reflect on the texture of the strokes to be imposed on the canvas, to be given rhythm and sound, weighted toward the top or the bottom of the picture. I consider the ranges available to the musician—the creation of a space—upward, the possibility of transparency, the diaphanous and downward, somber hues, intensity. The colors of the musician are nourished by numerous timbres and their clever interplay, by the structure of sounds and occasionally by a very free modality, universal, almost elementary, which creates a feeling, an emotion, or even some simple intervals connected, which themselves transform into timbres. All is possible.

Messiaen told his students, "You can do everything." We talked about his work, his ideas concerning sound and color, his catalogue of birds. Total liberty of language, no barriers. The same is true for the painter.

We listened to Stravinsky, an extract from *The Rite of Spring, Petrouchka*. Then Boulez, Xenakis, Ligeti...

Joan was a master of color. And she was perfectly at home in certain worlds of sound. At her request I spoke to her about *Sterne,* a work for a full orchestra that she heard live in concert.[14] We talked about white noise, certain frequencies that together effaced colors in the manner of white ground on an unpainted canvas.

A full orchestra provides the possibility of filtering sound material, producing harmonic fields, territories of color, possible energies. So *Sterne* sometimes uses strings *très divisées,* with many woodwinds and brasses, a piano, and six percussionists. The history of the work begins with a dedication, a tribute to Dubonnet, the goldfish that belonged to the little girl who lived in Chicago. Joan had told me about his disappearance down the toilet, her mother having emptied the bowl too quickly. So poor Dubonnet perished by drowning, a tragic end for a fish.

We gazed at the Seine; we listened to the rain. Barges glided by in a slow, endless procession. The Seine, sometimes lost in mists, invisible, the fog suddenly breaking to reveal a deep black penetrating the woolly white clouds. Barges carrying coal, a thousand charcoal pencils. Deep tones. A drumstick, its sound muffled by thick, tender wool but also very high sounds, no vibrato.

Rain, rains, strong west winds... *Little Rain* (1989, plate 121), *Rained On, No Rain* (1976, plate 89), *Rain, Blue Rain*...[15]

I am struck by the percussive nature of some of her paintings—*Salut Patou, Clinging Vine, Sarrians* (1977, plate 94), and others. They demonstrate a different vitality, a distinctive use of color. It is a bit like the story of *Little Rain,* a work for two percussionists that adds keyboards to the other instruments. Joan took up this title later for a painting. It is also the story of *Rained On,* a work for three percussionists that contains a hidden reference to the *Grande Vallée*—another moment of sharing, this time in homage to the painting *Rained On,* an earlier work by the painter.

Complicity with titles, underground meanings.

And then there is the wonderful diptych *Blue Rain*. It inspired a composition by the same title for two pianists and two percussionists following the painter's death. It was followed by *Rain,* a work for four percussionists that likewise pays tribute to the painter and her work. These pieces followed one another like a series of paintings, limitlessly exploring and revisiting themes and variations.

La Grande Vallée was another part of our shared story. A valley of childhood, of vibrations, where one can hear the sounds of nature, the origin of many percussive works. A lyrical, poetic valley, reuniting life and death. The first concerts with blades of grass or straw acting as flutes, very basic xylophones formed by pieces of cardboard affixed in a bicycle's wheels. And then the metallic buzzing of insects, certain bird songs, the croaking of frogs, the whispering winds and the water lapping. Here there is the feeling of a landscape in which sound and color are one.

Joan asked me again and again to tell her about *La Grande Vallée*—"and the colors." I spoke to her of *Fritillaires damier*—thousands of them, in fields of purple.[16] The brilliant yellow of dandelions. A sky that is cloudy until an explosion of blue. I described the greenness of the meadows, the waters of the Tlalocs, the ecstasy of love, this land in motion, this spiraling world that reaches up endlessly toward the sky. Joan entered into this mysterious valley accompanied by a very long retinue of poets. She made this valley her own and provided these dearest friends a home.

It was a time of intense creation—feverish, meaningful, and life enhancing, painting after painting. Sound masses moving forward and backward, counterpoints producing the same imperious energy as a work by Bach—such as his overture to the Passion of Saint John, as its initial tempo, so difficult to comprehend, finally reaches the dramatic perfection of the narrative. And then the first shattering cry of the great choir—as sudden and violent as a tube of paint spurting its color onto the canvas.

A rule we shared: music must remain something alive; painting too. It was a sort of ascetic quest in our two studios. And all around were pacific deities such as Charchoune, who makes no distinction between music and painting, or Feldman, who does the same in his unforgettable *Rothko Chapel*.

While Joan listened to Billie Holiday or perhaps Purcell and *Dido's Lament,* I dreamed of didgeridoos, Tibetan trumpets, bass trombones and pedal sounds, African percussions and drums rolling forever, rhythms of life. I pondered the hypnotic modes of Bali, in fast and slow motion, the music of Gamelan, the cries of the wandering Bauls of Bengal, the *cencerros* (cowbells), a vibrant land, a thousand colors, a thousand sounds, the song—harsh tones—of an old woman, a gypsy tune suspended to the fierce G string of a violin, a world in motion but also an impression of quiet joy.

And then Curie . . . the hospital . . . The curtain half-open, for now it was time . . . And then again, a new dawn, a sunrise, dripping with fire, and the promises of Frank O'Hara: "We shall have everything we want and there'll be no more dying . . ."[17]

And so the painter went away with all her colors, on a very long journey, this journey with no end. And I continued the story, a story with no beginning. I composed, in tribute, *Un jardin pour Audrey*; along with *I Shin Den Shin,* a message of love; then a *Petit Matin*; then *Un autre jardin.*[18]

Joan, now very busy in her great studio, which she had described before taking the barque, Charon's barque that she loved so much to point to on the Seine, a mysterious old boat opposite our studios and to the left. Joan paints: "The studio is larger, with my dogs on the grass. *The Sky is Blue, the Grass is Green*."[19] And I hear Callas, and the beam quivers, and all is perfection.

I gaze at *Two Pianos* again and again. I listen to the tones, shared and secret, magnetic waves, crashing loudly, wave after wave, without beginning or end . . .

The song . . .

A song . . .

And all is perfection.

Translated from French by Alastair Gunn

To a Sunflower

Joyce Pensato

FIG 1 Left to right: Gisèle Barreau, Joan Mitchell, and Joyce Pensato on the patio at La Tour, Vétheuil, France, ca. 1983. Courtesy the Estate of Joyce Pensato

FIG 2 Joyce Pensato and Joan Mitchell with Mitchell's German shepherds at La Tour, Vétheuil, France, ca. 1983. Courtesy the Estate of Joyce Pensato

I met Joan Mitchell in the late 1970s, when I was in my sixth year at the New York Studio School. Another student, Hollis Jeffcoat, recommended she come see my work. I heard a knock on the door, and when I opened it a woman who looked to me like the '40s, from the movies, like Lauren Bacall with a fur coat, was standing there. And someone said, "This is Joan." My anger went out of me, and I said, "Oh my God, it's Joan Mitchell!" At that time I was doing Batman and Mickey drawings. They were covering the whole floor, and I loaded her up with them. She had glasses, she was tough looking, and I wanted to be just like her. She said, "Why don't we go up the block to Shakespeare for a drink." I didn't have any money, and as a shy student I felt like I couldn't order any food. I didn't eat and I had six martinis. By nine o'clock, I had passed out. After that she called me "Six Martinis Joyce." That was our first meeting.

Joan would come into town and take us everywhere—Fourcade, the bars—and at night we would take her home to St. Mark's. When [Jean Paul] Riopelle left her, there was all this drama, screaming. But then she was free of a man who had always gotten all the fucking attention. *La Vie en rose*—that fantastic, huge painting—is her saying, "Now I can be who I am, I have nothing left to lose" (1979, plate 99). She started inviting us to come to France in the summer—she wanted to give to young people. There was nothing going on in Brooklyn, and she had this incredible place in France, and she was paying my way. Carl [Plansky] and I called it the Fresh Air Fund. She called me "Joycie," and she'd make fun of my Brooklyn accent. The first time she invited me for the summer, it ended up being March to September. I got brainwashed for six months, and that's how I found out who I am.

Joan would say to me, "It's like ice-skating: color and light." Van Gogh was her boy. New York was about drawing; when she went to France, she found her color and light. The *Petit Matin* paintings are so beautiful. *La Lande* was on the wall, in a room looking out at the Seine, and it never came down—it was so important to her. She had a connection to the linden tree outside the house. All of this connected to painting, and it was all inside her head—she didn't have to go outside. We spent most of our time indoors, working and talking, but we did walk in the garden. Gisèle's small garden was very important to her, and she was also really proud of her squashes. But mostly on those walks, she would point out all the different sunflowers: that one's a teenager, there's a young one, there's an old one. And then, the dying sunflowers—she would bring them into the studio. These things also became important to me. I got out of myself, and she made me see things. I think she was doing her best work then.

And yet she was so dark, she could be so heavy. Joan was such a tough bitch. She would demand, "Do you want to be one of those German Expressionists, or do you want to have French color?" I would parrot back, "Joan, I don't want to be one of those German Expressionists, I want to have French color." I realized later that I was a German Expressionist. What she gave me was intensity. When she was depressed, it was painting, doggies, what you love. Painting would make her feel great—*any* painting, even bad painting. "Put your feelings in there." She repeated that over and over. "Don't just paint some shit, like you don't care." Feelings were something very deep, and they gave you something more than just paintings. Her paintings conveyed her own very deep, deep feelings—about the Seine, about her sister's death, about her friends dying—she knew ahead of time, while she was working, that the paintings were for them, what their colors were, how she felt about them. Some of the *Grande Vallée* paintings are dedicated to friends.

We were all connected to Edrita Fried. Joan said, "Carl has to go to a shrink." He was my best friend, and he went to Edrita, and then Edrita recommended her daughter Jacqui. I saw Jacqui for twenty-five years. In Vétheuil, we knew to go to bed by midnight or there would be group therapy 'til 6 a.m. Joan would write morning notes critiquing our psychology, our behavior. She would take out Edrita's book, *The Courage to Change,* and read from it, and we would pass it around like the Bible. I remember her making the painting for Edrita. I remember the colors, the blue and the orange and gold—Edrita's colors. Edrita was beautiful and she had so much strength. A classic European shrink, very impressive. Those colors had her mood—even and stable, calm. Edrita was Joan's lifeline for thirty years. We talked about her all the time. I met her at Jacqui's office once. She came out into the waiting room and said, "You remind me of Gisèle." Gisèle had that intensity, a deep passion for music and the garden and life—Joan saw that in her.

We were the little Joanie family for a few years, in New York and France, in letters and late-night Sunday phone calls. At La Tour, we'd go into her studio at night and it was like a party, with music blasting—she loved Maria Callas and she loved jazz. There was Scotch. Carl and Joan dancing. The three dogs. Joan laughing and drinking. That's what I miss. She gave me her studio for part of that first summer in Vétheuil. I'd go there in the morning and scream to get my anger out and my feelings and energy up, ready to paint. The neighbors started complaining, so I would crank up the Patti Smith record *Horses* so they couldn't hear me. I was trying to paint myself, but Joan always said, "You have veils on, you are hiding yourself." And she tried to get me to love something—a tree, a bird, a flower—outside myself. She didn't want to be known as just "a woman artist." There were so few women in the '70s whom I could point to and say, "Wow, she's not one of the guys, there she is—a strong woman." But that was Joan. She meant so much to me.

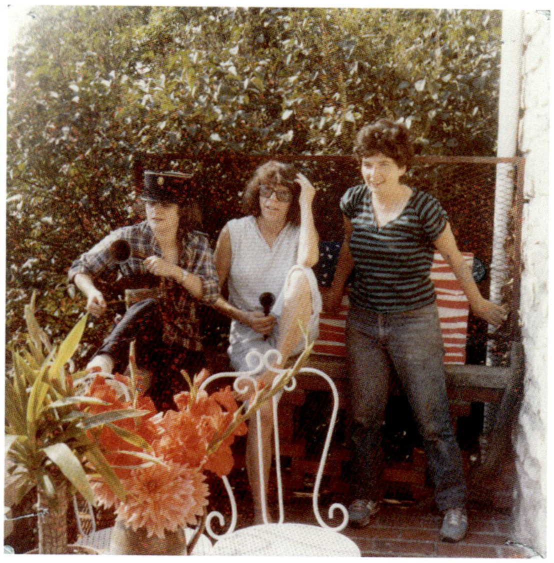

1

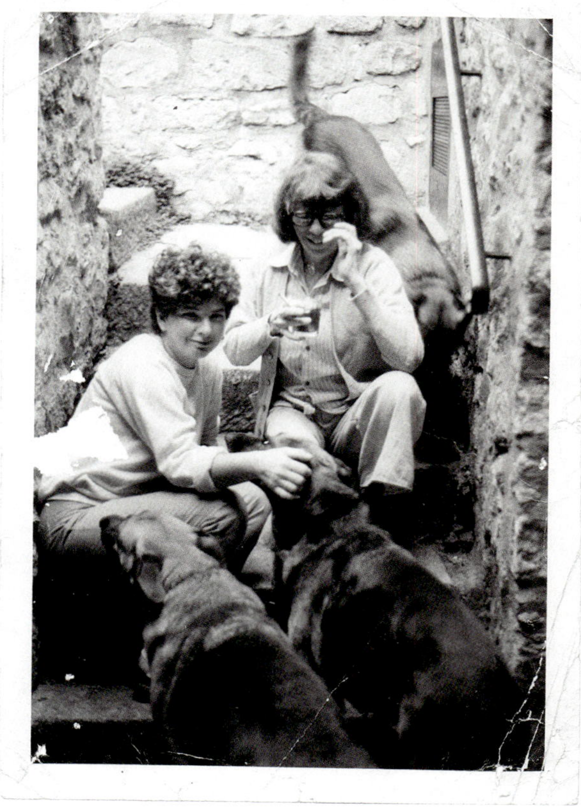

2

This text was developed in consultation with Joyce Pensato based on a series of interviews conducted by Katy Siegel between January and June 2019 for exhibition research purposes.

October 30, 1992

Joan died last night!

I'll miss calling you,
you giving me a hard time,
making me feel special
My past
Knowing you were there!

. . .

You were my art mother. Mostly you taught me how to see. You taught me who I was not.

After that 6 months, you were my board that I could go against so that I could become. I know I wasn't a French painter (color & light). I'm just a girl from Brooklyn, an American, who loves to draw and draws well. You tried Joan—to make a French painter out of me. I still have those drawings—I'll miss you—I know when I would call you—you gave me your full attention like I was the only one existing. I'll always remember you—the Grammar lady—most of all when I look back I laugh.

FIG 3 Letter from Joyce Pensato to Joan Mitchell, ca. November 8, 1979. Joan Mitchell Foundation Archives, New York

. . .

I'll miss you—
there is no one to call in France knowing you could call late because Joan is up painting & would be happy to talk to you. "Give you a hard time." I know you're with your dogs, you have your shrink, your sister there, some friends. I hope you get a good studio.

I'll be thinking of you—you were my mentor that women were just as good as men & could be out there as a painter who breathes it eats it lived for her dogs, music & to paint. I will remember & always, always when Mozart comes on, or Maria Callas. I will always remember you.

To a Sunflower
To a painter who I respect

Love,
Joyce

From Joyce Pensato's journal

There are so few women painters one
can look up to. (Your one of them)
Keep the brushes going!
Looking forward to seeing you +
your work

Love
Joyce

PS I may be the first to paint in
a fur coat!

Carl said I looked
like Lauren Bacall
at the easel

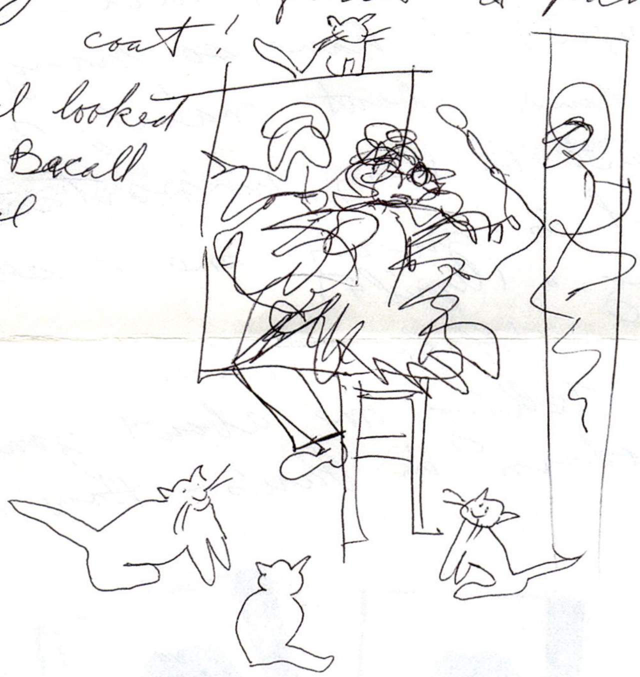

3

Eight Poems and Joan Mitchell's *City Landscape*

Eileen Myles

City Landscape is illustrated as plate 14.

The cab driver was a cute young man with a rasping voice. He picked me up at Toyota and he was taking me way across town. Last day in town doing my errands. The guy had an accent, and I tried to locate him, being self-excited about what a world traveler I am, and how political. He grew up in Brooklyn.

We philosophized. How is your day. Each day is pretty good he espoused a casual gratitude, what is ever so bad. It's good, he smiled. Excuse me. His phone was ringing. Do you mind if I take it, no I allowed just as long as we *get there*. He spoke to someone. My cousin died, he told me when he got off.

I'm sorry. Was it sudden. Was he sick. He hesitated. He was shot. Silence filled the cab. I'm sorry I said helplessly when I got out. Anything I said was impotent, impossible in relation to his news. I continued my day.

When Shaw wrote *Saint Joan,* he never knew her. "He had never seen her walk, never heard her talk, could never have been haunted by any of those infinitesimal, inimitable tones, turns, tics, quirks, which are different in every human being . . ." wrote James Baldwin who had known Malcolm X and was struggling to write a screenplay about him after his death, and apparently it was really hard.

I never met Joan. It strikes me that I *could* have met her and more than once I'm sure we were in the same room. She visited Joe LeSueur who lived right around the corner from me on Second Ave and Robert Harms who's a painter and a friend met her there for the first time one night in 1982 and *I* will forever insist I was home that night and if my phone rang of course I would have come running.

I've stood outside her building on St. Mark's Place, the New York address she lived in the most and I've thought about the building. It's a nice one. I think of it as Zen because of the gates on the first floor windows that pass beyond simple function into desire. The building is cool, gray green, which is probably not true, but I'm painting from memory. Baldwin says Ray Charles said tell the truth as an anthem, but that's easier in singing than painting. Right? Does painting tell the truth. Poetry doesn't, I'll say that.

Both dour and showgirl

bit of a car

honking yet

hellenistic

I mean if there were really

formal lipstick

pure thought

uttering the carnal truth

of philosophy

he comes and

goes and there's nothing

hotter than that

a cloudy day

and then she

lifts the blinds

It strikes me that I didn't meet her because of misogyny. Imagine misogyny in New York. City full of us (women) loving and bouncing off each other. Moving around each other, ignoring each other, meeting each other a lot, straight or gay, despite men. As long as she lived the men I knew who knew her would say Myles, or hey Ei-leen, have you met J-O-O-A-A-N. Then there was a kind of silent double take, like they were imagining what that would be like and it made them laugh. What did they see. I felt it, for sure. And it gave them pleasure.

I'm talking about the terror of Joan, or perhaps the terror of Eileen. The terror behind all artists, probably humans. Female artists for sure. It was impossible to know which terror they meant. Because the laughter at our imagined encounter meant that this was something that should never happen. And so it did not. The laughter meant these creatures would claw at each other somehow, and it wouldn't be fun. Or it was more fun to imagine. There was a particular architecture to the imaginary meeting, a building that couldn't get built without some fur flying, some skin, some blood on the floor. Some body parts for sure would wind up deep in the cement. That was the legend, the myth. I always of course assumed it was about her, though I didn't ignore the snark and go ahead and find Joan Mitchell for myself and say hi I'm Eileen, because obviously I knew what they meant.

We all lived in New York. Every woman is one of "them" right. We come to the city fangs out, and everyone tells you not to act that way. Don't be a monster, a shrew, a bitch. I love this big horny red painting (*City Landscape*) because it's bitch work. It's tooth and claw.

Took a hot bike ride one day in late July around New York to look at all of her apartments.

one day I imagine

it sails past

so all the structure

holds the

impertinence

if I can have

that or a sword

First place she lived was 267 West 11th. I admire the newel, the curling metal grip of the balustrade, the handrail leading up to the fancy ass door of the building. By that I mean an extremely ornamental black one, all kinds of braided sunbursts, tree escutcheons and raised stuff on it. The door had to have been there then, almost seventy years ago. She moved in the week I was born! When Joan Mitchell walked up to that building she probably said wow, I'll take it. Barney look at *that door*.

Turns out there's a tiny metal gate to the right of the building, itself full of grates and scrolls, and it leads to the single-story building behind 267 West 11th, where Joan and Barney actually wound up living. There's a landmark case going on right now, and if it goes the owner's way the small building will soon be a teardown.

Out front there's a flyer on a post. It says:

Horoscopes for Dogs
Wellness for Dogs

And a dog face, of course.

Then it says:

CHEAP
CHEAP
CHEAP

In New York I think at this same time Joan Mitchell lived with a brown poodle named George. As well as Barney Rosset.

The apartment's near where St. Vincent's Hospital used to be. It's loaded with churches, two red ones on her block and as you walked toward Greenwich Ave you can see the green spire of the Jefferson Library over on 6th Ave, right next door to the Women's House of Detention, richly described by Tom Wolfe but for everybody else it was just part of the scene.

St. Vincent's was many different things. In the '70s it's where you didn't want to go. Very violent lots of shootings in that emergency room. Later, it was the AIDS hospital. Christine Quinn a city councilor who aspired to be mayor let her girlfriend a realtor sell it. Huge mistake. It's why she didn't win. So it's gone.

Greenwich Avenue's sidewalk is interrupted by grilles venting the subway below and the rumble of the trains is a lot of what you know about this street apart from its angle, Greenwich Ave veering always, which is useful since everything else (Charles, Perry) comes off of it and it's heading east.

59 West 9th was on a tree-lined block. The building was branded with "1839." It had black gates round the stoop. People used to sit out there on summer nights drinking beers. Now only the tenants can sit. This apartment's right around the corner from the Women's House of Detention, now long gone but definitely there when Joan stepped out on the avenue to get the subway, catch a cab or walk cross town she could hear those women scream. This was the last stop before she and Barney broke up.

He stayed on West 9th and Joan moved into her studio at 51 West 10th, an address which now is totally gone. It was apparently eaten up by the Peter, green and nondistinctive, which covers about three addresses now. My friend suggested it's a translation of the Pierre uptown which is so New York in its sheer tackiness and it *is* pretty funny. But do developers have a sense of humor?

Across the street from her gone apartment there's one building that is blue and orange, and parked in front of it, twee-ly enough, is a scooter of the same two bright colors. It's not good. It's Pappagallo bad. Next to it a white building bears a roughened sign that says GROSVENOR PRIVATE BOARDING STABLE.

I got pretty excited about this, wondering if Joan rode, and *here*. Wouldn't that be cool and she *was* a jock. But the stable was actually gone by the end of the 19th century so the sign is merely for charm. Edward Albee lived there after he made some money on *Who's Afraid of Virginia Woolf* which happened in 1962.

But they also I think wouldn't have liked each other and Joan would've been gone by then.

interior brain
which is
color

jaws leeching

what
mumbled
memory

making a portrait of a place that has violence and grace

climbing
up New York
for a time

if I stare too
long I lose
what it
says which
is once

I began wondering if any old stones from the earlier buildings made the Peter. Of course there's a word for that phenomenon, the repurposed bricks, here it is: *spolia*. Because it was once a stable street I thought about cobblestones which were largely designed for the size of horseshoes (4 × 5 inches) so the horses would be secure as they stepped.

You can't think about cobblestones and horses without hearing them in your mind somehow if only from movies.

Only 15 miles of cobblestoned streets remain in New York today, unlike 1949 when there were 140. So many of these addresses of Joan's are in prime cobblestone territory. Greenwich Avenue must have been cobblestoned. The east village was, 2nd Ave. She was a drinker, and I'm thinking of the sound and the reality of walking home drunk on cobblestones talking loudly about the night. And being young. Joan painted *City Landscape* when she was thirty, really a perfect age. For a woman, having a little bit of authority then.

Pretty
much a nature
painting of
New York
whatever
the plug
gy buil
dings
or else two
rivers dirty &
beige like
cartons of eggs
the island
is a slash of
depravity & want
and an unfair
exchange if we re
member that
tobacco
& beads

in fact the bouquet
is extended
every day in a dirty
hand, the river
gets cleaner
the light is the
point the incred
ible bounce
that makes
all the sad ads
and the ready legs
softer than
they should & the tables
at night full of us are fun
you can hear
this painting.

In a 1957 piece called "Mitchell Paints a Picture," Irving Sandler says that she lived in a 4th-floor walk-up on the lower east side, which is what they called it then.

From that I know she lived high which I bet she always did, which will take us in a minute to Chicago. But I also think Sandler was a friend because the walk up sounds poor and I can't help thinking that not only was her gender a problem, as a young female painter, but her wealth. But the combination plus the love of a man caused her to move to Paris just like James Baldwin (who I and all of New York are reading now) who I also think she wouldn't have been friends with though they had a lot in common I believe. They shared a timing, a discomfort, an analytic. I think both of them understood the limits on who they were and when they were. New York was his home, it wasn't hers, but both of them for different reasons just as compelling had to get out.

Joan as I imagined liked to get down and dirty but she didn't want to live there. But that's New York.

This brash pancake. All those blocks of colourless sections invaded by tiny runnels of colour (pools of rain). Wonder what to do with the muscularity, cause something pedestalizes, it slows everything down right beneath the splashing wad of colour.

Think furniture: is it a chair, a body, a lap. Stand back. A fountain. I don't mean so much to see things but to describe their effect. I'll say it. It's such physical work. Years later in France she'd go outside and absorb the light and then she'd come back inside her studio. It's why she liked dogs. They had it all.

Here she squares the thing off almost to give elbow room to the portrait, the red profile, this battering bash of colour—what is it, a landscape, an inventory of the feeling of a place, an infernal busyness not a noun but *so many* people around, the acts, such blaring, the ever-incessant calendaring, seasons, the self, always the *need*. It's such a human painting.

The traffic up above (this is imaginary) trimming the shape.

First admittedly I thought the subject of *City Landscape* was the lake, cause I was *in* Chicago, but no it (the painting) is definitely New York: the river, rivers, and the sky upside either or the other hanging down.

Then there are all those bars, these clumpy slashes, black on top measuring time, also beneath the mess and it, its heart, its bunched up maroon beating heart, it has raucous heft. And when you think of it—walking through the city (cause the painting holds everything), the various lit scenes, dim, radiant, actually finally (truly the worst word in the world) *creative*. The city is creative. But Joan felt squeezed. This is that. It's a party but it's also a bright ripe incredible squeezure. Who can do this dance exactly. One becomes drunken. I mean how many dead men are walking around. City full of ghosts. Bright, sneering, trashy color, that's Joan, inexcusably exact, a source of upending forcefulness.

I look to the left and the right standing *in* the Art Institute of Chicago. Am I allowed to take a picture. It's something I've been thinking for a while. Was there a Black Joan. A Black Joan of Arc. Condola Rashad played her on Broadway in 2018. I'm staring at that time code again (the black thing on the top, and blackness in painting is power) when I first thought "clouds," if it's not this city. Argh, of course not. Not Chicago, it's New York. It's America. Looking at clouds, the dirty flower, rivers, the fist. Not so much a heart. A fist. Think muscular. The cream advancing to the bottom, then she bends the *J* of her name like an *L*. It hovers like a sign without import above that small swath of black holding up. Just holding, holding.

Meanwhile all the docents are waving around. I pull back to admire the pillows, the collages, the tiles of her background, these units that forge the incredible squalor called *City Landscape*: this.

It strikes me that this beautiful painting is ugly.

I mean at first I thought since I was *here* I would write about her great painting *The Lake,* but then I learned it's not here, it's in a museum in Japan, and they are renovating, so *The Lake* is in storage.

trains
units
way
oh awesome
nothing
a beach
a dinosaur
Joan you
tremble
city beach
warped
peeing
looking down
on the drake
1 million
dollar apartments
down there
blurry
cross-eyed
wide ribbon
swathe
you don't
read
all of Proust
at once
you don't
the cars
stream
north
doodle
Peter gestures
there's so many
good buildings
in Chicago

Peter used to live in New York. A lawyer, he once dated a friend of mine, Anne, and today I ran into him on Halstead. We decided to get a drink and went to one of those big-view places, Chicago's loaded with them. We went to this top of a building called 360 Chicago. It was night and we saw it of course, Lake Michigan, like a gilded scar, a bog with traffic streaming (it sizzled) like a single sprawling limb, and that made Joan want to paint when she was young day and night most likely and all year it changes.

I found a way up into the building where she lived. Lo! One "unit" was *available*. The young agent, Harry, enthusiastically took us up. I'm with a Chicago artist, Karolina Gnatowski. We wandered its endless procession of rooms, and always there was that big blue sucker down there, leering, on the lit side of that apartment. I leaned my hip on several casements, kneeling, stretching with my phone and notebook, trying to get what she saw.

The gesture was pointless, but you have to put your body through the work to not be a ghost.

She saw a blue lake. It was a feeling. Weirdly, today or yesterday was Joan Mitchell's birthday. I thought of that picture of her diving into a pool. Phallic woman pierces the pool. The lake is just out there. I will paint. Probably a rich girl's need to escape. Not just breaking the surface, but making it. It's either that or into the ether.

Harry hovered for a while, then he left, he said feel free so after a while as we began to leave I kept stopping the elevator at each funereal entrance, gold yellow brown, there were twelve floors, each as big as a football field and each entrance different yet you couldn't be more staid. Clearly the rich prefer to be dead. Each plant each pot, all had its own deep suburban theme. And of course while we ogled each floor (I took pictures) we held the elevator hostage forcing the tenants to take the freight elevator. Harry flamed at me later on when I thanked him for the access. He put me in my place. I thought you were *legit*. Back to New York where we are a bunch of bastards. Past the river, leaving the city, but always coming back.

can't exactly write
a poem at
that
fisted
so that what she grasped
is muscular
statuesque
this is a foisted
map of a red
and hungry
island. It's fish
that populate
the borders
dead fish & old
condoms, bodies
balloons caught in trees

the occasional pa
rade, the lurch of bus
iness, a good fun
eral brings everyone
out, a lunch

let's have a drink
even that synagogue
facing chinatown

at night and fog

Manhattan Island is pretty much shimmer all day long, we manage to live in the effect of that echoing light.

What's that? River light he said and just think of the action of two moving bands of water reflecting the sky, tossing that up into the air.

Though the buildings broke it, the skyscrapers were named after the tallest mast of a ship too damn many ships now but if you look at the right time of day down the right street that's shooting across the island you can see it still almost green like Joan's painting hovers violently true. An incantation: light the day and the suffusion cooling as you head toward the river at dusk in summer. The city empties and moves toward the edges, supple and slippery and those squares of greenish and stained husks of color support, her painting *it, its* wavering musculature.

There's just one last thing to say about Chicago: it wants to tower and see its own single body in flames like a saint and the wind comes down from the north and that's in this painting too a high grandiosity against the plains whereas it takes a certain kind of intelligence, New York does. Really, here we're just all pushed around like cattle, here we either splay or play. So the painting's both. Both cities now.

I do it from memory now the painting and the island I remember framed by the two rivers, early mapmakers named both shores Manahatta, a double, but they were just copying something wrong from earlier as the heated city exploded into a raggedy exaggerated confection of pain, enjoyment, embarrassment, crisis, and commerce.

fear of the atom
bomb makes

colors recklessly

wide like a ship
wreck, con
fetti fix the ex
cess by voting

business en
velopes
have their own
velocity, the teeth

bite down
on a sandwich
of love, her maw
makes men
feel both
excited and alone
her body's not in it,

no myth but
a pith, flagrant and pomp
ous, are we
there yet, did we
miss

O you who take cabs up and across the island, you'd def be smoking in one though we don't do that anymore. Joan did. You could just take a checker. Flip down the seats, open the windows, smoking your cigs, everyone pile in.

David Rattray told me long ago (in the 20th century) that *Manhattan* meant "isle of general intoxication" because the white people gave the Native people whiskey but it's actually not true. We have better indigenous translators now. It actually means "the place where bows are gathered." Manhattan (before contact and still for a while) had a lot of hickory trees, which are perfect for that purpose. Making bows not arrows. Arrows are made from a single branch and a different wood. Inwood Hill Park remains an old growth forest, and there's part of the original salt marsh there which used to surround the island and up there are still some of those very same trees, the ones since from before the arrival of the Dutch. It's where you'd go to get your bow, Joan did, and left.

This city landscape is nothing but social. It's the direct approach of somebody giving you flowers now let's go out. It's the bloodied road called Broadway that once was an Indian trail.

Brooklyn's over here possibly under the painting there's no that's west and this is north. There's a thrust to the painting, so this is positioned, positioning.

Did you know the Carnasee Lenape were the original tribe never mind the punk clubs in the '80s nights at Dave's Luncheonette on Canal after the Mudd Club but I don't have a cent. Take a boat at the tip to get off Manahatta, try it one night late on the water the greatest relief imagine coming for a solid century with no visas no green cards by the way hordes kept storming its colors. Gate to come or gate to go? Joan left. Sort of. Every horse falling in Five Points and someone sticks a handbill on the poor dead animal's body and began thrusting flyers into the crowd there gaping here's your next opportunity, a deal. In London at the Tate we bivouacked this way and that everyone excited to see one another, a crowd this local monster here this town of coteries would actually be happier outside smoking I hate a crowd everyone says it and dives back in or on to the next. Uncontainable probably cause the city's not a swarm, more of a slice. This squirting island. We are squeezed like that small fish grasped upside down shimmering within our own screaming limits, shivering, caught in the air that's the firmament so it's nothing but want.

a shower
a pile
of mistakes
Writ large

elevation so squashed
almost
a crated day
desiring

you're what
I want

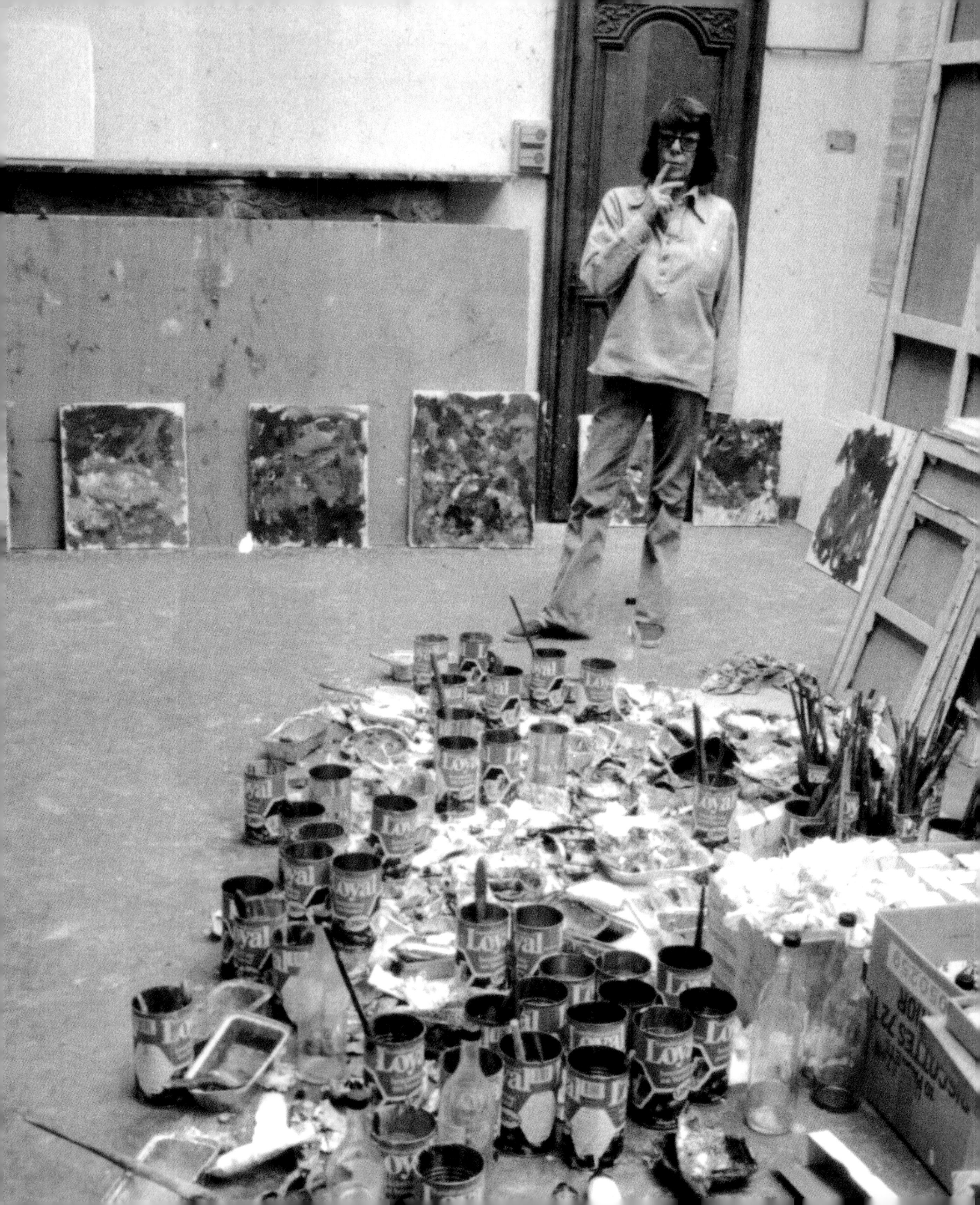
Loyal

References

Note to the Reader

In order to fully understand Joan Mitchell's historical and social context, the authors of this book have drawn not only from published accounts but also from a range of primary sources, including materials held at the Joan Mitchell Foundation Archives and in other personal and institutional archival collections, as well as personal recollections of those who knew the artist. Transcripts of interviews conducted by the curatorial team and other original research files will be made available through the institutional archives at The Baltimore Museum of Art and the San Francisco Museum of Modern Art.

In quotations from primary documents, orthography has been standardized throughout this publication. For example, following the multivolume catalogue raisonné authored by Yseult Riopelle et al. and published by Hibou beginning in 1999, "Jean-Paul Riopelle" is rendered "Jean Paul Riopelle." All other omissions (denoted by ellipses) or additions (set in brackets) are indicated. Translations appearing throughout these texts were made by the authors unless otherwise noted. The names of artworks by Mitchell titled in French are capitalized following Académie française guidelines, as this was the style most commonly followed in publications during her lifetime.

Abbreviations for frequently cited sources:

AAA: Archives of American Art, Smithsonian Institution, Washington, D.C.

Albers Papers: Patricia Albers personal papers

Fourcade Archives: Xavier Fourcade, Inc. Archives Materials were made available for our research by Jill Weinberg Adams, New York.

Goldberg Papers, AAA: Michael Goldberg Papers, 1942–1981, Archives of American Art, Smithsonian Institution, Washington, D.C.

Note: Most of Mitchell's letters to Goldberg are undated. Where possible, we have assigned dates (indicated in brackets) based on our research and the contents of the letters. As an aid to future research, the first line of the cited material is included when first cited for letters with uncertain dates.

GRI: Getty Research Institute, Los Angeles

Jackson Gallery Archives: Martha Jackson Gallery Archives, UB Anderson Gallery, University at Buffalo

JMFA: Joan Mitchell Foundation Archives, New York

Frequently cited collections are identified in the following pages by collection number only.

JMFA001: Joan Mitchell Papers

JMFA003: Joan Mitchell letters to Barney Rosset

JMFA004: Joan Mitchell Exhibition Records

JMFA008: Joan Mitchell letters to Patricia Molloy

JMFA018: Joan Mitchell letters to Joanne Von Blon

Munro Papers, AAA: Eleanor Munro Papers, Archives of American Art, Smithsonian Institution, Washington, D.C.

Munro interview transcript, [1977], Munro Papers, AAA: Joan Mitchell, interview by Eleanor Munro, "Joan Mitchell" transcript by Pat King, box 31, folder 25, Eleanor Munro Papers, Archives of American Art, Smithsonian Institution, Washington, D.C.

Munro typewritten interview notes, [1977], Munro Papers, AAA: Joan Mitchell, typescript interview notes by Eleanor Munro, n.p., box 31, folder 26, Eleanor Munro Papers, Archives of American Art, Smithsonian Institution, Washington, D.C.

Nochlin, AAA oral history: "Oral history interview with Joan Mitchell, conducted by Linda Nochlin," April 16, 1986, Archives of American Art, Smithsonian Institution, Washington, D.C., https://www.aaa.si.edu/collections/interviews/oral-history-interview-joan-mitchell-12183

Riopelle Archives: Yseult Riopelle Archives, Montreal

Sandler Papers, GRI: All documents cited are held in box 22, folder 14, Irving Sandler Papers, Getty Research Institute, Los Angeles. Citations differentiate between handwritten notes made during the interview, and the subsequent, and slightly revised, typewritten version.

Seckler, AAA oral history: "Oral history interview with Joan Mitchell, conducted by Dorothy Gees Seckler," May 21, 1965, Archives of American Art, Smithsonian Institution, Washington, D.C., https://www.aaa.si.edu/collections/interviews/oral-history-interview-joan-mitchell-16086

Beautiful Weed

Sarah Roberts and Katy Siegel

12–15

1. Here we are thinking of the reassessment of individual women artists, as well as brilliant recent writing on the conditions of being a woman artist. For example, see Jia Tolentino, "The Cult of the Difficult Woman," in *Trick Mirror: Reflections on Self-Delusion* (New York: Random House, 2019), 235–62; on overshadowed women, see Zadie Smith, "The Muse at Her Easel," *New York Review of Books* 66, no. 18 (November 21, 2019): 61–65.

2. The question of whether a woman can be a great artist is haunted and inspired by Linda Nochlin's 1971 essay "Why Are There No Great Women Artists?," *Art News* 69, no. 9 (January 1971): 22–39, 67–71. It has been particularly interesting to consider Mitchell's relationship to Nochlin's work in the 1970s and their shared interest in contemporary feminism, painting, and nineteenth-century art.

3. Simone de Beauvoir, *The Second Sex* [1949], trans. H. M. Parshley (London: Jonathan Cape, 1956). It is clear from correspondence with Marion Strobel and others that Mitchell knew Beauvoir's work.

4. Ibid., 671.

5. Ibid.

6. Mitchell identified with "les mauvaises herbes" in an interview. See Catherine Lawless, "Le territoire de Joan Mitchell," in *Artistes et ateliers,* ed. Yves Michaud (Paris: Éditions Jacqueline Chambon, 1990), 22. Painters Monique Frydman, Frédérique Lucien, and Philippe Richard all describe Mitchell calling herself a "mauvaise herbe."

7. Letter from Jean Paul Riopelle to Mitchell, December 13, 1956, JMFA001.

8. For example, in her case study of six artists, only Tina Mandell (a pseudonym for a patient who bears a striking resemblance to Mitchell) escapes the "grandiose ideas concerning their talents and their products" that distorts the thinking of the five male artists. Edrita Fried, *Artistic Productivity and Mental Health* (Springfield, IL: Charles C. Thomas, 1964), 168.

9. Eileen Myles, "Being Female," *The Awl,* February 14, 2011, https://www.theawl.com/2011/02/being-female/.

10. T. S. Eliot, "Baudelaire," in *T.S. Eliot, Selected Essays, 1917–1932* (London: Faber and Faber, 1932), 390.

I Painter

Sarah Roberts

16–25

Epigraph: George H. Dillon, "Fall of Stars," *Poetry* 28, no. 5 (August 1926): 242, reprinted in Dillon, *Boy in the Wind* (New York: Viking Press, 1927).

1. Mitchell, quoted in Munro typewritten interview notes, [1977], 4. Munro Papers, AAA.

2. Ibid.

3. Marion Strobel Mitchell used her maiden name professionally. For ease of distinguishing her from her daughter, she is referred to as Strobel throughout this volume.

4. Letter from Mitchell to George Dillon, December 12, 1935, box 8, folder: Mitchell, Joan, 1936, 1966, 1967, undated, George Dillon Papers, Special Collections Research Center, Syracuse University Libraries.

5. The Potter Palmer Collection, 1922; the Helen Birch Bartlett Memorial Collection, 1926; the Arthur Jerome Eddy Memorial Collection, 1931; the Mr. and Mrs. Martin A. Ryerson Collection, 1933; and the Mr. and Mrs. Lewis Larned Coburn Memorial Collection, 1933.

6. "J'ai appris à Chicago, à l'Art Institute. Quand j'étais jeune, les leçons avaient lieu dans le sous-sol de l'institut, sous les salles du musée. Et dans les salles, Seurat, Cézanne, Van Gogh, Lautrec, Monet . . . Quand j'étais enfant, je croyais que toute la peinture était française à cause des noms." Philippe Dagen, "La fureur de Joan Mitchell: de Chicago aux bords de la Seine, la recherche d'une indépendance absolue" (interview), *Le Monde* (Paris), August 2–3, 1992, 11.

7. Jill Weinberg Adams noted that on a visit to the Art Institute in 1988, it seemed that Mitchell, walking briskly through the galleries, knew the paintings so well that she did not need to look at them. In contrast, during their visit to see the Mellon collection of French paintings in the National Gallery earlier in the year, Mitchell had spent considerable time looking deeply. Weinberg Adams, email to the author, August 20, 2019.

8. Mitchell, quoted in Munro interview transcript, [1977], 23, Munro Papers, AAA.

9. She also saw *Paintings and Drawings by Vincent van Gogh,* an exhibition organized by the Museum of Modern Art, New York, when it traveled to the Art Institute (August 26–September 23, 1936).

10. Mitchell, in *Joan Mitchell: Portrait of an Abstract Painter,* directed by Marion Cajori (New York: Arthouse Films, 1992), DVD, 5:56 min.

11. Paul Richard, interview with Patricia Albers, August 16, 2002, Albers Papers. Richard grew up in Chicago and his mother taught Mitchell French at the Francis Parker School. He later became a writer for the *Washington Post.* For Mitchell's thoughts on Hackett, see Paul Richard, "Joan Mitchell's Bleak Horizons," *Washington Post,* February 27, 1988. Hackett is also discussed in Patricia Albers's interview with Herbert Katzman, a School of the Art Institute classmate of Mitchell's, July 23, 2001, Albers Papers.

12. Mitchell, quoted in Paul Richard, "Joan Mitchell's Bleak Horizons."

13. Mitchell, quoted in Munro typewritten interview notes, [1977], Munro Papers, AAA.

14. Ibid.

15. Mitchell won the Midwest Junior pairs championship in 1941, and then competed solo in 1942, taking the Midwest Senior Ladies title and progressing to the U.S. National Junior Figure Skating Championships, where she finished in a disappointing fourth place.

16. Eleanor Munro, *Originals: American Women Artists* (New York: Simon and Schuster, 1979), 239.

17. Mitchell's mother noted her proclivity for art when she was just four years old, writing to Harriet Munroe: "Joan has a talent for drawing. Of course it's too early to tell much, but she gets all flushed and absorbed and snappy if she's interrupted . . . and it looks like something! (something a bit drunk, but most deliciously, tipsily colorful)." Letter from Marion Strobel to Harriet Monroe, April 10, 1929, box 24, folder 27, Poetry: A Magazine of Verse Records, Gen. 1912–1936, Special Collections Research Center, University of Chicago Library.

18. Mitchell, quoted in Munro typewritten interview notes, [1977], 7, Munro Papers, AAA.

19. Nochlin, AAA oral history.

20. Mitchell, quoted in Munro interview transcript, [1977], 2, Munro Papers, AAA.

21. Mitchell, quoted in Munro typewritten interview notes, [1977], 9, Munro Papers, AAA.

22. Von Neumann gained recognition for Regionalist scenes of fishermen and laborers, but by the 1940s had moved into landscapes rendered with a clear debt to Paul Cézanne. Ritman had lived and worked primarily in Paris and Giverny from 1909 to 1929, specifically to be in proximity to Claude Monet. There he developed his own variation of Impressionist brushwork and specialized in contemplative female figures in gardens overflowing with color and flecked with sunlight and shadows.

23. Letter from Mitchell to Martha Bertolette, n.d. [ca. 1944–45], JMFA001. Lines early in the letter make it clear that Mitchell is just settling into Chicago after leaving Smith.

24. The term is Barney Rosset's, who attributed Mitchell's political shift to his own influence, but Bowman's affiliation with communism and Mitchell predates Rosset's. Rosset, notes for autobiography, box 2, folder 33, Barney Rosset Papers, Series II: Chronological Materials, Rare Book and Manuscript Library, Columbia University Library.

25. See Richard Bowman, interview with Patricia Albers, August 26, 2001, Albers Papers. See also Eldon Danhausen, interview with Patricia Albers, November 24, 2001, Albers Papers.

26. Letter from Daniel Catton Rich to Mitchell, June 13, 1946, Correspondence series: Art Institute of Chicago, JMFA001.

27. Zuka Booyakovitsch Mitelberg, interview with Jane Livingston, September 26, 1999, Jane Livingston personal papers.

28. Philip Guston was on the jury, and though Mitchell does not seem to have met him at the time, his involvement was later a point of pride for her. The *Art News* and *Chicago Tribune* reviews of the exhibition list the winning print as *Subway*. "Youth Wins in the Windy City," *Art News* 46, no. 4 (June 1947): 20; *Chicago Tribune,* June 3, 1947. However, the Art Institute's official catalogue for the exhibition illustrates and lists *Tired Children,* as does a second notice in the *Chicago Tribune* by critic Eleanor Jewett. *51st Annual Exhibition by Artists of Chicago and Vicinity,* exh. cat. (Art Institute of Chicago, 1947), n.p., Mitchell's *Tired Children* listed as cat. 106, plate 7; Eleanor Jewett, "Local Artists' Annual Exhibit Incredibly Bad," *Chicago Tribune,* June 4, 1947. Art Institute curator Frederick A. Sweet wrote to congratulate Mitchell on winning the prize for *Tired Children*. Letter from Sweet to Mitchell, June 3, 1947, Correspondence series: Art Institute of Chicago, JMFA001.

29. On the impact of Kollwitz during this period, see Jean Owens Schaefer, "Kollwitz in America: A Study of Reception, 1900–1960," *Woman's Art Journal* 15, no. 1 (Spring–Summer 1994): 29–34. Articles Mitchell likely saw include Jakob Rosenberg, "German Expressionist Printmaking," *Magazine of Art* 38, no. 8 (December 1945): 300–305; Karl Kup, "Prints," *American Artist* 11, no. 1 (January 1947): 30–31, 40–41; and Howard Devree, "Käthe Kollwitz: Friend of Humanity," *New York Times Magazine,* November 18, 1945, 16–17.

30. Letter from Mitchell to Barney Rosset, February 3, 1947, JMFA003.

31. Letter from Mitchell to Rosset, n.d. [postmarked March 18, 1947], JMFA003.

32. "Ritman says I should go to New York more often because I'm doing a good painting." Letter from Mitchell to Rosset, n.d. [postmarked March 20, 1947], JMFA003.

33. Nochlin, AAA oral history. Mitchell likely was referring to *Arshile Gorky* at Julien Levy Gallery, New York (February 29–March 20, 1948); and *Roberto Matta* at Pierre Matisse Gallery (November 4–22, 1947). The Pollock reference is less certain, but he had an exhibition at Art of This Century in January 1947. Letters from Mitchell to Rosset in late January suggest that she accompanied Rosset on his trip to New York that month, so she may have seen Pollock's show then.

34. Barney Rosset photographs, JMFA002.

35. Transcriptions of Rosset's journal, September 30–October 15, 1950, box 3, folder 27, Barney Rosset Papers, Series II, Rare Book and Manuscript Library, Columbia University Library.

36. Letter from Mitchell to Joanne Von Blon, February 8, 1949, JMFA018.

37. Details noted in Marion Strobel's reply to a letter from Mitchell that is apparently lost. "Of course your having finished 18 canvases, in spite of all the difficulties, impresses me. I wish I could see the ones of the stove—in fact, all of them." Letter from Strobel to Mitchell, December 14, 1948, JMFA001.

38. "See, everybody, to do modern art then, seemed to me, when you were going 'modern' (both chuckle), it was Picasso. I mean, everybody. But I avoided that like the plague. I thought . . . I loved Picasso, but it just wasn't for me." Nochlin, AAA oral history.

39. Ibid.

40. Letter from Mitchell to Von Blon, February 8, 1949, JMFA018.

41. This conclusion is drawn from the selection of works that are known to have been made in Paris and Le Lavandou because of their appearance in contemporaneous correspondence and photographs, or in definitive statements in interviews with Mitchell and Rosset.

42. Rosset, notes for autobiography, "Joan and Barney," 7–8, box 3, folder 5, Barney Rosset Papers, Series II, Rare Book and Manuscript Library, Columbia University Library.

43. Ibid.

44. Seckler, AAA oral history; and Munro interview transcript, [1977], 10, Munro Papers, AAA.

Sketchbook drawings, ca. 1948
Karli Wurzelbacher

26–27

1. Letter from Mitchell to Barney Rosset, n.d. [postmarked March 18, 1947], JMFA003.

2. Letter from Mitchell to Rosset, n.d. [postmarked September 21, 1948], JMFA003.

3. Mitchell sketchbook, ca. 1948, n.p., JMFA.

4. Letter from Mitchell to Rosset, July 22, 1948, JMFA003.

5. Letter from Mitchell to Rosset, July 23, 1948, JMFA003.

2 St. Mark's
Katy Siegel

30–37

Epigraph: Mitchell quoted this Billie Holiday song to Michael Goldberg in two letters, recalling time spent together at his place on Second Street. Letter from Mitchell to Michael Goldberg, n.d. [ca. summer 1955], first line: "Darling—The records—christ I went out of my head listening—+ 'The mood that I'm in,'" and letter from Mitchell to Goldberg, n.d. [June 1955], first line: "Stupid Letter Darling I'm Sorry. There are times, so seldom, when the world is meaningful," Goldberg Papers, AAA.

1. Mitchell, quoted in Munro interview transcript, [1977], 10, Munro Papers, AAA.

2. Ibid.

3. At times their colors are similar enough to suggest the possibility of shared paint, as is true of their respective works chosen for the Ninth Street exhibition (particularly a brownish yellow); Goldberg later dated his untitled Ninth Street painting to 1949, but it is quite possible that he may have pushed the date earlier.

4. She also continued to pursue more formal education, taking classes at New York University, Columbia University, and the New School.

5. Of the three, Mitchell met Guston first while she was in Paris sometime between 1948 and 1949. Munro typewritten interview notes, [1977], 10, Munro Papers, AAA. Then, in 1950, she met Kline, as frequently recounted. See, for example, Munro interview transcript, [1977], 16, Munro Papers, AAA; and Nochlin, AAA oral history.

6. Mitchell's New York residences and studios from 1950 to 1955 include the Chelsea Hotel, 267 W. Eleventh Street, 57 W. Ninth Street, 51 W. Tenth Street, and 60 St. Mark's Place.

7. Kline seems to have introduced her to de Kooning, and while there are many contradictory accounts of precisely how and when they met (with both Rosset and Goldberg taking credit), Mitchell saw *Attic* (1949) in the 1949 Whitney Annual and may have seen *Excavation* (1950) and *Woman I* (1950–52) in progress that same year. *Woman I* is mentioned in the interview about de Kooning she did for the Centre Georges Pompidou, conducted by Claire Stoullig on October 12, 1983, Dossier documentaire Willem de Kooning: BVAP DEKOONING 3: textes de l'artiste (photocopies), textes sur l'artiste (photocopies), entretiens

(photocopies). Thanks to Laura Morris, Joan Mitchell Foundation, for sharing the transcription with me. In Munro interview transcript, [1977], 17–18, Munro Papers, AAA, Mitchell implies that she saw the first *Woman* painting before abruptly switching to talking about female artists' struggle to break into the male group: "they didn't accept women." Mitchell often stipulated that Kline and de Kooning were supportive of her as a female painter, but also clearly felt stigmatized in the larger social context of the New York painters.

8. Munro interview transcript, [1977], 16, Munro Papers, AAA.

9. Sandler typewritten interview notes, March 21, 1957, n.p., Sandler Papers, GRI. Mitchell spoke of "Kline's immediate image" to Irving Sandler, according to his typewritten interview notes, March 14, 1957, n.p., Sandler Papers, GRI.

10. On Gorky, Kline, and de Kooning, Mitchell said: "The two words that are important in their painting are crudeness and accuracy. This sounds contradictory." Sandler typewritten interview notes, March 21, 1957, n.p., Sandler Papers, GRI. For "accuracy" in de Kooning alone, see Irving Sandler typewritten interview notes, February 18, 1957, 2, Sandler Papers, GRI.

11. Michael Goldberg mentioned these weekly visits in an unpublished interview with Patricia Albers, June 20, 2002, Albers Papers. Mitchell stated, "I saw the big Gorky retrospective at the Whitney and I was crazy mad for the late turpentine things." Mitchell, quoted in Sandler typewritten interview notes, February 18, 1957, 2, Sandler Papers, GRI.

12. Goldberg also provides insight into Mitchell's relation to Hans Hofmann, the other great older figure of New York painting. Though she attended his school for a single day, perhaps two, before going to Paris in 1948, critics and scholars made a general association between Mitchell and Hofmann throughout her life. Goldberg studied with Hofmann at two different moments, and in Mitchell's letters to him, we see that she has picked up some of the language, criticizing "tonal painting" (which Hofmann saw as an academic degradation of color); landing on the word "mysticism" as a refutation of a more theoretical attitude to painting; and, of course, referencing "push and pull"—all familiar Hofmannisms. For example, Mitchell wrote to Goldberg of "push + pull" and said, "I feel painting physically + maybe mystically and that's about all." Letter from Mitchell to Goldberg, n.d. [ca. 1951], first line: "Monday, Darling I can't look at you enough or feel you enough—it was wonderful," Goldberg Papers, AAA.

13. Thaw opened the gallery with a business partner, Jack Landau, who left the partnership soon after Mitchell's exhibition. My thanks to Alexandra Tagami Vargo of the Joan Mitchell Catalogue Raisonné for pointing this out.

14. Betty Holliday, "Reviews and Previews: Joan Mitchell," *Art News* 50, no. 9 (January 1952): 46.

15. Critic Thomas B. Hess dubbed one small related painting "Homage to Gorky." Joanne Von Blon recalled Hess's titling of this painting in an interview with Patricia Albers, March 22, 2005, Albers Papers.

16. Conservator Jennifer Hickey in conversation with the author, November 27, 2018, at a convening organized by the curatorial team, Joan Mitchell Foundation, New York. Conservator Benoît Dagron pointed out in a February 28, 2019, viewing at the Fondation Louis Vuitton, Paris, that this was a device employed by Picasso and other European Modernists.

17. The future MoMA curator William Rubin sold two clarinets to pay for the painting, which he purchased after the exhibition, perhaps to avoid buying it from Thaw (who later saw the work in Rubin's apartment). Letter from Rubin to Mitchell, n.d. [postmarked May 29, 1952], JMFA001.

18. Mitchell largely blamed Clement Greenberg for keeping her out of the Tibor de Nagy Gallery, although she also laid the blame alternately at the feet of his then girlfriend, Helen Frankenthaler (whose aesthetic was associated with Pollock), and Grace Hartigan (who was very close to O'Hara, and also, according to Mitchell, "cut-throat"). Munro typewritten interview notes, [1977], 12, Munro Papers, AAA; Eric Brown (former gallery assistant at Tibor de Nagy Gallery; became co-owner in 1993), email to the author, May 9, 2019. She also described the galleries as having a quota system: Mitchell in Stephen Westfall, "Then and Now: Six of the New York School Look Back," *Art in America* 73, no. 6 (June 1985): 114.

19. John Ashbery, foreword to *Joan Mitchell, 1992* (New York: Robert Miller Gallery, 1993), n.p.

20. Greenberg's remark was quoted by Phyllis Tuchman in an interview with the author and Sarah Roberts, April 17, 2019, New York; Grace Hartigan, "Jan 15" [1952] entry, *The Journals of Grace Hartigan, 1951–1955,* ed. William T. La Moy and Joseph O. McCaffrey (Syracuse: Syracuse University Press, 2009), 22.

21. Mitchell finished the statement with a tart, "now they call me the opposite." Sandler handwritten interview notes, n.d. [ca. 1957], Sandler Papers, GRI. In a slightly later interview with Sandler, she spoke of the 1950s paintings as expressing a wild time in her life, a mode of "freedom and spontaneity and a tremendous control," and acknowledged that "analysis also helped in allowing her to be freer in her work." Irving Sandler typewritten interview notes, July 4, 1958, Sandler Papers, GRI.

22. Throughout his criticism of the 1940s and 1950s, Greenberg regularly used the word "cuisine," stressing the French connection, to describe attention to the details of materialist painting.

23. Letter from Mitchell to Sally Perry, April 12, 1982, courtesy Sally Perry.

24. Letter from Mitchell to Joanne Von Blon, December 1–8, 1952, JMFA018.

25. Her mother attended the opening. Letter from Marion Strobel to Mitchell, April 23, 1953, courtesy Peter Soriano. Mitchell, describing the 1953 Stable Gallery exhibition, said that is when "the white really came in." Munro interview transcript, [1977], 17, Munro Papers, AAA. Paul Brach, who was close to Mitchell, called the paintings "buoyant," saying, "These new canvases seem to have their own light." Paul Brach, "57th Street: Joan Mitchell," *Art Digest* 27, no. 14 (April 15, 1953): 16.

26. Brach, "57th Street," 16; Robert Goodnough, "Reviews and Previews: Joan Mitchell," *Art News* 52, no. 2 (April 1953): 41; James Fitzsimmons, "Art," *Arts & Architecture* 70, no. 5 (May 1953): 8.

27. Thanks to Harry Cooper of the National Gallery of Art, Washington, D.C., and Sally Radic of the Guston catalogue raisonné project for sharing images and discussing the artists' relationship. It is worth noting that Mitchell swung back and forth between dismissing and admiring Guston; the question of influence was generally complicated for her, and perhaps particularly in his case.

28. Guston's interiority was something Mitchell objected to, as stated by painter Howard Kanovitz, a friend in the 1950s. Howard Kanovitz, interview (typewritten) with Patricia Albers, July 18, 2002, Albers Papers.

29. Fairfield Porter, "Reviews and Previews: Philip Guston's [*sic*]," *Art News* 51, no. 10 (February 1953): 55.

30. Ibid.; Frank O'Hara, "Nature and the New Painting," *Folder 3,* 2, no. 1 (1954–55): n.p.; Elaine de Kooning, "Subject: What, How or Who?" *Art News* 54, no. 2 (April 1955): 26–29, 61–62; and Thomas B. Hess, "U.S. Painting: Some Recent Directions," *Art News Annual* 1956: 25th Christmas Edition, part 2, 54, no. 7 (November 1955): 74–98, 174-80, 192–99.

31. Many scholars in recent years have mistakenly credited Greenberg alone for the "revival" of Impressionism, with his embrace of late Monet.

32. As O'Hara writes, "Because of the ferocity of modern life, man and nature have become one. A scientist can be an earthquake." O'Hara, "Nature and the New Painting," n.p. The idea was widespread, the result of humans seeming to play God

with the advent of atomic science. The fusing of the human and natural worlds as a matter of perception was also a dominant metaphysical concept, as in Maurice Merleau-Ponty's *Phénoménologie de la perception* (Paris: Gallimard, 1945).

33. Sandler typewritten interview notes, February 18, 1957, 3, Sandler Papers, GRI.

34. In 1955 (likely late spring), Mitchell wrote a letter to Goldberg complaining about having to give Hess a statement for a roundup on contemporary painting; it was published in late 1955 with a quote, "semi-abstractly from nature." Letter from Mitchell to Goldberg, n.d. [ca. late spring 1955], first line: "Dearest Michael, I miss you—miss you—c'est affreux," Goldberg Papers, AAA. See Hess, "U.S. Painting," 82.

35. By the later 1950s, she would cavil about "nature" as a term, taken in a "bird-watching sense," a disdain born of the prescriptive critical fashion and her distaste for broad categories. Sandler typewritten interview notes, February 18, 1957, 3, Sandler Papers, GRI.

36. For example: "I start with landscape ideas." Mitchell, quoted in ibid., 1.

37. Elaine de Kooning's sympathetic definition of the topic included this subjectivity: "Today, for the artist with a signature, there is no simple *what*—no reality, no subject, that does not include *who* he is and *how* he perceives it. . . . nature includes his way of looking at it." De Kooning, "Subject: What, How or Who?," 62.

38. Although she loved painting, Mitchell describes being bored in art history class by the memorizing and the march of names and recalls looking at the view out the library window instead of at her books. Letter from Mitchell to Goldberg, n.d. [ca. spring 1951], first line: "Monday Darling, Christ I missed you Sunday and got depressed and miserable and it seems so long now." Goldberg Papers, AAA. Mitchell criticizes the "cataloguing" impulse generally in letters to Goldberg at least three times in these years.

39. Full statement quoted from Sandler typewritten interview notes, February 18, 1957, 3, Sandler Papers, GRI. See published extract in Irving Sandler, "Mitchell Paints a Picture," *Art News* 56, no. 6 (October 1957): 44.

40. Letters from Mitchell to Goldberg, n.d. [postmarked August 10 and 19, 1954], Goldberg Papers, AAA. The rallying against cliché in language and in relations with the world, and for the revitalizing effects of novelty of expression, was a major theme of the published work of Mitchell's therapist, Edrita Fried—and, one would imagine, a theme of their therapy sessions.

41. As Mitchell later said, "I used a lot more color in the high school than I did for a long time after—you know, yellow and red." Munro interview transcript, [1977], 22–23, Munro Papers, AAA.

42. Letter from Mitchell to Goldberg, n.d. [postmarked July 31, 1954], Goldberg Papers, AAA.

43. Letter from Mitchell to Goldberg, n.d. [postmarked August 13, 1954], Goldberg Papers, AAA.

44. Letter from Mitchell to Goldberg, n.d. [postmarked August 20, 1954], Goldberg Papers, AAA.

45. "Discord" is the word Mitchell used in ibid. Edrita Fried wrote a case study of a woman ("Barbara"), clearly based on Mitchell, who sought emotional friction to feel alive; see Fried, *On Love and Sexuality* (New York: Grune & Stratton, 1960), 23–24, 40–42. Fried generally believed in active contact in relationships as a vivifying force, specifically contradicting Freud's tenet that tension be reduced for better psychic functioning; see Fried, *Active/Passive: The Crucial Psychological Dimension* (New York: Grune & Stratton, 1970).

46. Letter from Mitchell to Goldberg, n.d. [postmarked August 13, 1954], Goldberg Papers, AAA.

47. The painting's reproduction in Hess's "U.S. Painting" makes it likely that this was the work shown in *U.S. Painting: Some Recent Directions,* Stable Gallery, New York (November 29–December 23, 1955). In October, Hess wrote Mitchell in Paris to thank her for participating, and to let her know that the work was going to be published, and that they were going to make a show of it and would need to add a larger painting, which he would get from the Stable Gallery. Letter from Hess to Mitchell, October 13, 1955, box 2, folder 13, Stable Gallery Records, AAA.

48. Letter from Mitchell to Goldberg, n.d. [postmarked August 20, 1954], Goldberg Papers, AAA.

49. Letter from Mitchell to Evans Herman, August 30, 1954, courtesy Patricia Albers.

50. Al Newbill, "Fortnight in Review: Joan Mitchell," *Art Digest* 29, no. 11 (March 1, 1955): 28; and Dorothy Gees Seckler, "Reviews and Previews: Joan Mitchell," *Art News* 54, no. 1 (March 1955): 51.

51. A fate that Helen Frankenthaler did not escape, because of her painting style, and perhaps her personal style as well. See Katy Siegel, ed., *"The Heroine Paint": Art after Frankenthaler* (New York: Gagosian, 2015).

52. Letter from Mitchell to Goldberg, n.d. [dated in pencil June 10, 1954], first line: "Friday Afternoon Darling Mike, I miss you—sitting in front of one blue and one yellow pitcha," Goldberg Papers, AAA.

53. Hal Fondren wrote that for him, *City Landscape* would have the subtitle "In Winter," recalling seeing the work in her studio in the cold of late 1954/early 1955; see Fondren, "Sunday Afternoons with Joan," in *Joan Mitchell: Paintings, 1950–1955, from the Estate of Joan Mitchell* (New York: Robert Miller Gallery, 1998), n.p. Reviewers described the works as "huge sprawling city-scapes seen from vast distances" (Newbill, "Fortnight in Review," 28) and "wall-sized, landscape-inspired abstractions which add a new range of color intensity to the style" (Seckler, "Reviews and Previews: Joan Mitchell," 51).

54. Mitchell's version of action painting was largely walking that distance between the two facing walls, as she wryly observed, and "hard on the shoes." Sandler handwritten interview notes, n.d. [1957], Sandler Papers, GRI.

Untitled, ca. 1950
Tracey Bashkoff

38–39

I am grateful to David Max Horowitz, Jamie Danis, Carlyn Thomas, and Marin Sarvé-Tarr for their assistance with research.

1. Irving Sandler, "Is Today's Artist with or against the Past? Interviews with David Smith, Frederick Kiesler, Franz Kline, Joan Mitchell," *Art News* 57, no. 5 (September 1958): 41.

2. Ibid.

3. Ibid.

4. Patricia Albers, *Joan Mitchell: Lady Painter, a Life* (New York: Alfred A. Knopf, 2011), 192. The Kandinsky memorial exhibition, which ran November 2–30, 1945, included thirty-one works lent by Solomon Guggenheim and an additional seven by Rebay. See folded brochure printed by the Hilla Von Rebay Foundation.

5. The Museum of Non-Objective Painting was located at 24 E. Fifty-Fourth Street from 1939 to 1947, and at 1071 Fifth Avenue from 1948 to 1952. Special exhibitions featuring Kandinsky were presented throughout the years, but of note during Mitchell's early years in New York were *Tenth Anniversary Exhibition* (May 31–October 10, 1949) and *Evolution in Painting from 1900 to 1952—Academicism, Impressionism, Expressionism, Cubism, Abstraction—to Non-objectivity* (opened April 29, 1952). According to Albers, during Mitchell's "winter with Barney [Rosset] in Brooklyn," she frequented the Museum of Non-Objective Painting; see Albers, *Joan Mitchell,* 192. Gail Levin discusses the role Rebay and the Museum of Non-Objective Painting played in the promotion and accessibility of Kandinsky's work to the New York School painters and others in Levin, "Kandinsky and Abstract Expressionism," in *Theme and Improvisation: Kandinsky and the American Avant-Garde, 1912–1950*, exh. cat., ed. Gail Levin and Marianne Lorenz (Boston: Little,

Brown, 1992). The M. Knoedler & Co. gallery on E. Seventieth Street also hosted *Kandinsky,* a 1952 exhibition that originated at the Institute of Contemporary Art in Boston and traveled that year to the San Francisco Museum of Art (July 20–August 26), the Walker Art Center, Minneapolis (September 14–October 26), and the Cleveland Museum of Art (November 6–December 7).

6. James Johnson Sweeney organized MoMA's Mondrian memorial exhibition. He would go on, in 1952, to become the director of the Guggenheim Museum, where he organized a 1957 exhibition of thirty-nine Mondrian paintings and works on paper.

7. Letter from Mitchell to Michael Goldberg, n.d. [ca. 1951], first line: "Darling Michael, Christ it was wonderful to see you . . .," Goldberg Papers, AAA.

8. In 1948, the Knoedler gallery exhibited sixteen paintings found in Mondrian's studio upon his death, some unfinished. From 1949 through 1957, Sidney Janis Gallery repeatedly featured the artist's work in solo exhibitions and group presentations. In 1949, Mondrian's work was installed at Rose Fried's Pinacotheca Gallery and at the Museum of Non-Objective Painting, where four canvases were included in the tenth anniversary exhibition. For a recounting of Mondrian's legacy in the United States, see Nancy J. Troy, *The Afterlife of Piet Mondrian* (Chicago: University of Chicago Press, 2013). Troy notes the significance of the circulation of publications in shaping the artist's influence.

9. In 1951, eleven Mondrian paintings from the collection of John Senior Jr. were on view at MoMA, and in 1952–53, the museum showed eight Mondrian works in the exhibition *De Stijl*; see Troy, *The Afterlife,* 191.

10. No correspondence or record of this visit exists in the Guggenheim's archives, but conclusions should not be drawn from incomplete files.

11. Levin posits that an interest in Kandinsky, and in the intellectual currents of "primitivism, anarchism, and mysticism," links the first generation of American Modernists to the formation of the Abstract Expressionists in the 1930s and 1940s; see Levin, "Kandinsky and Abstract Expressionism."

12. Klaus Kertess, *Joan Mitchell* (New York: Harry N. Abrams, 1987), 18.

13. Kandinsky rarely wrote about specific canvases or his process of painting, but did in this instance. As if to underscore the break with compositions of the past, Kandinsky writes that the work has two centers, "separated, and at the same time linked." Wassily Kandinsky, "The Picture with the White Edge," in *Kandinsky: Complete Writings on Art,* ed. Kenneth C. Lindsay and Peter Vergo (1982; repr., New York: Da Capo Press, 1994), 390. Mitchell's Territories canvases from the early 1970s similarly adopt an aerial viewpoint.

14. Ibid.

15. Sandler, "Is Today's Artist with or against the Past?," 41.

16. Ibid.

3 Par Avion
Katy Siegel

40–47

Epigraph: Letter from Frank O'Hara to Mitchell, July 30, 1957, JMFA001. Published as René Char, "À *** (see p. 41 epigraph)" in *Poèmes et prose choisis de René Char* (Paris: Gallimard, 1957), 166–67. O'Hara noted that he had been trying to emulate Char for years, and his poem "To the Harbormaster" may be a successful response to the older French poet. See O'Hara, "To the Harbormaster," in *Meditations in an Emergency* (New York: Grove Press, 1957), 1.

1. Letter from Mitchell to Michael Goldberg, n.d. [ca. mid-August 1955], first line: "Lousy letter—forgive Darling. The shit hits the site of the fan here too—I've moved—26, rue Jacob-Paris 6," Goldberg Papers, AAA.

2. Mitchell often described air travel in letters, with longing references to the Air France sign in Paris or New York, and the views of mountain and sea from planes. Both Sam Francis and Jean Paul Riopelle made works that referred to aerial views. See, for example, Pierre Schneider, "Du ciel ou presque," in *Sam Francis: les années parisiennes 1950–1961,* exh. cat. (Paris: Galerie nationale du Jeu de Paume, 1995), 11–39; and, on Riopelle, an early essay by Schneider, "Jean-Paul Riopelle," *L'oeil* 18 (June 1956): 36–41.

3. Dore Ashton, undated transcript, ca. 1955, 5, box 5, folder 38, Dore Ashton Papers, AAA. Ashton also published this line in Ashton, "Art," *Arts & Architecture* 73, no. 2 (February 1956): 11.

4. Thomas B. Hess, "U.S. Painting: Some Recent Directions," *Art News Annual* 1956: 25th Christmas Edition, part 2, 54, no. 7 (November 1955): 90.

5. Letter from Mitchell to Goldberg, n.d. [ca. June 1955], first line: "Darling—No word from you for so long—I feel you're gone," Goldberg Papers, AAA. This description echoes Gertrude Stein's assessment that "publicity in France is really not important, tradition and their private life and the soil which always produces something, that's what counts." Stein, *Paris France* (1940; new ed., New York: W. W. Norton, 2013), 12. Mitchell's copy of the book is in the JMFA library. In Mitchell's first letter to Goldberg from France, she refers to Paris as a "small town—half the Cedar running on half its fuel." Letter from Mitchell to Goldberg, n.d. [ca. May 1955], first line: "Sweetie Pie, How I miss you and often I wonder why I'm here at all," Goldberg Papers, AAA.

6. Letter from Mitchell to Barney Rosset, n.d. [1955], JMFA003.

7. Hotel Montalembert, rue de Montalembert (mid-May through mid-June); Kimber Smith's Batignolles studio (June 15–July 15); 26 rue Jacob (August); 150 avenue Émile Zola (September); and 5 rue Marcel Loyau, Boulogne-Billancourt (October, first half of November).

8. Letter from Mitchell to Barney and Loly Rosset, n.d. [postmarked September 5, 1955], JMFA003.

9. See, for example, letter from Mitchell to Goldberg, n.d. [ca. late October 1955], first line: "Dearest Michael—Well—enfin a letter—even the fuck you kind is OK—I reread it often," Goldberg Papers, AAA.

10. "It's strange to paint with other tubes—with other color names—to try to control them." Letter from Mitchell to Goldberg, n.d. [ca. August 1955], first line: "Darling I almost always smoke Gauloises now— I'm getting into bad habits," Goldberg Papers, AAA. "None of the colors are transparent." Letter from Mitchell to Goldberg, n.d. [ca. July 15, 1955], first line: "Michael—sweetie pie—Got your letter this morning under my door—and it was a nice letter," Goldberg Papers, AAA.

11. Letter from Mitchell to Goldberg, n.d. [ca. late October 1955], Goldberg Papers, AAA.

12. Letter from Mitchell to Goldberg, n.d. [ca. July 15, 1955], Goldberg Papers, AAA.

13. Letter from Mitchell (at St. Mark's Place) to Jean Paul Riopelle (in Paris), January 2, 1956, Mitchell-Riopelle correspondence, Riopelle Archives; accessed October 2017 by Amy Rahn. We are grateful to her for providing access to her transcriptions.

14. *Hudson River Day Line* was dated 1956 in a Jewish Museum exhibition (in 1957) and ca. 1956 in *School of New York: Some Younger Artists* (a 1959–61 touring exhibition); Alexandra Tagami Vargo, Joan Mitchell Catalogue Raisonné, suggests that the Stable Gallery inventory number indicates a 1955 date. Rather than celebrate the transparency she was achieving in these paintings, Mitchell complained to Riopelle that her work had become "drippy and thin"—the opposite of his own preference for heavy, knife-wrought impasto. Letter from Mitchell to Riopelle, February 6, [1956], Riopelle Archives.

15. Dorothy Seiberling, "Women Artists in Ascendance: Young Group Reflects Lively Virtues of U.S. Painting," *Life* 42, no. 19 (May 13, 1957): 74–77.

16. Letter from Riopelle to Mitchell, December 13, 1956, JMFA001. During these years, Riopelle often addressed her as "chère maître." He explicitly acknowledged the play on maître/maîtresse in a letter dated November 29, 1955.

17. Letter from Mitchell to Goldberg, n.d. [ca. July–August 1957], first line: "Sat. Sweetie Pie Had a silly feeling not hearing from you for so long—et enfin a note arrived," Goldberg Papers, AAA.

18. One year later, in October 1957, the artist's mother, Marion Strobel, wrote: "Are you in Paris? Is it cold? I do hope this year there won't be an 'October Island'—much as I admire that painting." Letter from Strobel to Mitchell, n.d. [ca. October 1957], JMFA001. Mitchell refers to Riopelle seeing *Hemlock* in a studio setting in an annotation of Irving Sandler's review (Irving Sandler, "Young Moderns and Modern Masters: Joan Mitchell," *Art News* 56, no. 1 [March 1957]: 32, 64), in a letter sent to Riopelle, n.d. [ca. spring 1957], Riopelle Archives. Thank you to Amy Rahn for pointing this out.

19. "The Vocal Girls," *Time* 75, no. 8 (May 2, 1960): 74.

20. Letter from Mitchell to Riopelle, n.d. [ca. December 1956], Riopelle Archives. Mitchell wrote to Riopelle about seeing his painting at MoMA, ca. December 1955, Riopelle Archives. In "The Vocal Girls," 74, she said that de Kooning joked that the dark green painting was a little like a Christmas tree.

21. Letter from Mitchell to Riopelle, n.d. [ca. December 1956].

22. Ragon cites himself as coining the term in 1956 in Ragon and Michel Seuphor, *L'art abstrait, 1939–1970,* 3 vols. (Paris: Maeght, 1973), 3:40.

23. John I. H. Baur, *Nature in Abstraction: The Relation of Abstract Painting and Sculpture to Nature in Twentieth-Century American Art,* exh. cat. (New York: Whitney Museum of American Art, 1958). Georges Limbour, "La nouvelle école de Paris," *L'oeil* 34 (October 1957), 64. Limbour specifically emphasized feeling over realism in paintings that "ne transposent pas une réalité ou un spectacle, mais un sentiment. C'est l'extériorisation d'une ferveur ou d'une illumination intérieure" (don't transpose a reality or a spectacle, but a feeling. It is the exteriorization of a passion, or of an interior illumination) (ibid., 65). While Mitchell was not given to referencing art criticism except as it touched her directly, she does seem to have kept up generally throughout her life, and in Paris, read "newspapers & *L'oeil* (a French *Art News*)," as she wrote Goldberg. Letter from Mitchell to Goldberg, n.d. [ca. early June 1955], first line: "Dearest Michael, I've sort of run the gamut + now hit rock bottom–spent a night of nightmares–the room turned into plaster casts," Goldberg Papers, AAA.

24. Both Francis and Riopelle titled works after Monet's *Nymphéas* in the mid-1950s, and Mitchell wrote to Riopelle in December 1955 that she had gone to MoMA to see the *Nymphéas,* indicating she was aware of this interest. She also told Irving Sandler that she admired the late—but not the early—Monet, an interest she was later at pains to deny. Sandler handwritten interview notes, n.d. [ca. 1957], Sandler Papers, GRI. While Clement Greenberg appears most prominently in the literature, his was one voice among many, including Fairfield Porter, Elaine de Kooning, Frank O'Hara, and Thomas B. Hess, as discussed in chapter 2 of this volume. Subsequent critics tended to brand and categorize more aggressively: Louis Finkelstein, "New Look: Abstract-Impressionism," *Art News* 55, no. 1 (March 1956): 36–39, 66–68; William Seitz, "Monet and Abstract Painting," *College Art Journal* 16, no. 1 (Fall 1956): 34–46; Clement Greenberg, "The Later Monet," *Art News Annual* 26 (1957): 132–48, 194–96; and Lawrence Alloway, *Abstract Impressionism,* exh. cat. (London: Arts Council of Great Britain, 1958). Most recently, Cécile Debray explored the topic in *Nymphéas: l'abstraction américaine et le dernier Monet,* exh. cat. (Paris: Musée de l'Orangerie, 2018).

25. Georges Duthuit, *A Painter of Awakening: Jean-Paul Riopelle, 1951–53,* exh. cat., trans. Samuel Beckett (New York: Pierre Matisse Gallery, 1954), n.p. The discourse concerning Riopelle is almost hysterically gendered around his singularity and physicality.

26. Letter from Sam Francis to Shirley Jaffe, n.d. [ca. 1956], cited in Debra Burchett-Lere and Aneta Zebala, *Sam Francis: The Artist's Materials* (Los Angeles: Getty Conservation Institute, 2019), 41. Duthuit used the word "cosmological" in a letter, as noted by Natalie Adamson, "Sam Francis and Painting in Paris," in "In Focus: *Around the Blues* 1957, 1962–3 by Sam Francis," July 2019, https://www.tate.org.uk/research/publications/in-focus/around-the-blues/painting-in-paris. On his critical discourse on Francis, see Éric de Chassey's text in this volume, page 92, and Adamson, "Sam Francis and Painting in Paris." For an extended discussion of Francis and space, see Elizabeth Buhe, "Space without Place: Sam Francis's Travel Paintings," in "In Focus: *Around the Blues,*" https://www.tate.org.uk/research/publications/in-focus/around-the-blues/francis-travel-paintings. It is worth noting that while Mitchell did not share this sense of immersion in the painting, her letters repeatedly describe a fantasy or experience of being in a room totally lined in white surfaces, drawing paper, or canvas.

27. Mitchell read Sartre and Beauvoir, and she referred to existentialism as part of the intellectual fashion in the late 1940s and 1950s, an interest she shared with many others, including Rosset, Marion Strobel, Elaine de Kooning, and Janice Biala.

28. Rosenberg, in particular, read and corresponded with Sartre, Beauvoir, and Merleau-Ponty. There is no evidence that Mitchell read Merleau-Ponty; she may have come in contact with his ideas as a general intellectual topic at The Club in New York, or through more specific interactions with Rosenberg, Francis, Jacobs, Duthuit, and Schneider. Rachel Jacobs is likely the "Rachel" occasionally mentioned in Mitchell's letters during these years; Jacobs also discussed Mitchell in a 1958 article; Rachel Jacobs and Yvonne Hagen, "L'académie délinquante," *Aujourd'hui,* no. 20 (December 1958): 36–38. Meyer Schapiro engaged with Merleau-Ponty early on, and Mitchell may have read Schapiro's *Vincent van Gogh* (New York: Harry N. Abrams, 1950), a book mentioned in her Columbia lecture notes. Joan Mitchell notebook, Joyce Pensato Papers, courtesy the Estate of Joyce Pensato.

29. Rosenberg originally wrote "The American Action Painters" for *Les temps modernes,* withdrawing it after a conflict with Sartre and giving it instead to his friend Thomas B. Hess at *Art News*; see Christa Noel Robbins, "Harold Rosenberg on the Character of Action," *Oxford Art Journal* 35, no. 2 (June 2012): 195–214; and Robert Slifkin, "The Tragic Image: Action Painting Refigured," *Oxford Art Journal* 34, no. 2 (June 2011): 227–46. Merleau-Ponty referred to Rosenberg (and Schapiro) as American "friends" in "The Adversary Is Complicit," published in *Les temps modernes* (1950), reprinted in *The Merleau-Ponty Reader,* ed. Ted Toadvine and Leonard Lawlor (Evanston, IL: Northwestern University Press, 2007), 140. Hess's account of de Kooning just a few months later was sympathetic to Rosenberg and highly Francophile; he used the phrase "phenomenological 'thereness'" in Hess, "Jean-Paul Riopelle," in *Riopelle, Paintings from 1970–1973 and the Le Roi de Thulé Series, 1973* (New York: Pierre Matisse Gallery, 1974), n.p. I thank Natalie Adamson for her generosity in pointing me toward Merleau-Ponty at a February 2019 Paris conference on Mitchell.

30. For an account of the division between Sartre's freedom (of pure consciousness) and Merleau-Ponty's embodiment as it affected postwar art in Europe, see Frances Morris's introduction, and Sarah Wilson, "Paris Post War: In Search of the Absolute," both in *Paris Post War: Art and Existentialism,* exh. cat., ed. Francis Morris (London: Tate Gallery, 1993), 15–24, 25–52. See also Maurice Merleau-Ponty, "Sensorium commune," in *Phenomenology of Perception,* trans. Donald A. Landes (New York: Routledge, 2013), 244; originally published in French as *Phénoménologie de la perception,* 1945. For Beauvoir, the taste of black-currant candy set off a colored light; see Simone de Beauvoir, *Memoirs of a Dutiful Daughter,* trans. James Kirkup (1958; repr., New York: Harper Perennial, 2005), 7. Mitchell read Beauvoir's *The Mandarins*; we don't know whether she read the

author's memoirs, although Marion Strobel did, as mentioned in a letter to Mitchell, and so did Elaine de Kooning. Mitchell, letter to Goldberg n.d. [ca. September 1955], first line: "Darling—I loved your pictures—sweet little boy—and your letters," Goldberg Papers, AAA, and Strobel, letter to Mitchell n.d. [ca. 1953], JMFA001.

31. Letter from Mitchell to Rosset, n.d. [postmarked March 18, 1947], JMFA003, as discussed in chapter 1 of this volume.

32. This relationship, as one between subject and object, would be developed by Schneider in relation to Mitchell in the 1960s. Mitchell's childhood curtains, mentioned several times by the artist, were discussed by Edrita Fried in psychoanalytic terms of overidentification in her case study of "Barbara," in *The Ego in Love and Sexuality* (New York: Grune & Stratton, 1960), 40–41. For Mitchell's invocation of curtains, see Cora Cohen and Betsy Sussler, "Joan Mitchell" (interview), *BOMB*, no. 17 (Fall 1986): 24.

33. On perception as expression, see Donald A. Landes, *Merleau-Ponty and the Paradoxes of Expression* (New York: Bloomsbury, 2013). Mitchell, quoted in Sandler, handwritten interview notes, n.d. [1957], Sandler Papers, GRI.

34. For Merleau-Ponty on the continuity of subject through time, see *Phenomenology of Perception,* 442–44.

35. The importance of Marcel Proust to these discussions of memory is obvious, but still significant. Mitchell read Proust's *In Search of Lost Time,* referring to him infrequently but consistently, and stressed his ideas with respect to memory in one of her studio sessions with Irving Sandler. Sandler typewritten interview notes, February 18, 1957, 4, Sandler Papers, GRI.

36. Of those New York memories, Mitchell wrote: "Hal Fondren lived on 73rd St & gave pleasant—lovely dinners." Mitchell, response to questionnaire from Herbert Johnson Museum of Art, 1986, Fourcade Archives. See also Correspondence series: Herbert F. Johnson Museum of Art, Cornell University, JMFA001. The moments of contact could be brief; the landings and leavings were often marked by poems—as Joe LeSueur quipped, if it weren't for these occasions, Frank O'Hara might never have written a poem. LeSueur, *Digressions on Some Poems by Frank O'Hara* (New York: Farrar, Straus and Giroux, 2004), 122.

37. Irving Sandler, "Mitchell Paints a Picture," *Art News* 56, no. 6 (October 1957): 44–47, 69–70. See also Sandler typewritten interview notes, March 14, March 21, and February 18, 1957, and handwritten interview notes, n.d. [1957], n.p., Sandler Papers, GRI.

38. See Mary Gabriel, *Ninth Street Women: Lee Krasner, Elaine de Kooning, Grace Hartigan, Joan Mitchell, and Helen Frankenthaler: Five Painters and the Movement That Changed Modern Art* (New York: Back Bay Books, 2018), 624–25.

39. Sandler, "Mitchell Paints a Picture," 45. Some version of this statement was also voiced by Willem de Kooning, Hans Hofmann, and Helen Frankenthaler early on, but with less consistency and centrality over the years.

40. Mitchell, quoted in Sandler typewritten interview notes, "Conversation 4," n.d. [ca. March 7, 1957], Sandler Papers, GRI.

41. Ibid.

42. Mitchell, quoted in Sandler typewritten interview notes, February 20, 1957, Sandler Papers, GRI.

43. Mitchell, quoted in Sandler typewritten interview notes, "Conversation 4," Sandler Papers, GRI. Somewhat infuriatingly, Rosenberg takes this observation and ascribes it to his experience of Hofmann, which he subsequently used as an almost page-long footnote in his republication of "The American Action Painters"—without referencing Mitchell, who seems to have influenced his ideas of action painting, along with Merleau-Ponty. The cited excerpts (from his 1957 article "Hans Hofmann: Nature into Action," *Art News* 56, no. 8 [May 1957]: 34–36, 55–56)—which include a quote from Rainer Maria Rilke, the statement that "a stroke of pigment, for example 'works' within us in the same way as a bridge across the Hudson," and a reference to line as "figure skating"—strongly evoke Mitchell, not Hofmann. Rosenberg, "The American Action Painters," in *The Tradition of the New* (New York: Horizon Press, 1959), 27.

44. See Sandler handwritten interview notes, n.d. [1957], Sandler Papers, GRI.

45. Mitchell, quoted in ibid.

46. Mitchell, quoted in ibid.

47. See Sandler handwritten interview notes, ibid. On the next page, Sandler mentions that she stated that the word "accurate" connoted "delicacy of line." Mitchell values a deliberateness and fine-tuning not usually associated with gestural paintings. Sandler seems to have made these notes on unlined paper in Mitchell's studio as she worked on the early failed *Bridge* painting in February 1957.

48. Marion Strobel is quoting Mitchell back to herself: "Strong and lyrical is a wonderful target to shoot for." Letter from Strobel to Mitchell, October 26, 1957, JMFA001.

49. In France, *lyricism* as a painting term had origins in 1947 exhibitions featuring Wols and Georges Mathieu; it seems to describe a general romantic quality, against the more systematic abstractions of prewar Europe; see Natalie Adamson, "'An ambiguous meaning links us to history': Reconsidering the Situation of *la jeune peinture* in Paris, 1956," *Third Text* 20, no. 2 (March 2006): 143. In the United States, "lyricism" connotes loveliness or decorativeness, and was often used to describe the work of women and gay men. In the late 1960s, the term "lyrical abstraction" would become a category used by critics to describe decorative, color-based abstraction; see Katy Siegel, "Another History is Possible," in *High Times, Hard Times: New York Painting, 1967–1975,* exh. cat., ed. Katy Siegel (New York: Independent Curators International, 2006), 32, 88n9.

50. *Piano mécanique* seems to have certainly been started, and possibly finished, in late 1957. As Mitchell wrote from Paris in January 1958: "Enclosed are some of the pictures for the show. I didn't have them sooner because the first batch was bad. . . . Probably in reality the best or most important is *Piano Mechanique* [*sic*] except for another which is not photographed." Letter from Mitchell to Eleanor Ward, January 17, 1958, box 2, folder 13, Stable Gallery Records, AAA.

51. As recognized by reviewers in 1960. See "Les expositions à Paris," *Connaissance des arts* 98 (April 1960): 41.

52. Mitchell and Riopelle corresponded in a brief, elliptical way about some of the practicalities of these exhibitions, with Riopelle supporting Mitchell by speaking about her and sharing her work during her absences from Paris, and also by helping to facilitate some of the shipping. See, for example, letter from Riopelle to Mitchell, n.d. [likely April 1959], first line: "Paris 10 [drawing of fish] 69/ Joan Cherie: Je suis au Falstaff en compagnie d'un vieux bifsteak," JMFA001.

53. On the relations between France and Italy, Galerie Arnaud, and Pierre Restany, see Julie Verlaine, *Les galeries d'art contemporain à Paris: une histoire culturelle du marché de l'art, 1944–1970* (Paris: Publications de la Sorbonne, 2012); on the relation between Jackson and Michel Tapié, see correspondence in the Jackson Gallery Archives on international connections between Italy, France, New York, Osaka, and Tokyo, see Ming Tiampo, "The Politics of Geography and Gutai Exhibitions" and "International Contemporaneity and Gutai Exhibitions," in *Gutai: Decentering Modernism* (Chicago: University of Chicago Press, 2011), 99–144. Other significantly connected figures in these networks included dealers Samuel Kootz, Lawrence Rubin, Beatrice Monti, and Pierre Matisse, and director Arnold Rüdlinger of the Kunsthalle Basel.

54. The catalogue called this section "France et Communauté Française," defined as French artists living in France or abroad and "artistes étrangers" living in France for more than three years. *Première biennale de Paris,* exh. cat. (Paris: Musée d'art moderne de la ville de Paris, 1959), 121. Some observers saw this category as symptomatic of the Paris art world's wish to redefine itself as cosmopolitan; see Natalie

Adamson, *Painting, Politics and the Struggle for the École de Paris, 1944–1964* (Farnham, England: Ashgate, 2009), 242.

55. Letter from Mitchell to Paul Jenkins, n.d. [ca. January–February, 1959], box 7, folder 4, Paul Jenkins Papers, AAA. Mitchell wrote, "Frémicourt is finished demolished Mar 15," in a letter to Patricia Molloy, March 7, 1975, JMFA008.

56. "Adieu to Norman, Bon Jour to Joan and Jean Paul," in letter from Frank O'Hara to Mitchell, August 7, 1959, JMFA001.

The Bridge, 1956
Marin Sarvé-Tarr

48–49

1. *Joan Mitchell* (New York: Stable Gallery, 1957).

2. Mitchell, quoted in Irving Sandler typewritten interview notes, February 27, 1957, n.p., Sandler Papers, GRI.

3. Mitchell, quoted in Sandler typewritten interview notes, February 18, 1957, 3, Sandler Papers, GRI. Typographic errors corrected.

4. Mitchell, quoted in Sandler handwritten interview notes, n.d. [ca. February 20, 1957], n.p., Sandler Papers, GRI.

5. Letter from Mitchell to Barney Rosset, July 22, 1948, JMFA003.

6. Mitchell, quoted in Irving Sandler, "Is Today's Artist with or against the Past? Interviews with David Smith, Frederick Kiesler, Franz Kline, Joan Mitchell," *Art News* 57, no. 5 (September 1958): 41.

7. See Katy Siegel, interview with Joyce Pensato, May 12, 2019, New York.

8. The bridge theme stemmed from multilayered references. A few months before her 1952 New Gallery exhibition, which featured *Cross Section of a Bridge*, Mitchell listed possible painting titles around themes of water and landscape on the back of a notebook. This list included "Bridge," and appears above the names of authors and titles of literary works. The notation "Crane–Bridge" suggests she connected this title to Hart Cane's *The Bridge*, which opens with "To Brooklyn Bridge." Joan Mitchell notebook cover, September 4, 1951, Joyce Pensato Papers, courtesy the Estate of Joyce Pensato.

9. Letter from Mitchell to Jean Paul Riopelle, n.d. [ca. December 1956], Riopelle Archives.

10. Mitchell, quoted in Sandler typewritten interview notes, February 18, 1957, 4, Sandler Papers, GRI.

A Country of Her Own: Joan Mitchell and France, 1948–1967
Éric de Chassey

86–95

1. Nochlin, AAA oral history.

2. Letter from Mitchell to Barney Rosset, n.d. [postmarked July 10, 1948], JMFA003.

3. Nochlin, AAA oral history.

4. Letter from Mitchell to Michael Goldberg, n.d. [ca. June 1955], first line: "Darling—No word from you for so long," Goldberg Papers, AAA.

5. "Pourquoi être venue? Pas à cause des Français en tout cas. . . . Évidemment ici, il y a d'autres avantages, les paysages, les bistrots, tout ce que vous appelez la qualité de la vie." Mitchell, quoted in Philippe Dagen, "La fureur de Joan Mitchell: de Chicago aux bords de la Seine, la recherche d'une indépendance absolue" (interview), *Le Monde* (Paris), August 2–3, 1992.

6. Letter from Mitchell to Rosset, n.d. [postmarked July 10, 1948], JMFA003.

7. "Je n'ai pas d'affinités particulières avec la peinture française." Mitchell, quoted in Suzanne Pagé and Béatrice Parent, eds., *Joan Mitchell: Choix de peintures 1970–1982* (Paris: Musée d'art moderne de la ville de Paris, 1982), n.p.

8. "Je ne suis pas du tout intégrée à la scène française. Je ne fais pas partie d'un groupe . . . Ma relation avec le monde de l'art est lointaine. . . . Je connais beaucoup miux New York qu'ici." Mitchell, quoted in ibid.

9. On this exhibition, see April Paul, "Introduction à la peinture moderne américaine: Six Young American Painters of the Samuel Kootz Gallery: An Inferiority Complex in Paris," *Arts Magazine* 60, no. 6 (February 1986): 65–71.

10. On Galerie Huit, see *Galerie Huit: American Artists in Paris 1950–52*, exh. cat. (New York: Studio 18 Gallery, 2002).

11. D. G. S. [Dorothy Gees Seckler], "Reviews and Previews: Joan Mitchell," *Art News* 54, no. 1 (March 1955): 51.

12. Éric de Chassey, "Paris/New York: The Rivalry and the Refusal," in *Paris, Capital of the Arts*, exh. cat., ed. Sarah Wilson (London: Royal Academy, 2002), 344–51.

13. Letter from Nicolas de Staël to Douglas Cooper, January 1955, in *Lettres 1926–1955*, ed. Germain Viatte (Paris: Le bruit du temps, 2014), 654.

14. This similarity was noted by Robert Storr, "Joan Mitchell: Pastorale furieuse," in *Joan Mitchell*, exh. cat., ed. Françoise Bonnefoy (Nantes: Musée des beaux-arts de Nantes; Paris: Galerie nationale du Jeu de Paume, 1994), 15.

15. Natalia Dumitresco, personal file for the Centre de documentation des artistes, April 1966, quoted by Anne Bariteaud in *Les sujets de l'abstraction: peinture non-figurative de la seconde École de Paris. 101 chefs-d'oeuvre de la Fondation Gandur pour l'Art*, exh. cat., Éric de Chassey and Eveline Notter (Milan: 5 Continents, 2011), 234n1.

16. On this double bind, see Éric de Chassey, "L'impossible deuil de l'expressionnisme abstrait ou Comment être un peintre américain après Pollock" (2005), in *L'abstraction, avec ou sans raisons* (Paris: Gallimard, 2017), 147–71.

17. See Alexandra Charvier, "La non-figuration—Un essai de définition: L'idée de non-figuration en France, 1931–1964" (master's thesis, Université François Rabelais, 2009); and Jean-Paul Ameline, "Non-figuration, abstraction lyrique, informel, tachisme: émergence d'une abstraction non-géométrique à Paris (1945–1960)," in de Chassey and Notter, *Les sujets de l'abstraction*, 33–45.

18. "Cette force [la force étrange des souvenirs oubliés], combien de fois l'ai-je subie? Telle texture de paysage de Lorraine [totalement oublié mais lié au souvenir du froid et de l'inquiétude], resurgie dix ans plus tard dans une toile—*L'Hiver*—qui n'avait nulle prétention à être figurative." Jean Bazaine, "Exercice de la peinture" (1957), in *Le temps de la peinture (1938–1998)* (Paris: Flammarion [Champs], 2002), 205.

19. "Si par la figuration une peinture introduit des rapports de terme à terme avec le monde, la peinture qui n'est pas figurative introduit d'autres relations; pour le spectateur comme pour le peintre, le monde est non plus regardé mais vécu, il est passé dans l'expérience qu'ils en ont. Cette expérience s'éprouve elle-même à travers les significations qui, par elle, viennent se faire et se défaire sur la toile. Ainsi cette peinture qui se prive de la représentation est cernée par le monde et lui doit son sens." Pierre Soulages, "Écrits d'artistes: Soulages," *Cimaise* (Paris), no. 1 (November 1953): 17.

20. Nochlin, AAA oral history.

21. Michel Martin, ed., *Mitchell/Riopelle: Nothing in Moderation*, exh. cat. (Montreal: Musée national des beaux-arts du Québec; Milan: 5 Continents, 2017).

22. Yves Michaud, "Passions Shared, Passions Compared," in Martin, *Mitchell/Riopelle*, 118.

23. Letter from Jean Paul Riopelle to Mitchell, January 10, 1956, JMFA001. As translated in Michel Martin, "Mitchell/Riopelle: Painting Bears Witness," in Martin, *Mitchell/Riopelle*, 26n24.

24. Pierre Schneider, quoted by Riopelle in a letter to Mitchell, March 2, 1957, JMFA001. As translated in Martin, *Mitchell/Riopelle*, 28.

25. Letter from Mitchell to Riopelle, n.d. [ca. 1958], Riopelle Archives.

26. Martin, "Mitchell/Riopelle," 30.

27. Nochlin, AAA oral history.

28. Norman Bluhm explained that "they set themselves up as a sort of, you know 'Americana.' They were kind of a boring group, boring because they became more nationalistic." "Oral history interview with Norman Bluhm, conducted by Paul Cummings," October 23–November 12, 1969, AAA. Throughout the 1950s, Mitchell was friends with Paul Jenkins, who had shown at Galerie Huit in 1951 and gained a reputation in Paris as one of the foremost "tachiste" painters through exhibitions at Studio Paul Facchetti and Galerie Stadler.

29. On those artists, see Elisa Capdevila, "Les artistes américains à Paris de 1945 à la fin des années soixante" (PhD diss., Institut d'études politiques de Paris, 2012), 226–39, 335–39.

30. "S'imposent comme une broussaille de sensations encore indifférenciées." Georges Duthuit, "Le paysage en friche" (1949–55), in *L'image en souffrance, I: Coulures* (Paris: Georges Fall, 1961), 15.

31. "La forme se déterminera pour ainsi dire d'elle-même, comme si le créateur était en quelque sorte un goulot dont le rôle serait simplement d'assumer et de contenir la pression du torrent qui, à travers lui, par lui, fuse, contre la toile, imprévisible,—lyrique." Duthuit, "D'une épiphanie élémentaire" (1950–60), in *L'image en souffrance,* 37.

32. "Je persiste à croire que la peinture a d'autres possibilités, dont celle de nous aider à connaître un peu mieux les choses et nous-mêmes à travers elles, à nous pencher sur un certain coeur du monde qui continue à battre quand du nôtre a sonné le glas." Duthuit, "Le dialogue inimaginable" (1953–60), in *L'image en souffrance,* 66.

33. In 1981, Jaffe remembered: "I was also looking at the *nuagistes,* I was interested in [Frédéric] Benrath, [Claude] Bellegarde, the painting of [Hans] Hartung, the large very colored formats of [Serge] Charchoune." Shirley Jaffe, "Entretien avec Xavier Girard," in *Shirley Jaffe,* exh. cat., ed. Xavier Girard (Chambéry: Musée savoisien, 1981), n.p.

34. Letter from Mitchell to Barney and Loly Rosset, n.d. [postmarked June 17, 1955], JMFA003.

35. Letter from Mitchell to Goldberg, n.d. [ca. May 1955], first line: "Sweetie Pie How I miss you and often I wonder why I'm here at all," Goldberg Papers, AAA.

36. Letter from Mitchell to Harold Rosenberg, April 24, 1959, box 2, folders 1–7, Harold Rosenberg Papers, GRI.

37. Serge Guilbaut has pitted New York's "dripping" against Paris's "staining." See Guilbaut, "Disdain for the Stain: Abstract Expressionism and Tachisme," in *Abstract Expressionism: The International Context,* ed. Joan Marter (New Brunswick, NJ: Rutgers University Press, 2007), 39.

38. Charles Estienne, "Une révolution: le Tachisme," *Combat-Art* (Paris), no. 4 (March 1, 1954): 1.

39. Michel Ragon wrote, for instance, about the "current academism of the stain, the sign, and thick paint." Ragon, "Petit bilan pour tous," *Cimaise* (Paris) 5, no. 1 (September–October 1957): 26.

40. "La tache colorée naît, se développe, s'organise à partir du travail de la brosse; et tout cela ... est tension lyrique et création d'un langage." Charles Estienne, *Loubchansky,* exh. cat. (Paris: Galerie Kléber, 1960), n.p.

41. Julien Alvard, "School's Out for Paris," *Cimaise* (Paris) 3, no. 10 (October–November 1955): 5 (article originally published in English).

42. Alain Jouffroy, "Situation de la jeune peinture à Paris," *Preuves* (Paris), (October 1956): 24–25.

43. Mitchell met Tapié in the summer of 1955, three years after he had organized the exhibition *Un art autre,* part of a scheme to internationalize the École de Paris (with Pollock and Riopelle, among others). He invited her to participate in a group show at Galerie Rive Droite in March 1956.

44. Herta Wechser, "School of Paris Influence over American Painters Vitality of Paris," *Cimaise* (Paris) 4, no. 2 (November–December 1956): 45 (article originally published in English). On the "*Cimaise* debate," see Natalie Adamson, *Painting, Politics and the Struggle for the École de Paris, 1944–1964* (Farnham, England: Ashgate, 2009), 200–204. It should be emphasized that this position was mirrored in New York, as can be gauged by reading "Symposium: Is the French Avant Garde Overrated?," *Art Digest* 27, no. 20 (September 1953): 12–13, 27, where Clement Greenberg wrote: "If 'abstract expressionism' embodies a vision all its own, that vision is tamed in Paris—not, as the French themselves may think, disciplined."

45. "On pourrait donc dire, sans chauvinisme, qu'il n'existe pas actuellement d'autre art que celui qui se fait à Paris." Michel Ragon, *L'aventure de l'art abstrait* (Paris: Robert Laffont, 1956), 131–32.

46. "Paris est-il toujours la capitale des arts? Oui. Et c'est même plus vrai que jamais.... Si nous en doutons nous-mêmes, les jeunes artistes étrangers n'en doutent pas." Yvan Jouannet and Jacques Mousseau, "Une enquête," *En Français dans le texte,* aired September 23, 1960, on ORTF (Radiodiffusion Télévision Française).

47. "Paris n'est plus la ville d'une carrière unique. A Paris on vient faire un stage ... qui entraîne la reconnaissance dans les pays nationaux et qui permet une carrière internationale.... Paris est la ville indispensable à l'acquisition d'un langage universel dans les arts." Pierre Restany, quoted in ibid.

48. Pierre Schneider, unpublished lecture, 1994, at the Galerie nationale du Jeu de Paume, Paris.

49. William Rubin, "Younger American Painters," *Art International* (Lugano), 4, no. 1 (January 1960): 26.

50. Joan Mitchell, quoted in Michael Brenson, "Three Who Were Warmed by the City of Light," *New York Times,* June 25, 1989. I have the feeling that when Linda Nochlin emphasized Mitchell's "rage, violence, anger" in her essay for Mitchell's first retrospective in a major New York museum, it was largely—consciously or unconsciously—as a way to anticipate and resist prejudices against the "Frenchness" of her work. See Nochlin, "Joan Mitchell: A Rage to Paint," in *The Paintings of Joan Mitchell,* exh. cat., ed. Jane Livingston (New York: Whitney Museum of American Art, 2002), 49–59.

51. "Joan Mitchell était une vraie amie. Je la voyais à Vétheuil plus tard. Et bien avant et après sa rupture avec Riopelle. Joan et Simon s'appréciaient l'un l'autre. Ce qui était bien rare pour eux." Zsuzsa Hantaï, email to the author, August 9, 2019.

52. Mitchell, quoted in Judith E. Bernstock, *Joan Mitchell,* exh. cat. (New York: Hudson Hills, 1988), 33.

53. "Dans ces conditions l'instant indéfinissable est la signification, d'où l'impossibilité de significations préfixées et l'importance des notions: absence de gestes et de formes préconçus, de la vitesse d'exécution." Simon Hantaï, "Notes confusionnelles accélérantes et autres pour une avant-garde réactionnaire non réductible," leaflet for the exhibition *Hantaï: peintures récentes du 3 mars au 30 mars 1958* (Paris: Galerie Kléber, 1958), n.p.

54. After research revealed that the untitled triptych was shown in this exhibition, it was redated 1963.

55. I heard Fournier make this remark about Mitchell, Hantaï, and Francis on numerous occasions between 1991 and his death in 2006.

56. Mitchell and Hantaï's somehow paradoxically creative relationship lasted until Mitchell's death but is outside the chronological scope of this essay. I tend to see the "veil of lilac color" that Yves Michaud noticed in Mitchell's paintings for her exhibition at Fournier in June 1992, which she knew was certainly her last one, as an emulation of and an homage to Hantaï's *Tabulas lilas,* the paintings he presented in 1982 as his last ones. Michaud's text was printed on the invitation for the exhibition.

57. Letter from Mitchell to Joanne and Philip Von Blon, n.d. [ca. January 1981], JMFA018.

58. Nochlin, AAA oral history, 60–61.

4 Frémicourt
Sarah Roberts

96–103

Epigraph: Barbara Guest, *The Location of Things* (New York: Tibor de Nagy, 1960), 3. Mitchell knew Guest through her New York poetry circles and she titled a 1960 painting *The Green Book of Barbara Guest,* a reference to *The Location of Things,* which was published with a green cover. Mitchell's copy of Guest's book was inscribed, "For Joan—who paints her own locale—with Love, Barbara, New York 1969."

1. Letter from Mitchell to Eleanor Ward, n.d. [ca. December 1958], box 2, folder 12, Stable Gallery Records, 1916–1999 (bulk 1953–1970), AAA.

2. Notable examples include the following: *À propos du baroque: Jean Degottex, Marcelle Ferron, Sam Francis, Simon Hantaï, Shirley Jaffe, Marcelle Loubchansky, Joan Mitchell, Judit Reigl, Jean-Paul Riopelle,* Galerie Kléber, Paris (November–December 1958); *XXIX Esposizione Biennale Internazionale d'Arte,* International Young Artists Section, Palazzo Centrale, Venice, Italy (June 14–October 19, 1958); *Première biennale de Paris,* Musée d'art moderne de la ville de Paris (October 2–25, 1959); *V Bienal do Museu de Arte Moderna de São Paulo,* Museu de Arte Moderna, São Paulo, Brazil (September 21–December 31, 1959); and *Documenta II: Kunst nach 1945,* Internationale Ausstellung, Museum Fridericianum, Kassel, West Germany (July 11–October 11, 1959).

3. In the same letter in which she asked Ward to send money to secure her new studio, Mitchell mentioned that she sold individual works to the Gimpel Fils Gallery of London, Arnold Rüdlinger (then director of the Kunsthalle Basel), and Galerie Kléber in Paris, and that she had no interest in showing with the U.S. Information Service or with a Brussels gallery that also offered showings. Letter from Mitchell to Ward, n.d. [ca. December 1958], Stable Gallery Records, AAA.

4. Ibid. Schneider also noted that Mitchell was not interested in pursuing Paris galleries and that financial success was seen as despicable on some level within her circle. Pierre Schneider, interview with Patricia Albers, September 24, 2006, Albers Papers.

5. William Rubin interview with Jane Livingston, October 27, 1999. Jane Livingston Personal Papers.

6. A note on dates: Mitchell writes to Ward in March 1960 that she has been working and now has enough paintings for her Paris and Milan shows. As was her habit, she made a big push to have new work for these April and May 1960 exhibitions. She was traveling constantly from April to early September 1959, and it is unlikely that she painted them while in New York because Paul Jenkins was living in and using her St. Mark's studio. Therefore, she likely painted much of this group between when she finally moved into Frémicourt, around September 1959, and March 1960, giving them some time to dry before the May exhibitions. Letter from Mitchell to Ward, n.d. [ca. March 1960], box 2, folder 12, Stable Gallery Records, AAA.

7. The haystack connection to Monet did not go unnoticed by the reviewer for *Connaissance des arts,* who referenced hay and the humor in Mitchell's title; see "Les expositions à Paris," *Connaissance des arts* 98 (April 1960): 41.

8. Pierre Restany's "Constitutive Declaration of New Realism" was signed by eight artists in Yves Klein's studio that October.

9. "La foule anonyme des action-painters new-Yorkais" and "une consistance organique, une tenue interne rarement égalée chez les expressionistes abstraits (ce qui fait totalement défaut au De Kooning actuel . . .)." Pierre Restany, "Joan Mitchell," *Cimaise* (Paris) 48, no. 3 (April–June 1960): 90.

10. "C'est une solution possible à l'impasse de la peinture d'action . . ." Ibid.

11. On the discourse around abstract painting and the political and social forces that impacted French abstraction and the École de Paris, see Natalie Adamson's introduction and "Is the École de Paris Condemned to Death?," in *Painting, Politics, and the Struggle for the École de Paris, 1944–1964* (Farnham, England: Ashgate, 2009), 1–15, 217–65. I am grateful to Marin Sarvé-Tarr for sharing her insights on this period with me in the development of this chapter.

12. On the unsettled state of the art market, see Julie Verlaine's introduction and "Les marchands d'art: médiation et promotion," in *Les galeries d'art contemporain à Paris: une histoire culturelle du marché de l'art 1944–1970* (Paris: Publications de la Sorbonne, 2012), 7–17, 383–403.

13. Rubin described cultivating relationships with Alfred Schmela in Düsseldorf and Beatrice Monti in Milan in order to generate interest in his artists. Lawrence Rubin, interview with Elisa Capdevila, September 2, 2009, Elisa Capdevila personal papers. See also Elisa Capdevila, "Les artistes américains à Paris de 1945 à la fin des années soixante" (PhD diss., Institut d'études politiques de Paris, 2012).

14. Artist Marc Berlet, quoted in Hélène de Billy, *Riopelle* (Montreal: Art Global, 1996), 157.

15. Mitchell wrote to Michael Goldberg that Beckett had called and she would meet him the following week. Letter from Mitchell to Michael Goldberg, n.d. [ca. June 1955], Goldberg Papers, AAA. Berlet, who was among the regular lunch group at the rue Frémicourt studio that included Beckett, described Beckett as being infatuated with Mitchell and noted the intensity of the relationship. Marc Berlet, interview with Patricia Albers, August 5, 2006, Albers Papers.

16. In 1959, Beckett wrote to Barney Rosset that he had recently seen Mitchell and Riopelle, and that he "admired her work enormously." See letter from March 20, 1959, in George Craig, Martha Dow Fehsenfeld, Dan Gunn, and Lois More Overbeck, eds., *The Letters of Samuel Beckett, Volume III: 1957–1965* (Cambridge: Cambridge University Press, 2014), 215. The overall time line of Beckett and Mitchell's relationship is cloudy, as very little correspondence exists. As evidenced in Marion Strobel's replies, Mitchell seems to have written of Beckett regularly to her mother from 1962 to 1964; Mitchell's half of this correspondence is, regrettably, missing or lost. She also wrote to Rosset about her nights with Beckett in 1967, suggesting that from 1962 to 1967 or 1968, perhaps when she moved to Vétheuil, was the most intense period of their relationship.

17. Mitchell, quoted in Judith E. Bernstock, *Joan Mitchell,* exh. cat. (New York: Hudson Hills, 1988), 106.

18. Letter from Mitchell to Barney and Loly Rosset, n.d. [postmarked June 17, 1955], JMFA003.

19. *Water Gate, The Green Book of Barbara Guest,* and *Bridge Stop* are mentioned in Irving Sandler's review of Mitchell's 1961 Stable Gallery exhibition. *The Green Book of Barbara Guest* and *County Clare* similarly are noted in a review by Sidney Tillim. Sandler and Tillim likely had been given previews of the show so that their reviews could appear while the show was still open. See Sandler, "Joan Mitchell," *Artnews* 60, no. 3 (May 1961): 11; and Tillim, "Joan Mitchell," *Arts Magazine* 35, nos. 8–9, (May–June 1961): 84–85. None of these four paintings appeared on the final exhibition checklist, however, and it seems likely they were swapped out for a group Mitchell shipped from Paris in late March 1961, per correspondence with Ward. Letter from Mitchell to Ward, n.d. [ca. March 1961], box 2, folder 12, Stable Gallery Records, AAA; and response from Ward to Mitchell, April 3, 1961, box 2, folder 13, Stable Gallery Records, AAA. The four paintings noted in the reviews were not part of this group shipped from Paris, and the fact that they were readily available to Ward in New York before the exhibition suggests they may have been painted in Paris and shipped earlier, or, more likely, painted in Easthampton in summer 1960 and stored locally. Either way, they were among Mitchell's first successes in her new mode. I am grateful to Alexandra Tagami Vargo, Joan Mitchell Catalogue

Raisonné, for her assistance with teasing out the details of this complex chronology.

20. Letter from Mitchell to Sam Francis, n.d. [ca. 1961], box 6, folder 2, Sam Francis Papers, 1916–2010, GRI.

21. Linda Nochlin, "Joan Mitchell: A Rage to Paint," in *The Paintings of Joan Mitchell,* exh. cat., ed. Jane Livingston (New York: Whitney Museum of American Art, 2002), 49–59.

22. On Riopelle being stopped, see Barney Rosset, interview with Patricia Albers, January 18, 2001, Albers Papers; and Sally Perry's travel diary from 1962, courtesy her daughter, Sally Perry. In reference to bombings, see postcard from Mitchell to Eleanor Ward, February 17, 1962, box 2, folder 13, Stable Gallery Records, AAA. Bill Berkson recalled Mitchell telling of nearby explosions when he visited in fall 1960. Berkson, "Tiger, Tiger: A Few Days with Joan," *Poetry* 201, no. 5 (February 2013): 538.

23. Letter from Mitchell to Goldberg, n.d., first line: "I feel at such a distance and somewhat atrophied," Goldberg Papers, AAA.

24. Letter from Mitchell to Jean Paul Riopelle, n.d. [May 1960], Riopelle Archives; copy accessed October 2017 by Amy Rahn.

25. "Je suis de mon côté très malheureux de ton pessimisme au sujet de tes derniers tableaux . . . je disais à G. Duthuit que . . . tu étais le plus important peintre actuel, baby, c'est à mon avis tout au fond de ma pensée." Letter from Riopelle to Mitchell, n.d. [ca. 1959], JMFA001.

26. See Katy Siegel's discussion of this mark in chapter 2, page 36.

27. On Riopelle's separation of colors and layers, see Marie-Claude Corbeil, Kate Helwig, and Jennifer Poulin, *Jean Paul Riopelle: The Artist's Materials* (Los Angeles: Getty Conservation Institute, 2011), 40–41.

28. Mitchell, in *Joan Mitchell: Portrait of an Abstract Painter,* directed by Marion Cajori (New York: Arthouse Films, 1992), DVD, 28:56 min.

29. Notably, his name does not appear once in her 1965 oral history. See Seckler, AAA oral history.

30. Letter from Mitchell to Goldberg, n.d. [ca. early June 1955], first line: "Sweetie Pie Your letter came enfin with the teeth things," Goldberg Papers, AAA.

31. The jointly arranged exhibitions at the two galleries stand out as somewhat anomalous for Paris at the time. Perhaps the arrangement was a way of smoothing over her transition from Rubin to Dubourg. Letters between Mitchell and Ward confirm that Dubourg had begun working with her in spring 1961, and this May 1962 show was her first with him. In her 1986 oral history interview, Mitchell blamed the split with Rubin on Clement Greenberg telling him to get rid of her because she was too gestural. But the Mitchell-Ward correspondence suggests that working with Rubin may have been rocky, and not just for Mitchell. See Nochlin, AAA Oral History, and letter from Ward to Mitchell, April 15, 1961, box 2, folder 13, Stable Gallery Records, AAA.

32. Letter from Mitchell to Goldberg, n.d. [postmarked June 4, 1962], Goldberg Papers, AAA.

33. "À travers les galeries," *Le Monde* (Paris), May 18, 1962; Jean-Jacques Lévêque, "Les expositions à Paris: Joan Mitchell," *Aujourd'hui* 37 (June 1962): 40; and Pierre Restany, "Joan Mitchell," *Cimaise* (Paris) 60 (July–August 1962): 92–93.

34. Pierre Schneider, "Art News from Paris," *Art News* 61, no. 4 (Summer 1962): 43.

35. John Ashbery, "Paris Letter: May–June 1962," *Art International* 6, no. 7 (September 25, 1962): 58.

36. Pierre Schneider, untitled essay, in *Joan Mitchell* (Paris: Jacques Dubourg and Galerie Lawrence, 1962), n.p., reprinted as "From Confession to Landscape" in *Art News* 67, no. 2 (April 1968): 42–43, 72–73 (in English), and as "Pour Joan Mitchell" in *XXe siècle* 40 (June 1973): 116–19 (in French), 192 (in English).

Mud Time, 1960
Amy Rahn

104–5

1. Joan Mitchell Correspondence ca. 1954–1979, box 2, folder 12, Stable Gallery Records, 1916–1999 (bulk 1953–1970), AAA.

2. Exhibition files, 1961 Stable Gallery exhibition, JMFA004.

3. Sidney Tillim, "Joan Mitchell," *Arts* 35, nos. 8–9 (May–June 1961): 85.

4. Robert Frost, "Two Tramps in Mud Time" [1934], in *The Poetry of Robert Frost: The Collected Poems, Complete and Unabridged*, ed. Edward Connery Lathem (New York: Holt, Rinehart and Winston, 1979), 276.

5. Frost, "Two Tramps in Mud Time," 275.

6. Seckler, AAA oral history.

7. Linda Nochlin, "Joan Mitchell: A Rage to Paint," in *The Paintings of Joan Mitchell,* exh. cat., ed. Jane Livingston (New York: Whitney Museum of American Art, 2002), 52.

5 Voyages
Sarah Roberts

108–15

Epigraph: "Astonishing voyagers! What splendid stories/ We read in your eyes as deep as the seas!/ Show us the chest of your rich memories,/ Those marvelous jewels, made of ether and stars./ We wish to voyage without steam and without sails!/ To brighten the ennui of our prisons,/ Make your memories, framed in their horizons,/ Pass across our minds stretched like canvasses./ Tell us what you have seen." Charles Baudelaire, "The Voyage," in *The Flowers of Evil,* trans. William Aggeler (Fresno, CA: Academy Library Guild, 1954), January 2020 version https://fleursdumal.org/poem/231. Originally published as *Les fleurs du mal,* 1857.

1. Letter from Mitchell to Michael Goldberg, n.d. [postmarked June 4, 1962], Goldberg Papers, AAA.

2. Ibid.

3. Letter from Mitchell to Goldberg, n.d. [postmarked July 8, 1965], Goldberg Papers, AAA.

4. On this broader trend, see Elisa Capdevila, "De Paris à l'Europe: sur les traces des 'Américains à Paris,' entre mobilités récréatives et quêtes artistiques en Europe (de l'après-Seconde Guerre mondiale aux années 1960)," *Artl@s Bulletin* 4, no. 2 (2016), article 7.

5. In a letter from ca. 1961, Mitchell refers to artist Joan Miró, Paris gallery owner Aimé Maeght, and Riopelle's New York gallerist Pierre Matisse. Soby is most likely U.S. curator James Thrall Soby, who also traveled in their circles in Paris and the South of France. Letter from Mitchell to Shirley Jaffe, n.d. [ca. 1961], Shirley Jaffe papers, 1950s–2011, AAA.

6. Nochlin, AAA oral history.

7. Letter from Mitchell to Goldberg, n.d. [postmarked November 5, 1965], Goldberg Papers, AAA.

8. Marc Berlet, interview with Patricia Albers, August 5, 2006, Albers Papers.

9. Seckler, AAA oral history.

10. Ibid. Although *Girolata* has been consistently dated 1964, Mitchell's comments to Seckler, made in reference to Ashbery's review of the 1965 Stable Gallery exhibition, suggest that the painting might be dated 1963–65.

11. Mitchell noted, for example, that she made one panel of *Girolata* into a separate work and created a new panel to complete the triptych. Seckler, AAA oral history.

12. *Cross Section of a Bridge* (1951, plate 9), in her New Gallery exhibition of 1952, and *The 14th of July* (1956) and *The Sink* (1956), in her 1957 Stable Gallery show, are two instances of such centerpiece horizontals.

13. Currently known examples from 1964 range in size from 38 by 64 inches to 44¾ by 76¾ inches.

14. Other than Francis, very few U.S. painters made multipanel works in the 1960s. Ellsworth Kelly, Robert Rauschenberg, and James Rosenquist come to mind as exceptions, but they used the format to completely different ends.

15. Françoise Choay, "Jackson Pollock," *L'oeil* 43–44 (July–August 1958): 42–47. For an overview of Pollock's reception in France, see Claire Stoullig, "Jackson Pollock et la presse," in *Jackson Pollock,* ed. Daniel Abadie (Paris: Centre Georges Pompidou, 1982), 357–58.

16. I am grateful to Richard Shiff, Pierre Wat, Éric de Chassey, Natalie Adamson, Katy Siegel, Marin Sarvé-Tarr, and Elisa Capdevila for their illuminating exchange on verticality versus horizontality during the February 2019 convening funded by the Terra Foundation and held in their offices in Paris as part of the curatorial team's exhibition research. Our conversations critically informed this chapter. Transcript in BMA and SFMOMA curatorial research files.

17. Mitchell, quoted in Irving Sandler, "Mitchell Paints a Picture," *Art News* 56, no. 6 (October 1957): 45.

18. Sandler typewritten interview notes, March 21, 1957, 1, Sandler Papers, GRI.

19. In a letter to their mother, who then relayed the sentiment to Mitchell, the artist's sister, Sally Perry, reacted to the idea of Mitchell and Riopelle crossing the Atlantic: "She will come out of it painting the sea because there will be so much sea that she will have no time to have impressions of it." Perry's remark, though somewhat ambiguous, suggests the experience would be so absorbing that Mitchell would inevitably end up painting the water. Letter from Marion Strobel to Mitchell, November 6, 1961, JMFA001.

20. Although none of these paintings is actually black, Mitchell referred to them in remarks to Ashbery for his *Art News* review of the exhibition as her new "black paintings." She did not repeat the designation, and, though they are often referred to as her black paintings as a shorthand for the group, they are not an official series in the manner of Mitchell's *La Grande Vallée* paintings. John Ashbery, "An Expressionist in Paris," *Art News* 64, no. 2 (April 1965): 63.

21. Seckler, AAA oral history.

22. Ibid.

23. As noted by numerous previous authors, Mitchell titled *Hemlock* with reference to the 1916 Wallace Stevens poem "Domination of Black." See page 44 in this volume and Judith E. Bernstock, *Joan Mitchell,* exh. cat. (New York: Hudson Hills, 1988), 40.

24. Seckler, AAA oral history.

25. Stable Gallery "Joan Mitchell" checklist, 1965, box 2, folder 12, Stable Gallery Records, AAA.

26. Mitchell specifically states that the metro paintings came out of the cypress and blue tree series. Seckler, AAA oral history.

27. This group may nod loosely to Monet's 1877 *Gare St. Lazare* series, much as the *Cercando un Ago* paintings make sly reference to his haystacks. The Paris Métro system, which had undergone significant renewal in the late 1950s and early 1960s, was frequently in the news. In addition to being an inconvenience, the construction led to the redevelopment of neighborhoods of artists' studios, including that of Larry Rivers, among Mitchell's acquaintances; see "Studios: Atelier Crisis," *Time* 86, no. 9, August 27, 1965, 62. This activity might also have prompted Mitchell's interest in the subject/title. On the subway renovations, see Elisa Capdevila, *Des Américains à Paris: artistes et bohèmes dans la France de l'après-guerre* (Malakoff, France: Armand Colin, 2017), 115.

28. Ashbery, "An Expressionist in Paris," 44.

29. For a thorough and nuanced reading of the historical context of the term "apatride" and its political implications, see Amy Rahn, "In and Between: Joan Mitchell in Paris and New York, 1955–1965" (PhD diss., Stony Brook University, 2019), 251–58.

30. Ashbery, "An Expressionist in Paris," 63.

31. Ibid.

32. John Yau identifies this championing of art that exists outside language as the defining concern of Ashbery's criticism. Yau, "The Poet as Critic," *American Poetry Review* 34, no. 3 (May/June 2005): 49.

33. John Ashbery, "Grey Eminence," *Art News* 71, no. 1 (March 1972): 64. Yau also cites this review.

34. Bernstock makes this point in *Joan Mitchell,* 120–21, as does Richard Francis in "Mnemotechny," in *Joan Mitchell: Memory Abstracted* (New York: Edward Tyler Nahem Fine Art, 2002), 14–15.

35. Mitchell, transcript of an interview with Yves Michaud, n.d. [August 7, 1989], with Mitchell's edits, JMFA001. Later published dated August 7, 1989, as "Entretiens," in *Joan Mitchell,* exh. cat., ed. Françoise Bonnefoy (Nantes: Musée des beaux-arts de Nantes; Paris: Galerie nationale du Jeu de Paume, 1994), 31.

36. Ashbery, "An Expressionist in Paris," 64.

37. Thomas B. Hess casts de Kooning's painting and repainting his *Woman I* (1950–52) as a Baudelairean voyage, proceeding on belief in the value of the journey over the end result; see Hess, "De Kooning Paints a Picture," *Art News* 52, no. 1 (March 1953): 32, 64–67. Michael Goldberg and Frank O'Hara's engagement with Baudelaire is palpable in their 1960 limited-edition book *Odes* (published by Tiber Press in the same series as *The Poems,* Mitchell's collaboration with Ashbery). Also notable are the earlier three albums of photographs by Rudy Burckhardt documenting observations of the decay and life of New York: *New York, N. Why?* (ca. 1939, Metropolitan Museum of Art); *An Afternoon in Astoria* (1940, Museum of Modern Art); and *A Walk through Astoria and Other Places in Queens, with poems by Edwin Derby* (1943, collection unknown). I am grateful to Katy Siegel for her suggestions in fleshing out this argument.

38. Sandler, "Mitchell Paints a Picture." Also, letter from Frank O'Hara to Mitchell, October 24, 1957, JMFA001, congratulating her for Sandler's "Mitchell Paints a Picture" article in *Art News.*

39. Bernstock, *Joan Mitchell,* 120–21.

40. Jonathan Culler, introduction to Charles Baudelaire, *The Flowers of Evil,* trans. James McGowan (New York: Oxford University Press, 1993), xxix–xxx.

41. Charles Baudelaire, "Spleen (II)," in Baudelaire, *The Flowers of Evil,* 147.

Girolata Triptych, 1963
Meredith George Van Dyke

116–17

1. Mitchell mentions her first visits to Corsica in a letter to Grace Hartigan, n.d. [postmarked August 19, 1958], Grace Hartigan Papers, Special Collections Research Center, Syracuse University Libraries; and a letter to Paul Jenkins, n.d. [ca. 1958], box 7, folder 4, Paul Jenkins Papers, AAA. Later, she describes the excursions as *yearly* visits. Unsent letter from Mitchell to Patricia Molloy, n.d. [ca. 1968], JMFA001.

2. Dorothy Carrington, *Corsica: Portrait of a Granite Island* (New York: John Day, 1971), 231. Mitchell's friends Betsy Jolas and Gabriel Illouz rented a house near Saint Florent, prompting Mitchell and Jean Paul Riopelle's additional visits to the island. Enamored by their time there, the two couples considered buying property on Corsica together. Betsy Jolas, interview with Patricia Albers, March 26, 2003, Albers Papers.

3. Letter from Mitchell to Michael Goldberg, July 27, 1965, Goldberg Papers, AAA.

4. Sally Perry's 1962 journal, courtesy her daughter, Sally Perry.

5. Although no one remembers her drawing at sea, Mitchell recalled making watercolors "en bateau." Catherine Lawless, "Le territoire de Joan Mitchell," in *Artistes et ateliers,* ed. Yves Michaud (Nîmes: Jacqueline Chambon, 1990), 16.

6. Letter from Mitchell to Goldberg, July 27, 1965, Goldberg Papers, AAA.

7. On the black paintings, see chapter 5 of this volume.

8. Mitchell worried about the whites shifting on the "notably smaller triptych," as well as "some earlier on stretchers," and asked Ward to put the paintings in the "light to make the white return to white for a few days" before going on view. Letter from Mitchell to Eleanor Ward, n.d. [ca. March 1965], box 2, folder 12, Stable Gallery Records, AAA. *Girolata Triptych* was likely included in the 1965 exhibition at Stable Gallery. Thanks to Laura Morris for confirming a Martha Jackson Gallery label on the painting that shows its Stable Gallery inventory number. Email to the author, September 10, 2019.

9. John Ashbery, "An Expressionist in Paris," *Art News* 64, no. 2 (April 1965): 63, 64.

6 Vétheuil
Katy Siegel

118–25

Epigraph: John Ashbery, "A Blessing in Disguise," in *Rivers and Mountains* (New York: Holt, Rinehart and Winston, 1966), 26. The book was in Mitchell's library, see JMFA Library title-page photocopies. Bill Berkson also brought this poem along with him for their 1988 interview, in response to her request for "early, lyrical" Ashbery. Letter from Bill Berkson to Mitchell, June 23, 1988, JMFA001.

1. Edward Clark in Jack Whitten, "Edward Clark by Jack Whitten" (interview), *BOMB,* June 2, 2014, http://bombmagazine.org/articles/edward-clark/.

2. Betsy Jolas, interview with the author, October 10, 2018, Paris. The two couples had talked about buying a home together in Corsica, so Jolas knew that Mitchell and Riopelle were looking for a country house. Confirmed in Betsy Jolas, interview with Patricia Albers, March 26, 2003, Albers Papers.

3. Letter from Mitchell to Barbara Guest, June 23, 1968, box 25, folder 522, Barbara Guest Papers, Yale Collection of American Literature, Beinecke Rare Book and Manuscript Library, Yale University.

4. Letter from Mitchell to Olivier Bernier, January 29, 1967, Jackson Gallery Archives.

5. Mitchell, quoted in Philippe Dagen, "La fureur de Joan Mitchell: de Chicago aux bords de la Seine, la recherche d'une indépendance absolue" (interview), *Le Monde* (Paris), August 2–3, 1992, 11. Interviewed by Dagen very near the end of her life, Mitchell stated that this freedom was what Vétheuil represented to her.

6. Letter from Mitchell to Bernier, January 29, 1967, Jackson Gallery Archives.

7. Ibid.

8. By 1968, when Pierre Schneider published the English translation of his 1962 text on Mitchell (see chapter 4, note 36), he was at work on a book on Matisse, as noted in his byline. Schneider, "From Confession to Landscape," *Art News* 67, no. 2 (April 1968): 43. Schneider was likely also preparing for his 1970 Matisse exhibition at the Grand Palais, at which Mitchell reportedly "wept with emotion." Andreas Freund, "Paris Unveils a Grand Matisse Exhibition," *New York Times,* April 21, 1970, 48.

9. Mitchell's other exhibition prospects, as mentioned in her letters to Bernier and others, were confirmed by Alexandra Tagami Vargo, Joan Mitchell Catalogue Raisonné. For Riopelle and Mitchell's gallery negotiations, see Hélène de Billy, *Riopelle* (Montreal: Art Global, 1996), 184–85.

10. Andre Fermigier, "Sommeil heureux," *Le nouvel observateur,* May 31, 1967, press clipping, JMFA exhibitions files. "Joan Mitchell à la galerie Fournier," *Le nouveau dimanche,* aired October 1, 1967, on ORTF (Office de Radiodiffusion Télévision Française). Footage of the exhibition from this brief news report shows *Woods/Country.*

11. Chicago's Shedd Aquarium opened in 1930. MoMA featured *Woman before an Aquarium* in *Henri Matisse* (November 13, 1951–January 13, 1952). Clearly the painting was important to Mitchell even late in life, and she mentioned it to others. On a postcard sent to Mitchell by Marabeth Cohen-Tyler from Chicago: "Went to Art Institute. They are still all hanging. Girl watching fish in fishbowl. Matisse. Van Gogh. Intense and beautiful Cézanne's apples of course." Postmark not fully legible [1990], JMFA001.

The premature death of Mitchell's goldfish, Dubonnet, when Mitchell's mother cleaned out the water and dumped the fish in the toilet, was a related touchstone; close friend Gisèle Barreau would later dedicate her composition *Sterne* to Dubonnet. Gisèle Barreau, interview with the author, Sarah Roberts, and Marin Sarvé-Tarr, February 21, 2019, Paris.

12. Mitchell mentions that *My Landscape I* was in the Fournier show; letter from Mitchell to Bernier, n.d. [ca. November 1967], Jackson Gallery Archives.

13. For the use of "my landscape" in relation to his memory of Russia, see letter from Rainer Maria Rilke to Paula [Modersohn] Becker, October 18, 1900, in *Letters of Rainer Maria Rilke, 1892–1910,* trans. Jane Bannard Greene and M. D. Herter Norton (New York: W. W. Norton, 1969), 46. For an example of the "inner equivalents" stirred by his time in Toledo, Spain, see Rainer Maria Rilke to Ellen Delp, October 27, 1915, in *Wartime Letters* (New York: W. W. Norton, 1964), 50. For an example of the simultaneity of the observed and subjective landscape, see Rilke's letter of October 9, 1907, in trans. Joel Agee, *Letters on Cézanne,* ed. Clara Rilke (New York: Fromm International Publishing Corp., 1985), 34. We do not know whether Mitchell owned or read Rilke's earlier letters (including the one to Modersohn-Becker), but she could have, as they were first published in English in 1945, and it is likely, considering the depth of her interest; we do know that she owned *Wartime Letters* and *Letters on Cézanne.* JMFA Library title-page photocopies. See chapter nine, note 34.

14. The reference to her own territory, object, or space is a leitmotif throughout Mitchell's life. For a sensitive discussion of the implications of "mine," see Judith E. Bernstock, *Joan Mitchell, exh. cat.* (New York: Hudson Hills Press, 1988), 69–70.

15. "Bridge money" meant the inheritance issuing from the money her grandfather made as an engineer working on large-scale bridge projects. See Ed Clark, interview with Patricia Albers, June 21, 2002, Albers Papers. Check from Mitchell to Madam L. V. Schneider, May 26, 1967, Financial Records, JMFA. This first check was a deposit. A check dated June 29, 1967, for $70,808, was provided at closing, and another check, for $881, was issued to Mme. Schneider on October 13, 1967. Riopelle started to rent the garage/studio in 1969, and then purchased it in 1974.

16. Mitchell writes in a letter mailed from Frémicourt: "We go to the country house on weekends—it is nice & you would like it.… The bathrooms work & all & Sylvie & dogs feel they have a 'home.'" Mitchell also notes that she will spend "Xmas" there. Letter from Mitchell to Barney Rosset, n.d. [postmarked December 22, 1967], JMFA003.

17. Ed Clark, interview with Quincy Troupe, transcript, 1993, box 4, folders 1–6, Ed Clark Papers, 1923–2017, AAA. Later published in *Edward Clark: For the Sake of the Search,* ed. Barbara Cavaliere and George R. N'Namdi (Belleville Lake, MI: Belleville Lake Press, 1997), 21.

18. A list of works in a letter to Bernier seems to be in chronological order, with Mitchell dating *Vétheuil* 1967–68. Letter from Mitchell to Bernier, n.d. [ca. November 1967], Jackson Gallery Archives.

19. Mitchell writes to Bernier, "*My Landscape I* Jan '67 you can see the evolvement to the last pics.—or an intelligent critic could. Hess is using Pierre Schneider—the article has been written—so don't panic." Ibid.

20. Unsent letter from Mitchell to Patricia Molloy, 1968, Unsent Correspondence, JMFA001.

21. Joan Mitchell, interview with Phyllis Tuchman, June 10, 1971, "Selected audio recordings from Phyllis Tuchman interviews with artists, 1971–1979," box 4, cassette 38, Phyllis Tuchman Interviews with Artists, 1968–1987, GRI. Mitchell tells Tuchman

that the multipart paintings both addressed the lack of space for large works in her Frémicourt studio and were cheaper to ship than single-canvas works of equivalent size. At the end of her life, she would say that she liked the way that the vertical line disrupted the horizontal. Dagen, "La fureur de Joan Mitchell," 11.

22. Mitchell writes, "I have learned more about birds—feed them on terrace table & watch them as one might watch T.V.—color is much better—but the sweet ones—the gossipy—the nasty—etc—& those starlings—really. It's fun. Natch I'm sitting inside looking out." Letter from Mitchell to Joanne and Philip Von Blon, n.d. [postmarked January 2, 1987], JMFA018.

23. Pierre Schneider, "Joan Mitchell Notes Divers," Fonds Pierre Schneider, Institut Mémoires de l'édition contemporaine (IMEC), Caen, France.

24. Mitchell, interview with Tuchman, June 10, 1971, GRI.

25. Letter from Marion Strobel to Mitchell, September 29, 1965, JMFA001.

26. *Joan Mitchell—Recent Paintings* (April 2–27, 1968), press release, March 19, 1968, Martha Jackson Gallery, New York, JMFA004: Joan Mitchell Exhibition Records. Sixteen paintings total were exhibited.

27. Mitchell complains to Rosset, "The space is awful & I'm depressed & my paintings are very mixed in style—and won't look well there." Letter from Mitchell to Rosset, n.d. [postmarked December 22, 1967], JMFA003. Mitchell adds that she wishes she could postpone the show. There is a marked difference in the chronological presentation of paintings between Mitchell's gallery exhibitions at Fournier (1967, 1969) and Martha Jackson (1968) and the tighter, subject-based groupings exhibited in 1972 at *My Five Years in the Country: An Exhibition of Forty-Nine Paintings by Joan Mitchell,* Everson Museum of Art, Syracuse, New York (March 26–April 21), which traveled to the Martha Jackson Gallery in New York in two parts: *Blue Series 1970–1971* (April 26–May 13) and *The Fields Series 1971–1972* (May 16–June 3). The museum exhibition pleased Mitchell, and perhaps exhibiting clearer subject groups would have been her preference if she had been able to postpone the 1968 gallery show.

28. Unsent letter from Mitchell to Jean Lamouroux, 1968, Unsent Correspondence, JMFA001; unsent letter from Mitchell to Shirley Jaffe, 1968, JMFA001.

29. Gregory Battcock, "In the Galleries: Joan Mitchell," *Arts Magazine* 42, no. 6 (April 1968): 59; Hilton Kramer, "*John Heliker: Under Close Scrutiny*: Retrospective Given by Whitney Museum," *New York Times,* April 6, 1968, 35; and Max Kozloff, "New York: Joan Mitchell," *Artforum* 6, no. 10 (Summer 1968): 50. As a further marker of the changing fashion, her 1969 exhibition at Fournier does not seem to have garnered any critical attention.

30. On asking Clark to finish his series and then cede the large studio, see letter from Mitchell to Molloy, July 1968, JMFA001. Hedy Clark (who had returned to New York) sent a letter addressed to Ed at Vétheuil in late October. Letter from Hedy Clark to Ed Clark, October 25, 1968, box 2, folder 3, Ed Clark Papers, 1923–2017, AAA. Also, Hedy Clark, interview with the author, March 10, 2019, New York.

31. Unsent letter from Mitchell to Molloy, 1968, JMFA001.

32. Letter from Mitchell to Evans Herman, November 26, 1968, courtesy Patricia Albers.

33. Letter from Mitchell to Molloy, September 1, 1969, JMFA008; letter from Mitchell to Norman Bluhm, October 1969, Norman Bluhm Papers, 1956–1969, AAA; and letter from Mitchell to Rosset, n.d. [postmarked October 2, 1969], JMFA003.

34. Emily Cheng, interview with Karli Wurzelbacher, February 18, 2019, New York.

35. Letter from Mitchell to Molloy, September 1, 1969.

36. Munro interview transcript, [1977], 19, Munro Papers, AAA.

37. Letter from Mitchell to Karen Edwards, November 26, 1968, Karen Edwards papers, courtesy Zoe Jet Ellis.

38. She would make at least six works titled *Sunflower* that year, with the others going to group shows and the home of Patricia Matisse.

39. Although Mitchell painted "for" gallery exhibitions, her studio process was fluid, and she would cycle between and back to subjects within a period. In addition, titles often came later, in the context of sales and publications, and Martha Jackson's son David Anderson (who took over the gallery after Jackson's death in 1969) had a strong hand in shaping this during her time with Jackson. Correspondence around *My Five Years in the Country* explicates the gathering of the works from 1968–70 that were originally intermingled in three gallery shows: Fournier in 1967, Jackson in 1968, and Fournier in 1969. Anderson oversaw sorting them, with Mitchell's agreement, into subject-based series: La Seine, River and Tree, Sunflower, and Sans neige (together with other series from 1970–72, discussed in chapter 7 of this volume).

40. Seckler, AAA oral history; and Marcia Tucker, Joan Mitchell interview notes, December 1973, box 64, folder 14, Marcia Tucker Papers, 1957–2007, GRI. See also Marcia Tucker, *Joan Mitchell,* exh. cat. (New York: Whitney Museum of American Art, 1974), 17n10.

41. Pierre Schneider, "From Confession to Landscape," *Art News* 67, no. 2 (April 1968): 73.

Untitled, 1969
Mara Hoberman

126–27

1. Letter from Vincent van Gogh to Theo van Gogh, August 21 or 22, 1888, in *Vincent van Gogh: The Letters,* ed. Leo Jansen, Hans Luijten, and Nienke Bakker (Amsterdam & The Hague: Van Gogh Museum & Huygens, 2009), December 2010 version, http://www.vangoghletters.org/vg/letters/let666/letter.html.

2. "Les pétales tombés de l'harmonueux bouquet de pivoines se désintègrent en un chaos de pigments." Pierre Schneider, "Les bonheurs de Joan Mitchell," *L'Express,* June 14–20, 1975.

3. Yves Michaud, "Conversations with Joan Mitchell, January 12, 1986," in *Joan Mitchell: New Paintings,* exh. cat. (New York: Xavier Fourcade, 1986), n.p.

4. Barbara Rose, "Joan Mitchell: The Landscape of Light," *Vogue* (June 1981): 245.

5. Peter Schjeldahl, "Joan Mitchell: To Obscurity and Back," *New York Times,* April 30, 1972.

"Love Is the Condition of Arriving at Infinity": Joan Mitchell and Poetry
Jenni Quilter

188–97

1. Judith E. Bernstock, *Joan Mitchell,* exh. cat. (New York: Hudson Hills, 1997), 13. Mitchell's "Autumn" appeared in *Poetry* in 1935, after her tenth birthday.

2. Strobel returned Mitchell's gaze. In Strobel's first crime novel, *Ice before Killing* (New York: Charles Scribner's Sons, 1943), the protagonist, Liz Soames, is a young figure skater contemplating whether or not to turn professional. She is the same age (eighteen) as Mitchell was when Strobel was writing the book. Strobel's description of skating pays particular attention to the visual coherency of the scene, as if it were an abstract painting: "Then the lights went on. The dark luster of the ice became mother of pearl, the skaters who had stood or leaned or perched as shadowy shapes took on color like plumage, all together, in their violent reds and purples, in their greens and yellows and electric blues, swooped on the ice. In a few minutes there was order, and the noise had died down. In its place was rhythm and symmetry. Liz, frowning, became one of the smoothest of the component parts of this of unified whole." Not

only did Strobel consider the ice rink as a visual field, she briefly accounted for the absorbed concentration that comes from any creative process. Her description of Liz skating could be of Mitchell painting—or herself writing: "Her eyes were lowered to watch what she was doing. After a half hour of concentration, she stooped over, brushed the snowy particles from the surface and examined her tracings. They were as clean as the scratch of a diamond on glass" (ibid., 39). In later years, Mitchell was reluctant to concede that skating might be a calligraphic precursor to her own painting, but it is obvious that Strobel was intrigued enough with the analogy to quietly play with it.

3. Back jacket copy for Marion Strobel, *Once in a Blue Moon* (New York: Harcourt, Brace, 1925).

4. In her letters to her daughter in the late 1940s, Strobel briefly described some of the editorial disagreements at *Poetry* over this topic: there were those who thought of poems as "intellectual observations," whereas Strobel and George Dillon's position was that "the spring-board for poetry *must* be emotion." Emphasis Strobel's, letter from Marion Strobel to Mitchell, July 2, 1948, JMFA001. Despite Strobel's concerns, she later noted that *Poetry* would still print the seminal "The New Criticism" across three issues of *Poetry*. The series, "cooked up by [Allen] Tate, [John Crowe] Ransom, [Robert Penn] Warren and their satellites," contends that "a poem can be written for instance on an ashcan—the words are what count, there need be no emotion behind them." Letter from Strobel to Mitchell, August 14–15, 1948, JMFA001.

5. Marion Strobel, *Lost City* (Boston: Houghton Mifflin, 1928), 57.

6. Laura Quinney, *The Poetics of Disappointment: Wordsworth to Ashbery* (Charlottesville: University Press of Virginia, 1999), 2.

7. The novels were tepidly reviewed. *Kirkus*, for example, considered Strobel's *Fellow Mortals* (New York: Farrar and Rinehart, 1935) "a more ambitious book than her previous novels, but still essentially a book for women and for rental libraries." *Kirkus Reviews,* February 21, 1935, https://www.kirkusreviews.com/book-reviews/marion-strobel-2/fellow-mortals/. The echoes between Strobel's life and the characters were obvious, though quite possibly shallow. *Saturday Afternoon* features a forty-year-old female protagonist who was obviously modeled in part on Harriet Monroe, the founder of *Poetry*. The novel opens in Pease's living room, where a group of "Chicago literati—an anemic crowd, underweight and over-sexed" are enjoying her "home-made spice-cake, her tea, her strawberry jam, hot rolls, and buttered toast." Pease (unlike Monroe) comes from money. She has offered $10,000 to the first "good" Chicago novel in order to jumpstart a "renaissance of literature in Chicago." Marion Strobel, *Saturday Afternoon* (New York: Farrar and Rinehart, 1930), 8.

8. If the environment of Strobel's novels was socially conservative, she was not. In the hundreds of letters Strobel wrote to Joan from the mid-1940s to the mid-1960s, she staunchly stood by her daughter's decisions about love and marriage, however unorthodox they might be in her own social set in Chicago. For instance, Strobel conveyed to Mitchell her conversation with Barney Rosset's father, who was expecting the two of them to marry: "He repeatedly said that you kept telling B to wait. He said that you felt 'misunderstood at home' and that we did not like B. When I said that I thought you were seriously interested in painting, which made a decision about marriage more difficult than it would be ordinarily, he said: 'You mean, at present, painting comes before sex?'" Letter from Strobel to Mitchell, June 5, 1949, JMFA001. That Strobel advanced this argument speaks volumes about her support of her daughter's career.

9. Joan Mitchell biographical materials: Smith College English 211 exam book, January 15, 1943, JMFA001.

10. Irving Sandler, "Mitchell Paints a Picture," *Art News* 56, no. 6 (October 1957): 45.

11. Bernstock, *Joan Mitchell*, 41.

12. Mitchell referred to Rilke in her paintings *My Plant* (1966) and *My Other Plant* (1965) and *My Landscape I* and *II* (both 1967, plate 55).

13. William Wordsworth, *"Lyrical Ballads" and Other Poems, 1797–1800,* ed. James Butler and Karen Green (Ithaca, NY: Cornell University Press, 1993), 756.

14. Joan Mitchell, artist's statement in *Nature in Abstraction: The Relation of Abstract Painting and Sculpture to Nature in Twentieth Century American Art,* exh. cat., ed. John I. H. Baur (New York: Whitney Museum of American Art, 1958), 75.

15. Bernstock, *Joan Mitchell,* 35.

16. *The Poems* by John Ashbery, prints by Joan Mitchell; *Permanently* by Kenneth Koch, prints by Alfred Leslie; *Odes* by Frank O'Hara, prints by Michael Goldberg; and *Salute* by James Schuyler, prints by Grace Hartigan (New York: Tiber Press, 1960). (The publication date has been printed as 1960 and 1961, but the books were actually bound and distributed in 1963.)

17. Fairfield Porter, "Poets and Painters in Collaboration" (1961), reprinted in Porter, *Art in Its Own Terms: Selected Criticism 1935–1975,* ed. Rackstraw Downes (Boston: Museum of Fine Arts, Boston, 1979), 225.

18. Fairfield Porter, "Wyndham Lewis on Picasso: A Letter to the 'Kenyon Review,'" in Porter, *Art in Its Own Terms,* 239.

19. Frank O'Hara, Elaine de Kooning, Norman Bluhm, Michael Goldberg, and Joan Mitchell, "5 Participants in a Hearsay Panel," *It Is* 3 (Winter/Spring 1959): 59.

20. "Ma relation avec le monde de l'art est lointaine, elle passe surtout à travers les individus." Mitchell, quoted in Suzanne Pagé and Béatrice Parent, eds., *Joan Mitchell: choix de peintures 1970–1982* (Paris: Musée d'art moderne de la Ville de Paris, 1982), n.p. Translation by Éric de Chassey.

21. Larry Rivers, "Speech Read at Frank O'Hara's Funeral, Springs, Long Island, July 27, 1966," in *Homage to Frank O'Hara,* ed. Bill Berkson and Joe LeSueur (Bolinas, CA: Big Sky, 1978), 138.

22. Letter from Frank O'Hara to Mitchell, August 7, 1959, JMFA001. For discussion of the accompanying poem, see chapter 3 of this volume.

23. Joe Brainard, "I Remember," reprinted in *The Collected Writings of Joe Brainard,* ed. Ron Padgett (New York: Library of America, 2012), 17.

24. Frank O'Hara, "Poem Read at Joan Mitchell's," reprinted in *The Collected Poems of Frank O'Hara,* ed. Donald Allen (Berkeley: University of California Press, 1995), 265.

25. Frank O'Hara, "Adieu to Norman, Bon Jour to Joan and Jean-Paul," reprinted in *The Collected Poems of Frank O'Hara,* 328.

26. Mitchell was very fond of Hugo von Hofmannsthal's "The Letter of Lord Chandos," which she showed to Bernstock, and the essay is an excellent example of a lyric expression of the consolations of a failed language. See Hugo von Hofmannsthal, *The Lord Chandos Letter and Other Writings,* trans. Joel Rotenberg (New York: New York Review of Books, 2005). This text is a hypothetical letter written by the youngest son of the Earl of Bath to Francis Bacon, "apologizing for his complete abandonment of literary activity" (ibid., 117). Chandos's self-diagnosis is that he has lost the "ability to think or speak coherently about anything at all" (ibid., 121) but, rather perversely, he writes of this failure extremely coherently. His paralysis begins with an intolerance for abstractions, for words like "spirit," "soul," or "body," and then begins to broaden like "spreading rust" (ibid.). Even in a treatise on the corruption of language, Hofmannsthal didn't meet an analogy he could refuse, and most of these metaphors have to do with sight. Indeed, objects turn out to be Chandos's salvation, and he provides a list that could serve as an inventory of nineteenth-century painting: "a watering can, a harrow left in a field, a dog in the sun, a shabby churchyard, a cripple, a small farmhouse ... past which the eye

ordinarily glides with natural indifference, can ... [be] filled to the brim with ... a steeply rising tide of heavenly feeling" (ibid., 123). It is a salvation that comes from seeing (which suited Mitchell) and a salvation whose value was proportionate to its own awareness of failure.

27. John Ashbery's poem "Europe" began: "To employ her/ construction ball/ Morning fed on the/ light blue wood/ of the mouth/ Cannot understand/ feels deeply." It appeared deliberately incomprehensible, exulting in rather than mourning a failure of language.

28. Bill Berkson, "Tiger, Tiger: A Few Days with Joan," *Poetry* 201, no. 5 (February 2013): 538.

29. Letter from Bill Berkson to Mitchell, May 23, 1988, JMFA001. It is worth noting what Berkson picked out, trying to anticipate Mitchell's taste: John Ashbery's "The Grapevine," "The Painter," "Some Trees," and "A Blessing in Disguise"; Frank O'Hara's "To the Harbormaster," "Ode to Joy," "Adieu to Norman, Bon Jour to Joan and Jean-Paul," and "The Day Lady Died"; and James Schuyler's "Footnote," "The Bluet," "Cornflowers," and "Sunset."

30. James Schuyler, "A Few Days," reprinted in *Collected Poems* (New York: Farrar, Straus and Giroux, 1993), 356, 354.

31. Mitchell observed, "Much of Pollock's painting, almost all of it, I would say, is excessively lyric, and I think he thought of it as violent. They were extremely lyric paintings. Whether they're beautiful or not, they're lyric, which is now a dirty word." Bernstock, *Joan Mitchell,* 38. Of "nature," she commented, "nature was a dirty word in the fifties." Ibid., 67.

32. Letter from Frank O'Hara to Kenneth Koch, quoted in Brad Gooch, *City Poet: The Life and Times of Frank O'Hara* (New York: Alfred A. Knopf, 1993), 261. In 1957, O'Hara also wrote to Mitchell about his "periodic summer affair with French poetry," noting that she flew off to Paris each year "about the same time as I fly away from Pound and Williams and Whitman into the cool arms of Char and Reverdy and Verlaine." Letter from O'Hara to Mitchell, July 30, 1957, JMFA001.

33. Interestingly enough, to Harriet Monroe in 1917, Ezra Pound wrote, "The only thing I can see for strengthening the prose section of *Poetry* is a series of essays on French poets." *Poetry* magazine included very few translations of French poems in the early twentieth century. It was not necessarily a tradition with which Strobel would have been well acquainted, though it was available to Mitchell's generation through a number of translations by her peers (including Ashbery, Auster, and Beckett) in other magazines and anthologies.

34. Paul Auster, introduction to *The Random House Book of Twentieth Century French Poetry* (New York: Random House, 1982), xxxii.

35. Bernstock, *Joan Mitchell,* 106. Bernstock notes that Mitchell also admired "his ability to create an atmosphere without resorting to literal description" (ibid.).

36. Anecdote noted by Auster, introduction to *The Random House Book,* xxxii.

37. Bernstock, *Joan Mitchell,* 41.

38. Bernstock refers to these pieces as "color abstracts," though they are now commonly referred to as "poem pastels" (ibid., 137).

39. Frank O'Hara, "Personism: A Manifesto," in *The Collected Poems of Frank O'Hara,* 498–99.

7 Territories
Sarah Roberts

198–205

Epigraph: "waiting not too slow regretting not too long the absence/ in the service of presence/ a few tatters of azure in the head the points finally/ dead of the heart." Samuel Beckett, excerpt from "à elle l'acte calme," in *Collected Poems in English and French: Samuel Beckett* (New York: Grove Press, 1977), 40. First published in *Les temps modernes* 2, no. 14 (November 1946). English translation by "P.N.," published in *Poetry Magazine* 91, no. 5 (February 2008): 385.

1. Letter from Mitchell to Karen Edwards, n.d. [postmarked February 11, 1971], Karen Edwards papers, courtesy Zoe Jet Ellis.

2. Letter from Mitchell to Edwards, February 9, 1974, Karen Edwards papers, courtesy Zoe Jet Ellis.

3. Letter from Mitchell to Patricia Molloy, February 21, 1971, JMFA008. Letter from Mitchell to Edwards, February 11, 1971, Karen Edwards papers, courtesy Zoe Jet Ellis.

4. Letter from Mitchell to Leon Arkus of the Carnegie Museum of Art, June 21, 1971, typed copy, Jackson Gallery Archives.

5. Pierre Schneider, "Pour Joan Mitchell" in *XXe siècle,* no. 40 (June 1973): 116–19 (in French), 192 (in English). For previous printings, see chapter 4, note 36.

6. Though it has been proposed that the title *Three Seasons* was drawn from a Christina Rossetti poem, it more likely derived from the Alice Clay Judson poem "Three Seasons of Growth," which was published in *Poetry* 73, no. 1 (April 1948): 17. The poem describes the difficult passage of a woman through three phases of life. The third stanza begins: "Bewildered woman/ Now mature/ Uncertain touch becoming sure." Judson was a family friend in Chicago when she and Mitchell were children, and they attended Francis Parker School together. Mitchell had her mother's library shipped to Vétheuil after her death, which may have contributed to the resurgence of her interest in reading poetry.

7. Mitchell did not necessarily paint the canvas with Dupin's poem in mind; it is more likely that she titled it after it was completed, in recognition of the resonance she felt between the painting and a poem she knew well and loved. See Judith E. Bernstock, *Joan Mitchell,* exh. cat. (New York: Hudson Hills, 1988), 98. Among the volumes in Mitchell's library were Dupin's *Gravir* (1963) and *Fits and Starts* (translated by Paul Auster, 1974), as well as a clothbound, accordion-fold artist's book with his poem, "La ligne de rupture" written in Dupin's hand, with a dedication to Mitchell. See page 319 in this volume.

8. Richard Stamelman, *Lost beyond Telling: Representations of Death and Absence in Modern French Poetry* (Ithaca, NY: Cornell University Press, 1990), see especially 161–63.

9. Letter from Mitchell to Jon Schueler, n.d. [ca. December 1971], Jon Schueler Archives, courtesy the Jon Schueler Estate.

10. Fournier wrote, "Je vous adresse cette image, chère Joan en hommage à celle de votre rivière vue un peu du haut de votre jardin, en sortant de votre atelier" (I send you this image, dear Joan, in homage to that of your river seen almost from the top of your garden, coming out of your studio). Postcard from Jean Fournier to Mitchell, June 27, 1973, JMFA001. See page 198.

11. Munro typewritten interview notes, [1977], 16, Munro Papers, AAA.

12. Anderson arranged much of the checklist and oversaw the catalogue for the Everson exhibition. The Territories designation was not included in the Everson catalogue, but was added for the presentations at the Martha Jackson Gallery. See Anderson correspondence with Mitchell for his introduction of the series titles to her. Letter from David Anderson to Mitchell, February 8, 1971, Jackson Gallery Archives.

13. Mitchell, quoted in Marcia Tucker, *Joan Mitchell,* exh. cat. (New York: Whitney Museum of American Art, 1974), 8–9. The remark also appears with slightly different wording in Tucker, Joan Mitchell interview notes, December 1973, box 64, folder 14, Marcia Tucker Papers, 1957–2007, GRI: "I like to have my paintings keep still, hold one image despite all the activity."

14. Munro typewritten interview notes, [1977], 16, Munro Papers, AAA.

15. Carter Ratcliff, "Joan Mitchell's Envisionments," *Art in America* 62, no. 4 (July–August 1974): 37.

16. Mitchell in Tucker, interview notes, December 1973.

17. Ellen Lubell, "New York Galleries," *Arts Magazine* 46, no. 8 (Summer 1972): 60. See also Gordon Muck, "King James Version of Everson Really Jumps," *Syracuse Post Standard*, April 3, 1972, 11.

18. Peter Schjeldahl, "Joan Mitchell: To Obscurity and Back," *New York Times,* April 30, 1972.

19. Tucker, *Joan Mitchell,* 15. In her endnote 20, Tucker cites the quote within her statement as follows: Christian Norberg-Schulz, *Existence, Space and Architecture* (Boston: Beacon Press, 1969), 72.

20. Nochlin, AAA oral history.

21. *Joan Mitchell* (March 26–May 5, 1974), press release, Whitney Museum of American Art, New York, JMFA004.

22. Tucker, Mitchell interview notes, December 1973.

23. Harold Rosenberg, "The Art World: Artist against Background," *New Yorker* 50, no. 10 (April 29, 1974): 74.

24. April Kingsley, "New York Letter," *Art International* 18, no. 6 (Summer 1974): 43.

25. Hans Hofmann, "Plastic Creation" (1932), reprinted in *Hans Hofmann,* ed. Sam Hunter (New York: Harry N. Abrams, 1964), 37.

26. Kingsley, "New York Letter," 43. See also Barbara Rose, "First-Rate Art by the Second Sex," *New York,* April 8, 1974, 80; and Hayden Herrera, "Reviews and Previews: Joan Mitchell," *Art News* 73, no. 6 (Summer 1974): 111.

27. Rosalind Krauss, "Painting Becomes Cyclorama," *Artforum* 12, no. 10 (June 1974): 50.

28. Letter from Mitchell to Michael Goldberg, n.d. [postmarked July 13, 1974], Goldberg Papers, AAA. Notably, she did not object to Krauss's invocation of Monet.

29. Marcia Tucker, *A Short Life of Trouble: Forty Years in the New York Art World* (Berkeley: University of California Press, 2010), 105–7.

30. Photocopy of letter from Mitchell to Sally Perry, December 18, 1973, JMFA001 (whereabouts of original unknown).

31. This exhibition also traveled to the National Arts Club, New York.

32. Letter from Mitchell to Molloy, February 21, 1971, JMFA008.

33. Letter from Mitchell to Edwards, January 21, 1974, Karen Edwards papers, courtesy Zoe Jet Ellis.

34. Letter from Chris Larson to Mitchell, February 12, 1973, JMFA001.

35. Ibid.

36. Mitchell mentions the invitation in a letter to Edwards: "Have been asked to represent *France* at the Venice Biennale—pretty funny—don't know but have to decide by Thursday." Letter from Mitchell to Edwards, January 21, 1974, Karen Edwards papers, courtesy Zoe Jet Ellis. The Venice invitation is also reported in handwritten notes of a telephone call from Fourcade to the Arts Club of Chicago: "She is very anxious to have a show, *however,* she has been chosen to represent France in the Venice Biennale which will take place in September." Phone call 4/16 to Mr. Fourcade, Arts Club of Chicago Papers, box 80, folder 932, Newberry Library. The three-month lag between the letter to Edwards, when she had to decide within days, and the phone call suggest that she had committed to participating.

37. Letter from Mitchell to Edwards, November 17, 1975, Karen Edwards papers, courtesy Zoe Jet Ellis.

38. Letter from Mitchell to Xavier Fourcade, August 1, 1974, Fourcade Archives.

Poem pastels
Erin Kimmel

206–7

1. Nochlin, AAA oral history.

2. Nochlin, AAA oral history.

3. Letter from Mitchell to Xavier Fourcade, March 27, 1975, Fourcade Archives.

4. Letter from Frank O'Hara to Mitchell, October 24, 1957, JMFA001.

5. Letter from Joe LeSueur to Mitchell, February 7, 1977, JMFA001.

6. James Schuyler, "Letter to a Friend: Who is Nancy Daum?" in *Collected Poems* (New York: Farrar, Straus and Giroux, 1993), 128.

7. Carl Little, "An Interview with James Schuyler," *Agni,* no. 37 (1992): 169.

8. James Schuyler, "Daylight," in *Hymn to Life* (New York: Random House, 1974), 71.

8 Green
Katy Siegel

208–15

Epigraph: Francis Ponge, *The Making of the Pré (La fabrique du pré),* trans. Lee Fahnestock (Columbia: University of Missouri Press, 1979), 99. Ponge would have known people in Mitchell's Paris social circles in the 1960s and 1970s, but we do not know whether she read his work. He worked on the poem "Le Pré" during the early 1960s, when Mitchell used the title *Vert comme pré* for a 1962 painting. The poem was published in *Tel Quel* 18 (Summer 1964), and in 1971 Ponge published *La fabrique du pré,* a small book with notes and drawings around the process of writing the poem.

1. Letter from Mitchell to Patricia Molloy, n.d. [postmarked September 18, 1976], JMFA008.

2. Jean Fournier, interview with Patricia Albers, March 27, 2003, Albers Papers.

3. Letter from Mitchell to Xavier Fourcade, March 27, 1975, Fourcade Archives.

4. "Key" painting, in Eleanor Munro, "Joan Mitchell," in *Originals: American Women Artists* (New York: Simon and Schuster, 1979), 238.

5. Letter from Mitchell to Betsy Jolas, March 1968, Betsy Jolas Papers, Beinecke Rare Book and Manuscript Library, Yale University.

6. Donal Henahan, "Betsy Jolas Winning Recognition in U.S.," *New York Times,* August 30, 1976, 15. Upon first meeting, Mitchell reportedly said to Jolas, "You are a lady composer and I am a lady painter." Betsy Jolas, interview with the author, October 10, 2018, Paris.

7. Munro, "Joan Mitchell," 238.

8. "That painting . . . has—the first ups and downs. . . . These verticals rather than round sunflowers or something—and that was the beginning of a new phase." Munro interview transcript, [1977], 8, Munro Papers, AAA.

9. Mitchell said of *Quatuor II,* "I worked on for about a year. Off and on, you know, I kept looking at it, changing the panels." Ibid., 10.

10. Speaking about the spaces between, see, for example, ibid., 9. Gisèle Barreau also mentioned Mitchell saying this to her; Barreau, interview with the author, Sarah Roberts, and Marin Sarvé-Tarr, February 19, 2019, Paris. For "space-feelings," see Linda Nochlin, "Joan Mitchell: Art and Life at Vétheuil," *House & Garden* 156, no. 11 (November 1984): 228.

11. Letter from Mitchell to Cristina and Barney Rosset, June 1976, with copy of exhibition announcement included, JMFA003.

12. Mitchell wrote to Fourcade that the show was all large work, and also that MoMA or Beaubourg (that is, the Centre Georges Pompidou [CGP]) had shown interest. Letter from Mitchell to Fourcade, May 13, 1976, Fourcade Archives. The CGP acquired *Sylvie's Sunday* from Fournier in 1976. Thanks to Jean-Pierre Criqui and Odile Rousseau of the CGP for confirming this in an email to the author, October 4, 2019.

13. The period was so productive that many significant works, such as *Red Tree* (plate 93) and *Sarrians* (plate 94), were not shown at the time; the gallery exhibitions simply could not accommodate the number of strong paintings. See letter from Fourcade to Mitchell, September 18, 1976, Fourcade Archives.

14. Letter from Mitchell to Molloy, July 4, 1977, JMFA008.

15. Writing about the Fourcade exhibition, her close friend Tom Hess called them "studio pictures." Thomas B. Hess, "Sensations of Landscape," *New York,* December 20, 1976, 78.

16. Letter from Mitchell to Fourcade, October 19, 1976, Fourcade Archives.

17. Mitchell, interviewed in "Joan Mitchell à Vétheuil," in *American Artists in Europe,* directed by Angeliki Haas (Paris, 1976), 8mm, 30 min.

18. Mitchell would have seen van Gogh's drawings in museums throughout her life, and likely was particularly aware of the drawings van Gogh included in his letters, as her edition of the letters included tipped-in plates of those sketches. We know that she owned the French edition; it is quite likely that she owned the English edition as well. It appears that van Gogh's work from 1898 and 1899, and in particular, the gardens at Arles and St-Rémy, relates to Mitchell's from 1976 to 1978. See Vincent van Gogh, *Correspondance complète de Vincent van Gogh enrichie de tous les dessins originaux,* 3 vols., trans. M. Beerblock and L. Röelandt, with an introduction and notes by Georges Charensol (Paris: Gallimard-Grosset, 1960); Mitchell's copy remains with her library in the Joan Mitchell Foundation Archives.

19. Apparently speaking about a 1977 work in the Munro interview in New York that fall, Mitchell jokes that it was an "homage to Vincent perhaps. There are no crows." Munro interview transcript, [1977], 9, Munro Papers, AAA. Mitchell would title a 1987 painting *No Birds*; the title perhaps also recalls *Sans neige* and its negative reference to Monet (see chapter 6 of this volume). Two other paintings from 1976 may refer to van Gogh: *Tournesols* (van Gogh's original title for the sunflower paintings), and *Loom,* possibly a reference to van Gogh's images of weavers, a subject that Linda Nochlin was researching and writing about during her visits to France in the mid-1970s.

20. Linda Nochlin made notes while interviewing Mitchell in 1984 that an "artist can go dead—then come back. VG [Van Gogh]—1st favorite—now back to where [he] was as [a] child." Linda Nochlin, dedicated 1984 notebook, box 19, folder 23, Linda Nochlin Papers, AAA.

21. On van Gogh's letters, see note 18. For the Musée de l'Orangerie exhibition, see *Vincent van Gogh: collection du Musée national Vincent van Gogh à Amsterdam,* exh. cat. (Paris: Réunion des musées nationaux, 1972).

22. Letter from Fourcade to Mitchell, February 4, 1976, Fourcade Archives.

23. For van Gogh, see for example, letter from Vincent van Gogh to Theo van Gogh, September, 18, 1888, in *Vincent van Gogh: The Letters,* ed. Leo Jansen, Hans Luijten, and Nienke Bakker (Amsterdam & The Hague: Van Gogh Museum & Huygens, 2009), December 2010 version, http://www.vangoghletters.org/vg/letters/let682/letter.html. For Mitchell, see letter from Mitchell to Molloy, n.d. [postmarked June 12, 1976], JMFA008. Written in the form of a brochure for the "Funny Farm," it details the daily routine at Vétheuil, which she believes would be healing for Molloy in its regularity, and also the grounding in nature rather than in social conventions.

24. Letter from Mitchell to Fourcade, October 29, 1976, Fourcade Archives.

25. Letter from Vincent van Gogh to Theo van Gogh, May 1, 1890, in *Vincent van Gogh: The Letters,* http://vangoghletters.org/vg/letters/let865/letter.html.

26. Meyer Schapiro's book on van Gogh emphasized the painter's directness in both color and brushstroke, and his engagement with the natural world. Paul Brach stated that Mitchell studied with Schapiro at Columbia but there is no evidence that he was her professor; she did, however, mention his volume on van Gogh in her notebook. Schapiro, *Van Gogh* (New York: Harry N. Abrams, 1950); Joan Mitchell, 1951 Columbia notebook, Joyce Pensato Papers, courtesy the Estate of Joyce Pensato. Linda Nochlin's interview notes on Mitchell include her dislike of printmaking because of its indirectness, and her preference for direct art making. Linda Nochlin, dedicated 1984 notebook, box 19, 23, Linda Nochlin Papers, AAA.

27. Jeanne Siegel, "The Whitney Biennial: 'A Firmer Position on Current Esthetic Trends,'" *Art News* 72, no. 3 (March 1973): 68.

28. Claude Viallat [1974], quoted in *Oeuvres contemporaines des collections nationales: Accrochage II* (Paris: Centre Georges Pompidou, 1979), n.p.

29. Munro, "Joan Mitchell," 235. Emily Cheng, interview with Karli Wurzelbacher, February 18, 2019, New York.

30. Mitchell to Leon Arkus, director of the Carnegie Museum, June 21, 1971, Jackson Gallery Archives.

31. Mitchell met Lynda Benglis in the mid-1970s through Michael Goldberg. See Klaus Kertess, interview with Jane Livingston, September 14, 1999, Jane Livingston personal papers; Benglis, interview with the author, October 29, 2019, New York.

32. Galerie Jean Fournier, *Peinture, couleurs Lefranc-Bourgeois* (Bishop, Degottex, Francis, Hantaï, Jaffe, Mitchell, Viallat) (November 13–December 12, 1973).

33. There were four exhibitions of the collection in these years: *Oeuvres contemporaines des collections nationales: Accrochage galeries contemporaines* (December 13, 1978–January 22, 1979), brochure (8 pages) with preface by Bernard Anthonioz and Pontus Hulten; *Oeuvres contemporaines des collections nationales—Accrochage II* (February 7–April 2, 1979), brochure with preface by Bernard Anthonioz, Pontus Hulten, and Alfred Pacquement; *Oeuvres contemporaines des collections nationales: Accrochage III: Galeries contemporaines* (October 10–November 19, 1979); and *Ateliers aujourd'hui: Oeuvres contemporaines des collections nationales—Accrochage IV: Galeries contemporaines* (April 9–June 1, 1980). Early on, Paul Auster also showed slides of the work of his friend David Reed to Mitchell, to her approval. See letter from Paul Auster to David Reed, November 19, 1973, courtesy David Reed.

34. Letter from Mitchell to Fourcade, October 29, 1976, Fourcade Archives.

35. Peter Schjeldahl, "Joan Mitchell: To Obscurity and Back," *New York Times,* April 30, 1972, 23. Harold Rosenberg, "The Art World: Artist against Background," *New Yorker,* April 29, 1974, 71–72, 74, 76, 78; Paul Brach, "Review of Exhibitions: New York. Joan Mitchell at Fourcade," *Art in America* 66, no. 2 (March–April 1978): 135, 143.

36. These statements come amidst a review of her rising and falling professional fortunes in Munro typewritten interview notes, [1977], 15–16, Munro Papers, AAA. Munro, who shows a certain lack of insight into Mitchell in the published piece, ascribes bitterness to the artist herself, despite the fact that Mitchell is criticizing the bitterness of other artists. Mitchell was likely responding to statements like those from a 1974 interviewer, who asked, "How do you feel about this very recent rebirth in your work?" Lyn Blumenthal (interviewer) and Kate Horsfield (camera), *Joan Mitchell: An Interview* (Chicago: Video Data Bank, School of the Art Institute of Chicago, 1974).

37. There were many small exhibitions of work by women artists; two of the more significant include *Women's Work: American Art 1974,* Museum of the Philadelphia Civic Center, Philadelphia (April 27–May 26, 1974); and *Langage au féminine, Création feminine Rhône-Alpes,* Espace lyonnais d'art contemporain, Lyon (November 1978–January 8, 1979). Mitchell told both Linda Nochlin and Peter Soriano, with pleasure, that her work was on the cover of *La part des femmes dans l'art contemporain,* Galerie municipale, Vitry-sur-Seine, France (March 1984). Dedicated 1984 notebook, box 19, folder 23, Linda Nochlin Papers, AAA. Soriano, interview with the author, September 28, 2018, New York.

38. Cindy Nemser, "An Afternoon with Joan Mitchell," *Feminist Art Journal* 3, no. 1 (Spring 1974): 5–6, 24. Blumenthal and Horsfield, *Joan Mitchell: An Interview.*

39. There are many entries in Nochlin's datebooks during the 1970s to call or see Joan Mitchell, as well as Shirley Jaffe and Zuka Mitelberg. See Nochlin, datebooks, box 2, folders 4–7, Linda Nochlin Papers, AAA. It is worth noting that during these years, Nochlin was teaching feminist art history and broad questions of the nineteenth century, as well as the work of younger artists such as Elizabeth Murray and Pat Steir. See, for example, the syllabus for the seminar

Monet, Cézanne and the Modern Imagination, 1979, box 24, folder 42, Linda Nochlin Papers, AAA.

40. See Nochlin, datebooks, box 2, folder 7, Linda Nochlin Papers, AAA. Munro interview transcript, [1977] 23, Munro Papers, AAA. Mitchell refers to the exhibition as being at Brooklyn; it was originally curated with Ann Sutherland Harris for the Los Angeles County Museum of Art and traveled to three venues, with the Brooklyn Museum as its final stop, in late 1977, during Mitchell's visit for her exhibition at Fourcade. Mitchell mentions the exhibition to Munro after discussing Anne Ryan as an early role model: "I mean how many are there?" Munro interview transcript, [1977], 23, Munro Papers, AAA.

41. Munro typewritten interview notes, [1977], 17, Munro Papers, AAA.

42. Check from Mitchell to *Women Artists Newsletter*, Midmarch Assoc., February 14, 1976, JMFA001: Financial records. There was also a phone number and note about a subscription to *Ms.* magazine from Kate Millet, n.d., JMFA001: Correspondence.

43. Zuka Mitelberg described the shift: "She didn't want to be with women in groups at the beginning of feminism. Later she changed." Mitelberg, interview with Patricia Albers, March 24, 2003, Albers Papers.

44. Mitchell's buoyant and yet frank letters to Edwards are instructive in revealing her propensity to tailor her voice to different correspondents. Karen Edwards papers, courtesy Zoe Jet Ellis.

45. Letter from Mitchell to Fourcade, October 19, 1976, Fourcade Archives.

46. For de Kooning's visit in 1975, see letter from Joe LeSueur to Mitchell, August 29, 1975, JMFA001. Mitchell also visited the Studio School in New York in 1977 (and almost certainly at other times in the 1970s, speaking and going to see studios, including that of Joyce Pensato). Joyce Pensato, interview with the author and Karli Wurzelbacher, January 30, 2019, New York.

47. Letter from Mitchell to Molloy, July 4, 1977, JMFA008. "Elaine de Kooning & her students bothering me." Letter from Mitchell to Molloy, August 13, 1976, JMFA008. By the following month, Mitchell wrote that "[Haas] did a film on me.... Phyllis helped a great deal." Letter from Mitchell to Molloy, n.d. [postmarked September 18, 1976], JMFA008.

48. Postcard from Phyllis Hailey and Hollis Jeffcoat to Mitchell, n.d. [postmarked May 18, 1977], JMFA001. Mitchell also tells a friend that Jeffcoat plays "Gertrude," while she is "Mildred"; it is unclear whether the reference is to Gertrude Stein and friend Mildred Aldrich, or more generally, to old-fashioned, spinsterish women's names. Letter from Mitchell to Molloy, July 4, 1977, JMFA008.

49. Postcard from Hailey and Jeffcoat to Mitchell, n.d. [postmarked May 18, 1977], JMFA001. On another subsidized trip the following year, Phyllis would die in a car accident, and many years later, Mitchell dedicated a painting to her: *L'Arbre de Phyllis* (1991).

50. Munro interview transcript, [1977], 9, Munro Papers, AAA.

51. Chris Larson noted her "front-door linden tree" in a poem to "Dear, dearer, dearissima Joan" dated February 12, as cited in Roberts, chapter 7, note 33, which Mitchell would then use in an untitled poem pastel dated 1975. The poem is a list of her daily pleasures that make life worth living. Letter from Chris Larson to Mitchell, February 12, 1973, JMFA001.

52. See, for example, Jean Fournier, interview with Patricia Albers, March 27, 2003, Albers Papers.

53. Mitchell, interviewed in "Joan Mitchell à Vétheuil," in *American Artists in Europe*, directed by Haas.

Weeds, 1976
Cecilia Wichmann

216–17

1. John Russell, "Joan Mitchell," *New York Times*, December 3, 1976.

2. Letter from Xavier Fourcade to Mitchell, October 8, 1976, Fourcade Archives.

3. Letter from Mitchell to Fourcade, October 19, 1976, Fourcade Archives. Phil Patton, "Reviews. New York: Joan Mitchell," *Artforum* 15 (February 1977): 71–72.

4. Allen Ellenzweig, "Joan Mitchell, Xavier Fourcade," *Arts* 51, no. 6 (February 1977): 22.

5. Letter from Mitchell to Patricia Molloy, September 1, 1969, JMFA008.

6. Note from Mitchell to Molloy, n.d. [ca. September 1976], JMFA008.

7. Gisèle Barreau, "Porte adieu, Joan Mitchell, souvenirs," in *Joan Mitchell: la pittura dei due mondi/la peinture des deux mondes* (Milan: Skira, 2009), 140.

8. Ann Sargent Wooster, "New York Reviews: Joan Mitchell," *Art News* 76 (February 1977): 125–26.

Add Red, or Not
Richard Shiff

282–91

I thank Katy Siegel for introducing me to the Mitchell project and facilitating my participation in multiple ways. For memories of Mitchell and welcome advice, I am grateful to Peter Soriano, Adrienne Farb, Bill Scott, and Mark Schlesinger. For generous aid in research, I thank Laura Morris, Sarah Roberts, Karli Wurzelbacher, Andrew Beccone, Liza Kirwin, Joan Levy Hepburn, Gilles Heno-Coe, John Semlitsch, and Alexandra Boiarsky.

1. "Don't cover up the lake," Mitchell told a patron with a similar prospect. Nochlin, AAA oral history.

2. Mitchell, transcript of an interview with Yves Michaud, n.d. [August 7, 1989], with Mitchell's edits, JMFA001; published in French translation as Yves Michaud, "Entretiens," in *Joan Mitchell*, exh. cat. (Paris: Réunion des musées nationaux, 1994), 29–31.

3. Yves Bonnefoy, interview with Shusha Guppy, "Yves Bonnefoy: The Art of Poetry LXIX," *Paris Review* 36 (Summer 1994): 122 (emphasis in the original). Samuel Beckett, Mitchell's friend in Paris, also invoked the value of poetic silence: "To restore silence is the role of objects." *Molloy*, trans. Samuel Beckett and Patrick Bowles, in *Three Novels by Samuel Beckett: Molloy, Malone Dies, The Unnamable* (New York: Grove Press, 1955), 13.

4. Mitchell, transcript of an interview with Yves Michaud, n.d. [January 12, 1986], with Mitchell's edits, JMFA001; published as Yves Michaud, "Conversation with Joan Mitchell, January 12, 1986," *Joan Mitchell: New Paintings*, exh. cat. (New York: Xavier Fourcade, 1986), n.p.

5. Letter from Mitchell to Michael Goldberg, n.d. [postmarked July 8, 1965], Goldberg Papers, AAA.

6. Mitchell, in Michaud interview transcript, n.d. [January 12, 1986].

7. Seckler, AAA oral history.

8. Mitchell, in Michaud interview transcript, n.d. [January 12, 1986] (emphasis added), and August 7, 1989.

9. Mitchell, in *Joan Mitchell: Portrait of an Abstract Painter*, directed by Marion Cajori (New York: Arthouse Films, 1992), DVD, 30:37 min.

10. Mitchell, in Michaud interview transcript, n.d. [January 12, 1986]. Mitchell would likely have been irritated by a philosophical reference; her statements nevertheless bear comparison with those of Maurice Merleau-Ponty: "It becomes impossible to distinguish between what sees and what is seen, what paints and what is painted.... The painter's vision is a continued birth"—a first moment of consciousness at which subject and object remain one ("Eye and Mind" [1961], trans. Carleton Dallery, in *The Primacy of Perception*, ed. James M. Edie [Evanston, IL: Northwestern University Press, 1964]: 167–68). See also, Maurice Merleau-Ponty, "Cézanne's Doubt" (1945), in *Sense and Non-Sense*, trans. Hubert L. Dreyfus and Patricia A. Dreyfus (Evanston, IL: Northwestern University Press, 1964), 17–18. Merleau-Ponty stresses the capacity of one's consciousness *of* an object to become the equivalent of attributing consciousness *to* an object, so that a thing might "think itself"

within the perceptual experience. Mitchell's appreciation of Hugo von Hofmannsthal strikes a similar note; Nochlin, AAA oral history. She signals this passage: "I could no longer comprehend [daily life] with the simplifying glance of habit. . . . It seemed impossible to contain anything at all within a single concept," from Hofmannsthal, "The Letter of Lord Chandos" (1902), trans. Tania and James Stern, in *The Whole Difference: Selected Writings of Hugo von Hofmannsthal,* ed. J. D. McClatchy (Princeton, NJ: Princeton University Press, 2008), 74.

11. For example, "Joan is evasive, turning things back around to the interviewer." Betsy Sussler, introduction to Cora Cohen and Betsy Sussler, "Joan Mitchell" (interview), *BOMB* (Fall 1986), https://bombmagazine.org/articles/joan-mitchell/. And "Her strange inarticulateness . . . left most people at a loss." Jane Livingston, "The Paintings of Joan Mitchell," in *The Paintings of Joan Mitchell,* exh. cat., ed. Jane Livingston (New York: Whitney Museum of American Art, 2002), 38.

12. See, for example, Harold Rosenberg, "Joan Mitchell: Artist against Background" (1974), in *Art on the Edge: Creators and Situations* (New York: Macmillan, 1975), 84, 86.

13. Mitchell, artist's statement in *Nature in Abstraction: The Relation of Abstract Painting and Sculpture to Nature in Twentieth-Century American Art,* exh. cat., ed. John I. H. Baur (New York: Whitney Museum of American Art, 1958), 75. Mitchell's attitude was relatively common during the 1950s. By the chance of alphabetical order, her statement in Baur's book immediately precedes one by Hans Moller, which reads similarly.

14. Mitchell, quoted in Michaud interview transcript, n.d. [January 12, 1986]. Henri Matisse had established a precedent: "I am unable to distinguish between the feeling I have about life and my way of translating it. . . . I am forced to interpret nature and submit it to the spirit of the picture." Matisse, "Notes of a Painter" (1908), *Matisse on Art,* ed. and trans. Jack Flam (Berkeley: University of California Press, 1995), 38, 40.

15. Mitchell's title derives from Frank O'Hara's poetry.

16. Mitchell recounted the phrase in Nochlin, AAA oral history.

17. Mitchell, quoted in Michaud interview transcript, n.d. [August 7, 1989].

18. Ibid.

19. In the Michaud interview transcript, n.d. [August 7, 1989], Mitchell follows the previously quoted passages with "Now the surface is felt too," a sentence eliminated in her editing process.

20. "Give me a dead color. It's dead because of what's next to it. Then if it's not a color, then move something to make it into a color." Mitchell, in *Joan Mitchell: Portrait of an Abstract Painter,* directed by Marion Cajori, 28:55 min.

21. Mitchell, interview with Marcia Tucker, December 1973, quoted in Tucker, *Joan Mitchell* (New York: Whitney Museum of American Art, 1974), 9.

22. Curated by Judith E. Bernstock, organized by the Herbert F. Johnson Museum of Art, Cornell University. Bernstock's monograph, *Joan Mitchell* (New York: Hudson Hills, 1988), became the catalogue.

23. "She absolutely loved the Cézanne painting." Bill Scott, who accompanied Mitchell at the time, email to Karli Wurzelbacher and Laura Morris, July 1, 2019.

24. "On ne peut pas entrer dans un Cézanne, parce qu'il repousse. L'oeil est repoussé à la surface immédiatement. Voilà pourquoi je l'aime." Mitchell, in Philippe Dagen, "La fureur de Joan Mitchell: de Chicago aux bords de la Seine, la recherche d'une indépendance absolue" (interview), *Le Monde* (Paris), August 2–3, 1992, 11.

25. Émile Bernard, "Paul Cézanne," *L'Occident* 6 (July 1904): 21.

26. Maurice Denis, "Le peintre Paul Sérusier," *L'Occident* 14 (December 1908): 279. For the context and related examples, see Richard Shiff, "Dream of Abstraction," in *Paths to Abstraction 1867–1917,* ed. Terence Maloon (Munich: Prestel, 2010), 52–69; and Shiff, "He Painted," in *Cézanne's Card Players,* ed. Barnaby Wright (London: Courtauld Institute, 2010), 72–91.

27. Thadée Natanson, "Paul Cézanne," *La revue blanche* 9 (December 1, 1895): 498.

28. Mitchell, quoted in Michaud interview transcript, n.d. [August 7, 1989].

29. Letter from André Derain to Henri Matisse, March 15–16, 1906, quoted in Rémi Labrusse, *Matisse: la condition de l'image* (Paris: Gallimard, 1999), 53.

30. Mitchell, quoted in Michaud interview transcript, n.d. [August 7, 1989].

31. Ibid. This passage is incorrectly rendered in the 1994 French translation (see note 2, above). Mitchell provided Marion Cajori with a crude chart of the letter-to-color correspondences, shown on-screen in *Joan Mitchell: Portrait of an Abstract Painter,* 27:41 min. *S*, for example, was the only pure red.

32. Mitchell, quoted in Michaud interview transcript, January 12, 1986. The word "blank" presented the same difficulty; see Mitchell's comments in Cohen and Sussler, "Joan Mitchell" (interview).

33. Mitchell, quoted in Michaud interview transcript, August 7, 1989.

34. By 1975, "a whole mode, painting, [had] been dropped gradually from avant-garde writing." Max Kozloff, "Painting and Anti-Painting: A Family Quarrel," *Artforum* 14 (September 1975): 37. On the critical fortune of painting during the later decades of Mitchell's career, see Richard Shiff, "Optiken [Optics]," in *New York Painting,* ed. Christoph Schreier (Cologne: Snoeck, 2015), 28–52.

35. Seckler, AAA oral history.

36. Mitchell, interview with Marcia Tucker, in Tucker, *Joan Mitchell,* 6.

37. Mitchell, quoted in Bernstock, *Joan Mitchell,* 86 (interviews conducted June 27–July 4, 1986).

38. Mitchell, interview with Marcia Tucker, in Tucker, *Joan Mitchell,* 8.

39. Color "is not a question of change of mood." Mitchell, quoted in Michaud interview transcript, August 7, 1989.

40. Émile Verhaeren, "Le salon des Indépendants," *L'art moderne* (Brussels) 11 (April 5, 1891): 112.

41. Thoré-Bürger (Théophile Thoré), "Salon de 1847," *Les salons,* 3 vols. (Brussels: Lamertin, 1893), 1:536–37. See also, 1:447: "In the arts, the subject is absolutely indifferent." The bronze addition to Clésinger's marble, observed by Thoré, no longer adorns the work; it may have been present solely for Salon purposes. I thank Adrienne Farb for first-hand inspection of the sculpture and am grateful to both Nadège Horner (consulting conservator's notes by Anne Pingeot) and Joel Shapiro for confirming aspects of the history of the work.

42. Théophile Thoré, "Galerie de M. le Comte de Morny," *L'artiste,* ser. 4, 10/4 (July 25, 1847): 52. Here, too, Thoré referred to the relative insignificance of representational subject matter.

43. Thoré, "Salon de 1845," *Les salons,* 1:105.

44. Sensitive to what was fashionable, Mitchell often designated her aesthetic as "old hat" or "AEOH," Abstract Expressionist Old Hat. See Nochlin, AAA oral history; also, Bernstock, *Joan Mitchell*, 53. In 1965 (and subsequently), Mitchell noted the increasing influence of Marcel Duchamp, whom *Time* magazine quoted prominently: "Oil painting is old hat and should be discarded forever. . . . Abstract Expressionism was not intellectual at all for me." "Pop's Dada," *Time,* February 5, 1965, 85. For Mitchell's references to Duchamp at the time, see John Ashbery, "An Expressionist in Paris," *Art News* 64, no. 2 (April 1965): 64; and Seckler, AAA oral history.

45. Paul Mantz, *Salon de 1847* (Paris: Ferdinand Sartorius, 1847), 96.

46. Seckler, AAA oral history. See also Ashbery, "An Expressionist in Paris," 63. At an earlier date, Mitchell associated dark green with loneliness; see her letter to Barney Rosset, n.d. [postmarked October 14, 1948], JMFA003. We

would nevertheless lapse into pathetic fallacy to insist that Mitchell's interest in this color reflected her psychological state. Mantz's account of reciprocal projection accords better with Mitchell's ambivalence over attributing meaning to feeling.

47. Ashbery ("An Expressionist in Paris," 63) quotes Mitchell stating that her cypress images contain no black pigment. She may have been referring to a select few. Laura Morris (email to the author, July 9, 2019) reports that Mitchell did occasionally use a black, such as ivory black, within this series of works. Mitchell may or may not have known that van Gogh prided himself in making "a painting of night without black." Letter from Vincent van Gogh to Willemien van Gogh, September 9 and ca. 14, 1888, in *Vincent van Gogh: The Letters,* ed. Leo Jansen, Hans Luijten, and Nienke Bakker (Amsterdam & The Hague: Van Gogh Museum & Huygens, 2009), December 2010 version, http://www.vangoghletters.org/vg/letters/let678/letter.html.

48. Letter from Vincent van Gogh to Theo van Gogh, June 25, 1889, in *Vincent van Gogh: The Letters,* http://www.vangoghletters.org/vg/letters/let783/letter.html.

49. Letter from Vincent van Gogh to Albert Aurier, February 9 or 10, 1890, in *Vincent van Gogh: The Letters,* http://www.vangoghletters.org/vg/letters/let853/letter.html.

50. Ibid.

51. "Des cyprès dressant leurs cauchemardantes silhouettes de flammes, qui seraient noires." Albert Aurier, "Les isolés: Vincent van Gogh," *Mercure de France* 1 (January 1890): 24.

52. Letter from Vincent van Gogh to Albert Aurier, February 9 or 10, 1890, in *Vincent van Gogh: The Letters.*

53. Seckler, AAA oral history.

54. Mitchell, in *Joan Mitchell: Portrait of an Abstract Painter,* 24:50 min.

55. Antonin Artaud, "Van Gogh: The Man Suicided by Society," trans. Bernard Fretchman, in *The Trembling Lamb,* ed. John Fles (New York: H. Gantt, 1959), 20. Originally published as *Van Gogh: le suicidé de la société,* 1947. See also Bernstock, *Joan Mitchell,* 87–88.

56. Mitchell, quoted in Michaud interview transcript, August 7, 1989. This passage remains legible, though Mitchell crossed it out.

57. "I don't like fields of sunflowers. I like them alone or, of course, painted by van Gogh." Mitchell, quoted in Michaud interview transcript, January 12, 1986. Mitchell had several opportunities to become familiar with van Gogh's *Rain,* through exhibitions and reproductions. (I thank Bill Scott, Karli Wurzelbacher, and Sarah Roberts for confirmation.)

58. Seckler, AAA oral history.

59. Mitchell, quoted in Michaud interview transcript, January 12, 1986.

60. Ibid.

61. On the tendency to abandon quality as a criterion for aesthetic judgment, see Barbara Rose, "Twilight of the Superstars," *Partisan Review* 41 (Winter 1974): 568–69.

62. Mitchell, quoted in Michaud interview transcript, January 12, 1986.

9 La Vie en rose
Katy Siegel

292–99

Epigraph: Mitchell listened to Kiri Te Kanawa's 1979 recording of Strauss's *Four Last Songs* very often in the early 1980s, and mentioned them in letters (see, for example, note 41 of this chapter).

1. Note from Edrita Fried to Mitchell, n.d., JMFA001.

2. Letter from Sally Perry to Mitchell, March 9, 1979, JMFA001.

3. Letter from Mitchell to Carl Plansky, April 23, 1979, courtesy the Estate of Carl Plansky.

4. She wrote to Karen Edwards on May 10, referencing the lilacs, that she had been doing pastels and, one week before, had returned to painting on a daily basis. Edwards replied, "Dear Joan—You sound terrific! Organized, too. . . . From what you said in N.Y. seems like you've had to deal with this for about 9 months, so maybe you've been through the worst." Letter from Mitchell to Karen Edwards, May 10, 1979, Karen Edwards papers, courtesy Zoe Jet Ellis; letter from Edwards to Mitchell, May 25, 1979, JMFA001; and Franck Maubert, "Les lilas de Vétheuil," *L'Express,* May 24–30, 1980, 53.

5. Mitchell referred to Piaf repeatedly; Gisèle Barreau recalls Mitchell's description of the concert: "Petite femme; tailleur noir maigrissant, la petite femme avec force de voix, non seulement chanteuse, aussi une personnage. Tragique, comique" (A small woman; her black suit highlighting her slightness, the small woman with a strong voice, not only a singer, but a personage. Tragic and comic). Barreau, interview with the author, Sarah Roberts, and Marin Sarvé-Tarr, February 21, 2019, Paris.

6. Mitchell was just finishing the painting, and Barreau viewed it with the left and right panels angled in a kind of accordion position, because the three panels could not be placed side by side within the studio. Barreau, interview with the author and Sarah Roberts, June 6, 2018, Paris. Rebecca Purdum, too, remembers seeing works staged in the studio with the panels at right angles. Purdum, email to Karli Wurzelbacher, March 9, 2019. On timing, see letter from Mitchell to Patricia Molloy, January 17, 1980, JMFA008, referring to struggling with a quadriptych and hoping it would go as quickly as one the previous year.

7. Jean Boivin, *La classe de Messiaen* (Paris: Christian Bourgois, 1995), 429–31; and Gisèle Barreau, "Olivier Messiaen, en hommage," in *Messiaen 2008: Messiaen au conservatoire,* ed. Anne Bongrain (Paris: Centre de recherche et d'édition du Conservatoire, 2008), 63–64.

8. Unsent letter from Mitchell to Perry, May 13, 1979, JMFA001.

9. "Notes biographiques et distinctions internationales," composer file on Gisèle Barreau, Centre de documentation de la musique contemporaine, Paris. Thanks to Gisèle Barreau, Betsy Jolas, and Yves Balmer of the Conservatoire national supérieur de musique et de danse de Paris for discussing French new music with me. For Mitchell's comparison to Beckett, see note from Mitchell to Gisèle Barreau, n.d., JMFA001.

10. Having studied with, among others, Pierre Schaeffer at the Groupe de Recherches Musicales, the leading electronic music studio in France.

11. Program including *Sterne,* December 2, 1983, sent to Joanne and Philip Von Blon, December 23, 1983, JMFA018.

12. Letter from Barreau to Joyce Pensato, n.d., Joyce Pensato Papers, courtesy the Estate of Joyce Pensato.

13. Mitchell wrote Karen Edwards in late 1980 to say the exhibition was coming up the next year. The dates apparently shifted in 1980–82, amidst what seems to have been a complex situation: she told Pensato and Plansky during the eventual installation in late spring 1982 that she had canceled the exhibition twice. Letter from Mitchell to Edwards, November 11, 1980, Karen Edwards papers, courtesy Zoe Jet Ellis. Letter from Mitchell to Pensato and Plansky, n.d. [ca. June 1982], courtesy the Estate of Carl Plansky.

14. Letter from Mitchell to Molloy, n.d. [ca. 1980], JMFA008.

15. "Have little time now but have two high middle blue pics which I thought were perfect but they need two wide sides & I keep thinking can I do it—like last year or why don't you come & make me & do my mail. Am waiting for the 2 sides to be delivered & keep thinking I can do it in 3 weeks like last year. Thank God it's not last year & there are lots of other pics." Letter from Mitchell to Molloy, January 17, 1980, JMFA008. In a letter from Mitchell to Elisabeth Kley, n.d. [ca. November 1983], courtesy Elisabeth Kley, Mitchell wrote of *La Grande Vallée:* "They're all single pics except for a dip that I might add 2 big wide ones to—I don't know." A Fourcade list of paintings coming from France, dated December 11, 1980, notes that two diptychs, *Monday* and *Thursday,* "cam [*sic*] be put

together as a quadriptych." "Paintings by Joan Mitchell coming from France," December 11, 1980, Fourcade Archives.

16. Mitchell, quoted in Linda Nochlin, "Joan Mitchell: Art and Life at Vétheuil," *House & Garden* 156, no. 11 (November 1984): 232.

17. Barreau identifies the plant growing up the fence as morning glory. Barreau, interview with the author, Roberts, and Sarvé-Tarr, February 26, 2019, Paris. Philippe Richard remembered the compositional effect as enduring throughout Mitchell's life. Richard, interview with the author, Roberts, and Sarvé-Tarr, February 23, 2019, Paris. For Mitchell's complaint to Nochlin that the photographer for *House & Garden* did not recognize the value of apparently commonplace plants, such as Barreau's daisies, see letter from Mitchell to Nochlin, n.d. [ca. 1976], Linda Nochlin Papers, AAA.

18. Letter from Mitchell to Joyce Pensato, n.d. [ca. 1981], Joyce Pensato Papers, courtesy the Estate of Joyce Pensato. The press release for the February 1981 Xavier Fourcade exhibition calls the painting "a 9½ × 23½" long mural." Xavier Fourcade, Inc., "Joan Mitchell: New Paintings," press release, 1981, Fourcade Archives.

19. As recounted by Barreau, interview with the author, Roberts, and Sarvé-Tarr, February 26, 2019, Paris. Mitchell wrote to Zuka Mitelberg, "The blue forget-me-nots are smashing with the yellow & black tulips in Gizee's small garden." Letter from Mitchell to Zuka Mitelberg, May 6, 1985, JMFA017.

20. Mitchell wrote to Nochlin that after Riopelle left, she finally began to settle into Vétheuil, and that Barreau helped her occupy the house and garden. Letter from Mitchell to Nochlin, n.d. [ca. 1986], Linda Nochlin Papers, AAA.

21. Letter from Mitchell to Perry, April 12, 1982, courtesy Sally Perry.

22. Letter from Barreau to Mitchell, May 28 [1982], JMFA001.

23. Letter from Mitchell to Plansky and Pensato, n.d. [ca. June 1982], courtesy the Estate of Carl Plansky. Letter from Mitchell to Mitelberg, n.d. [postmarked March 21, 1985], JMFA017: "My goodness—how you fill *my landscape—my life*."

24. Letter from Mitchell to Perry, April 25, 1982, courtesy Sally Perry; and letter from Mitchell to Perry, April 12, 1982, courtesy Sally Perry. "Recall" refers to Mitchell's ability to remember the past in great detail, a quality she saw as foundational and characteristic.

25. Letter from Mitchell to Perry, n.d. [ca. 1981–82], courtesy Sally Perry.

26. Pierre Schneider, "Mitchell: la conscience et la terre," *L'Express*, September 3, 1982, 13.

27. Letter from Mitchell to Plansky, n.d. [ca. 1984], courtesy the Estate of Carl Plansky.

28. Letter from Barreau to Mitchell, n.d., JMFA001.

29. Edrita Fried, *Artistic Productivity and Mental Health* (Springfield, IL: Charles C. Thomas, 1964), 88. In a gendered interpretation, among the book's six case studies of artists, the sole woman (a figure for Mitchell) is the only one who is able to put aside the external pressures and measures of ego and career success—the delusion of "omnipotence," a word frequently used by Mitchell to critique younger artists—in order to attend to a real material experience of the world.

30. Letter from Mitchell to Pensato, n.d., Joyce Pensato Papers, courtesy the Estate of Joyce Pensato.

31. While Mitchell responded positively to the context of contemporary painting in the early 1970s, she did not react favorably to Neo-Expressionism in the 1980s. She was certainly aware of Georg Baselitz, whose exhibition at Fourcade in 1983 followed immediately on the heels of her own. Her attention may also have been focused by articles that mentioned her work in context with that of Julian Schnabel and other younger painters. See, for example, Carter Ratcliff, "The Short Life of the Sincere Stroke," in "Expressionism, II," ed. Elizabeth C. Baker, special issue, *Art in America* 71, no. 1 (January 1983): 73–79, 137. Mitchell mentioned Schnabel by name, criticizing the gimmick of broken plates and his outsize scale. See, for example, Joan Mitchell, lecture at the New York Studio School, March 2, 1988; recording accessed at the JMFA.

32. Nochlin, AAA oral history. In the interview, Mitchell showed Nochlin von Hofmannsthal's book *The Lord Chandos Letter and Other Writings,* of which she owned more than one copy. Earlier that year, Yves Michaud mentioned the book to Mitchell, promising to pick it up when he had a chance to visit Gallimard. Letter from Yves Michaud to Mitchell, February 28, 1986, JMFA001.

33. In the 1986 Nochlin interview, Mitchell seemed to have Rilke's *Letters on Cézanne* on her table, along with the von Hofmannsthal. Nochlin, AAA oral history.

34. Letter from Rainer Maria Rilke to Ellen Delp, October 27, 1915, in *Wartime Letters* (New York: W. W. Norton, 1964), 50–51. Mitchell owned *Wartime Letters,* along with Rilke's *Letters on Cézanne*, *Duino Elegies,* his novel *Notebooks,* and several other volumes. *Wartime Letters* and others remain in Mitchell's library at JMFA; his *Notebooks* were mentioned throughout her life.

35. "Et puis le merveilleux, l'inénarrable moment fasciné devant la réalité, et le surnaturel qui se dégageait de ton atelier, porté, ravi par l'intensité de l'émotion, des couleurs [fleuris?] les yeux, l'or et le voile rose, et le frissonnement et le danse, le duo de la cantate de Bach. . . . Et tu as parlé de ta sœur et j'ai parlé de la mort, de Dieu, de la vie, de l'amour et de . . . la contemplation." Letter from Philippe le Thomas to Mitchell, February 20, 1983, JMFA001.

36. The significance of this music for Mitchell and her circle is evident in the fact that Barreau sent her a postcard with a bar of music labeled "C. A. 78 (J. S. Bach)." Letter from Barreau to Mitchell, n.d., JMFA001.

37. "I painted 11 big paintings all entitled 'La Grand Vallée' from that day you & I both cried separately when she—Gisèle—was talking about her cousin. Anyway it's—the grand valley—quite a vast space the way I've envisaged it." Letter from Mitchell to Kley, n.d. [ca. November 1983], courtesy Elisabeth Kley.

38. Cora Cohen and Betsy Sussler, "Joan Mitchell" (interview), *BOMB,* no. 17 (Fall 1986): 24.

39. But sufficiently abstract, apparently, that it was reproduced upside down in *BOMB* magazine. Cohen and Sussler, "Joan Mitchell" (interview), 23.

40. For Proust, see chapter 3, note 35, citing Sandler. Writing to her sister, she reiterates the connection between her "recall" and Proust's. Letter from Mitchell to Perry, April 12, 1982, courtesy Sally Perry. For Rilke, Mitchell told Michael Goldberg at Christmas 1954 that, restless in the Chicago family home, she again picked up his *The Notebooks of Malte Laurids Brigge*. Letter from Mitchell to Goldberg, n.d. [postmarked December 27, 1954], Goldberg Papers, AAA.

41. In a letter to Mitchell, Hal Fondren enthused about Kiri Te Kanawa's 1979 recording of Strauss's *Four Last Songs*: "I love those doom ridden songs and she is particularly good in them." Letter from Hal Fondren to Mitchell, June 1, 1982, JMFA001. Mitchell wrote, "I'm still listening to Kiri—Strauss—beautiful dawn," in a late-night note she left for Kley at Vétheuil later that summer. Note from Mitchell to Kley, n.d. [ca. late July 1982], courtesy Elisabeth Kley. Years later, in 1988, when writer Harry Gaugh visited, she offered to play the Te Kanawa recording of Strauss for him. Gaugh, "Dark Victories," *Art News* 87, no. 6 (Summer 1988): 159.

42. Letter from Mitchell to Cora Cohen about the trip to New York earlier that spring, n.d. [postmarked May 5, 1986], courtesy Cora Cohen.

43. Ibid.

44. As Barreau alluded in a note from the time, encouraging Mitchell: "Please keep the head out of water./ glou – glou – glou . . . I will not let you go down." Letter from Barreau to Mitchell, n.d., JMFA001.

45. Letter from Mitchell to Joanne and Philip Von Blon, n.d. [postmarked January 2, 1987], JMFA018. She is listening to Bach's *Cantata no. 78* as she writes.

46. See Gisèle Barreau's essay in this volume.

47. Yves Michaud, "Conversation with Joan Mitchell, January 12, 1986," in *Joan Mitchell: New Paintings,* exh. cat. (New York: Xavier Fourcade, 1986), n.p.

48. Letter from Mitchell to Nochlin, n.d. [ca. 1986], box 6, folder 48, Linda Nochlin Papers, AAA. Mitchell is making a play on the names of artists Al Held and Clyfford Still.

La Grande Vallée XVI, pour Iva, 1983
David Max Horowitz

300–301

1. Nochlin, AAA oral history.

2. Yvette T. Lee, "'Beyond Life and Death': Joan Mitchell's *Grande Vallée* Suite," in *The Paintings of Joan Mitchell,* exh. cat., ed. Jane Livingston (New York: Whitney Museum of American Art, 2002), 62.

3. Nochlin, AAA oral history.

4. The relevant works are *La Grande Vallée XVI, pour Iva*; *La Grande Vallée XVII (Carl)*; *La Grande Vallée XVIII (Luc)*; *La Grande Vallée XIX (Yves)*; and *La Grande Vallée XX (Jean)*. Though the numbering does not necessarily reflect the order in which the paintings were made, the higher numbers and fact that none of these was included in the first show of works from the suite, held at Galerie Jean Fournier, Paris (May 29–July 15, 1984), suggest that at least the titles can be associated with the latest stages of the suite's development. For the identification of "Luc," see Patricia Albers, *Joan Mitchell: Lady Painter, a Life* (New York: Alfred A. Knopf, 2011), 372.

5. Mitchell discusses "soul baring" to her dogs in a letter from Mitchell to Patricia Molloy, n.d. [postmarked June 12, 1976], JMFA008. Iva's general importance to Mitchell is encapsulated in her claim, "She's a total extension of me, or I am of her," which appears in Judith E. Bernstock, *Joan Mitchell,* exh. cat. (New York: Hudson Hills, 1988), 134. Mitchell's feelings about Iva are perhaps most powerfully expressed in a letter written after Iva's death in 1986. Letter from Mitchell to Joanne and Philip Von Blon, n.d. [postmarked January 2, 1987], JMFA018. I would like to thank Laura Morris for her guidance within the Joan Mitchell Foundation's archival collections.

6. Mitchell was known to allow only her dogs to watch her paint. For a brief description of the interspecies dynamic of the studio, see Cora Cohen and Betsy Sussler, "Joan Mitchell" (interview), *BOMB,* no. 17 (Fall 1986): 25; and Yves Michaud, "Conversation with Joan Mitchell, January 12, 1986," in *Joan Mitchell: New Paintings* (New York: Xavier Fourcade, 1986), n.p.

7. Letter from Mitchell to Molloy, October 19, 1977, JMFA008; Albers, *Joan Mitchell: Lady Painter,* 368; and Bernstock, *Joan Mitchell,* 181.

8. Such readings, which are compelling but, as I argue here, incomplete, can be found, for instance, in Bernstock, *Joan Mitchell*, 188; and Klaus Kertess, *Joan Mitchell* (New York: Harry N. Abrams, 1997), 57.

9. Mitchell, in Michaud, "Conversation with Joan Mitchell."

10. Coincidentally, *La Grande Vallée XVI, pour Iva* was first shown at the Grand Palais in October 1984, alongside six other *Grande Vallée* paintings, as part of the Galerie Jean Fournier presentation at Foire internationale d'art contemporain (FIAC).

11. Mitchell, in Michaud, "Conversation with Joan Mitchell."

12. The desire to affirm life within these paintings is borne out in their lush, jubilant colors.

13. Mitchell, in Cohen and Sussler, "Joan Mitchell" (interview), 24.

14. I would like to thank Heather C. Whitehead, Joan Mitchell Foundation, who initially directed my attention to many of these oddities within the painting.

15. Yves Michaud, "The Colors of Feeling," trans. James Scarborough, in *Joan Mitchell: La Grande vallée* (Paris: Galerie Jean Fournier, 1984), n.p.

10 Painting
Sarah Roberts

302–9

Epigraph: T. S. Eliot, "Silence," in *Inventions of the March Hare: Poems 1909–1917,* ed. Christopher Ricks (New York: Harcourt, Brace, 1996), 18.

1. Deborah Solomon, "In Monet's Light," *New York Times,* November 24, 1991.

2. In conversation with Ora Lerman, Mitchell confirmed that she saw the exhibition *Van Gogh in Saint-Rémy and Auvers* at the Metropolitan Museum of Art, New York (November 25, 1986–March 22, 1987) and that it stimulated in her a renewed focus on van Gogh. Ora Lerman, "The Elusive Subject: Joan Mitchell's Reflections on van Gogh," *Arts Magazine* 65, no. 1 (September 1990): 44.

3. Joan Mitchell, lecture at the New York Studio School, March 2, 1988; 11:13 min, side B; recording accessed at the JMFA.

4. Mitchell, interviewed in "Joan Mitchell à Vétheuil," in *American Artists in Europe,* directed by Angeliki Haas (Paris, 1976), 8mm, 30 min. This quote appears at approximately 9:30 in the excerpt housed at the JMFA. She is likely referring to a letter from Vincent van Gogh to Willemien van Gogh, February 19, 1890, in *Vincent van Gogh: The Letters,* ed. Leo Jansen, Hans Luijten, and Nienke Bakker (Amsterdam & The Hague: Van Gogh Museum & Huygens, 2009), December 2010 version, http://www.vangoghletters.org/vg/letters/let856/letter.html.

5. Antonin Artaud, *Van Gogh: le suicidé de la société* (Paris: k éditeur, 1947). The JMFA retained a subset of Mitchell's library at the time of her death, including several Artaud publications. This volume is not among the books in the archives, but Frédérique Lucien reports that Mitchell still referred to her original 1947 edition in the late 1980s. Frédérique Lucien, interview with Marin Sarvé-Tarr, February 19, 2019, Paris.

6. In her conversations with Judith E. Bernstock in 1987, Mitchell noted that she thought Artaud's text, which she had first read in the 1950s, was one of few outstanding commentaries on art. Judith E. Bernstock, *Joan Mitchell,* exh. cat. (New York: Hudson Hills, 1988), 87. Hélène de Billy references this text as meaningful to Jean Paul Riopelle and Mitchell in the 1950s in *Riopelle* (Montreal: Art Global, 1996), 67, 126.

7. On her fear of death, see Klaus Kertess, "Her Passion Was Abstract but No Less Combustible," *New York Times,* June 16, 2002. See also Yves Michaud, "Conversation with Joan Mitchell, January 12, 1986," in *Joan Mitchell: New Paintings,* exh. cat. (New York: Xavier Fourcade, 1986).

8. Literally, "it smells like fir" (the wood used for coffins). Michaële-Andréa Schatt, interview with Marin Sarvé-Tarr and the author, February 20, 2019, Paris.

9. Laura Morris, email to the author, November 16, 2019. In the future, there may be paintings currently dated to 1987 or 1989 that will be determined to have been made in 1988. However, it does seem clear that Mitchell's production dipped dramatically that year, given the practical consideration of her extensive time away from Vétheuil and the frequency with which friends report that she was not working.

10. Mitchell, transcript of an interview with Yves Michaud, n.d. [August 7, 1989], with Mitchell's edits, JMFA001. Later published

dated August 7, 1989, as "Entretiens," in *Joan Mitchell,* exh. cat., ed. Françoise Bonnefoy (Nantes: Musée des beaux-arts de Nantes; Paris: Galerie nationale du Jeu de Paume, 1994), 29–31.

11. Mitchell used pastel as well as water-soluble wax crayon, a drawing medium with similarly dense pigment and vivid color capable of being made into a wash either by directly brushing water over drawn lines or by mixing a color wash in advance. She referred to both as "pastel" in conversation. The first known works using the latter date from 1967–68. She preferred the density of the pigment in the water-soluble crayon to watercolor. See Nochlin, AAA oral history. For simplicity, "pastel" is used here to refer to both. For a thorough chronology and examination of Mitchell's use of both drawing media, see Rachel Mochon, "Joan Mitchell: Drawings by a 'Painter's Painter'" (master's thesis, Institute of Fine Arts, New York University, May 2019), and Mochon's essay on pages 310–11, this volume.

12. For additional discussion of these red marks, see chapter 2 in this volume, and Thomas B. Hess, "Sensations of Landscape," *New York,* December 20, 1976, 76.

13. Philippe Dagen, "La fureur de Joan Mitchell: de Chicago aux bords de la Seine, la recherche d'une indépendance absolue" (interview), *Le Monde* (Paris), August 2–3, 1992, 11.

14. "On ne peut pas entrer dans un Cézanne, parce qu'il repousse. L'oeil est repoussé à la surface immédiatement. Voilà pourquoi je l'aime." Ibid.

15. Two other paintings from this moment, *Land* and *Mountain* (both 1989), approach the doubling of *South.* But in neither are the two panels as fully distinct. In both, the joining of the panels merges their compositions more than it highlights their distinctions.

16. Philippe Richard, interview with Katy Siegel and the author, October 25, 2018, Paris. Similarly, Jean Fournier reported that Mitchell had asked him the word for trees that had been pruned in the French manner when she was making the *Tilleuls,* and he had replied "moignons," which translates loosely to "stumps." Fournier then noted that the word "moignons" was changed to "trees" when the paintings were shown in the United States. The *Tilleuls* were not shown as *Trees,* but the *Taillade* paintings were, at Robert Miller Gallery in 1991. Fournier may have confused *Tilleuls* and *Taillades* in conversation, or perhaps Mitchell's interest in these severe pruning practices was present already when she painted the *Tilleuls* in the late 1970s. Fournier interview with Patricia Albers, March 27, 2003, Albers Papers.

17. A number of van Gogh's cypress paintings were on view in the Metropolitan Museum of Art, New York, in 1986–87, including *Cypresses* (1889, Metropolitan Museum of Art) and *Country Road in Provence by Night,* formerly *Road with Cypress and Star* (1890, Kröller-Müller, Otterlo, Netherlands). See Ronald Pickvance, *Van Gogh in Saint-Rémy and Auvers,* exh. cat. (New York: Metropolitan Museum of Art, 1986).

18. Catherine Flohic, interview with Katy Siegel and the author, October 19, 2018, Paris.

19. Bill Scott confirmed stretchers were made of a lightweight wood in his interview with Karli Wurzelbacher, June 6, 2019, Philadelphia.

20. Klaus Kertess, "Joan Mitchell: The Last Decade," *Art in America* 80, no. 12 (December 1992): 96.

21. "La solitude que je trouve dans mon atelier est alors une plénitude. Je m'y suffis à moi-même. J'y vis pleinement." Catherine Lawless, "Le territoire de Joan Mitchell," in *Artistes et ateliers,* ed. Yves Michaud (Nîmes: Jacqueline Chambon, 1990), 15.

Late pastels
Rachel Mochon

310–11

1. Jill Weinberg Adams, *Joan Mitchell: Paintings and Pastels 1973–1983* (New York: Lennon, Weinberg, 2008), 7.

2. Weinberg Adams, *Joan Mitchell,* 8.

3. Jill Weinberg Adams, in conversation with the author, March, 26, 2019.

4. Gisèle Barreau, email to Laura Morris, February 22, 2019.

5. Joyce H. Townsend, "Analysis of Pastel and Chalk Materials," *Paper Conservator* 22, no. 1 (1998): 21.

6. Joan Mitchell, artist's statement in *Nature in Abstraction: The Relation of Abstract Painting and Sculpture to Nature in Twentieth-Century American Art,* exh. cat., ed. John I. H. Baur (New York: Whitney Museum of American Art, 1958), 75.

7. Thea Burns and Philippe Saunier, *The Art of the Pastel* (New York: Abbeville, 2015), 7.

8. Doreen Bolger, et al., *American Pastels in the Metropolitan Museum of Art* (New York: Harry N. Abrams, 1989), 24–25.

Joan and "la musique à peindre"
Gisèle Barreau

320–25

1. *Piano-Piano* is an ensemble work by Gisèle Barreau, commissioned by the French government and published by Éditions Salabert in 1982.

2. *Two Pianos* is a painting by Joan Mitchell.

3. *La Lande* is a painting by Joan Mitchell.

4. Paul Verlaine, excerpt from *Sagesse* (1881).

5. Paul Verlaine, excerpt from *Romance sans paroles* (ca. 1873).

6. "Les filles" (the girls) was the nickname given by Joan to her three German shepherds: Iva, the mother, and her pups Marion and Madeleine. "On y va qui mal y pense" was Joan's twist on the motto of the Order of the Garter: "Honi soit qui mal y pense" (Evil to him who evil thinks).

7. *Tlaloc* is a work for two percussionists by Barreau, published by Éditions Salabert in 1977. It was titled after the Aztec god of rain, earthly fertility, and water.

8. Mitchell created several works known as *Petit Matins.* Barreau also composed a work with this title.

9. *Belle Bête* (1973) is a painting by Mitchell that was named for her Brittany spaniel. Sally was Mitchell's older sister.

10. *Aires pour Marion* (1975–76) is a painting by Mitchell. Barreau composed a work by this title for an amplified choir (twelve soloists) and six percussionists in 1986.

11. *Chasse Interdite, Fields,* and *Champs* are titles or parts of titles of several paintings by Mitchell.

12. "La Vie en Rose" is a song famously performed by Édith Piaf. Mitchell titled a painting after this song in 1979 (plate 99). "Allez venez, Milord" is another notable song in Piaf's repertoire.

13. "La Reine de la Nuit" (The Queen of the Night) is a character in Mozart's opera *The Magic Flute.*

14. *Sterne* is a work for full orchestra by Barreau, commissioned by Radio-France.

15. *Little Rain, Rained On, Rain,* and *Blue Rain* are the titles of works by Mitchell and Barreau. Mitchell also used the title *No Rain.*

16. *Fritillaires damier,* also known as *Fritillaria meleagris,* are wildflowers.

17. Frank O'Hara, excerpt from the poem "Ode to Joy" (1957).

18. Both Mitchell and Barreau used the title *Un Jardin pour Audrey,* and titled works *Petit Matin.*

19. *The Sky is Blue, the Grass is Green* is a painting by Mitchell.

Contributors

SARAH ROBERTS is the Andrew W. Mellon Foundation Curator and Head of Painting and Sculpture at the San Francisco Museum of Modern Art (SFMOMA). She was the primary author and editor of the Rauschenberg Research Project, SFMOMA's first scholarly digital publication, and she co-organized the museum's 2017 presentation of the Robert Rauschenberg retrospective. She oversees The Doris and Donald Fisher Collection at SFMOMA, and her recent exhibitions include *Carol Bove and John Chamberlain: Converse* and *Louise Bourgeois Spiders*.

KATY SIEGEL is the senior programming and research curator at the Baltimore Museum of Art and the Eugene V. and Clare E. Thaw Endowed Chair in Modern American Art at Stony Brook University, New York. Her exhibitions include *Postwar: Art Between the Pacific and the Atlantic, 1945–1965,* curated with Okwui Enwezor and Ulrich Wilmes at the Haus der Kunst, Munich; and Mark Bradford's presentation at the United States Pavilion for the 2017 Venice Biennale, curated with Christopher Bedford. She has written extensively on modern and contemporary art.

PAUL AUSTER met Joan Mitchell in Paris in the early 1970s, and they remained close for the next two decades. Auster is the bestselling author of *4 3 2 1, Winter Journal, Sunset Park, Invisible,* and *The Book of Illusions,* among many other works. He lives in Brooklyn.

GISÈLE BARREAU and Joan Mitchell were close friends, sharing La Tour and its grounds and inspiring and supporting each other's respective practices of music and painting. Barreau studied at the Paris Conservatory with Olivier Messiaen, Betsy Jolas, André Boucourechliev, and Claude Ballif, as well as with the Groupe de Recherches Musicales directed by Pierre Schaeffer. Over the years she met several times with Ivo Malec and Maurice Ohana.

TRACEY BASHKOFF is senior director of collections and senior curator at the Solomon R. Guggenheim Museum, New York. Bashkoff joined the Guggenheim in 1993 and has organized exhibitions covering a range of twentieth-century subjects, including retrospectives of the work of Wassily Kandinsky, Hilma af Klint, and Agnes Martin. In 2014, she was a fellow at the Center for Curatorial Leadership, New York.

ÉRIC DE CHASSEY has been general director of the Institut national d'histoire de l'art (INHA), Paris, since 2016, and professor of art history at the École normale supérieure de Lyon since 2012. He has published numerous articles, essays, and catalogues and other books, including studies of transnational artistic relations and twentieth- and twenty-first-century abstraction.

JENNIFER HICKEY is the paintings conservator for the Hirshhorn Museum and Sculpture Garden, Smithsonian Institution, Washington, D.C. She specializes in the study, treatment, and stewardship of modern and contemporary paintings.

MARA HOBERMAN is an art historian and critic based in Paris, where she is currently conducting research for the Joan Mitchell catalogue raisonné. She is a regular contributor to *Artforum* and has authored texts for catalogues published by the Swiss Institute, New York; the Indianapolis Museum of Art; the Essl Museum, Klosterneuburg, Austria; the Middelheim Museum, Antwerp; and the Palais de Tokyo, Paris.

DAVID MAX HOROWITZ is an assistant curator at the Solomon R. Guggenheim Museum, New York. He was curator of *Marking Time: Process in Minimal Abstraction* and co-curator of *R. H. Quaytman: + ×, Chapter 34,* and he was part of the curatorial team for *Hilma af Klint: Paintings for the Future* and *Agnes Martin*.

ERIN KIMMEL is a PhD candidate in art history at Stony Brook University, New York, where she is writing a dissertation on the relationship of American postwar landscape painting to emergent technologies of vision and the speculative development of land. Her writing has been published by the Museum of Modern Art, New York, *Artforum,* and *Art in America*.

RACHEL MOCHON is a graduate student specializing in the conservation of works on paper at the Conservation Center of the Institute of Fine Arts, New York University.

She began working with the Joan Mitchell Foundation in 2017 on the examination of works on paper, which prompted her to write her master's thesis on Mitchell's drawings and materials.

EILEEN MYLES is a poet, novelist, and art journalist. Their twenty-two books include *evolution, Afterglow (a dog memoir), I Must Be Living Twice: New and Selected Poems, Chelsea Girls,* and *For Now*. Myles has received numerous prizes and awards, including a Guggenheim Fellowship, grants from the Andy Warhol Foundation/Creative Capital and the Foundation for Contemporary Arts, the Clark Prize for Excellence in Arts Writing, and an award from the American Academy of Arts and Letters. They live in New York and Marfa, Texas.

JOYCE PENSATO met Joan Mitchell, whom she would grow to consider a friend and mentor, during a studio visit at the New York Studio School in the late 1970s. Pensato's paintings have been exhibited widely, including at the Museum of Contemporary Art, St. Louis; the Modern Art Museum of Fort Worth; and the Santa Monica Museum of Art. Her work is in the collections of the Hammer Museum, Los Angeles; the Dallas Museum of Art; the San Francisco Museum of Modern Art; and the Museum of Modern Art, New York, among others.

JENNI QUILTER teaches at New York University. Her most recent book is *New York School Painters and Poets: Neon in Daylight*.

AMY RAHN is an assistant professor of art history and the director of the Charles Danforth Gallery at the University of Maine at Augusta. She wrote the first English-language dissertation on Joan Mitchell and is currently researching the art historical consequences of contemporary women artists' networks of understanding and camaraderie.

DAVID REED got to know many of the artists in Mitchell's generation as a young painter at the New York Studio School. Reed's paintings have been exhibited at MoMA PS1, the Kunstmuseum Bonn, and the Hamburger Bahnhof. He is represented in the collections of the Art Institute of Chicago; the Centre Georges Pompidou, Paris; the Solomon R. Guggenheim Museum, New York; the Museum of Contemporary Art, San Diego; the Museum für Moderne Kunst, Frankfurt; and the Museum of Modern Art, New York, among others. He lives in New York.

MARIN SARVÉ-TARR is an assistant curator of painting and sculpture at the San Francisco Museum of Modern Art. She has written on modern and contemporary art in France and the United States and co-organized the exhibition *Interiors and Exteriors: Avant-Garde Itineraries in Postwar France* at the University of Chicago's Smart Museum of Art.

RICHARD SHIFF is the Effie Marie Cain Regents Chair in Art at the University of Texas at Austin, where he directs the Center for the Study of Modernism. His books include *Between Sense and de Kooning* and, most recently, *Sensuous Thoughts: Essays on the Work of Donald Judd*.

MEREDITH GEORGE VAN DYKE is a curatorial assistant in the Department of Painting and Sculpture at the San Francisco Museum of Modern Art. She has worked on a wide array of exhibitions, including *Robert Rauschenberg: Erasing the Rules.* She wrote *Richard Diebenkorn: Drawing from Ocean Park* and has contributed to publications on Rauschenberg, Jay DeFeo, and Bay Area art.

CECILIA WICHMANN is an associate curator of contemporary art at the Baltimore Museum of Art. She has worked on major exhibitions, including *Generations: A History of Black Abstract Art* and *Odyssey: Jack Whitten Sculpture, 1963–2017*. Her curated exhibitions include *Ellen Lesperance: Velvet Fist* and *Hitching Their Dreams to Untamed Stars: Joyce J. Scott & Elizabeth Talford Scott*.

KARLI WURZELBACHER is curator of The Heckscher Museum of Art in Huntington, New York. She has contributed to such publications as the exhibition catalogue for *Odyssey: Jack Whitten Sculpture, 1963–2017,* the *Journal of Glass Studies,* and *Charles Burchfield 1920: The Architecture of Painting*.

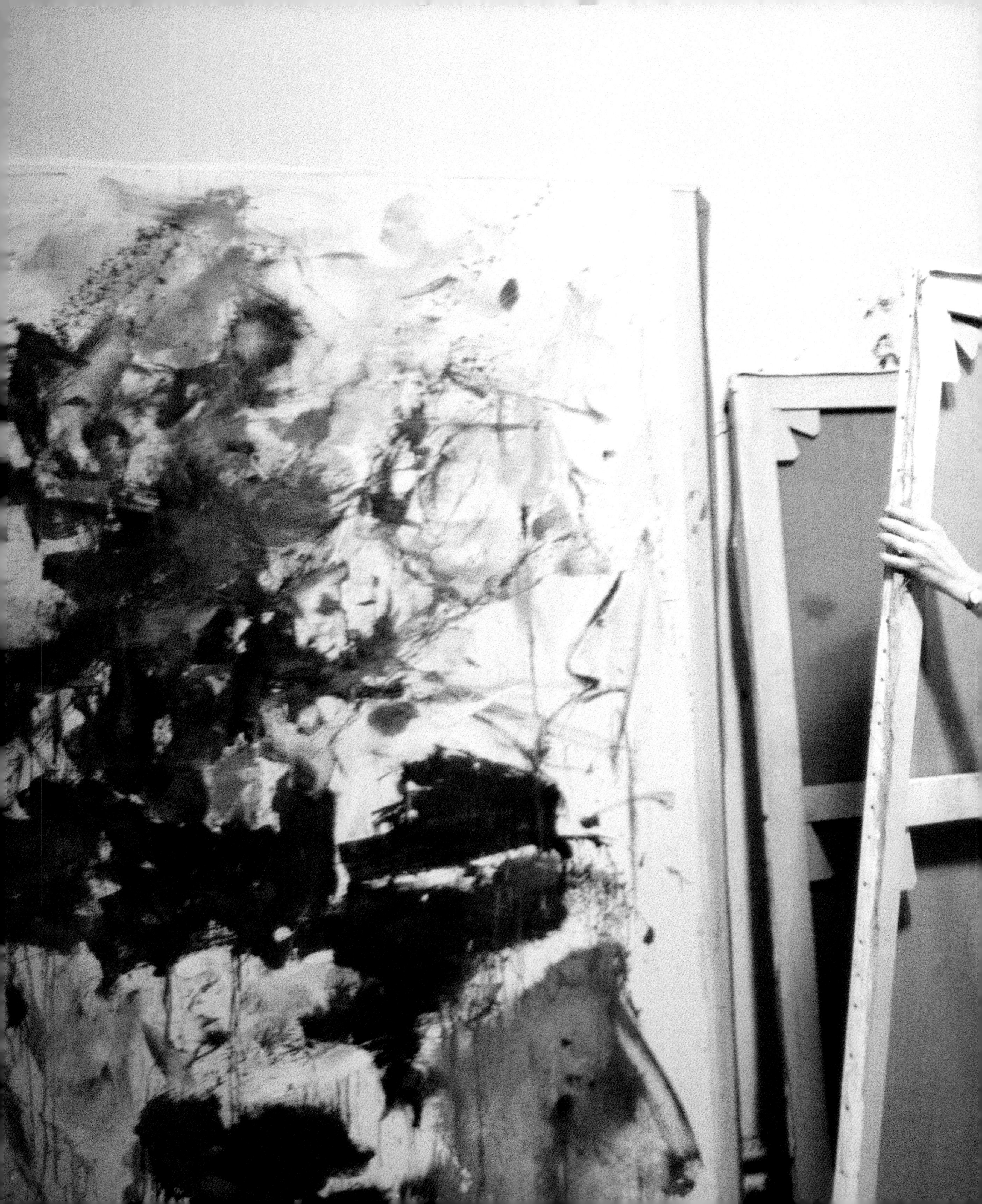

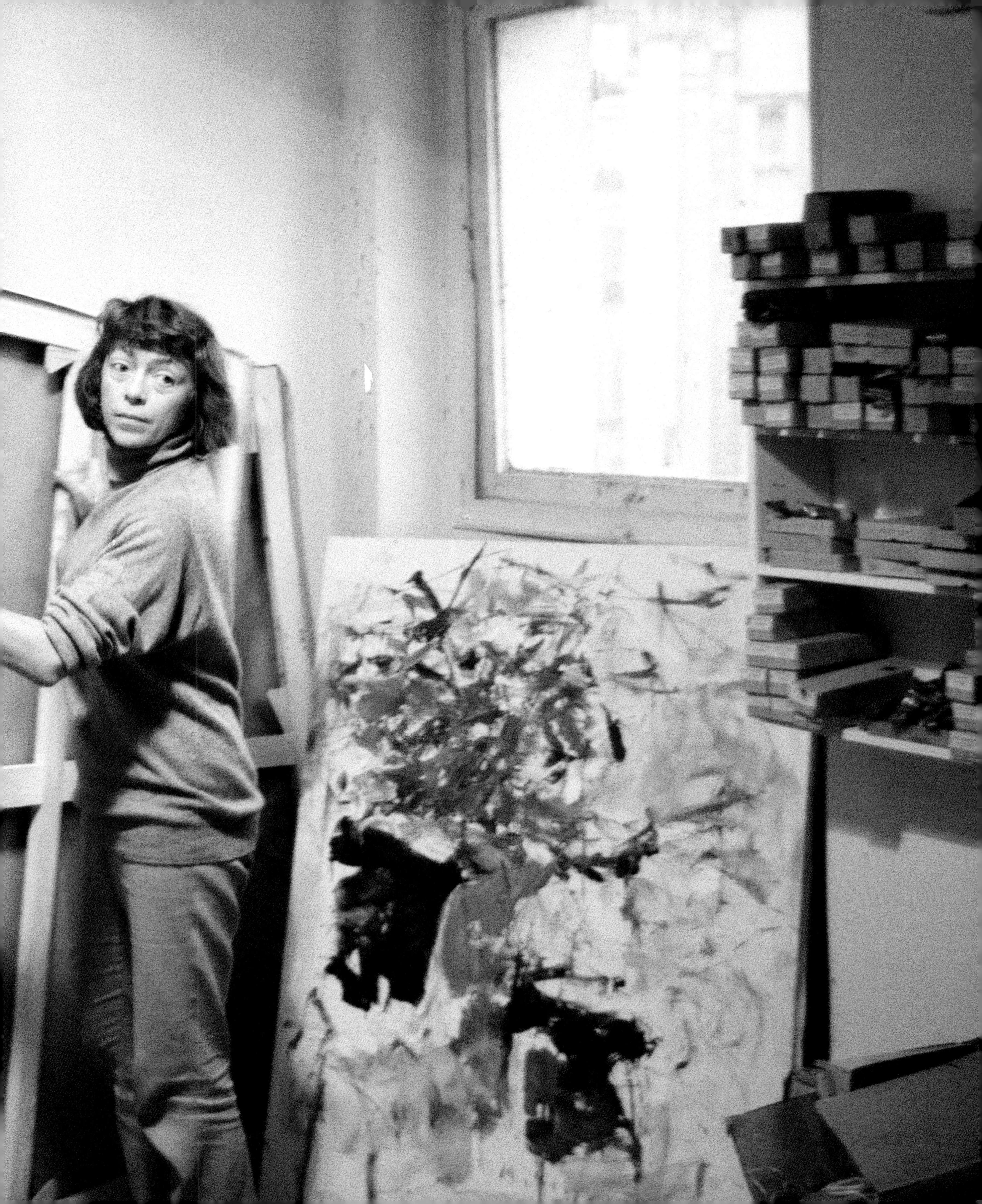

Acknowledgments

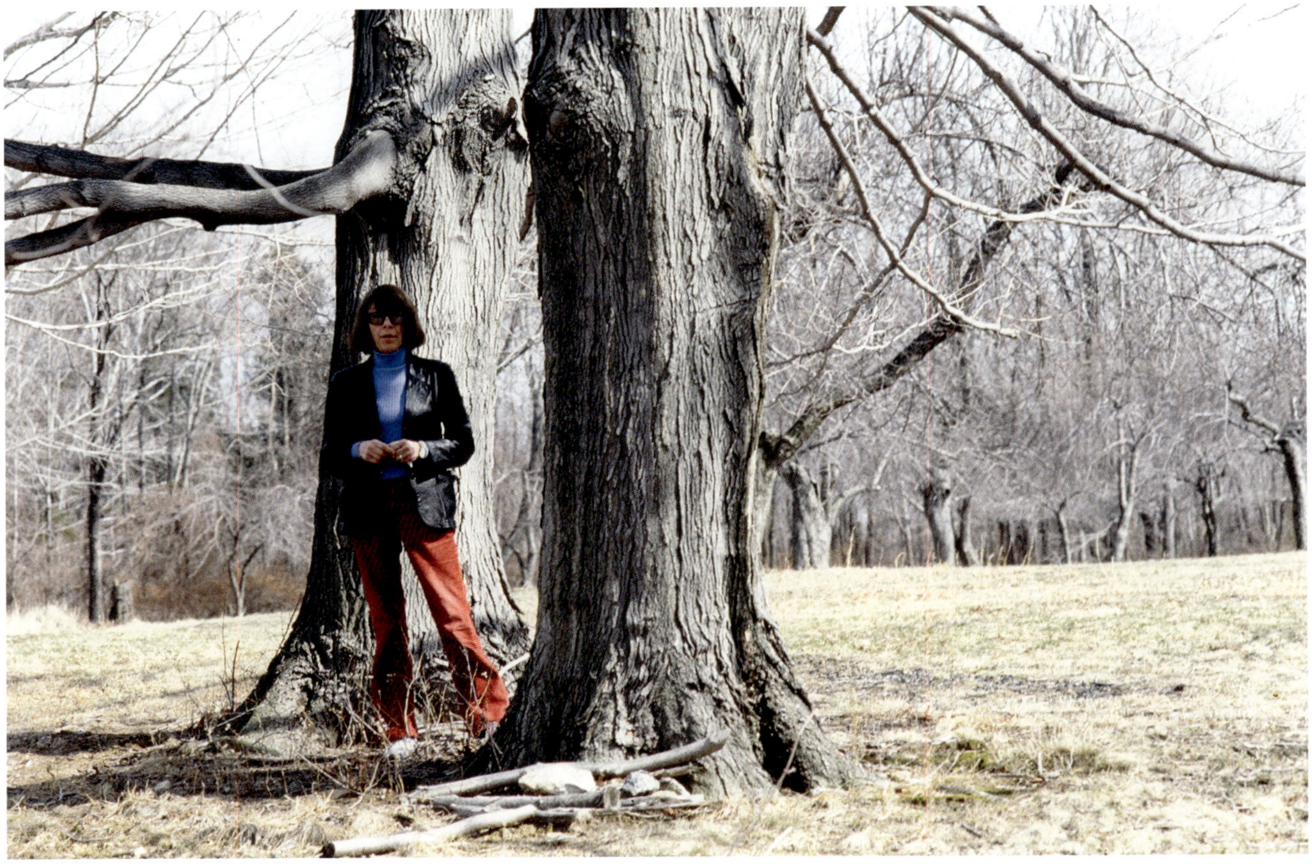

Realizing a project of this scope requires an institutional commitment of the highest order over a period of many years. For their belief in this undertaking and their dedication to seeing it to completion, we extend our gratitude to Christopher Bedford, Dorothy Wagner Wallis Director, and Asma Naeem, Eddie C. and C. Sylvia Brown Chief Curator, The Baltimore Museum of Art (BMA), and to Neal Benezra, Helen and Charles Schwab Director, and Janet Bishop, Thomas Weisel Family Chief Curator and Curator of Painting and Sculpture, San Francisco Museum of Modern Art (SFMOMA).

This publication reflects the exhibition *Joan Mitchell* and its themes as well as a broader story of Mitchell, her work, and her wider historical context. As such, the plates encompass many works not included in any of the museum presentations. At the time this book went to press, the extraordinary events related to the COVID-19 pandemic were just beginning to unfold, their ultimate impacts on the exhibition unknown. The lender acknowledgments below reflect the exhibition as it was planned and understood in April 2020.

We are deeply indebted to all of our lenders for the enormous generosity they have demonstrated in parting with their magnificent paintings and drawings. Without their support, the exhibition would not have been feasible. Those at public museums and institutions include the following: Jason Linetzky, Anderson Collection at Stanford University, Stanford, California; James Rondeau, Ann Goldstein, and Caitlin Haskell, Art Institute of Chicago; Graham C. Boettcher and Hallie Ringle, Birmingham Museum of Art; Simone Wicha and Carter Foster, Blanton Museum of Art at the University of Texas at Austin; Eric Crosby, Carnegie Museum of Art, Pittsburgh; Jeff Fleming, Alison Ferris, and Jared Ledesma, Des Moines Art Center; Bernard Arnault, Suzanne Pagé, and Olivier Michelon, Fondation Louis Vuitton, Paris; Melissa Chiu, Andrea Jain, and Jennifer Hickey, Hirshhorn Museum and Sculpture Garden, Smithsonian Institution, Washington, D.C.; Nancy Richner, Hofstra University Museum of Art, Hempstead, New York; Helen Chason, The Kreeger Museum, Washington, D.C.; Mary-Kay Lombino, Frances Lehman Loeb Art Center, Vassar College, Poughkeepsie, New York; Richard Aste and René Barilleaux, McNay Art Museum, San Antonio; Max Hollein and Sheena Wagstaff, The Metropolitan Museum of Art, New York; Marla Price and Andrea Karnes, Modern Art Museum of Fort Worth; John W. Smith and Dominic Molon, Museum of Art, Rhode Island School of Design, Providence; Glenn Lowry, Ann Temkin, and Paulina Pobocha, The Museum of Modern Art, New York; Kaywin Feldman and Harry Cooper, National Gallery of Art, Washington, D.C.; Doris Fisher and Laura Satersmoen, The Doris and Donald Fisher Collection at the San Francisco Museum of Modern Art; Stephanie Stebich and Melissa Ho, Smithsonian American Art Museum, Washington, D.C.; Robert Scalise, University at Buffalo Art Galleries; Adam Weinberg, Scott Rothkopf, David Breslin, and Jane Panetta, Whitney Museum of American Art, New York; Pamela Franks and Lisa Dorin, Williams College Museum of Art, Williamstown, Massachusetts; and Matthias Waschek, Claire Chandler Whitner, and Erin Corrales-Diaz, Worcester Art Museum, Massachusetts.

Mitchell collectors treasure living with these beautiful paintings and drawings, and many have generously lent more than one work to the exhibition. We extend our heartfelt thanks to the individuals who have allowed us to borrow their greatly valued works for such an extended period of time. This group includes the following as well as those who wish to remain anonymous: AKS Art, John Cheim, Joan and Preston Haskell, Nathan Kernan, Richard and Mary Jo Kovacevich, The Long View Legacy LLC, Komal Shah and Gaurav Garg, Alyssa and Gregory Shannon II, Jon Shirley, and Josh and Suzy Tanzer.

For their assistance with locating works and securing loans, we warmly thank John Cheim, Stephen Truax, Sara Hutchins, and Olena Whipple, Cheim & Read, New York; Emmanuel Clavé and Amandine Baumgartner, Emmanuel Clavé Art Conseil, Paris; Emilie Ovaere-Corthay, Galerie Jean Fournier, Paris; Abigail Asher and Barbara Guggenheim, Guggenheim, Asher Associates, New York and Los Angeles; Nadine Zuni and Sarah Lili Frey, Hauser & Wirth Collection Services; Marc Payot and Laura Bechter, Hauser & Wirth Gallery; Kirk Homeyer; Mike Killackey; Ekaterina Klimochkina; Christopher Eykyn, Nicholas Maclean, and Susan Wallach, Eykyn Maclean Gallery; Robert McClain and Erin Dorn, McClain Gallery, Houston; David Moos, David Moos Art Advisory, Toronto;

Andrew Arnot, Tibor de Nagy Gallery, New York; Edward Tyler Nahem and Stacie Khandros, Edward Tyler Nahem Fine Art, New York; Adam Sheffer, Pace Gallery, New York; Robert Manley, Phillips, New York; Erica Samuels, Samuels Creative & Co., New York; and David Leiber and David Zwirner, David Zwirner Gallery, New York. Numerous individuals at Christie's kindly aided our efforts at every stage of this project, and we are especially grateful to Katherine Drake, Allison Immergut, Laura Nagle, Ellanor Notides, Joanna Szymkowiak, and Allison Whiting for their committed assistance. For their help with research and their counsel regarding potential loans, we are very grateful to Stephanie Barron, Los Angeles County Museum of Art; Mary Ceruti and Pavel Pyś, Walker Art Center, Minneapolis; Andrea Gyorody, Allen Memorial Art Museum at Oberlin College, Ohio; Christine Macel, Centre Pompidou, Paris; and Courtney Kremers and Nina Buhne, Sotheby's, New York.

We are deeply grateful to the scholars, curators, artists, and conservators who shared their insights with us at two convenings organized to discuss Mitchell and scholarship on her work in France and the U.S. In New York, speakers, panelists, and participants included Elise Archias, Andrianna Campbell, John Elderfield, Romy Golan, Suzanne Hudson, Courtney J. Martin, Laura Morris, Eileen Myles, Eleanor Nairne, Maggie Nelson, Jenni Quilter, Amy Rahn, David Reed, Sarah Rich, Richard Shiff, Amy Sillman, Peter Soriano, Charline von Heyl, and Jill Weinberg Adams. Katy Siegel thanks the Eugene V. and Clare E. Thaw Chair in Modern American Art at Stony Brook University for supporting this New York gathering as well as her travel throughout the exhibition research process. In Paris, we benefited enormously from two days of focused conversation and looking at paintings with Natalie Adamson, Elisa Capdevila, Éric de Chassey, Benoît Dagron, Cécile Debray, Nathalie Ogé, Richard Shiff, Ming Tiampo, Julie Verlaine, and Pierre Wat. We offer our thanks to Jim Coddington for his participation in New York and for his valuable counsel on questions of methods and materials that arose during the writing process. For her warmth, patience, and two years of commitment to helping us understand the many nuances of Mitchell's exceptional painting practices, we sincerely thank Jennifer Hickey.

We offer heartfelt thanks to Patricia Albers and Jane Livingston for generously sharing with us their extensive knowledge of Mitchell and the invaluable interview transcripts they produced for their own important Mitchell projects. Others who aided our research immensely by providing access to primary materials and fielding a variety of queries include Judith Bernstock, Hedy and Melanca Clark, Cora Cohen, Larry Elder, Zoe Jet Ellis, Daisy Friedman, Elisabeth Kley, the Estate of Joyce Pensato, Amy Rahn, and Yseult Riopelle. We also offer our appreciation to the many staff members of the institutional archives upon which we relied heavily: Archives of American Art, Smithsonian Institution, Washington, D.C.; Les Archives de la critique d'art, Rennes, France; Archives & Special Collections at the Thomas J. Dodd Research Center, University of Connecticut Library, Storrs; Bibliothèque-Archives, Musée d'art moderne de la ville de Paris; Bibliothèque Kandinsky at the Centre Pompidou, Paris; Everson Museum of Art, Syracuse, New York; Fales Library and Special Collections, New York University; Fondation Marguerite et Aimé Maeght, Saint-Paul-de-Vence, France; Sam Francis Foundation, Pasadena, California; Getty Research Institute, Los Angeles; L'Institut Mémoires de l'édition contemporaine, Saint-Germain-la-Blanche-Herbe, France; Institut national de l'audiovisuel, Bry-sur-Marne, France; Institutional Archives of the Art Institute of Chicago; Martha Jackson Gallery Archives at the University at Buffalo Art Galleries; Morgan Library & Museum, New York; Newberry Library, Chicago; New York Public Library; Rare Book and Manuscript Library at Columbia University, New York; Stuart A. Rose Manuscript, Archives, and Rare Book Library, Emory University, Atlanta; Special Collections Research Center, Syracuse University Libraries, New York; Special Collections Research Center, University of Chicago Library; Special Collections and University Archives at Rutgers University Libraries, New Brunswick, New Jersey; Yale University Music Library, New Haven, Connecticut; and Zao Wou-Ki Foundation, Geneva. We are enormously grateful to interns and research assistants Sara Carrillo, May Peterson, Nina Vukic, Elise Armani, Alexandra Zoë Dostal, Sofia Kofodimos, and Katherine Manansala, all of whom helped with focused research projects in libraries and archives.

Our knowledge of Mitchell has been immeasurably enhanced through extensive dialogues with individuals who knew her. We are deeply grateful to Gisèle Barreau, who patiently participated in extensive interviews, offered photographs, answered our many questions, and generously shared her unique perspective on the artist and her work. Jill Weinberg Adams graciously provided us with access to documents and photos, assisted with finding works, and offered her extensive insights. Frédérique Lucien, Philippe Richard, and Peter Soriano similarly gave their time to interviews, conversations, and emails; their perspectives as artists greatly informed our understanding. Sally Perry kindly shared her memories and allowed us to leaf through her fascinating boxes of Mitchell family photos and history. Yseult and Sylvie Riopelle thoughtfully contributed their stories, photographs, and archival documents to our project. Yseult in particular fielded numerous queries with her keen insight and sharp memory.

We extend our warm appreciation to the many other individuals who shared photos, letters, and memories with us in formal interviews and in informal conversations. They include Jean-Max Albert, David Amram, Sally Apfelbaum, Paul Auster, Lynda Benglis, John Bennett, Carole Benzaken, Reed Bertolette Jr., Guy Bloch-Champfort, Christopher Campbell, John Cheim, Emily Cheng, Katy Crowe, Christine Dupin, Elisabeth Dupin, Hélène Dupin, Louise Fishman, Catherine Flohic, Jacqueline Fried, Monique Frydman, James Harithas, Robert Harms, Elga Heinzen, Sara Holt, Betsy Jolas, Nathan Kernan, Anne Madden, Françoise Maki, Heidi Meister, Joyce Pensato, J. Mitch Perry, Newt Perry, Bernard Piffaretti, Rebecca Purdum, Christiane Rousseaux-Mosettig, Magda Salvesen, Michaële-Andréa Schatt, Bill Scott, Billy Sullivan, Phyllis Tuchman, Kate Van Houten, Joanne Von Blon, and Mâkhi Xenakis. We also thank Hervé Chandès, Annie Claustres, Catherine Francblin, Sébastien Gokalp, and Francesca Rose for valuable intellectual exchange that signficantly aided us in the research and development of the exhibition.

We thank our many colleagues at the BMA and SFMOMA who have dedicated their time and expertise to all aspects of this endeavor. At the BMA, the management of this large-scale project was expertly administered by Steven Mann, senior director of exhibitions, and supported at every stage through the leadership of Christine Dietze, chief operating officer. On the curatorial team, Carlyn Thomas managed the myriad organizational details with diligence, intelligence, and equanimity, and Cecilia Wichmann contributed her own meticulous scholarly research as well as collaborating on installation and interpretation. Senior registrar Melanie Harwood masterfully helmed the registration effort for the exhibition, supported by Giselle Pique and David Felts. Mary Sebera, Scott Homolka, and Lauren Ross in Conservation consulted on the paintings and works on paper, as well as their shipping and framing, guiding the travel and care for these important artworks. In Advancement, Elizabeth Courtemanche, Allison Baldwin, Alexa Milroy, Brandy Wolfe, and particularly Clair Zamoiski Segal, the museum's board chair, secured support that made the exhibition possible. The Education team led by Gamynne Guillotte collaborated on every aspect of visitor experience; Verónica Betancourt in particular brought the show to life through thoughtful interpretation, as did Tracey Beale through energetic public programs, Elizabeth Benskin through teacher programs, and Suzy Wolffe in collaboration with the museum's dedicated docents. With Acoustiguide, Guru, and sg scripts, this team also developed the evocative soundscape within the exhibition. Betty Fisher Wiggins created the beautiful and lucid exhibition design. Special thanks for managing a complex installation go to David Verchomin and David Zimmerman, to Greg St. Pierre for his AV expertise, to Maggie Robbins for the impeccable lighting, and to an outstanding team of art handlers. In Marketing and Experience, Melanie Martin shaped the public face of the exhibition, working with senior graphic designer Lindsey Bridwell; Anne Mannix-Brown skillfully managed media relations with support from Sarah Pedroni; Jessica Novak guided print and digital content strategy with the aid of Andrea Boston; and Meghan Gross handled image rights. We are grateful to all the other many key contributors, including members of the security, facilities, membership, BMA shop, and visitor experience teams.

At SFMOMA, the Exhibitions Department's management of the project was overseen first by Emily Lewis and then skillfully brought to completion by Jessica Woznak, with the assistance of Jillian Aubrey and Tanya Gayer, and with the leadership of Tsugumi Maki. On the curatorial team, Marin Sarvé-Tarr and Meredith George Van Dyke conducted impeccable research and managed monumental amounts of information critical to the realization of both the book and exhibition. Paintings conservator Paula De Cristofaro skillfully helped us secure loans of fragile paintings and carefully tended them as they moved from venue to venue. Jennifer Hing masterfully and graciously handled the registration needs of the show, with the vital support of Olga Charyshyn. Special thanks are due to Jess Kreglow, who expertly oversaw the installation of the show, and to Steve Dye, who managed technical needs, along with our team of dedicated art handlers, all of whom worked diligently to make the exhibition look its very best. The superb exhibition design was conceived and executed by Bosco Hernández, Kiddee Charoenpanitkul, Sarah Choi, and Michelle Thomas. Tobey Martin enthusiastically developed beautiful products for the Museum Store that helped cement certain lender commitments. We extend warm thanks to other key contributors, including current and former members of SFMOMA's Philanthropy team Samantha Leo, Caroline Stevens, Misty Youmans, Kathleen Brennan, Elizabeth Waller, Sydney Blumenkranz, and Amanda Spector; Chad Coerver, Julie Charles, Erica Gangsei, Tomoko Kanamitsu, Christo Oropeza, and Claire Bradley in Education and Public Engagement; Ann von Germeten, Gina Yrrizarry, Maria Castro-Dara, Janet Ozzard, Cristina Chan, Jill Lynch, and Clara Hatcher Baruth in Marketing and Communications; Sriba Kwadjovie Quintana and Ian Gill in Collections Information and Access; Leigh Brawer, Emily Quist, Julie Knight, and their indispensable teams in Membership and Visitor Experience; Anna Tang in Finance; Mike Chominski, Courtney Costello, Walter Logue, and Tim Tengonciang in Operations; and many other valued colleagues who joined the exhibition project team after this publication went to press.

We warmly thank our colleagues at the Fondation Louis Vuitton, Paris, where this exhibition will travel after Baltimore and San Francisco. Our sincere thanks go to Bernard Arnault, president; Jean-Paul Claverie, advisor to the president; Suzanne Pagé, artistic director; Sophie Durrleman, executive director; and Olivier Michelon and Angeline Scherf, curators.

This beautiful and complex catalogue was produced by SFMOMA's Publications Department under the exceptional management of Amanda Glesmann, senior editor, with the dedicated assistance of Brianna Nelson, publications associate. We thank them profusely for their meticulousness, patience, good cheer, and cunning use of GIFs. We also thank Kristin Swan for her sharp editorial insights and editor Jennifer Boynton for her keen eye and rigorous tracking of innumerable facts and details during manuscript proofing and galley review. Kathleen Preciado prepared a comprehensive index. Translator Sharon Grevet added crucial nuance to our French translations. For their razor-sharp eyes for color and their expertise in making every painting look its best on the page, we warmly thank Tony Manzella and his team at Echelon Color. We are also grateful to Sergio Brunelli, Zeno Ferrandini, Nancy Freeman, and the press team at Verona Libri. We offer profound thanks to Tracey Shiffman and James Ihira for their tremendously thoughtful and powerful book design. Katherine Boller and her colleagues at Yale University Press were enthusiastic supporters of this project from the start; we cannot imagine better copublishing partners.

For their valuable contributions to scholarship on Mitchell, we extend our gratitude to essayists Éric de Chassey, Jenni Quilter, and Richard Shiff. The book is further enriched by contributions from Paul Auster, Gisèle Barreau, Tracey Bashkoff, Jennifer Hickey and David Reed, Mara Hoberman, David Max Horowitz, Erin Kimmel, Rachel Mochon, Eileen Myles, Amy Rahn, Marin Sarvé-Tarr, Meredith George Van Dyke, Cecilia Wichmann, and Karli Wurzelbacher. Joyce Pensato shared archival materials and memories with a characteristically tough, profound, and joyful spirit during the final months and weeks of her life.

The leadership and staff of the Joan Mitchell Foundation and Joan Mitchell Catalogue Raisonné have supported archival research, made their collection available to us for study, and generously lent numerous works and archival materials to the exhibition. They have responded to endless queries and gone to extraordinary lengths to ensure the quality and fidelity of the images in this volume. Additionally, their support of a year-long research residency at the Joan Mitchell Foundation Archives for fellow Karli Wurzelbacher was critical to the success of this project. For their commitment to our work and to enriching Joan Mitchell's legacy, we extend our deepest gratitude to Christa Blatchford, executive director; Laura Morris, director of archives and research; Heather Whitehead, collection manager; Joey Cabrera, associate archivist; Andrew Beccone, database and digital asset manager; Courtney Lynch, former assistant archivist; Jenny Gill, communications manager; and Janice Teran, administrative associate. We are equally thankful for the detailed research assistance of Suzi Villiger, project director, and Mara Hoberman, Marley Lewis, and Alexandra Tagami Vargo, researchers, at the Joan Mitchell Catalogue Raisonné.

Finally, this exhibition and book stand on an extraordinary foundation of collaborative thinking and primary research built by Karli Wurzelbacher, Erin Kimmel, Gabriella Shypula, Cecilia Wichmann, Marin Sarvé-Tarr, and Meredith George Van Dyke. The shape and content of this entire endeavor owe everything to their exceptional research skills, collective spirit, and, most importantly, their intellectual engagement and commitment to this project.

For their constant support and patience with our many months of being away as we conducted research over the past three years, we offer our deepest thanks to our families. Katy salutes Paul and Felix Mattick, who read chapter drafts, made lunch for the research team, listened to the Joan Mitchell playlist, and generally kept her company in Mitchell land. Sarah thanks Keith, Jackson, Eleanor, and Meredith Roberts, for pulling off moving to a new house as she wrote her last book chapters and for the laughter, great cooking, and long walks that sustain her always. We are forever grateful.

SARAH ROBERTS AND KATY SIEGEL

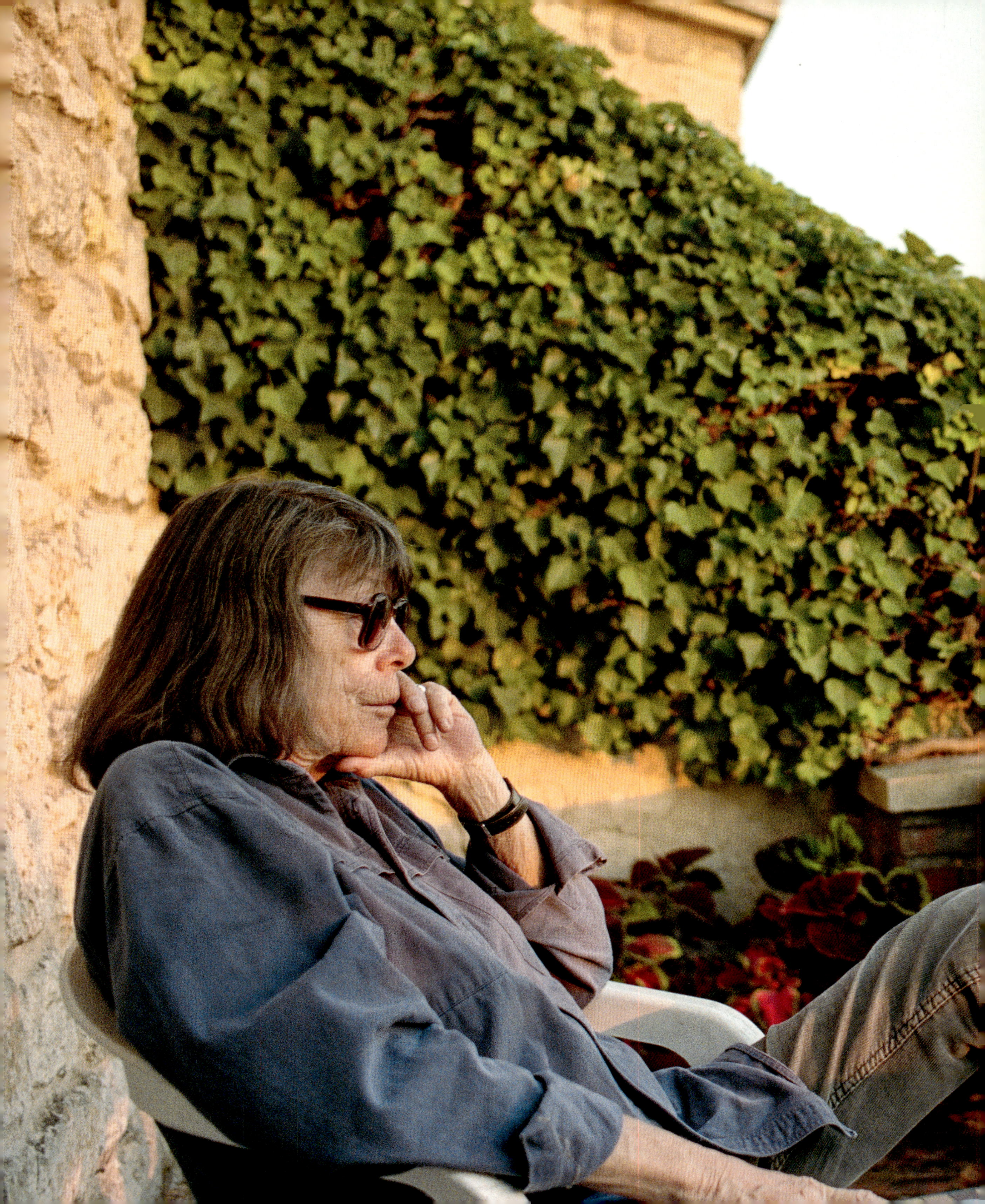

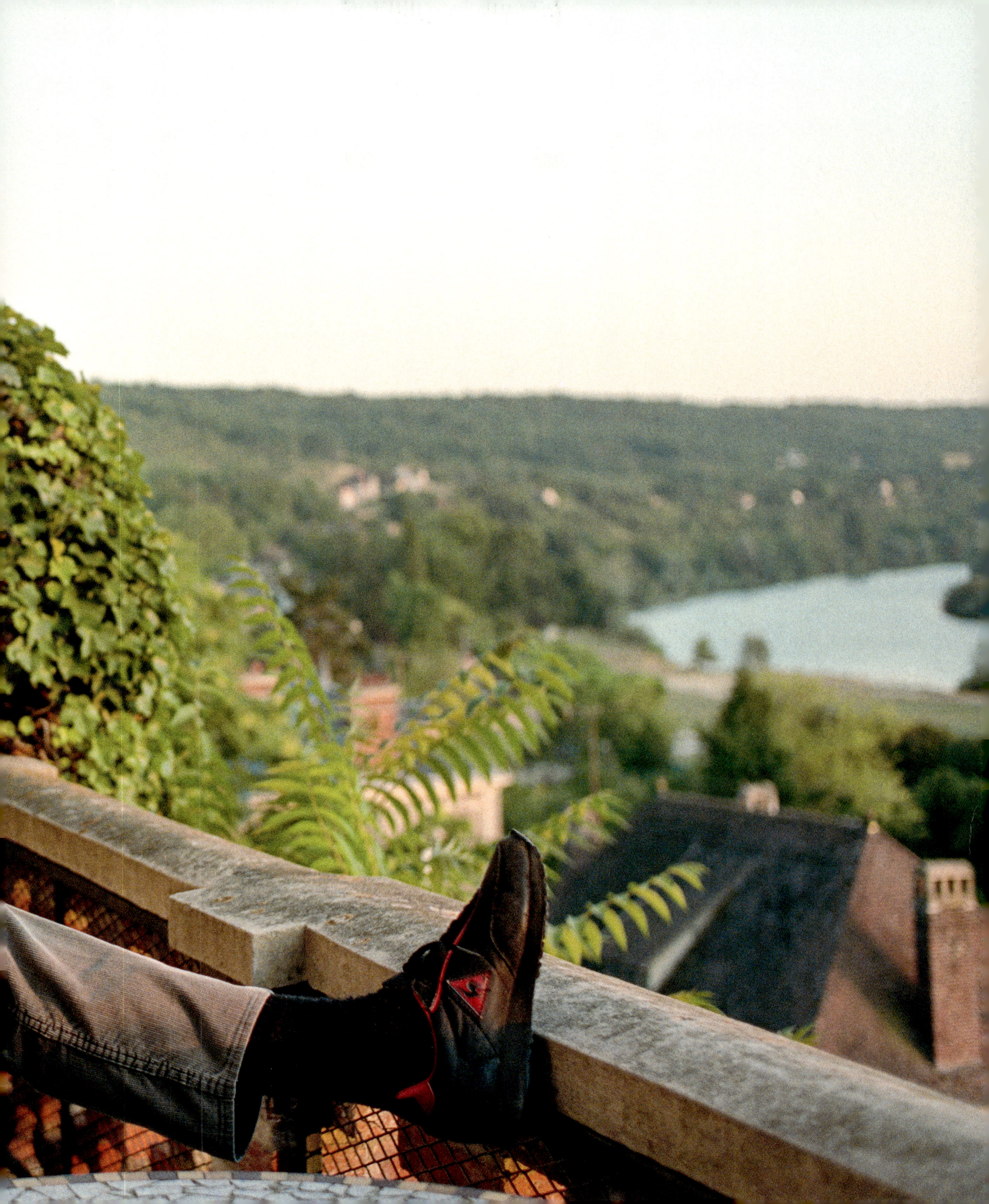

Index

Numbers in *italics* refer to illustrations. Plate numbers, where applicable, are provided in parentheses.

Image Credits

All works by Joan Mitchell © Estate of Joan Mitchell. Images of Mitchell's work were provided by the Joan Mitchell Foundation unless otherwise noted. Additional image credits appear below.

PLATES

Listings are identified by plate number.

1, 2, 3, 12, 16, 49, 50, 64, 84, 85: Brian Buckley. **4, 5, 7, 13, 18, 56, 57, 60, 96, 97, 104, 105, 106, 109, 110, 111, 118 (and detail), 131, 132:** Kris Graves. **6, 39, 54, 65, 70, 72, 81, 95, 117:** Christian Baraja. **8:** Chip Porter. **9:** Courtesy Nakanoshima Museum of Art, Osaka. **11:** Edward C. Robison III, courtesy Crystal Bridges Museum of American Art, Bentonville, Arkansas. **14:** Aimee Marshall. **19:** Don Ross, courtesy the San Francisco Museum of Modern Art. **20, 123, 134:** Courtesy Cheim & Read, New York. **21:** Cameron Wittig. **22, 102, 115:** Kerry McFate. **23:** Courtesy The Doris and Donald Fisher Collection at the San Francisco Museum of Modern Art. **25:** Tom Loonan. **26, 32, 34:** Paul Hester. **27 (and detail), 77:** Tony Prikryl. **28, 38, 58, 59:** Digital Image © The Museum of Modern Art / Licensed by SCALA / Art Resource, New York. **29, 100:** Courtesy the National Gallery of Art, Washington, D.C. **30, 43:** Spike Mafford. **31:** Colin Doyle. **33:** Kevin Ryan. **35, 44:** Stefan Altenburger Photography, Zürich. **36:** Courtesy the Modern Art Museum of Fort Worth. **37:** Courtesy the Currier Museum of Art, Manchester, New Hampshire. **40:** Jacek Gancarz. **41:** Courtesy Lennon Weinberg, New York. **42:** Worcester Art Museum, Massachusetts, USA / Bridgeman Images. **46:** Jonathan Sherman. **47:** Rich Sanders, Des Moines, Iowa. **48:** Jeff McLane, courtesy the San Francisco Museum of Modern Art. **51, 90, 121:** Courtesy Sotheby's. **52:** Courtesy the McNay Art Museum, San Antonio, Texas. **53:** Photo © 2013 Christie's Images Limited. **55:** Courtesy the Smithsonian American Art Museum, Washington, D.C. **61, 62, 63:** Jens Nober, courtesy Museum Folkwang, Essen, Germany. **66, 99 (and detail):** Image copyright © The Metropolitan Museum of Art, New York. Image source: Art Resource, New York. **67:** Petegorsky / Gipe Photo. **68:** Ron Amstutz. **69:** Lee Stalsworth. **71:** Courtesy Christie's. **73:** Courtesy the Carnegie Museum of Art, Pittsburgh. **74:** Clint Jenkins. **75:** Biff Henrich, IMG_INK, Buffalo, New York. **76:** Courtesy Museum of Art, Rhode Island School of Design, Providence. **79:** Bertrand Prévost. Photo © CNAC / MNAM / Dist. RMN-Grand Palais / Art Resource, New York. **80:** Jason Mandella, courtesy the San Francisco Museum of Modern Art. **87:** Philippe Migeat. Photo © CNAC / MNAM / Dist. RMN-Grand Palais / Art Resource, New York. **88:** Courtesy Preston Haskell. **92, 108:** Ian Lefebvre. **93, 98, 120, 122:** Photo © Primae / David Bordes. **103:** Gary Mamay. **112, 125, 129:** Josh Nefsky. **113:** Eric Caillet. **114:** Ian Reeves. **119:** Katherine Du Tiel, courtesy the San Francisco Museum of Modern Art. **126:** Courtesy Alexandra Mollof Fine Art, London. **127:** Justyna Badach. **133:** Courtesy David Zwirner, New York.

FIGURE ILLUSTRATIONS

Listings are identified by page and figure number. Photographers with a personal connection to Mitchell are named in the image captions.

16, 23, 29 (figs. 6 and 7), 31, 40, 41, 106 (figs. 3, 4, and 6), 107 (figs. 7, 8, 10, and 11), 108, 109, 110 (fig. 5.3), 113 (fig. 5.6), 118 (bottom), 119, 121, 122, 189 (fig. 1), 198, 199, 205 (fig. 7.3), 208, 209, 217 (fig. 8.7), 218 (fig. 4), 219 (fig. 10), 292 (top), 293, 299, 301 (fig. 9.9), 312 (fig. 4), 313 (figs. 6 and 8), 319: JMFA001: Joan Mitchell Papers. **19, 22:** Kris Graves. JMFA001: Joan Mitchell Papers. **20:** Artwork © Estate of Robert Von Neumann. Courtesy White Crow Fine Paintings, Milwaukee. **21, 123 (fig. 6.5):** Brian Buckley. **27 (figs. 1.8 and 1.9):** Brian Buckley. JMFA001: Joan Mitchell Papers. **28 (figs. 2 and 4), 29 (fig. 5), 34 (fig. 2.4):** © Joan Mitchell Foundation. JMFA002: Barney Rosset Photographs. **30 (top):** Walt Silver. © 2020 Larry Rivers Foundation. **30 (bottom):** Courtesy Stuart A. Rose Manuscript, Archives, and Rare Book Library, Emory University, Atlanta. **33 (fig. 2.2):** Hans Namuth. © 1991 Hans Namuth Estate, courtesy the Center for Creative Photography, University of Arizona. JMFA001: Joan Mitchell Papers. **33 (fig. 2.3), 37, 99, 107 (fig. 9), 192 (top and bottom):** Walt Silver. © Photography Collection, The New York Public Library. **34 (fig. 2.5):** Walt Silver, courtesy the Miriam Schapiro Estate. **36 (fig. 2.7):** Yoshitaka Uchida, Nomadic Studio. **39 (fig. 2.9):** Artwork © 2020 Estate of Wassily Kandinsky / Artists Rights Society (ARS), New York. Photo © Solomon R. Guggenheim Museum, New York. **39 (fig. 2.10):** Artwork © 2020 Mondrian / Holtzman Trust. Photo © Solomon R. Guggenheim Museum, New York. **42:** Carol Haerer, courtesy the Sam Francis Foundation, California. **43 (fig. 3.3), 218 (fig. 1):** Courtesy the Getty Research Institute, Los Angeles. **47 (fig. 3.5):** Loomis Dean / The LIFE Picture Collection via Getty Images. **47 (fig. 3.6), 49, 219 (fig. 8):** Don Ross, courtesy the San Francisco Museum of Modern Art. **50 (fig. 1):** Max Margulis. **50 (fig. 2):** Artwork © 2020 The Arshile Gorky Foundation / Artists Rights Society (ARS), New York. Digital Image © The Museum of Modern Art / Licensed by SCALA / Art Resource, New York. **50 (fig. 3):** Artwork © The Franz Kline Estate / Artists Rights Society (ARS), New York. Photo © President and Fellows of Harvard College. **50 (fig. 4):** Artwork © Estate of Michael Goldberg. Courtesy Michael Rosenfeld Gallery LLC, New York. **50 (fig. 5):** Artwork © The Estate of Philip Guston. Image copyright © The Metropolitan Museum of Art, New York. Image source: Art Resource, New York. **51 (fig. 6):** Artwork © 2020 Estate of Jean Paul Riopelle / Artists Rights Society (ARS), New York / SOCAN, Montreal. Digital Image © The Museum of Modern Art, New York / Licensed by SCALA / Art Resource, New York. **51 (fig. 7):** Artwork © 2020 Sam Francis Foundation, California / Artists Rights Society (ARS), New York. Courtesy the Sam Francis Foundation, California. **51 (fig. 8):** Jerry Cooke. © 2020 Jerry Cooke Archive. **51 (fig. 9):** Artwork © Estate of Judit Reigl / Artists Rights Society (ARS), New York / ADAGP, Paris. Courtesy Janos Gat Gallery, New York. **51 (fig. 10), 95, 218 (fig. 2), 311 (fig. 10.9):** © Galerie Jean Fournier, Paris. **89:** Artwork © 2020 The Estate of Natalia

Dumitresco / Artists Rights Society (ARS), New York / SIAE, Rome. Photo: Sandra Pointet, © Fondation Gandur pour l'Art, Genève. **90:** Artwork © 2020 Estate of Jean Paul Riopelle / Artists Rights Society (ARS), New York / SOCAN, Montreal. Photo: Elie Posner, © The Israel Museum, Jerusalem. **91, 111, 205 (fig. 7.4):** Ian Lefebvre. **92:** Artwork © Estate of Marcelle Loubchansky / Artists Rights Society (ARS), New York / ADAGP, Paris. Photo © Bruun Rasmussen Auctioneers. **94:** Artwork © Estate of Simon Hantaï / Artists Rights Society (ARS), New York / ADAGP, Paris. **96, 214, 219 (fig. 7), 295 (fig. 9.4):** Courtesy the Archives of American Art, Smithsonian Institution, Washington, D.C. **97, 102 (fig. 4.3), 103, 106 (figs. 1 and 2):** Heidi Meister. **102 (fig. 4.4):** Artwork © 2020 Estate of Jean Paul Riopelle / Artists Rights Society (ARS), New York / SOCAN, Montreal. Image courtesy Art Gallery of Hamilton, Ontario, Canada. **105 (fig. 4.6):** JMFA004: Joan Mitchell Exhibition Records. **105 (fig. 4.7):** Paul Hester. **110 (fig. 5.2):** © 2020 Estate of Jean Paul Riopelle / Artists Rights Society (ARS), New York / SOCAN, Montreal. JMFA001: Joan Mitchell Papers. **113 (fig. 5.5), 117 (fig. 5.8):** Courtesy Lennon Weinberg, New York. **117 (fig. 5.7):** © 2020 Estate of Jean Paul Riopelle / Artists Rights Society (ARS), New York / SOCAN, Montreal. JMFA005: Jean Paul Riopelle Papers. **120:** Artwork © 2020 Succession H. Matisse / Artists Rights Society (ARS), New York. Photo: The Art Institute of Chicago / Art Resource, New York. **123 (fig. 6.6):** Kerry McFate. **127 (fig. 6.7):** Christian Baraja. **127 (fig. 6.8), 219 (fig. 9):** © Nancy Crampton. **196, 312 (fig. 2):** Robert A. Freson. © Robert A. Freson. JMFA010: Robert Freson Photographs. **207 (fig. 7.6):** Jason Mandella, courtesy the San Francisco Museum of Modern Art. **211:** Courtesy the Philadelphia Museum of Art. **213 (fig. 8.4), 218 (fig. 3):** © Centre Pompidou, MNAM-CCI. **215:** Courtesy The New York Studio School of Drawing, Painting & Sculpture. **217 (fig. 8.8), 306 (fig. 10.4):** Kris Graves. **218 (fig. 5):** JMFA017: Zuka Mitelberg Papers. **219 (fig. 6):** Jesse A. Fernandez. © Jesse A. Fernandez—Collection France Mazin Fernandez. **286:** Courtesy the Albright-Knox Art Gallery, Buffalo, New York. **289:** Courtesy The Phillips Collection, Washington, D.C. **290 (fig. 3):** Rik Klein, Gotnik, Harderwijk. Photo © 2020 Kröller-Müller Museum, Otterlo, The Netherlands. **290 (fig. 4), 305 (fig. 10.2), 309:** Courtesy the Van Gogh Museum, Amsterdam (Vincent van Gogh Foundation). **291 (fig. 5):** Josh Nefsky. **295 (fig. 9.3), 298:** Photo © Primae / David Bordes. **301 (fig. 9.8):** André Morain. © Galerie Jean Fournier, Paris. **302:** © David Seidner Archive / International Center of Photography. **303, 313 (fig. 10):** David Turnley / Corbis / VCG via Getty Images. **305 (fig. 10.3):** Mitro Hood, courtesy the Baltimore Museum of Art. **306 (fig. 10.5):** Digital image © Whitney Museum of American Art, New York / Licensed by SCALA / Art Resource, New York. **311 (fig. 10.8):** Bill Scott. **312 (figs. 1 and 3):** Christopher Campbell. **312 (fig. 5):** Guy Bloch-Champfort. **315 (and details):** Courtesy Cheim & Read, New York. **322:** Elga Heinzen.

This catalogue is published on the occasion of the exhibition *Joan Mitchell,* co-organized by The Baltimore Museum of Art and the San Francisco Museum of Modern Art.

Presenting support for *Joan Mitchell* is provided by the Henry Luce Foundation.

HENRY LUCE FOUNDATION

Major support is provided by the Terra Foundation for American Art, sponsor of the international tour.

TERRA
FOUNDATION FOR AMERICAN ART

At The Baltimore Museum of Art, *Joan Mitchell* is sponsored by Bank of America.

BANK OF AMERICA

The exhibition is generously supported by The Alvin and Fanny B. Thalheimer Exhibition Endowment Fund. The project is also supported in part by an award from the National Endowment for the Arts. Additional support is provided by the Sigmund M. and Mary B. Hyman Fund for American Art, The Stoneridge Fund of Amy and Marc Meadows, and Komal Shah and Gaurav Garg.

NATIONAL ENDOWMENT for the ARTS
arts.gov

At the San Francisco Museum of Modern Art, leadership support is provided by Helen and Charles Schwab.

Major support is provided by Sanford Robertson.

Generous support is provided by Richard and Mary Jo Kovacevich, the Joan Mitchell Foundation, the Bernard and Barbro Osher Fund, Komal Shah and Gaurav Garg, and the Wyeth Foundation for American Art.

JOAN MITCHELL FOUNDATION

WYETH FOUNDATION FOR AMERICAN ART

San Francisco Museum of Modern Art
151 Third Street
San Francisco, CA 94103
sfmoma.org

Published in association with Yale University Press
302 Temple Street
P.O. Box 209040
New Haven, CT 06520-9040
yalebooks.com/art

This book was produced by the publications department at the San Francisco Museum of Modern Art (Kari Dahlgren, director of publications; Amanda Glesmann, senior editor; Lucy Medrich, editor; Brianna Nelson and Jessica Ruiz DeCamp, publications associates).

Project editor: Amanda Glesmann
Editors: Kristin Swan with Jennifer Boynton
Assistant editor and image coordinator: Brianna Nelson
Designers: Tracey Shiffman and James Ihira, Shiffman & Kohnke
Indexer: Kathleen Preciado
Color separations by Echelon, Santa Monica, California
Printed in Italy by VeronaLibri

Set in Theinhardt and Didonesque
Printed on Perigord 150gsm

Library of Congress Control Number: 2020934248

ISBN: 978-0-300-24727-5

COVER: Joan Mitchell, *Sans Pierre,* 1969 (detail). Oil on canvas, 102½ × 78½ in. (260.4 × 199.4 cm). Collection of The Long View Legacy LLC. Artwork © Estate of Joan Mitchell. Photo: Lee Stalsworth, courtesy the San Francisco Museum of Modern Art. See plate 89. PAGE 1: Letter from Joan Mitchell to Joyce Pensato, July 14, 1981. Courtesy the Estate of Joyce Pensato. PAGE 2: Joan Mitchell, 1954. Joan Mitchell Foundation Archives, New York. Photo: Walt Silver. PAGES 6–7: Joan Mitchell at La Tour, Vétheuil, France, 1984. Joan Mitchell Foundation Archives, New York. Photo: Édouard Boubat. © Estate of Édouard Boubat. PAGES 10–11: Iva in front of *Garden for Audrey* (1975) in Joan Mitchell's studio at La Tour, Vétheuil, France, 1975. Joan Mitchell Foundation Archives, New York. PAGE 13: Joan Mitchell at La Tour, Vétheuil, France, 1991. Photo: David Turnley / Corbis / VCG via Getty Images. PAGE 338: Joan Mitchell in her studio at La Tour, Vétheuil, France, 1984. Joan Mitchell Foundation Archives, New York. Photo: Édouard Boubat. © Estate of Édouard Boubat. PAGES 368–69: Joan Mitchell in her studio at 10 rue Frémicourt, Paris, 1962. Photo: Jean-Pierre Biot / Paris Match via Getty Images. PAGE 370: Joan Mitchell, 1981. Photo: Hans Namuth. © 1991 Hans Namuth Estate, courtesy Center for Creative Photography, University of Arizona. PAGES 376–77: Mitchell on the balcony at La Tour, Vétheuil, France, 1991. Photo: Christopher Campbell.